América del Sur

PEARSON
myspanishlab ¡Hola!

Part of the award-winning MyLanguageLabs suite of online learning and assessment systems for basic language courses, MySpanishLab brings together—in one convenient, easily navigable site—a wide array of language-learning tools and resources, including an interactive version of the *¡Anda! Curso elemental para estudiantes avanzados* student text, an online Student Activities Manual, and all materials from the audio and video programs. Chapter Practice Tests, tutorials, and English grammar Readiness Checks personalize instruction to meet the unique needs of individual students. Instructors can use the system to make assignments, set grading parameters, listen to student-created audio recordings, and provide feedback on student work. MySpanishLab can be packaged with the text at a substantial savings. For more information, visit us online at http://www.mylanguagelabs.com/books.html.

A GUIDE TO ¡ANDA! CURSO ELEMENTAL PARA ESTUDIANTES AVANZADOS ICONS

✓	**Readiness Check for MySpanishLab**	This icon, located in each chapter opener, reminds students to take the Readiness Check in MySpanishLab to test their understanding of the English grammar related to the Spanish grammar concepts in the chapter.
¡Hola!	**MySpanishLab**	This icon indicates that additional resources for pronunciation and grammar are available in MySpanishLab.
🔊	**Text Audio Program**	This icon indicates that recorded material to accompany *¡Anda! Curso elemental* is available in MySpanishLab (www.mylanguagelabs.com), on audio CD, or on the Companion Website (www.pearsonhighered.com/anda).
👥	**Pair Activity**	This icon indicates that the activity is designed to be done by students working in pairs.
👥	**Group Activity**	This icon indicates that the activity is designed to be done by students working in small groups or as a whole class.
🌐	**Web Activity**	This icon indicates that the activity involves use of the Internet.
🎬	**Video icon**	This icon indicates that a video episode is available for the *Ambiciones siniestras* video series that accompanies the *¡Anda! Curso elemental* program. The video is available on DVD and in MySpanishLab.
📖	**Student Activities Manual**	This icon indicates that there are practice activities available in the *¡Anda! Curso elemental* Student Activities Manual. The activities may be found either in the printed version of the manual or in the interactive version available through MySpanishLab. Activity numbers are indicated in the text for ease of reference.
📖	**Workbooklet**	This icon indicates that an activity has been reproduced in the *Workbooklet* available as a print supplement or in MySpanishLab.
🌍	**Interactive Globe**	This icon indicates that additional cultural resources in the form of videos, web links, interactive maps, and more, relating to particular countries, are organized on an interactive globe in MySpanishLab.
e	**eText Activities**	This icon indicates that the activity is only available online and can be found in students' MySpanishLab course.

Curso elemental para estudiantes avanzados

Curso elemental para estudiantes avanzados

ANNOTATED INSTRUCTOR'S EDITION

Curso elemental para estudiantes avanzados

¡Anda!

AUDREY L. HEINING-BOYNTON
GLYNIS S. COWELL
The University of North Carolina at Chapel Hill

WITH

Jean LeLoup

María del Carmen Caña Jiménez

PEARSON

Boston   Columbus   Indianapolis   New York   San Francisco   Upper Saddle River
Amsterdam   Cape Town   Dubai   London   Madrid   Milan   Munich   Paris   Montréal   Toronto
Delhi   Mexico City   São Paulo   Sydney   Hong Kong   Seoul   Singapore   Taipei   Tokyo

Senior Vice President: Steve Debow
Executive Editor, Spanish: Julia Caballero
Editorial Assistant: Jessica Finaldi
Executive Marketing Manager: Kris Ellis-Levy
Senior Marketing Manager: Denise Miller
Development Coordinator: Celia Meana
Development Editor, ¡Anda!: Janet García-Levitas
Development Editor, Spanish: Meriel Martínez
Senior Managing Editor for Product Development:
   Mary Rottino
Associate Managing Editor (Production): Janice Stangel
Senior Production Project Manager: Nancy Stevenson
Executive Editor, MyLanguageLabs: Bob Hemmer
Senior Media Editor: Samantha Alducin

Development Editor, MyLanguageLabs: Bill Bliss
Editorial Coordinator, World Languages:
   Regina Rivera
Senior Art Director: Maria Lange
Cover Design: DePinho Design
Operations Manager: Mary Fischer
Operations Specialist: Alan Fischer
Full-Service Project Management: Michael Packard,
   PreMediaGlobal
Composition: PreMediaGlobal
Printer/Binder: R.R. Donnelley
Cover Printer: Lehigh - Phoenix Color
Cover Image: Shutterstock Images

This book was set in 10/12 Janson Roman.

Credits and acknowledgments borrowed from other sources and reproduced, with permission, in this textbook appear on appropriate pages within the text (or on page A47).

Student Edition, ISBN-10: 0-205-90571-4
Student Edition, ISBN-13: 978-0-205-90571-3

Annotated Instructor's Edition, ISBN-10: 0-205-95517-7
Annotated Instructor's Edition, ISBN-13: 978-0-205-95517-6

10 9 8 7 6 5 4 3 2 1

PEARSON

Brief Contents

PARA EMPEZAR

(The numbers next to the grammar and vocabulary sections indicate their location in the **eText**, which can be found in **MySpanishLab**.)

	CAPÍTULO A Preliminar	CAPÍTULO 1 ¿Quiénes somos?	CAPÍTULO 2 La vida universitaria
Vocabulary sections	**1** Saludos, despedidas y presentaciones p. 4 **2** Expresiones útiles para la clase p. 8 **4** Los cognados p. 10 **7** Los adjetivos de nacionalidad p. 14 **8** Los números 0–30 p. 16 **9** La hora p. 18 **10** Los días, los meses y las estaciones p. 20 **11** El tiempo p. 23	**1** La familia p. 32 **6** Gente p. 40 **9** Los números 31–100 p. 47	**1** Las materias y las especialidades p. 62 **2** La sala de clase p. 65 **5** Los números 100–1.000 p. 72 **6** En la universidad p. 74 **8** Las emociones y los estados p. 79 **10** Los deportes y los pasatiempos p. 81
Grammar sections	**3** El alfabeto p. 9 **5** Los pronombres personales p. 11 **6** El verbo **ser** p. 13 **12** *Gustar* p. 25	**2** El verbo **tener** p. 34 **3** Sustantivos singulares y plurales p. 36 **4** El masculino y el femenino p. 37 **5** Los artículos definidos e indefinidos p. 38 **7** Los adjetivos posesivos p. 41 **8** Los adjetivos descriptivos p. 43	**3** Presente indicativo de verbos regulares p. 67 **4** La formación de preguntas y las palabras interrogativas p. 70 **7** El verbo **estar** p. 76 **9** El verbo **gustar** p. 80
Pronunciation		Vowels p. 33	Word stress and accent marks p. 63
Cultural readings and country focus	• **Nota cultural** Cómo se saluda la gente p. 7 • **Nota cultural** ¿Tú o usted? p. 12 • **Nota cultural** Los hispanos p. 16 • **Nota cultural** El mundo hispano p. 17	• **Nota cultural** Los apellidos en el mundo hispano p. 33 • **Nota cultural** El español, lengua diversa p. 46	• **Nota cultural** Las universidades hispanas p. 64 • **Nota cultural** Los deportes en el mundo hispano p. 84
Cultura		**LOS ESTADOS UNIDOS** p. 52	**MÉXICO** p. 88
Escucha		Presentaciones p. 49 **Estrategia:** Determining the topic and listening for words you know p. 49	Una conversación p. 86 **Estrategia:** Listening for the gist p. 86
¡Conversemos!		Communicating about people you know p. 50	Communicating about university life p. 86
Escribe		Un poema p. 50 **Estrategia:** Organizing ideas / Preparing to write p. 50	Una descripción p. 87 **Estrategia:** Creating sentences p. 87
Ambiciones siniestras		**Lectura:** *Conexiones* p. 54 **Estrategia:** Recognizing cognates p. 54 **Video:** *¿Quiénes son?* p. 56	**Lectura:** *Las solicitudes* p. 90 **Estrategia:** Skimming p. 90 **Video:** *La aventura comienza* p. 92

viii

CAPÍTULO 3 Estamos en casa	CAPÍTULO 4 Nuestra comunidad	CAPÍTULO 5 ¡A divertirse! La música y el cine	CAPÍTULO 6 ¡Sí, lo sé!
1 La casa p. 98 **3** Los muebles y otros objetos de la casa p. 106 **4** Los quehaceres de la casa p. 109 **5** Los colores p. 111 **7** Los números 1.000–100.000.000 p. 116	**1** Los lugares p. 134 **3** ¿Qué tienen que hacer? ¿Qué pasa? p. 140 **7** Servicios a la comunidad p. 149	**1** El mundo de la música p. 172 **6** El mundo del cine p. 184	**Reviewing strategies** p. 206
2 Algunos verbos irregulares p. 101 **6** Algunas expresiones con *tener* p. 113 **8** *Hay* p. 119	**2** *Saber* y *conocer* p. 137 **4** Los verbos con cambio de raíz p. 142 **5** El verbo *ir* p. 146 **6** *Ir* + *a* + infinitivo p. 147 **8** Las expresiones afirmativas y negativas p. 151 **9** Un repaso de *ser* y *estar* p. 154	**2** Los adjetivos demostrativos p. 175 **3** Los pronombres demostrativos p. 177 **4** Los adverbios p. 179 **5** El presente progresivo p. 180 **7** Los números ordinales p. 187 **8** *Hay que* + infinitivo p. 188 **9** Los pronombres de complemento directo y la "*a*" personal p. 189	**Comunicación** Recycling of **Capítulo Preliminar A** to **Capítulo 5**
The letters *h, j,* and *g* p. 99	The letters *c* and *z* p. 135	Diphthongs and linking p. 173	
• **Nota cultural** ¿Dónde viven los españoles? p. 105 • **Nota cultural** Las casas "verdes" p. 119	• **Nota cultural** Actividades cotidianas: Las compras y el paseo p. 136 • **Nota cultural** La conciencia social p. 151	• **Nota cultural** La música latina en los Estados Unidos p. 178 • **Nota cultural** La influencia hispana en el cine norteamericano p. 186	
ESPAÑA p. 124	**HONDURAS, GUATEMALA Y EL SALVADOR** p. 161	**NICARAGUA, COSTA RICA Y PANAMÁ** p. 195	**Cultura**
Una descripción p. 121 **Estrategia:** Listening for specific information p. 121	El voluntariado p. 157 **Estrategia:** Paraphrasing what you hear p. 157	Planes para un concierto p. 192 **Estrategia:** Anticipating content p. 192	
Communicating about homes and life at home p. 122	Communicating about ways to serve the community p. 158	Communicating about music and film p. 193	
Un anuncio p. 123 **Estrategia:** Noun → adjective agreement p. 123	Una tarjeta postal p. 159 **Estrategia:** Proofreading p. 159	Una reseña p. 194 **Estrategia:** Peer review/editing p. 194	
Lectura: *El concurso* p. 126 **Estrategia:** Scanning p. 126 **Video:** *¡Tienes una gran oportunidad!* p. 128	**Lectura:** *Las cosas no son siempre lo que parecen* p. 164 **Estrategia:** Skimming and Scanning (II) p. 164 **Video:** *¿Quiénes son en realidad?* p. 166	**Lectura:** *La búsqueda de Eduardo* p. 198 **Estrategia:** Anticipating content p. 198 **Video:** *Se conocen* p. 200	Recap of Episodes 1–5

(The numbers next to the grammar and vocabulary sections indicate their location in the **eText**, which can be found in **MySpanishLab**.)

	CAPÍTULO 7 ¡A comer!	CAPÍTULO 8 ¿Qué te pones?	CAPÍTULO 9 Estamos en forma
Vocabulary sections	**1** La comida p. 256 **5** La preparación de las comidas p. 269 **7** En el restaurante p. 277	**1** La ropa p. 294 **5** Las telas y los materiales p. 309	**1** El cuerpo humano p. 334 **3** Algunas enfermedades y tratamientos médicos p. 341
Grammar sections	**2** Repaso del complemento directo p. 261 **3** El pretérito (Parte I) p. 263 **4** El pretérito (Parte II) p. 265 **6** Algunos verbos irregulares en el pretérito p. 272	**2** Los pronombres de complemento indirecto p. 299 **3** *Gustar* y verbos como *gustar* p. 302 **4** Los pronombres de complemento directo e indirecto usados juntos p. 305 **6** Las construcciones reflexivas p. 312 **7** El imperfecto p. 317	**2** Un resumen de los pronombres de complemento directoe indirecto y reflexivos p. 337 **4** **¡Qué!** y **¡cuánto!** p. 346 **5** El pretérito y el imperfecto p. 349 **6** Expresiones con *hacer* p. 356
Pronunciation	The different pronunciations of *r* and *rr* p. 257	The letters *ll* and *ñ* p. 295	The letters *d* and *t* p. 335
Cultural readings and country focus	• **Nota cultural** Las comidas en el mundo hispano p. 261 • **Nota cultural** La comida hispana p. 271	• **Nota cultural** Zara: la moda internacional p. 298 • **Nota cultural** Los centros comerciales en Latinoamérica p. 316	• **Nota cultural** El agua y la buena salud p. 346 • **Nota cultural** Las farmacias en el mundo hispanohablante p. 356
Cultura	**CHILE Y PARAGUAY** p. 284	**ARGENTINA Y URUGUAY** p. 324	**PERÚ, BOLIVIA Y ECUADOR** p. 363
Escucha	Las compras en el mercado p. 281 **Estrategia:** Combining strategies p. 281	En el centro comercial p. 321 **Estrategia:** Guessing meaning from context p. 321	Síntomas y tratamientos p. 360 **Estrategia:** Asking yourself questions p. 360
¡Conversemos!	Communicating about food shopping and party planning p. 282	Communicating about clothing and fashion p. 322	Communicating about ailments and healthy living p. 361
Escribe	Una descripción p. 283 **Estrategia:** Topic sentence and conclusion p. 283	Un email p. 323 **Estrategia:** Circumlocution p. 323	Un resumen p. 362 **Estrategia:** Sequencing events p. 362
Ambiciones siniestras	**Lectura:** *El rompecabezas* p. 286 **Estrategia:** Predicting p. 286 **Video:** *¡Qué rico está el pisco!* p. 288	**Lectura:** *¿Quién fue?* p. 326 **Estrategia:** Guessing meaning from context p. 326 **Video:** *El misterio crece* p. 328	**Lectura:** *¡Qué mentira!* p. 366 **Estrategia:** Asking yourself questions p. 366 **Video:** *No llores por mí* p. 368

CAPÍTULO 10 ¡Viajemos!	CAPÍTULO 11 El mundo actual	CAPÍTULO 12 Y por fin, ¡lo sé!
1 Los medios de transporte p. 374 **4** El viaje p. 388	**1** Los animales p. 412 **2** El medio ambiente p. 416 **4** La política p. 426	**Reviewing strategies** p. 452
2 Los mandatos informales p. 379 **3** Los mandatos formales p. 383 **5** Otras formas del posesivo p. 392 **6** El comparativo y el superlativo p. 394	**3** El subjuntivo p. 419 **5** *Por* y *para* p. 429 **6** Las preposiciones y los pronombres preposicionales p. 432 **7** El infinitivo después de preposiciones p. 436	**Comunicación** Recycling of **Capítulo Preliminar B** to **Capítulo 11**
The letters *b* and *v* p. 375	Review of Word Stress and Accent Marks p. 413	
• **Nota cultural** ¿Cómo nos movemos? p. 386 • **Nota cultural** Venezuela, país de aventuras p. 391	• **Nota cultural** El Yunque: tesoro tropical p. 419 • **Nota cultural** La política en el mundo hispano p. 428	
COLOMBIA Y VENEZUELA p. 402	**CUBA, PUERTO RICO Y LA REPÚBLICA DOMINICANA** p. 441	**Cultura**
Las vacaciones p. 399 **Estrategia:** Listening for linguistic cues p. 399	Un anuncio político p. 438 **Estrategia:** Using visual organizers p. 438	
Communicating about travel plans p. 400	Communicating about world issues p. 439	
Un reportaje p. 401 **Estrategia:** Using linking words p. 401	Un anuncio de servicio público p. 440 **Estrategia:** Persuasive writing p. 440	
Lectura: *¿Qué sabía?* p. 404 **Estrategia:** Skipping words p. 404 **Video:** *Falsas apariencias* p. 406	**Lectura:** *Celia* p. 444 **Estrategia:** Using visual organizers p. 444 **Video:** *El desenlace* p. 446	Recap of Episodes 7–11

Preface

WELCOME TO *¡ANDA! CURSO ELEMENTAL PARA ESTUDIANTES AVANZADOS*

The program designed for high beginner courses that provides *all* that your students need in one semester to prepare them for a successful entry to an intermediate level of language study!

¡Anda! Curso elemental para estudiantes avanzados is a research-based, class-tested, accelerated beginning Spanish program entirely grounded in the National Standards. This dynamic and motivating one-semester program provides the tools, practice, and support your students need to achieve their goals. It also provides the support that *you*, the instructor, need to help your students achieve success.

Who are the students who benefit from *¡Anda! Curso elemental para estudiantes avanzados?*

There are a variety of student populations that benefit from the *¡Anda! Curso elemental para estudiantes avanzados* program.

✔ **Students who studied Spanish in K–12 schools:** These learners have had formal study in the K–12 schools, but do not place directly into college intermediate courses. What these learners need is a refresher before continuing their studies of the Spanish language. The thorough review with *¡Anda! Curso elemental para estudiantes avanzados* brings these diverse learners to the perfect launching point for intermediate Spanish language courses.

✔ **Students who are heritage speakers of Spanish:** Many heritage speakers need a more formal, accelerated approach to the language and culture they inherited from their families. These heritage language learners may come directly from high school, they may be learners who decide during their undergraduate or graduate programs that they want to learn more about their home language, or they may be inspired, non-traditional learners who are interested in pursuing their heritage language either for career goals or for pleasure. *¡Anda! Curso elemental para estudiantes avanzados* delivers an abundance of support they need to achieve their goals.

✔ **Spanish for special purposes learners:** Course offerings with titles such as *Business Spanish, Spanish for Law Enforcement,* or *Spanish for Health Care Providers* are usually one semester in duration. These courses need a foundation in Spanish language structures and cultures. Teaching the specialized vocabulary for the multitude of careers is not enough. *¡Anda! Curso elemental para estudiantes avanzados* provides the structure that creates the essential scaffolding for the curriculum.

- ✔ **Adult learners:** As the importance of Spanish continues to rise in the worlds of commerce, national security, and travel, more adults are interested in pursuing Spanish in an individualized, self-study, or small group setting. Unlike other commercial products that make unreasonable claims regarding what the learner will be able to do, *¡Anda! Curso elemental para estudiantes avanzados* sets realistic, achievable goals.

- ✔ **Learners whose native language is neither English nor Spanish:** These international students usually are competent in English as a foreign language as well as their home language. Since they are already at least bilingual, they are familiar with language learning and how they learn a language. *¡Anda! Curso elemental para estudiantes avanzados* is the perfect learning environment for them to continue their multilingual paths.

Why *¡Anda! Curso elemental para estudiantes avanzados*?

We were pleased by the enthusiastic response to the first edition of *¡Anda!*, and we are honored that so many schools have chosen to adopt it for use in their introductory Spanish courses. The response confirmed our sense that many schools were feeling a need for a new kind of Spanish textbook program.

We wrote *¡Anda!* originally because Spanish instructors had told us that their courses were changing. In survey after survey, in focus group after focus group, they had said that they were finding it increasingly difficult to accomplish everything they wanted in their elementary Spanish courses. They also told us that they needed a version of *¡Anda!* specifically designed for the accelerated/high-beginner student. They told us that their lives and their students' lives were busier than ever. And as a result, they told us, there simply wasn't enough time available to do everything they wanted to do. Some reported that they felt compelled to gallop through their text in order to cover all the grammar and vocabulary, omitting important cultural topics and limiting their students' opportunities to develop and practice communication skills. Many instructors were looking for new ways to address the challenges they and their students were facing. We created *¡Anda! Curso elemental para estudiantes avanzados* to solve these challenges.

The challenges we heard about from all these Spanish instructors still exist today, and thus our goals and guiding principles for the second edition of the *¡Anda!* program remain the same as they were in the first edition. Nevertheless we have made many changes in response to helpful suggestions from users of the first edition, and we have created a power-paced program even more focused on the needs of students and instructors in the High Beginner/Accelerated Elementary course.

The *¡Anda!* Story

The *¡Anda!* program was developed to provide practical responses to the challenges today's Spanish instructors are facing. Its innovations center around three key areas:

1. Realistic goals with a realistic approach

2. Focus on student motivation

3. Tools to promote success

Realistic goals with a realistic approach

¡Anda! **Curso elemental para estudiantes avanzados** was created and organized specifically for learners with language talents and /or previous language learning experiences. In the opening Para empezar chapter, *¡Anda! Curso elemental para estudiantes avanzados* moves the learner quickly and efficiently through basic vocabulary and grammar that is familiar from previous studies. After this jump-start chapter, the program proceeds with realistic goals and a realistic pace. The ultimate goal is to lead students successfully toward the American Council on the Teaching of Foreign Languages (ACTFL) Oral Proficiency Interview (OPI) level of narrating in the major time frames. *¡Anda! Curso elemental para estudiantes avanzados* provides an abundance of practice that helps learners achieve their goals.

The scope and sequence has been carefully designed, based on research and feedback from instructors and users at a wide variety of institutions. The vocabulary in *¡Anda! Curso elemental para estudiantes avanzados* is high frequency, and the number of new words is controlled. The grammar scope and sequence is the result of extensive research in which hundreds of Spanish instructors across the country responded. Well over 80% of the respondents agree with the placement of the grammar topics for the *Curso elemental para estudiantes avanzados* program. This careful planning and attention to chunking of material results in students having adequate time throughout the program to focus on communication, culture, and skills development, and to master the vocabulary and grammar concepts to which they are introduced.

Para empezar, the initial chapter of *¡Anda! Curso elemental para estudiantes avanzados,* is comprised of four mini-chapters: Preliminar and Chapters 1–3. These brief chapters are meant to jump-start the learners with basic vocabulary and grammatical structures. Then, Chapters 4 through 11 of *¡Anda! Curso elemental para estudiantes avanzados* provide a realistic approach for the achievement of realistic goals.

- New material is presented in manageable amounts, or **chunks,** allowing students to assimilate and practice without feeling overwhelmed.

- Each chapter contains a **realistic** number of new vocabulary words.

- Vocabulary and grammar explanations are interspersed, each **introduced at the point of need.**

- Grammar explanations are clear and concise, utilizing either deductive or inductive presentations, and include many supporting examples followed by practice activities. The inductive presentations provide students with examples of a grammar concept. They then must formulate the rule(s) through the use of guiding questions. The inductive presentations are accompanied by a new *Explícalo tú* heading and an icon that directs them to Appendix 1, where answers to the questions in the presentations may be found.

- Practice begins with **mechanical** exercises, for which there are correct answers, progresses through more **meaningful,** structured activities in which the student is guided but has some flexibility in determining the appropriate responses, and ends with **communicative** activities in which students are manipulating language to create personalized responses.

Focus on student motivation

The many innovative features of *¡Anda!* that have made it such a successful program continue in *¡Anda! Curso elemental para estudiantes avanzados* to help instructors generate and sustain interest on the part of their students, whether they be of traditional college age or adult learners:

- Chapters are organized around themes that reflect **student interests** and tap into students' **real-life experiences.**

- Basic **vocabulary** has been selected and tested through *¡Anda!'s* development for its relevance and support, while additional words and phrases are offered so that **students can personalize** their responses and acquire the vocabulary that is most meaningful to them. Additional vocabulary items are found in *Vocabulario útil* boxes throughout the chapters as well as in Appendix 3 (*También se dice…*).

- Activities have been designed to foster active participation by students. The focus throughout is on giving students opportunities to speak and on allowing instructors to **increase the amount of student "talk time"** in each class period. The majority of activities **elicit students' ideas and opinions,** engaging them to respond to each other on a variety of levels. Abundant pair and group activities encourage students to learn from and support each other, creating a comfortable arena for language learning.

- Each activity is designed to begin with **what the student already knows.**

- A **high-interest mystery story,** *Ambiciones siniestras*, runs through each chapter. Two episodes are presented in each regular chapter, one as the chapter's reading selection (in the *Lectura* section), the other in a corresponding video segment (in the *Video* section).

- Both **"high" and "popular" culture** are woven throughout the chapters to enable students to learn to recognize and appreciate cultural diversity as they explore behaviors and values of the Spanish-speaking world. They are encouraged to think critically about these cultural practices and gifts to society.

Tools to promote success

The *¡Anda! Curso elemental para estudiantes avanzados* program includes many unique features and components designed to help students succeed at language learning and their instructors at language teaching.

Student learning support

- A **"walking tour"** of the *¡Anda! Curso elemental para estudiantes avanzados* text and supplements helps students navigate their language program materials and understand better the whys and howls of learning Spanish.

- Explicit, systematic **recycling boxes with page references** help students link current learning to previously studied material in earlier chapters or sections.

- **Periodic review and self-assessment** boxes (*¿Cómo andas? I* and *¿Cómo andas? II*) help students gauge their understanding and retention of the material presented. A final assessment in each chapter (*Y por fin, ¿cómo andas?*) offers a comprehensive self-assessment.

- **Student notes** provide additional explanations and guidance in the learning process. Some of these contain cross-references to other student supplements. Others offer learning strategies (*Estrategia*) and additional information (*Fíjate*).

- **MySpanishLab** offers students all the resources and support for a complete learning program. The asynchronous learning environment includes the e-book sections and practice activities as well as English and Spanish grammar tutorials, vocabulary tutorials, pre-assessments, and individualized study plans. Hints, verb charts, instructional games, a glossary, and other resources are available as well.

- A **Workbooklet,** available separately, allows students to complete the activities that involve writing without having to write in their copies of the textbook.

Instructor teaching support

One of the most important keys to student success is instructor success. The *¡Anda!* program has all of the support that you have come to expect and, based on our research, it offers many other enhancements!

- The **Annotated Instructor's Edition** of *¡Anda!* offers a wealth of materials designed to help instructors teach effectively and efficiently. Strategically placed annotations explain the text's methodology and function as **a built-in course in language teaching methods.**

- **Estimated time indicators** for presentational materials and practice activities help instructors create lesson plans.

- Other annotations provide **additional activities** and suggested answers.

- **The annotations are color-coded** and labeled for ready reference and ease of use.

- A treasure trove of supplemental activities, available for download in the **Extra Activities** folder of MySpanishLab, allows instructors to choose additional materials for in-class use.

Teacher Annotations

The teacher annotations in the *¡Anda!* fall into a variety of categories:

- **Methodology:** A deep and broad set of methods notes designed for the novice instructor.

- **Section Goals:** Set of student objectives for each section.

- **National Standards:** Information containing the correlation between each section with the National Standards as well as tips for increasing student performance.

- **21st Century Skills:** Interpreting the new Partnership for the 21st Century skills and the National Standards. These skills enumerate what is necessary for successful 21st century citizens.

- **Planning Ahead:** Suggestions for instructors included in the chapter openers to help prepare materials in advance for certain activities in the chapter. Also provided is information regarding which activities to assign to students prior to them coming to class.

- **Warm-up:** Suggestions for setting up an activity or how to activate students' prior knowledge relating to the task at hand.

- **Suggestion:** Teaching tips that provide ideas that will help with the implementation of activities and sections.

- **Note:** Additional information that instructors may wish to share with students beyond what is presented in the text.

- **Expansion:** Ideas for variations of a topic that may serve as wrap-up activities.

- **Follow-up:** Suggestions to aid instructors in assessing student comprehension.

- **Notes:** Information on people, places, and things that aid in the completion of activities and sections by providing background knowledge.

- **Additional Activity:** Independent activities related to the ones in the text that provide further practice than those supplied in the text.

- **Alternate Activity:** Variations of activities provided to suit each individual classroom and preferences.

- **Heritage Language Learners:** Suggestions for the heritage language learners in the classroom that provide alternatives and expansions for sections and activities based on prior knowledge and skills.

- **Audioscript:** Written script of all *Escucha* recordings.

- **Recap of *Ambiciones siniestras:*** A synopsis of both the *Lectura* and *Video* sections for each episode of *Ambiciones siniestras.*

The authors' approach

Learning a language is an exciting, enriching, and sometimes life-changing experience. The development of the *¡Anda!* program, now its second edition, is the result of many years of teaching and research that guided the authors independently to make important discoveries about language learning, the most important of which center on the student. Research-based and pedagogically sound, *¡Anda! Curso elemental para estudiantes avanzados* is also the product of extensive information gathered firsthand from numerous focus group sessions with students, graduate instructors, adjunct faculty, full-time professors, and administrators in an effort to determine the learning and instructional needs of each of these groups.

The Importance of the National Foreign Language Standards in *¡Anda!*

The *¡Anda! Curso elemental para estudiantes avanzados* program is based on the *National Foreign Language Standards.* The five organizing principles (the 5 Cs) of the Standards for language teaching and learning are at the core of *¡Anda!:* **Communication, Cultures, Connections, Comparisons,** and **Communities.** Each chapter opener identifies for the instructor where and in what capacity each of the 5 Cs is addressed. The **Weave of Curricular Elements** of the *National Foreign Language Standards* provides additional organizational structure for *¡Anda!* Those components of the **Curricular Weave** are: **Language System, Cultural Knowledge, Communication Strategies, Critical Thinking Skills, Learning Strategies, Other Subject Areas,** and **Technology.** Each of the Curricular Weave elements is omnipresent and, like the 5 Cs, permeates all aspects of each chapter of *¡Anda!*

- The *Language System*, which comprises components such as grammar, vocabulary, and phonetics, is at the heart of each chapter.

- The *Comunicación* sections of each chapter present vocabulary, grammar, and pronunciation at the point of need and maximum usage. Streamlined presentations are utilized that allow the learner to be immediately successful in employing the new concepts.

- *Cultural Knowledge* is approached thematically, making use of the chapter's vocabulary and grammar. Many of the grammar and vocabulary activities are presented in cultural contexts. Cultural presentations begin with the two-page chapter openers and always start with what the students already know about the cultural themes/concepts from their home, local, regional, or national cultural perspective. The *Nota cultural* and *Les presento mi país* sections provide rich cultural information about each Hispanic country.

- *Communication and Learning Strategies* are abundant with tips for both students and instructors on how to maximize studying and in-class learning of Spanish, as well as how to utilize the language outside of the classroom.

- *Critical Thinking Skills* take center stage in ***¡Anda! Curso elemental para estudiantes avanzados.*** Questions throughout the chapters, in particular tied to the cultural presentations, provide students with the opportunities to answer more than discrete point questions. The answers students are able to provide do indeed require higher-order thinking, but at a linguistic level completely appropriate for a beginning language learner.

- With regard to *Other Subject Areas,* ***¡Anda! Curso elemental para estudiantes avanzados*** diligently incorporates **Connections** to other disciplines via vocabulary, discussion topics, and suggested activities. This edition also highlights a **Communities** section, which includes experiential and service learning activities in the Student Activities Manual.

- Finally, *technology* is taken to an entirely new level with **MySpanishLab** and the *Ambiciones siniestras* DVD. The authors and Pearson Education believe that technology is a means to the end, not the end in and of itself, and so the focus is not on the technology per se, but on how that technology can deliver great content in better, more efficient, more interactive, and more meaningful ways.

By embracing the National Foreign Language Standards and as a result of decades of experience teaching Spanish, the authors believe that:

- A **student-centered classroom** is the best learning environment.

- Instruction must **begin where the learner is,** and all students come to the learning experience with prior knowledge that needs to be tapped.

- All students can learn in a **supportive environment** where they are encouraged to take risks when learning another language.

- **Critical thinking** is an important skill that must constantly be encouraged, practiced, and nurtured.

- **Learners** need to **make connections** with other disciplines in the Spanish classroom.

With these beliefs in mind, the authors have developed hundreds of creative and meaningful language-learning activities for the text and supporting components that employ students' imagination and engage the senses. For both students and instructors, they have created an instructional program that is **manageable, motivating,** and **clear.**

Comparison of Chapters in ¡Anda!
Curso elemental para estudiantes avanzados

Many of you have successfully used or are using *¡Anda! Curso elemental*. What follows is a correspondence of the chapters in that edition with those in this *¡Anda! Curso elemental para estudiantes avanzados* edition.

Para empezar	This is a condensed chapter containing content from chapters Preliminar A through 3 from the full edition. Vocabulary presentations are preserved in their entirety. All grammar explanations, along with many activities, have been pulled out and placed in **MySpanishLab** for online review and practice. Vocabulary and Grammar summaries for each chapter are included at the end of *Para empezar* for easy student reference.
Capítulo 4	Same content as Capítulo 4 in the full edition. *Nota cultural* readings and *Ambiciones siniestras* readings and video can be found in the eText in **MySpanishLab**. Activities for these sections can also be completed online.
Capítulo 5	Same content as Capítulo 5 in the full edition. *Nota cultural* readings and *Ambiciones siniestras* readings and video can be found in the eText in **MySpanishLab**. Activities for these sections can also be completed online.
Capítulo 6	Reduced to include only the *Un poco de todo* activities.
Capítulos 7–11	Same content as the corresponding chapters in the full edition. *Nota cultural* readings and *Ambiciones siniestras* readings and video can be found in the eText in **MySpanishLab**. Activities for these sections can also be completed online.
Capítulo 12	Reduced to include only the *Un poco de todo* activities.

The Authors

Audrey Heining-Boynton

Audrey Heining-Boynton received her Ph.D. from Michigan State University and her M.A. from The Ohio State University. Her career spans K-12 through graduate school teaching, most recently as Professor of Education and Spanish at The University of North Carolina at Chapel Hill. She has won many teaching awards, including the prestigious ACTFL Anthony Papalia Award for Excellence in Teacher Education, the Foreign Language Association of North Carolina (FLANC) Teacher of the Year Award, and the UNC ACCESS Award for Excellence in Working with LD and ADHD students. Dr. Heining-Boynton is a frequent presenter at national and international conferences, has published more than one hundred articles, curricula, textbooks, and manuals, and has won nearly $4 million in grants to help create language programs in North and South Carolina. Dr. Heining-Boynton has also held many important positions: President of the American Council on the Teaching of Foreign Languages (ACTFL), President of the National Network for Early Language Learning, Vice President of Michigan Foreign Language Association, board member of the Foreign Language Association of North Carolina, committee chair for Foreign Language in the Elementary School for the American Association of Teachers of Spanish and Portuguese, and elected Executive Council member of ACTFL. She is also an appointed two-term *Foreign Language Annals* Editorial Board member and guest editor of the publication.

Glynis Cowell

Glynis Cowell is the Director of the Spanish Language Program in the Department of Romance Languages and Literatures and an Assistant Dean in the Academic Advising Program at The University of North Carolina at Chapel Hill. She has taught first-year seminars, honors courses, and numerous face-to-face and hybrid Spanish language courses. She also team-teaches a graduate course on the theories and techniques of teaching foreign languages. Dr. Cowell received her M.A. in Spanish Literature and her Ph.D. in Curriculum and Instruction, with a concentration in Foreign Language Education, from The University of North Carolina at Chapel Hill. Prior to joining the faculty at UNC-CH in August 1994, she coordinated the Spanish Language Program in the Department of Romance Studies at Duke University. She has also taught Spanish at both the high school and community college level. At UNC-CH she has received the Students' Award for Excellence in Undergraduate Teaching as well as the Graduate Student Mentor Award for the Department of Romance Languages and Literatures.

Dr. Cowell has directed teacher workshops on Spanish language and cultures and has presented papers and written articles on the teaching of language and literature, the transition to blended and online courses in language teaching, and teaching across the curriculum. She is the co-author of two other college textbooks.

Faculty Reviewers

Silvia P. Albanese, *Nassau Community College*
Ángeles Aller, *Whitworth University*
Nuria Alonso García, *Providence College*
Carlos Amaya, *Eastern Illinois University*
Tyler Anderson, *Colorado Mesa University*
Aleta Anderson, *Grand Rapids Community College*
Ines Anido, *Houston Baptist University*
Inés Arribas, *Bryn Mawr College*
Tim Altanero, *Austin Community College*
Bárbara Ávila-Shah, *University at Buffalo*
Ann Baker, *University of Evansville*
Ashlee Balena, *University of North Carolina–Wilmington*
Amy R. Barber, *Grove City College*
Mark Bates, *Simpson College*
Charla Bennaji, *New College of Florida*
Georgia Betcher, *Fayetteville Technical Community College*
Christine Blackshaw, *Mount Saint Mary's University*
Marie Blair, *University of Nebraska*
Kristy Britt, *University of South Alabama*
Isabel Zakrzewski Brown, *University of South Alabama*
Eduardo Cabrera, *Millikin University*
Majel Campbell, *Pikes Peak Community College*
Paul Cankar, *Austin Community College*
Monica Cantero, *Drew University*
Aurora Castillo, *Georgia College & State University*
Tulio Cedillo, *Lynchburg College*
Kerry Chermel, *Northern Illinois University*
Carrie Clay, *Anderson University*
Alyce Cook, *Columbus State University*
Jorge H. Cubillos, *University of Delaware*
Shay Culbertson, *Jefferson State Community College*
Cathleen G. Cuppett, *Coker College*
Addison Dalton, *Virginia Tech*
John B. Davis, *Indiana University, South Bend*
Laura Dennis, *University of the Cumberlands*
Lisa DeWaard, *Clemson University*
Sister Carmen Marie Diaz, *Silver Lake College of the Holy Family*
Joanna Dieckman, *Belhaven University*
Donna Donnelly, *Ohio Wesleyan University*
Kim Dorsey, *Howard College*
Mark A. Dowell, *Randolph Community College*
Dina A. Fabery, *University of Central Florida*
Jenny Faile, *University of South Alabama*
Juliet Falce-Robinson, *University of California, Los Angeles*
Mary Fatora-Tumbaga, *Kauai Community College*
Ronna Feit, *Nassau Community College*
Irene Fernandez, *North Shore Community College*
Erin Fernández Mommer, *Green River Community College*
Rocío Fuentes, *Clark University*

Judith Garcia-Quismondo, *Seton Hill University*
Elaine Gerber, *University of Michigan at Dearborn*
Andrea Giddens, *Salt Lake Community College*
Amy Ginck, *Messiah College*
Kenneth Gordon, *Winthrop University*
Agnieszka Gutthy, *Southeastern Louisiana University*
Shannon Hahn, *Durham Technical Community College*
Nancy Hanway, *Gustavus Adolphus College*
Sarah Harmon, *Cañada College*
Marilyn Harper, *Pellissippi State Community College*
Mark Harpring, *University of Puget Sound*
Dan Hickman, *Maryville College*
Amarilis Hidalgo de Jesus, *Bloomsburg University*
Charles Holloway, *University of Louisiana Monroe*
Anneliese Horst Foerster, *Queens University of Charlotte*
John Incledon, *Albright College*
William Jensen, *Snow College*
Qiu Y. Jimenez, *Bakersfield College*
Roberto Jiménez, *Western Kentucky University (Glasgow Regional Center)*
Valerie Job, *South Plains College*
Michael Jones, *Schenectady County Community College*
Dallas Jurisevic, *Metropolitan Community College*
Hilda M. Kachmar, *St. Catherine University*
Amos Kasperek, *University of Oklahoma*
Melissa Katz, *Albright College*
Lydia Gil Keff, *University of Denver*
Nieves Knapp, *Brigham Young University*
Melissa Knosp, *Johnson C. Smith University*
Pedro Koo, *Missouri State University*
Allison D. Krogstad, *Central College*
Courtney Lanute, *Edison State College*
Rafael Lara-Martinez, *New Mexico Institute of Mining and Technology*
John Lance Lee, *Durham Technical Community College*
Roxana Levin, *St. Petersburg College: Tarpon Springs Campus*
Penny Lovett, *Wake Technical Community College*
Paula Luteran, *Hutchinson Community College*
Katie MacLean, *Kalamazoo College*
Eder F. Maestre, *Western Kentucky University*
William Maisch, *University of North Carolina, Chapel Hill*
H.J. Manzari, *Washington and Jefferson College*
Lynne Flora Margolies, *Manchester College*
Anne Mattrella, *Naugatuck Valley Community College*
Maria R. Matz, *University of Massachusetts, Lowell*
Sandra Delgado Merrill, *University of Central Missouri*
Lisa Mershcel, *Duke University*
Geoff Mitchell, *Maryville College*
Charles H. Molano, *Lehigh Carbon Community College*
Javier Morin, *Del Mar College*
Noemi Esther Morriberon, *Chicago State University*
Gustavo Obeso, *Western Kentucky University*

Elizabeth Olvera, *University of Texas at San Antonio*
Michelle Orecchio, *University of Michigan*
Martha T. Oregel, *University of San Diego*
Cristina Pardo-Ballister, *Iowa State University*
Edward Anthony Pasko, *Purdue University, Calumet*
Joyce Pauley, *Moberly Area Community College*
Gilberto A. Pérez, *Cal Baptist University*
Beth Pollack, *New Mexico State University*
Silvia T. Pulido, *Brevard Community College*
JoAnne B. Pumariega, *Penn State Berks*
Lynn C. Purkey, *University of Tennessee at Chattanooga*
Aida Ramos-Sellman, *Goucher College*
Alice S. Reyes, *Marywood University*
Rita Ricaurte, *Nebraska Wesleyan University*
Geoffrey Ridley Barlow, *Purdue University, Calumet*
Daniel Robins, *Cabrillo College*
Sharon D. Robinson, *Lynchburg College*
Ibis Rodriguez, *Metropolitan University, SUAGM*
David Diego Rodríguez, *University of Illinois, Chicago*
Mileta Roe, *Bard College at Simon's Rock*
Donna Boston Ross, *Catawba Valley Community College*
Marc Roth, *St. John's University*
Kristin Routt, *Eastern Illinois University*
Christian Rubio, *University of Louisiana at Monroe*
Claudia Sahagún, *Broward College*
Adán Salinas, *Southwestern Illinois College*
Ruth Sánchez Imizcoz, *The University of the South*
Love Sánchez-Suárez, *York Technical College*
Gabriela Segal, *Arcadia University*
Diana Semmes, *University of Mississippi*
Michele Shaul, *Queens University of Charlotte*
Steve Sheppard, *University of North Texas, Denton*
Roger K. Simpson, *Clemson University*
Carter Smith, *University of Wisconsin–Eau Claire*
Nancy Smith, *Allegheny College*
Ruth Smith, *University of Louisiana at Monroe*
Margaret L. Snyder, *Moravian College*
Wayne Steely, *Saint Joseph's College*
Irena Stefanova, *Santa Clara University*
Benay Stein, *Northwestern University*
Gwen H. Stickney, *North Dakota State University*
Erika M. Sutherland, *Muhlenberg College*
Carla A. Swygert, *University of South Carolina*
Sarah Tahtinen-Pacheco, *Bethel University*
Luz Consuelo Triana-Echeverria, *St. Cloud State University*
Cynthia Trocchio, *Kent State University*
Elaini Tsoukatos, *Mount St. Mary's University*
Robert Turner, *Shorter University*
Ivelisse Urbán, *Tarleton State University*
Maria Vallieres, *Villanova University*

Sharon Van Houte, *Lorain County Community College*
Yertty VanderMolen, *Luther College*
Kristi Velleman, *American University*
Gayle Vierma, *University of Southern California*
Phoebe Vitharana, *Le Moyne College*
Richard L.W. Wallace, *Crowder College*
Martha L. Wallen, *University of Wisconsin–Stout*
Mary H. West, *Des Moines Area Community College*
Michelangelo Zapata, *Western Kentucky University*
Theresa Zmurkewycz, *Saint Joseph's University*

Faculty Focus Groups

Stephanie Aaron, *University of Central Florida*
María J. Barbosa, *University of Central Florida*
Ileana Bougeois-Serrano, *Valencia Community College*
Samira Chater, *Valencia Community College*
Natalie Cifuentes, *Valencia Community College*
Ana Ma. Diaz, *University of Florida*
Aida E. Diaz, *Valencia Community College*
Dina A. Fabery, *University of Central Florida*
Ana J. Caldero Figueroa, *Valencia Community College*
Pilar Florenz, *University of Central Florida*
Stephanie Gates, *University of Florida*
Antonio Gil, *University of Florida*
José I. González, *University of Central Florida*
Victor Jordan, *University of Florida*
Alice A. Korosy, *University of Central Florida*
Joseph Menig, *Valencia Community College*
Odyscea Moghimi-Kon, *University of Florida*
Kathryn Dwyer Navajas, *University of Florida*
Julie Pomerleau, *University of Central Florida*
Anne Prucha, *University of Central Florida*
Lester E. Sandres Rápalo, *Valencia Community College*
Arcadio Rivera, *University of Central Florida*
Elizabeth Z. Solis, *University of Central Florida*
Dania Varela, *University of Central Florida*
Helena Veenstra, *Valencia Community College*
Hilaurmé Velez-Soto, *University of Central Florida*
Roberto E. Weiss, *University of Florida*
Robert Williams, *University of Central Florida*
Sara Zahler, *University of Florida*

Acknowledgments

¡Anda! Curso elemental para estudiantes avanzados is the result of careful planning between ourselves and our publisher and ongoing collaboration with students and you, our colleagues. We look forward to continuing this dialogue and sincerely appreciate your input. We owe special thanks to the many members of the Spanish-teaching community whose comments and suggestions helped shape the pages of every chapter—you will see yourselves everywhere. We gratefully acknowledge the reviewers and we thank in particular our *¡Anda! Advisory Board* for their invaluable support, input, and feedback. The Board members are:

Megan Echevarría, *University of Rhode Island*

Luz Font, *Florida State College at Jacksonville*

Yolanda Gonzalez, *Valencia College*

Linda Keown, *University of Missouri*

Jeff Longwell, *New Mexico State University*

Gillian Lord, *University of Florida*

Dawn Meissner, *Anne Arundel Community College*

María Monica Montalvo, *University of Central Florida*

Markus Muller, *Long Beach State University*

Joan Turner, *University of Arkansas – Fayetteville*

Donny Vigil, *University of North Texas, Denton*

Iñigo Yanguas, *San Diego State University*

Special thanks go to Esther Castro for her important input and support. We are also grateful to those who have collaborated with us in the writing of *¡Anda! Curso elemental para estudiantes avanzados.*

We owe many thanks to Megan Echevarría for her superb work on the Student Activities Manual. We also owe great thanks to Donny Vigil for his authoring of the Testing Program as well as Anastacia Kohl for her important Testing Program authoring contributions.

Equally important are the contributions of the highly talented individuals at Pearson Education. We wish to express our gratitude and deep appreciation to the many people at Pearson who contributed their ideas, tireless efforts, and publishing experience for *¡Anda! Curso elemental para estudiantes avanzados.* First, we are indebted to Pearson Vice President Steve Debow for his invaluable expertise, guidance, motivation, and leadership with this program. Additionally we thank Phil Miller, Publisher, and Julia Caballero, Executive Editor, whose support and guidance have been essential. We are indebted to Janet García-Levitas, Development Editor, for all of her hard work, suggestions, attention to detail, and dedication to the programs. We have also been fortunate to have Celia Meana, Development Coordinator, bring her special talents to the project, helping to create the outstanding final product. We would also like to thank Bob Hemmer and Samantha Alducin for all of the hard work on the integration of technology for the *¡Anda!* program with MySpanishLab.

Our thanks to Meriel Martínez, Development Editor, for her efficient and meticulous work in managing the preparation of the Student Activities Manual and the Testing

Program. Thanks to Samantha Pritchard, Editorial Assistant, for attending to many administrative details.

Our thanks also go to Denise Miller, Senior Marketing Manager, for her strong support of *¡Anda!,* creating and coordinating all marketing and promotion for this high beginner program.

Many thanks are also due to Nancy Stevenson, Senior Production Editor, who guided *¡Anda!* through the many stages of production, and to our Art Manager, Gail Cocker. We continue to be indebted to Andrew Lange for the amazing illustrations that translate our vision.

We would like to sincerely thank Mary Rottino, Senior Managing Editor for Product Development, for her unwavering support and commitment to *¡Anda!* and Janice Stangel, Associate Managing Editor, Production, for her support and commitment to the success of *¡Anda!* We also thank our colleagues and students from across the country who inspire us and from whom we learn.

And finally, our love and deepest appreciation to our families for all of their support during this journey: David; John, Jack, and Kate.

Audrey L. Heining-Boynton

Glynis S. Cowell

A WALKING TOUR

I'm Audrey
Heining-Boynton

¡Hola!
¡Bienvenidos!

and I'm
Glynis Cowell

We are the authors of *¡Anda! Curso elemental para estudiantes avanzados* and we were thinking that when you visit a new place, one of the best ways to get to know your new environment quickly is to consult your guidebook before you take the trip! We thought it would be a good idea for you to join us on a "walking tour" of your new Spanish textbook and supplementary materials because we know from experience that language texts have a unique organization that is different from that of other textbooks. . . . They use terminology that you might not be familiar with, and lots of the material is written in the language you don't know yet. So let's get on with the tour!

Here it is!

Curso elemental para estudiantes avanzados

¡Anda!

STOP 1

Do you know what each section of a Spanish textbook is about?
Do you know what you're being asked to read, memorize, and practice, and why? Here's an outline of a typical chapter (Chapters 4–11) in *¡Anda!* followed by some actual chapter sections so that you can see what they look like. And we couldn't resist . . . we made lots of notes for you!

COMUNICACIÓN I

Vocabulary and grammar	(in manageable chunks, as needed, each numbered consecutively throughout the chapter)
Pronunciation practice	(after first vocabulary list, located in your Student Activities Manual [SAM] / MySpanishLab)
Nota cultural box	(brief, contextualized readings, relevant to chapter theme)
¿Cómo andas? I	(first self-assessment box)

COMUNICACIÓN II

Vocabulary and grammar	(in manageable chunks, as needed, each numbered consecutively throughout the chapter)
Nota cultural box	(brief, contextualized readings, relevant to chapter theme)
Escucha	(a focus on listening)
¡Conversemos!	(fun, contextualized activities where you "put it all together" orally)
Escribe	(a focus on writing)
¿Cómo andas? II	(second self-assessment box)

CULTURA

(a focus on one or more Spanish-speaking countries—what the people do, what they make, and how they think)

AMBICIONES SINIESTRAS

(a mystery story told through reading and video)

Y por fin, ¿cómo andas?	(cumulative self-assessment box)
Vocabulario activo	(a two-page list of all of the essential vocabulary of the chapter)

xxvi

CHAPTER OPENER

STOP 2

The chapter title announces the theme of the chapter, which is reflected in the visual on the right.

The questions are designed to get you to think about the topic for the chapter—not to get you to search for THE right answer. Bringing the topic to the forefront of your mind will help you make educated guesses about the meanings of Spanish words. Remember the topic as you work your way through the chapter.

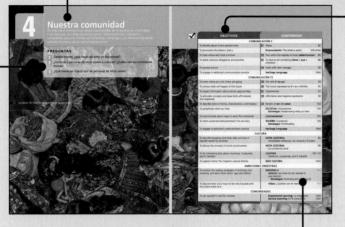

There is a list of goals for the communication, culture, and mystery story sections under *Objetivos*. You will also see other goals such as those for using Spanish outside of your classroom and in the community. Notice how the goals relate to the chapter theme!

The content related to the goals is listed under *Contenidos,* with page numbers. It's in English so that you can understand it clearly!

COMUNICACIÓN

STOP 3

Comunicación I and II are divided into manageable chunks of what you need to learn: vocabulary (the words you need) and grammar (the structures that you use to put the words together). Vocabulary and grammar are two of the most important tools for communication! By the way, we didn't invent this—research indicates that the best presentation of language separates vocabulary and grammar for a manageable progression especially when combined with recycling and reintroduction of previously studied material—more on that later.

The vocabulary sections are numbered consecutively throughout the chapter.

The vocabulary chunks introduce new vocabulary through art.

A lot of the vocabulary is presented without translations so that you can try to figure out the meanings of the Spanish words.

Communicative goals are listed for each vocabulary and grammar section.

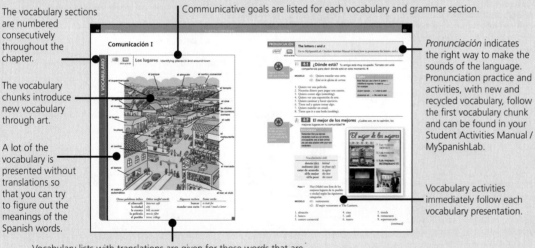

Pronunciación indicates the right way to make the sounds of the language. Pronunciation practice and activities, with new and recycled vocabulary, follow the first vocabulary chunk and can be found in your Student Activities Manual / MySpanishLab.

Vocabulary activities immediately follow each vocabulary presentation.

Vocabulary lists with translations are given for those words that are hard to illustrate and, therefore, hard for you to guess the meanings.

xxvii

GRAMMAR

The grammar sections introduce new grammar concepts.

STOP 4

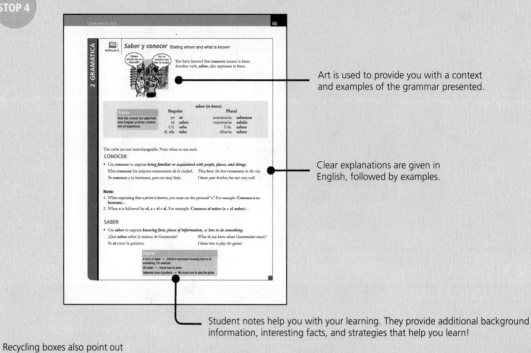

Art is used to provide you with a context and examples of the grammar presented.

Clear explanations are given in English, followed by examples.

Student notes help you with your learning. They provide additional background information, interesting facts, and strategies that help you learn!

Recycling boxes also point out when we have deliberately reused materials from a previous chapter—or from earlier in the same chapter—to help you build upon what you have already studied. Page references are provided so that you can return to that section of the book if you need and/or want to.

Icons indicate when to work in pairs or groups, and also refer you to other resources (e.g., MySpanishLab, audio, corresponding activity numbers in the Student Activities Manual) when you need them.

You'll find a blend of activities that practice individual words and verb forms, as well as activities in which you focus on putting everything together to use the language for purposes of communication.

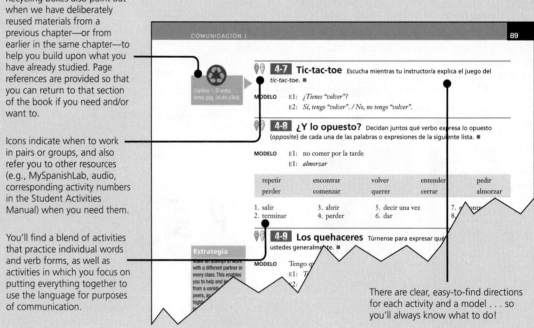

There are clear, easy-to-find directions for each activity and a model . . . so you'll always know what to do!

STOP 5

The second **Comunicación** provides listening comprehension (**Escucha**), more interactive oral activities (**¡Conversemos!**), and writing activities (**Escribe**) prior to the self-assessment check (**¿Cómo andas?**).

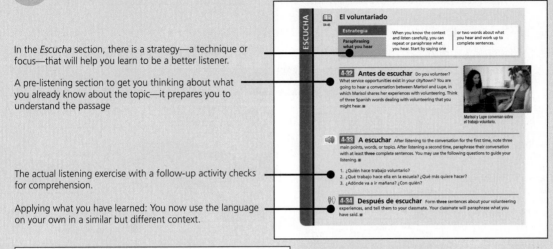

In the *Escucha* section, there is a strategy—a technique or focus—that will help you learn to be a better listener.

A pre-listening section to get you thinking about what you already know about the topic—it prepares you to understand the passage

The actual listening exercise with a follow-up activity checks for comprehension.

Applying what you have learned: You now use the language on your own in a similar but different context.

The *¡Conversemos!* section provides you with even more oral practice. In this section you put together all the grammar and vocabulary you have learned in the current chapter along with opportunities to recycle your Spanish knowledge from previous chapters. These are real-life scenarios in which you interact with a classmate or present on your own.

Escribe is also related to the chapter theme, includes a strategy that will help you learn to be a better writer, and walks you through the writing process with pre-writing and post-writing activities.

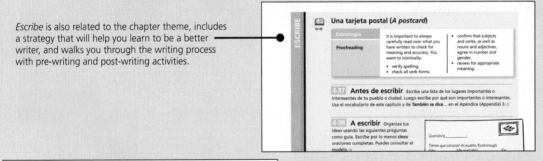

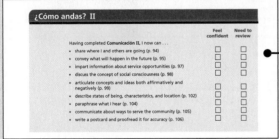

The final activity in each *Comunicación* section is the self-assessment, called *¿Cómo andas?* (How are you doing?). Here you can do a quick check to see how well you have mastered the topics and structures in that section. At the end of the chapter, *Y por fin, ¿cómo andas?* (So, finally, how are you doing?), is the cumulative self-assessment which allows you to determine what you have mastered in that chapter and what you need to review prior to moving on to the next chapter.

CULTURE

Time for a break to grab a cup of **café con leche**?

STOP 6 Between the second **Comunicación** and **Ambiciones siniestras** (the ongoing mystery story) is **Cultura,** designed to provide key facts and high-interest information concerning Spanish-speaking countries and peoples.

You'll find lots of photos with short captions in Spanish.

Read/listen to a native speaker explain a little bit about his or her country . . . what folks do there, what they think, and what they like. We hope you'll want to learn more about these countries and maybe even visit some of them.

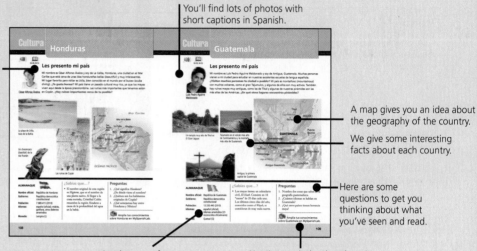

A map gives you an idea about the geography of the country.

We give some interesting facts about each country.

Here are some questions to get you thinking about what you've seen and read.

An almanac of country statistics is given for each country presented.

Here's a reminder that there is more information about this country on MySpanishLab.

Also appearing at pertinent points throughout the *Comunicación* sections are brief cultural presentations (**Nota cultural**) that seamlessly connect the Spanish language with the culture of its speakers. You will find the text of two Nota cultural readings in your eText on MSL.

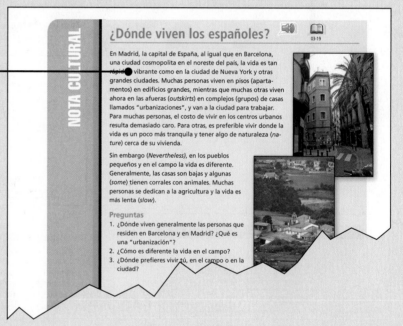

NOTA CULTURAL

¿Dónde viven los españoles?

03-19

En Madrid, la capital de España, al igual que en Barcelona, una ciudad cosmopolita en el noreste del país, la vida es tan rápida y vibrante como en la ciudad de Nueva York y otras grandes ciudades. Muchas personas viven en pisos (apartamentos) en edificios grandes, mientras que muchas otras viven ahora en las afueras (*outskirts*) en complejos (grupos) de casas llamados "urbanizaciones", y van a la ciudad para trabajar. Para muchas personas, el costo de vivir en los centros urbanos resulta demasiado caro. Para otras, es preferible vivir donde la vida es un poco más tranquila y tener algo de naturaleza (*nature*) cerca de su vivienda.

Sin embargo (*Nevertheless*), en los pueblos pequeños y en el campo la vida es diferente. Generalmente, las casas son bajas y algunas (*some*) tienen corrales con animales. Muchas personas se dedican a la agricultura y la vida es más lenta (*slow*).

Preguntas

1. ¿Dónde viven generalmente las personas que residen en Barcelona y en Madrid? ¿Qué es una "urbanización"?
2. ¿Cómo es diferente la vida en el campo?
3. ¿Dónde prefieres vivir tú, en el campo o en la ciudad?

READING AND VIDEO

STOP 7

A mystery story called **Ambiciones siniestras** is presented through readings and videos. It reuses many of the grammar structures and vocabulary words presented in the chapter. In your eText on MSL you will see the following features.

Strategies give you ideas and techniques to help you become a better reader.

The pre-reading activity helps you prepare for what you are about to read. It gets you thinking about topics that will be presented in the story so that the context will help you figure out what is going on.

The reading activity asks you to apply the strategies to the reading.

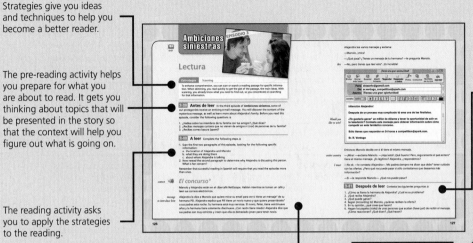

The post-reading activity helps you check your comprehension.

The sequence of activities for the video episode is the same: pre-, during, and post-. The story that was started in the reading is continued in the video. To understand the story, you'll have to read first and then watch the video.

VOCABULARY SUMMARIES

STOP 8

The **Vocabulario activo** section at the end of each chapter is where you have all the new vocabulary from the chapter in one place. The words and phrases are organized by topic, in alphabetical order.

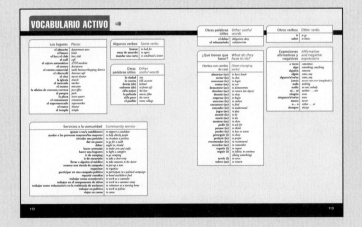

Meet the cast of the video:

Alejandra

Cisco

Manolo

Eduardo

Marisol

Lupe

Sr. Verdugo

SUPPLEMENTARY MATERIALS

STOP 9 Before we finish our walking tour, we want to walk through the many supplements that we provide. Your instructor may have selected some of them to be used in your course.

Student Activities Manual	The Student Activities Manual (SAM for short) contains practice activities that were designed as homework to reinforce what you learn in class. Your pronunciation activities are also found in the SAM as well as ideas on how to practice Spanish in your community. Additionally, there are activities that can be done by all students and/or those who have a Hispanic heritage. Although instructors may use the SAM in different ways, one thing is constant: the SAM is assigned as homework. So we make no assumptions . . . we know you probably won't have an instructor around to answer any questions when you're doing your homework at 2:00 A.M.!
Answer Key for the Student Activities Manual	Some instructors want their students to have this answer key; other instructors don't. We'll sell you the answer key only if your instructor requests it.
Workbooklet	We know that most students don't want to write in their textbooks, but we also know that writing is a great method for helping you to learn Spanish! So, we've created a **Workbooklet,** in which we have reproduced all of the activities in *¡Anda!* where writing is an important part of the activity (e.g., you need to gather information in writing from classmates and then report back to the class orally).
Ambiciones siniestras DVD	The DVD of **Ambiciones siniestras** allows you to watch or rewatch the video at any point during your busy 24/7 life. This is a great tool for helping you practice your comprehension and listening skills!
Audio CD for the student text	This audio CD contains the listening passages that correlate with sections of your textbook. A listening icon appears in your text with a cross-reference to help you locate the audio.
Audio CDs for the Student Activities Manual	These audio CDs contain the listening passages you'll need for some of the activities in the SAM.
Vistas culturales DVD	If you want to listen to native speakers of Spanish and learn more about each of the Spanish-speaking countries, this is the DVD for you!
MySpanishLab	MySpanishLab contains all of the above supplements and more. It's a state-of-the-art learning management system, designed specifically for language learners and teachers. You'll need an access code to get in, but the price is very reasonable, considering how much you receive. For more information, go to www.myspanishlab.com.

SIGNPOSTS!

When traveling, it's always helpful to watch out for the signposts. Here is a list of signposts that we've used in *¡Anda!*

STOP 10

 You will find this first icon in each chapter opener to remind you to take the Readiness Check in MySpanishLab to test your understanding of the English grammar related to the Spanish grammar concepts in the chapter.

 Accompanying the activity instructions, this pair icon indicates that the activity is designed to be completed in groups of two.

 This group icon indicates that the activity is designed to be completed in small groups or as a whole class.

 This icon indicates that an activity involves listening and that the audio is provided for you either on the Companion Website (CW) or, if you are using MySpanishLab, in the eBook.

 Activities that ask you to write have been duplicated in a separate *Workbooklet* so that you don't have to write in your text if you don't want to. This icon indicates that an activity has been reproduced in the *Workbooklet*.

 The activity references below this icon tell you which activities in the Student Activities Manual (SAM) are related to that particular section of the textbook. You may have the printed SAM or the electronic version in MySpanishLab.

 This icon tells you where to find the **Ambiciones siniestras** video: on DVD or in MySpanishLab.

 This icon tells you where to find the **Vistas culturales** video and other cultural resources in MySpanishLab.

 This icon means that the activity that it accompanies requires you to use the Internet.

 This icon indicates that additional resources for pronunciation, practice activities, and Spanish/English tutorials related to the Spanish grammar topic that you are studying are available in MySpanishLab.

 This icon indicates that the activity is only available online and can be found in students' MySpanishLab course.

¡Qué disfruten! Enjoy!

xxxiii

Instructor Resources
- IRM: Syllabi and Lesson Plans

NATIONAL STANDARDS

COMUNICACIÓN
- To greet, say good-bye, and introduce someone (Communication, Cultures, Comparisons, Communities)
- To understand and respond appropriately to basic classroom expressions and requests (Communication)
- To spell in Spanish (Communication)
- To identify cognates (Communication, Comparisons)
- To express the subject pronouns (Communication)
- To use *to be* (Communication)
- To state nationalities (Communication, Connections)
- To count from 0–30 (Communication)
- To state the time (Communication, Comparisons)
- To elicit the date and season (Communication, Comparisons)
- To report the weather (Communication, Comparisons)
- To share personal likes and dislikes (Communication)
- To engage in additional communication practice (Communication)

CULTURA
- To compare and contrast greetings in the Spanish-speaking world and in the United States (Cultures, Comparisons)
- To explain when to use the familiar and formal *you* (Cultures, Comparisons)
- To summarize the diversity of the Spanish-speaking world (Cultures, Comparisons)
- To name the continents and countries where Spanish is spoken (Cultures, Comparisons)
- To explore further the chapter's cultural themes (Cultures)

COMUNIDADES
- To use Spanish in real-life contexts (Communities)

INTRODUCTION to *Chapter opener*

Each chapter has a two-page Chapter opener. These pages help to orient your students regarding the content of the chapter and access any prior knowledge they may have regarding the theme. The intention is for the instructor to spend no more than 5 to 7 minutes on these openers.

PRELIMINAR

A 1 2 3

Para empezar

Welcome to *¡Anda! Curso elemental para estudiantes avanzados.* As you know, learning a language is a skill much like learning to ski or playing an instrument. Developing these skills takes practice and commitment. Since you have had experiences in Spanish or other world languages, *¡Anda! Curso elemental para estudiantes avanzados* will be your guide. It will provide you with key essentials in your journey to become successful communicating in Spanish. This program will support you as you complete the review and study of essential first-year concepts, preparing you for successful study at the intermediate level and beyond.

Spanish is one of the most widely spoken languages in the world. You will find that knowledge of the Spanish language is a useful professional and personal tool.

This *Para empezar* chapter is comprised of four mini chapters: Capítulo Preliminar A, and Capítulos 1, 2 and 3. The vocabulary and grammar in these four short chapters of *Para empezar* are basic concepts of beginning Spanish that will successfully jump-start your one semester introductory Spanish experience.

PREGUNTAS

1 What are some characteristics of successful language learners?
2 Why is it important to study Spanish?
3 How might Spanish play a role in your future?

METHODOLOGY FOR HIGH BEGINNERS: Getting started
In MySpanishLab, you will find a series of pre-assessments created especially for *¡Anda! Curso elemental para estudiantes avanzados*. These assessments were created both for you and your students to determine what your students already know. By using these assessments, you can customize your class, moving quickly beyond concepts your students already know and starting where your students are. These assessments represent the essence of educational philosopher John Dewey, who espoused starting where the learner is. Since our high-beginner learners are not true beginners, we must honor their current linguistic abilities and individualize our programs to meet their needs.

METHODOLOGY: Individualized study plans
In assigning the pre-assessments available in MySpanishLab for every vocabulary and grammar segment, you facilitate the review process for your students. Upon completion of each assessment, the student will either have mastered the concept or will receive an individualized study plan to achieve mastery.

OBJETIVOS	CONTENIDOS	
COMUNICACIÓN - CAPÍTULO PRELIMINAR A		
To greet, say good-bye, and introduce someone	**1** Greetings	4
To understand and respond appropriately to basic classroom expressions and requests	**2** Useful classroom expressions	6
To spell in Spanish	**3** Alphabet	7
To identify cognates	**4** Cognates	8
To express the subject pronouns	**5** Subject pronouns	8
To use *to be*	**6** The verb **ser** (*to be*)	9
To state nationalities	**7** Adjectives of nationality	10
To count from 0–30	**8** Numbers 0–30	11
To state the time	**9** Telling time	12
To elicit the date and season	**10** Days, months, and seasons	14
To report the weather	**11** Weather	16
To share personal likes and dislikes	**12** The verb **gustar** (*to like*)	17
CULTURA		
To compare and contrast greetings in the Spanish-speaking world and in the United States	**NOTA CULTURAL** Cómo se saluda la gente	6
To explain when to use the familiar and formal *you*	**NOTA CULTURAL** ¿Tú o usted?	9
To summarize the diversity of the Spanish-speaking world	**NOTA CULTURAL** Los hispanos	11
To name the continents and countries where Spanish is spoken	**NOTA CULTURAL** El mundo hispano	12
To explore further the chapter's cultural themes	**MÁS CULTURA**	SAM

ANSWERS to *Preguntas*

1. *Answers may include:* Like any skill, successful language learners practice and review on a daily basis. This includes reviewing grammar and vocabulary, using learning and reviewing strategies, being a good listener, completing homework assignments, working with a partner, etc.
2. *Some of the many reasons to study Spanish (or any language in addition to English) include:* increased awareness and appreciation of others; enhancement for any career choice; learning one's native language more thoroughly by acquiring Spanish grammar and vocabulary; learning more about the culture (art, music, cuisine, etc.) firsthand and in-depth, etc.
3. *Answers may include:* travel to a Spanish-speaking country; volunteering in a hospital or other community setting; job requirements, etc.

3

INTRODUCTION to *Objetivos*

The chapter objectives are an organizational tool for you and your students. They allow you to see the main points of the chapter at a glance, and they serve as a way for you to assess whether your students have mastered the main ideas and skills from every chapter. You can use the chapter objectives to preview what the students will be learning in a particular chapter and to review what you taught. Encourage your students to preview the chapter by reading the objectives, and to use the objectives from each chapter when they prepare for an assessment. Also encourage your students to use the *¿Cómo andas?* and *Y por fin, ¿cómo andas?* features to help them self-assess their accomplishments and needs.

EXPANSION for *Preguntas*

Ask your students the following questions:
1. If you could speak fluent Spanish, how would your life change?
2. How could Spanish be relevant for you now?

SUGGESTION for *Chapter opener*

You may wish to get a paper copy of the ADFL (MLA) brochure *Why Learn Another Language?* or have students download a PDF version from the MLA web site. Lead a discussion of the ways students will use Spanish in their careers, communities, personal growth, and travel.

METHODOLOGY FOR HIGH BEGINNERS: Individualizing instruction

At the beginning of the semester, it is always crucial to determine what Spanish knowledge your students already possess. Some of you may ascertain that with only three or four days of review your students can move directly into Chapter 4. Within those days of quick review, students will also read and then view the first three episodes of *Ambiciones siniestras*, a high-interest, i+1 engaging mystery that incorporates the vocabulary and grammar they have learned in the chapters.

THE NATIONAL STANDARDS
National Standards: Standards for Foreign Language Learning in the 21st Century
¡Anda! Curso elemental is committed to and based on the *Standards for Foreign Language Learning in the 21st Century*. These national foreign language standards are sometimes referred to as *the 5 Cs*, and they represent five goal areas: Communication, Cultures, Connections, Comparisons, and Communities. Each goal area has corresponding standards, which in turn promote attainment of the specific goal. The beginning of each chapter will highlight how the standards underlying each of the 5 Cs will be addressed in that chapter of the text, as well as in the *Student Activities Manual*. In particular, the standards and goals highlighted throughout the textbook are taken from the *Standards for Learning Spanish*. These are language-specific standards that reflect the goals as they relate to the teaching and learning of Spanish. Throughout the rest of *¡Anda! Curso elemental,* we will refer to the standards as the National Standards.

21ST CENTURY SKILLS • DEFINITION
The Partnership for 21st Century Skills (P21) is a multidisciplinary project. The group, housed in Washington, D.C., has brought together the key national organizations representing the core academic subjects. The American Council on the Teaching of Foreign Languages (ACTFL) collaborated for a year developing the 21st Century Skills Map. The map, created by hundreds of world language educators, reflects the integration of languages and the necessary skills for a successful 21st century citizen.

Instructor Resources
• Textbook images, PPT, Extra Activities

INTRODUCTION to *Comunicación*

The *Comunicación* section is designed to foster interaction and communication using the target language. Each *Comunicación* section will include objectives that identify what a student will be able to do at the end of the section. Communication is a multifaceted process. There are 3 communicative modes highlighted in the National Standards: interpersonal, interpretive, and presentational. The Communication Goal of the *Standards for Learning Spanish* (*Communicate in Spanish*) has three corresponding standards, and each standard corresponds to a communicative mode. Standard 1.1 (the interpersonal mode) states that "Students engage in conversations, provide and obtain information, express feelings and emotions, and exchange opinions" (p. 434). Standard 1.2 (the interpretive mode) states that "Students understand and interpret written Spanish on a variety of topics" (p. 434). Standard 1.3 (the presentational mode) states that "Students present information, concepts, and ideas in Spanish to an audience of listeners or readers on a variety of topics" (p. 434). *¡Anda! Curso elemental* provides activities that use each communicative mode.

SECTION GOALS for *Comunicación*

By the end of the *Comunicación* section, students will be able to:
• greet others and talk about how they are feeling.
• begin and end conversations politely.
• introduce themselves and others.
• compare how to greet people in the Spanish-speaking world and in the United States.
• understand and respond appropriately to basic classroom expressions and requests.
• spell in Spanish.
• distinguish between the sounds each letter makes and sound out new words.
• recognize cognates.
• understand when to use *tú* and when to use *usted*.
• match the subject pronouns with the appropriate forms of the verb *ser*.
• describe nationalities using *ser*.
• summarize the diversity of the Spanish-speaking world.
• count from 0 to 30.
• name the continents and countries where Spanish is spoken.
• tell time using expressions for A.M. and P.M.
• identify the months and the seasons and describe the weather in a particular month, season, or region.
• express basic likes and dislikes using *gustar*.

---

1 VOCABULARIO

Comunicación
Capítulo Preliminar A

Estrategia

For a complete list of vocabulary for *Para empezar*, refer to the Vocabulary summary beginning on page 70. You will notice that all of the vocabulary for *Capítulos Preliminar A, 1, 2* and *3* are there for you to consult.

¡Hola! eText 4 A-01 to A-04

Saludos, despedidas y presentaciones
Greeting, saying good-bye, and introducing someone

Los saludos	Greetings
¡Hola!	Hi! Hello!
Buenos días.	Good morning.
Buenas tardes.	Good afternoon.
Buenas noches.	Good evening; Good night.
¿Cómo estás?	How are you? (familiar)
¿Cómo está usted?	How are you? (formal)
¿Qué tal?	How's it going?
Más o menos.	So-so.
Regular.	Okay.
Bien, gracias.	Fine, thanks.
Bastante bien.	Just fine.
Muy bien.	Really well.
¿Y tú?	And you? (familiar)
¿Y usted?	And you? (formal)

Las despedidas	Farewells
Adiós.	Good-bye.
Chao.	Bye.
Hasta luego.	See you later.
Hasta mañana.	See you tomorrow.
Hasta pronto.	See you soon.

Las presentaciones	Introductions
¿Cómo te llamas?	What is your name? (familiar)
¿Cómo se llama usted?	What is your name? (formal)
Me llamo…	My name is . . .
Soy…	I am . . .
Mucho gusto.	Nice to meet you.
Encantado/Encantada.	Pleased to meet you.
Igualmente.	Likewise.
Quiero presentarte a…	I would like to introduce you to . . . (familiar)
Quiero presentarle a…	I would like to introduce you to . . . (formal)

METHODOLOGY FOR HIGH BEGINNERS: Building Community in the Classroom

Even though you may determine that your class is linguistically beyond *Preliminar A* of *Para empezar*, you will still want to build community within your classroom. By building community from the inception of the semester, your students will gain confidence to interact orally with their classmates. Research affirms that students learn best from students, and they do so when they are in a non-threatening atmosphere. An important activity that you can

do to help facilitate building community in your classroom is A-5. Students have the opportunity to introduce themselves to each other, and thus start the process of them feeling comfortable working with each other. After they spend a minute with one group of 5 students, have them change groups to meet another 5 students. Then change the groups again until all students have introduced themselves to each other.

- The expressions **¿Cómo te llamas?** and **¿Cómo se llama usted?** both mean *What is your name?* but the former is used among students and other peers (referred to as *familiar*). You will learn about the differences between these *familiar* and *formal* forms later in this chapter. Note that **Encantado** is said by a male, and **Encantada** is said by a female.
- Spanish uses special punctuation to signal a question or an exclamation. An upside-down question mark begins a question and an upside-down exclamation mark begins an exclamation, as in **¿Cómo te llamas?** and **¡Hola!**

Estrategia

Activities with the *e* icon can be found in your MySpanishLab course. The activities provide practice as you review, develop, and refine your Spanish knowledge and abilities. These activities to be done online, outside of class help prepare you for the pair and group activities that will take place during your class.

e **A-1** Saludos y despedidas

e **A-2** ¡Hola! ¿Qué tal?

e **A-3** ¿Cómo te llamas?

e **A-4** Quiero presentarte a…

Estrategia

This icon signifies that you will be working with a group of students. Working with your classmates affords you extra practice speaking Spanish.

A-5 **Una fiesta** Imagine that you are at a party. In groups of five, introduce [2:00] yourselves to each other. Use the model as a guide. ■

MODELO   AMY: *Hola, ¿qué tal? Soy Amy.*
          ORLANDO: *Hola, Amy. Soy Orlando. ¿Cómo estás?*
          AMY: *Muy bien, Orlando. ¿Y tú?*
          ORLANDO: *Bien, gracias. Amy, quiero presentarte a Tom.*
          TOM: *Encantado.*
          E4:   *…*

Instructor Resources
- PPT, Extra Activities

NATIONAL STANDARDS
Communication
Communication is the first "C" of the National Standards. Communication encompasses all aspects of interaction, including speaking, listening, reading, and writing. Vocabulary is essential to communicating and *¡Anda!* will present high-frequency vocabulary throughout the program.

METHODOLOGY: Students taking responsibility
While we always hope that students take responsibility for their learning, it is especially critical in the high-beginner course. These students come from a variety of language-learning backgrounds, and what they know and don't know varies greatly. Encourage your students to prepare well for class by completing all assignments and spending necessary study time to arrive ready to actively participate in class. This will allow you to move efficiently and effectively through *Para empezar* and beyond.

INTRODUCTION to
Vocabulario Presentations
Vocabulary is presented in what we refer to as *chunks*. The words are always presented via a stimulating and contextualized drawing as a context. The drawings can assist you in the presentation, review, and reinforcement of the vocabulary. All of these drawings are available for download from MySpanish Lab or the Instructors Resource Center (IRC). There are also additional activities in the *Extra Activities* folder under Instructor Resources.

NOTE for
Heritage Language Learners
In your classes you may have heritage language learners. Unlike bilingual Spanish-English speakers, heritage language learners have a greater command of speaking and listening skills, but their writing and reading skills may not match their level of conversational and listening skills. *¡Anda!* will provide activities and suggestions for the heritage language learners in the *Student Activities Manual.*

METHODOLOGY: Maximizing asynchronous learning
MySpanishLab can be an invaluable tool for the advanced beginner course, and when used efficiently, will allow instructors to reduce greatly the amount of time spent actively teaching the basic vocabulary topics and grammar concepts students need to review quickly at the beginning of the course and beyond.

NOTE for *Los saludos*
You will find additional greetings in the *También se dice…* section in Appendix 3.

METHODOLOGY • Lesson Planning
We have provided suggested amounts of time for you to devote to each in-class activity. It is not appropriate to redo all of the activities that students have completed with partners. Explain to students that they need to help each other and to self-correct within their small groups.

METHODOLOGY • Pair Work
The authors of *¡Anda!* strongly believe in the research that says "students learn best from students." Hence, there is an abundance of pair and group activities in *¡Anda!*. For this chapter, simply have students turn to a partner.

HERITAGE LANGUAGE LEARNERS
Ask your heritage language learners if there are any other greetings they use at home. See if the greetings vary by country or region.

METHODOLOGY • Timing Activities

You will have noted that each activity in the Annotated Instructors' Edition has a time clock. These clocks are suggestions of how long to spend on each activity. These are approximations, as you will have some students progress more quickly and others more slowly. You will also have classes in which you assign group activities to be completed as a whole, and will not need additional time for creating pairs. Nor will all activities necessitate a direct follow-up. Use these as a guide for your lesson planning and classroom activities. They are meant to be helpful, not prescriptive. Also remember never to wait until all students have completed all items of an activity. Rather, consider assigning several activities at once so that partners who finish one activity move on to the next.

INTRODUCTION to *Nota cultural boxes*

Each regular chapter has two *Nota cultural* boxes, available only online in MySpanishLab. They are meant to be brief and are always contextualized and relevant to the theme of the chapter.

METHODOLOGY • Planning Ahead

We recommend assigning *all* culture sections to be read in advance. We also recommend assigning students to read *all* the grammar explanations before class since they are written in a very clear, concise fashion. The instructor's role then becomes that of clarifying or reviewing any points that the students read in advance.

EXPANSION for *Nota cultural* (Online)

Additional questions to ask your students are:
1. How do your male friends greet your female friends?
2. How do your parents greet their friends?
3. How do you greet your family members?

INTRODUCTION to *Chunks / Chunking*

The concept of *chunks* of material and *chunking* of material is a major notion that drove the development of ¡Anda! Curso elemental. Learning theory and the subsequent research of literally thousands of studies on general learning of any and all subject areas confirm that students learn best when information is grouped into smaller chunks. Giving students *all* of the rules and *all* of the ways to express an idea

---

NOTA CULTURAL

 ¡Hola!
eText 7   A-05 to A-07

Cómo se saluda la gente
NOTE for *Nota cultural*
See eText pg. 7 for complete *Nota cultural* reading and *Preguntas*.

Estrategia
The *¡Hola!* icon indicates that the reading for *Nota cultural* can be found in the eText in your MySpanishLab course. The number indicates the page for the cultural information and activity.

---

2 VOCABULARIO

 ¡Hola!
eText 8   A-08 to A-10

Expresiones útiles para la clase
Understanding and responding appropriately to basic classroom expressions and requests

The following list provides useful expressions that you and your instructor will use frequently.

Preguntas y respuestas	*Questions and answers*	Expresiones de cortesía	*Polite expressions*
¿Cómo?	*What? How?*	**De nada.**	*You're welcome.*
¿Cómo se dice... en español?	*How do you say . . . in Spanish?*	**Gracias.**	*Thank you.*
¿Cómo se escribe... en español?	*How do you write . . . in Spanish?*	**Por favor.**	*Please.*
¿Qué significa?	*What does it mean?*		*Classroom instructions (commands)*
¿Quién?	*Who?*	**Mandatos para la clase**	
¿Qué es esto?	*What is this?*	**Abra(n) el libro en la página...**	*Open your book to page . . .*
Comprendo.	*I understand.*	**Cierre(n) el/los libro/s.**	*Close your book/s.*
No comprendo.	*I don't understand.*	**Conteste(n).**	*Answer.*
Lo sé.	*I know.*	**Escriba(n).**	*Write.*
No lo sé.	*I don't know.*	**Escuche(n).**	*Listen.*
Sí.	*Yes.*	**Lea(n).**	*Read.*
No.	*No.*	**Repita(n).**	*Repeat.*
		Vaya(n) a la pizarra.	*Go to the board.*

In Spanish, commands can have two forms. The singular form (**abra, cierre, conteste,** etc.) is directed to one person, while the plural form (those ending in **-n: abran, cierren, contesten,** etc.) is used with more than one person.

---

can be overwhelming. When information is not chunked, learners tend to shut down, since they find the amount of information that needs to be learned overwhelming. Hence, chunking is the best way to insure that students see success and progress and are motivated to learn more.

METHODOLOGY • Teaching Vocabulary

We have attempted to streamline the vocabulary. A variety of words and expressions can become confusing for some students. For example, at this time, we are only introducing *De nada* rather than including expressions such as *No hay de que.* If you wish to include additional vocabulary, please do so.

METHODOLOGY • Teaching Commands

It is intentional that we have introduced lexically only the *usted/ustedes* commands. The similarity in their endings makes it a more streamlined choice since the goal at this stage is to simplify language and to jump start your students, which aids greatly in motivation.

METHODOLOGY • Use of Commands

You will note that at this very early point in the learning process only the formal commands are presented lexically. If you prefer to use familiar commands, please do so. A formal presentation of commands will appear in *Capítulo 10.*

🔑 **Instructor Resources**
• PPT, Extra Activities

TPR Activity for *Expresiones útiles para la clase*
You can use Total Physical Response (TPR) with some of the classroom expressions, e.g., *abra el libro, cierre el libro*. Students can also act out expressions such as *escuchen, escriban, lean, vaya(n) a la pizarra*, etc.

NOTE on *El alfabeto*
In December, 2010, the Real Academia Española issued some changes to the alphabet. Among the changes/additions to the language, the RAE states that *ch, ll,* and *rr* are no longer considered letters. They have also added *ye* for the letter *y*.

SUGGESTION for *El alfabeto*
Make flashcards for each letter of the alphabet. Read the alphabet aloud and have the students repeat each letter. Have the students recite the alphabet without your assistance. Then have your students form a circle. Pass out a letter to each member of the class, and have them practice pronouncing each letter A–Z. As they do, they hold up the cards for the class to see. Then practice Z–A (reverse alphabetical order). This requires them to pay attention, and they learn the sounds at the same time.

EXPANSION for *El alfabeto*
For extra practice, you can write additional words on the board for your students to spell. Encourage your students to ask, *¿Qué significa?, ¿Qué es…?*

---

e **A-6** **Práctica**

e **A-7** **Más práctica**

---

iHola! eText 9   A-11 to A-16

El alfabeto   Spelling in Spanish

The Spanish alphabet is quite similar to the English alphabet except in the ways the letters are pronounced. Learning the proper pronunciation of the individual letters in Spanish will help you pronounce new words and phrases.

3 GRAMÁTICA | 2:00

Estrategia

For a summary of this and all of the grammar points, go to the eText or refer to *Capítulo Preliminar A* in the Grammar summary at the end of *Para empezar*, beginning on page 74. You will also note that all of the grammar points for mini chapters 1, 2, and 3 are referenced there to assist you.

LETTER	LETTER NAME	EXAMPLES	LETTER	LETTER NAME	EXAMPLES
a	a	adiós	ñ	eñe	mañana
b	be	buenos	o	o	cómo
c	ce	clase	p	pe	por favor
d	de	día	q	cu	qué
e	e	español	r	ere	señora
f	efe	por favor	s	ese	saludos
g	ge	luego	t	te	tarde
h	hache	hola	u	u	usted
i	i	señorita	v	uve	nueve
j	jota	julio	w	doble ve o uve doble	Washington
k	ka	kilómetro	x	equis	examen
l	ele	luego	y	ye o i griega	yo
m	eme	madre	z	zeta	pizarra
n	ene	noche			

---

e **A-8** **En español**

---

e **A-9** **¿Qué es esto?**

Instructor Resources
• Textbook images, PPT, Extra Activities

NATIONAL STANDARDS
Comparisons
The fourth goal area of the National Standards is Comparisons. The Comparisons Goal is to "Develop Insight into the Nature of Language and Culture." This goal has two corresponding standards: Standards 4.1 and 4.2. In the *Standards for Learning Spanish*, Standard 4.1 states that "Students demonstrate understanding of the nature of language through comparisons between Spanish and English" (p. 434). Standard 4.2 states that "Students demonstrate understanding of the concept of culture through comparisons between Hispanic cultures and their own" (p. 434). Language and culture are interconnected, and the standards under Goal Four promote awareness about the similarities and differences between Spanish and English.

INTRODUCTION to
Gramática Presentations
Grammar is introduced, as is vocabulary, in *chunks:* small, manageable amounts of information. The presentations are always in English and employ either deductive or inductive approaches. A very conscious effort has been made to present only the most basic information on each topic and not to burden beginning Spanish students with exceptions to the rules. The more sophisticated nuances of the language are reserved for intermediate levels and beyond. The goal is to build learners' confidence that Spanish is manageable and that they can communicate in the language. English and Spanish tutorials are also available on MySpanishLab to provide students with additional support.

NOTE for *Los pronombres personales*
¡Anda! I will present, but not actively practice, the *vosotros* forms. If you wish to practice these forms, please add them to your classroom drills or to any of the exercises in this program.

METHODOLOGY • Teaching Concepts at the Point of Need
Our philosophy is to provide students with grammatical information they need to be successful at the moment, and not to overburden them. Hence, we delay the explanation of *it* until gender is introduced and they have noun subjects (in addition to people) to practice. E.g., *El libro es aburrido. No, es interesante.*

---

4 VOCABULARIO

1:00 | ¡Hola! eText 10 | A-17 to A-19 |

Los cognados Identifying cognates

Cognados, or *cognates*, are words that are similar in form and meaning to their English equivalents. As you learn Spanish you will discover many cognates. Can you guess the meanings of the following words?

    inteligente   **septiembre**   **familia**   **universidad**

---

e **A-10 Práctica**

---

e **A-11 ¿Hablas español?**

---

5 GRAMÁTICA

4:00 | ¡Hola! eText 11 | A-20 to A-21

Los pronombres personales
Expressing the subject pronouns

NOTA CULTURAL

 ¡Hola! eText 12   📖 A-22 to A-25   **¿Tú o usted?**

NOTE for *Nota cultural*
See eText pg. 12 for complete *Nota cultural* reading and *Preguntas*.

e **A-12** **¿Cómo se dice?**

e **A-13** **¿Tú o usted?**

3:00

6 GRAMÁTICA

 ¡Hola! eText 13   📖 A-26 to A-31   **El verbo *ser*** Using *to be*

ser (*to be*)					
Singular			**Plural**		
yo	**soy**	*I am*	nosotros/as	**somos**	*we are*
tú	**eres**	*you are*	vosotros/as	**sois**	*you are*
Ud.	**es**	*you are*	Uds.	**son**	*you are*
él, ella	**es**	*he/she is*	ellos/as	**son**	*they are*

e **A-14** **Vamos a practicar**

e **A-15** **"Ser o no ser... "**

At this point in the textbook, you can explain the use of *you all* as a way to express the plural of *you*.

NOTE for *El verbo ser*
As we instructors know, the pronoun and the concept *it* is not identical in Spanish and English. In many ways, it is an advanced structural concept. The *¡Anda! Curso elemental* recommendation would be the simple approach, which would be to tell beginning students that the subject pronoun *it* does not have an equivalent in Spanish.

 Instructor Resources
• PPT, Extra Activities

NOTE for *Nota cultural* (Online)
You may wish to explain to your students that in some Spanish-speaking countries, parents and children address each other using *usted*. Grandchildren often use *usted* with grandparents, even when grandparents use *tú* with them.

EXPANSION for *Nota cultural* (Online)
Additional questions to ask your students are:
1. What are some regional language differences in the United States? What differences in language occur between the United States and England? What differences in language occur between the United States and Canada? Can the British, Canadians, and Americans understand each other?
2. In the past century, what new words have been added to English?
3. What are some English words that have changed in meaning?

(**Answers:** 1. *soda* vs. *pop* vs. *Coke; lift* vs. *elevator; water fountain* vs. *bubbler*. Yes, the British, Canadians, and Americans can understand each other. 2. Words dealing with transportation, electronics, and household appliances, like *airplane, jet, car, truck, van, television, video recorder, vacuum cleaner, microwave oven*, etc. 3. *cool, gay*, etc.)

NOTE for *Los pronombres personales*
In this section, usage is mechanical, and students will have ample opportunities to use the pronouns in context in the coming activities.

NOTE for *El verbo ser*
The verb *ser* is the first verb presented in this chapter. Accordingly, the verb *to be* is presented in English with its corresponding subject pronouns. Note that *usted* and *ustedes* have been separated from the other third-person singular and plural subject pronouns. This has been done throughout *¡Anda!* for clarity. You will also note that in the verb chart for *to be*, the authors have used the words *you all* in the translation of *vosotros, vosotras*, and *Uds.* to indicate that this is the plural of the word *you*.

🗝 **Instructor Resources**
• Extra Activities

METHODOLOGY • Beginning Language Learning
The philosophy of *¡Anda!* is to have beginning language learners engage in meaningful communication as soon as possible. The adjectives of nationality should provide an overview of the nationalities represented in your classes so that students can say *Soy…* or so that they can speak about their friends. Please adapt this list as needed.

SUGGESTION for *Los adjetivos de nacionalidad*
You may wish to share additional adjectives of nationality from other Spanish-speaking countries. Or perhaps you have a diverse group of international students and you could introduce their nationalities. Also, share other nationalities with students that they may want to know that aren't listed. You will also find additional adjectives of nationality in the *También se dice…* section in *Appendix 3.*

NATIONAL STANDARDS
Connections
Goal 3 of the National Standards is Connections. The *Standards for Learning Spanish* defines this goal as "Connect with Other Disciplines and Acquire Information." There are 2 standards that define this goal: Standards 3.1 and 3.2. Standard 3.1 states that "Students reinforce and further their knowledge of other disciplines through Spanish." Standard 3.2 states that "Students acquire information and recognize distinctive viewpoints that are only available through the Spanish language and its cultures." In *¡Anda! Curso elemental,* we will provide opportunities for including other disciplines and showing your students how language can be combined with any life aspiration.

NOTE for *Los adjetivos de nacionalidad*
Adjective agreement and making nouns plural are presented in detail in *Capítulo 1.* Word stress and rules on written accents will be presented in *Capítulo 2* on MySpanishLab and in the *Student Activities Manual.*

NOTE for *Los adjetivos de nacionalidad*
You may wish to explain to students that *canadiense* and *estadounidense* are both masculine and feminine.

---

7 VOCABULARIO

[2:00]   ¡Hola! eText 14   📖 A-32 to A-34

Los adjetivos de nacionalidad Stating nationalities

> Me llamo Sonia. Soy puertorriqueña.

> Encantado. Yo soy John. Soy estadounidense.

Nacionalidad	Estudiantes		Nacionalidad	Estudiantes
alemán	Hans		**francés**	Jean-Paul
alemana	Ingrid		**francesa**	Brigitte
canadiense	Jacques/Alice		**inglés**	James
chino	Tsong		**inglesa**	Diana
china	Xue Lan		**japonés**	Tabo
cubano	Javier		**japonesa**	Yasu
cubana	Pilar		**mexicano**	Manuel
español	Rodrigo		**mexicana**	Milagros
española	Guadalupe		**nigeriano**	Yena
estadounidense	John/Kate		**nigeriana**	Ngidaha
(norteamericano/a)			**puertorriqueño**	Ernesto
			puertorriqueña	Sonia

EXPANSION for *Los adjetivos de nacionalidad*
If you have a diverse student population, you may wish to practice having students say *Me llamo… Soy* (nationality). *¿Y tú? Yo soy…* or bring in a map of the world and have students mark their countries of origin on the map. The class can take turns guessing: *¿Quién es de…?* and answering _____ *es de…*

In Spanish:

- adjectives of nationality are not capitalized unless one is the first word in a sentence.
- most adjectives of nationality have a form for males, and a slightly different one for females. (You will learn more about this in **Capítulo 1.** For now, simply note the differences.)
- when referring to more than one individual, you make the adjectives plural by adding either an **-s** or an **-es.** (Again, in **Capítulo 1** you will formally learn more about forming plural words.)
- some adjectives of nationality have a written accent mark in the masculine form, but not in the feminine, like **inglés/inglesa** and **francés/francesa.** For example: **Mi papá es** *inglés* **y mi mamá es** *francesa*.

e **A-16** ¿Cuál es tu nacionalidad?

e **A-17** ¿Qué son?

NOTA CULTURAL

¡Hola!   eText 16   A-35   **Los hispanos**

NOTE for *Nota cultural*
See eText pg. 16 for complete *Nota cultural* reading and *Preguntas*.

8 VOCABULARIO

1:00

¡Hola!   eText 16   A-36 to A-39   **Los números 0–30**   Counting from 0–30

0	cero	7	siete	13	trece	19	diecinueve	25	veinticinco
1	uno	8	ocho	14	catorce	20	veinte	26	veintiséis
2	dos	9	nueve	15	quince	21	veintiuno	27	veintisiete
3	tres	10	diez	16	dieciséis	22	veintidós	28	veintiocho
4	cuatro	11	once	17	diecisiete	23	veintitrés	29	veintinueve
5	cinco	12	doce	18	dieciocho	24	veinticuatro	30	treinta
6	seis								

e **A-18** ¿Qué número?

e **A-19** ¿Cuál es la secuencia?

Instructor Resources
- PPT, Extra Activities

CULTURAL BACKGROUND for *Nota cultural* **(Online)**
- Regarding the controversy surrounding the terms *Hispanic* and *Latino,* refer to the results of a *Time* magazine survey, cited in the August 13, 2005, article: "The 25 Most Influential Hispanics in America." The results of the poll of Hispanic adults reported 42% said they choose to be called Hispanic, only 17% said Latino and 34% had no particular preference (p. 43).
- *Latino* refers to Latin as an origin: Spanish, French, Portuguese, Italian, and Romanian are Latin-derived languages.

HERITAGE LANGUAGE LEARNERS
Most heritage language learners will know the information in this chapter, but they may have interesting comments to share regarding their experiences using the language, such as with *tú* and *usted*.

SUGGESTION for *Nota cultural* **(Online)**
Using a map, review the countries that comprise Latin America. Bring in photos of famous Hispanic personalities or use the web to show celebrities' personal fan sites. Find out the origin of each celebrity. Ask the students to determine whether their favorite celebrity is Hispanic or Latino, and why they used the chosen term.

EXPANSION for *Los números*
Create basic math problems so your students can practice *son,* e.g., *Tres más tres son seis.*

Instructor Resources
• Extra Activities

NATIONAL STANDARDS

Cultures

Goal 2 of the *Standards for Foreign Language Learning* is Cultures. The Cultures Goal is to "Gain Knowledge and Understanding of Spanish-Speaking Cultures," and it is defined by 2 standards. Standard 2.1 of the *Standards for Learning Spanish* states that "Students demonstrate an understanding of the relationship between the practices and perspectives of Hispanic cultures." Standard 2.2 states that "Students demonstrate an understanding of the relationship between the products and perspectives of Hispanic cultures." This goal encompasses and embraces the similarities and differences between the many cultures that share a common language.

Note the plural use of the word. It is meant, in the case of Spanish, for us as instructors to guide and encourage our students to learn about and embrace the plurality of the Spanish-speaking world. The goals of the accompanying questions are to have students practice the numbers, and to become familiar with the countries where Spanish is spoken.

CULTURAL EXPANSION for
Nota cultural **(Online)**

Spanish is an official language in the countries listed in the chart with the reading.

Spanish is a major second language, and Spanish speakers are a sizable minority of up to 30% in Andorra, Aruba, Belize, Brazil, Gibraltar (British territory in the Iberian Peninsula), the Netherlands Antilles, Trinidad and Tobago, the United States, and the Virgin Islands.

ANSWERS to *Nota cultural* (Online)

1. América del Norte: 2 (México y Estados Unidos); Centroamérica: 6 (Costa Rica, El Salvador, Guatemala, Honduras, Nicaragua y Panamá); El Caribe: 3 (Cuba, Puerto Rico y La República Dominicana); América del Sur: 9 (Argentina, Bolivia, Chile, Colombia, Ecuador, Paraguay, Perú, Uruguay y Venezuela); Europa: 1 (España); África: 1 (Guinea Ecuatorial); en total, 22 países.
2. 4: América del Norte, América del Sur, Europa y África.
3. 7: Argentina, Colombia, Perú, Venezuela—América del Sur; España—Europa; Estados Unidos, México—América del Norte.

EXPANSION for *Nota cultural* (Online)

Additional questions to ask your students are:

1. Where are the majority of the Spanish-speaking countries located?

NOTA CULTURAL

eText 17   A-40 to A-41   **El mundo hispano**

NOTE for *Nota cultural*
See eText pg. 17 for complete *Nota cultural* reading and *Preguntas*.

[3:00]   9 VOCABULARIO   eText 18   A-42 to A-44   ## La hora   Stating the time

Es (la) medianoche.   Es (el) mediodía.   Es la una.   Son las diez y cinco.

Son las tres y cuarto.   Son las seis y media.   Son las nueve menos cuarto.   Son las diez menos veinticinco.

La hora	Telling time		
¿Qué hora es?	*What time is it?*	...de la noche	*. . . in the evening, at night*
Es la una. / Son las...	*It's one o'clock. / It's . . . o'clock.*	la medianoche	*midnight*
¿A qué hora... ?	*At what time . . . ?*	el mediodía	*noon*
A la... / A las...	*At . . . o'clock.*	menos cinco	*five minutes to the hour*
...de la mañana	*. . . in the morning*	y cinco	*five minutes after the hour*
...de la tarde	*. . . in the afternoon, early evening*		

---

2. In which country did the Spanish language originate?
3. How did the Spanish language spread to the Americas (North, Central, and South) as well as to Africa?

(**Answers:** 1. Sudamérica, 2. España, 3. Exploration by individuals such as Cristobal Colón, Ponce de León, Hernán Cortez, etc.)

CULTURAL BACKGROUND for *Nota cultural* (Online)

Through numerous conquests, the Spanish Empire and the Spanish language expanded to various parts of the world, including Equatorial Guinea and the Philippines. The Spaniards named the Philippines after King Phillip II.

SUGGESTION for *Nota cultural* (Online)

Lead a discussion with your students regarding the number of Spanish-speaking countries across the world with your students. Questions could include: *Why are there so many countries whose official language is Spanish? What are other languages spoken in those countries?* To discover the current numbers of Spanish speakers worldwide, check web sites such as www.actfl.org. Also, to find out other names of indigenous languages spoken in Spanish-speaking countries, search the particular country you are interested in and type "languages." You could also ask a student to research how many Spanish speakers are in the United States.

When telling time in Spanish:

- use **Es la…** to say times between 1:00 and 1:59.
- use **Son las…** to say times *except* between 1:00 and 1:59.
- use **A la…** or **A las…** to say *at* what time.
- use **la** with **una** (**a la una**) for hours between 1:00 and 1:59.
- use **las** for hours greater than *one* (**a las ocho**).
- use the expressions **mediodía** and **medianoche** to say *noon* and *midnight*.
- **de la tarde** tends to mean from noon until 7:00 or 8:00 P.M.
- **cuarto** and **media** are equivalent to the English expressions *quarter* (fifteen minutes) and *half* (thirty minutes). **Cuarto** and **media** are interchangeable with the numbers **quince** and **treinta**.
- use **y** for times that are before and up to the half-hour mark.
- use **menos** for times that are beyond the half-hour mark.

e **A-20** **¿Qué hora es?**

A-21 **Tu horario** Think about your daily schedule. Then, take turns asking and telling your partner at what times you do the following activities. ■

MODELO E1: *¿A qué hora?*
        E2: *a la una y media*

1.
2.
3.
4.

5.
6.
7.
8.

A-22 **¿Y el fin de semana?** What is your schedule for the weekend? Take turns telling your partner at what times you plan to do the activities from **A-21** this coming weekend. ■

Instructor Resources
- PPT, Extra Activities

SUGGESTION for *La hora*
You may wish to tell your students that in some countries, a typical way to ask for the time is: *¿Qué hora tienes?* A typical response could be: *Faltan… para las siete.* You may also wish to mention the use of 24-hour time in airports, train and bus stations, and schedules for movie, musical, and theater productions.

NOTE for *La hora*
You may wish to point out that some Spanish speakers say *un cuarto para,* rather than *menos,* to state the time.

METHODOLOGY for *La hora*
You may wish to explain to your students that the words in parentheses are optional.

NOTE for A-21
Note that we suggest having Student 1 simply ask, *¿A qué hora?* There is no need to translate to English. Student 1's question is used as a prompt for Student 2 and gives your students practice with asking the time.

METHODOLOGY • Content Taught in *Capítulo Preliminar A*
As mentioned previously, this chapter is meant to jump-start learners. Some students will not be true beginners, and so this vocabulary may be a review for them. For those who are learning this material for the first time, it will be recycled throughout the rest of the program.

METHODOLOGY: Maximizing instruction
The majority of your students are actively reviewing outside of class, allowing you to assess mastery rapidly in class with check activities like A-22. Address any common doubts quickly and invite individuals who appear to need more clarification to see you after class or to attend office hours.

Instructor Resources
- Textbook images, PPT, Extra Activities

NOTE for *Los días, los meses y las estaciones*
This presentation is based on the northern hemisphere. You may wish to point out to your students that the seasons are reversed in the southern hemisphere.

SUGGESTION for *Los días, los meses y las estaciones*
Have students play Ping-Pong with the days and months. This fast-paced game consists of partners taking turns saying the days and months quickly (back and forth) in order.

MODELO
E1:   *lunes*
E2:   *martes*
E1:   *miércoles*
E2:   *jueves*

10 VOCABULARIO

¡Hola!   eText 20   A-45 to A-51   2:00

Los días, los meses y las estaciones
Eliciting the date and season

Los meses y las estaciones (*Months and seasons*)

la primavera

marzo, abril y mayo

el verano

junio, julio y agosto

el otoño

septiembre, octubre y noviembre

el invierno

diciembre, enero y febrero

Los días de la semana	*Days of the week*	Expresiones útiles	*Useful expressions*
lunes	*Monday*	¿Qué día es hoy?	*What day is today?*
martes	*Tuesday*	¿Cuál es la fecha de hoy?	*What is today's date?*
miércoles	*Wednesday*	Hoy es lunes.	*Today is Monday.*
jueves	*Thursday*	Hoy es el 1° (primero)	*Today is September first.*
viernes	*Friday*	de septiembre.	
sábado	*Saturday*	Mañana es el 2 (dos)	*Tomorrow is September second.*
domingo	*Sunday*	de septiembre.	

Unlike in English, the days of the week and the months of the year are not capitalized in Spanish. Also, in the Spanish-speaking world, in some countries, Monday is considered the first day of the week. On calendars the days are listed from Monday through Sunday.

e **A-23** **Antes y después**

e **A-24** **Y los meses**

[3:00] 🍦🍦 **A-25** **¿Cuándo es?** Look at the activities included in the **Guía del ocio**. Take turns determining what activity takes place and at what time on the following days. ■

Fijate

In Spanish, *h* is the abbreviation for *hora*.

GUÍA DEL OCIO MADRID

MÚSICA

Sábado 4
• **XVI Festival de Jazz:**
 Joe Henderson
La Riviera. 21 h.
• **Alonso y Williams**
La Madriguera. 24 h.

Domingo 5
• **Pedro Iturralde**
Clamores. Pases: 22.45 y 0.45 h. Libre.

Lunes 6
• **Moreiras Jazztet**
Café Central. 22 h.

CINE

Las vidas de Celia
(2005, España)****
Género: Drama
Director: Antonio Chavarrías
Interpretación: Najwa Nimri, Luis Tosar…
Najwa Nimri da vida a una mujer que intenta suicidarse la misma noche que otra joven es asesinada.

Mujeres en el parque
(2006, España)*****
Género: Drama
Director: Felipe Vega
Interpretación: Adolfo Fernández, Blanca Apilánez…
Una película llena de pequeños misterios, donde los personajes se enfrentan a lo difícil de las relaciones personales.

Volver (2006, España)*****
Género: Comedia dramática
Director: Pedro Almodóvar
Interpretación: Penélope Cruz, Carmen Maura…
Se basa en la vida y los recuerdos del director sobre su madre y el lugar donde se crió.

EXPOSICIONES

• **Museo Nacional Centro de Arte Reina Sofía**
Santa Isabel, 52.
Metro Atocha
Tel. 91 4675062
Horario: de 10 a 21 h. Domingo de 10 a 14.30 h.
Martes cerrado.

Un recorrido del arte del siglo XX, desde Picasso. Salas dedicadas a los comienzos de la vanguardia. Además, exposiciones temporales.

• **Museo del Prado**
Paseo del Prado, s/n. Metro Banco de España.
Tel. 91 420 36 62 y 91 420 37 68
Horario: martes a sábado de 9 a 19 h. Domingo de 9 a 14 h. Lunes cerrado.

Todas las escuelas españolas, desde los frescos románicos hasta el siglo XVIII. Grandes colecciones de Velázquez, Goya, Murillo, etc. Importante representación de las escuelas europeas (Rubens, Tiziano, Durero, etc.). Escultura clásica griega y romana y Tesoro del Delfín.

MODELO   E1: el lunes por la noche
              E2: *El Moreiras Jazztet es a las veintidós horas / a las diez.*

1. el sábado por la noche
2. el miércoles por la mañana
3. el domingo
4. el sábado por la noche
5. el martes por la tarde

11 VOCABULARIO

¡Hola!
eText 23   A-52 to A-56

El tiempo Reporting the weather

¿Qué tiempo hace? (*What's the weather like?*)

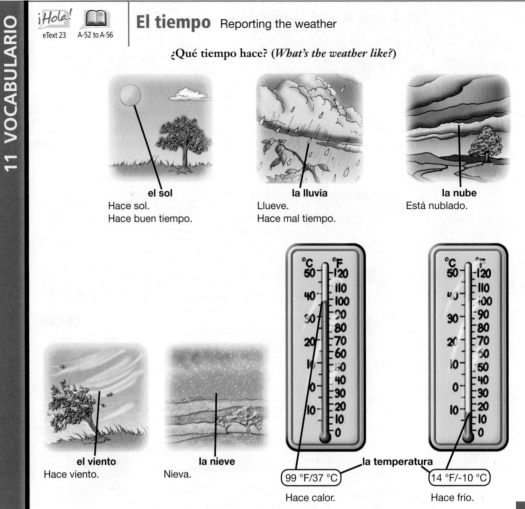

el sol
Hace sol.
Hace buen tiempo.

la lluvia
Llueve.
Hace mal tiempo.

la nube
Está nublado.

el viento
Hace viento.

la nieve
Nieva.

la temperatura

99 °F/37 °C

14 °F/-10 °C

Hace calor.

Hace frío.

e **A-26** ¿Qué tiempo hace?

e **A-27** España

2:00 **A-28** **Y América del Sur** Take turns making statements about the weather based on the map of South America. You can say what the weather is like, and also what it is not like. Follow the model. ■

MODELO   E1: *Llueve en Bogotá.*
           E2: *No hace frío en Venezuela.*

Fijate

To make a negative statement, simply place the word no before the verb: *No llueve en Caracas. No nieva en Buenos Aires. No hace calor en Punta Arenas.*

Possible answers include: Llueve en Bogotá. Hace sol y hace calor en Caracas. Hace viento en Buenos Aires y está nublado. Nieva en Punta Arenas. Está nublado en Lima.

2:00 **12 GRAMÁTICA**

¡Hola! eText 25   A-57 to A-59

Gustar   Sharing personal likes and dislikes

Me gusta la primavera.

No me gusta el invierno.

Me gustan los viernes.

No me gustan los lunes.

EXPANSION for A-28
You may want to bring a map of Central America to class or use the maps provided in the text in order to name the countries and capitals in that region as well.

EXPANSION for A-28 Physical map:
Divide the class in 2 teams. Make a set of cards with the name of each Spanish-speaking country on a different card. Give each group a set. Groups are instructed to place themselves or the cards appropriately to create an accurate physical map. The group that does so first, or that is the most accurate, wins. For the second round, the students must write the name of each capital on the back of the card. The group that gets the most capitals correct wins.

NOTE for *Gustar*
Gustar is introduced here in an abbreviated fashion with the goal of having students state their likes and dislikes. In this chapter, *gustar* is presented lexically. Then, there is an expanded presentation in *Capítulo 2*. Finally, *gustar* is reviewed and then presented in a complete fashion along with verbs like *gustar* in *Capítulo 8*.

NOTE for *Gramática*
This is an inductive grammar presentation in which the students are given examples of a grammar concept and then guiding questions. By answering the questions, they formulate the rule in their own words. They are then to check their answers in *Appendix 1*. Research indicates that students remember and internalize grammar rules better when they construct their own knowledge.

SUGGESTION for *Gustar*
Review the months and seasons with the class. Then discuss what the weather is like in your area for each season. Ask the students to describe the pictures in the text. What is the weather like in each picture? Using *gustar*, have students state why they like or dislike the weather in each picture. You might want to include some new verbs in infinitive form such as *tomar el sol, nadar, esquiar,* or *correr en el parque*. That way, students can explain why they like certain weather patterns.

SUGGESTION for A-30
You may wish to point out the number of words that look like their English equivalents in this activity to reinforce the presentation on cognates.

e **A-29** ¿Qué te gusta?

 **A-30** ¿Qué más te gusta? Take turns asking your partner about the following places and things. ■

MODELO   E1: *¿Te gustan las hamburguesas?*
         E2: *No, no me gustan las hamburguesas.*

1.
Las Vegas, Nevada

2.
las guitarras

3.
las camionetas

4.
la pizza

5.
San Antonio, Texas

6.

7.
el béisbol

8.
el fútbol

los teléfonos celulares

¿Cómo andas?

Each of the coming chapters of *¡Anda! Curso elemental para estudiantes avanzados* will have self-check sections for you to assess your progress. In this chapter, a **¿Cómo andas?** (*How are you doing?*) section will appear after each *Comunicación*. Use the checklists to measure what you have learned in the chapter. Place a check in the *Feel confident* column of the topics you feel you know, and a check in the *Need to review* column of those that you need to practice more. Be sure to go back and practice because it is the key to your success!

	Feel confident	Need to review
Having completed this section of *Para empezar*, I now can . . .		
Comunicación - Capítulo Preliminar A		
• greet, say good-bye, and introduce someone (p. 4)	☐	☐
• understand and respond appropriately to basic classroom expressions and requests (p. 6)	☐	☐
• spell in Spanish (p. 7)	☐	☐
• identify cognates (p. 8)	☐	☐
• express the subject pronouns (p. 8)	☐	☐
• use *to be* (p. 9)	☐	☐
• state nationalities (p. 10)	☐	☐
• count from 0 to 30 (p. 11)	☐	☐
• state the time (p. 12)	☐	☐
• elicit the date and season (p. 14)	☐	☐
• report the weather (p. 16)	☐	☐
• share personal likes and dislikes (p. 17)	☐	☐
Cultura		
• compare and contrast greetings in the Spanish-speaking world and in the United States (p. 6)	☐	☐
• explain when to use the familiar and formal *you* (p. 9)	☐	☐
• summarize the diversity of the Spanish-speaking world (p. 11)	☐	☐
• name the continents and countries where Spanish is spoken (p. 12)	☐	☐

Instructor Resources
• PPT, Extra Activities

INTRODUCTION to ¿Cómo andas?

Throughout the textbook, you will encounter three sections per chapter that allow the students to self-assess. The *¿Cómo andas?* section has a chart listing the concepts from the chapter. For each concept, students can check off whether they feel confident about it or whether they need to review it. As students complete the *¿Cómo andas?* section, you can survey the class to see which areas students need to review. If the majority of students are having difficulties, you may want to review the concept in class. As an instructor, you can suggest that students make appointments for extra help on any concepts they need to review. This checklist is especially helpful if students have a peer tutor or study group, because they can keep a record of the concepts that are difficult. Peer tutors will appreciate having a checklist of concepts they should review for each tutoring session. Each chapter will normally have three self-checks, but since *Para empezar* is meant to be a quick review, there is only one self-check in each *Comunicación*. Encourage students to use these self-checks, since they help them become accountable for their own learning and promote self-actualization.

METHODOLOGY FOR HIGH BEGINNERS: ¿Cómo andas? Self-assessments

The *¿Cómo andas?* self-assessments are particularly important in a high beginner course. Completing the equivalent of two semesters of course work in one semester requires self-actualized learners. The *¿Cómo andas?* and the *¿Y por fin cómo andas?* sections starting in Chapter 4 help build self-actualized learners.

SUGGESTION for ¿Cómo andas?

We recommend that students complete these self-assessments outside of class. You may want to spot-check some students and ask how they are doing (e.g., "How many of you feel confident with greeting, saying good-bye, and introducing someone?"). For those students who do not raise their hands, remind them that they need to consult the pages listed to review the material.

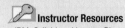

Instructor Resources
• IRM: Syllabi and Lesson Plans

NATIONAL STANDARDS

COMUNICACIÓN

- To describe families (Communication)
- To pronounce vowels (Communication)
- To express what someone has (Communication)
- To use singular and plural nouns (Communication)
- To identify masculine and feminine nouns (Communication)
- To convey *the, a, one,* and *some* (Communication)
- To give details about yourself and others (Communication)
- To state possession (Communication)
- To supply details about people, places, and things (Communication)
- To count from 31 to 100 (Communication, Cultures)
- To determine the topic and listen for known words (Communication)
- To communicate about people you know (Communication)
- To organize ideas to write a poem (Communication, Cultures)
- To engage in additional communication practice (Communication)

CULTURA

- To illustrate formation of Hispanic last names (Cultures, Comparisons, Communities)
- To compare and contrast several regional and national differences in the English and Spanish languages (Communication, Comparisons, Communities)
- To discuss the size, location, and makeup of the Hispanic population in the United States (Cultures, Connections)
- To explore the chapter's cultural themes further (Cultures)

AMBICIONES SINIESTRAS (Online)

- To recognize cognates when reading and to meet the six protagonists (Communication, Cultures)
- To discover more about the protagonists' classes and their lives (Communication)

COMUNIDADES

- To use Spanish in real-life contexts (Communication, Communities)

OBJETIVOS	CONTENIDOS	
COMUNICACIÓN - CAPÍTULO 1		
To describe families	**1** The family	21
To pronounce vowels	**Pronunciación:** Vowels	MSL / SAM
To express what someone has	**2** The verb **tener**	22
To use singular and plural nouns	**3** Singular and plural nouns	24
To identify masculine and feminine nouns	**4** Masculine and feminine nouns	24
To convey *the, a, one,* and *some*	**5** Definite (*the*) and indefinite (*a, an, some*) articles	25
To give details about yourself and others	**6** People	26
To state possession	**7** Possessive adjectives (*my, your, our,* etc.)	27
To supply details about people, places, and things	**8** Descriptive adjectives	28
To count from 31 to 100	**9** Numbers 31–100	30
To determine the topic and listen for known words	**ESCUCHA:** Family introductions **Estrategia:** Determining the topic and listening for words you know	32
To communicate about people you know	**¡Conversemos!**	32
To organize ideas to write a poem	**ESCRIBE:** A poem **Estrategia:** Organizing ideas/Preparing to write	32
To engage in additional communication practice	**Heritage Language**	SAM
CULTURA		
To illustrate formation of Hispanic last names	**NOTA CULTURAL** Los apellidos en el mundo hispano	22
To compare and contrast several regional and national differences in the English and Spanish languages	**NOTA CULTURAL** El español, lengua diversa	30
AMBICIONES SINIESTRAS		
To recognize cognates when reading and to meet the six protagonists	**EPISODIO 1** **Lectura:** *Conexiones* **Estrategia:** Recognizing cognates	33
To discover more about the protagonists' classes and their lives	**Video:** *¿Quiénes son?*	33
COMUNIDADES		
To use Spanish in real-life contexts	**Experiential Learning:** Familias famosas **Service Learning:** Familia, cultura y niños	SAM SAM

METHODOLOGY • Starting Where the Learner Is
Beginning with what students themselves already know best helps to build interest in the chapter. John Dewey's philosophy encourages instructors to start where the learners are, which includes what they already know about the subject. Being able to share about what they already know helps motivate the learners and put them in an anticipatory state for the chapter's content.

NATIONAL STANDARDS *Communities*
Ask students to identify areas in your community where large populations of Spanish speakers live. What do these communities offer? What types of services do these Spanish speakers need? What services could your students provide? Is there an activity that the students and the community members should share?

Some ideas of service learning projects in your area might include: collections of food and clothing for shelters; educational services, such as tutoring or after-school enrichment programs; music; reading to those who cannot; and simply keeping someone company. Remind students that everyone shares basic necessities that need to be fulfilled, regardless of nationality or culture.

NOTE for *Contenidos*
The Heritage Language activities, available in the Student Activities Manual (SAM), are not only for heritage learners, but for all of your students. The activities either require students to reflect on the usage of Spanish, or to use Spanish in ways that encompass all of the 5 Cs. The end product will vary from student to student, which is an expected outcome of performance-based activities.

Comunicación

Capítulo 1 ¿Quiénes somos?

¡Hola! eText 32   01-01 to 01-05

La familia   Describing families

la abuela
Carmen Jiménez
de Martín

el abuelo
Manuel Martín García

el tío
Enrique
Martín
Jiménez

la madre
Rosario
Domínguez
de Martín

la tía
Francisca
Ávila de
Martín

el padre
Pedro
Martín
Jiménez

el hermano
Antonio
Martín
Domínguez

Eduardo Martín
Domínguez

casados (married)

la hermana Adriana
Martín Domínguez

la prima Sonia
Martín Ávila

Más miembros de la familia	More family members
los abuelos	grandparents
la esposa	wife
el esposo	husband
los hermanos	brothers and sisters; siblings
la hija	daughter
el hijo	son
los hijos	sons and daughters; children
la madrastra	stepmother

la mamá	mom
el nieto	grandson
la nieta	granddaughter
el padrastro	stepfather
el papá	dad
los padres	parents
el primo	cousin (male)
los primos	cousins
los tíos	aunts and uncles

HERITAGE LANGUAGE LEARNERS
Encourage your heritage language learners to make family trees, adding additional vocabulary to what is presented in the book. Allow them to use terms of endearment such as *abuelita* or *titi* for their family members.

METHODOLOGY • Using English in the Classroom
The philosophy of *¡Anda!* regarding the use of English is as follows:
1. Grammar explanations are brief and in English.
2. Critical-thinking questions or those tapping students' prior knowledge start in English due to the limited nature of the students' Spanish language capability. As the program progresses, these questions will be in Spanish.

3. Directions for activities are in English until *Capítulo 3*, when students are eased into Spanish and weaned away from English.

The use of Spanish in *¡Anda!* is based on Stephen Krashen's Input Hypothesis (*i* + 1), which states that students acquire more language when exposed to structures that are a little beyond (+1) what they completely comprehend (*i*).

SECTION GOALS
By the end of the *Contenidos* 1 through 5, students will be able to:
- describe their family members.
- explain the relationships between members of the family.
- pronounce vowels in Spanish.
- contrast the use of surnames in Spanish and English.
- express possession using the forms of the verb *tener*.
- narrate the characteristics of someone else's family using *tener* and vocabulary from *la familia*.
- form the plural of nouns and adjectives.
- distinguish between masculine and feminine endings of nouns and adjectives.
- practice identifying cognates.
- differentiate between the definite and indefinite articles.

METHODOLOGY • Vocabulary
For new instructors (and as a reminder for those of us who have been teaching), whenever introducing new vocabulary, say the word, have students repeat after you, then say the word again, having them repeat once again. Even though the words are pronounced in MySpanishLab, the Student Activities Manual, and the *¡Anda!* CD, reinforcement in class helps novice learners. Spend approximately three minutes introducing new vocabulary.
Note: Do not repeat in unison with your students since you will be unable to monitor their pronunciation.

METHODOLOGY • *También se dice…* Appendix 3
The *También se dice…* appendix provides additional words that pertain to each topic. Words presented in introductory courses may not be the exact words that students wish to use; even native speakers sometimes search for additional vocabulary. *También se dice…* is meant to serve as an amplification of vocabulary for all students. The list should not be included on chapter assessments.

NOTE for *La familia*
The terms *madrastra* and *padrastro*, as in English, can sometimes take on negative connotations. Many children would prefer to say "la esposa de mi padre/el esposo de mi madre."

INTRODUCTION to *Pronunciación*
Each chapter has a brief presentation on Spanish pronunciation in MySpanishLab and in the Student Activities Manual after the initial vocabulary section. These presentations are concise, taking examples from vocabulary both just presented and previously learned, as well as from cognates. The presentations are brief so that students can focus on small portions of Spanish pronunciation without feeling overwhelmed. Encourage your students to practice these sections several times.

SECTION GOALS for *Pronunciación*
By the end of the *Pronunciación* section, students will be able to:
• pronounce the Spanish vowels *a, e, i, o,* and *u.*
• practice pronouncing cognates and new vocabulary by sounding out each letter.

NATIONAL STANDARDS
Cultures, Comparisons, Communities
In the *Nota cultural* online presentation *Los nombres en el mundo hispano,* you will find an explanation of how names and surnames are written in Spanish. This cultural reading addresses Standard 2.1, because it explains the differences between how people are named in Hispanic countries and how people in the United States are named. This cultural difference is important when communicating with Spanish speakers, because students may incorrectly assume that a Hispanic woman is single or divorced if her last name differs from that of her husband. Similarly, Hispanic children and their mothers may use different last names. Standard 4.1 asks students to make comparisons between their own language and Spanish. You can point out that sometimes, for professional or personal reasons, married women in the United States keep their maiden names, while others hyphenate both last names or use both names without a hyphen. When students understand how to address someone correctly, they are more likely to communicate effectively. Standard 5.1 encourages the use of Spanish skills beyond the school setting. Mastering the use of surnames in Spanish allows students to connect with Spanish speakers.

ANSWERS to *Nota cultural* **(Online)**
1. Hyphenated last names, double last names (e.g., Hillary Rodham Clinton).
2. *Some answers may include:* less confusion in phone books with common names, family last names

---

Vowels

01-06 to 01-08

Go to MySpanishLab / Student Activities Manual to learn about the pronunciation of vowels.

Fíjate
You will find this *Pronunciación* section, and accompanying activities, on MySpanishLab and in the Student Activities Manual.

Estrategia
Remember that activities with the *e* icon can be found in your MySpanishLab course. The activities provide practice as you review, develop, and refine your Spanish knowledge and abilities.

e **1-1** La familia de Eduardo

e **1-2** Mi familia

NOTA CULTURAL

¡Hola!   **Los apellidos en el mundo hispano**
eText 33   01-09 to 01-11

NOTE for *Nota cultural*
See eText pg. 33 for complete *Nota cultural* reading and *Preguntas.*

2 GRAMÁTICA

1:00   *¡Hola!*
eText 34   01-12 to 01-16

El verbo *tener* Expressing what someone has

Tengo una hermana y un hermano.

Estrategia
As a reminder, you will find a summary of this and all of the grammar points in the eText or refer to *Capítulo Preliminar A* in the Grammar summary at the end of *Para empezar,* beginning on page 74. You will also note that all of the grammar points for mini chapters 1, 2, and 3 are referenced there to assist you.

---

are not lost as quickly, and potentially easier reconstruction of a family's heritage.

EXPANSION for *Nota cultural* **(Online)**
Additional questions and projects for your students are:
1. What is your full name in the Spanish style? Write it out, and then write the names of five family members or friends *a la española.* For example, Gail Parker's mother's maiden name is Smith. Her name *a la española* would be *Gail Parker Smith.*
2. Ask students to bring the wedding announcement page of a newspaper to class. Have them work in pairs to decide what the names of five new brides would be *a la española* if they took their new husbands' last names.

METHODOLOGY • Recycling
We know from thousands of educational research studies that learners need material to be recycled in order to acquire the concepts. The authors of *¡Anda!* firmly believe in recycling previously introduced material and do so frequently throughout every chapter.

METHODOLOGY • Deductive Presentations of Grammar
Verb presentations such as the one for *tener* are done *deductively* (give students the rules/forms and go directly to practice) to streamline presentation time. All grammar presentations in this chapter are deductive.

e **1-3** ¿Quién tiene familia?

e **1-4** ¡Apúrate!

[3:00] **1-5** **La familia de José** Complete the paragraph with the correct forms of **tener.** Then share your answers with a partner. Finally, based on what you learned in the previous culture presentation regarding last names, what is José's father's last name? What is José's mother's maiden name? ■

Yo soy el primo de José. Él (1) ___tiene___ una familia grande. (2) ___Tiene___ tres hermanos, Pepe, Alonso y Tina. Su hermano Pepe está casado (*is married*) y (3) ___tiene___ dos hijos. También José y sus hermanos (4) ___tienen___ muchos tíos, siete en total. La madre de José (5) ___tiene___ tres hermanos y dos están casados. El padre de José (6) ___tiene___ una hermana y ella está casada con mi padre: ¡es mi madre! Nosotros (7) ___tenemos___ una familia grande. ¿Y tú?, ¿(8) ___tienes___ una familia grande?

José Olivo Peralta y su familia

[3:00] **1-6** **De tal palo, tal astilla** Create **three** sentences with **tener** based on the family tree that you sketched for **1-2,** page 22. Tell them to your partner, who will then share what you said with another classmate. ■

based on the family tree that you sketched for **1-2,** page 22.

> **Fíjate**
> The word *un* in the *modelo* for **1-6** is the shortened form of the number *uno.* It is used before a masculine noun—a concept that will be explained later in this chapter.

MODELO   E1 (ALICE):   *Tengo un hermano, Scott. Tengo dos tíos, George y David. No tengo abuelos.*

E2 (JEFF):   *Alice tiene un hermano, Scott. Tiene dos tíos, George y David. No tiene abuelos.*

METHODOLOGY • Interpretive, Interpersonal, and Presentation Modes of Communication

There are three modes of communication: *interpretive, interpersonal,* and *presentational.* The *interpretive* mode of communication includes reading and listening. It is deciphering linguistic code. The *interpersonal* mode of communication is a core concept of *¡Anda!* It is oral communication between two or more individuals. It can also be communicating via writing. Finally, the *presentational* mode of communication is when an individual makes a presentation to an individual or group, usually orally. *¡Anda!* balances all three modes of communication to provide learners with ample opportunities to grow in the language. For example, when students are working in pairs on the activities in the text, they are employing the interpretive and interpersonal modes of communication. When the activity has students speaking in extended discourse (three or more sentences) to a partner, that is the presentational mode. The *¡Conversemos!* sections of each chapter as well as Chapters 6 and 12 also incorporate extensively all three modes of communication.

NATIONAL STANDARDS
Communication
This series of activities uses oral communication to move from highly structured to more open-ended, personalized activities.

Standard 1.1 requires students to use Spanish by engaging in conversations and providing and obtaining information in an interpersonal mode. The *Preguntas* in the chapter opener allow students to work with a partner and exchange information about their heritage.

Students practice asking and answering questions, and they can share this information with other members of the class. You will find other interpersonal activities that encourage your students to work in pairs, or groups, to practice communicating in Spanish.

ADDITIONAL ACTIVITY for
El verbo tener
Practica conmigo Take turns saying the following subject pronouns with the corresponding forms of **tener.** Practice in random order until you can say them quickly with no errors.
1. tú
2. ustedes
3. yo
4. nosotros
5. ella
6. ellas
7. él
8. ellos
9. usted
10. tú y yo

METHODOLOGY •
Cooperative Learning
Pair and cooperative learning is a proven technique for increasing student performance. Research is emphatic regarding the benefits of students learning from students. It is recommended that you have them change partners frequently; daily is ideal. Physically separate groups as much as space permits. Students are less prone to be distracted by other groups the farther apart they sit.

METHODOLOGY • Reporting
Back What One Hears
In **1-6,** students are required to actively listen to their partners and then report what they heard. This type of activity occurs frequently in *¡Anda! Curso elemental* and helps students practice switching between first and third person verb forms. It also reinforces active listening and helps with classroom management, since it requires both partners to take active roles.

Instructor Resources
• PPT, Extra Activities

SUGGESTION for *Los sustantivos singulares y plurales*

Have students create a friendly challenge where they take turns making as many nouns as possible both singular and plural. Encourage them to use active vocabulary as well as cognates.

METHODOLOGY • Instructional Delivery

There are many ways to make instructional delivery more efficient. One way is pairing your students for the day. Put the activities that you want them to do on the board. You suggest the amount of time they may want to spend. Some partners will need more time than others. Give directions in advance for any activities that require additional explanations. Otherwise, the students should be permitted to negotiate meaning together. Finally, always have one or more activities ready for groups that finish early. This may include reviewing the vocabulary from previous chapters, or you may want to list activities from previous chapters that they should go back and redo.

METHODOLOGY • A Non-Threatening Atmosphere

Students of all ages enjoy activities that are game-like in nature. These types of activities reinforce grammar and vocabulary in a non-threatening atmosphere.

METHODOLOGY • Teaching Written Accent Marks

Rules for stress and accent marks will be formally presented in the *Capítulo 2 Pronunciación* section in MySpanishLab and in the Student Activities Manual. The philosophy of *¡Anda! Curso elemental* is to present concepts in small chunks. We encourage students to process and master one set of rules first, and then proceed to additional information, such as rules for written accent marks. Therefore, we suggest postponing detailed explanations regarding accent marks and accentuation until *Capítulo 2*.

METHODOLOGY • False Cognates

The concept of *false cognates* is presented at the point of need and usage, again, with the goal of streamlining and presenting only essential information at the beginning to help students build confidence.

---

3 GRAMÁTICA

[3:00] eText 36 01-17 to 01-20

Sustantivos singulares y plurales
Using singular and plural nouns

Raúl tiene dos primas y Jorge tiene una prima.

e **1-7** Te toca a ti

e **1-8** De nuevo

---

4 GRAMÁTICA

[5:00]  eText 37 01-21 to 01-22

El masculino y el femenino
Identifying masculine and feminine nouns

El abuelo y las tías.

e **1-9** ¿Recuerdas?

METHODOLOGY • Grammar for Beginners

Based on decades of experience, the authors of *¡Anda! Curso elemental* believe that the initial presentation of grammar rules needs to be basic. Too many exceptions to the rule may confuse and frustrate true beginners. Hence, additional exceptions, such as *el agua*, are presented at the point of introduction of the vocabulary. If you have heritage language learners or false beginners, you may expand the presentation to suit their needs.

ADDITIONAL ACTIVITY for *Los artículos definidos e indefinidos*

Use the correct definite article with the following active vocabulary words and cognates, and then repeat the activity with indefinite articles.

1. primavera
2. norteamericanos
3. teléfono
4. sol
5. temperatura
6. nubes
7. domingo
8. viento
9. otoño
10. mañanas

5 GRAMÁTICA

5:00

 **1-10 Para practicar**

¡Hola! eText 38   01-23 to 01-27

Los artículos definidos e indefinidos

Conveying *the*, *a*, *one*, and *some*

Eduardo tiene una hermana. La hermana de Eduardo se llama Adriana.

 1-11 Vamos a practicar

1-12 Una concordancia

3:00

 1-13 ¿Quiénes son? Fill in the blanks with the correct form of either the definite or indefinite article. Then take turns sharing your answers and explaining your choices. You may want to refer to the family tree on page 21. ■

MODELO   Adriana es _la_ hermana de Eduardo.

(1) ___Los (the)___ abuelos se llaman Manuel y Carmen. Eduardo tiene (2) ___un (the)___ tío.

(3) ___El (the)___ tío se llama Enrique. Eduardo tiene (4) ___una (the)___ prima; se llama Sonia.

(5) ___El (the)___ hermano de Eduardo se llama Antonio.

Estrategia

To say "Eduardo's sister" or "Eduardo's grandparents," you add *de Eduardo* to each of your sentences: *Es la hermana de Eduardo. Son los abuelos de Eduardo.*

Instructor Resources
• PPT, Extra Activities

SECTION GOALS

By the end of *Contenidos* 6 through 9, students will be able to:
• describe themselves and others.
• distinguish between people of different ages and use titles of respect accordingly.
• show possession, using possessive adjectives.
• report characteristics about various family members.
• identify famous people and describe characteristics of each person.
• express the opposites of certain characteristics (e.g., nice, mean).
• make true and false statements.
• understand linguistic variations in vocabulary across regions of the world.
• count from 31 to 100.
• report demographics from Hispanic countries.

NOTE for *Gente*

The terms "boy/girl" in Spanish can vary from region to region. *El niño/la niña* is often interchangeable with *el chico/la chica. El muchacho/la muchacha* may also be interchanged with *el/la joven.* These terms are not limited to the age depicted in the images presented.

NATIONAL STANDARDS
Communication

There are many ways to describe yourself and others. If students are in pairs or small groups, sharing information about themselves and asking follow-up questions, the standard this activity addresses is Standard 1.1. You could vary the activity by asking students to create posters of themselves with photos or drawings and captions using simple phrases in Spanish to describe themselves. You could showcase the posters in the classroom to an audience of readers, or students could present the information from the posters orally to the class. Communication Standard 1.3 addresses the presentational mode.

EXPANSION for 1-15

Ask your students the following questions:
¿Cómo se llaman los jóvenes?
¿Cómo se llama la niña?
¿Cómo se llaman los niños?
¿Cómo se llama la señorita?
¿Cómo se llaman los amigos?
¿Cómo se llaman los chicos?

---

6 VOCABULARIO

[2:00]   eText 40   01-28 to 1-31

Gente   Giving details about yourself and others

Miguelito/Clarita

el niño/la niña

Daniel/Mariela

**el chico, el muchacho/
la chica, la muchacha**

Javier/Ana

el joven/la joven

la Sra. Torres/
la Srta. Sánchez/
el Sr. Martín

Manuel/Manuela

el hombre/la mujer

**la señora/
la señorita/el señor**

Manolo/Pilar

el amigo/la amiga

Roberto/Pepita

el novio/la novia

---

e **1-14** **Los opuestos**

---

e **1-15** **¿Cómo se llama?**

---

7 GRAMÁTICA

 ¡Hola! eText 41 01-32 to 01-36

Los adjetivos posesivos Stating possession

> Mis padres se llaman Juan y María. ¿Cómo se llaman tus padres?

e **1-16** ¿De quién es?

e **1-17** Relaciones familiares

Estrategia
Using your own friends and family will help you remember the vocabulary. Write the names of your immediate family or your best friends. Then write a description of how those people are connected to each other. E.g., *Karen es la madre de Brian* or *Brian es el hijo de Karen.*

 1-18 **Tu familia** Using at least **three** different possessive adjectives, talk to your partner about your family. ■

MODELO   En mi familia somos cinco personas. Mi padre se llama John y mi madre es Marie. Sus amigos son Mary y Dennis. Tengo dos hermanos, Clark y Blake. Nuestros tíos son Alice y Ralph y nuestras primas se llaman Gina y Glynis.

SUGGESTION for *Los adjetivos posesivos*
You may want to physically demonstrate the use of possessive adjectives. For example, bring something unusual to class, like a chocolate bar. Hold it up and say, *¿Es mi chocolate?* Move around the room, repeating the sentence as you look at students, emphasizing the *mi*. Then, stop and present the bar to a student. He/she takes it. Then say to the student, *¿Es tu* (emphasize) *chocolate?* Turn to the other students and say, *X tiene el chocolate. No es mi* (exaggerate) *chocolate, es su* (exaggerate) *chocolate.* Then ask the student, *¿Es tu chocolate?* Guide the student into saying, *Sí, es mi chocolate.* At this point you can take the bar away and say "no" and go through the routine quickly with another student. Now open the bar (or several bars, if you like) and break it into a few pieces, sharing the pieces with your students. Say, *Ahora es nuestro chocolate, ¿no, clase?* Have them respond, *Sí, es nuestro chocolate.*

SUGGESTION for *Los adjetivos posesivos*
Tell the students you are going to play a game. You can bring in objects that are familiar to students or use the students' possessions (the textbook, a backpack, paper, pencils, etc.). "Rob" the students and move the possessions around the room to different students and have them act out whose possession it is. One student can be the police officer and the other students can "report" what's theirs, or simply "steal" the possessions back, stating, *No, ¡es MI libro!*

METHODOLOGY • Student Accountability
When students are working in class, either with partners or by themselves, always circulate around the room to ensure they are on task. We suggest giving a daily class participation grade for student accountability. Also, spotcheck activity answers not only for comprehension, but also for accountability. It sends a strong message to students that they must stay on task, as does allotting a brief but appropriate time for each activity.

EXPANSION for 1-18
As a follow-up, have at least one student present his/her family to the entire class. Tell students that they will have to listen carefully. When he/she finishes, ask comprehension questions like, *¿Cúantos hermanos tiene?, ¿Cómo se llama su hermana?, ¿Cómo se llaman sus padres?* Holding students accountable for what others say helps them to become better listeners and keeps them actively engaged in class.

8 GRAMÁTICA

 ¡Hola! eText 43   01-37 to 01-42

Los adjetivos descriptivos
Supplying details about people, places, and things

Las características físicas, la personalidad y otros rasgos

alto   alta   bajo   baja   guapo   guapa   delgado delgada   gordo gorda

débil   fuerte   inteligente   joven   mayor   pobre   rico rica

La personalidad	Personality
aburrido/a	boring
antipático/a	unpleasant
bueno/a	good
cómico/a	funny; comical
interesante	interesting
malo/a	bad
paciente	patient
perezoso/a	lazy
responsable	responsible
simpático/a	nice
tonto/a	silly; dumb
trabajador/a	hard-working

Las características físicas	Physical characteristics
bonito/a	pretty
feo/a	ugly
grande	big; large
pequeño/a	small

Otras palabras útiles	Other useful words
muy	very
(un) poco	(a) little

e **1-19** ¿Cómo son?

EXPANSION for 1-20
Have students name famous Hispanics and describe them.

METHODOLOGY • Student Accountability
When students are working in class, either with partners or by themselves, always circulate around the room to ensure they are on task. We suggest giving a daily class participation grade for student accountability. Also, spotcheck activity answers not only for comprehension, but also for accountability. It sends a strong message to students that they must stay on task, as does allotting a brief but appropriate time for each activity.

METHODOLOGY • The Active Listener
Note that once again in 1-22, students are asked to be active listeners and to compare what they have heard each other say.

  1-20 ¿Cómo los describes?

[2:00] **1-21** **Al contrario** Student 1 creates a sentence using the cues provided, and Student 2 expresses the opposite. Pay special attention to adjective agreement. ■

MODELO   los hermanos González/guapo
E1: *Los hermanos González son guapos.*
E2: *¡Ay no, son muy feos!*

1. los abuelos / pobre
2. la señora López / muy antipático
3. Jaime / delgado

4. la tía Claudia / mayor
5. Tomás y Antonia / alto
6. nosotros / perezoso

[5:00] **1-22** **¿Cómo eres?** Imagine you are applying to a dating service. ■

Paso 1 Describe yourself to your partner using at least **three** adjectives, and then describe your ideal date.

MODELO *Me llamo Julie. Soy joven, muy inteligente y alta. Mi hombre ideal es inteligente, paciente y cómico.*

Paso 2 How similar are you and your partner and how similar are your ideal mates?

MODELO *Rebeca y yo somos jóvenes, altas y muy inteligentes. Nuestros hombres ideales son cómicos y pacientes.*

matchideal.com

Soy inteligente, cómico y responsable.
No soy muy rico pero soy trabajador.
¿Eres inteligente, simpática y cómica?

Contacta con matchideal.com/chucho.

[5:00] **1-23** **¿Es cierto o falso?** Describe **five** famous (or infamous!) people or characters. Your partner can react by saying **Es verdad** (*It's true*) or **No es verdad** (*It's not true*). If your partner disagrees with you, he/she must correct your statement. ■

Estrategia

Being an "active listener" is an important skill in any language. *Active listening* means that you hear and understand what someone is saying. Being able to repeat what someone says helps you practice and perfect the skill of active listening.

MODELO   E1: *Santa Claus es gordo y un poco feo.*
E2: *No es verdad. Sí, es gordo pero no es feo. Es guapo.*

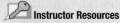
NATIONAL STANDARDS
Communication, Comparisons, Communities

El español, lengua diversa offers insight into the many ways in which communication takes place. Communicating in Spanish is Goal One, and Standard 1.1 encourages students to engage in conversations. The fact that Spanish vocabulary varies by country reinforces the awareness of linguistic variations in English. Students are able to make comparisons, as defined in Standard 4.1, between regional and linguistic differences that occur in English and Spanish. Students can apply this knowledge when interacting with Hispanic people in the United States and abroad. Standard 5.1 encompasses using Spanish within and beyond an academic environment, and taking risks with the language by communicating with Spanish speakers from all over the world is part of being a successful language learner.

ANSWERS to *Nota cultural* (Online)

1. *Possible answers:* Accents and pronunciation; Different words such as *lift* for *elevator*, *flat* for *apartment*, *barbie* for *barbeque*, etc.
2. *Possible answers:* Bayou in Texas and other places in the South; *arroyo* in the Southwest; *put up* versus *put away*; pronunciation differences for words like *roof*, *creek*, etc.

SUGGESTION for *Los números 31–100*

Although all vocabulary is pronounced for your students on the accompanying *¡Anda! Curso elemental* MySpanishLab, as well as on CD, it can be helpful to pronounce the numbers in class and have students repeat after you. Additional practice can include having them count by twos or fives or count backwards.

METHODOLOGY • Teaching Numbers

An easy way to introduce numbers is to have visuals with numbers that you can then take out of numerical order. Students need practice with numbers out of sequence. Using visuals helps to accommodate different learning styles.

 1-24 **¿Cuáles son sus cualidades?** Think of the qualities of your best friend and those of someone you do not particularly like (**una persona que no me gusta**). Using adjectives that you know in Spanish, write at least **three** sentences that describe each of these people. Share your list with a partner. ■

MODELO | MI MEJOR (*BEST*) AMIGO/A | UNA PERSONA QUE NO ME GUSTA
| 1. Es trabajador/a. | 1. Es antipático/a.
| 2. Es inteligente. | 2. No es paciente.
| 3. … | 3. …

Capítulo Preliminar A. Los pronombres personales, pág. 11 del eText.

1-25 **Describe a una familia** Bring family photos (personal ones or some taken from the Internet or a magazine) to class and describe the family members to a classmate, using at least **five** sentences. ■

MODELO   *Tengo dos hermanas, Kate y Ana. Ellas son simpáticas y bonitas. Mi papá no es aburrido y es muy trabajador. Tengo seis primos…*

NOTA CULTURAL

  El español, lengua diversa

eText 46   01-43 to 01-44

NOTE for *Nota cultural*
See eText pg. 46 for complete *Nota cultural* reading and *Preguntas*.

 **9 VOCABULARIO**

  Los números 31–100 Counting from 31 to 100

eText 47   01-45 to 01-48

The numbers 31–100 function in much the same way as the numbers 0–30. Note how the numbers 30–39 are formed. This pattern will repeat itself up to 100.

31	treinta y uno	37	treinta y siete	51	cincuenta y uno…
32	treinta y dos	38	treinta y ocho	60	sesenta
33	treinta y tres	39	treinta y nueve	70	setenta
34	treinta y cuatro	40	cuarenta	80	ochenta
35	treinta y cinco	41	cuarenta y uno…	90	noventa
36	treinta y seis	50	cincuenta	100	cien

Estrategia
Practice the numbers in Spanish by reading and pronouncing any numbers you see in your daily routine (e.g., highway signs, prices on your shopping receipts, room numbers on campus, phone numbers, etc.).

e **1-26** **Examen de matemáticas**

e **1-27** **¿Qué número es?**

(3:00) **1-28** **¿Quiere dejar un recado?** Imagine that you work in a busy office. You take messages with the following phone numbers. Say the numbers to a partner who will write them down. Then switch roles, mixing the order of the numbers. ■

MODELO E1: 223-7256

E2: *dos, veintitrés, setenta y dos, cincuenta y seis*

1. 962-2136   3. 871-4954   5. 761-7920
2. 615-9563   4. 414-4415   6. 270-2325

Capítulo Preliminar A.
Los números 0–30,
pág. 16 del eText.

Fíjate

In most of the Spanish-speaking world, commas are used where the English-speaking world uses decimal points, and vice versa. For example, in English one says "six point four percent," in Spanish, *seis coma cuatro por ciento.*

(2:00) **1-29** **Los hispanos en los EE.UU.** Use the information from the pie chart to answer the following questions in Spanish. ■

Vocabulario útil	
por ciento	*percent*

PORCENTAJE DE POBLACIÓN HISPANA

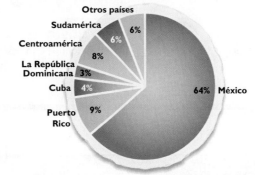

Otros países
Sudamérica — 6%
Centroamérica — 6%
8%
La República Dominicana — 3%
Cuba — 4%
Puerto Rico — 9%
64% México

Source: US Census Bureau State & County Quick Facts

1. What percentage of U.S. Hispanics is from Cuba? 4%
2. What percentage of U.S. Hispanics is from Puerto Rico? 9%
3. What percentage of U.S. Hispanics is from Mexico? 64%
4. What percentage of U.S. Hispanics is from South America? 6%
5. What percentage of U.S. Hispanics comes from countries other than Mexico? 36%

CAPÍTULO 1

🔑 **Instructor Resources**
• PPT, Extra Activities

NOTE for 1-28
Explain that when reading a long list of numbers, such as phone numbers or serial numbers, Spanish speakers often group the numbers in pairs. For example, in a seven-digit phone number, the first number is said alone and the remainder is said as 3 two-digit numerals. Thus, the phone number 919-4827 in Mexico is said as *nueve, diecinueve, cuarenta y ocho, veintisiete.*

NATIONAL STANDARDS
Communication, Cultures
Activities **1-27** and **1-28** allow students to provide and exchange information (Standard 1.1) in an interpersonal mode. Students are asked to work in pairs as they practice pronouncing the numbers and listening to whose number the partner is saying. Each person is responsible for the exchange of information.

EXPANSION for 1-29
You may wish to ask your students the information from the additional countries in the chart.

EXPANSION for 1-29
You may wish to have your students check local populations using the Census Bureau's American Fact Finder.

INTRODUCTION to *Escucha*

A listening section entitled *Escucha* appears approximately two thirds of the way through each regular chapter. In the *Para empezar* chapter, *Escucha* is available only online in MySpanishLab. These presentations utilize examples from the vocabulary and grammar presented in the current, as well as previous, chapters. The passages are brief to help students focus on and practice one strategy at a time so they will not feel overwhelmed.

SECTION GOALS for *Escucha* (Online)

By the end of the *Escucha* section, students will be able to:
- identify cognates.
- report about Alejandra's family.
- discuss characteristics of their families.

ANSWERS to 1-30, (Online)

Answers may vary. Some possibilities include: who her family members are, their names, what they are like.

ANSWERS to 1-31, (Online)

b. *Possible answers:* grande, hermanos, hermanas, dos.
1. grande
2. Raúl y Pilar
3. tres/dos

AUDIOSCRIPT for 1-3, (Online)

What follows is the audio script that the students will hear when completing the *Escucha* section. The audioscripts will appear in the AIE margins for every *Escucha* section. *Hola. Soy Alejandra. Mi familia es muy grande. Mis padres son Raúl y Pilar. Tengo dos hermanas y tres hermanos.*

NATIONAL STANDARDS

Communication

The strategy *listening for cognates* facilitates communication in the interpretive mode. Standard 1.2 requires that students understand and interpret spoken Spanish on a variety of topics. In *Capítulo 1*, students listen for a description of family members and they focus on cognate recognition. The short conversations that students have about their own families are interpersonal communication: Standard 1.1.

INTRODUCTION to *¡Conversemos!*

Toward the end of each chapter the section *¡Conversemos!* appears. These sections "put it all together" by combining all of the vocabulary and grammar of the current chapter, as well as offer the student the opportunity to recycle vocabulary and grammar from previous chapters.

SECTION GOALS for *¡Conversemos!*

By the end of the *¡Conversemos!* section, students will be able to:
- introduce themselves and others.
- describe themselves.

NATIONAL STANDARDS

Communication

These activities will focus on interpersonal communication, Standard 1.1, as well as the presentational mode, Standard 1.3.

ESCUCHA

¡Hola! **Presentaciones**
eText 49   01-49 to 01-50

NOTE for *Escucha*
See eText pg. 49 for *Estrategia* and accompanying activities for *Escucha*.

Estrategia

The *¡Hola!* icon indicates where you can find the *Estrategia* and activities for *Escucha* in the eText in your MySpanishLab course.

¡CONVERSEMOS!
01-51

1-33 Jefe nuevo With a partner, imagine that your new boss came to your office today to introduce himself/herself. Call your best friend, and describe your new boss in at least **four** sentences. ■

1-34 Mucho gusto You have just met a new neighbor. Imagine that your partner is your new neighbor, and describe yourself and your family to him/her. Use at least **six** sentences. In addition to **ser** and **tener**, create sentences using *Me gusta / No me gusta*, etc. ■

ESCRIBE

¡Hola! **Un poema**
eText 50   01-52

NOTE for *Escribe*
See eText pg. 50 for *Estrategia* and accompanying activities for *Escribe*.

Estrategia

The *¡Hola!* icon indicates where you can find the *Estrategia* and activities for *Escribe* in the eText in your MySpanishLab course.

INTRODUCTION to *Escribe*

Escribe, a process writing section, appears toward the end of each chapter. In the *Para empezar* chapter, *Escribe* is available only online in MySpanishLab. Students will be given a strategy, and are then led to write step by step, using vocabulary and grammatical structures from the current chapter as well as previous ones.

SECTION GOALS for *Escribe* (Online)

By the end of the *Escribe* section, students will be able to:
- organize ideas.
- compile a list of nouns and adjectives that define themselves.
- write an acrostic poem.
- match letters with the beginning sounds of words.
- modify the poems to create sentences using *ser* and *tener*.

NATIONAL STANDARDS

Communication

Después de escribir asks students to present their poems. Depending on how you implement the activity, it could satisfy Standard 1.1 or 1.3. Standard 1.1 asks students to express feelings and emotions and share opinions. They are reporting things about themselves to a classmate, and the classmate can offer opinions about the poem. This might include agreement or disagreement with the adjectives used, or what the classmate likes or dislikes about the poem. Implemented in this way, the activity becomes an interpersonal exchange. On the other hand, Standard 1.3 requires students to present to an audience of readers or listeners. Students could write the poems and display them in a collection of class poems, or students could have a poetry reading, where they read their poems aloud to the class. This way of using the poems requires the presentational mode of communication.

¡Hola!
eText 54   01-57

Ambiciones siniestras

EPISODIO 1

Lectura y video

Estrategia

The ¡Hola! icon indicates where you can find the video, reading and corresponding activities for *Ambiciones sinestras* in the eText in your MySpanishLab course.

¿Cómo andas?

	Feel confident	Need to review
Having completed this section of *Para empezar*, I now can . . .		
Comunicación - Capítulo 1		
• describe families (p. 21)	☐	☐
• pronounce vowels (MSL / SAM)	☐	☐
• express what someone has (p. 22)	☐	☐
• use singular and plural nouns (p. 24)	☐	☐
• identify masculine and feminine nouns (p. 24)	☐	☐
• convey *the, a, one,* and *some* (p. 25)	☐	☐
• give details about myself and others (p. 26)	☐	☐
• state possession (p. 27)	☐	☐
• supply details about people, places, and things (p. 28)	☐	☐
• count from 31 to 100 (p. 30)	☐	☐
• determine the topic and listen for known words (p. 32)	☐	☐
• communicate about people I know (p. 32)	☐	☐
• organize ideas to write a poem (p. 32)	☐	☐
Cultura		
• illustrate formation of Hispanic last names (p. 22)	☐	☐
• compare and contrast several regional and national differences in the English and Spanish languages (p. 30)	☐	☐
Ambiciones siniestras		
• recognize cognates when reading and meet the six protagonists (p. 33)	☐	☐
• discover more about the protagonists' classes and their lives (p. 33)	☐	☐
Comunidades		
• use Spanish in real-life contexts (SAM)	☐	☐

33

METHODOLOGY • Student Self-Assessments

For a number of years our profession has moved in the direction of student self-assessments in addition to assessments by teachers. These self-assessments help students determine where they are with regard to their learning, and what individual remediation is needed. Research contends that instructors have to make students ultimately responsible for their own learning and one of the ways to do this is by having them self-assess. Research also finds that students tend to be overly critical of what they do and do not know, and periodic self-assessments help them to self-evaluate realistically.

METHODOLOGY • Assessment Domains

With regard to assessment, as previously noted, there are two main types of assessment: *formal* and *informal*. Within those two types, there are three domains/modes by which we can assess our students: *interpretive, interpersonal,* and *presentational*. When students read a passage, as with the chapter opener, and then respond to comprehension and critical thinking questions, you are employing the *interpretive* mode. When students work in pairs/groups, you are able to assess them in the *interpersonal* mode. Finally, when students present an assignment to partners/groups or the class, they are using the *presentational* mode.

CAPÍTULO 1

Instructor Resources
• PPT, Extra Activities

INTRODUCTION to
Ambiciones siniestras

In *Ambiciones siniestras*, you will meet a group of college students. They have become accidentally involved in an international plot. This section will be repeated throughout the regular chapters, beginning with a reading episode, followed by a video episode that continues the storyline. These episodes contextualize the vocabulary and grammar presented in the chapter. In the *Para empezar* chapter, *Ambiciones siniestras*, reading and video, is available only online in MySpanishLab.

SECTION GOALS for
Lectura y video

By the end of the *Ambiciones siniestras* reading and video sections, students will be able to:
• highlight cognates in the passage.
• read brief e-mails in Spanish.
• understand the main idea of each e-mail.
• distinguish between the characters.
• match the faces and voices of the characters to what they know about each character.
• provide background information about each character.
• compare the lives of the characters with their own.

NATIONAL STANDARDS
Communication, Cultures

The reading passage of *Ambiciones siniestras* provides an authentic text in Spanish. The format of this reading uses e-mail messages, a medium familiar to students. This reading highlights Standard 1.2 because the students are required to understand and interpret written Spanish, and the *Ambiciones siniestras* video segment that follows the reading also requires students to understand and interpret spoken Spanish. The reading provides a glimpse into the practices and perspectives of Hispanic cultures (Standard 2.2) because it highlights advertisements written in an e-mail format. Students are able to visualize where this advertisement might be posted in a Hispanic country.

NATIONAL STANDARDS
Comparisons

The reading from *Ambiciones siniestras* contains many cognates. Students of Spanish should recognize that there are many cognates between English and Spanish. Students use Standard 4.1 when they understand the nature of Spanish by making comparisons between Spanish and their own language. By scanning any reading passage to find cognates, students are focusing on how much they already know in Spanish instead of what they have yet to learn.

Instructor Resources
• IRM: Syllabi and Lesson Plans

NATIONAL STANDARDS

COMUNICACIÓN

- To share information about courses and majors (Communication)
- To indicate the stressed syllables in words (Communication)
- To describe your classroom and classmates (Communication)
- To relate daily activities (Communication)
- To create and answer questions (Communication)
- To count from 100–1,000 (Communication)
- To elaborate on university places and objects (Communication)
- To express *to be* (Communication)
- To articulate emotions and states of being (Communication)
- To convey likes and dislikes (Communication)
- To offer opinions on sports and pastimes (Communication)
- To glean the main idea (Communication)
- To communicate about university life (Communication)
- To craft a personal description (Communication)
- To engage in additional communication practice (Communication)

CULTURA

- To examine Hispanic university life (Cultures, Comparisons)
- To compare and contrast sports (Cultures, Comparisons)
- To exchange information regarding Mexico (Cultures, Comparisons)
- To explore the chapter's cultural themes further (Cultures)

AMBICIONES SINIESTRAS (Online)

- To skim a reading and note facts about the protagonists' lives (Comparisons)
- To discover more about the protagonists (Communication, Cultures)

COMUNIDADES

- To use Spanish in real-life contexts (Communities)

OBJETIVOS	CONTENIDOS	
COMUNICACIÓN - CAPÍTULO 2		
To share information about courses and majors	**1** School subjects and majors	35
To indicate the stressed syllables in words	**Pronunciación:** Word stress and accent marks	MSL/SAM
To describe your classroom and classmates	**2** The classroom	37
To relate daily activities	**3** Present tense of regular verbs	38
To create and answer questions	**4** Question formation and interrogative words	39
To count from 100–1,000	**5** Numbers 100–1,000	40
To elaborate on university places and objects	**6** Academic life	41–42
To express *to be*	**7** The verb **estar** (*to be*)	43
To articulate emotions and states of being	**8** Emotions and states	45
To convey likes and dislikes	**9** The verb **gustar** (*to like*)	46
To offer opinions on sports and pastimes	**10** Sports and pastimes	46–47
To glean the main idea	**ESCUCHA:** A conversation with a parent **Estrategia:** Listening for the gist	49
To communicate about university life	**¡Conversemos!**	49
To craft a personal description	**ESCRIBE:** A description **Estrategia:** Creating sentences	49
To engage in additional communication practice	**Heritage Language**	SAM
CULTURA		
To examine Hispanic university life	**NOTA CULTURAL** Las universidades hispanas	36
To compare and contrast sports	**NOTA CULTURAL** Los deportes en el mundo hispano	48
To explore further the chapter's cultural themes	**MÁS CULTURA**	SAM
AMBICIONES SINIESTRAS		
To skim a reading and note facts about the protagonists' lives	**EPISODIO 2** **Lectura:** *Las solicitudes* **Estrategia:** Skimming	50
To discover more about the protagonists	**Video:** *La aventura comienza*	50
COMUNIDADES		
To use Spanish in real-life contexts	**Experiential Learning:** Compras en línea **Service Learning:** Estudiantes hispanohablantes	SAM SAM

34

NATIONAL STANDARDS
Communities

College students can be a valuable resource in the community. Consider asking students from different disciplines and majors to make presentations to local high schools and middle schools. This presentation could be bilingual in nature, and they can talk about the number of hours they take at the university, what types of classes are required, how many hours they spend studying per week, and the kind of jobs (and salaries) they anticipate upon graduation. They might spend a semester mentoring a student group from a high school or middle school that shares the same future career plans. Standard 5.1 encourages students to use their Spanish in and beyond the school setting.

Comunicación
Capítulo 2 La vida universitaria

1 VOCABULARIO

3:00

¡Hola! eText 62 02-01 to 02-05

Las materias y las especialidades
Sharing information about courses and majors

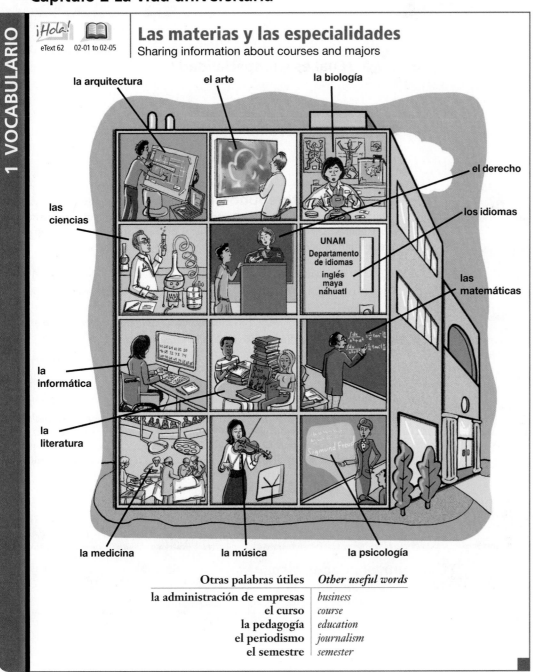

la arquitectura

el arte

la biología

el derecho

las ciencias

los idiomas

UNAM
Departamento
de idiomas
inglés
maya
náhuatl

las matemáticas

la informática

la literatura

la medicina

la música

la psicología

Otras palabras útiles	*Other useful words*
la administración de empresas	*business*
el curso	*course*
la pedagogía	*education*
el periodismo	*journalism*
el semestre	*semester*

Instructor Resources
• Textbook images, Extra Activities

SECTION GOALS
By the end of the *Contenidos* 1 through 5 students will be able to:
• report about their courses of study and their daily academic schedules.
• accent words using the rules for word stress.
• differentiate between words spelled the same that change meaning when accented.
• pronounce words correctly to indicate the stressed syllables.
• discuss common stereotypes.
• list classroom objects using *hay*.
• form regular verbs that end in *-ar*, *-er*, and *-ir*.
• ask questions using interrogative words and question marks.
• answer questions affirmatively and negatively.
• count from 100–1,000.

NATIONAL STANDARDS
Connections

What is obvious to us as instructors is not always obvious to students. It is important to help students realize the importance of studying Spanish and other languages as well. As you discuss the vocabulary for majors, have students share how they could use Spanish in their future careers. If they are uncertain of the connection, encourage other students to help them brainstorm how they will be able to do so.

The information presented in *Capítulo 2* is about university life. The cultural readings, vocabulary, and grammar (e.g., *gustar*) provide a starting point from which students can make connections between their courses of study and Spanish (Standard 3.1). This chapter also introduces rules for accents, stereotypes, and sports, which allow students to connect different viewpoints through the lens of a Spanish speaker (Standard 3.2). Some of the grammar presentations, such as *gustar* and regular verbs in the present, also promote making comparisons between English and Spanish (Standard 4.1).

21ST CENTURY SKILLS • CORE SUBJECTS
There are nine core subjects that are required for a learner to be prepared for work and life in the 21st century. The core subjects are *English, reading or language arts, world language, the arts, mathematics, economics, science, geography, history, government and civics.* It is important to note that world languages are listed as #2 in the list of nine core subjects. This fact can be shared with your students to help support their decision to study Spanish.

NOTE for *Las materias y las especialidades*
There is a great deal of variety in vocabulary throughout the Spanish-speaking world. We have attempted to use the most common words in the text, and variations appear in the *También se dice...* section in Appendix 3. For example, the Spanish equivalent of "business" could be *la administración de empresas* or *los negocios,* and "computer science" could be *la computación* or *la informática.* Feel free to use the words that are most familiar to you.

METHODOLOGY • Teaching Vocabulary
If you have a local "rival" university, start out by making comparisons in Spanish between that university and yours. For example, *Universidad X es*

muy pequeña, pero nuestra universidad es grande. Then ask students to recall certain adjectives by asking whether *grande* refers to your university or the rival university. Brainstorm to see how they think their university differs from universities in Latin America or Spain.

SUGGESTION for *Las materias y las especialidades*
Sometimes students take required interdisciplinary courses with special names like Western Humanities. When they talk about what they study, they want to translate the exact name of the course. Instead, ask them to think about what subject that course belongs to.

SECTION GOALS for *Pronunciación*

By the end of the *Pronunciación* section, students will be able to:
- distinguish the differences in pronunciation between accented and non-accented words.
- emphasize the accented syllable.
- pronounce question words and emphasize the stress on the proper syllable.

SUGGESTION for *Pronunciación*

Students should be encouraged to practice pronunciation both in and out of the classroom. In class, the most effective way to practice is for the instructor to say the sound, word, or phrase, and then have the students repeat it. Then say the sound, word, or phrase again and have students repeat it once again. Not repeating with the students allows you to hear how well they are imitating the sounds of the words.

SUGGESTION for *Las materias y las especialidades*

Always have a map of your campus available, as a hard copy or bookmarked on the Internet. Ask students to identify where on campus one studies each major. By personalizing the instruction to their campus, they are more likely to remember the information. This promotes learning about what majors other people study, instead of only what each student studies.

SUGGESTION for *Las materias y las especialidades*

Get to know the students in your class. If the class is composed of mostly first-year students, secondary (high school) students, part-time students, or community members taking the course for fun, recognize that they might not have majors or they might not have declared a major yet. Ask them to report about which classes they are currently taking, and ask them to identify to what majors those classes belong.

EXPANSION for 2-3

You may wish to have students each select a Spanish-speaking country, and then have them research a university in that country on the Internet. They can then share the facts they discovered with their classmates.

NATIONAL STANDARDS
Communication

Activity **2-3** promotes communication in the interpersonal mode. Students pair up, engage in conversation, provide and obtain information, and exchange opinions (Standard 1.1).

PRONUNCIACIÓN

02-06 to 02-08

Word stress and accent marks

Go to MySpanishLab / Student Activities Manual to learn about word stress and accent marks.

---

e **2-1** ¿Cuál es su especialidad?

---

e **2-2** ¿Qué clases tienes?

2-3 **Unos estereotipos** Do you think stereotypes exist just at your university? In your opinion, the following characteristics are stereotypically associated with students majoring in which fields? Share your responses with your group of three or four students, then report the group findings to the class. ■

Capítulo 1. El verbo *tener,* pág. 34 del eText; Los adjetivos descriptivos. pág. 43 del eText.

Estrategia

Go to Appendix 3, *También se dice…,* for an expanded list of college majors. *También se dice… includes* additional vocabulary and regional expressions for all chapters. Although not exhaustive, the list will give you an idea of the variety and richness of the Spanish language.

MODELO   Los estudiantes de _____ son ricos.

E1:   *Tengo "Los estudiantes de administración de empresas son ricos". ¿Qué tienes tú?*

E2:   *También tengo "Los estudiantes de administración de empresas son ricos".*

E3:   *Tengo "Los estudiantes de informática son ricos".*

GRUPO: *Tenemos "Los estudiantes de administración de empresas y los estudiantes de informática son ricos".*

Los estudiantes de…

1. _____ son ricos.
2. _____ son simpáticos.
3. _____ son trabajadores.
4. _____ son cómicos.
5. _____ son responsables.
6. _____ son pacientes.
7. _____ son interesantes.
8. _____ son muy inteligentes.

NOTA CULTURAL

eText 64   02-09

Las universidades hispanas

NOTE for *Nota cultural*
See eText pg. 64 for complete *Nota cultural* reading and *Preguntas.*

ADDITIONAL ACTIVITY for *Las materias y las especialidades*

The following activity will help students practice with creating memory devices. Group the students in pairs and have them create two lists based on the vocabulary for *Las materias y las especialidades.* Under List 1, have them write all the cognates they find in the new vocabulary words. Under List 2, have them write the remaining words. Students should create a memory device for each word in List 2. For example: *la informática:* "I save a lot of information on my computer." Other sample memory devices:

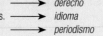

Dere *cho*se to study law. ⟶ *derecho*
I would be an *idiot* not to study languages. ⟶ *idioma*
*Periodi*cally I dabble in journalism. ⟶ *periodismo*

2 VOCABULARIO

4:00

¡Hola! eText 65 02-10 to 02-13

La sala de clase Describing your classroom and classmates

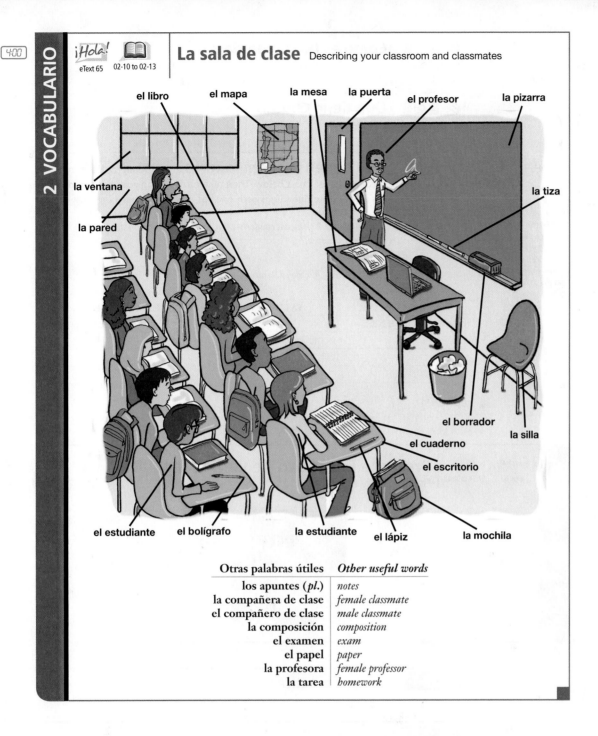

el libro · el mapa · la mesa · la puerta · el profesor · la pizarra · la ventana · la pared · la tiza · el borrador · la silla · el cuaderno · el escritorio · el estudiante · el bolígrafo · la estudiante · el lápiz · la mochila

Otras palabras útiles	Other useful words
los apuntes (*pl.*)	*notes*
la compañera de clase	*female classmate*
el compañero de clase	*male classmate*
la composición	*composition*
el examen	*exam*
el papel	*paper*
la profesora	*female professor*
la tarea	*homework*

 Instructor Resources
• Textbook images, Extra Activities

HERITAGE LANGUAGE LEARNERS
Some heritage language learners may be self-conscious about knowing Spanish and do not wish to be identified as "knowing" Spanish already. If you have more than one heritage language learner, you might want to pair them for some (but certainly not all) speaking activities. Initially, the very shy students may be nervous or intimidated working with a heritage language learner, but if you explain to students that they will all benefit by working with each other, your shy students will gain confidence.

21ST CENTURY SKILLS • FRAMEWORK
The Framework of P21 is depicted by connected circles. The divisions of the framework are: *Core Subjects-3Rs and 21st Century Themes; Life and Career Skills; Learning and Innovation Skills-4Cs (Critical Thinking, Communication, Collaboration, Creativity); Information, Media and Technology Skills.* Also connected by circles are Standards and Assessments; Curriculum and Instruction; Professional Development; Leaning Environments. All of these aspects are connected leading to the needs for 21st century teaching and learning.

SUGGESTION for *La sala de clase*
You may want to bring a shopping bag to class with some of the items from the vocabulary presentation inside. Practice the words by having students name the items you take out, one by one; or ask students each to reach in, draw an item, and then name it (or call on another student to name it).

ADDITIONAL ACTIVITY for *La sala de clase*

Asociación libre
The following is a list of words associated with school. Take turns calling out the words from the list and naming your associations.

MODELO
E1: *la mochila*
E2: *los libros*

1. los apuntes
2. el lápiz
3. la pizarra
4. la silla
5. la composición
6. la literatura
7. la tarea
8. el/la estudiante
9. la tiza
10. el cuaderno

EXPANSION for 2-5
In groups of 3 or 4, students should brainstorm a list of 4 things that each person in the group has brought to class and at least one thing no one brought.

NOTE for 2-6
Activities like **2-6** require students to write. *¡Anda! Curso elemental* offers various writing activities per chapter. Some require recording personal information that will be shared; others require gathering information from others. Students do not need to write in their books. These activities are available in the Workbooklet, or they may write on separate sheets of paper.

NATIONAL STANDARDS
Comparisons
Most grammar explanations in *¡Anda! Curso elemental* will encourage students to consider English grammar as the point of departure for understanding Spanish grammar.

NOTE for *Presente indicativo de verbos regulares*
Preferences vary regarding the presentation of *-ar, -er,* and *-ir* verbs separately or together. We believe that presenting them at the same time, but in progression (first *-ar,* then *-er,* then *-ir*), allows students to learn the *-ar* conjugation and then build on that knowledge, substituting the changes for *-er* and then *-ir* conjugations.

SUGGESTION for *Presente indicativo de verbos regulares*
You may want to use these drawings after you have reviewed the present tense conjugations. Have students describe Mario's schedule in more detail. You can also return to these drawings to practice question formation.

HERITAGE LANGUAGE LEARNERS
Your heritage language learners will most likely not understand the concept of "regular" and "irregular" verbs, just as many English speakers do not recognize that the concept of conjugation exists in English. They probably have not had to conjugate verb forms in Spanish before, but they will be able to determine whether something sounds right or not. They might substitute *usted* command forms for the present tense (e.g., *hable* instead of *habla*) because that is something they have heard at home.

SUGGESTION for *Presente indicativo de verbos regulares*
Have students practice the following verbs by quickly saying the correct forms using the following nouns and pronouns.

 2-4 ¿Cómo es tu sala de clase?

2-5 ¿Qué tiene Chucho?

 Workbooklet

2-6 ¿Qué tienen tus compañeros? Randomly choose three students and complete the chart below. Then take turns having your partner identify the classmates as you state **five** things each one has or does not have for class. ■

MODELO   E1: *La estudiante 1 tiene dos cuadernos, un libro, un bolígrafo y dos lápices. ¡No tiene la tarea!*
E2: *¿Es Sarah?*
E1: *Sí, es Sarah. / No, no es Sarah.*

ESTUDIANTE 1 _____	ESTUDIANTE 2 _____	ESTUDIANTE 3 _____
(NO) TIENE...	(NO) TIENE...	(NO) TIENE...
1.	1.	1.
2.	2.	2.
3.	3.	3.
4.	4.	4.
5.	5.	5.

 **3 GRAMÁTICA**

¡Hola! eText 67   02-14 to 02-18

Presente indicativo de verbos regulares
Relating daily activities

2-7 Vamos a practicar

2-8 El email de Carlos

Verbs: *estudiar, hablar, comer, correr, escribir, vivir*
Subjects: *tú, nosotros, Marco, usted, ustedes, Juan y Eva, yo, ellas, Mariela, ella*

NOTE for 2-9
Remind students that when they are working in pairs, there will sometimes be an odd number of students. Instead of using the *tú* form, they could ask the same questions of the other two students in a group in the *ustedes* form.

EXPANSION for 2-9
This can be expanded into a listening activity. Students take turns reading their sentences to a partner. While one student reads, the other student listens carefully and connects the items mentioned. Then they can check each other's work to see whether the lines match what was read.

HERITAGE LANGUAGE LEARNERS
Feel free to modify the directions of an activity for heritage language learners in order for them to practice their writing and reading skills. In particular, the mechanical practice of writing out each question will alert them to the punctuation and accent marks used in questions.

Workbooklet

`4:00`

  2-9 **Dime quién, dónde y cuándo** Look at the three columns below. Then, connect a pronoun to an activity, and then to a class, to create **five** sentences. Share your answers with a classmate. ■

MODELO E1: *nosotros / usar un microscopio / clase de ciencias*

E2: Usamos un microscopio en la clase de ciencias.

Fíjate

Remember that subject pronouns (*yo, tú, él, ella*, etc.) are used for emphasis or clarification, and therefore do not always need to be expressed.

PRONOMBRE	ACTIVIDAD	CLASE
yo	preparar una presentación	matemáticas
nosotros/as	leer mucho	literatura
ellos/as	necesitar una calculadora	español
ella	estudiar leyes (*laws*)	periodismo
tú	escribir muchas composiciones	historia
Uds.	contestar muchas preguntas	derecho
él	aprender mucho	arquitectura

`8:00` **2-10** **¿A quién conoces que...?** Who do you know who displays the following characteristics? Complete the following questions. Then, take turns asking and answering in complete sentences to practice the new verbs. ■

MODELO ¿Quién _____ (hablar) mucho?

E1: *¿Quién habla mucho?*

E2: *Mi hermano Tom habla mucho. También mis hermanas hablan mucho.*

1. ¿Quién ___corre___ (correr) mucho?
2. ¿Quién ___estudia___ (estudiar) muy poco (*very little*)?
3. ¿Quién ___escribe___ (escribir) muchos emails?
4. ¿Quién ___llega___ (llegar) siempre tarde a la clase?
5. ¿Quién ___abre___ (abrir) su mochila?
6. ¿Quién ___usa___ (usar) los apuntes de sus amigos?
7. ¿Quién ___comprende___ (comprender) todo (*everything*) cuando el/la profesor/a habla español?
8. ¿Quién ___cree___ (creer) en Santa Claus?

`5:00`

4 GRAMÁTICA

 ¡Hola! eText 70   02-19 to 02-23

La formación de preguntas y las palabras interrogativas Creating and answering questions

Antonio: ¿Cuántos idiomas hablas?

Silvia: Hablo dos, español y francés. ¿Y tú?

Antonio: Solo hablo español, pero mi loro habla cinco idiomas.

 Instructor Resources
• PPT, Extra Activities

NOTE for *Las palabras interrogativas*
As students are not familiar with the personal *a*, "whom" is not introduced at this point.

METHODOLOGY • The Natural Approach
This sequence of activities is a good example of the *Natural Approach* for language acquisition, taking students from simple yes/no questions to slightly longer sentence utterances.

ADDITIONAL ACTIVITY for *Las palabras interrogativas*
 Split the class into groups made up of 2 or 3 students; then have each group create and write 6 questions (2 addressed to someone's best friend, 2 addressed to 2 of their professors, and 2 asking about any 1 or 2 of their classmates) using the verbs and vocabulary of the chapter. Once the questions are formulated, they are to exchange them with another group and answer the other group's questions. This drill should be performed several times per term.

SUGGESTION for 2-13
Encourage students to circulate around the classroom, interviewing as many different people as possible.

NOTE for 2-14
Actividad **2-14** allows students to create their own questions without cues.

NOTE for Los números 100–1.000
Remind students that the numbers 16–19 and 21–29 are written as single words: *dieciséis, diecisiete, veintiuno, veintidós,* etc.

e **2-11** ¿Sí o no?

e **2-12** Preguntas, más preguntas

[8:00] **2-13** ¿Y tú? Interview your classmates using the following questions about Spanish class. ■

MODELO   E1:   ¿Cuántas sillas hay en la clase?
         E2:   *Hay veinte sillas.*

1. ¿Quién enseña la clase?
2. ¿Dónde enseña la clase?
3. ¿Quiénes hablan en la clase generalmente?
4. ¿Cuántos estudiantes hay en la clase?
5. ¿Qué libro(s) usas en la clase?
6. ¿Tomas muchos apuntes en la clase?
7. ¿Es la clase fácil o difícil?
8. ¿Trabajas mucho en la clase de español?

Vocabulario útil	
difícil	*difficult*
fácil	*easy*

♻ [8:00] **2-14** ¿Y tu familia o amigos? Write five questions you could ask classmates about their families or friends, then move around the room asking those questions of as many people as possible. ■

Capítulo 1. La familia, pág. 32 del eText; El verbo *tener*, pág. 34 del eText; Los adjetivos descriptivos, pág. 43 del eText.

MODELO   E1:   *¿Cómo se llaman tus padres? ¿Dónde viven tus abuelos?*
         E2:   *¿Cuántos hermanos tienes?...*

[3:00] **5 VOCABULARIO**   ¡Hola! 📖   eText 72   02-24 to 02-27

Los números 100–1.000   Counting from 100–1,000

100	cien	200	doscientos	600	seiscientos
101	ciento uno	201	doscientos uno	700	setecientos
102	ciento dos	300	trescientos	800	ochocientos
116	ciento dieciséis	400	cuatrocientos	900	novecientos
120	ciento veinte	500	quinientos	1.000	mil

6 VOCABULARIO

e **2-15** ¡Dinero!

e **2-16** Vamos a adivinar

5:00

¡Hola!
eText 74   02-28 to 02-32

En la universidad   Elaborating on university places and objects

Los lugares

el cuarto

Otras palabras útiles	Other useful words
el apartamento	*apartment*
el edificio	*building*
el laboratorio	*laboratory*
la tienda	*store*

NOTE for *Television*
The RAE accepts the use of both *televisor* and *televisión* to mean "television set." The authors of *¡Anda! Curso elemental* have elected to use only *televisión*.

NOTE for *Radio*
Please note that the radio can be feminine or masculine (la radio/el radio) depending of the country. Some Spanish-speaking students may say "la radio". The broadcast is always feminine.

SUGGESTION for *En la universidad*
Have students state the names of the buildings on your campus, e.g., *el gimnasio Woolen, etc.*

SUGGESTION for *En la universidad*
Have students tell their partners which of the items they have and do not have in their rooms/apartments, e.g., *Tengo una computadora; no tengo un radio.*

La residencia

Fíjate
El radio is the radio; *la radio* is the broadcast.

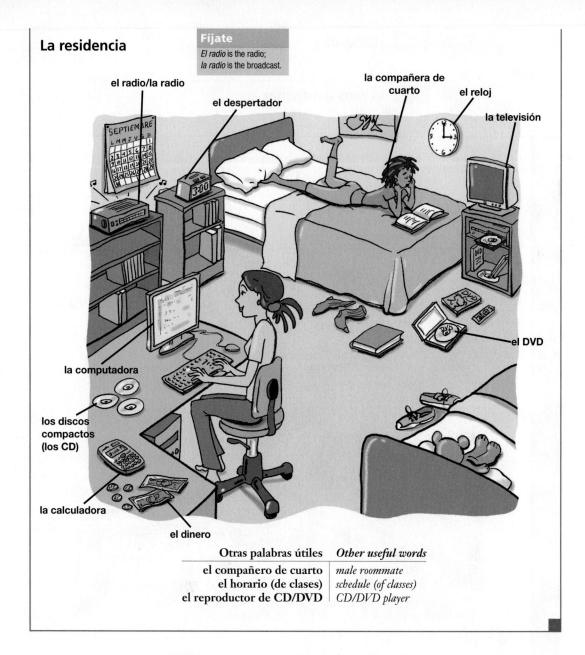

el radio/la radio · el despertador · la compañera de cuarto · el reloj · la televisión · la computadora · los discos compactos (los CD) · la calculadora · el dinero · el DVD

Otras palabras útiles	*Other useful words*
el compañero de cuarto	*male roommate*
el horario (de clases)	*schedule (of classes)*
el reproductor de CD/DVD	*CD/DVD player*

e **2-17** ¡Lo sé!

e **2-18** En mi cuarto...

Instructor Resources
• PPT, Extra Activities

[10:00] **2-19** **Datos personales** You are a foreign exchange student in Mexico, living with a family. Your Mexican little "brother" wants to know all about you! Answer his questions, which follow, then ask a classmate the same questions. ■

1. ¿De dónde eres?
2. ¿Qué estudias?
3. ¿Dónde estudias?
4. ¿Dónde comes?
5. ¿Dónde compras tus libros?
6. ¿Dónde vives?
7. ¿Qué necesitas para tu clase de español?
8. ¿Qué necesitas para una clase de matemáticas?
9. ¿Qué tienes en tu mochila?

METHODOLOGY • Grammar
It is helpful to have your students read through the grammar explanations prior to coming to class. In addition, you can assign 2–3 mechanical activities from the Student Activities Manual, the Extra Activities folder found in the Instructor Resources Manual, or other practice activities available on MySpanishLab for students to complete to practice the new grammar point. This allows students to come to class better prepared and more confident. ¡Anda! Curso elemental offers a great deal of student support and additional practice on MySpanishLab.

7 GRAMÁTICA

[3:00]

 ¡Hola! eText 76   02-33 to 02-37

El verbo *estar* Expressing *to be*

¿Dónde está mi hijita?

Estoy aquí, papi, ¡en el armario!

 **2-20** ¿Cuál es la palabra?

2-21 Busco...

ADDITIONAL ACTIVITY for *El verbo* estar
¿Dónde están?
Determine together where the following people are based on the statements given. Give as many possibilities as you can.

MODELO
La profesora Salgado contesta las preguntas de los estudiantes.
E1: La profesora Salgado está en la sala de clase.
E2: La profesora Salgado está en el laboratorio.
1. Cristina y Nico comen y ven la televisión.
2. Selma necesita comprar un libro para la clase de inglés.
3. Gregorio y David necesitan una calculadora.
4. Pedro termina la tarea.
5. Nosotros tenemos una reunión (meeting) con otros estudiantes.

[5:00] **2-22** **¡Ahora mismo!** With a partner, determine what the following people may be doing, using the following verbs. ■

aprender	comprar	comer	escribir	estudiar
hablar	leer	preparar	tomar	trabajar

MODELO E1: Marta está en la sala de clase.
E2: *Toma apuntes.*

1. Juan y Pepa están en la biblioteca.
2. Mi hermana está en la librería.
3. El profesor está en su casa.
4. Los estudiantes están en la cafetería.
5. María está en su apartamento.
6. Patricia está en el centro estudiantil.
7. Tú estás en el laboratorio.
8. Mi amiga y yo estamos en la clase de español.

METHODOLOGY • Pair Work
For 2-22 through 2-23, you may want Student 1 to do the even-numbered items while Student 2 does the odd items. It is important for you to overtly tell students to take turns when working in pairs. If not, one student may monopolize the pair work.

ADDITIONAL ACTIVITY for *El verbo* estar
Working in pairs, have students say whether the following places are *cerca* or *lejos*. For example: destination vs. where the student is now: la biblioteca/la sala de clase de español;
La biblioteca está lejos.
1. la biblioteca/la cafetería
2. la residencia estudiantil (o apartamento/casa)/la librería de la universidad
3. un laboratorio de computadoras/el centro estudiantil
4. el gimnasio/el estadio
5. un laboratorio de ciencias/la biblioteca
6. la casa de tu familia/tu residencia estudiantil (o el lugar donde vives)
7. el centro estudiantil/el estadio

2-23 La clase de geografía Take turns asking a partner in which countries the following capitals are located. ■

MODELO   E1: *¿Dónde está Washington, D.C.?*
         E2: *Washington, D.C., está en los Estados Unidos.*

Fíjate

Knowledge of geography is increasingly important in our global community. Activity **2-23** presents an opportunity to review the countries and capitals of the Spanish-speaking world.

1. Madrid	6. Buenos Aires
2. México, D.F.	7. Santiago
3. Lima	8. Tegucigalpa
4. San Juan	9. Santo Domingo
5. La Paz	10. La Habana

8 VOCABULARIO

3:00

¡Hola!
eText 79   02-38 to 02-41

Las emociones y los estados
Articulating emotions and states of being

Chema/Gloria **aburrido/a**

Roberto/Mayra **cansado/a**

Samuel/Tina **contento/a**

Ruy/Carmen **enfermo/a**

Memo/Eva **enojado/a**

Carlos/Patricia **nervioso/a**

Ramón/Raquel **preocupado/a**

Fernando/Silvia **triste**

Carlos/Rebeca **feliz**

---

e **2-24** ¿Cómo están?

---

e **2-25** ¿Qué pasa?

3:00 👥👥 **2-26** **¿Dónde y cómo?** Together, look at the following drawings and determine where the people are, what they are doing, and how they might be feeling. ■

 Tomás

 Tina

 Ana y Mirta

 El profesor Martín y sus estudiantes

MODELO   E1: El profesor Martín
                E2: *El profesor Martín está en la clase. Enseña matemáticas. Está contento.*

1. Tomás
2. Tina

3. Ana y Mirta
4. Los estudiantes del profesor Martín

🔑 **Instructor Resources**
• Textbook images, Extra Activities

SUGGESTION for *Las emociones y los estados*
Poll students to see which ones are tired, sick, happy, nervous, worried, etc.

SUGGESTION for *Las emociones y los estados*
Ask students when they experience the emotions and states of being presented. Then have students ask each other the question *¿Cuándo estás…?*

ANSWERS to 2-26
1. Tomás está en la biblioteca. Estudia/ Lee. Está aburrido.
2. Tina está en su cuarto. Está enferma.
3. Ana y Mirta están en una tienda. Compran un disco compacto (CD). Están contentas.
4. Están en la clase. Aprenden matemáticas/Tienen un examen. Están nerviosos.

METHODOLOGY • Lexical Presentations at the Point of Need

In *¡Anda! Curso elemental*, we have made the conscious decision to teach *gustar* in a very brief introduction. Educational psychologists inform us that all humans like to talk about themselves. We love to express our likes and dislikes early on in conversation. In order for your students to express their personal feelings and those of their friends or family members, it is important for them to be able to say at the very least *I like . . .* in order to practice vocabulary in complete sentences. *In ¡Anda! Curso elemental*, we have decided to introduce the pronouns *I, you, he/she,* and *it* with *gustar*. Indirect object pronouns and a more in-depth explanation of *gustar* will appear in *Capítulo 8*. You may also choose to present "to please" as a possible equivalent to *gustar*.

NOTE for *Gramática*

This is an inductive grammar presentation in which the students are given examples of a grammar concept and, through the use of guiding questions, they formulate the rule in their own words. Research indicates that students remember and internalize grammar rules better when they construct their own knowledge.

METHODOLOGY • Presentation and Practive of Infinitives

To reinforce the presentation of *gustar*, the students will practice with the infinitives of *los deportes y los pasatiempos*. Feel free to practice the regular verbs with directed questions such as: *¿Bailas bien?, ¿Cuándo nadas?, ¿Quiénes montan en bicicleta?*, etc.

NOTE for *Los deportes y los pasatiempos*

Remind students that they have already learned several *deportes y pasatiempos* such as *correr* and *leer*.

---

9 GRAMÁTICA

⏲ 3:00

eText 80   02-42 to 02-46

El verbo *gustar*   Conveying likes and dislikes

---

e **2-27** ¿Qué te gusta?

---

e **2-28** Te toca a ti

---

10 VOCABULARIO

⏲ 4:00

¡Hola!
eText 81   02-47 to 02-50

Los deportes y los pasatiempos
Offering opinions on sports and pastimes

bailar

caminar

escuchar música

ir de compras

jugar al básquetbol

jugar al béisbol

jugar al fútbol

jugar al fútbol americano

jugar al golf

montar en bicicleta

jugar al tenis

nadar

ver la televisión

patinar

tocar un instrumento

tomar el sol

Otras palabras útiles	*Other useful words*
el equipo	*team*
hacer ejercicio	*to exercise*
la pelota	*ball*

SUGGESTION for *Los deportes y los pasatiempos*
Ask students to name the sport or activity depicted in each photo.

SUGGESTION for *Los deportes y los pasatiempos*
Poll students regarding their favorite activities/pastimes and tally the results on the board.

EXPANSION for *Los deportes y los pasatiempos*
Have students play charades or *Pictionary* to practice the new vocabulary words.

ADDITIONAL ACTIVITY for *Los deportes y los pasatiempos*
Instruct students, working in pairs, to make three lists, referring to the vocabulary for *Los deportes y los pasatiempos*. In the first list, they should write the names of activities that are normally done in teams. In the second list, they write the names of the activities that can be done alone, and in the third list, the names of the activities that work best with partners. Have students determine which activities appear on more than one list.

2-29 ¿En qué mes te gusta...?

 2-30 ¿Cuánto te gusta?

NOTA CULTURAL

 ¡Hola! eText 84   02-51   **Los deportes en el mundo hispano**

NOTE for *Nota cultural*
See eText pg. 84 for complete *Nota cultural* reading and *Preguntas.*

 2-31 **¿Eres activo/a?** Just how active are you? Complete the chart with activities that should, or do, occupy your time. Share your results with a partner. So . . . are you leading a well-balanced life? ■

Vocabulario útil	
a menudo	*often*
a veces	*sometimes; from time to time*
nunca	*never*

A MENUDO	A VECES	NUNCA	NECESITO HACERLO (*DO IT*) MÁS
1.	1.	1.	1.
2.	2.	2.	2.
3.	3.	3.	3.
4.	4.	4.	4.
5.	5.	5.	5.

   2-32 **Tus preferencias** Select your **three** favorite sports and/or pastimes (**que más me gustan**) and then select your **three** least favorite (**que menos me gustan**) from **2-31**. ■

Paso 1 Write your choices in the chart. Then, create **two** sentences summarizing your choices.

LOS DEPORTES/PASATIEMPOS QUE MÁS ME GUSTAN	LOS DEPORTES/PASATIEMPOS QUE MENOS ME GUSTAN
1. patinar	1.
2. bailar	2.
3. leer	3.

MODELO *Los deportes o pasatiempos que más me gustan son patinar, bailar y leer. Los deportes o pasatiempos que menos me gustan son…*

Paso 2 Circulate around the classroom to find classmates with the same likes and dislikes as you. Follow the model. When you find someone with the same likes or dislikes, write his/her name in the chart that follows.

MODELO
E1: *¿Qué deporte o pasatiempo te gusta más?*
E2: *El deporte que me gusta más es el tenis.*
E1: *¿Qué deporte o pasatiempo te gusta menos?*
E2: *El pasatiempo que me gusta menos es ir de compras.*

LOS/LAS COMPAÑEROS/AS	EL DEPORTE/PASATIEMPO QUE MÁS LES GUSTA
1.	
2.	
3.	
LOS/LAS COMPAÑEROS/AS	EL DEPORTE/PASATIEMPO QUE MENOS LES GUSTA
1.	
2.	
3.	

ESCUCHA

eText 86   02-52 to 02-53

Una conversación

NOTE for *Escucha*
See eText pg. 86 for *Estrategia* and accompanying activities for *Escucha*.

¡CONVERSEMOS!
02-54

2-36 **La vida universitaria** Imagine that you are at a gathering on campus for exchange students from Mexico. Introduce yourself. ■

Paso 1 Create at least **five sentences** about you. Then create at least **five questions** to ask the person you are meeting. Include the following information:

- Introductions from *Capítulo Preliminar A* (p. 4)
- Vocabulary including majors, courses, professions, campus places, emotions and states of being, and sports and pastimes
- New **-ar**, **-er**, and **-ir** verbs from this chapter.

Paso 2 Take turns playing the roles of the student on your campus and the visiting Mexican student.

ESCRIBE

eText 87   02-55

Una descripción

NOTE for *Escribe*
See eText pg. 87 for *Estrategia* and accompanying activities for *Escribe*.

NATIONAL STANDARDS
Communication, Communities
The *¡Conversemos!* section affords students the opportunity to communicate in extended discourse in Spanish (Standard 1.3). Students can also be using the language in the community or simulating a real-life scenario (Standard 5.3).

METHODOLOGY • Building and Creating Sentences
We are committed to helping students work toward building and creating sentences. These kinds of descriptions and activities help to move them in that direction.

SECTION GOALS for *Escribe*
By the end of the *Escribe* section, students will be able to:
- organize their pre-writing thoughts by creating sentences.
- create a description of themselves and their likes/dislikes.
- write a brief summary using complete sentences to form a paragraph.

SECTION GOALS for *Escucha* **(Online)**
By the end of the *Escucha* section, students will be able to:
- distinguish between speakers in a telephone conversation.
- listen for the main idea.
- recognize questions in a conversation.
- retell the main points of the conversation by role-playing.

NATIONAL STANDARDS
Communication
In *Capítulo 2*, students practice listening for the gist, or main idea, of a listening passage. Students must understand and interpret spoken Spanish (Standard 1.2) each time they complete the *Escucha* section. The follow-up activity, **2-35**, encompasses the interpersonal communicative mode and the presentational communicative mode. In small groups or pairs, students provide alternate endings to the conversation (Standard 1.1) and present the endings as if they were Eduardo and his mother. If they present the dialogue to the class they can also meet Standard 1.3.

AUDIOSCRIPT for *A Escuchar* **(Online)**
(Sound of phone ringing)
mamá: *(mother answers)* Dígame.
eduardo: *(sleepily)* Hola, mamá. ¿Cómo estás?
mamá: *(lovingly)* Ay, Eduardo. Buenos días. Yo estoy muy bien, ¿y tú, mi vida?
eduardo: Bien, mamá. Muy bien. Mira… *(mother interrupts)*
mamá: Eduardo, son las nueve de la mañana. ¿No tienes clases hoy?
eduardo: *(uncertain)* Pues sí. A ver… hoy es martes… A las diez tengo psicología. Y a las dos tengo la clase de literatura inglesa… creo.
mamá: *(excitedly)* Bueno hijo. Gracias por llamar, pero tú tienes clase. Hablamos luego. ¡Adiós!
eduardo: *(frustrated)* Pero, mamá, necesito dinero… *(click—call is ended)*

SECTION GOALS for *¡Conversemos!*
By the end of the *¡Conversemos!* section, students will be able to:
- introduce themselves.
- describe themselves.
- describe their campus.
- share information about their classes.
- enumerate their schedules.
- state likes and dislikes.
- create questions to ask others the same information.

Instructor Resources
• PPT, Extra Activities

SECTION GOALS for *Lectura y video* (Online)

By the end of the *Lectura y video* sections, students will be able to:

• summarize information about each character.
• distinguish between when the narrator gives background information and when Sr. Verdugo is speaking.
• read a text that includes cognates, new vocabulary, and unfamiliar words.
• organize the information they have read into a chart.
• describe the characters in more detail.
• recap the events in chronological order.
• make predictions about the next episode.

METHODOLOGY • Video

The video and reading episodes in each chapter contextualize new vocabulary and grammatical structures. This feature is a critical part of the ¡Anda! program, as both episodes end in a mini-cliffhanger that is continued or resolved in the subsequent episode. If either is omitted, students will not be able to follow the story and a learning opportunity will be missed.

RECAP of *Ambiciones siniestras* Episodio 1

Lectura: In the first episode, there were three e-mail messages from some of the characters to various people. The first message was from Alejandra to her mother. In the e-mail, she described how handsome her new friend Manolo was, and she asked after her family. In the second, Eduardo wrote to Cisco about a *macroeconomía* assignment where he needed Cisco's help. In the last e-mail Marisol forwarded an e-mail to her cousin Ligia asking her if she should respond to the personal ad.

Video: In the video episode, the main characters (Marisol, Lupe, Alejandra, Manolo, Cisco, and Eduardo) were introduced. The students attend 3 different universities. At the northeastern university, Cisco and Eduardo discussed the macroeconomics homework; at the midwestern university, Marisol introduced Phillip (not a recurring character) to Lupe; and at the western university, Alejandra talked to Manolo.

ANSWERS to 2-42, *Lectura* (Online)

1. Three applications; Alejandra, Manolo, Francisco (Cisco)
2. Alejandra es de San Antonio, Texas; tiene muchos hermanos; su posible especialidad es el arte; sus actividades son pintar, escribir poesía y viajar. Manolo es de San Diego, California; tiene cuatro hermanos y

---

eText 90   02-60

Ambiciones siniestras

EPISODIO 2

Lectura y video

¿Cómo andas?

Having completed this section of *Para empezar*, I now can . . .

	Feel confident	Need to review
Comunicación - Capítulo 2		
• share information about courses and majors (p. 35)	☐	☐
• indicate the stressed syllables in words (MSL/SAM)	☐	☐
• describe my classroom and classmates (p. 37)	☐	☐
• relate daily activities (p. 38)	☐	☐
• create and answer questions (p. 39)	☐	☐
• count from 100–1,000 (p. 40)	☐	☐
• elaborate on university places and objects (pp. 41–42)	☐	☐
• express *to be* (p. 43)	☐	☐
• articulate emotions and states of being (p. 45)	☐	☐
• convey likes and dislikes (p. 46)	☐	☐
• offer opinions on sports and pastimes (pp. 46–47)	☐	☐
• glean the main idea (p. 49)	☐	☐
• communicate about university life (p. 49)	☐	☐
• craft a personal description (p. 49)	☐	☐
Cultura		
• examine Hispanic university life (p. 36)	☐	☐
• compare and contrast sports (p. 48)	☐	☐
Ambiciones siniestras		
• skim a reading and note facts about the protagonists' lives (p. 50)	☐	☐
• discover more about the protagonists (p. 50)	☐	☐
Comunidades		
• use Spanish in real-life contexts (SAM)	☐	☐

50

---

sus padres están divorciados; su posible especialidad es la medicina; sus actividades son jugar a los deportes, especialmente el fútbol americano. Cisco es de West Palm Beach, Florida; su posible especialidad es la informática; sus actividades son estudiar y trabajar.

3. Alejandro, Manolo y Cisco son similares porque son estudiantes. Son diferentes porque sus familias son diferentes y viven en ciudades diferentes, etc.

ANSWERS to 2-44, *Video* (Online)

1. *Possible answers:* joven, alto, fuerte, impaciente, guapo, curioso
2. An Internet café; No

3. *Possible facts about Eduardo:* third year student; major is Economics; speaks Spanish, English, and Portuguese; likes to play tennis and swim; volunteers to help poor children; spends time with his family
   Possible facts about Lupe: 25 years old; history and journalism major; spent 3 months in Brazil; speaks Spanish, English, German, and Portuguese; likes to write; family is important to her
   Possible facts about Marisol: born in New York; psychology major; junior; only child; likes to play golf and read detective novels; works as a volunteer in a hospital and in an elementary school
4. He reads it and thinks about it.
5. He is writing and sending an e-mail message.

OBJETIVOS	CONTENIDOS	
COMUNICACIÓN - CAPÍTULO 3		
To describe homes	**1** The house	52
To pronounce the letters **h, j,** and **g**	**Pronunciación:** The letters **h, j,** and **g**	MSL/SAM
To express actions	**2** Some irregular verbs	54
To elaborate on rooms	**3** Furniture and other household objects	57
To share information about household chores	**4** Household chores	59
To illustrate objects using color	**5** Colors	60
To depict states of being using **tener**	**6** Expressions with **tener**	61
To count from 1.000–100.000.000	**7** Numbers 1,000–100,000,000	63
To state *There is / There are*	**8** **Hay** (*There is, There are*)	64
To listen for specific information	**ESCUCHA:** A home description **Estrategia:** Listening for specific information	65
To communicate about homes and life at home	**¡Conversemos!**	66
To create an ad	**ESCRIBE:** An ad **Estrategia:** Noun → adjective agreement	66
To engage in additional communication practice	**Heritage Language**	SAM
CULTURA		
To relate general differences in housing in Spain	**NOTA CULTURAL** ¿Dónde viven los españoles?	56
To discover green initiatives	**NOTA CULTURAL** Las casas "verdes"	64
To exchange information about Mexico and Spain	**CULTURA** México y España	67–68
To explore further the chapter's cultural themes	**MÁS CULTURA**	SAM
AMBICIONES SINIESTRAS		
To scan a passage consisting of an enticing e-mail message received by Alejandra and Manolo	**EPISODIO 3** **Lectura:** *El concurso* **Estrategia:** Scanning	69
To determine who else receives the mysterious e-mail and their reactions to the message	**Video:** *¡Tienes una gran oportunidad!*	69
COMUNIDADES		
To use Spanish in real-life contexts	**Experiential Learning:** Las viviendas en España	SAM
	Service Learning: Casas para todos	SAM

51

NATIONAL STANDARDS
Communities
Use the community in which you teach as a resource for your students. Standard 5.1 states that students use Spanish both within and beyond the school setting. If students have not learned the appropriate vocabulary for these ideas, you will need to provide them a list of vocabulary for situations they might encounter. If your institution or community has a branch of Habitat for Humanity or another service organization, consider giving credit for volunteering for building projects for Spanish-speaking residents. Another idea would be to consider assisting senior citizens who might need help with a seasonal cleaning of their houses, with moving from residences to assisted-living facilities, or with getting ready to market and sell their property. Ask students to find a Spanish-speaking realtor, skilled laborer, architect, construction manager, housekeeper, building superintendent, etc., who lives and works in the community. Have the students shadow that person on the job and see how that job impacts the community.

21ST CENTURY SKILLS • DEFINITION
The Partnership for 21st Century Skills (P21) is a multidisciplinary project. The group, housed in Washington, D.C., has brought together the key national organizations representing the core academic subjects. The American Council on the Teaching of Foreign Languages (ACTFL) collaborated for a year developing the 21st Century Skills Map. The map, created by hundreds of world language educators, reflects the integration of languages and the necessary skills for a successful 21st century citizen.

NATIONAL STANDARDS
Connections
Question #3 of *Preguntas* connects the chapter theme to the disciplines of architecture, design, and construction as well as other disciplines such as geography, environmentalism, and anthropology.

SECTION GOALS

By the end of *Contenidos* 1 through 3, students will be able to:

- compare the features of their houses with the houses of others.
- explain how floors or stories of buildings are numbered in other countries.
- form the irregular verbs *dar, conocer, hacer, poner, salir, traer,* and *ver.*
- recognize patterns in the verbs with irregular *yo* forms.
- conjugate the stem-changing verbs *decir, oír, poder, venir,* and *querer.*
- express preferences using *querer.*
- combine *poder* with other infinitives.
- report on the activities of classmates.
- talk about the housing options available in Spain.
- describe the interior and exterior spaces of a house.

NATIONAL STANDARDS
Comunicación

The activities in this *Comunicación* section address Standard 1.1. Students can partner with classmates and engage in conversations about their houses. A simple summary sheet containing the vocabulary related to a house, the number of rooms, and/or its square footage can provide the basis for giving and obtaining information and exchanging opinions. Students can draw diagrams or write inventories of the things in their houses and present short narrations to the class using the new vocabulary (Standard 1.3). The students in their seats can listen to the presenter and compare their summary sheets with the information given by the speaker (Standard 1.2).

NOTE for *La casa*

Remind students that across the Spanish-speaking world there are many variations in vocabulary depending on where you are and with whom you are speaking. For example, the English word "bedroom" can mean *el dormitorio, la alcoba, la habitación, la recámara,* etc.

Comunicación
Capítulo 3 Estamos en casa

1 VOCABULARIO

`4:00`

¡Hola! eText 98   03-01 to 03-07

La casa   Describing homes

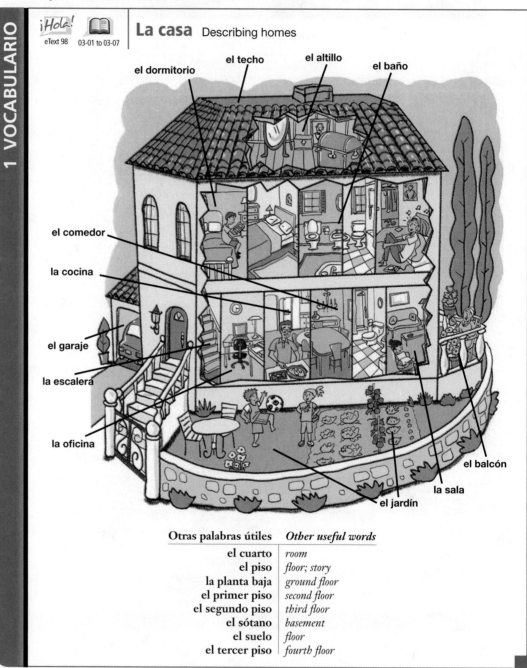

el dormitorio · el techo · el altillo · el baño · el comedor · la cocina · el garaje · la escalera · la oficina · el jardín · la sala · el balcón

Otras palabras útiles	*Other useful words*
el cuarto	*room*
el piso	*floor; story*
la planta baja	*ground floor*
el primer piso	*second floor*
el segundo piso	*third floor*
el sótano	*basement*
el suelo	*floor*
el tercer piso	*fourth floor*

METHODOLOGY • Teaching Vocabulary

With beginning language students, we believe in presenting vocabulary that is the most commonly used, and giving few, if any, country/regional variations. Presenting several ways to say the same thing becomes too complicated for the novice learner. Having said that, as Spanish language instructors, we all know it is difficult to determine exactly which words have the highest frequency of usage among Spanish-speakers in the world. In *¡Anda! Curso elemental,* we have attempted to select what appear to be the most commonly used words, but please feel free to use whatever words you may prefer. We encourage you to direct students to the *También se dice…* section in *Appendix 3,* for variations and additional vocabulary to enrich the basic *Vocabulario activo.*

PRONUNCIACIÓN

The letters *h*, *j*, and *g*

03-08 to 03-11

Go to MySpanishLab/Student Activities Manual to learn to pronounce the letters **h, j,** and **g.**

 3-1 **¿Dónde están?**

 3-2 **Las partes de la casa**

[4:00] 🍦🍦 **3-3** **¿Y tu casa...?** Túrnense para describir sus casas (o la de un miembro de su familia o de un amigo) y compararlas con la casa de la página 52. Usen el modelo para crear por lo menos (*at least*) **cinco** oraciones (*sentences*). ■

MODELO *En la casa del dibujo, la sala está en la planta baja y mi sala está en la planta baja también. En la casa del dibujo, el dormitorio está en el segundo piso, pero mi dormitorio está en la planta baja. No tenemos un altillo...*

Fíjate
In the directions, words like *miren, túrnense, comparen,* and *usen* are plural—they refer to both you and your classmate.

[4:00] 🍦🍦 **3-4** **Es una casa interesante...** Look at the following photos and together, create a short description of one of the houses. Imagine the interior, and the person(s) who may live there. Share your description with the class. ■

MODELO *La casa está en México y es grande y muy moderna. Tiene seis dormitorios, cuatro baños, una cocina grande y moderna, una sala grande y un balcón. Gastón y Patricia viven allí. Tienen tres hijos. Ellos trabajan en la ciudad...*

Vocabulario útil	
antiguo/a	*old*
la calle	*street*
el campo	*country*
la ciudad	*city*
contemporáneo/a	*contemporary*
humilde	*humble*
moderno/a	*modern*
nuevo/a	*new*
tradicional	*traditional*
viejo/a	*old*

SUGGESTION for 3-4
Remind of students, or help them brainstorm, useful vocabulary they already know in addition to the *Vocabulario útil* listed, e.g., *alto, bajo, grande, pequeño, pobre, rico, bueno, malo, fuerte, débil, el edificio,* etc.

EXPANSION for 3-4
Bring in a photo of a recognizable house or building, such as the White House, Trump Towers, or some other famous example of architecture in your area. Ask students to compare these buildings with the photos, or with the places in which they live.

SUGGESTION for *La casa*
Encourage students to use this location strategy to learn the parts of a house: Imagine that you are in your house, or a house that is familiar to you, and you learn the vocabulary by arranging the list in the order that you see the rooms. You might enter through *la puerta,* then see *la sala,* then *el comedor, la cocina,* and *el baño.* If you can, walk through the house and pronounce the vocabulary as you enter each room or hang a sign in each room with the corresponding vocabulary word. When it is time to take your test, close your eyes and remember the order in which you learned the rooms, just as they appear when you walk through them.

SECTION GOALS for *Pronunciación*
By the end of the *Pronunciación* section, students will be able to:
- distinguish between the English *h* sound and the silent Spanish *h.*
- pronounce the Spanish letter *j.*
- distinguish between the hard *g* and soft *g* sounds.
- use *refranes* as a way to integrate culture and pronunciation practice.

NOTE for *La casa*
Remind students that when communicating with native speakers from different Spanish-speaking areas of the world, they can combine words that they may have learned already with new vocabulary to express their ideas. You can use the word *el cuarto* to describe a room in general and then tell what function the room has. For example, you can refer to a bedroom as *un cuarto de dormir,* etc.

HERITAGE LANGUAGE LEARNERS
Ask your heritage language learners if they have any words related to the house that they use on a regular basis. Add those words to your vocabulary list so other students are familiar with them.

METHODOLOGY • Writing
Research strongly supports our belief that class time should be spent engaging students almost exclusively in meaningful *oral* activities. Virtually all of the activities in *¡Anda! Curso elemental* are meant to be done orally in pairs or groups. This maximizes students' opportunities to speak and use Spanish in confidence-building *i + 1* settings. Research confirms that strong oral skills translate into better writing skills. Therefore, students need a controlled environment to practice speaking so that outside of class, they will be more successful and confident writers. For more mechanical writing activities, please refer your students to the Student Activities Manual, Extra Activities, and MySpanishLab.

NOTE for 3-4
This activity exposes students to more variety on the subject of housing in the Spanish-speaking world. Further discussion may include housing in other parts of the Spanish-speaking world that are not represented here, the typical organization around the centralized urban state vs. provinces, economic disparity in Latin America, urban immigration and ghettos, etc.

1.

2.

México

3.

Oviedo, España

Guanajuato, México

4.

5.

6.

Cartagena, Colombia

Las islas flotantes de los Uros, Perú

Luarca, España

2 GRAMÁTICA

5:00

¡Hola!
eText 101   03-12 to 03-18

Algunos verbos irregulares   Expressing actions

> Necesito un apartamento para este semestre. ¿Qué hago?

> ¿Por qué no pones un anuncio en el periódico?

> Quiero comprar esta casa. ¿Qué dices?

> Me gusta. ¡Yo digo que sí!

e **3-5** La ruleta

e **3-6** Combinaciones

 `12:00` **3-7** **Otras combinaciones** Completa los siguientes pasos. ■

Paso 1 Escribe una oración lógica con cada (*each*) verbo, combinando elementos de las tres columnas.

MODELO (A) nosotros, (B) hacer, (C) la tarea en el dormitorio
Nosotros hacemos la tarea en el dormitorio.

COLUMNA A	COLUMNA B	COLUMNA C
Uds.	(no) hacer	estudiar en el balcón
mamá y papá	(no) ver	programas interesantes en la
yo	(no) conocer	televisión los domingos
tú	(no) oír	de la casa
el profesor	(no) querer	la tarea en el dormitorio
nosotros/as	(no) salir	los libros al segundo piso
ellos/ellas	(no) traer	ruidos (*noises*) en el altillo por la noche
		bien el arte de España

Paso 2 En grupos de tres, lean las oraciones y corrijan (*correct*) los errores.

Paso 3 Escriban juntos (*together*) **dos** oraciones nuevas y compártanlas (*share them*) con la clase.

Capítulo 2. La formación de preguntas y las palabras interrogativas, pág. 70 del eText.

 `6:00` **3-8** **Confesiones** Time for true confessions! Take turns asking each other how often you do the following things. ■

siempre (*always*)	a menudo (*often*)	a veces (*sometimes*)	nunca (*never*)

MODELO venir tarde (*late*) a la clase de español
E1: *¿Vienes tarde a la clase de español?*
E2: *Nunca vengo tarde a la clase de español. ¿Y tú?*
E1: *Yo vengo tarde a veces.*

1. querer estudiar
2. oír lo que (*what*) dice tu profesor/a
3. poder contestar las preguntas de tu profesor/a de español
4. escuchar música en la clase de español

5. hacer preguntas tontas en clase
6. traer tus libros a la clase
7. salir temprano (*early*) de tus clases
8. querer comer en la sala para ver la televisión

---

context. A level higher than *i + 1* is not comprehensible; it causes confusion and frustrates many learners, causing them to shut down to a point where they cannot comprehend anything. By the end of the first semester, virtually all direction lines will be in Spanish.

METHODOLOGY • Teaching Techniques
Most of the vocabulary and grammar activities are designed to be completed either in pairs or small groups. Krashen's Affective Filter Hypothesis states that students need a non-threatening environment, and having students work with each other provides just such an environment.

SUGGESTION for 3-8
Remind students that for **3-8**, they can confess what other people do. Sometimes shy students are more willing to participate if they can talk about other people, instead of themselves. They could say: *Yo no vengo tarde, pero mi hermana siempre viene tarde.* That way, they also practice the other verb forms.

INSTRUCTIONS for
La ruleta
Form groups of 2 to 4 students. Each group will need either a die or six small pieces of paper on which the numbers 1 through 6 have been written. Number 1 = *yo*; 2 = *tú*; 3 = *él, ella*; 4 = *Ud.*; 5 = *nosotros, nosotras*; 6 = *ellos, ellas.* The first person in the group rolls the die (or selects a numbered piece of paper) and gives the correct verb form, matching the number rolled. Other group members must verify the answer. After the correct verb form is given, the player passes the die to the next person. Players continue until the forms come quickly and automatically.

You may wish to keep 10 dice on hand to provide to students for activities like **3-5**.

 ADDITIONAL ACTIVITY for
Algunos verbos irregulares
Jugar a la pelota
Use a softball or make one out of paper. Say an infinitive and a subject, then toss the ball to a student. The student must give the correct form of the verb. At this point, you can either remain in control of the ball by having the student toss it back to you so that you can continue as before, or students can take over the game. If students take control, then the one who catches the ball and gives the correct answer (sometimes with some coaching by the teacher or other students) then says another infinitive and subject and tosses the ball to a different student, who must give the correct verb form.

Be sure to say the infinitive and subject before tossing the ball, so that all students formulate the answer instead of only the one who catches the ball.

NOTE for 3-5
Activities like *La ruleta* and *Jugar a la pelota* can be used regularly in class. The first time you give directions, a more detailed explanation may be required, but thereafter, set-up for the activity is minimal.

SUGGESTION for 3-7
Paso 3 could also be used to follow up and summarize group work.

METHODOLOGY • Direction Lines
Beginning in this chapter, direction lines will be in Spanish if they are *i + 1*. The nomenclature *i + 1* comes from research by Stephen Krashen known as the Input Hypothesis. (See Krashen, Stephen. *Principles and Practice in Second Language Acquisition.* New York: Pergamon Press, 1982, pp. 9–32.) The Input Hypothesis states that learners can comprehend input (language) based on words they already know plus a few additional words they may not know, but can intuit from

SUGGESTION for 3-9

As a follow-up, instead of just asking questions such as: *¿Quién ve la televisión todas las noches?* also ask *¿Quiénes ven la televisión todas las noches?* Or, after gathering some answers, check to make sure students are listening by asking questions like *¿Tom ve la televisión todas las noches? ¿Shirley y Steve ven la televisión todas las noches?*

NATIONAL STANDARDS
Communication, Cultures, Comparisons

By reading texts in Spanish (Standard 1.2), students are exposed to the culture of the people whose language they study. An article on Spanish housing provides a glimpse into one important aspect of the culture (Standard 2.1) while simultaneously reinforcing the reading comprehension and communication skills of the learners. The reading online is short, it includes definitions for unfamiliar vocabulary, and it includes appropriate cognates. University students are familiar with different types of housing, and they can make comparisons between typical housing arrangements in the United States and abroad (Standard 4.2). They understand the cost of housing as part of their room and board at school or by paying rent in an off-campus apartment. This background knowledge helps them compare the cultural differences.

METHODOLOGY • Students Taking Responsibility

We recommend assigning *all* culture sections to be read in advance. Additionally, we recommend assigning students to read *all* the grammar explanations before class since they are written in a very clear, concise fashion. The instructor's role then becomes that of clarifying or reviewing any points that the students read in advance.

Finally, we suggest assigning the *Escribe* sections as homework, as well as the *Ambiciones siniestras* text and video episodes. You may also want to assign pages from the book for students to study for homework. Remind them to read through the activities, including direction lines, so that less class time is spent setting up activities and more time can be spent with students actively engaged.

Workbooklet

3-9 Firma aquí Complete the following steps. ■

Paso 1 Circulate around the room, asking your classmates appropriate questions using the cues provided. Ask those who answer **sí** to sign on the corresponding line in the chart.

MODELO venir a clase todos los días

E1: *Roberto, ¿vienes a clase todos los días?*
E2: *No, no vengo a clase todos los días.*
E1: *Amanda, ¿vienes a clase todos los días?*
E3: *Sí, vengo a clase todos los días.*
E1: *Muy bien. Firma aquí, por favor.* ___*Amanda*___

Fíjate

Part of the enjoyment of learning another language is getting to know other people. Your instructor structures your class so that you have many opportunities to work with different classmates.

¿QUIÉN… ?	
1. ver la televisión todas las noches	_____
2. hacer la tarea siempre	_____
3. salir con los amigos los jueves por la noche	_____
4. estar enfermo/a hoy	_____
5. conocer Madrid	_____
6. poder estudiar con música fuerte (*loud*)	_____
7. querer ser arquitecto	_____
8. tener una nota muy buena en la clase de español	_____

Paso 2 Report some of your findings to the class.

MODELO *Joe ve la televisión todas las noches. Toni siempre hace la tarea. Chad está enfermo hoy…*

3-10 Entrevista Complete the following steps. ■

Paso 1 Ask a classmate you do not know the following questions. Then change roles.

1. ¿Haces ejercicio? ¿Con quién? ¿Dónde?
2. ¿Cuándo ves la televisión? ¿Cuál es tu programa favorito?
3. ¿Con quién(es) sales los fines de semana (*weekends*)? ¿Qué hacen ustedes?
4. ¿Qué días vienes a la clase de español? ¿A qué hora?
5. ¿Dónde pones tus libros?
6. ¿Siempre dices la verdad?

Paso 2 Share a few of the things you have learned about your classmate with the class.

MODELO *Mi compañero sale los fines de semana con sus amigos y no hace ejercicio.*

NOTA CULTURAL

¡Hola!
eText 105   03-19

¿Dónde viven los españoles?

NOTE for *Nota cultural*
See eText pg. 105 for complete *Nota cultural* reading and *Preguntas.*

METHODOLOGY • Reading

Prior to assigning a reading, always activate students' schemata, e.g., tap into their pre-existing knowledge. For example, prepare students for this reading by asking:

1. where most people live in New York City (or a large city near your university).
2. what types of dwellings are found out in the country.

You can also brainstorm with them words they know that relate to housing. You may want to pick out a few key words from the reading and ask what they mean.

EXPANSION for *Nota cultural*

Additional questions to ask your students are: *¿En qué se diferencian las casas del campo y de la ciudad? ¿Qué tipo de casas hay en tu ciudad/pueblo? ¿Hay barrios de inmigrantes? En el futuro, ¿dónde quieres vivir? ¿en la ciudad o en el campo? ¿Cuáles son las ventajas y las desventajas de vivir en un apartamento en la ciudad?*

ANSWERS to *Nota cultural* (Online)

1. Viven en pisos/apartamentos. Una urbanización es un grupo de casas en las afueras de una ciudad.
2. La vida en el campo es más lenta.
3. *Answers may vary.*

3 VOCABULARIO

4:00

¡Hola!
eText 106   03-20 to 03-25

Los muebles y otros objetos de la casa
Elaborating on rooms

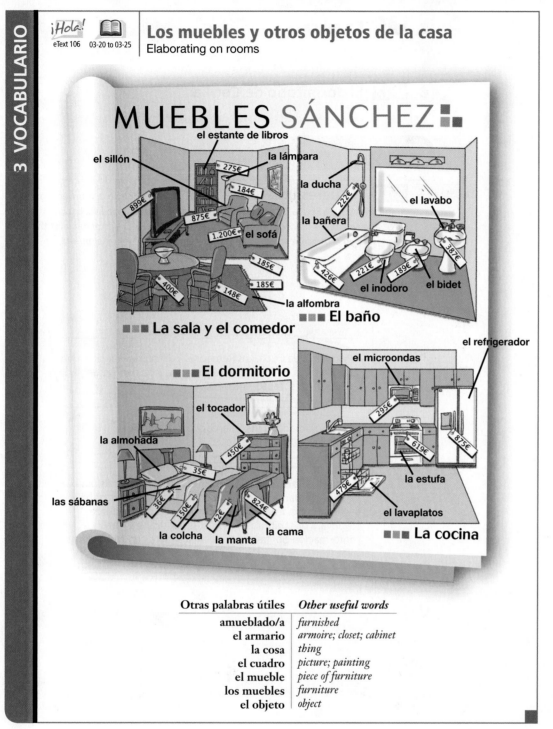

MUEBLES SÁNCHEZ

el estante de libros
el sillón
la lámpara
275€
184€
899€
875€
1.200€   el sofá
185€
400€
185€
148€
la alfombra
■■■ La sala y el comedor

la ducha
la bañera
222€
el lavabo
426€   221€   189€   387€
el inodoro   el bidet
■■■ El baño

■■■ El dormitorio

el microondas
el refrigerador
el tocador
la almohada
295€
450€
35€
las sábanas   875€
36€
619€
150€   42€   824€
la estufa
la colcha   la manta   la cama
el lavaplatos
■■■ La cocina

Otras palabras útiles	Other useful words
amueblado/a	*furnished*
el armario	*armoire; closet; cabinet*
la cosa	*thing*
el cuadro	*picture; painting*
el mueble	*piece of furniture*
los muebles	*furniture*
el objeto	*object*

EXPANSION for 3-11

Several additional activity ideas include:

1. Have students bring in images of rooms from the Internet, or catalogs and magazines, to describe to a partner.

2. As homework, or quickly in class, have students draw a floor plan of an ideal house, labeling the furniture. For students in CAD (Computer Assisted Design) classes, they could bring in an assignment from class to describe.

3. Have students bring in an image of an ideal room that they describe to their partner. The partner draws what he/she hears. The images are then compared when they are finished.

EXPANSION for 3-13

Ask each student to write an ad to "sell" his/her own apartment or the apartment of a friend or family member.

e **3-11** **En mi casa**

e **3-12** **El dormitorio de Cecilia**

Capítulo 2. El verbo *gustar*, pág. 80 del eText.

`8:00` ♥♥ **3-13** **¿Quieres una casa estupenda?** You have received a grant to study abroad in Sevilla, Spain! Now you need to find a place to live. Look at the three apartment ads below, and select one of them. Give your partner at least **three** reasons for your choice. Use expressions like **Me gusta(n)…** or **Tiene un/una…** Be creative! ■

MODELO   *Me gusta el edificio nuevo y tiene muebles. No me gustan…*

> Piso. Plaza de Cuba, Los Remedios. Edificio nuevo: dos dormitorios, baño, cocina, sala grande y balcón. Amueblado. 750€ al mes. Tel. 95 446 04 55.

> Piso. Colonia San Luis. Sala, cocina, dormitorio y baño. Sin muebles. 400€ al mes. Tel. 95 448 85 32.

> Alquilo piso de lujo en casa patio rehabilitada del siglo XVIII. Dos plantas, sala, cocina con zona de comedor, baño y dormitorio. Totalmente amueblado (junto a la Plaza Nueva, a dos minutos de la Catedral, Alcázar). Para más información por favor ponte en contacto con Teresa Rivas. Tel. 95 422 47 03.

4 VOCABULARIO

¡Hola! eText 109   03-26 to 03-29

Los quehaceres de la casa
Sharing information about household chores

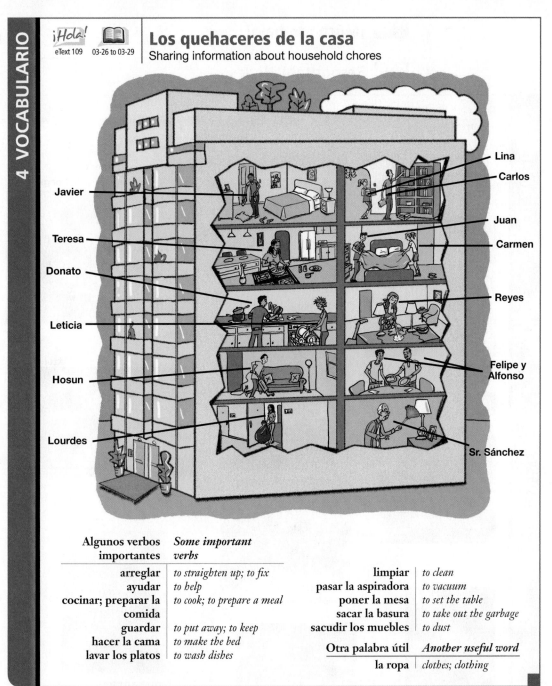

Labels on illustration: Javier, Teresa, Donato, Leticia, Hosun, Lourdes, Lina, Carlos, Juan, Carmen, Reyes, Felipe y Alfonso, Sr. Sánchez

Algunos verbos importantes	*Some important verbs*		
arreglar	*to straighten up; to fix*	limpiar	*to clean*
ayudar	*to help*	pasar la aspiradora	*to vacuum*
cocinar; preparar la comida	*to cook; to prepare a meal*	poner la mesa	*to set the table*
guardar	*to put away; to keep*	sacar la basura	*to take out the garbage*
hacer la cama	*to make the bed*	sacudir los muebles	*to dust*
lavar los platos	*to wash dishes*	**Otra palabra útil**	*Another useful word*
		la ropa	*clothes; clothing*

METHODOLOGY • *Tener que* + infinitive
Tener que + infinitive is introduced lexically in **3-15** and then introduced on page 115, *Algunas expresiones con* tener.

SUGGESTION for *Los colores*
Ask students to identify any additional colors they see in the photos.

NOTE for *Los colores*
Although "beige" is spelled the same in both English and Spanish, reinforce the proper Spanish pronunciation.

EXPANSION for *Los colores*
For further practice with colors, use the photos *El dormitorio de Cecilia*, from **3-12,** and *¿Cómo son?* **3-17.** Ask specific questions like *¿Qué colores ves en la foto? ¿De qué color es la alfombra? ¿De qué color es la lámpara?* or ask students to describe the two rooms orally and/or in writing.

Additional questions include: *¿De qué color es tu dormitorio? ¿De qué color es tu silla favorita? ¿Qué color te gusta más? ¿Qué color no te gusta?* etc.

ANSWER to question in *Los colores* presentation
Un refrigerador negro, un sofá blanco, una cocina verde, unas sillas amarillas.

HERITAGE LANGUAGE LEARNERS
Remind students that so far they have been using colors as descriptive adjectives. They are also used as nouns when they do not describe objects, just as in English: e.g., the brown one (*el marrón*), the blue ones (*los azules*), etc.

ADDITIONAL ACTIVITY for *Los colores*
Túrnense para decir cuáles son sus colores favoritos y qué cosas de esos (*those*) colores hay en la sala de clase.

MODELO
E1: *Mis colores favoritos son el marrón, el azul y el verde. En la clase hay veinte escritorios marrones y un libro azul.*
E2: *Sí, y también hay una puerta marrón.*

---

e **3-14** ¡Mucho trabajo!

e **3-15** Responsabilidades

5 VOCABULARIO

3:00

¡Hola! eText 111   03-30 to 03-33

Los colores Illustrating objects using colors

una casa sevillana
amarillo · *marrón*

una casa urbana española
beige

el puerto de Ribadeo
anaranjado

Los Picos de Europa
blanco · *negro*

el mar al lado de Baiona
azul

la catedral en Bilbao
gris

Un viñedo en La Rioja
morado

una casa privada
rosado

un autobús
rojo

las botellas para la sidra
verde

 **3-16 La casa ideal**

e **3-17 ¿Cómo son?**

4:00 **3-18 Buena memoria** Bring in colorful pictures of a house or rooms in a house. Select one picture and take a minute to study it carefully. Turn it over and relate to a partner as much detail as you can remember about the picture, especially pertaining to colors. Then listen to your partner talk about his or her picture. Who remembers more? ■

5:00 **3-19 En la casa de Dalí** Go to the Internet to take a virtual tour of the home of a famous Spaniard, such as the house of the famous artist Salvador Dalí, the Castillo Gala Dalí in Púbol, Spain. While you are exploring his house, or the house of another Spaniard, answer the following questions. Then compare your answers with those of a classmate. ■

1. ¿Qué ves en el jardín?
2. ¿Qué muebles ves o imaginas en cada cuarto?
3. ¿Cuáles son los colores principales de cada cuarto?
4. ¿Qué te gusta más de esta casa? ¿Qué te gusta menos?

El Castillo Gala Dalí

6 GRAMÁTICA

5:00

¡Hola! eText 113   03-34 to 03-37

Algunas expresiones con *tener*
Depicting states of being using *tener*

Susana tiene 19 años.

The verb **tener,** besides meaning *to have,* is used in a variety of expressions.

tener... años	*to be . . . years old*
tener calor	*to feel hot*
tener cuidado	*to be careful*
tener éxito	*to be successful*
tener frío	*to be cold*
tener ganas de + (infinitive)	*to feel like + (verb)*
tener hambre	*to be hungry*
tener miedo	*to be afraid*
tener prisa	*to be in a hurry*
tener que + (infinitive)	*to have to + (verb)*
tener razón	*to be right*
tener sed	*to be thirsty*
tener sueño	*to be sleepy*
tener suerte	*to be lucky*
tener vergüenza	*to be embarrassed*

EXPANSION for 3-20

EXPANSION for 3-20
Other ideas to expand upon are:
1. Have students say what they have to do this week, next week, etc.
2. Have students say what they think their instructor has to do today, tomorrow, etc.
3. Have students say what their parents have to do.

Note that these expansion options encourage students to use other forms of the verb *tener.*

ANSWERS to 3-22
1. Temprano en la mañana tengo sueño.
2. Los viernes por la tarde tengo ganas de salir.
3. Después de correr mucho tengo sed.
4. En el verano tengo calor.
5. En el invierno tengo frío.
6. Cuando tengo tres minutos para llegar a clase tengo prisa.
7. Cuando saco una "A" en un examen tengo suerte/éxito.
8. Cuando leo un libro de Stephen King o veo una película de terror tengo miedo.

NOTE for 3-23
These vignettes are based on Pablo, a character from Madrid, Spain. Some students may need more information about the few cultural nuances that appear in the vignettes (e.g., grades). This can also lend itself to cultural comparison.

HERITAGE LANGUAGE LEARNERS
Have students create a complete narrative of Pablo's day, including as many details as possible.

 3-20 ¿Qué pasa?

3-21 ¿Qué haces cuando...?

 3-22 ¿Qué tengo yo? Expresa cómo te sientes (*you feel*) en las siguientes ocasiones usando (*using*) expresiones con **tener.** Compara tus respuestas con las de un/a compañero/a. ■

Capítulo Preliminar A. Los días, los meses y las estaciones, pág. 20 del eText; Capítulo 2. Presente indicativo de verbos regulares, pág. 67 del eText.

MODELO   E1: antes de comer
            E2: *Antes de comer tengo hambre.*

1. temprano en la mañana
2. los viernes por la tarde
3. después de correr mucho
4. en el verano
5. en el invierno
6. cuando tienes tres minutos para llegar a clase
7. cuando sacas una "A" en un examen
8. cuando lees un libro de Stephen King o ves una película (*movie*) de terror

3-23 Pobre Pablo Poor Pablo, our friend from Madrid, is having one of those days! With a partner, retell his story using **tener** expressions. ■

MODELO

El despertador de Pablo no funciona (*does not work*). Tiene una clase a las 8:00 y es tarde. Sale de casa a las 8:10.

Pablo tiene prisa.

1. Es invierno y Pablo no tiene abrigo (*coat*).

2. Pablo tiene un insuficiente (60% en los Estados Unidos) en un examen.

3. Pablo recibe una oferta (*offer*) de trabajo increíble.

4. Pablo ve que no tiene dinero para comer.

5. Pablo está en casa y quiere una botella de agua. En el refrigerador no hay ninguna (*none*).

[4:00] **3-24** **Datos personales** Túrnense para hacerse esta entrevista (*interview*). ∎

1. ¿Cuántos años tienes?
2. ¿Qué tienes que hacer hoy?
3. ¿Tienes ganas de hacer algo diferente? ¿Qué?
4. ¿En qué clase tienes sueño?
5. ¿En qué clase tienes mucha suerte?
6. ¿Siempre tienes razón?
7. ¿Cuándo tienes hambre?
8. ¿Cuándo tienes sueño?
9. Cuando tienes sed, ¿qué tomas?
10. ¿En qué tienes éxito?

 [4:00]

7 VOCABULARIO

¡Hola! eText 116   03-38 to 03-42

Los números 1.000–100.000.000
Counting from 1,000 to 100,000,000

1.000	mil	**100.000**	cien mil
1.001	mil uno	**400.000**	cuatrocientos mil
1.010	mil diez	**1.000.000**	un millón
2.000	dos mil	**2.000.000**	dos millones
30.000	treinta mil	**100.000.000**	cien millones

e **3-25** ¿Cuánto cuesta?

e **3-26** ¿Cuál es su población?

 Instructor Resources
• Textbook images, PPT, Extra Activities

NATIONAL STANDARDS
Communication
Students work with partners using *tener* expressions to communicate how they feel. They are able to express feelings and emotions with their partners in an interpersonal exchange. This dialogue also allows them to exchange opinions about things such as fears, obligations, and how they react to a changing environment. The *Datos personales* activity, **3-24,** facilitates conversation because students have to provide and obtain information. This type of activity facilitates Goal One, Communicate in Spanish, by using Standard 1.1.

SUGGESTION for 3-24
As a follow-up, encourage your students to circulate, ask others the same questions, and report back to their groups in order to practice the third-person forms.

SUGGESTION for *Los números 1.000–100.000.000*
Have students review numbers 100–1,000 prior to beginning chunk 7.

SUGGESTION for *Los números 1.000–100.000.000*
Pronounce the numbers and have students repeat after you. Then write sample numbers on the board and have individuals say them.

NOTE for *Los números 1.000–100.000.000*
Many Latin American countries have experienced dramatic inflation over the past decades; therefore, prices of everyday items are often expressed in thousands of *soles, colones, pesos,* etc. Explain to your students that learning the numbers, especially the larger ones, will help them become a successful consumer in the Spanish-speaking world.

NOTE for *Los números 1.000–100.000.000*
You may wish to practice stating dates by placing a series of dates on the board and having students in groups express the dates to their partners. There is more practice with dates in the Student Activities Manual.

[4:00]   **3-27** **¿Qué compras?** Your rich uncle left you an inheritance with the stipulation that you use the money to furnish your house. Refer to the pictures on page 57 to spend 3.500€ on your house. Make a list of what you want to buy, assigning prices to any items without tags. Then share your list with your partner, who will keep track of your spending. Did you overspend? ■

MODELO   *Quiero comprar una televisión por* (for) *ochocientos noventa y nueve euros.*

> **Fíjate**
> The sentence in the model includes two verbs; the second verb is an infinitive (*-ar, -er, -ir*).
>
> Quiero compr**ar**   *I want to buy*
> una televisión.   *a television.*

NOTA CULTURAL

eText 119   03-46   **Las casas "verdes"**

NOTE for *Nota cultural*
See eText pg. 119 for complete *Nota cultural* reading and *Preguntas.*

[2:00]   **8 GRAMÁTICA**

¡Hola!   📖
eText 119   03-43 to 03-45

Hay Stating *There is / There are*

¿Qué hay en ese cuarto?

e **3-28** ¡Escucha bien!

e **3-29** ¿Qué hay en tu casa?

 Capítulo Preliminar A. Los números 0–30, pág. 16 del eText; Capítulo 2. La formación de preguntas y las palabras interrogativas, pág. 70 del eText.

[4:00] 👥 **3-30** **¿Cuántos hay?** Túrnense para preguntar y contestar cuántos objetos y personas hay en su clase aproximadamente. ■

MODELO   libros de español

E1: *¿Cuántos libros de español hay?*

E2: *Hay treinta libros de español.*

1. puertas
2. escritorios
3. mochilas azules
4. cuadernos negros
5. estudiantes contentos
6. estudiantes cansados
7. computadoras
8. estudiantes a quienes les gusta jugar al fútbol
9. estudiantes a quienes les gusta ir a fiestas (*parties*)
10. estudiantes a quienes les gusta estudiar

ESCUCHA

  ¡Hola! eText 121   03-47 to 03-48

Una descripción

NOTE for *Escucha*
See eText pg. 121 for *Estrategia* and accompanying activities for *Escucha*.

SECTION GOALS for
Escucha **(Online)**
By the end of the *Escucha* section, students will be able to:

- practice pre-listening strategies.
- prepare questions they might ask a real estate agent.
- complete checklists of features of houses.
- listen for specific details.
- use the information from a listening passage to relay information to others.

NATIONAL STANDARDS
Communication
Once students are able to listen for cognates and the main idea, the next strategy they can apply is listening for specific information. The communicative mode is interpretive (Standard 1.2) as they understand and interpret spoken Spanish. The *Después de escuchar* activity allows students to practice role-playing, and the communication is interpersonal (Standard 1.1). If the students describe the house in front of an audience of listeners, they are also communicating in the presentational mode (Standard 1.3).

AUDIOSCRIPT for *Escucha*
AGENTE: Tengo la casa perfecta para usted y su familia. Es una casa bella de un solo piso. Tiene cuatro dormitorios —uno grande y los otros tres más pequeños— y tres baños. La cocina es enorme y muy moderna.
SR. GARRIDO: ¿Y la sala? Siempre tenemos muchos amigos en casa.
AGENTE: La sala es grande y está al lado de la cocina. Hay mucho espacio para su familia y sus amigos.
SR. GARRIDO: ¿Cuál es el precio de la casa?
AGENTE: Es muy razonable. Solo 204.000 dólares.

ANSWERS to 3-32 (Online)
1. Number of floors: 1
2. Number of bedrooms: 4
3. Number of bathrooms: 3
4. Size of kitchen: large
5. Size of living room: large
6. Price: $204,000.

¡CONVERSEMOS!

03-49

 3-34 **Su casa** Look at the drawing below, and create a story about the family who lives there. Your partner will ask you the following questions as well as additional ones he/she may have. ■

- When does your story take place?
- What is the weather?
- What is the name of the family?
- Describe furniture and household objects using colors.

Also make sure that your story includes the following components.

- Include at least *eight* different verbs.
- Use at least *three* new **tener** expressions (p. 61).

3-35 **Mi casa ideal** Describe tu casa ideal. Di por lo menos (*at least*) **diez** oraciones, usando palabras descriptivas (adjetivos) en cada oración. Tu compañero/a de clase va a hacer por lo menos **tres** preguntas sobre tu descripción. ■

ESCRIBE

 ¡Hola!
eText 123

03-50

Un anuncio (*ad*)

NOTE for *Escribe*
See eText pg. 123 for *Estrategia* and accompanying activities for *Escribe*.

¡Hola!
eText 88   02-56 to 02-59

Les presento mi país

Gabriela García
Cordera

Mi nombre es Gabriela García Cordera y soy de Monte Albán, México. Soy una estudiante de la Universidad Nacional Autónoma de México (la UNAM) que está en la Ciudad de México. Vivo cerca de (*near*) la universidad con la familia de mi tía porque normalmente hay pocas residencias estudiantiles en las universidades y muchos estudiantes viven con sus parientes (*relatives*). La UNAM es la universidad más grande de México y de América Latina. **¿Cuántos estudiantes hay en tu universidad?** En la UNAM, tenemos un equipo de fútbol, los "Pumas". El fútbol es muy popular en mi país: es el pasatiempo nacional. **¿Qué deporte es muy popular en tu país?** Monte Albán está en el estado de Oaxaca, un centro famoso de artesanía. En particular, hay hojalatería (*tin work*), cerámicas de barro negro (*black clay*), cestería (*basket making*), fabricación de textiles y de alebrijes (*painted wooden animals*) y mucho más. **¿Qué tipo de artesanía hay en tu región?**

La biblioteca de la Universidad Nacional Autónoma de México. La fachada tiene un mosaico de la historia de México.

El tianguis de Tepotzlán en Morelia se instala los sábados y domingos con una variedad de artículos como comida y ropa.

ALMANAQUE

Nombre oficial:	Estados Unidos Mexicanos
Gobierno:	República federal
Población:	111.211.789 (2010)
Idiomas:	español (oficial); maya, náhuatl
Moneda:	peso mexicano ($)

¿Sabías que...?

- El origen del chicle (*gum*) es el látex del chicozapote (*sapodilla tree* en inglés), un árbol tropical de la península de Yucatán. Los mayas, tribu antigua y muy importante de Yucatán, usaban (*used*) el látex como chicle.
- La planta "cabeza de negro", del estado mexicano de Veracruz, forma la base del proceso para crear la cortisona y "la píldora", el contraceptivo oral.

Preguntas

1. What is the most popular sport in Mexico?
2. What is a "tianguis"? What do we have in the United States that is similar?
3. What are the origins of cortisone and the birth control pill?
4. What are some of the hand-crafted items from Mexico? What are similar handcrafted items made in your region?
5. What are some differences between the UNAM and your school?

 Amplía tus conocimientos sobre México en MySpanishLab.

---

coat of arms evolved from an Aztec legend. In the legend, the Aztec supreme deity, Huitzilopochtli, instructed the Aztec people to seek a place where they would find an eagle sitting on a prickly pear cactus eating a snake. In that place, they were to construct their city. After many years of wandering, they found this "sign" in Lake Texcoco, a swampy place. They established the city of Tenochtitlán (Place of the Prickly Pear Cactus), and it remained an important Aztec city until these people suffered defeat at the hands of the Spaniards in 1521. Mexico City is built on the ruins of this site.

ANSWERS to *Preguntas*
1. Soccer is the most important sport in Mexico.
2. It is a market. In the United States we have flea markets.

3. It comes from a plant from the state of Veracruz.
4. *Possible answers include:* woven blankets, hand carved objects, hand-made furniture, handmade baskets, etc.
5. *Possible answers include:* entrance requirements and size.

Instructor Resources
- Text images (of map)

SECTION GOALS for *Cultura*
By the end of the *Cultura* section, students will be able to:
- scan the reading for important information about Mexico.
- compare the UNAM and Oaxaca with where they attend school.
- list several popular forms of *artesanía*.
- comprehend brief background information from the *almanaque*.
- compare housing options in Spain.
- recognize the *tortilla*.
- discover the importance of el *fútbol*.
- discuss pastimes.
- identify La Alhambra and some of its architectural influences.
- summarize the statistics about Spain and its government.
- identify los *castillos*.

NATIONAL STANDARDS
Cultures, Comparisons
The information about Mexico and Spain in the cultural reading addresses the Cultures and Comparisons goals. Standard 2.2 is about understanding the relationship between the practices and perspectives of Hispanic cultures. Students learn that, in Mexico, unlike in the United States, there are fewer student residences on campus; therefore, many students live with their immediate family or with other family members. The reading also describes some of the common regional *artesanía*. Students can make comparisons between university housing options and products in the United States and Mexico (Standard 4.2).

The cultural information about la *tortilla*, La Alhambra, and the *Almanaque* section provide an excellent resource for making comparisons between the English language and Spanish (Standard 4.1). You could discuss the *influencia árabe* and the inclusion of words beginning with al into the Spanish language, the difference between the Mexican *tortilla* and the Spanish *tortilla* (Standard 4.2), and the frequency of "borrowed" words between the languages. The topics of *tapas*, nightlife, and soccer lend themselves well to comparing other cultural differences such as the hours for eating, the size of portions, the drinking age, the *discotecas*, the way Spaniards socialize, and their zeal for soccer (Standard 2.1).

CULTURAL BACKGROUND for *Almanaque*
The Mexican flag is a vertical tricolor flag with bands of green, white, and red (from left to right). In the center is a coat of arms, with a well-known emblem. The emblem contains an eagle holding a serpent in its talon, perched on top of a prickly pear cactus. The cactus is situated on a rock that rises above a lake. This

Cultura

España

   ¡Hola! eText 124 03-51 to 03-53

Les presento mi país

Mariela Castañeda Ropero

Mi nombre es Mariela Castañeda Ropero y soy de Madrid, la capital de España. Vivo con mis padres en un piso en el centro. **¿Dónde vives tú? ¿En una casa, en un apartamento o en una residencia estudiantil?** Me gusta la vida en la capital porque hay mucha actividad. A veces, me gusta salir con mis amigos por la tarde para comer tapas y tomar algo. La Plaza Mayor es uno de los lugares típicos para ir de tapas. **¿Cuál es tu lugar favorito para conversar y pasar tiempo con tus amigos?** Frecuentemente, hablamos de los deportes, sobre todo del fútbol y de los equipos españoles. ¡Cada uno tiene su favorito! **¿Cuál es tu deporte preferido? ¿Eres aficionado o jugador?**

Los ganadores de la Copa Mundial 2010

El patio de los leones de La Alhambra muestra la influencia árabe en Granada.

ALMANAQUE

Nombre oficial:	Reino de España
Gobierno:	Monarquía parlamentaria
Población:	46.505.963 (2010)
Idiomas oficiales:	español, catalán, gallego, euskera (vasco)
Moneda:	euro (€)

¿Sabías que...?

• España tiene una diversidad de culturas, regiones y arquitectura. Para un país el doble del estado de Oregon, tiene una gran variedad.

• Los *castells* forman parte de una tradición empezada en Cataluña en el siglo (*century*) XVIII que consiste en competir por hacer la torre (*tower*) humana más alta. ¡Actualmente el récord es un castillo de nueve pisos!

Preguntas

1. ¿Qué es una tapa?
2. ¿Qué evidencia hay de la presencia histórica de los árabes en España?
3. ¿Por qué son impresionantes los *castells*? Nombra una competencia famosa de tu país.
4. ¿Qué tienen en común México y España en cuanto a los deportes?

Amplía tus conocimientos sobre España en MySpanishLab.

Ambiciones siniestras

EPISODIO 3

¡Hola!
eText 126   03-57

Lectura y video

¿Cómo andas?

	Feel confident	Need to review
Having completed this section of *Para empezar*, I now can . . .		

Comunicación - Capítulo 3

	Feel confident	Need to review
• describe homes (p. 52)	☐	☐
• pronounce the letters **h, j,** and **g** (MSL/SAM)	☐	☐
• express actions (p. 54)	☐	☐
• elaborate on rooms (p. 57)	☐	☐
• share information about household chores (p. 59)	☐	☐
• illustrate objects using colors (p. 60)	☐	☐
• depict states of being using **tener** (p. 61)	☐	☐
• count from 1,000–100,000,000 (p. 63)	☐	☐
• state *There is / There are* (p. 64)	☐	☐
• listen for specific information (p. 65)	☐	☐
• communicate about homes and life at home (p. 66)	☐	☐
• create an ad (p. 66)	☐	☐

Cultura

	Feel confident	Need to review
• describe general differences in housing in Spain (p. 56)	☐	☐
• discover green initiatives (p. 64)	☐	☐
• exchange information about Mexico and Spain (pp. 67–68)	☐	☐

Ambiciones siniestras

	Feel confident	Need to review
• scan a passage consisting of an enticing e-mail message received by Alejandra and Manolo (p. 69)	☐	☐
• determine who else receives the mysterious e-mail and their reactions to the message (p. 69)	☐	☐

Comunidades

	Feel confident	Need to review
• use Spanish in real-life contexts (SAM)	☐	☐

Video: The mystery man from the reading, el Sr. Verdugo, commented as he read various essays. He was pleased with the applications of three students: Eduardo, Lupe, and Marisol, because they had Hispanic surnames (which meant they probably could speak Spanish), and they seemed to be curious students. El Sr. Verdugo plans to e-mail the 3 students. He ends by commenting aloud that the adventure is just beginning.

ANSWERS to 3-41, *Lectura* (Online)
1. Pili. Su novio, Peter, tiene 29 años.
2. Recibe un e-mail sobre un concurso.
3. Puede ganar un millón de dólares.
4. El país entero.
5. *Answers will vary.*
6. *Answers will vary.*

ANSWERS to 3-43, *Video* (Online)
1. *Possible answers may include:* Es bonito y grande. Su dormitorio tiene una ventana, etc.
2. Un e-mail sobre un concurso. También recibe el mismo e-mail.
3. En la biblioteca. Estudian matemáticas *(or whatever your students reply that would have mathematical problems).*
4. *Possible answers may include:* Es bastante grande con una cama grande, un armario, un sillón y una mesa para su computadora.
5. *Possible answers may include:* Es muy grande con una piscina grande. Es impresionante.
6. Eduardo y Cisco reciben el mismo e-mail que reciben Marisol, Lupe, Alejandra y Manolo.

CAPÍTULO 3

SECTION GOALS for *Lectura y video* (Online)
By the end of the *Lectura y video* section, students will be able to:
- engage in pre-reading activities.
- organize the information presented in the reading and scan for relevant information.
- utilize reading strategies such as focusing their attention and re-reading the passage.
- differentiate between the characters and who is speaking to whom.
- compare el Sr. Verdugo's e-mail with the junk e-mail they receive.
- role play how they would react if they received a similar e-mail.
- predict how Alejandra's parents might react to Peter, using the *tener* expressions.
- recognize the living space of Lupe.
- listen for specific pieces of information, such as the phrase *tal vez.*
- describe the homes and/or rooms of Eduardo and Cisco.
- narrate the characters' activities.
- summarize the messages the characters receive.
- arrange the events of the video in chronological order.

NATIONAL STANDARDS
Comparisons
The *Antes de leer* questions are created to spark students' interest, as well as to engage them in critical thinking and hypothesizing.

The reading from *Ambiciones siniestras* takes place in an Internet café. The characters discuss an e-mail they have received and what to do about it. Students can make comparisons about how they use e-mail for correspondence, what they do about unwanted e-mail, and how they protect themselves online from spam and scams. The e-mail format of the reading allows students to compare the informal writing style of e-mails and the different style of advertisements and junk mail (Standard 4.1).

NATIONAL STANDARDS
Communication, Comparisons
Note that the readings are kept at a level of comprehensible input that still entices students to read. Also, follow-up questions encourage students to think beyond the story content and to make informed guesses about what they would do in the same circumstance.

RECAP of *Ambiciones Siniestras Episodio 2*
Lectura: In *Capítulo* 2, a mysterious man used his computer to hack into the university web sites, and he read the college application essays of various students. In particular he read essays from Alejandra, Manolo, and Cisco. From their essays he found out their backgrounds, where they live, what years they are in college, and what their majors are.

CAPÍTULO 3   **69**

Vocabulary summary *Para empezar*

Capítulo Preliminar A

Los saludos *Greetings*

Bastante bien. *Just fine.*
Bien, gracias. *Fine, thanks.*
Buenos días. *Good morning.*
Buenas noches. *Good evening.;*
    Good night.
Buenas tardes. *Good afternoon.*
¿Cómo está usted? *How are you?*
    (formal)
¿Cómo estás? *How are you?* (familiar)
¡Hola! *Hi!; Hello!*
Más o menos. *So-so.*
Muy bien. *Really well.*
¿Qué tal? *How's it going?*
Regular. *Okay.*
¿Y tú? *And you?* (familiar)
¿Y usted? *And you?* (formal)

Las despedidas *Farewells*

Adiós. *Good-bye.*
Chao. *Bye.*
Hasta luego. *See you later.*
Hasta mañana. *See you tomorrow.*
Hasta pronto. *See you soon.*

Las presentaciones *Introductions*

¿Cómo te llamas? *What is your name?*
    (familiar)
¿Cómo se llama usted? *What is your name?*
    (formal)
Encantado/a. *Pleased to meet you.*
Igualmente. *Likewise.*
Me llamo… *My name is . . .*
Mucho gusto. *Nice to meet you.*
Quiero presentarte a… *I would like to*
    introduce you to . . . (familiar)
Quiero presentarle a… *I would like to*
    introduce you to . . . (formal)
Soy… *I am . . .*

Expresiones útiles para la clase *Useful classroom expressions*

Preguntas y respuestas *Questions and answers*

¿Cómo? *What?; How?*
¿Cómo se dice… en español? *How do you*
    say . . . in Spanish?

¿Cómo se escribe… en español? *How do*
    you write . . . in Spanish?
Lo sé. *I know.*
No. *No.*
No comprendo. *I don't understand.*
No lo sé. *I don't know.*
Sí. *Yes.*
¿Qué es esto? *What is this?*
¿Qué significa? *What does it mean?*
¿Quién? *Who?*

Expresiones de cortesía *Polite expressions*

De nada. *You're welcome.*
Gracias. *Thank you.*
Por favor. *Please.*

Mandatos para la clase *Classroom instructions (commands)*

Abra(n) el libro en la página… *Open your*
    book to page . . .
Cierre(n) el/los libro/s. *Close your book/s.*
Conteste(n). *Answer.*
Escriba(n). *Write.*
Escuche(n). *Listen.*
Lea(n). *Read.*
Repita(n). *Repeat.*
Vaya(n) a la pizarra. *Go to the board.*

Las nacionalidades *Nationalities*

alemán/alemana *German*
canadiense *Canadian*
chino/a *Chinese*
cubano/a *Cuban*
español/a *Spanish*
estadounidense (norteamericano/a)
    American
francés/francesa *French*
inglés/inglesa *English*
japonés/japonesa *Japanese*
mexicano/a *Mexican*
nigeriano/a *Nigerian*
puertorriqueño/a *Puerto Rican*

Los números 0–30 *Numbers 0–30*

cero *0*
uno *1*

dos *2*
tres *3*
cuatro *4*
cinco *5*
seis *6*
siete *7*
ocho *8*
nueve *9*
diez *10*
once *11*
doce *12*
trece *13*
catorce *14*
quince *15*
dieciséis *16*
diecisiete *17*
dieciocho *18*
diecinueve *19*
veinte *20*
veintiuno *21*
veintidós *22*
veintitrés *23*
veinticuatro *24*
veinticinco *25*
veintiséis *26*
veintisiete *27*
veintiocho *28*
veintinueve *29*
treinta *30*

La hora *Telling time*

A la… / A las… *At . . . o'clock.*
¿A qué hora… ? *At what time . . . ?*
… de la mañana *. . . in the morning*
… de la noche *. . . in the evening*
… de la tarde *. . . in the afternoon, early*
    evening
¿Cuál es la fecha de hoy? *What is today's*
    date?
Es la… / Son las… *It's . . . o'clock.*
Hoy es… *Today is . . .*
Mañana es… *Tomorrow is . . .*
la medianoche *midnight*
el mediodía *noon*
¿Qué día es hoy? *What day is*
    today?
¿Qué hora es? *What time is it?*
y cinco *five minutes after the hour*

Los días de la semana *Days of the week*

lunes *Monday*
martes *Tuesday*
miércoles *Wednesday*
jueves *Thursday*
viernes *Friday*
sábado *Saturday*
domingo *Sunday*

Los meses del año *Months of the year*

enero *January*
febrero *February*
marzo *March*
abril *April*
mayo *May*
junio *June*
julio *July*
agosto *August*
septiembre *September*
octubre *October*
noviembre *November*
diciembre *December*

Las estaciones *Seasons*

el invierno *winter*
la primavera *spring*
el otoño *autumn; fall*
el verano *summer*

Expresiones del tiempo *Weather expressions*

Está nublado. *It's cloudy.*
Hace buen tiempo. *The weather is nice.*
Hace calor. *It's hot.*
Hace frío. *It's cold.*
Hace mal tiempo. *The weather is bad.*
Hace sol. *It's sunny.*
Hace viento. *It's windy.*
Llueve. *It's raining.*
la lluvia *rain*
Nieva. *It's snowing.*
la nieve *snow*
la nube *cloud*
¿Qué tiempo hace? *What's the weather like?*
el sol *sun*
la temperatura *temperature*
el viento *wind*

Algunos verbos *Some verbs*

gustar *to like*
ser *to be*

Capítulo 1 ¿Quiénes somos?

La familia *Family*

el/la abuelo/a *grandfather/grandmother*
los abuelos *grandparents*
el/la esposo/a *husband/wife*
el/la hermano/a *brother/sister*
los hermanos *brothers and sisters; siblings*
el/la hijo/a *son/daughter*
los hijos *sons and daughters; children*
la madrastra *stepmother*
la madre / la mamá *mother / mom*
el/la nieto/a *grandson/grandaughter*
el padrastro *stepfather*
el padre / el papá *father / dad*
los padres *parents*
el/la primo/a *cousin*
los primos *cousins*
el/la tío/a *uncle/aunt*
los tíos *aunts and uncles*

La gente *People*

el/la amigo/a *friend*
el/la chico/a *boy/girl*
el hombre *man*
el/la joven *young man/young woman*
el/la muchacho/a *boy/girl*
la mujer *woman*
el/la niño/a *little boy/little girl*
el/la novio/a *boyfriend/girlfriend*
el señor (Sr.) *man; gentleman; Mr.*
la señora (Sra.) *woman; lady; Mrs.*
la señorita (Srta.) *young woman; Miss*

Los adjetivos *Adjectives*

La personalidad y otros rasgos
  Personality and other characteristics

aburrido/a *boring*
antipático/a *unpleasant*
bueno/a *good*
cómico/a *funny; comical*
inteligente *intelligent*
interesante *interesting*
malo/a *bad*
paciente *patient*
perezoso/a *lazy*
pobre *poor*
responsable *responsible*
rico/a *rich*
simpático/a *nice*
tonto/a *silly; dumb*
trabajador/a *hard-working*

Las características físicas *Physical characteristics*

alto/a *tall*
bajo/a *short*
bonito/a *pretty*
débil *weak*
delgado/a *thin*
feo/a *ugly*
fuerte *strong*
gordo/a *fat*
grande *big; large*
guapo/a *handsome/pretty*
joven *young*
mayor *old*
pequeño/a *small*

Los números 31–100 *Numbers 31–100*

treinta y uno *31*
treinta y dos *32*
treinta y tres *33*
treinta y cuatro *34*
treinta y cinco *35*
treinta y seis *36*
treinta y siete *37*
treinta y ocho *38*
treinta y nueve *39*
cuarenta *40*
cuarenta y uno *41*
cincuenta *50*
cincuenta y uno *51*
sesenta *60*
setenta *70*
ochenta *80*
noventa *90*
cien *100*

Un verbo *A verb*

tener *to have*

Otras palabras útiles *Other useful words*

muy *very*
(un) poco *(a) little*

Vocabulario útil *Useful vocabulary*

más *plus*
menos *minus*
son *equals*
por ciento *percent*
por *times; by*
dividido por *divided by*

Capítulo 2 La vida universitaria

Las materias y las especialidades *Subjects and majors*

la administración de empresas *business*
la arquitectura *architecture*
el arte *art*
la biología *biology*
las ciencias (*pl.*) *science*
el derecho *law*
los idiomas (*pl.*) *languages*
la informática *computer science*
la literatura *literature*
las matemáticas (*pl.*) *mathematics*
la medicina *medicine*
la música *music*
la pedagogía *education*
el periodismo *journalism*
la psicología *psychology*
el semestre *semester*

En la sala de clase *In the classroom*

los apuntes (*pl.*) *notes*
el bolígrafo *ballpoint pen*
el borrador *eraser*
el/la compañero/a de clase *classmate*
la composición *composition*
el cuaderno *notebook*
el escritorio *desk*
el/la estudiante *student*
el examen *exam*
el lápiz *pencil*
el libro *book*
el mapa *map*
la mesa *table*
la mochila *book bag; knapsack*
el papel *paper*
la pared *wall*
la pizarra *chalkboard*
el/la profesor/a *professor*
la puerta *door*
la sala de clase *classroom*
la silla *chair*
la tarea *homework*
la tiza *chalk*
la ventana *window*

Los verbos *Verbs*

abrir *to open*
aprender *to learn*
comer *to eat*
comprar *to buy*
comprender *to understand*
contestar *to answer*
correr *to run*
creer *to believe*
enseñar *to teach; to show*
escribir *to write*
esperar *to wait for; to hope*
estar *to be*
estudiar *to study*
hablar *to speak*

leer *to read*
llegar *to arrive*
necesitar *to need*
preguntar *to ask (a question)*
preparar *to prepare; to get ready*
recibir *to receive*
regresar *to return*
terminar *to finish; to end*
tomar *to take; to drink*
trabajar *to work*
usar *to use*
vivir *to live*

Las palabras interrogativas *Interrogative words*

¿Adónde? *To where?*
¿Cómo? *How?*
¿Cuál? *Which (one)?*
¿Cuáles? *Which (ones)?*
¿Cuándo? *When?*
¿Cuánto/a? *How much?*
¿Cuántos/as? *How many?*
¿Dónde? *Where?*
¿Por qué? *Why?*
¿Qué? *What?*
¿Quién? *Who?*
¿Quiénes? *Who?*

Los números 100–1.000 *Numbers 100–1,000*

cien *100*
ciento uno *101*
ciento dos *102*
ciento dieciséis *116*
ciento veinte *120*
doscientos *200*
doscientos uno *201*
trescientos *300*
cuatrocientos *400*
quinientos *500*
seiscientos *600*
setecientos *700*
ochocientos *800*
novecientos *900*
mil *1,000*

Los lugares *Places*

el apartamento *apartment*
la biblioteca *library*
la cafetería *cafeteria*
el centro estudiantil *student center; student union*
el cuarto *room*
el edificio *building*
el estadio *stadium*
el gimnasio *gymnasium*
el laboratorio *laboratory*
la librería *bookstore*
la residencia estudiantil *dormitory*
la tienda *store*

La residencia *The dorm*

la calculadora *calculator*
el/la compañero/a de cuarto *roommate*
la computadora *computer*
el despertador *alarm clock*
el dinero *money*
el disco compacto (el CD) *compact disk*
el DVD *DVD*
el horario (de clases) *schedule (of classes)*
el radio/la radio *radio*
el reloj *clock; watch*
el reproductor de CD/DVD *CD/DVD player*
la televisión *television*

Los deportes y los pasatiempos *Sports and pastimes*

bailar *to dance*
caminar *to walk*
el equipo *team*
escuchar música *to listen to music*
hacer ejercicio *to exercise*
ir de compras *to go shopping*
jugar al básquetbol *to play basketball*
jugar al béisbol *to play baseball*
jugar al fútbol *to play soccer*
jugar al fútbol americano *to play football*
jugar al golf *to play golf*
jugar al tenis *to play tennis*
montar en bicicleta *to ride a bike*
nadar *to swim*
patinar *to skate*
la pelota *ball*
tocar un instrumento *to play an instrument*
tomar el sol *to sunbathe*
ver la televisión *to watch television*

Otras palabras útiles. *Other useful words*

a menudo *often*
a veces *sometimes; from time to time*
difícil *difficult*
fácil *easy*
hay *there is; there are*
nunca *never*
pero *but*
también *too; also*
y *and*

Emociones y estados *Emotions and states of being*

aburrido/a *bored (with* estar)
cansado/a *tired*
contento/a *content; happy*
enfermo/a *ill; sick*
enojado/a *angry*
feliz *happy*
nervioso/a *upset; nervous*
preocupado/a *worried*
triste *sad*

72

Capítulo 3 Estamos en casa

La casa *The house*

el altillo *attic*
el balcón *balcony*
el baño *bathroom*
la cocina *kitchen*
el comedor *dining room*
el cuarto *room*
el dormitorio *bedroom*
la escalera *staircase*
el garaje *garage*
el jardín *garden*
la oficina *office*
el piso *floor; story*
la planta baja *ground floor*
el primer piso *second floor*
la sala *living room*
el segundo piso *third floor*
el sótano *basement*
el suelo *floor*
el techo *roof*
el tercer piso *fourth floor*

Los verbos *Verbs*

conocer *to be acquainted with*
dar *to give*
decir *to say; to tell*
hacer *to do; to make*
oír *to hear*
poder *to be able to*
poner *to put; to place*
querer *to want; to love*
salir *to leave; to go out*
traer *to bring*
venir *to come*
ver *to see*

Los muebles y otros objetos de la casa *Furniture and other objects in the house*

La sala y el comedor *The living room and dining room*

la alfombra *rug; carpet*
el estante *bookcase*
la lámpara *lamp*
el sillón *armchair*
el sofá *sofa*

La cocina *The kitchen*

la estufa *stove*
el lavaplatos *dishwasher*
el microondas *microwave*
el refrigerador *refrigerator*

El baño *The bathroom*

la bañera *bathtub*
el bidet *bidet*

la ducha *shower*
el inodoro *toilet*
el lavabo *sink*

El dormitorio *The bedroom*

la almohada *pillow*
la cama *bed*
la colcha *bedspread; comforter*
la manta *blanket*
las sábanas *sheets*
el tocador *dresser*

Otras palabras útiles en la casa *Other useful words in the house*

amueblado/a *furnished*
el armario *armoire; closet; cabinet*
la cosa *thing*
el cuadro *picture; painting*
el mueble *piece of furniture*
los muebles *furniture*
el objeto *object*

Los quehaceres de la casa *Household chores*

arreglar *to straighten up; to fix*
ayudar *to help*
cocinar, preparar la comida *to cook*
guardar *to put away; to keep*
hacer la cama *to make the bed*
lavar los platos *to wash dishes*
limpiar *to clean*
pasar la aspiradora *to vacuum*
poner la mesa *to set the table*
sacar la basura *to take out the garbage*
sacudir los muebles *to dust*

Los colores *Colors*

amarillo *yellow*
anaranjado *orange*
azul *blue*
beige *beige*
blanco *white*
gris *gray*
marrón *brown*
morado *purple*
negro *black*
rojo *red*
rosado *pink*
verde *green*

Expresiones con *tener* *Expressions with* tener

tener... años *to be . . . years old*
tener calor *to be hot*
tener cuidado *to be careful*

tener éxito *to be successful*
tener frío *to be cold*
tener ganas de + *(infinitive) to feel like + (verb)*
tener hambre *to be hungry*
tener miedo *to be afraid*
tener prisa *to be in a hurry*
tener que + *(infinitive) to have to + (verb)*
tener razón *to be right*
tener sed *to be thirsty*
tener sueño *to be sleepy*
tener suerte *to be lucky*
tener vergüenza *to be embarrassed*

Los números 1.000– 100.000.000 *Numbers 1,000–100,000,000*

mil *1,000*
mil uno *1,001*
mil diez *1,010*
dos mil *2,000*
treinta mil *30,000*
cien mil *100,000*
cuatrocientos mil *400,000*
un millón *1,000,000*
dos millones *2,000,000*
cien millones *100,000,000*

Otras palabras útiles *Other useful words*

a la derecha (de) *to the right (of)*
a la izquierda (de) *to the left (of)*
al lado (de) *beside*
a menudo *often*
a veces *sometimes*
antiguo/a *old*
la calle *street*
el campo *country*
la ciudad *city*
contemporáneo/a *contemporary*
desordenado/a *messy*
encima (de) *on top (of)*
humilde *humble*
limpio/a *clean*
moderno/a *modern*
nuevo/a *new*
la ropa *clothes; clothing*
siempre *always*
sucio/a *dirty*
tradicional *traditional*
viejo/a *old*

73

Grammar summary *Para empezar*

El alfabeto

The Spanish alphabet is quite similar to the English alphabet except in the ways the letters are pronounced. Learning the proper pronunciation of the individual letters in Spanish will help you pronounce new words and phrases.

Letter	Letter Name	Examples
a	a	adiós
b	be	buenos
c	ce	clase
d	de	día
e	e	español
f	efe	por favor
g	ge	luego
h	hache	hola
i	i	señorita
j	jota	julio
k	ka	kilómetro
l	ele	luego
m	eme	madre
n	ene	noche
ñ	eñe	mañana
o	o	cómo
p	pe	por favor
q	cu	qué
r	ere	señora
s	ese	saludos
t	te	tarde
u	u	usted
v	uve	nueve
w	doble ve o uve doble	Washington
x	equis	examen
y	ye o i griega	yo
z	zeta	pizarra

Los pronombres personales

The chart below lists the subject pronouns in Spanish and their equivalents in English. As you will note, Spanish has several equivalents for *you*.

yo	*I*	nosotros/as	*we*
tú	*you (fam.)*	vosotros/as	*you (pl., Spain)*
usted	*you (form.)*	ustedes	*you (pl.)*
él	*he*	ellos	*they (masc.)*
ella	*she*	ellas	*they (fem.)*

Generally speaking, **tú** (you, singular) is used for people with whom you are on a first-name basis, such as family members and friends.

Usted, abbreviated **Ud.,** is used with people you do not know well, or with people with whom you are not on a first-name basis. **Usted** is also used with older people, or with those to whom you want to show respect.

Spanish shows gender more clearly than English. **Nosotros** and **ellos** are used to refer to either all males or to a mixed group of males and females. **Nosotras** and **ellas** refer to an all-female group.

El verbo *ser*

You have already learned the subject pronouns in Spanish. It is time to put them together with a verb. First, consider the verb *to be* in English. The *to* form of a verb, as in *to be* or *to see* is called an *infinitive*. Note that *to be* has different forms for different subjects.

to be			
I	am	we	are
you	are	you (all)	are
he, she, it	is	they	are

Verbs in Spanish also have different forms for different subjects.

ser (*to be*)					
Singular			**Plural**		
yo	soy	*I am*	nosotros/as	somos	*we are*
tú	eres	*you are*	vosotros/as	sois	*you are*
Ud.	es	*you are*	Uds.	son	*you are*
él, ella	es	*he/she is*	ellos/as	son	*they are*

- In Spanish, subject pronouns are not required, but rather used for clarification or emphasis. Pronouns are indicated by the verb ending. For example:

  Soy means *I am.*

  Es means either *he is, she is,* or *you* (formal) *are.*

- If you are using a subject pronoun, it will appear first, followed by the form of the verb that corresponds to the subject pronoun, and then the rest of the sentence, as in the examples:

  Yo **soy** Mark.   **Soy** Mark.

  Él **es** inteligente.   **Es** inteligente.

Capítulo 1 ¿Quiénes somos?

El verbo *tener*

In **Capítulo Preliminar A** you learned the present tense of **ser.** Another very common verb in Spanish is **tener** (*to have*). The present tense forms of the verb **tener** follow.

tener (*to have*)				
Singular		**Plural**		
yo	**tengo** *I have*	nosotros/as	**tenemos** *we have*	
tú	**tienes** *you have*	vosotros/as	**tenéis** *you have*	
Ud.	**tiene** *you have*	Uds.	**tienen** *you all have*	
él, ella	**tiene** *he/she has*	ellos/as	**tienen** *they have*	

Sustantivos singulares y plurales

To pluralize singular nouns and adjectives in Spanish, follow these simple guidelines.

1. If the word ends in a vowel, add **-s.**
   hermana → hermana**s**   abuelo → abuelo**s**
   día → día**s**   mi → mi**s**

2. If the word ends in a consonant, add **-es.**
   mes → mes**es**   ciudad → ciudad**es**
   televisión → televisiones   joven → jóvenes

3. If the word ends in a **-z**, change the **z** to **c**, and add **-es.**
   lápiz → lápi**ces**   feliz → feli**ces**

El masculino y el femenino

In Spanish, all nouns (people, places, and things) have a gender; they are either masculine or feminine. Use the following rules to help you determine the gender of nouns. If a noun does not belong to any of the following categories, you must memorize the gender as you learn that noun.

1. Most words ending in **-a** are feminine.

   la hermana, la hija, la mamá, la tía

   *Some exceptions: **el día, el papá,** and words of Greek origin ending in -**ma,** such as **el problema** and **el programa.**

2. Most words ending in **-o** are masculine.

   el abuelo, el hermano, el hijo, el nieto

   *Some exceptions: **la foto** (*photo*), **la mano** (*hand*), **la moto** (*motorcycle*)
   *Note: **la foto** and **la moto** are shortened forms for **la fotografía** and **la motocicleta.**

3. Words ending in **-ción** and **-sión** are feminine.

   la discusión, la recepción, la televisión

   *Note: The suffix **-ción** is equivalent to the English *-tion.*

4. Words ending in **-dad** or **-tad** are feminine.

   la ciudad (*city*), **la libertad, la universidad**

   *Note: these suffixes are equivalent to the English *-ty.*

As you learned in **Capítulo Preliminar A,** words that look alike and have the same meaning in both English and Spanish, such as **discusión** and **universidad,** are known as *cognates.* Use them to help you decipher meaning and to form words.

Los artículos definidos e indefinidos

Like English, Spanish has two kinds of articles, definite and indefinite. The definite article in English is *the;* the indefinite articles are *a, an,* and *some.*

In Spanish, articles and other adjectives mirror the gender (masculine or feminine) and number (singular or plural) of the nouns to which they refer. For example, an article referring to a singular masculine noun must also be singular and masculine. Note the forms of the articles in the following charts.

Los artículos definidos			
el hermano	*the brother*	**los** hermanos	*the brothers / the brothers and sisters*
la hermana	*the sister*	**las** hermanas	*the sisters*

Los artículos indefinidos			
un hermano	*a / one brother*	**unos** hermanos	*some brothers / some brothers and sisters*
una hermana	*a / one sister*	**unas** hermanas	*some sisters*

75

1. *Definite articles* are used to refer to **the** person, place, or thing.

2. *Indefinite articles* are used to refer to **a** or **some** person, place, or thing.

Adriana es **la** hermana de Eduardo y **los** abuelos de él se llaman Carmen y Manuel.	*Adriana is Eduardo's sister, and his grandparents' names are Carmen and Manuel.*
Jorge tiene **una** tía y **unos** tíos.	*Jorge has an aunt and some uncles.*

Los adjetivos posesivos

You have already used the possessive adjective **mi** (*my*). Other forms of possessive adjectives are also useful in conversation.

Look at the following chart to see how to personalize talk about your family (*our* dad, *his* sister, *our* cousins, etc.) using possessive adjectives.

Los adjetivos posesivos

mi, mis	*my*	nuestro/a/os/as	*our*
tu, tus	*your*	vuestro/a/os/as	*your*
su, sus	*your*	su, sus	*your*
su, sus	*his, her, its*	su, sus	*their*

Note:

1. Possessive adjectives agree in form with the person, place, or thing possessed, *not with the possessor.*

2. Possessive adjectives agree in number (singular or plural), and in addition, **nuestro** and **vuestro** indicate gender (masculine or feminine).

3. The possessive adjectives **tu/tus** (*your*) refer to someone with whom you are familiar and/or on a first name basis. **Su/sus** (*your*) is used when you are referring to people to whom you refer with *usted* and *ustedes*, that is, more formally and perhaps not on a first-name basis. **Su/sus** (*your* plural or *their*) is used when referring to individuals whom you are addressing with *ustedes* or when expressing possession with *ellos* and *ellas.*

mi	*my*	**mis**	*my brothers /*
hermano	*brother*	hermanos	*siblings*
tu primo	*your cousin*	**tus** primos	*your cousins*
su tía	*her/his/your/ their aunt*	**sus** tías	*her/his/your/their aunts*
nuestra familia	*our family*	**nuestras** familias	*our families*
vuestra mamá	*your mom*	**vuestras** mamás	*your moms*
su hija	*your/their daughter*	**sus** hijas	*your (plural)/ their daughters*

Eduardo tiene una novia.	*Eduardo has a girlfriend.*
Su novia se llama Julia.	*His girlfriend's name is Julia.*
Nuestros padres tienen dos amigos.	*Our parents have two friends.*
Sus amigos son Jorge y Marta.	*Their friends are Jorge and Marta.*

Los adjetivos descriptivos

Descriptive adjectives are words that describe people, places, and things.

1. In English, adjectives usually come before the words they describe (e.g., **the** *red* **car**), but in Spanish, they usually follow the word (e.g., **el coche** *rojo*).

2. Adjectives in Spanish agree with the nouns they modify in number (singular or plural) and in gender (masculine or feminine).

Carlos es un **chico** simpático.	*Carlos is a nice boy.*
Adela es una **chica** simpática.	*Adela is a nice girl.*
Carlos y Adela son (unos) **chicos** simpáticos.	*Carlos and Adela are (some) nice children.*

3. A descriptive adjective can also follow the verb **ser** directly. When it does, it still agrees with the noun to which it refers, which is the subject in this case.

Carlos es simpático.	*Carlos is nice.*
Adela es simpática.	*Adela is nice.*
Carlos y Adela son simpáticos.	*Carlos and Adela are nice.*

Las características físicas, la personalidad y otros rasgos

La personalidad	*Personality*		
aburrido/a	*boring*	interesante	*interesting*
alto/a	*tall*	joven	*young*
antipático/a	*unpleasant*	malo/a	*bad*
bajo/a	*short*	mayor	*old*
bueno/a	*good*	paciente	*patient*
cómico/a	*funny; comical*	perezoso/a	*lazy*
débil	*weak*	pobre	*poor*
delgado/a	*thin*	responsable	*responsible*
fuerte	*strong*	rico/a	*rich*
gordo/a	*fat*	simpático/a	*nice*
guapo/a	*handsome/pretty*	tonto/a	*silly; dumb*
inteligente	*intelligent*	trabajador/a	*hard-working*

Las características físicas	Physical characteristics
bonito/a	pretty
feo/a	ugly
grande	big; large
pequeño/a	small

Otras palabras útiles	Other useful words
muy	very
(un) poco	(a) little

Capítulo 2 La vida universitaria

Presente indicativo de verbos regulares

Spanish has three groups of verbs which are categorized by the ending of the infinitive. Remember that an infinitive is expressed in English by the word *to: to have*, *to be*, and *to speak* are all infinitive forms of English verbs. Spanish infinitives end in **-ar**, **-er**, or **-ir**.

Verbos que terminan en *-ar*

comprar	to buy	preguntar	to ask (a question)
contestar	to answer	preparar	to prepare; to get ready
enseñar	to teach; to show	regresar	to return
esperar	to wait for; to hope	terminar	to finish; to end
estudiar	to study	tomar	to take; to drink
hablar	to speak	trabajar	to work
llegar	to arrive	usar	to use
necesitar	to need		

Verbos que terminan en *-er*

aprender	to learn	correr	to run
comer	to eat	creer	to believe
comprender	to understand	leer	to read

Verbos que terminan en *-ir*

abrir	to open	recibir	to receive
escribir	to write	vivir	to live

To talk about daily or ongoing activities or actions, you need to use the present tense. You can also use the present tense to express future events.

Mario **lee** en la biblioteca.
- *Mario reads in the library.*
- *Mario is reading in the library.*

Mario **lee** en la biblioteca mañana. — *Mario will read in the library tomorrow.*

To form the present indicative, drop the **-ar**, **-er**, or **-ir** ending from the infinitive, and add the appropriate ending. The endings are highlighted in the following chart. Follow this simple pattern with all regular verbs.

	hablar (*to speak*)	comer (*to eat*)	vivir (*to live*)
yo	habl**o**	com**o**	viv**o**
tú	habl**as**	com**es**	viv**es**
Ud.	habl**a**	com**e**	viv**e**
él, ella	habl**a**	com**e**	viv**e**
nosotros/as	habl**amos**	com**emos**	viv**imos**
vosotros/as	habl**áis**	com**éis**	viv**ís**
Uds.	habl**an**	com**en**	viv**en**
ellos/as	habl**an**	com**en**	viv**en**

La formación de preguntas y las palabras interrogativas

Asking yes/no questions

Yes/no questions in Spanish are formed in two different ways:

a. Adding question marks to the statement.

Antonio habla español. → ¿Antonio habla español?

Antonio speaks Spanish. — *Does Antonio speak Spanish?* or *Antonio speaks Spanish?*

As in English, your voice goes up at the end of the sentence. Remember that written Spanish has an upside-down question mark at the beginning of a question.

b. Inverting the order of the subject and the verb.

Antonio habla español. → ¿Habla Antonio español?

SUBJECT + VERB — VERB + SUBJECT

Antonio speaks Spanish. — *Does Antonio speak Spanish?*

Answering yes/no questions

Answering questions is also like English.

¿Habla Antonio español?	*Does Antonio speak Spanish?*
Sí, habla español.	*Yes, he speaks Spanish.*
No, no habla español.	*No, he does not speak Spanish.*

Notice that in the negative response to the question above, both English and Spanish have two negative words.

Information questions

Information questions begin with interrogative words. Study the list of question words below and remember, accents are used on all interrogative words and also on exclamatory words: **¡Qué bueno!** (*That's great!*)

Las palabras interrogativas

¿Qué?	What?	¿Qué idioma habla Antonio?	What language does Antonio speak?
¿Por qué?	Why?	¿Por qué no trabaja Antonio?	Why doesn't Antonio work?
¿Cómo?	How?	¿Cómo está Antonio?	How is Antonio?
¿Cuándo?	When?	¿Cuándo es la clase?	When is the class?
¿Adónde?	To where?	¿Adónde va Antonio?	(To) Where is Antonio going?
¿Dónde?	Where?	¿Dónde vive Antonio?	Where does Antonio live?
¿De dónde?	From where?	¿De dónde regresa Antonio?	Where is Antonio coming back from?
¿Cuánto/a?	How much?	¿Cuánto estudia Antonio para la clase?	How much does Antonio study for the class?
¿Cuántos/as?	How many?	¿Cuántos idiomas habla Antonio?	How many languages does he speak?
¿Cuál?	Which (one)?	¿Cuál es su clase favorita?	Which is his favorite class?
¿Cuáles?	Which (ones)?	¿Cuáles son sus clases favoritas?	Which are his favorite classes?
¿Quién?	Who?	¿Quién habla cinco idiomas?	Who speaks five languages?
¿Quiénes?	Who? (pl.)	¿Quiénes hablan cinco idiomas?	Who speaks five languages?

Note that, although it is not always necessary, when the subject is included in the sentence it follows the verb.

El verbo *estar*

Another verb that expresses *to be* in Spanish is **estar**. Like **tener** and **ser**, **estar** is not a regular verb; that is, you cannot simply drop the infinitive ending and add the usual **-ar** endings.

estar (to be)

Singular		Plural	
yo	estoy	nosotros/as	estamos
tú	estás	vosotros/as	estáis
Ud.	está	Uds.	están
él, ella	está	ellos/as	están

Ser and **estar** are not interchangeable because they are used differently. Two uses of **estar** are:

1. To describe the location of someone or something.

   Manuel **está** en la sala de clase. — *Manuel is in the classroom.*

   Nuestros padres **están** en México. — *Our parents are in Mexico.*

2. To describe how someone is feeling or to express a change from the norm.

   Estoy bien. ¿Y tú? — *I'm fine. And you?*

   Estamos tristes hoy. — *We are sad today. (Normally we are upbeat and happy.)*

Capítulo 3 Estamos en casa

Algunos verbos irregulares

Look at the present tense forms of the following verbs. In the first group, note that they all follow the same patterns that you learned in **Capítulo 2** to form the present tense of regular verbs, *except* in the **yo** form.

Group 1

	conocer (to be acquainted with)	dar (to give)	hacer (to do; to make)	poner (to put; to place)
yo	conozco	doy	hago	pongo
tú	conoces	das	haces	pones
Ud.	conoce	da	hace	pone
él, ella	conoce	da	hace	pone
nosotros/as	conocemos	damos	hacemos	ponemos
vosotros/as	conocéis	dais	hacéis	ponéis
Uds.	conocen	dan	hacen	ponen
ellos/as	conocen	dan	hacen	ponen

	salir (*to leave; to go out*)	traer (*to bring*)	ver (*to see*)
yo	salgo	traigo	veo
tú	sales	traes	ves
Ud.	sale	trae	ve
él, ella	sale	trae	ve
nosotros/as	salimos	traemos	vemos
vosotros/as	salís	traéis	veis
Uds.	salen	traen	ven
ellos/as	salen	traen	ven

Group 2

In the second group, note that **venir** is formed similarly to **tener**.

venir (*to come*)	
yo	vengo
tú	vienes
Ud.	viene
él, ella	viene
nosotros/as	venimos
vosotros/as	venís
Uds.	vienen
ellos/as	vienen

Group 3

In the third group of verbs, note that all of the verb forms have a spelling change except in the **nosotros** and **vosotros** forms.

	decir (*to say; to tell*)	oír (*to hear*)
yo	digo	oigo
tú	dices	oyes
Ud.	dice	oye
él, ella	dice	oye
nosotros/as	decimos	oímos
vosotros/as	decís	oís
Uds.	dicen	oyen
ellos/as	dicen	oyen

	poder (*to be able to*)	querer (*to want; to love*)
yo	puedo	quiero
tú	puedes	quieres
Ud.	puede	quiere
él, ella	puede	quiere
nosotros/as	podemos	queremos
vosotros/as	podéis	queréis
Uds.	pueden	quieren
ellos/as	pueden	quieren

Algunas expresiones con *tener*

The verb **tener**, besides meaning *to have*, is used in a variety of expressions.

tener... años	*to be . . . years old*
tener calor	*to be hot*
tener cuidado	*to be careful*
tener éxito	*to be successful*
tener frío	*to be cold*
tener ganas de + (*infinitive*)	*to feel like + (verb)*
tener hambre	*to be hungry*
tener miedo	*to be afraid*
tener prisa	*to be in a hurry*
tener que + (*infinitive*)	*to have to + (verb)*
tener razón	*to be right*
tener sed	*to be thirsty*
tener sueño	*to be sleepy*
tener suerte	*to be lucky*
tener vergüenza	*to be embarrassed*

—Mamá, **tengo hambre.** ¿Cuándo comemos?

Mom, I'm hungry. When are we eating?

—**Tienes suerte,** hijo. Salimos para el restaurante Tío Tapas en diez minutos.

You are lucky, son. We are leaving for Tío Tapas Restaurant in ten minutes.

Hay

In **Capítulo 2,** you became familiar with **hay** when you described your classroom. To say *there is* or *there are* in Spanish you use **hay.** The irregular form **hay** comes from the verb **haber.**

Hay un baño en mi casa.

There is one bathroom in my house.

Hay cuatro dormitorios también.

There are also four bedrooms.

—¿**Hay** tres baños en tu casa?

Are there three bathrooms in your house?

—No, no **hay** tres baños.

No, there aren't three bathrooms.

Instructor Resources
• IRM: Syllabi and Lesson Plans

NATIONAL STANDARDS

COMUNICACIÓN I
• To identify places in and around town (Communication, Cultures, Connections, Comparisons, Communities)
• To pronounce the letters *c* and *z* (Communication, Cultures)
• To state whom and what is known (Communication)
• To relate common obligations and activities (Communication)
• To express actions (Communication)
• To engage in additional communication practice (Communication)

COMUNICACIÓN II
• To share where you and others are going (Communication)
• To convey what will happen in the future (Communication)
• To impart information about service opportunities (Communication, Cultures, Connections, Comparisons, Communities)
• To articulate concepts and ideas both affirmatively and negatively (Communication, Comparisons)
• To describe states of being, characteristics, and location (Communication)
• To paraphrase what you hear (Communication)
• To communicate about ways to serve the community (Communication, Connections)
• To write a postcard and proofread it for accuracy (Communication, Comparisons)
• To engage in additional communication practice (Communication)

CULTURA
• To describe shopping and other daily activities in Spanish-speaking countries (Cultures, Comparisons)
• To discuss the concept of social consciousness (Communication, Connections, Comparisons)
• To list interesting facts about Honduras, Guatemala, and El Salvador (Cultures, Comparisons)
• To explore further the chapter's cultural themes (Cultures)

AMBICIONES SINIESTRAS
• To practice the reading strategies of skimming and scanning, and learn more about Lupe and Marisol (Communication, Comparisons)
• To discover that Cisco may not be who Eduardo and the others think he is (Communication)

COMUNIDADES
• To use Spanish in real-life contexts (Connections, Comparisons, Communities)

4 Nuestra comunidad

No importa si vivimos en el campo (*countryside*), en un pueblo, en una ciudad o en otro país, tenemos mucho en común. Todos comemos, trabajamos, compramos, pasamos tiempo con la familia y los amigos y ayudamos a los demás (*others*). Nuestra vida en comunidad es similar.

PREGUNTAS

1 Generalmente, ¿qué haces durante un día normal?

2 ¿Conoces a personas de otros países o culturas? ¿Cuáles son sus actividades típicas?

3 ¿Qué tienes en común con las personas de otros países?

La plaza de Chichicastenango en Guatemala

80

SECTION GOALS for *Chapter opener*
By the end of the Chapter opener section, students will be able to:
• discuss their daily routines.
• reflect about what they have in common with people from other countries.
• identify what it means to be part of a global community.

SUGGESTION for the *Chapter opener*
Ask students to define *la comunidad*. Write their ideas on the board. Is it the people in the area? Is it the physical location? Is it the architecture and the landmarks? Is it the blending of cultures? Find out what they think the word *community* encompasses and explain that this chapter includes all aspects of community. Ask students to think about what their school community is noted for.

EXPANSION for *Preguntas*
You may also want to ask your students additional questions regarding the Chapter opener, and we have included a suggestion for a question in Spanish. Remember that they will understand the question in Spanish, but some of your beginning students may need to answer in English. That is pedagogically acceptable, since the goal is for them to demonstrate that they comprehend the question as well as the reading. Additionally, the following question will give you insight into which Spanish-speaking countries interest your students: *¿Qué países quieres conocer? ¿Por qué?*

NATIONAL STANDARDS
Communities

The goal of this chapter is for students to learn that although people have different backgrounds and life experiences, each person has similar needs and responsibilities. Volunteerism is a great way to get your students involved in the community, and through doing so they can learn that people are more alike than different. You could start by asking them to brainstorm ideas about what jobs they think are most important to the running of a community (e.g., services such as fire and police, transportation, food, etc.) and then ask them to find a Spanish-speaking person who has each job. You could assign each student to shadow someone with a different job or career so that they may acquire a broader perspective of the jobs that contribute to the success of the community. Depending on the scope and sequence of the assignment, you could also invite community members to class as guest speakers or as members of a panel, or ask that students submit videos of their time on the job which they can post using MediaShare in MySpanishLab.

PLANNING AHEAD

You may want to assign **4-3** and **4-14** as homework so that students come prepared to do the tasks in class. For **4-31**, it is useful to have large sheets of newsprint paper and markers for your students, one sheet for every two students. Additionally, as a reminder, it is recommended that you assign the grammar explanations and the culture sections to be read before class. They are written in clear language so that the students will be able to understand them. Then you can maximize use of class time for students to ask for any possible clarification of the grammar and to answer the comprehension and critical-thinking questions that accompany the culture readings.

METHODOLOGY • Checking for Reading Comprehension

The text and questions for this chapter opener are completely in Spanish. The reading is at an *i + 1* level for your students. Regarding checking for comprehension, you can use several techniques. If your students are true beginners, allow them to answer in English, since they will be learning new vocabulary in the chapter to help them answer the questions. Some of your beginning students will be able to answer the questions in Spanish, perhaps not as completely as they would like, but they will still be able to communicate. Your heritage language learners will be able to answer the questions in a complete fashion in Spanish.

81

SECTION GOALS for *Comunicación I*

By the end of the *Comunicación* section, students will be able to:

• identify common buildings and services in a typical city.
• talk about the places they go or errands they run in a city.
• use prepositions to describe where buildings are located in relation to other buildings.
• correctly pronounce the letters *c* and *z*.
• distinguish between *saber* and *conocer*.
• report what chores or tasks they do using *tener* + *que* + infinitive.
• form stem-changing verbs in the present tense.

NATIONAL STANDARDS
Communication

The activities that follow provide an excellent range that allows students to personalize their new vocabulary. The activities that ask students to name the places in their town, tell where they are located, and explain what services they provide are all communicative in nature. Many of the activities follow Standard 1.1, which asks students to engage in conversations, provide and obtain information, and exchange opinions about various topics. Activity **4-2** can also fulfill Standard 1.3 if you ask students to present the information about "the best of the best." They could each take a photo of their favorite place, create a written document stating why this place is their favorite, and present it to the class. If several students have the same favorite restaurant, you could have them generate an award certificate to the business voted the best by the Spanish class of University X. They might also select their favorite products or services from "the best of the best" and make flyers in Spanish telling why these are their favorite items. This activity is excellent for encouraging discussion and disagreement among your students as they share their opinions.

Comunicación I

1 VOCABULARIO

🔊 📖
04-01 to 04-04

⏱ 3:00

Los lugares Identifying places in and around town

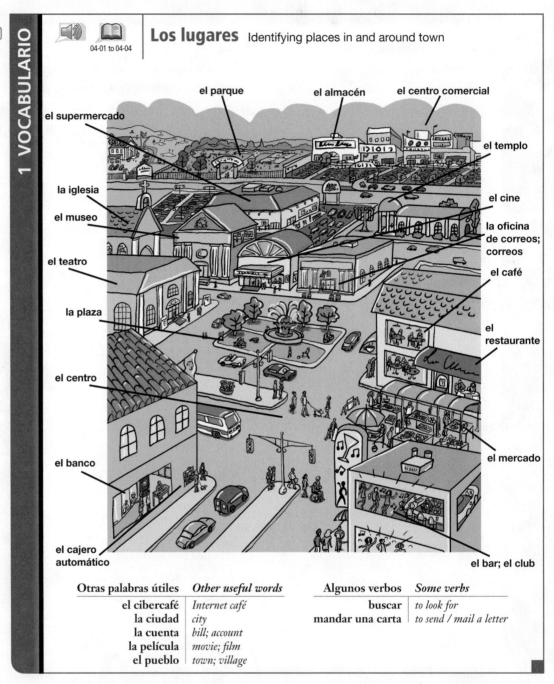

el parque · el almacén · el centro comercial · el supermercado · el templo · la iglesia · el cine · el museo · la oficina de correos; correos · el teatro · el café · la plaza · el restaurante · el centro · el banco · el mercado · el cajero automático · el bar; el club

Otras palabras útiles	*Other useful words*	Algunos verbos	*Some verbs*
el cibercafé	*Internet café*	buscar	*to look for*
la ciudad	*city*	mandar una carta	*to send / mail a letter*
la cuenta	*bill; account*		
la película	*movie; film*		
el pueblo	*town; village*		

SECTION GOALS for *Pronunciación*

By the end of the *Pronunciación* section, students will be able to:
• state the rules of pronunciation for the letter *c*.
• distinguish between the sounds the letters *c* and *z* make.

NOTE for *Pronunciación*

MySpanishLab provides pronunciation practice for students with a wide array of native speakers from across the Spanish-speaking world. If your students will have multiple instructors throughout their language coursework, you can also explain that they will hear different accents depending on the instructor.

METHODOLOGY • Progression of Activities

In planning your lessons it is important to follow a progression of activities: move from *mechanical* (highly structured, focus on form, one correct answer) to *meaningful* (structured but focus of activity shifts more toward creation of meaning) to *communicative* activities (the learner is afforded the opportunity for true, self-directed communication). In doing so, students are not only better equipped to follow along and succeed, but they also build their confidence.

CAPÍTULO 4

PRONUNCIACIÓN

The letters *c* and *z*

Go to MySpanishLab / Student Activites Manual to learn how to pronounce the letters *c* and *z*.

04-05 to 04-06

Capítulo 2. El verbo *estar*, pág. 76 del eText.

2:00

4-1 ¿Dónde está? Tu amigo está muy ocupado. Túrnate con un/a compañero/a para decir dónde está en este momento. ■

MODELO E1: Quiere mandar una carta.

E2: *Está en la oficina de correos.*

1. Quiere ver una película.
2. Necesita dinero para pagar una cuenta.
3. Quiere comer algo (*something*).
4. Quiere ver una exposición de arte.
5. Quiere caminar y hacer ejercicio.
6. Tiene sed y quiere tomar algo.
7. Quiere mandar un email.
8. Tiene que ir a una boda (*wedding*).

> **Fíjate**
>
> Note that you use a form of *querer* + *infinitive* to express "to want to _____."
> For example:
>
> *Quiero mandar…* = I want to send …
>
> *Queremos ver…* = We want to see …

7:00

4-2 El mejor de los mejores ¿Cuáles son, en tu opinión, los mejores lugares en tu comunidad? ■

Capítulo Preliminar A. El verbo *ser*, pág. 13 del eText; Capítulo 2. El verbo *estar*, pág. 76 del eText.

> **Estrategia**
>
> Remember that you learned vocabulary such as *a la derecha*, *a la izquierda*, and *al lado de* that you can also practice with your new vocabulary.

Vocabulario útil

detrás (de)	*behind*
enfrente (de)	*in front (of)*
estar de acuerdo	*to agree*
el/la mejor	*the best*
el/la peor	*the worst*

El mejor de los mejores

✳ **Las mejores TIENDAS**

✳ **Los mejores CINES**

✳ **Los mejores RESTAURANTES**

Paso 1 Haz (*Make*) una lista de los mejores lugares de tu pueblo o ciudad según las siguientes categorías.

MODELO E1: restaurante

E2: *El mejor restaurante es* The Lantern.

1. almacén
2. banco
3. centro comercial
4. cine
5. café
6. teatro
7. tienda
8. restaurante
9. supermercado

(continued)

Paso 2   Compara tu lista con las listas de los otros estudiantes de la clase. ¿Están de acuerdo?

MODELO   E1: *En mi opinión, el mejor restaurante es* The Lantern. *¿Estás de acuerdo?*

E2: *No, no estoy de acuerdo. El mejor restaurante es* The Cricket.

Paso 3   Túrnense para explicar dónde están los mejores lugares.

MODELO   E1: *Busco el mejor restaurante.*

E2: *El mejor restaurante es* The Lantern.

E1: *¿Dónde está?*

E2: *Está al lado del Banco Nacional.*

Fíjate
Remember that the preposition *de* combines with the masculine singular definite article *el* to form the contraction *del*. The feminine article *la* does not contract.

  4-3 **Chiquimula y mi ciudad…**
Chiquimula es un pueblo de 24.000 personas que está en el este de Guatemala. ■

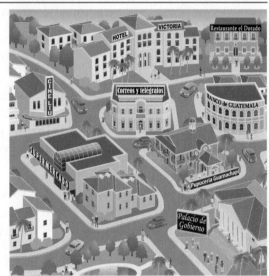

Paso 1   Túrnense para describir el centro del pueblo. Mencionen dónde están los edificios principales.

MODELO   *El Hotel Victoria está al lado del Restaurante el Dorado…*

Paso 2   Ahora dibuja (*draw*) un mapa del centro de tu pueblo o ciudad. El dibujo debe incluir los edificios principales. Después, túrnense para describirlo oralmente.

Paso 3   Túrnense para describir sus dibujos mientras tu compañero/a dibuja lo que dices.

NOTA CULTURAL

¡Hola!   📖   **Actividades cotidianas: Las compras y el paseo**
eText 136   04-07 to 04-08
                    NOTE for *Nota cultural*
                    See eText pg. 136 for complete *Nota cultural* reading and *Preguntas*.

2 GRAMÁTICA

04-09 to 04-12

Saber y conocer Stating whom and what is known

¿Sabes dónde hay un cibercafé?

No, no conozco muy bien la ciudad.

You have learned that **conocer** means *to know.* Another verb, **saber,** also expresses *to know.*

saber (*to know*)

	Singular		Plural
yo	**sé**	nosotros/as	**sabemos**
tú	**sabes**	vosotros/as	**sabéis**
Ud.	**sabe**	Uds.	**saben**
él, ella	**sabe**	ellos/as	**saben**

Fíjate

Note that *conocer* and *saber* both have irregular *yo* forms: *conozco* and *sé* respectively.

The verbs are not interchangeable. Note when to use each.

CONOCER

• Use **conocer** to express *being familiar or acquainted with people, places, and things.*

Ellos **conocen** los mejores restaurantes de la ciudad.
They know the best restaurants in the city.

Yo **conozco** a tu hermano, pero no muy bien.
I know your brother, but not very well.

Note:

1. When expressing that *a person* is known, you must use the personal "a." For example: **Conozco** *a* **tu hermano**…

2. When **a** is followed by **el, a + el = al.** For example: **Conozco al señor (a + el señor)**…

SABER

• Use **saber** to express *knowing facts, pieces of information*, or *how to do something.*

¿Qué **sabes** sobre la música de Guatemala?
What do you know about Guatemalan music?

Yo **sé** tocar la guitarra.
I know how to play the guitar.

Fíjate

A form of *saber* + *infinitive* expresses knowing how to do something. For example:
Sé nadar. = I know how to swim.
Sabemos tocar la guitarra. = We know how to play the guitar.

[2:00] **4-4** **¿Sabes o conoces?** Completa las siguientes preguntas usando **sabes** o **conoces**. Después, túrnate con un/a compañero/a para hacer y contestar las preguntas. ■

MODELO
E1: *¿Conoces San Salvador?*
E2: *Sí, conozco San Salvador. / No, no conozco San Salvador.*

1. ¿ _Sabes_ usar una computadora?
2. ¿ _Conoces_ al presidente del Banco Central?
3. ¿ _Sabes_ dónde hay un cajero automático?
4. ¿ _Conoces_ Tegucigalpa, Honduras?
5. ¿ _Conoces_ el mejor restaurante mexicano?
6. ¿ _Sabes_ llegar a la oficina de correos?
7. ¿ _Conoces_ las películas de James Cameron?
8. ¿ _Sabes_ cuál es el mejor café de esta ciudad?

[4:00] **4-5** **¿Qué sabemos de Honduras?** Completen juntos el diálogo con las formas correctas de **saber** y **conocer**. ■

PROF. DOMÍNGUEZ: ¿Qué (1) _saben_ ustedes sobre Honduras?

DREW: Yo (2) _sé_ que la capital de Honduras es Tegucigalpa.

DREW Y TANYA: Nosotros (3) _sabemos_ mucho sobre el país.

PROF. DOMÍNGUEZ: ¿Y (4) _saben_ ustedes cómo se llaman las personas de Honduras?

TANYA: Sí, se llaman *hondureños.* (5) _Conocemos_ la cultura hondureña bastante bien. Nuestra hermana, Gina, es una estudiante de intercambio allí este año y nos manda muchas fotos y cartas. Ella (6) _conoce_ a mucha gente interesante, incluso al hijo del Presidente.

PROF. DOMÍNGUEZ: ¡No me digan! ¿Estudia allí su hermana? ¿(7) _Saben_ ustedes que hay dos universidades muy buenas en Tegucigalpa?

TANYA: Sí, el novio de Gina estudia allí, pero yo no (8) _sé_ en qué universidad. Él es salvadoreño y nuestros padres no lo (9) _conocen_ todavía. Gina dice que no quiere volver a los Estados Unidos. Yo (10) _sé_ que mis padres van a estar muy tristes si ella no vuelve.

PROF. DOMÍNGUEZ: Yo (11) _conozco_ a tu hermana y (12) _sé_ que es una mujer inteligente. Va a pensarlo bien antes de tomar una decisión.

[3:00] **4-6** **¿Me puedes ayudar?** Sofía acaba de llegar a San Salvador y se siente un poco perdida (*she is feeling a little lost*). Túrnense para hacer y contestar sus preguntas de manera creativa. Luego, creen (*create*) y contesten **dos** preguntas más usando **saber** y **conocer.** ∎

MODELO   SOFÍA: *¿Sabes dónde hay una iglesia?*

          TÚ: *Sí, sé que hay una iglesia en la plaza.*

1. ¿Conoces un buen restaurante típico?
2. ¿Sabes dónde está el restaurante?
3. ¿Sabes qué tipo de comida sirven en el restaurante?
4. ¿Conoces al cocinero (*chef*)?
5. ¿?
6. ¿?

Instructor Resources
• Textbook images, PPT, Extra Activities

METHODOLOGY • Chunking
A common pedagogical technique for breaking up complex tasks is to chunk information into manageable bits. We have done that with stem-changing verbs and the *¿Qué tienen que hacer? ¿Qué pasa?* presentation. These verbs are presented first as vocabulary and then as stem-changing verbs. Practicing them as infinitives first helps students focus on and learn their meanings. The next step will be to introduce them as stem-changing verbs in the following grammar presentation on page 142.

**METHODOLOGY •
Constructing Knowledge**
Since the 1940s and 1950s, educational researchers have explored how we learn and what assists in learning. We now know that when learners *construct knowledge,* the knowledge becomes internalized and transfers into long-term memory. On the other hand, memorizing lists, for example, goes into short-term memory but usually does not transfer into long-term memory. There are many learning devices that help students retain information. Mnemonic devices assist in learning. So does connecting vocabulary with visual images. The "*Where's Waldo?*" style visuals for *¿Qué tienen que hacer? ¿Qué pasa?* help students learn the new verbs. Students may need to consult the *Vocabulario activo* pages at the end of the chapter to clarify/negotiate meaning, but that task helps them associate a visual image with a vocabulary word and acquire the word. The same concept is true with the vocabulary in *Servicios a la comunidad* on page 149. These visuals will be excellent to use when you are introducing or practicing new tenses, since the students will have associated these verbs with the images.

NOTE for *Vocabulario*
Remind students that in *Capítulo 3* they learned some expressions with *tener.* They will recall that *tener + que + infinitive* means "to have to do something."

3 VOCABULARIO

[2:00] 04-13 to 04-16

¿Qué tienen que hacer? ¿Qué pasa?
Relating common obligations and activities

Capítulo 1. El verbo *tener,* pág. 34 del eText.

[2:00] **4-7** **Tic-tac-toe** Escucha mientras tu instructor/a explica el juego del *tic-tac-toe.* ▪

MODELO E1: *¿Tienes "volver"?*
E2: *Sí, tengo "volver". / No, no tengo "volver".*

[2:00] **4-8** **¿Y lo opuesto?** Decidan juntos qué verbo expresa lo opuesto (*opposite*) de cada una de las palabras o expresiones de la siguiente lista. ▪

MODELO E1: no comer por la tarde
E1: *almorzar*

repetir	encontrar	volver	entender	pedir
perder	comenzar	querer	cerrar	almorzar

1. salir volver
2. terminar comenzar
3. abrir cerrar
4. perder encontrar
5. decir una vez repetir
6. dar pedir
7. encontrar perder
8. no comprender entender

[2:00]   **4-9** **Los quehaceres** Túrnense para expresar qué tienen que hacer ustedes generalmente. ▪

MODELO Tengo que encontrar…
E1: *Tengo que encontrar mi libro de español.*
E2: *Tengo que encontrar los apuntes para la clase de español.*

1. Tengo que comenzar…
2. Tengo que repetir…
3. Tengo que pedir…
4. Tengo que recordar…
5. Tengo que almorzar…
6. Tengo que dormir…

Capítulo 2. La sala de clase, pág. 65 del eText; Presente indicativo de verbos regulares. pág. 67 del eText.

[7:00] **4-10** **Entrevistas** Entrevista a tres compañeros para averiguar si (*to find out whether*) hacen cosas similares. Después, comparte la información con la clase. ¿Qué tienen ustedes en común? ▪

1. ¿Qué tienes que hacer para prepararte bien para las clases?
2. ¿Qué tienes que hacer durante la clase de español para sacar buenas notas?
3. Generalmente, ¿qué tienes que hacer cuando terminas con tus clases?

4 GRAMÁTICA

04-17 to 04-24

Los verbos con cambio de raíz Expressing actions

¡Cierro la ventana, pido una pizza y empiezo a estudiar!

You have learned a variety of common verbs that are irregular. Two of those verbs were **querer** and **poder,** which are irregular due to some changes in their stems. Look at the following verb groups and answer the questions regarding each group.

Change e → ie

cerrar (*to close*)

Singular		Plural	
yo	cierro	nosotros/as	cerramos
tú	cierras	vosotros/as	cerráis
Ud.	cierra	Uds.	cierran
él, ella	cierra	ellos/as	cierran

¡Explícalo tú!
1. Which verb forms look like the infinitive **cerrar**?
2. Which verb forms have a spelling change that differs from the infinitive **cerrar**?

 Check your answers to the preceding questions in Appendix 1.

Other verbs like **cerrar** (**e → ie**) are:

comenzar	*to begin*	**mentir**	*to lie*	**preferir**	*to prefer*
empezar	*to begin*	**pensar**	*to think*	**recomendar**	*to recommend*
entender	*to understand*	**perder**	*to lose; to waste*		

Change e → i

pedir (*to ask for*)

Singular		Plural	
yo	pido	nosotros/as	pedimos
tú	pides	vosotros/as	pedís
Ud.	pide	Uds.	piden
él, ella	pide	ellos/as	piden

¡Explícalo tú!
1. Which verb forms look like the infinitive **pedir**?
2. Which verb forms have a spelling change that differs from the infinitive **pedir**?

 Check your answers to the preceding questions in Appendix 1.

Other verbs like **pedir** (**e → i**) are:

repetir *to repeat*   **seguir*** *to follow; to continue (doing something)*   **servir** *to serve*

*Note: The **yo** form of **seguir** is **sigo.**

Change o → ue

encontrar (*to find*)

Singular		Plural	
yo	encuentro	nosotros/as	encontramos
tú	encuentras	vosotros/as	encontráis
Ud.	encuentra	Uds.	encuentran
él, ella	encuentra	ellos/as	encuentran

¡Explícalo tú!

1. Which verb forms look like the infinitive **encontrar**?
2. Which verb forms have a spelling change that differs from the infinitive **encontrar**?

 Check your answers to the preceding questions in Appendix 1.

Other verbs like **encontrar** (**o → ue**) are:

almorzar	*to have lunch*	**dormir**	*to sleep*	**mostrar**	*to show*	**volver**	*to return*
costar	*to cost*	**morir**	*to die*	**recordar**	*to remember*		

Change u → ue

jugar (*to play*)

Singular		Plural	
yo	juego	nosotros/as	jugamos
tú	juegas	vosotros/as	jugáis
Ud.	juega	Uds.	juegan
él, ella	juega	ellos/as	juegan

¡Explícalo tú!

1. Which verb forms look like the infinitive **jugar**?
2. Which verb forms have a spelling change that differs from the infinitive **jugar**?
3. Why does **jugar** not belong with the verbs like **encontrar**?

 Check your answers to the preceding questions in Appendix 1.

¡Explícalo tú!

To summarize . . .

1. What rule can you make regarding all four groups of stem-changing verbs and their forms?
2. With what group of stem-changing verbs would you put **querer**?
3. With what group of stem-changing verbs would you put each of the following verbs?

demostrar	*to demonstrate*	**encerrar**	*to enclose*
devolver	*to return (an object)*	**perseguir**	*to chase*

✔ Check your answers to the preceding questions in Appendix 1.

4-11 Categorías

Paso 1 With a partner, write the stem-changing verbs that were just presented on individual slips of paper. Next, make a chart with four categories: **e → ie, e → i, o → ue,** and **u → ue.**

Paso 2 Join another pair of students. When your instructor says **¡Empieza!,** place each verb under the correct category (**e → ie, e → i, o → ue,** or **u → ue**). Do several rounds of this activity, playing against different doubles partners.

EXPANSION for 4-12
If you wish, you can ask your students to prepare one or two additional questions to ask their classmates.

  4-12 Nuestras preferencias Averigua cuáles son las preferencias de tu compañero/a. Luego, comparte tus respuestas con la clase. ■

MODELO el cine o el teatro

E1: *¿Qué prefieres, el cine o el teatro?*

E2: *Prefiero el cine.*

¿Qué prefieres,...?

1. correr en el parque o en el gimnasio
2. comer en un restaurante o en un café
3. visitar un gran almacén o un centro comercial
4. comprar comida (*food*) en un supermercado o en un mercado al aire libre (*open-air*)
5. trabajar en un banco o en una oficina de correos
6. conversar con amigos en un bar o en una plaza

EXPANSION for 4-13
Have the students take each item and create questions to ask their partners, e.g., *¿Quién pierde su tarea?* or *¿Pierdes tu tarea?* Remind students to use *no* twice if they answer negatively.

  4-13 ¿Quién hace qué? Túrnense para decir qué personas que ustedes conocen hacen las siguientes cosas. ■

MODELO E1: siempre perder la tarea

E2: *Mi hermano Tom siempre pierde la tarea.*

1. pensar ser profesor/a
2. almorzar en McDonald's a menudo
3. querer visitar Sudamérica
4. siempre entender al/a la profesor/a de español
5. preferir dormir hasta el mediodía
6. volver tarde a casa a menudo
7. perder dinero
8. pensar que Santa Claus existe
9. nunca mentir
10. comenzar a hacer la tarea de noche

[7:00] **4-14** **¿Quién eres?** Escribe las respuestas a las siguientes preguntas en forma de párrafos. ▪

Capítulo Preliminar A. La hora, pág. 18 del eText; Capítulo 2. Las materias y las especialidades, pág. 62 del eText; Los deportes y los pasatiempos, pág. 81 del eText.

Primer párrafo

1. ¿Qué clases tienes este semestre?
2. ¿A qué hora empieza tu clase preferida? ¿Cuándo termina?
3. ¿Qué prefieres hacer si (*if*) tienes tiempo entre (*between*) tus clases?
4. ¿A qué hora vuelves a tu dormitorio/ apartamento/casa?

Segundo párrafo

1. ¿Qué carro tienes (o quieres tener)? ¿Cuánto cuesta un carro nuevo?
2. ¿Cómo vienes a la universidad? (Por ejemplo, ¿vienes en carro?)
3. ¿Dónde prefieres vivir, en una residencia estudiantil, en un apartamento o en una casa?
4. ¿Dónde quieres vivir después de graduarte?

Tercer párrafo

1. ¿Qué deporte y/o pasatiempo prefieres?
2. Si es un deporte, ¿juegas a ese deporte? ¿Ves ese deporte en la televisión?
3. Normalmente, ¿cuándo y con quién(es) juegas el deporte / disfrutas (*enjoy*) el pasatiempo?
4. ¿Qué otros deportes y pasatiempos te gustan?

¿Cómo andas? I

Having completed **Comunicación I,** I now can . . .	Feel confident	Need to review
• identify places in and around town (p. 82)	☐	☐
• pronounce the letters *c* and *z* (MSL/SAM)	☐	☐
• describe shopping and other daily activities in Spanish-speaking countries (p. 84)	☐	☐
• state whom and what is known (p. 85)	☐	☐
• relate common obligations and activities (p. 88)	☐	☐
• express actions (p. 90)	☐	☐

METHODOLOGY • Recycling
Activity **4-14** is an excellent recycling activity for previously learned grammar structures. Recycling is extremely important, as it helps your students review and recombine vocabulary and structures that help increase their linguistics skills.

SUGGESTION for 4-14
Activity **4-14** should be assigned as homework to save time in class.

SUGGESTION for 4-14
Select and read as many of the writing samples from **4-14** as time permits. This can also be done during the warm-up segments of several subsequent classes. You may want to have students guess who wrote each one as you read them aloud.

SUGGESTION for 4-14
In the second paragraph, question 4, students will have to answer *Quiero vivir… después de graduarme.* Since they do not know about reflexive verbs yet, you can tell them in advance how to answer and explain that this will be presented at a later point. Otherwise you could tell them to say… *después de la graduación.*

ADDITIONAL ACTIVITY for
Los verbos con cambio de raíz
¡Preparados, listos, ya!
A practicar. Escucha mientras tu profesor/a explica esta actividad.
INSTRUCTIONS: Form teams of equal size with at least four people, but no more than six. Team members sit in a row, one behind the other, facing the chalkboard. The first team member writes the subject pronouns *out of order* on the left side of a piece of paper, as in the model *tú, nosotros, ella, yo, ustedes, ellos.* You, the instructor, write a stem-changing verb on the board. The first team member in each row writes the *tú* form of the verb next to the pronoun and quickly passes the paper to the team member behind him/ her. The next team member has to write the *nosotros* form and pass the paper to the next team member, and so on. Any team member may correct any of his/ her teammates' previous answers if they are incorrect. The final person in the row brings (or runs!) the team's answers to you. The first group to get all of the verb forms correct gets five points, the second group gets four, and so forth. This activity is extremely successful with all types of students. It is an excellent activity to repeat when reviewing any and all verb tenses.

A variation is: The first team to finish (Team A) gets five points, but the other team (Team B) has the opportunity to earn some points as well. Team B may ask Team A one form of any three verbs they choose. For any verb form that Team A gets incorrect, Team B gets a point.

SECTION GOALS for *Comunicación II*

By the end of the *Comunicación* section, students will be able to:
• form the verb *ir* correctly.
• combine what they have to do (*tener + que + infinitive*) with where they go (*ir*) to do it.
• construct sentences in the periphrastic future using *ir + a + infinitive*.
• discuss jobs and volunteer work.
• use negative and affirmative indefinite expressions.
• demonstrate their understanding of how *ser* and *estar* are used.

METHODOLOGY • Presenting Information as Needed

We instructors love the Spanish language and are eager to share what we know with our students, yet sometimes we share more than students can grasp at a time. Too much information can confuse students and can also cause a raising of what Stephen Krashen calls the *affective filter*, where the students become hesitant to produce language for fear of making a mistake with the vast amount of information they have been given. If you feel that your students will benefit from a more in-depth presentation (e.g., heritage language learners), then please provide it.

SUGGESTION for *El verbo ir*

After drilling *ir* forms mechanically by giving subjects and having students give the matching verb forms, practice with directed questions, such as *¿Adónde vas mañana? ¿Adónde vas de vacaciones? ¿Adónde van tus amigos este fin de semana?*

SUGGESTION for *El verbo ir*

Create a substitution drill for students to practice the different forms of *ir*. Highlight the portions of the sentence the students should replace with different information. Encourage them to be creative and create as many versions as possible.

MODELO

Esta mañana Li-Ling va a la biblioteca porque tiene que estudiar. Después de cuatro horas, su compañera de cuarto y ella van al banco. Esta noche Li-Ling y yo vamos a un restaurante para comer con nuestros amigos.

Comunicación II

5 GRAMÁTICA

04-25 to 04-27

El verbo *ir* Sharing where you and others are going

Another important verb in Spanish is **ir**. Note its irregular present tense forms.

ir (*to go*)			
Singular		**Plural**	
yo	voy	nosotros/as	vamos
tú	vas	vosotros/as	vais
Ud.	va	Uds.	van
él, ella	va	ellos/as	van

Voy al parque. ¿**Van** ustedes también?
No, no **vamos** ahora. Preferimos **ir** más tarde.

I'm going to the park. Are you all going too?
No, we're not going now. We prefer to go later.

Voy al almacén. ¿Adónde vas tú?

2:00 **4-15** **¿Adónde vas?** Túrnense para completar la conversación que tienen Memo y Esteban al salir de la clase de música. Usen las formas correctas del verbo **ir**. ■

MEMO: Hola, Esteban. ¿Adónde (1) ___vas___ ahora?

ESTEBAN: ¿Qué hay? Pues, (2) ___voy___ a la clase de física.

MEMO: Ah sí. Bueno, mi compañero de cuarto y yo (3) ___vamos___ al gimnasio. Tenemos un torneo (*tournament*) de tenis.

ESTEBAN: Buena suerte. Oye, ¿tú (4) ___vas___ a la fiesta de Isabel esta noche?

MEMO: No sé. ¿Quiénes (5) ___van___? Creo que (yo) (6) ___vay___ al cine para ver la película nueva de Steven Spielberg.

ESTEBAN: ¿Por qué no (7) ___vas___ primero a la fiesta y después al cine?

MEMO: Buena idea. ¿(8) ___Vamos___ (tú y yo) juntos?

ESTEBAN: Muy bien. Mi amigo Roberto (9) ___va___ también. Hablamos después del torneo.

MEMO: Bueno, hasta luego.

2:00 **4-16** **Los "¿por qué?"** Esperanza tiene una sobrina que está en la etapa de los "¿por qué?" Tiene muchas preguntas. Túrnense para darle las respuestas de Esperanza a Rosita. ■

MODELO ROSITA: ¿Por qué va mi papá al gimnasio?
ESPERANZA: *Tu papá va al gimnasio porque quiere hacer ejercicio.*

1. ¿Por qué va mi mamá al mercado?
2. ¿Por qué va mi hermana a la oficina de correos?
3. ¿Por qué van mis hermanos al parque?
4. ¿Por qué vas a la universidad?
5. ¿Por qué no vamos al cine ahora?

ADDITIONAL ACTIVITY for *El verbo ir*

Hoy es sábado y... En grupos de 6 a 8 personas, túrnense para decir adónde van. Luego, tienen que repetir lo que dice cada persona.

MODELO
E1: *Hoy es sábado y esta mañana voy al gimnasio.*
E2: *Hoy es sábado y Jim va al gimnasio y yo voy a Krispy Kreme para comer donas.*
E3: *Hoy es sábado y Jim va al gimnasio, Carla va a Krispy Kreme y yo voy a la biblioteca...*

Instructor Resources
• PPT, Extra Activities

EXPANSION for 4-17
Have students write out their own schedules for a particular day, or week, and share with classmates. Who is busiest? Who has the most exciting schedule? Who has more study time? Who goes to the most places? etc.

NOTE for Gramática
This is an inductive grammar presentation in which the students are given examples of a grammar concept and, through the use of guiding questions, they formulate the rule in their own words. Research indicates that students remember and internalize grammar rules better when they construct their own knowledge.

NATIONAL STANDARDS
Communication
Speaking in the future tense is one of the main time frames. When an individual can sustain communication in the present, future, and past tenses, they are emerging into the ACTFL Advanced Level of oral proficiency.

The new verb *ir* and the *ir + a + infinitive* construction allow students a greater range of communication, because they can talk about where they are going and what they are doing in the immediate future. Learning the new construction provides more opportunities for communication in the interpersonal mode (Standard 1.1), as they engage in conversations about their plans and provide and obtain information. The *ir + a + infinitive* construction works well with Standard 1.3, because students are able to present about their future plans to an audience of listeners or readers. With the appropriate vocabulary, they can communicate their weekend plans, what they want to do after they graduate, how they will spend the next 5 years, and the characteristics of their ideal mate. You could also ask them to predict what their hometown or university town will be like in 10 years.

SUGGESTION for *ir + a + infinitivo*
After the initial presentation, the following directed questions can be used to practice *ir + a + infinitive*. They can also be used as warm-up questions to begin a class: *¿Cuándo vas a almorzar? ¿Cuándo vas a trabajar? ¿Cuándo vas a hacer tu tarea? ¿Adónde vas a estudiar? ¿Qué vas a estudiar? ¿Cuándo vas a limpiar tu casa? ¿Cuándo vas a lavar los platos? ¿Adónde vas a ir este verano?*

Capítulo Preliminar A. La hora, pág. 18 del eText.

10:00 👥👥 **4-17** **¿Adónde van?** Miren los horarios de las siguientes personas. Túrnense para decir adónde van, a qué hora y qué hacen en cada (*each*) lugar. ■

Mis padres

Mi hermano

Yo

MODELO *A las diez mis padres van a la librería para comprar unos libros. Luego…*

3:00

6 GRAMÁTICA

04-28 to 04-30

Ir + a + infinitivo Conveying what will happen in the future

Study the following sentences and then answer the questions that follow.

—**Voy a mandar** esta carta. ¿Quieres ir?   *I'm going to mail this letter. Do you want to go?*
—Sí. Luego, **¿vas a almorzar?**   *Yes. Then, are you going to have lunch?*
—Sí, **vamos a comer** comida guatemalteca.   *Yes, we are going to eat Guatemalan food.*
—¡Perfecto! **Voy a pedir** unos tamales.   *Perfect! I am going to order some tamales.*
—Pero, primero, **¡vamos a ir** al banco.   *But first we are going to the bank!*

¡Explícalo tú!
1. When do the actions in the previous sentences take place: in the *past*, *present*, or *future*?
2. What is the first bold type verb you see in each sentence?
3. In what form is the second bolded verb?
4. What word comes between the two verbs? Does this word have an equivalent in English?
5. What is your rule, then, for expressing future actions or statements?

 Check your answers to the preceding questions in Appendix 1.

4-18 ¿Y en el futuro? Túrnense para contestar las siguientes preguntas sobre el futuro. ■

1. ¿Vas a dedicar más tiempo a tus estudios?
2. Después de terminar con tus estudios, ¿vas a vivir en una ciudad, un pueblo pequeño o en el campo?
3. ¿Vas a vivir en una casa grande?
4. ¿Tus amigos y tú van a visitar Honduras u otro país en Centroamérica?
5. ¿Vamos a encontrar la cura para el cáncer?
6. ¿Vamos a poder acabar con (*end*) el terrorismo?

 Capítulo Preliminar A. Los días de la semana, los meses y las estaciones, pág. 20 del eText.

4-19 Mi agenda ¿Qué planes tienes para la semana que viene? Termina las siguientes frases sin (*without*) repetir los quehaceres. ■

MODELO   E1: El lunes…
    E2: *El lunes voy a pasar la aspiradora.*

1. El lunes…
2. El martes…
3. El miércoles…
4. El jueves…
5. El viernes…
6. El sábado…
7. El domingo…
8. El fin de semana…

4-20 Qué será, será… ¿Qué tiene el futuro para ti, tus amigos y tu familia? Escribe **cinco** predicciones de lo que va a ocurrir en el futuro. ■

MODELO   *Mi primo va a ir a la Universidad Autónoma el año que viene. Mis padres van a limpiar el armario y el altillo este fin de semana. Yo voy a estudiar en Sudamérica…*

7 VOCABULARIO

3:00

04-31 to 04-36

Servicios a la comunidad
Imparting information about service opportunities

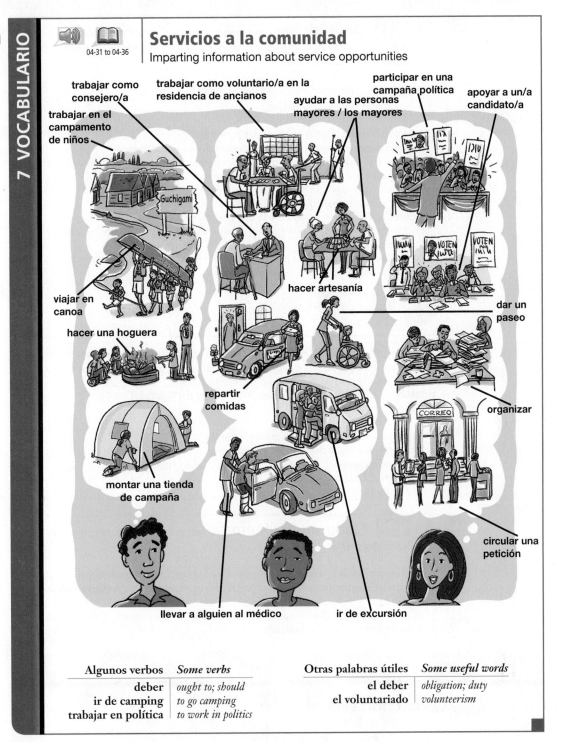

trabajar como consejero/a

trabajar como voluntario/a en la residencia de ancianos

trabajar en el campamento de niños

participar en una campaña política

ayudar a las personas mayores / los mayores

apoyar a un/a candidato/a

viajar en canoa

hacer artesanía

hacer una hoguera

dar un paseo

repartir comidas

organizar

montar una tienda de campaña

circular una petición

llevar a alguien al médico

ir de excursión

Algunos verbos	Some verbs
deber	ought to; should
ir de camping	to go camping
trabajar en política	to work in politics

Otras palabras útiles	Some useful words
el deber	obligation; duty
el voluntariado	volunteerism

NATIONAL STANDARDS
Communication, Connections, Communities
This vocabulary connects with other disciplines, such as health care professions. It also provides students with ideas of where they can use Spanish in their community. Some of your institutions require or encourage community service projects, and this vocabulary connects directly with many university offerings or initiatives. This vocabulary also ties in well with the chapter title Nuestra comunidad.

The vocabulary in the section, Servicios a la comunidad, provides a glimpse into the many types of volunteer work and paid work available to students. Ask the career center of your school what types of volunteer jobs are available and bring that information to class. Standards 1.1 and 1.3 apply to volunteer work because students can communicate interpersonally about the types of work they would like to do and they can present about the types of work. To integrate Standard 1.3, ask students each to research a particular volunteer position (or internship) available in their community and make a presentation to the class about their job. You could also invite a local organization in need of Spanish-speaking volunteers to present to students. Standard 3.1 states that students reinforce and further their knowledge of other disciplines through Spanish. Have the students research internships or volunteer positions that tie in with their majors so that they make connections and they are able to work in the community, applying their majors and the skills they have acquired in Spanish (Standard 5.1).

ANSWERS to 4-21

1. viajar en canoa
2. circular una petición
3. montar una tienda de campaña
4. llevar a alguien al médico
5. el/la consejero/a
6. el voluntariado
7. hacer artesanía
8. el campamento de niños
9. apoyar a un/a candidato/a, trabajar en política, participar en una campaña política
10. la residencia de ancianos

NOTE for 4-21

Give students the definitions on slips of paper and have them act out the definitions. You could also use the board for help on some of the items, or simply play charades.

NOTE for *Nota cultural* (Online)

The concept of volunteerism is expanding throughout the Spanish-speaking world, but still may not exist to the degree that it exists in the United States. In the United States, many schools and communities have highly developed programs for volunteering. In some schools, it is a requirement to volunteer a certain number of hours each year.

ANSWERS to *Nota cultural* (Online)

1. *Answers may include: participar en una campaña política, ayudar a las personas mayores, repartir comida, llevar a alguien al médico, trabajar como voluntario en un hospital, etc.*
2. *Answers will vary.*

NATIONAL STANDARDS
Communication, Connections, Communities

The *Nota cultural* reading online, *La conciencia social*, provides a starting point for discussing how students can help others in the community. Students can engage in conversations about how they contribute to the community and whether they feel they are doing enough to participate in their community (Standard 1.1). They can also brainstorm with other students to use what they are learning in their programs of study and apply their content knowledge to improving the community (3.1). Lastly, depending upon the size of the Hispanic population in your area, students could think of ways to serve the community now, during their experience as college students (Standard 5.1) or use *ir + a + infinitive* to talk about how they might combine their Spanish skills and their majors to serve the community after they graduate (Standard 5.2).

2:00   **4-21** **Definiciones** Túrnense para leer las siguientes definiciones y decir cuál de las palabras o expresiones del vocabulario de **Servicios a la comunidad** corresponde a cada una. ■

MODELO   E1: personas que tienen muchos años
             E2: *las personas mayores*

1. salir en un bote (*boat*) para una o dos personas
2. dar un documento a personas para obtener firmas (*signatures*)
3. "construir" una estructura portátil (no permanente) que se usa para dormir fuera de casa
4. acompañar a una persona a una cita (*appointment*) con el médico
5. trabajar con niños en un campamento
6. servir a las personas sin recibir dinero a cambio (*in exchange*)
7. disfrutar de (*enjoy*) un tipo de arte que puedes crear con materiales diversos
8. un lugar donde van los niños, generalmente en el verano, para hacer muchas actividades diferentes
9. trabajar para un candidato político
10. un lugar donde viven las personas mayores

Capítulo 2. El verbo gustar, p. 80 del eText.

4:00   **4-22** **En tu opinión…** Termina las siguientes oraciones sobre el voluntariado. Después, comparte tus respuestas con un/a compañero/a. ■

MODELO   *Yo soy una consejera perfecta porque me gustan los niños. También sé escuchar muy bien…*

1. Yo (no) soy un/a consejero/a perfecto/a porque…
2. Dos trabajos voluntarios que me gustan son…
3. Hay muchas residencias de ancianos en los Estados Unidos porque…
4. Yo apoyo al candidato _____ porque…
5. Cuando repartes comidas, puedes…

4:00   **4-23** **Elaborando el tema** En grupos de tres o cuatro, discutan las siguientes preguntas. ■

1. ¿Cuáles son las actividades más interesantes en los campamentos de niños?
2. ¿Cuáles son las oportunidades de voluntariado que existen en tu universidad/iglesia/templo?
3. ¿Cuáles son los trabajos voluntarios que se asocian más con apoyar a un candidato?
4. ¿Crees que servir a la comunidad es un deber?

NOTA CULTURAL

¡Hola!   **La conciencia social**
eText 151   04-37

NOTE for *Nota cultural*.
See eText pg. 151 for complete *Nota cultural* reading and *Preguntas*.

METHODOLOGY • Maximizing Class Time

None of us ever has enough class time to do what we feel is important and necessary. The authors of *¡Anda! Curso elemental* are committed to helping students spend as much of the class period as possible speaking Spanish. Hence, as was suggested from the beginning, we highly recommend that all of the culture readings are assigned to be read before class, especially as they become longer.

Instructor Resources
• PPT, Extra Activities

8 GRAMÁTICA

04-38 to 04-40 English Tutorial

Las expresiones afirmativas y negativas
Articulating concepts and ideas both affirmatively and negatively

Siempre me gusta hacer artesanía con los niños, ¡pero jamás voy a ir en una canoa con ellos!

In the previous chapters, you have seen and used a number of the affirmative and negative expressions listed on the following page. Study the list, and learn the ones that are new to you.

Expresiones afirmativas	
a veces	*sometimes*
algo	*something; anything*
alguien	*someone*
algún	*some; any*
alguno/a/os/as	*some; any*
siempre	*always*
o... o	*either . . . or*

Expresiones negativas	
jamás	*never; not ever* (emphatic)
nada	*nothing*
nadie	*no one; nobody*
ningún	*none*
ninguno/a/os/as	*none*
nunca	*never*
ni... ni	*neither . . . nor*

Look at the following sentences, paying special attention to the position of the negative words, and answer the questions that follow.

—¿Quién llama?   *Who is calling?*
—**Nadie** llama. (**No** llama **nadie**.)   *No one is calling.*
—¿Vas al gimnasio todos los días?   *Do you go to the gym every day?*
—No, **nunca** voy. (No, **no** voy **nunca**.) *No, I never go.*

Fíjate
Unlike English, Spanish can have two or more negatives in the same sentence. A double negative is actually quite common. For example, *No tengo nada que hacer* means *I don't have anything to do.*

¡Explícalo tú!

1. When you use a negative word (**nadie, nunca,** etc.) in a sentence, does it come before or after the verb?
2. When you use the word **no** and then a negative word in the same sentence, does **no** come before or after the verb? Where does the negative word come in these sentences?
3. Does the meaning change depending on where you put the negative word (e.g., **Nadie llama** *versus* **No llama nadie**)?

 Check your answers to the preceding questions in Appendix 1.

(continued)

NOTE for *Gramática*
This is an inductive grammar presentation in which the students are given examples of a grammar concept and, through the use of guiding questions, they formulate the rule in their own words. Research indicates that students remember and internalize grammar rules better when they construct their own knowledge.

NOTE for *Las expresiones afirmativas y negativas*
You may begin this presentation by asking students what they do on a regular basis and changing their affirmative responses to negative ones, stating that you do the opposite, e.g., *Yo voy al gimnasio. ¡Jamás voy al gimnasio!*

SUGGESTION for *Las expresiones afirmativas y negativas*
Say one of the affirmative or negative expressions to your students and have them write or say the opposite term: *siempre / nunca* or *jamás.* You can then take this exercise to the sentence level. Ask, *¿Siempre hacen ustedes trabajo voluntario?* and the students respond, *No, nunca hacemos trabajo voluntario.*

Algún and *ningún*

1. Forms of **algún** and **ningún** need to agree in gender and number with the nouns they modify.
2. **Alguno** and **ninguno** are shortened to **algún** and **ningún** when they are followed by *masculine, singular nouns.*
3. When no noun follows, use **alguno** or **ninguno** when referring to masculine, singular nouns.
4. The plural form **ningunos** is rarely used.

Study the following sentences.

MARÍA: ¿Tienes **alguna** clase fácil este semestre?
JUAN: No, no tengo **ninguna**. ¡Y **ningún** profesor es simpático!
MARÍA: Vaya, ¿y puedes hacer **algún** cambio?
JUAN: No, no puedo hacer **ninguno**. (No, no puedo tomar **ningún** otro curso.)

7:00   **4-24 ¿Con qué frecuencia?** Indica con qué frecuencia tus
Workbooklet   compañeros/as de clase hacen las siguientes actividades. Escribe el nombre de
cada compañero/a debajo de la columna apropiada y comparte los resultados
con la clase. ■

MODELO   ir de excursión con niños
          A veces Josefina va de excursión con niños.

	SIEMPRE	A VECES	NUNCA
1. ir de excursión con niños		Josefina	
2. participar en una campaña política			
3. hacer una hoguera			
4. circular una petición			
5. firmar una petición			
6. repartir comidas a los mayores			
7. visitar una residencia de ancianos			
8. trabajar en un campamento para niños			
9. trabajar como voluntario en un hospital o una clínica			
10. dormir en una tienda de campaña			

Capítulo 2. La sala de clase, pág. 65 del eText; En la universidad, pág. 74 del eText.

[2:00] **4-25 El/La profesor/a ideal** Túrnense para decir si las siguientes características son ciertas (*true*) o no en un/a profesor/a ideal. ■

MODELO

E1: a veces duerme en su trabajo

E2: *No. Un profesor ideal nunca duerme en su trabajo.*

E1: jamás va a clase sin sus apuntes

E2: *Sí, un profesor ideal jamás va a clase sin sus apuntes.*

Un/a profesor/a ideal…

1. siempre está contento/a en su trabajo.
2. a veces llega a clase cinco minutos tarde.
3. prepara algo interesante para cada clase.
4. piensa que sabe más que nadie.
5. falta (*misses*) a algunas clases.
6. nunca pone a los estudiantes en grupos.
7. jamás asigna tarea para la clase.
8. siempre prefiere leer sus apuntes.
9. no pierde nada (la tarea, los exámenes, etc.).
10. no habla con nadie después de la clase.

[3:00] **4-26 ¿Sí o no?** Túrnense para contestar las siguientes preguntas. ■

MODELO

E1: *¿Siempre almuerzas a las cuatro de la tarde?*

E2: *No, nunca almuerzo a las cuatro de la tarde. / No, no almuerzo nunca/jamás a las cuatro de la tarde.*

1. ¿Pierdes algo cuando vas de vacaciones?
2. ¿Siempre encuentras las cosas que pierdes?
3. ¿Siempre montas una tienda de campaña cuando vas de camping?
4. ¿A veces vas de excursión con tus amigos?
5. ¿Siempre almuerzas en restaurantes elegantes?
6. ¿Conoces a alguien de El Salvador?
7. ¿Siempre piensas en el amor (*love*)?
8. ¿Hay algo más importante que el dinero?

[2:00] **4-27 No tienes razón** Tu amigo/a es muy idealista. Túrnense para decirle (*tell him/her*) que debe ser más realista, usando expresiones negativas. ■

MODELO

1. Tengo que buscar una profesión sin estrés.
2. Quiero el carro perfecto, un Lexus.
3. Voy a tener hijos perfectos.
4. Pienso que no voy a estudiar la semana que viene.
5. Voy a encontrar unos muebles muy baratos (*cheap*) y elegantes.

SUGGESTION for 4-25
You may wish to simplify this activity by having students say the opposite of what is given.

EXPANSION for 4-25
This activity can be expanded in a few different ways. After students brainstorm the characteristics of the ideal professor, if you feel comfortable, ask them which characteristics they think you and the ideal professor have in common. You might also ask them to consider whether the characteristics vary across disciplines. As a follow-up, make a list of characteristics you think represent *el estudiante ideal*. Have the students write a list of characteristics they think the ideal student should have, and then compare your list to theirs. Discuss any differences between the lists.

NOTE for *Gramática*
This is an inductive grammar presentation in which the students are given examples of a grammar concept and, through the use of guiding questions, they formulate the rule in their own words. Research indicates that students remember and internalize grammar rules better when they construct their own knowledge.

NOTE for reviewing *Ser* and *estar*
Remind students that when using *ser* to say what or who someone or something is, as in the case of professions, they should omit the indefinite article (*un, una, unos, unas*) before the noun: *El Dr. Suárez es profesor de literatura* (Dr. Suárez is a professor of literature).

HERITAGE LANGUAGE LEARNERS
Remind heritage language learners that while *¡Anda! Curso elemental* has presented the basic rules about most concepts, there are subtle rules and exceptions that exist, for example, with *ser* and *estar*. The more subtle differences will be explained at a later point, although they may well be aware of those differences now. If you choose to individualize instruction, you may wish to spend a brief amount of time with your heritage language learners discussing some of the additional uses of *ser* and *estar*.

ADDITIONAL ACTIVITY for *Un repaso de ser y estar*
Pero yo... Completa los siguientes pasos.
Paso 1 Escribe una oración (verdadera para ti) para los siguientes usos de *ser* y *estar*.
1. your origin
2. what you are (student, brother, relationship to another person, etc.)
3. time of your first class (*primera clase*) on Monday
4. location of that class
5. what the professor of that class is like
6. brief description of you
7. brief description of how you feel today
8. location of an upcoming event on or around campus
Paso 2 Túrnense para compartir sus oraciones.

---

9 GRAMÁTICA

`5:00`   04-41 to 04-45

Un repaso de *ser* y *estar*
Describing states of being, characteristics, and location

You have learned two Spanish verbs that mean ***to be*** in English. These verbs, **ser** and **estar,** are contrasted here.

SER

Ser is used:

• **To describe physical or personality characteristics that remain relatively constant**

Gregorio **es** inteligente.	*Gregorio is intelligent.*
Yanina **es** guapa.	*Yanina is pretty.*
Su tienda de campaña **es** amarilla.	*Their tent is yellow.*
Las casas **son** grandes.	*The houses are large.*

• **To explain what or who someone or something is**

El Dr. Suárez **es** profesor de literatura.	*Dr. Suárez is a literature professor.*
Marisol **es** mi hermana.	*Marisol is my sister.*

• **To tell time, or to tell when or where an event takes place**

¿Qué hora **es**?	*What time is it?*
Son las ocho.	*It's eight o'clock.*
Mi clase de español **es** a las ocho y **es** en Peabody Hall.	*My Spanish class is at eight o'clock and is in Peabody Hall.*

• **To tell where someone is from and to express nationality**

Somos de Honduras.	*We are from Honduras.*
Somos hondureños.	*We are Honduran.*
Ellos **son** de Guatemala.	*They are from Guatemala.*
Son guatemaltecos.	*They are Guatemalan.*

ESTAR

Estar is used:

• **To describe physical or personality characteristics that can change, or to indicate a change in condition**

María **está** enferma hoy.	*María is sick today.*
Jorge y Julia **están** tristes.	*Jorge and Julia are sad.*
La cocina **está** sucia.	*The kitchen is dirty.*

• **To describe the locations of people, places, and things**

El museo **está** en la calle Quiroga.	*The museum is on Quiroga Street.*
Estamos en el centro comercial.	*We're at the mall.*
¿Dónde **estás** tú?	*Where are you?*

MODELO
E1: *Soy de Austin, Texas. ¿Y tú?*
E2: *Yo no soy de Austin. Soy de Little Rock, Arkansas. Soy estudiante. ¿Y tú?*
E1: *Soy estudiante, pero también soy mecánico. Los lunes tengo clase de biología a las ocho. ¿A qué hora es tu primera clase?...*

ADDITIONAL ACTIVITY for *Ser y estar*
Quiero conocerte mejor Túrnense para hacer y contestar las siguientes preguntas.
1. ¿De dónde eres?
2. ¿Cómo eres?
3. ¿Cómo estás hoy?
4. ¿A qué hora son tus clases?
5. ¿Cómo es tu casa?
6. ¿Dónde está tu casa?
7. ¿De qué color es tu casa?

8. ¿Dónde está tu dormitorio?
9. ¿Cómo es tu dormitorio?
10. ¿Cuál es tu color favorito?
11. Describe la persona más importante para ti.
12. ¿Dónde está él/ella ahora (*now*)?

You may wish to tell your students to interpret *casa* in this activity as either *casa, apartamento,* or *residencia estudiantil.*

¡Explícalo tú!

Compare the following sentences and answer the questions that follow.

Su hermano **es** simpático.
Su hermano **está** enfermo.

1. Why do you use a form of **ser** in the first sentence?
2. Why do you use a form of **estar** in the second sentence?

> ### Estrategia
> Review the forms of *ser* (p. 13 del eText) and *estar* (p. 76 del eText).

✓ Check your answers to the preceding questions in Appendix 1.

You will learn several more uses for **ser** and **estar** by the end of *¡Anda! Curso elemental*.

6:00 | **4-28 ¿Y Margarita?** Estér y Margarita son estudiantes de la Universidad Francisco Marroquín en la ciudad de Guatemala. Ellas tienen clase ahora pero Margarita no llega. Completen juntos el siguiente párrafo con las formas correctas de **ser** o **estar** para conocerla mejor. ■

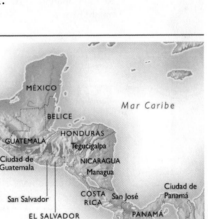

Paso 1

(1) _____Son_____ las siete y media de la mañana. Nuestra clase de física
(2) _____es_____ a las ocho y siempre vamos juntas. Bueno, ¿dónde (3) _____está_____ Margarita? Es raro porque ella (4) _____es_____ muy puntual y no le gusta llegar tarde.
Yo (5) _____soy_____ su mejor amiga y sé que (6) _____está_____ preocupada por sus abuelos.
Ellos (7) _____son_____ mayores y a veces (8) _____están_____ enfermos. Margarita
(9) _____es_____ muy responsable y ayuda mucho a sus abuelos. Toda su familia
(10) _____es_____ de la ciudad de Antigua y siempre piensa en ellos. Aqui viene Margarita, ¡menos mal!

Paso 2 Expliquen por qué usaron (*you used*) **ser** o **estar** en **Paso 1**.

MODELO 1. (*Son*) telling time

ANSWERS to 4-28
Paso 2
1. telling time
2. when an event takes place
3. location of people
4. personality characteristic
5. who someone is
6. condition
7. physical characteristic
8. physical condition
9. personality characteristic
10. tell where someone is from

1:00 | **4-29 Nuestro conocimiento** ¿Qué sabes de Guatemala, Honduras y El Salvador? Túrnense para hacerse y contestar las siguientes preguntas. ■

1. ¿Dónde están estos países: en Norteamérica, Centroamérica o Sudamérica?
2. ¿Cuál está más cerca de México? ¿Cuál está más cerca de Panamá?
3. ¿Son países grandes o pequeños?
4. ¿Cuáles son sus capitales?

ANSWERS to 4-29
1. Están en Centroamérica.
2. Guatemala está más cerca de México. Honduras está más cerca de Panamá.
3. Son países pequeños.
4. La capital de Guatemala es Ciudad de Guatemala. La capital de Honduras es Tegucigalpa. La capital de El Salvador es San Salvador.

5:00 | **4-30 ¡A jugar!** Vamos a practicar **ser** y **estar**. ■

Paso 1 Draw two columns on a piece of paper labeling one **ser** and the other **estar**. Write as many sentences as you can in the three minutes you are given.

Paso 2 Form groups of four to check your sentences and uses of the verbs.

SUGGESTION for 4-31

For **4-31,** pair students by their favorite colors. Also, for this activity, you can use notebook paper, but it is more enjoyable for the students if you use approximately 3 feet of newsprint and markers. They can hold up their work at the end of the activity and report to the rest of the class. If you are interested in acquiring a roll of newsprint, your local newspaper is usually happy either to donate or sell "end rolls" to educators at a very nominal price. The end rolls are wonderful for all sorts of classroom activities.

SECTION GOALS for *Escucha*

By the end of the *Escucha* section, students will be able to:
- paraphrase what they hear in short sentences.
- practice brainstorming in pre-listening activities for words they might hear.
- narrate how they volunteer and repeat what their classmates say about volunteering.

NATIONAL STANDARDS
Communication

The listening strategy for *Capítulo 4* is paraphrasing what you hear. This section represents Standard 1.2 as students listen, understand, and interpret what they have heard. Students also use Standard 1.1, the interpersonal mode, when they pair off and discuss volunteerism. The practice in a small group lends itself well to reinforcing the new strategy of paraphrasing.

AUDIOSCRIPT for 4-33

LUPE:	Marisol, ¿es verdad que tú haces trabajo voluntario?
MARISOL:	Sí, para mí el voluntariado es muy importante.
LUPE:	¿Qué tipo de trabajo haces?
MARISOL:	Pues, me gusta trabajar con los niños. Generalmente voy a la escuela y los ayudo con la tarea.
LUPE:	¿Qué más?
MARISOL:	Quiero trabajar en el hospital. Quiero visitar a los pacientes y llevarles las comidas.
LUPE:	¿Vas a hacer trabajo voluntario ahora que estás en la universidad?
MARISOL:	Pienso que sí. Mañana voy a ir al hospital. Quiero saber si hay oportunidades. ¿Quieres venir?
LUPE:	¡Sí! Quiero ir también.

⏱10:00 👥 **4-31** ## Somos iguales

Paso 1 Draw **three** circles, as per the model below, and ask each other questions to find out what things you have in common and what sets you apart. In the center circle write sentences using **ser** and **estar** about things you have in common, and in the side circles write sentences about things that set you apart.

MODELO
E1: *¿Cuál es tu color favorito?*
E2: *Mi color favorito es el negro.*
E1: *Mi color favorito es el negro también.*
E2: *Hoy estoy nerviosa. ¿Cómo estás tú?*
E1: *Yo estoy cansado.*

Paso 2 Share your diagrams with the class. What are some of the things that all of your classmates have in common?

Hoy estoy nerviosa.   Nuestro color favorito es el negro.   Hoy estoy cansado.

ESCUCHA

📖 04-46 ## El voluntariado

Estrategia

Paraphrasing what you hear

When you know the context and listen carefully, you can repeat or paraphrase what you hear. Start by saying one or two words about what you hear and work up to complete sentences.

4-32 ### Antes de escuchar Do you volunteer?

What service opportunities exist in your city/town? You are going to hear a conversation between Marisol and Lupe, in which Marisol shares her experiences with volunteering. Think of three Spanish words dealing with volunteering that you might hear. ∎

Marisol y Lupe conversan sobre el trabajo voluntario.

🔊 **4-33** ### A escuchar After listening to the conversation for the first time, note three main points, words, or topics. After listening a second time, paraphrase their conversation with at least **three** complete sentences. You may use the following questions to guide your listening. ∎

1. ¿Quién hace trabajo voluntario?
2. ¿Qué trabajo hace ella en la escuela? ¿Qué más quiere hacer?
3. ¿Adónde va a ir mañana? ¿Con quién?

🍦🍦 **4-34** ### Después de escuchar Form **three** sentences about your volunteering experiences, and tell them to your classmate. Your classmate will paraphrase what you have said. ∎

ANSWERS to 4-33

Answers may include: Marisol hace trabajo voluntario. En la escuela ayuda a los niños con la tarea. Quiere trabajar en el hospital y visitar a los pacientes y llevarles las comidas. Mañana va a ir con Lupe al hospital.

¡CONVERSEMOS!
04-47

👐 **4-35** **Mi comunidad** You and a partner are on the planning commission(s) of your town(s). Take turns sharing your ideas with the other commissioners, stating at least **five** positive aspects of your town and **five** areas that could be improved. You should also respond to your partner's ideas, agreeing or disagreeing. Use vocabulary words from *Los lugares,* on page 82, and verbs from page 88, *¿Qué tienen que hacer? ¿Qué pasa?* ■

4-36 **Servicio a nuestra comunidad** Your college has a community service component, and you are a coordinator for these services. With a partner, take turns describing the opportunities available to fellow students in your town(s) or school community. Create at least **ten** sentences using the vocabulary from *Servicios a la comunidad* on page 97. ■

SECTION GOALS for ¡Conversemos!
By the end of the *¡Conversemos!* section, students will be able to:
- express positive and negative aspects of their hometowns.
- describe service opportunities available to fellow students in and around campus.

NATIONAL STANDARDS
Communication, Communities
The *¡Conversemos!* section affords students the opportunity to communicate in extended discourse in Spanish (Standard 1.3). Students can also be using the language in the community or simulating a real-life scenario (Standard 5.3).

ESCRIBE

Una tarjeta postal (*A postcard*)

04-48

Estrategia	It is important to always carefully read over what you have written to check for meaning and accuracy. You want to minimally:	• confirm that subjects and verbs, as well as nouns and adjectives, agree in number and gender.
Proofreading	• verify spelling. • check all verb forms.	• review for appropriate meaning.

4-37 Antes de escribir Escribe una lista de los lugares importantes o interesantes de tu pueblo o ciudad. Luego escribe por qué son importantes o interesantes. Usa el vocabulario de este capítulo y de **También se dice…** en el Apéndice (*Appendix*) 3. ■

4-38 A escribir Organiza tus ideas usando las siguientes preguntas como guía. Escribe por lo menos **cinco** oraciones completas. Puedes consultar el modelo. ■

1. ¿Qué lugares hay en tu pueblo o ciudad?
2. ¿Por qué son importantes o interesantes?
3. Normalmente, ¿qué haces allí?
4. ¿Adónde vas los fines de semana?
5. ¿Qué te gusta de tu pueblo?

Querido/a_____:

Tienes que conocer mi pueblo, Roxborough. Hay _____. Me gusta(n) _____. Es interesante porque _____. Los fines de semana _____.

Con cariño,
__(Tu nombre)__

 4-39 Después de escribir Tu profesor/a va a recoger las tarjetas y "mandárselas" (*mail them*) a otros miembros de la clase para leerlas. Luego, la clase tiene que escoger los lugares que desean visitar. ■

¿Cómo andas? II

	Feel confident	Need to review
Having completed **Comunicación II,** I now can . . .		
• share where I and others are going (p. 94)	☐	☐
• convey what will happen in the future (p. 95)	☐	☐
• impart information about service opportunities (p. 97)	☐	☐
• discuss the concept of social consciousness (p. 98)	☐	☐
• articulate concepts and ideas both affirmatively and negatively (p. 99)	☐	☐
• describe states of being, characteristics, and location (p. 102)	☐	☐
• paraphrase what I hear (p. 104)	☐	☐
• communicate about ways to serve the community (p. 105)	☐	☐
• write a postcard and proofread it for accuracy (p. 106)	☐	☐

Instructor Resources
• Text images (maps), Video Resources

SECTION GOALS for Cultura
By the end of the *Cultura* section, students will be able to:
• identify the ruins of Copán in Honduras.
• describe how Honduras was named.
• identify the Mayan ruins and pyramids of Tikal, Guatemala.
• compare the indigenous populations and languages of Honduras, Guatemala, and El Salvador.
• discuss geographical features of Honduras, Guatemala, and El Salvador including coastal areas, mountains, and volcanoes.
• highlight the similarities and differences between Honduras, Guatemala, and El Salvador.

NATIONAL STANDARDS
Cultures, Comparisons
This three-page culture spread introduces students to basic information about Honduras, Guatemala, and El Salvador. Encourage students to compare and contrast these three Central American countries to each other as well as to the other feature countries up to this point.
  The *Les presento mi país* section compares the cultural information of Honduras, Guatemala, and El Salvador. Goal Two, Cultures, states that students gain knowledge and understanding of the cultures of the world. These readings encompass the practices, perspectives, and products of Hispanic cultures (Standards 2.1, 2.2). They present information about the indigenous people, the local economy, the tourism sector, pastimes, geography, and flora and fauna. Students are able to compare (Standard 4.2) the cultures of Honduras, Guatemala, and El Salvador with their own culture.

ANSWERS to Preguntas
1. Significa *profunda;* de Cristóbal Colón, por la profundidad del agua en la bahía
2. Los mayas en la época precolombina
3. Ruinas, la presencia maya (You may also want to discuss comparisons beyond the scope of the reading to geography, history, food, etc.)

NOTE for El charancaco
A *charancaco* (basilisk), also known as *monkey lala,* is one of most interesting animals on Roatan Island, Honduras. They move like miniature dragons on two legs with their finlike crests expanded. These long-toed relatives of the iguanas can actually hydroplane across water with their forelegs folded and the long tail lifted, creating the appearance of walking on water.

04-49, 04-52

Les presento mi país

César Alfonso Ávalos

Mi nombre es César Alfonso Ávalos y soy de La Ceiba, Honduras, una ciudad en el Mar Caribe que está cerca de unas islas hondureñas bellas (*beautiful*) y muy interesantes. Mi lugar favorito para visitar es Utila, bien conocido en el mundo por el buceo (*scuba diving*). **¿Te gusta bucear?** Mi país tiene un pasado cultural muy rico, ya que los mayas viven aquí desde la época precolombina. Las ruinas más importantes que tenemos están en Copán. **¿Hay ruinas importantes cerca de tu pueblo?**

La playa de Utila, Islas de la Bahía

Un charancaco (*basilisk*) de la isla Roatán

Las ruinas de Copán

ALMANAQUE

Nombre oficial:	República de Honduras
Gobierno:	República democrática constitucional
Población:	7.989.415 (2010)
Idiomas:	español (oficial); miskito, garífuna, otros dialectos amerindios
Moneda:	Lempira (L)

¿Sabías que...?

• El nombre original de esta región es *Higüeras,* que es el nombre de una planta nativa. Al llegar a la costa norteña, Cristóbal Colón renombra la región *Honduras* a causa de la profundidad del agua en la bahía.

Preguntas

1. ¿Qué significa *Honduras*? ¿De dónde viene el nombre?
2. ¿Quiénes son los habitantes originales de Copán?
3. ¿Qué semejanzas hay entre Honduras y México?

 Amplía tus conocimientos sobre Honduras en MySpanishLab.

NOTE for El charancaco
Honduras is home to a stunning array of animals:
• More than 210 species of mammals including monkeys, jaguars, pumas, anteaters, armadillos, coyotes, deer, foxes, peccaries, pocket gophers, porcupines, and tapirs.
• More than 95 species of amphibians and reptiles such as the bushmaster, coral snake, fer-de-lance, horned viper, rattlesnake, whip snake, caiman, crocodile, and iguana.
• 715 species of tropical birds including the toucan, black robin, hummingbird, macaw, nightingale, thrush, partridge, quail, quetzal, toucanet, and wren.
• Numerous varieties of freshwater and saltwater fish and turtles.

NOTE for La playa de Utila, Islas de la Bahía
The small island of Utila, part of the Honduran Bay Islands, is known for excellent scuba diving and snorkeling. It lies 18 miles off shore the Honduran port town of La Ceiba and is only 11 kilometers long and 4 kilometers wide.

EXPANSION for ¿Sabías qué...?
Ask students about names of places in the United States and their meanings. If your students are not native to the United States, ask about their home countries.

Cultura

Guatemala

04-50, 04-53

Luis Pedro Aguirre
Maldonado

Les presento mi país

Mi nombre es Luis Pedro Aguirre Maldonado y soy de Antigua, Guatemala. Muchas personas vienen a mi ciudad para estudiar en nuestras excelentes escuelas de lengua española. **¿Visitan muchas personas tu ciudad o pueblo?** Mi país es montañoso (*mountainous*) con muchos volcanes, como el gran Tajumulco, y algunos de ellos son muy activos. También hay ruinas mayas muy antiguas, como las de Tikal y algunas de nuestras pirámides son las más altas de las Américas. **¿En qué otros lugares encuentras pirámides?**

Un templo muy alto de Tikal es El Gran Jaguar.

Tajumulco es el volcán más alto de Centroamérica y la montaña más alta de Guatemala.

Antigua, la primera capital de Guatemala

ALMANAQUE

Nombre oficial: República de Guatemala

Gobierno: República democrática constitucional

Población: 13.550.440 (2010)

Idiomas: español (oficial); idiomas amerindios (23 reconocidos oficialmente)

Moneda: Quetzal (Q)

¿Sabías que...?

- Los mayas tienen un calendario civil, *El Haab*. Consiste en 18 "meses" de 20 días cada uno. Los últimos cinco días del año, conocidos como *el Wayeb*, se consideran de muy mala suerte.

Preguntas

1. Nombra dos cosas que sabes de la geografía guatemalteca.
2. ¿Cuántos idiomas se hablan en Guatemala?
3. ¿Qué otros países tienen herencia maya?

 Amplía tus conocimientos sobre Guatemala en MySpanishLab.

109

CAPÍTULO 4

 Instructor Resources
- Text images (maps), Video Resources

NOTE for *Tajumulco*
Tajumulco is the highest volcano in Central America and the highest elevation in Guatemala. It is 4,220 meters high, which is 13,845 feet. It is a peak in the Sierra Madre de Chiapas mountain range, which extends from southern Mexico into Guatemala. It is possible to climb this volcano.

SUGGESTION for *Tajumulco*
Ask students whether they have climbed a mountain or volcano. What was the experience like?

NOTE for *Tikal*
The Tikal National Park in northern Guatemala is a stunning archeological discovery. Covering an area of 222 square miles, much of the ruins are surrounded by jungle and have yet to be excavated. The University of Pennsylvania assisted in the initial excavation and restoration between 1956 and 1969. Work continued under the Proyecto Nacional Tikal, University of San Carlos in Guatemala, and the Instituto de Antropología e Historia. It is said to be the largest excavated site in the American continent.

ANSWERS to *Preguntas*
1. Hay muchas montañas y volcanes.
2. Español y 23 idiomas amerindios reconocidos oficialmente. En total, 24 oficialmente.
3. México y Honduras

NOTE for *Antigua*
A UNESCO World Heritage Site, the city is a gem of Spanish architecture and is full of historic buildings, monuments, fountains and ruins.

Instructor Resources
• Text images (maps), Video Resources

El Salvador

CULTURA • CULTURA • CULTURA • C

04-51, 04-54

Claudia Figueroa Barrios

Les presento mi país

Mi nombre es Claudia Figueroa Barrios. Soy de La Libertad, al sur de nuestra capital San Salvador. Mi ciudad está en la costa del Pacífico cerca de la playa El Sunzal, donde mucha gente practica los deportes acuáticos. **¿Te gustan los deportes acuáticos?** El Salvador es el único país de Centroamérica que no tiene costa caribeña. En mi casa viven tres generaciones de mi familia y nos gusta mucho la comida salvadoreña, como las pupusas. **¿Cuál es tu comida favorita?**

Las pupusas son la comida nacional de El Salvador.

La playa El Sunzal es un lugar excelente para el surfing, el snorkeling y el buceo.

En la antigüedad, los mayas usaron (*used*) granos de cacao como dinero.

ALMANAQUE

Nombre oficial: República de El Salvador
Gobierno: República democrática constitucional
Población: 6.052.064 (2010)
Idioma: español (oficial)
Moneda: Dólar estadounidense

¿Sabías que...?

• Algunos salvadoreños, sobre todo los que viven en las partes rurales del país, van a los curanderos (*folk healers*) para buscar ayuda médica.

Preguntas

1. ¿Qué importancia tiene el cacao en la historia maya?
2. ¿Qué deportes practican en El Salvador?
3. ¿Qué cosas de El Salvador son únicas o diferentes a las de otros países hispanos?

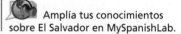 Amplía tus conocimientos sobre El Salvador en MySpanishLab.

EPISODIO 4

Ambiciones siniestras

¡Hola!
eText 164   04-59

Lectura y video

 Instructor Resources

• Video script

SECTION GOALS for *Lectura y video* (online)

By the end of the *Lectura y video* section, students will be able to:

• focus on pre-reading strategies like skimming and scanning.
• summarize the background information provided about Lupe and Marisol.
• make predictions about what will happen next.
• make predictions about the characters' volunteer activities.
• report the main events in chronological order.

Y por fin, ¿cómo andas?

	Feel confident	Need to review
Having completed this chapter, I now can . . .		
Comunicación I		
• identify places in and around town (p. 82)	☐	☐
• pronounce the letters *c* and *z* (MSL/SAM)	☐	☐
• state whom and what is known (p. 85)	☐	☐
• relate common obligations and activities (p. 88)	☐	☐
• express actions (p. 90)	☐	☐
Comunicación II		
• share where I and others are going (p. 94)	☐	☐
• convey what will happen in the future (p. 95)	☐	☐
• impart information about service opportunities (p. 97)	☐	☐
• articulate concepts and ideas both affirmatively and negatively (p. 99)	☐	☐
• describe states of being, characteristics, and location (p. 102)	☐	☐
• paraphrase what I hear (p. 104)	☐	☐
• communicate about ways to serve the community (p. 105)	☐	☐
• write a postcard and proofread it for accuracy (p. 106)	☐	☐
Cultura		
• describe shopping and other daily activities (p. 84)	☐	☐
• discuss the concept of social consciousness (p. 98)	☐	☐
• list interesting facts about Honduras, Guatemala, and El Salvador (pp. 108–110)	☐	☐
Ambiciones siniestras		
• practice the reading strategies of skimming and scanning, and learn more about Lupe and Marisol (p. 111)	☐	☐
• discover that Cisco may not be who Eduardo and the others think he is (p. 111)	☐	☐
Comunidades		
• use Spanish in real-life contexts (SAM)	☐	☐

RECAP OF *AMBICIONES SINIESTRAS* Episodio 3 (online)

Lectura: In the reading from *Capítulo 3, El concurso,* Manolo and Alejandra checked their e-mail in the Internet café, NetEscape. Both received an enticing e-mail from Sr. Verdugo about a contest in which they could win a million dollars. Alejandra was hesitant about replying, but Manolo wondered what could happen if they responded to the e-mail.

Video: In the *Capítulo 3* episode, *¡Tienes una gran oportunidad!,* Marisol, Lupe, Eduardo, and Cisco also received the mysterious e-mail about being finalists in the contest. Marisol received her message while she was at Lupe's apartment, and when Lupe checked her account, she had received the same e-mail. Eduardo and Cisco worked on their homework in the library, and when they checked their accounts, they realized that they, too, were finalists in a million-dollar contest.

NATIONAL STANDARDS
Communication

The *Ambiciones siniestras* section requires students to understand and interpret spoken (*Video*) and written (*Lectura*) Spanish (Standard 1.2) as they discover more about the characters and the plot. Depending on how you implement the activities that correspond to the reading and video sections, you can also encourage interpersonal communication in small groups or with partners (Standard 1.1). If you assigned the roles of the characters, students could act out a video scene and present their understanding of what happens in the video (Standard 1.3).

ANSWERS to 4-42, *Lectura*

1. Es un proyecto acerca de sus pueblos para la clase de sociología.
2. No quiere hablar de su familia.
3. Es una familia grande con muchos tíos y primos. Es hija única.
4. Vive en un pueblo cerca de Nueva York. Tiene de todo cerca de su casa.
5. Escribe sobre Los Ángeles, no sobre su pueblo en Ohio.

ANSWERS to 4-44, *Video*

1. Van a su apartamento.
2. *Answers may include:* Hablan de unos supermercados, de Centroamérica (y de Guatemala) y de sus trabajos como voluntarios.

3. Eduardo trabaja como voluntario. Ayuda a los niños.
4. Porque Eduardo toca sus papeles.
5. Eduardo va a un cibercafé y escribe un email.

NOTE for *Lectura*

Remember that the *Ambiciones siniestras* mystery offers a high-interest context in which students can practice the vocabulary and grammar they are acquiring in each chapter, as well as recycle previous material. It is important to complete both the *Lectura* and *Video* for each chapter because each segment builds on the previous segment. Sucessfully completing these segments, with the support of the strategies and pre- and post-reading/viewing activities, allows students to gain confidence in their ability to learn and use the language in meaningful ways.

ANSWERS to 4-41, *Lectura*

1. a. All of the characters, and in particular Marisol and Lupe.
   b. They are in an apartment.
2. a. country   b. small
   c. Akron

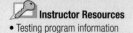

Instructor Resources
• Testing program information

VOCABULARIO ACTIVO

Los lugares	Places
el almacén	department store
el banco	bank
el bar; el club	bar; club
el café	café
el cajero automático	ATM machine
el centro	downtown
el centro comercial	mall; business/shopping district
el cibercafé	Internet café
el cine	movie theater
la iglesia	church
el mercado	market
el museo	museum
la oficina de correos; correos	post office
el parque	park
la plaza	town square
el restaurante	restaurant
el supermercado	supermarket
el teatro	theater
el templo	temple

Algunos verbos	Some verbs
buscar	to look for
estar de acuerdo	to agree
mandar una carta	to send/mail a letter

Otras palabras útiles	Other useful words
la ciudad	city
la cuenta	bill; account
detrás (de)	behind
enfrente (de)	in front (of)
el/la mejor	the best
la película	movie; film
el/la peor	the worst
el pueblo	town; village

Servicios a la comunidad	Community service
apoyar a un/a candidato/a	to support a candidate
ayudar a las personas mayores/los mayores	to help elderly people
circular una petición	to circulate a petition
dar un paseo	to go for a walk
deber	ought to; should
hacer artesanía	to make arts and crafts
hacer una hoguera	to light a campfire
ir de camping	to go camping
ir de excursión	to take a short trip
llevar a alguien al médico	to take someone to the doctor
montar una tienda de campaña	to put up a tent
organizar	to organize
participar en una campaña política	to participate in a political campaign
repartir comidas	to hand out/deliver food
trabajar como consejero/a	to work as a counselor
trabajar en el campamento de niños	to work in a summer camp
trabajar como voluntario/a en la residencia de ancianos	to volunteer at a nursing home
trabajar en política	to work in politics
viajar en canoa	to canoe

Otras palabras útiles	Other useful words
el deber	obligation; duty
el voluntariado	volunteerism

Otros verbos	Other verbs
ir	to go
saber	to know

¿Qué tienen que hacer?	What do they have to do?
(Verbos con cambio de raíz)	(Stem-changing verbs)
almorzar (ue)	to have lunch
cerrar (ie)	to close
comenzar (ie)	to begin
costar (ue)	to cost
demostrar (ue)	to demonstrate
devolver (ue)	to return (an object)
dormir (ue)	to sleep
empezar (ie)	to begin
encerrar (ie)	to enclose
encontrar (ue)	to find
entender (ie)	to understand
jugar (ue)	to play
mentir (ie)	to lie
morir (ue)	to die
mostrar (ue)	to show
pedir (i)	to ask for
pensar (ie)	to think
perder (ie)	to lose; to waste
perseguir (i)	to chase
preferir (ie)	to prefer
recomendar (ie)	to recommend
recordar (ue)	to remember
repetir (i)	to repeat
seguir (i)	to follow; to continue (doing something)
servir (i)	to serve
volver (ue)	to return

Expresiones afirmativas y negativas	Affirmative and negative expressions
a veces	sometimes
algo	something; anything
alguien	someone
algún	some; any
alguno/a/os/as	some; any
jamás	never; not ever (emphatic)
nada	nothing
nadie	no one; nobody
ni... ni	neither . . . nor
ningún	none
ninguno/a/os/as	none
nunca	never
o... o	either . . . or
siempre	always

CAPÍTULO 5

Instructor Resources
• IRM: Syllabi and Lesson Plans

NATIONAL STANDARDS

COMUNICACIÓN I

- To discuss music (Communication, Connections, Cultures, Comparisons)
- To practice pronouncing diphthongs and linking words (Communication, Cultures)
- To identify people and things (Part I) (Communication)
- To identify people and things (Part II) (Communication)
- To explain how something is done (Communication)
- To describe what is happening at the moment (Communication)
- To engage in additional communication practice (Communication)

COMUNICACIÓN II

- To share information about movies and television programs (Communication, Connections, Cultures)
- To rank people and things (Communication, Comparisons)
- To state what needs to be accomplished (Communication)
- To express *what* or *whom* (Communication)
- To anticipate content when listening (Communication)
- To communicate about music and film (Communication)
- To write a movie review and practice peer editing (Communication, Connections, Communities, Cultures)
- To engage in additional communication practice (Communication)

CULTURA

- To discuss Hispanic music in the United States (Communication, Cultures, Connections, Comparisons)
- To describe Hispanic influences in North American film (Communication, Cultures, Connections, Comparisons)
- To list interesting facts about Nicaragua, Costa Rica, and Panama (Cultures, Comparisons)
- To explore further the chapter's cultural themes (Cultures)

5 ¡A divertirse!
La música y el cine

En el mundo hispanohablante la gente trabaja pero también sabe divertirse (*enjoy themselves*). La música, el baile y el cine son formas de expresión y de distracción comunes. Estos pasatiempos, además de otros como los deportes o leer un buen libro, nos hacen la vida muy agradable. Sobre todo (*Above all*), es importante buscar maneras de relajarse y aliviar el estrés.

PREGUNTAS

1 ¿Qué haces cuando no estudias?

2 ¿Qué hacen tus amigos y tú para relajarse y aliviar el estrés?

3 Hay una expresión en español que dice: "Algunas personas viven para trabajar y otras trabajan para vivir". ¿Cuál es tu filosofía de la vida?

114

AMBICIONES SINIESTRAS

- To anticipate content when reading and discover what Cisco does in his search for Eduardo (Communication, Comparisons)
- To find out who is the second student to disappear (Communication)

COMUNIDADES

- To use Spanish in real-life contexts (Connections, Comparisons, Communities)

SECTION GOALS for *Chapter opener*
By the end of the *Chapter opener* section, students will be able to:
- name some forms of diversion in Hispanic countries.
- think about ways to alleviate stress.
- reflect on the concept of *trabajar para vivir* or *vivir para trabajar*.

NATIONAL STANDARDS
Communities
This chapter focuses on music and movies. Use the resources in your modern language department, the library, or audiovisual services to plan a foreign film festival. If you do not have videos or DVDs, you can rent them from teacher video rental companies, video stores, or from other video rental companies on the web. Compile several titles you feel may be appropriate for the community and its population, and ask students to plan a weekly or monthly movie that students and community members are invited to attend. You may require that students attend a certain number of films or that a certain number of students attend a particular film, to introduce themselves to the community members who attend. Standard 5.1 encourages the use of Spanish both within and beyond the school setting, and watching authentic movies and discussing them with the community members builds bridges between the campus and the community.

NOTE for *Chapter opener*
Note that the chapter introduction talks about other pastimes such as sports, reading, and ways to alleviate stress, but the main focus of the chapter is music and cinema. You might also want to expand on the importance of theater in Hispanic cultures, such as *El teatro campesino*, whose roots were in the United Farm Workers Union in California. It was started by Luis Valdez and featured Chicano themes. Other classic plays such as *La Celestina* or *La casa de Bernarda Alba* are offered throughout the United States by traveling theater groups. Browse the Internet for Spanish theater groups that might be coming to a city near you.

SUGGESTION for *Chapter opener*
Bring in a photo of your favorite Hispanic recording artist or group (or an American artist who sings in Spanish) and ask students to identify who they think the artist is. Play a track from your favorite CD or download the song and play a clip of the song. Ask your students to identify characteristics about the song and the artist from the clip. What genre of music do they think it is? Is this artist's music representative of his/her country? What is the tempo? What kinds of instruments do they hear?

PLANNING AHEAD
You will want to play music in class for the students to listen to, or ask students to bring in music they want to share. It is helpful to have access to a compact disc player or computer for music files, and blank CDs for students to bring in their music to share. You may also wish to plan on playing music daily in the background while students are working in their groups. Students find this technique adds to the immersion-style atmosphere.

METHODOLOGY • Making Topics Relevant for Students
The text and questions for this chapter opener are completely in Spanish, just as in *Capítulo 4*. Note that the questions begin with your learners and their preferences, something that we have learned from educational philosopher John Dewey. Try having your students each turn to a partner and answer the questions in pairs. Then have them share the answers their partners gave. This has them practice listening and paraphrasing.

PLANNING AHEAD
Remember that all grammar explanations and culture presentations should be assigned to be read before class. Class time should be spent answering clarification questions for the grammar presentations, or answering the comprehension/critical thinking questions that follow the culture presentations. Activities **5-4** and **5-9** can be assigned to be written at home and then shared in class.

🔑 **Instructor Resources**
• Textbook images, PPT, Extra Activities

SECTION GOALS for
Comunicación I

By the end of the *Comunicación* section, students will be able to:

• talk about the world of music, including genres and characteristics of each genre.
• pronounce strong vowels (*a, e, o*), weak vowels (*i, u*), and diphthongs.
• link words and pronounce identical vowels and consonants.
• discuss Hispanic music in the U.S.
• form demonstrative adjectives and demonstrative pronouns.
• review the agreement rules of nouns and adjectives.
• form adverbs from adjectives.
• produce the forms of the present progressive using regular and irregular gerunds.

NATIONAL STANDARDS
Communication, Cultures, Comparisons

If you have a collection of different types of music from the Spanish-speaking world, this chapter is an excellent opportunity for you to expose your students to a wide variety. Encourage them to compare and contrast the music within the Spanish-speaking world as well as with music from the English-speaking world.

The activities related to music provide you with multiple ways to address the Standards. In particular, you can address the Communication Goal (Standards 1.1, 1.2, and 1.3) by incorporating music into the class. Play your favorite Hispanic artist's music and have your students share their opinions and preferences about the artist and the music (Standard 1.1) in pairs or small groups. Give students a copy of the lyrics in Spanish, and ask them to interpret what the song is about. The combination of hearing the words and following along with the written lyrics facilitates interpretation (Standard 1.2). Ask students to present part of the song (reading aloud or singing in front of the class) or a different song of their choosing (Standard 1.3). They can bring in the Spanish lyrics for others to read along (Standard 1.2) as they present (Standard 1.3). Goal Two, Cultures, is also easily addressed through music. Highlight the different types of music in Spanish-speaking countries, how different cultures incorporate music into daily life, and the types of commercially produced music with which students might be familiar.

Comunicación I

1 VOCABULARIO

🔊 05-01 to 05-07 📖

El mundo de la música Discussing music

EL TEATRO NACIONAL RUBÉN DARÍO

el músico (la música)
la orquesta
el tambor
la trompeta
el trompetista (la trompetista)
el cantante (la cantante)
la guitarrista (el guitarrista)
el baterista (la baterista)
las grabaciones
la batería
el artista
la guitarra
la artista

el tamborista (la tamborista)
el pianista (la pianista)
el piano
la música
el empresario (la empresaria)
la gira
el conjunto
el concierto

Gira mundial de Las Piedras
¡Concierto a las 20h!

Encourage students to make comparisons (Standard 4.2) between what role music has in the United States and in Spanish-speaking countries, and among the different types of music available. When you analyze the lyrics, you can explain the literal meaning versus the figurative meaning, or how they translate versus what they mean. That allows students to make comparisons between Spanish and English (Standard 4.1).

Algunos géneros musicales	Some musical genres		Algunos verbos	Some verbs
el jazz	jazz		dar un concierto	to give/perform a concert
la música clásica	classical music		ensayar	to practice/rehearse
la música folklórica	folk music		grabar	to record
la música popular	pop music		hacer una gira	to tour
la música rap	rap music		sacar un CD	to release a CD
la ópera	opera		tocar	to play (a musical instrument)
el rock	rock			
la salsa	salsa		Otras palabras útiles	Some useful words
			el/la aficionado/a	fan
Algunos adjetivos	Some adjectives		la fama	fame
apasionado/a	passionate		el género	genre
cuidadoso/a	careful		la habilidad	ability; skill
fino/a	fine; delicate		la letra	lyrics
lento/a	slow		el ritmo	rhythm
suave	smooth		la voz	voice

PRONUNCIACIÓN

Diphthongs and linking

05-08 to 05-12

Go to MySpanishLab/Student Activities Manual to learn about diphthongs and linking.

[7:00] **5-1 Dibujemos** Escuchen mientras su profesor/a les da (gives you) las instrucciones de esta actividad. ■

[3:00] **5-2 Listas** Túrnate con un/a compañero/a para decir y escribir todas las palabras del vocabulario nuevo que recuerden (you both remember) de las tres categorías en el modelo. ¿Cuántas palabras pueden recordar? ■

MODELO

TIPOS DE MÚSICA	INSTRUMENTOS	OTRAS PALABRAS
el jazz	la trompeta	el conjunto

METHODOLOGY • Comprehensive input
Notice that virtually all of the direction lines in this chapter are in Spanish. For all students, this provides reading practice. You may choose to model some of the activities such as 5-2 to make sure that students understand what they are supposed to do with their partners.

METHODOLOGY • Visual Organizers
For 5-2, you may wish to project the image of the new vocabulary that does not have the words written on it. Students can then use the image as a visual organizer to assist them in remembering the vocabulary they have just learned.

METHODOLOGY • Working in Pairs
Remember that it is ideal for students to change partners daily. In this way, students have the opportunity to work with everyone in the class, and you build community within your classroom. At the very least, partners should be changed weekly.

NOTE for *Algunos géneros musicales*
You will notice that the genres listed here are mostly cognates. Students should be able to discuss the instruments and artists most commonly associated with each genre. *Salsa* is the genre that may require the most explanation. You can discuss the roots of *salsa* in the United States during the 1960s and 1970s, stemming from Puerto Rican immigration and Cuban influences. *Salsa* is quite popular in Latin America and is sometimes referred to as *música tropical* or Latin jazz. You may also want to add *el reggaetón, la soca, el norteño, el tejano, la cumbia,* etc. to the vocabulary list. An excellent source of types of popular music and musicians in the Spanish-speaking world is the Latin Grammys web site, http://www.latingrammy.com.

SECTION GOALS for *Pronunciación*
By the end of the *Pronunciación* section, students will be able to:
- differentiate between strong vowels and weak vowels.
- recognize diphthongs and how they are pronounced.
- link using the 4 rules: consonants to vowels, vowels to vowels, identical consonants, and identical vowels.
- pronounce new vocabulary using the rules for vowels and consonants.

SUGGESTION for *El mundo de la música*
Have students brainstorm 5 artists/musical groups from each decade and decide what musical genres dominated each decade. Depending on the age and composition of your class, you might start in the 1970s or later. Come prepared with a list of your most influential artists and see whether they match those of your students.

NOTE for 5-1
Activity **5-1** continues with the mechanical practice for your students to learn the new vocabulary. This activity can be used in other chapters as well, to either present or review vocabulary. It is also a good activity for pairs who finish early. Please give the following extended directions to your students: if you are familiar with the game *Pictionary,* it is very similar. It is like charades, but they have to draw pictures rather than act the words out.
INSTRUCTIONS: Divide your class into groups of 4. Each group of 4 will work as 2 teams of 2 students. "Captains" from each team select the word that they are going to draw. Their teammate needs to try to guess what the word is in Spanish as they draw. The round is over when one of the teams guesses the word. The roles are then switched, and the 2 team members who did the guessing now select the word that each will draw for his/her partner. We suggest doing this activity for at least 4 rounds. It is a motivating way to practice vocabulary.

NOTE for 5-3
Remind students that in **5-3** they are asked to share their answers with 2 other classmates. If they work in groups of 3, they can change the questions to the *ustedes* form.

CULTURAL BACKGROUND for 5-4
The Mejía brothers are among the most popular Nicaraguan artists; Ramón for his combination of rock, rap, and flamenco, and Luis for his salsa music. Ramón was politically active during the 2006 elections and wrote and performed a highly popular song, *Rompe el silencio*, that encouraged young Nicaraguans to get out and vote. Ramon's latest CD, *Canciones Populares Contestatarias*, was released in spring, 2010. Luis, also known as the "Príncipe de la Salsa," has recorded highly successful popular songs like *Yo no sé mañana*. In 2009, he won a Latin Grammy for his CD *Ciclos*.

SUGGESTION for 5-4
We suggest assigning the writing of the questions outside of class. Either show your students photos of the Mejia brothers or assign them to search for them on the Internet using the keywords "Luis Mejía," Ramón Mejía," "Perrozompopo". Encourage your students to go to the Internet to hear the Mejía brothers' music.

HERITAGE LANGUAGE LEARNERS
Ask your heritage language learners what types of Spanish-language music they enjoy. If the artists are not commonly known, ask them to bring in a sample of their music to share with the class.

METHODOLOGY • Having Students Create Questions
Research has confirmed what instructors have observed time and again: One of the most difficult skills for language learners is to create questions. Our classes tend to focus on questions we ask our students, but rarely are they asked to create their own questions. Activity **5-4** is excellent practice for your students.

METHODOLOGY • Peer Editing
You may wish to check your students' questions for **5-4** either with peer editing in pairs, or on the board. If you use the board, have each student write a question and let the class help edit them. Students will learn more about peer editing in the *Escribe* section of this chapter.

`7:00` **5-3** **Para conocerte mejor** Hazle las siguientes preguntas a un/a compañero/a. Toma apuntes y luego comparte las respuestas con otros dos compañeros. ■

Estrategia
When reporting your information, make complete sentences, and remember to use the *él* or *ella* form of the verb. Also, simply refer to your notes; do not read from them. This technique will help you to speak more fluidly and will help you speak in paragraphs, an important skill to perfect when learning a language.

1. ¿Con qué frecuencia vas a conciertos?
2. ¿Qué género de música prefieres?
3. ¿Cuál es tu grupo favorito?
4. ¿Cuál es tu cantante favorito/a? ¿Cómo es su voz?
5. ¿Qué instrumento te gusta?
6. ¿Cuál es tu canción favorita?
7. ¿Sabes tocar un instrumento? ¿Cuál?
8. ¿Sabes cantar bien? ¿Te gusta cantar? ¿Cuándo y dónde cantas?
9. ¿En qué tienes mucha habilidad o talento?
10. ¿Conoces algún conjunto o cantante hispano? ¿Cuál?

 Capítulo 2. La formación de preguntas y las palabras interrogativas, pág. 70 del eText.

`7:00` **5-4** **Los famosos** Completa los siguientes pasos. ■

Fíjate
Remember that if you are interviewing people whom you don't know, use the *usted/ustedes* form.

Paso 1 Como reportero/a de la revista *Rolling Stone* tienes la oportunidad de entrevistar a los hermanos Mejía, dos músicos populares de Nicaragua. Escribe por lo menos **cinco** preguntas que vas a hacerles.

Paso 2 Haz una investigación en el Internet para ver si puedes descubrir las respuestas a tus preguntas y para escuchar la música de Luis y Ramón Mejía. Después, comparte tus resultados y tu opinión con la clase; diles (*tell them*) qué canción te gusta más y por qué.

NATIONAL STANDARDS
Communities
One way of having some of your students use their Spanish in the community is to plan a talent show focusing on Hispanic music.

Spanish/ English Tutorials

05-13 to 05-15

Los adjetivos demostrativos
Identifying people and things (Part I)

> Esta mujer toca muy bien. Ese hombre toca bien y aquel hombre toca muy mal.

When you want to point out a specific person, place, thing, or idea, you use a ***demonstrative adjective***. In Spanish, they are:

DEMONSTRATIVE ADJECTIVES	MEANING	FROM THE PERSPECTIVE OF THE SPEAKER, IT REFERS TO . . .
este, esta, estos, estas	*this, these*	something nearby
ese, esa, esos, esas	*that, those over there*	something farther away
aquel, aquella, aquellos, aquellas	*that, those (way) over there*	something even farther away in distance and/or time . . . perhaps not even visible

Since forms of **este, ese,** and **aquel** are adjectives, they must agree in gender and number with the nouns they modify. Note the following examples.

Este conjunto es fantástico.	*This group is fantastic.*
Esta cantante es fenomenal.	*This singer is phenomenal.*
Estos conjuntos son fantásticos.	*These groups are fantastic.*
Estas cantantes son fenomenales.	*These singers are phenomenal.*
Ese conjunto es fantástico.	*That group is fantastic.*
Esa cantante es fenomenal.	*That singer is phenomenal.*
Esos conjuntos son fantásticos.	*Those groups are fantastic.*
Esas cantantes son fenomenales.	*Those singers are phenomenal.*
Aquel conjunto es fantástico.	*That group (over there) is fantastic.*
Aquella cantante es fenomenal.	*That singer (over there) is phenomenal.*
Aquellos conjuntos son fantásticos.	*Those groups (over there) are fantastic.*
Aquellas cantantes son fenomenales.	*Those singers (over there) are phenomenal.*

¡Explícalo tú!

In summary:

1. When do you use **este, ese,** and **aquel**?
2. When do you use **esta, esa,** and **aquella**?
3. When do you use **estos, esos,** and **aquellos**?
4. When do you use **estas, esas,** and **aquellas**?

✔ Check your answers to the preceding questions in Appendix 1.

SUGGESTION for *Los adjetivos demostrativos*
Use the demonstrative adjectives with classroom objects to indicate the distance from the speaker, using *this, that,* and *that one over there*: *Este lápiz es rojo, ese lápiz es azul y aquel lápiz es amarillo.* You can also use demonstrative adjectives as a way to review possession and possessive adjectives. Borrow various items from your students while the class is watching. Then ask *¿De quién es esta mochila?* and have them answer by using *ser + de* or an appropriate possessive adjective.

METHODOLOGY •
Streamlining the Syllabus
Based on research, as well as consultation with hundreds of instructors, the decision was made that *¡Anda! Curso elemental* will teach a more streamlined syllabus so that students may learn well (acquire) what is being presented. This is a departure from how it has been done in the past: to introduce everything and have students leave the course with little or nothing that they can do with the language. You have noticed that, when presenting grammar, we have not presented all of the exceptions to the rules or nuances of the language that can be presented at a later time so that students will comprehend the differences. Having said that, if you have heritage language learners or false beginners, feel free to present them. As always, we as instructors must ultimately decide what is best for our students.

SUGGESTION for *Los adjetivos demostrativos*
You may wish to use the following saying for students who need extra help with demonstratives: *This* and *these* both have *t*'s in Spanish; *that* and *those* do not in Spanish; (e.g., *Este, esta,* and *estos, estas* mean *this* and *these* and have *t*'s. *Ese, esa, esos,* and *esas* mean *that* and *those* and do not have *t*'s).

5-5 **Amiga, tienes razón** Tu amigo/a te da su opinión y tú respondes con una opinión similar. Cambia la forma de **este/a** a (*to*) **ese/a** y añade (*add*) la palabra **también**. ■

MODELO   TU AMIGO/A: Esta música es muy suave.
             TÚ: *Sí, y esa música es suave también.*

1. Este grupo es fenomenal.
2. Estos cantantes son muy jóvenes.
3. Esta gira empieza en enero.

4. Este CD sale ahora.
5. Estas canciones son muy apasionadas.
6. Estos pianistas tocan muy bien.

5-6 **En el centro estudiantil** Completen el diálogo de Lola y Tina con las formas correctas de **este, ese** y **aquel**. ■

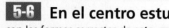

LOLA: Tina, mira (1) ___este___ (*this*) grupo de estudiantes que acaba de entrar.

TINA: Sí, creo que conozco a (2) ___este___ (*this*) hombre alto. Es guitarrista del trío de jazz *Ritmos*.

LOLA: Tienes razón. Y (3) ___esta___ (*this*) mujer rubia es pianista en la orquesta de la universidad.

TINA: ¿Quiénes son (4) ___esas___ (*those*) dos mujeres morenas?

LOLA: Están en nuestra clase de química. ¿No las conoces? Y (5) ___aquellos___ (*those over there*) dos hombres de las camisas rojas ¡son muy guapos!

Capítulo 2. El verbo *gustar*, pág. 80 del eText; Capítulo 4. Los verbos con cambios de raíz, pág. 142 del eText; Capítulo 3. La casa, pág. 98 del eText; Los colores, pág. 111 del eText.

5-7 **¿Qué opinas?** Miren el dibujo y expresen sus opiniones sobre las casas. Usen las formas apropiadas de **este, ese** y **aquel**. ■

MODELO   *Me gusta esta casa blanca, pero prefiero esa casa beige. Pienso que aquella casa roja es fea. También creo que este jardín de la casa blanca es bonito.*

3 GRAMÁTICA

  05-16 to 05-17 Spanish/English Tutorials

Los pronombres demostrativos
Identifying people and things (Part II)

Demonstrative pronouns take the place of nouns. They are identical in form and meaning to demonstrative adjectives.

¡Esta es muy buena! Ese no me gusta, pero ¡aquel es fenomenal!

Masculino	Femenino	*Meaning*
este	esta	*this one*
estos	estas	*these*
ese	esa	*that one*
esos	esas	*those*
aquel	aquella	*that one (way over there/not visible)*
aquellos	aquellas	*those (way over there/not visible)*

A demonstrative pronoun must agree in gender and number with the noun it replaces. Observe how demonstrative adjectives and demonstrative pronouns are used in the following sentences.

Yo quiero comprar **este CD,** pero mi hermana quiere comprar **ese.**

I want to buy this CD, but my sister wants to buy that one.

—¿Te gusta **esa guitarra**?
—No, a mí me gusta **esta.**

Do you like that guitar?
No, I like this one.

Estos instrumentos son interesantes, pero prefiero tocar **esos.**

These instruments are interesting, but I prefer to play those.

En **esta** calle hay varios cines. ¿Quieres ir a **aquel**?

There are several movie theaters on this street. Do you want to go to that one over there?

2:00   **5-8 Comparando cosas** Tu compañero/a te propone (*proposes*) una cosa pero tú siempre prefieres otra (*another one*). Responde a sus comentarios usando las formas correctas de **este, ese** y **aquel.** ■

MODELO   E1: ¿Quieres ir a este concierto?
          E2: *No, quiero ir a ese/aquel.*

1. ¿Quieres escuchar a estos músicos?
2. ¿Vamos a ir a ese teatro?
3. ¿Entiendes la letra de esta canción?
4. ¿Tus amigos tocan en aquel conjunto?
5. ¿Vas a comprar aquellas camisetas (*T-shirts*)?
6. ¿Piensas arreglar este cuarto para la fiesta?

 Instructor Resources
• PPT, Extra Activities

NOTE for *Los pronombres demostrativos*
The authors have chosen to present demonstrative adjectives and pronouns separately so that students can focus on one concept at a time. Once they understand the concept of demonstrative adjectives, then it is simpler for them to see how they then function as pronouns.

NOTE for *Los pronombres demostrativos*
In 1999, the Real Academia Española ruled that the use of a written accent to differentiate demonstrative pronouns from demonstrative adjectives is optional. In *¡Anda! Curso elemental,* we have omitted the accents on demonstrative pronouns.

NOTE for *Los pronombres demostrativos*
Your visual learners will benefit from sketching and sharing illustrations of sentence pairs, like the examples given in the grammar presentation.

SUGGESTION for *Los pronombres demostrativos*
Have students bring photos of instruments and musicians to class. Collect them and organize them in groups of 3. Then, ask 2 students to assist you. Give each of them one of the photos, with you holding the third. Position yourself nearest the remaining students, position one of the students a few feet behind, or to the side of you, and the other student by the door or in the back of the room. Have students vote on preferences (best musician, most interesting instrument, most famous, etc.) using *este/a, ese/a,* or *aquel/aquella.* You may want to use follow-up questions with individuals, e.g., *¿Cuál es tu instrumento favorito—este, ese o aquel?*

NATIONAL STANDARDS
Communication, Cultures, Connections, Comparisons

Determine whether you have any music majors or devotees among your students who may wish to do additional reports for class. You may wish to bring samples of the music of some of the genres listed as well as from several of the artists.

This reading online discusses various artists, genres, and influences in Latin music. Standard 1.2 requires communication through understanding and interpreting written Spanish, like the Spanish used in a cultural reading. The Cultures Goal is for students to gain knowledge and understanding of the cultures of the world through the practices, perspectives, and products of Hispanic cultures. The history of Latin music, the famous Latin artists, and the evolution of genres all contribute to Standards 2.1 and 2.2. Students can make connections (Standard 3.2) about how music has evolved in the United States and how religious festivals, indigenous populations, African influences, and political leaders have shaped Latin music. They can make comparisons (Standard 4.2) between the genres, how artists are rewarded for their music (Grammy awards), and the way music has changed over the past decades or eras.

SUGGESTION for Nota cultural
Remember to assign these readings in advance of class so that class time is spent discussing the answers to the questions.

ANSWERS to Nota cultural (Online)
1. La salsa, el merengue, el Tex-Mex, el merenhouse, el rock latino, el rap, el reggaetón, etc.
2. Answers may vary.

21ST CENTURY SKILLS • INFORMATION, MEDIA AND TECHNOLOGY SKILLS
!Anda! supports the development of information, media and technology skills in a variety of ways. MySpanishLab creates a robust platform to enhance learning, and teacher notes are provided so that instructors can guide students to access additional information on the Internet. Also, projects are suggested for students to use technology so that learners may demonstrate the interpretive, interpersonal, and presentational modes of communication.

`3:00`   **5-9** **¡Vamos a un concierto!**

¡Qué suerte! Tienes dos entradas gratis (*free tickets*) para ir a un concierto. ■

Paso 1   Haz una investigación en el Internet para escuchar la música de El Gran Combo, Marc Anthony, Juan Luis Guerra y Los Tigres del Norte.

Paso 2   Tu compañero/a y tú tienen que decidir a qué concierto quieren ir. Túrnense para describir a quién prefieren escuchar y por qué. Usen **este, ese** y **aquel** en sus descripciones.

MODELO   *Prefiero ir al concierto de Marc Anthony. ¡Él canta muy bien! Pero es difícil decidir porque los músicos de Los Tigres del Norte son muy buenos también. Estos saben tocar y cantar muy bien. Y aquellos…*

NOTA CULTURAL

¡Hola! eText p. 178   05-18 to 05-19   **La música latina en los Estados Unidos**
NOTE for *Nota cultural*
See eText pg. 178 for complete *Nota cultural* reading and *Preguntas.*

`3:00`

4 GRAMÁTICA

05-20 to 05-23   **¡Hola!** Spanish/ English Tutorials

Los adverbios
Explaining how something is done

An **adverb** usually describes a verb and **answers the question "how."** Many Spanish adverbs end in **-mente,** which is equivalent to the English *-ly.* These Spanish adverbs are formed as follows:

1. Add **-mente** to the *feminine singular* form of an *adjective.*

Este baterista toca horriblemente.

ADJETIVOS		ADVERBIOS
Masculino	**Femenino**	
rápido →	*rápida* + -mente →	**rápidamente**
lento →	*lenta* + -mente →	**lentamente**
tranquilo →	*tranquila* + -mente →	**tranquilamente**

2. If an *adjective* ends in a *consonant* or in **-e,** simply add **-mente.**

ADJETIVOS		ADVERBIOS
fácil →	*fácil* + -mente →	**fácilmente**
suave →	*suave* + -mente →	**suavemente**

NOTE: If an adjective has a written accent, it is retained when **-mente** is added.

Estrategia
Remember to first determine the *feminine singular* form of the adjective and then add *-mente*.

5-10 Lógicamente
Túrnense para transformar en adverbios los siguientes adjetivos. ■

MODELO E1: normal
E2: *normalmente*

1. interesante interesantemente
2. perezosos perezosamente
3. feliz felizmente
4. nervioso nerviosamente
5. fuertes fuertemente
6. claro claramente
7. seguro seguramente
8. apasionadas apasionadamente
9. difícil difícilmente
10. débil débilmente
11. rápida rápidamente
12. pacientes pacientemente

5-11 Para conocerte
Túrnense para hacerse y contestar las siguientes preguntas. Pueden usar los adjetivos de la lista. ■

| alegre | constante | paciente | difícil | divino |
| fácil | horrible | perfecto | rápido | tranquilo |

MODELO E1: ¿Cómo bailas? (divino)
E2: *Bailo divinamente.*

1. ¿Cómo cantas?
2. ¿Cómo duermes?
3. ¿Cómo hablas español?
4. ¿Cómo juegas al béisbol?
5. ¿Cómo tocas el piano?
6. ¿Cómo cocinas?
7. ¿Cómo lavas los platos?
8. ¿Cómo manejas (*drive*)?

5-12 Di la verdad
Hazle (*Ask*) a tu compañero/a las siguientes preguntas. Después, cambien de papel. ■

Estrategia
Answer in complete sentences when working with your partner. Even though it may seem mechanical at times, it leads to increased comfort speaking Spanish.

MODELO E1: ¿Qué haces diariamente (todos los días)?
E2: *Limpio mi dormitorio, voy a clase, estudio, como, hago ejercicio y duermo.*

1. ¿Qué haces perfectamente?
2. ¿Qué haces horriblemente?
3. ¿Qué haces fácilmente?
4. ¿Qué debes hacer rápidamente?
5. ¿Qué debes hacer lentamente?

NOTE for *Gramática*
This is an inductive grammar presentation in which the students are given examples of a grammar concept and, through the use of guiding questions, they formulate the rule in their own words. Research indicates that students remember and internalize grammar rules better when they construct their own knowledge.

SUGGESTION for *El presente progresivo*
Practice the formation of the present progressive orally with a mechanical drill such as giving a subject pronoun and an infinitive and having the students respond chorally with the correct form of the verb: e.g., *hablar, tú (estás hablando), comer, yo (estoy comiendo)*, etc.

METHODOLOGY • Presenting Grammar at the Point of Need
As you know, the authors of *¡Anda! Curso elemental* believe in presenting information in chunks at the point of need for your students, so as to not overwhelm them with information. *¡Anda!* will present the notion of verbs with the changes e → ie → i, o → ue → u, and e → i → i with the preterit in *Capítulo 7*.

EXPANSION for *El presente progresivo*
Additional questions to ask your students include: *1. Estás en la playa: ¿qué estás haciendo? 2. Estás en un concierto: ¿qué estás haciendo? 3. Juan está en el cine: ¿qué está haciendo? 4. María y Pablo están en el estudio de grabación: ¿qué están haciendo? 5. Nosotros estamos en la clase de español: ¿qué estamos haciendo? 6. Tú estás en la biblioteca: ¿qué estás haciendo?*

NOTE for *El presente progresivo*
The verbs *ir, poder,* and *venir* have irregular present participles: *yendo, pudiendo,* and *viniendo.* However, these 3 verbs are seldom used in the progressive.

---

5 GRAMÁTICA

`3:00`

  05-24 to 05-27 ¡Hola! Spanish/English Tutorials

El presente progresivo
Describing what is happening at the moment

So far you have been learning and using the present tense to communicate ideas. If you want to emphasize that an action is **occurring at the moment and is in progress,** you can use the *present progressive* tense.

The English present progressive is made up of a form of the verb *to be* **+ present participle (-ing)**. Look at the following sentences and formulate a rule for creating the present progressive in Spanish. Use the following questions to guide you.

—¿Qué *estás* **haciendo**?
—*Estoy* **ensayando.**

What are you doing?
I'm rehearsing.

—¿*Está* **escuchando** música tu hermano?
—No, *está* **tocando** la guitarra.

Is your brother listening to music?
No, he is playing the guitar.

—¿*Están* **viendo** ustedes la televisión?
—No, les *estamos* **escribiendo** una carta a nuestros padres.

Are you watching television?
No, we are writing a letter to our parents.

> **Fíjate**
> The present progressive is *not* used to express the future.
>
> Present progressive: *Estoy ensayando.* I am rehearsing (right now).
>
> Future: *Voy a ensayar mañana.* I am going to rehearse tomorrow.

¡Explícalo tú!

1. What is the infinitive of the first verb in each sentence that is in *italics*?
2. What are the infinitives of **haciendo, ensayando, escuchando, tocando, viendo,** and **escribiendo**?
3. How do you form the verb forms in **boldface**?
4. In this new tense, the *present progressive*, do any words come between the two parts of the verb?
5. Therefore, your formula for forming the *present progressive* is:
   a form of the verb _____ + a verb ending in _____ or _____.

✔ Check your answers to the preceding questions in Appendix 1.

NOTE: The following are some verbs that have irregular forms in this tense.

> **Fíjate**
> When the stem of an *-er* or *-ir* verb ends in a vowel, e.g. *creer* and *leer*, the present participle ends in *-yendo* (the *i* changes to *y*).

> **Fíjate**
> For the *-ir* stem-changing verbs only, these vowel changes occur in the stem: e → *i* (*diciendo*) and o → *u* (*durmiendo*).

decir → diciendo
mentir → mintiendo
pedir → pidiendo
preferir → prefiriendo
perseguir → persiguiendo
repetir → repitiendo
seguir → siguiendo
servir → sirviendo

dormir → durmiendo
morir → muriendo

creer → creyendo
leer → leyendo

NOTE and INSTRUCTIONS for 5-13

The authors of *¡Anda! Curso elemental* believe in offering highly creative activities while at the same time keeping the direction lines at an *i + 1* level. There are activities, such as this one, where it is more efficient for you to give the directions in English, unless you have a large number of heritage language learners or false beginners, in which case you may choose to give the following directions in Spanish.

INSTRUCTIONS: Work in groups of at least four students. One student makes a ball out of a piece of paper, says an infinitive and a subject (noun or pronoun), and then tosses the ball to someone in the group. The person who catches the ball must give the correct form of the verb in the present progressive. If correct, he or she receives a point. The activity continues until you, the teacher, call "time."

FOLLOW-UP for 5-14

If a student is absent, you can ask the class to predict what that student might be doing during the time when the other students are in class. If no one is absent, you might ask them what they think the university administrators are currently doing, or what the students in the other classes are doing.

`3:00` **5-13 Progresando** Escuchen mientras su instructor/a les da (*gives you*) las instrucciones de esta actividad. ¡Diviértanse! (*Enjoy!*) ■

MODELO
E1: *hablar, yo*
E2: *estoy hablando*
E2: *comer, nosotros*
E3: *estamos comiendo*

Capítulo 2. El verbo *gustar*, pág. 80 del eText.

`3:00` **5-14 ¿Tienes telepatía?** Es sábado. Túrnense para decir qué está haciendo su profesor/a en varios momentos del día. ■

MODELO
E1: Le gusta tomar café por la mañana.
E2: *Está tomando café en su terraza.*

1. Le gusta hacer ejercicio para comenzar su día.
2. Le gusta la música latina y está en una tienda.
3. Está cansado/a y tiene mucho sueño.
4. Trabaja en la computadora y tiene muchos mensajes de sus estudiantes.
5. Le gusta comer algo ligero (*light*) antes de ir a la fiesta.
6. Está con sus amigos en la fiesta y les gusta mucho la música que están tocando.

`2:00` **5-15 ¿Qué está ocurriendo?** Túrnense para decir qué están haciendo estas personas. ■

MODELO
E1: Felipe
E2: *Felipe está preparando su comida y está comiendo también.*

1. Manuel   Manuel está lavando los platos.
2. Sofía   Sofía está sacando la basura.
3. Raúl y Mari Carmen   Raúl y Mari Carmen están tocando música. Raúl está tocando el piano y Mari Carmen la flauta.
4. José   José está viendo la televisión.
5. Mercedes y Guillermo   Mercedes y Guillermo están escuchando música.

Felipe   Manuel   Sofía
Raúl y Mari Carmen   José   Mercedes y Guillermo

EXPANSION for 5-16
Find a photo (or assign students to bring a photo to class) of a group such as Calle 13 or Maxwell performing a concert. Using the present progressive, have students describe the photo.

NOTE for 5-17
Rather than having your students write songs, you may prefer to have them create dialogues.

2:00 **5-16** **No, ¡ahora mismo!** Contesten las siguientes preguntas para indicar que las personas están haciendo las acciones en este momento. ∎

MODELO   E1: ¿Ellos van a ver la nueva película de Javier Bardem mañana?

E2: *No, están viendo la película ahora mismo.*

1. ¿Tú vas a comprar el nuevo CD de Calle 13 la semana que viene?
2. ¿Maxwell va a hacer una gira mundial el próximo verano?
3. ¿Nosotros vamos a escuchar música rap esta noche?
4. ¿El conjunto va a vender muchas grabaciones el año que viene?
5. Este festival de música es impresionante. ¿Van a tocar Bebo y Chucho Valdés esta tarde?

8:00 **5-17** **¡Qué creativo!** Juntos escriban la letra de una canción popular usando **el presente progresivo** un mínimo de **seis** veces (*times*). Deben usar verbos de la siguiente lista. ∎

decir	dormir	repetir	creer	morir
mentir	leer	ir	seguir	servir

¿Cómo andas? I

	Feel confident	Need to review
Having completed **Comunicación I,** I now can . . .		
• discuss music (p. 116)	☐	☐
• practice pronouncing diphthongs and linking words (MSL/SAM)	☐	☐
• identify people and things (Part I) (p. 119)	☐	☐
• identify people and things (Part II) (p. 121)	☐	☐
• discuss Hispanic music in the United States (p. 122)	☐	☐
• explain how something is done (p. 122)	☐	☐
• describe what is happening at the moment (p. 124)	☐	☐

Comunicación II

Instructor Resources
• Textbook images, PPT, Extra Activities

6 VOCABULARIO

[3:00]

05-28 to 05-31

El mundo del cine
Sharing information about movies and television programs

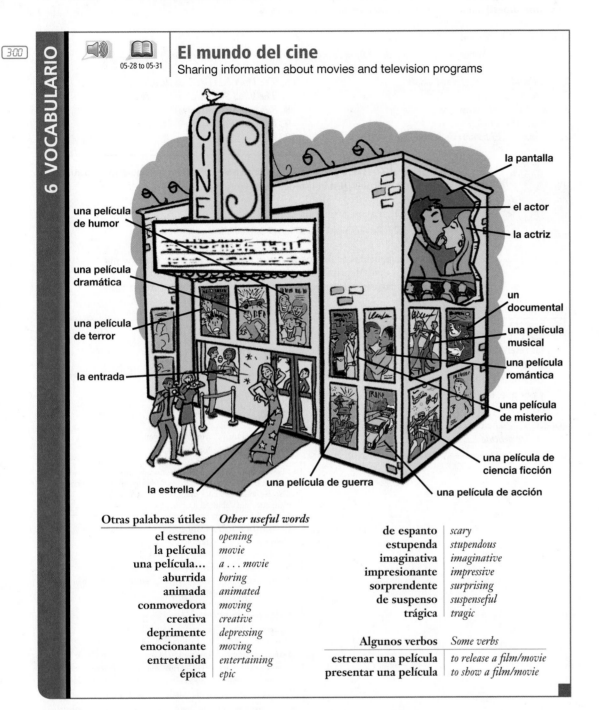

la pantalla

el actor

la actriz

un documental

una película musical

una película romántica

una película de misterio

una película de ciencia ficción

una película de acción

una película de guerra

la estrella

la entrada

una película de terror

una película dramática

una película de humor

Otras palabras útiles	Other useful words		de espanto	scary
el estreno	opening		estupenda	stupendous
la película	movie		imaginativa	imaginative
una película...	a . . . movie		impresionante	impressive
aburrida	boring		sorprendente	surprising
animada	animated		de suspenso	suspenseful
conmovedora	moving		trágica	tragic
creativa	creative			
deprimente	depressing		**Algunos verbos**	*Some verbs*
emocionante	moving		estrenar una película	to release a film/movie
entretenida	entertaining		presentar una película	to show a film/movie
épica	epic			

SECTION GOALS for
Comunicación II
By the end of the *Comunicación* section, students will be able to:
• discuss their favorite films and current releases.
• categorize films by genre.
• identify the Hispanic influence and presence in North American movies.
• rank items using ordinal numbers.
• construct sentences using the expression *hay* + *que* + *infinitive*.
• identify direct objects and use direct object pronouns.

NATIONAL STANDARDS
Communication
This vocabulary is optimal because so many of the words are cognates in English. Also, students enjoy talking about what interests them, and most students enjoy some genre of film. This vocabulary motivates students to share orally, which will then lead to meaningful communication in writing with the guidance that *¡Anda! Curso elemental* provides.

The activities in this *Comunicación* section provide opportunities for communication in the interpersonal and presentational modes. Students are encouraged to share their opinions and observations with others about their favorite movies and actors (Standard 1.1). Activities **5-19** and **5-20** can be adapted to address Standard 1.3 by having students each present a poster for their favorite movie and try to persuade others to see it. They can each vote for the movie they would most like to see, and then write a review of that movie in Spanish, practicing the new chapter vocabulary. If you have a particular movie that you like, you can write a description of the movie in Spanish, and students can practice listening as you present your movie. They could also practice reading if you make a pamphlet or jacket cover that summarizes what you said about the movie (Standard 1.2).

[3:00] **5-18** **¿Cuál es el género?** Clasifiquen las siguientes películas según su género y usen el mayor *(the largest)* número de palabras posibles para describirlas. ∎

MODELO   E1:   Avatar

E2:   Avatar *es una película dramática, de acción. Es emocionante, impresionante y entretenida…*

1. *The Social Network (La red social)*
2. *Inception (Origen)*
3. *Black Swan (El cisne negro)*
4. *Tangled (Enredados)*
5. *Ironman II (El hombre de hierro II)*
6. *The Hurt Locker (Zona de miedo)*
7. *The Blind Side (Un sueño posible)*
8. *Sanctum (El santuario)*
9. *Precious (Preciosa)*
10. ¿?

[3:00] **5-19** **En mi opinión** Túrnense para completar las siguientes oraciones sobre las películas. ¿Están ustedes de acuerdo? ∎

Capítulo Preliminar A.
El verbo *ser*, pág. 13
del eText.

MODELO   E1: La mejor película de terror…

E2: *La mejor película de terror es* Saw VI.

1. Las mejores películas de humor…
2. Una película épica deprimente…
3. Mis actores favoritos de las películas de acción…
4. La película de misterio que más me gusta…
5. Unas películas creativas…
6. El mejor documental…

[5:00] **5-20** **Mis preferencias** Lee las reseñas *(reviews)* de las tres películas. Después, túrnate con un/a compañero/a para describir la película que prefieres ver y por qué. ∎

MODELO   Prefiero ver _____. Es una película _____ y _____. Me gusta _____ porque _____ …

En el cine

Invictus (2010, EE.UU.)
Género: Drama
Director: Clint Eastwood
Interpretación: Morgan Freeman, Matt Damon
Basada en el libro de John Carlin, *The Human Factor: Nelson Mandela and the Game That Changed the World.* Mandela (Morgan Freeman) reconoce la importancia de tener la Copa del Mundo de Rugby en Sudáfrica en el año 1995, después de ser excluidos durante muchos años de las competiciones debido al apartheid.

El hombre lobo (2010, EE.UU.)
Género: Terror
Director: Joe Johnston
Interpretación: Benicio del Toro, Anthony Hopkins
Nueva versión del clásico del cine de terror en el que un hombre recibe la maldición del hombre lobo.

Origen (2010, EE.UU.)
Género: Ciencia ficción, Acción
Director: Christopher Nolan
Interpretación: Leonardo DiCaprio, Michael Caine
Dom Cobb (Leonardo DiCaprio) es un ladrón que roba secretos del subconsciente durante el estado de sueño en un tipo de espionaje corporativo, pero esto lo hace un fugitivo internacional.

5:00   **5-21** En nuestra opinión...

Paso 1 Habla de algunas películas que conoces con un/a compañero/a, usando las siguientes preguntas como guía (*guide*).

1. ¿Cuáles son las películas que más te gustan? ¿Por qué?
2. ¿Quiénes son tus actores y actrices favoritos?
3. ¿Qué películas que van a estrenar pronto quieres ver?

Paso 2 Ahora hablen sobre programas de televisión.

NOTA CULTURAL

¡Hola!
eText p. 186 05-32 to 05-33

 La influencia hispana en el cine norteamericano

NOTE for *Nota cultural*
See eText pg. 186 for complete *Nota cultural* reading and *Preguntas*.

2:00

7 GRAMÁTICA

 ¡Hola!
05-34 to 05-37 Spanish/English Tutorials

Los números ordinales Ranking people and things

An ordinal number indicates position in a series or order. The first ten ordinal numbers in Spanish are listed below. Ordinal numbers above *décimo* are rarely used.

¿Te gusta la primera sinfonía de Beethoven?

Sí, pero prefiero la novena.

primer, primero/a	*first*	**sexto/a**	*sixth*
segundo/a	*second*	**séptimo/a**	*seventh*
tercer, tercero/a	*third*	**octavo/a**	*eighth*
cuarto/a	*fourth*	**noveno/a**	*ninth*
quinto/a	*fifth*	**décimo/a**	*tenth*

1. Ordinal numbers are adjectives and agree in number and gender with the nouns they modify. They usually *precede* nouns.

   el **cuarto** año   *the fourth year*
   la **octava** sinfonía   *the eighth symphony*

2. Before masculine, singular nouns, **primero** and **tercero** are shortened to **primer** and **tercer**.

   el **primer** concierto   *the first concert*
   el **tercer** curso de español   *the third Spanish course*

3. After *décimo*, a cardinal number is used and *follows* the noun.

   el piso **catorce**
   el siglo (*century*) **veintiuno**

21ST CENTURY SKILLS • COMMUNICATION AND COLLABORATION
Two core elements of the Partnership for 21st (P21) Century Skills and ¡Anda! are to communicate clearly and to collaborate with others. P21 lists not only communicating thoughts and ideas effectively, but also listening effectively. ¡Anda! provides students with strategies on how to become good listeners. Also, ¡Anda! uses almost exclusively pair and group activities, supporting P21's goal of "demonstrating the ability to work effectively and respectfully with diverse teams, and to assume shared responsibility for collaborative work, valuing the individual contributions made by each team member."

SUGGESTION for Los números ordinales
Have students practice ordinal numbers by creating lists of favorites: novels, songs, movies, documentaries, television shows, actors, etc. Once they have their lists, they can order them from most favorite to least favorite, using ordinal numbers. This can be done in groups or individually.

SUGGESTION for Los números ordinales
Have students create questions using ordinal numbers, e.g., ¿Cuál es tu primera clase los lunes? Then, have them circulate to interview classmates.

CAPÍTULO 5
NATIONAL STANDARDS
Communication, Cultures, Connections, Comparisons
When discussing the National Standards, it is always interesting to note how the 5 Cs overlap. If you have a film festival at your school, you may wish to request either vintage movies or current films with Hispanic actors.

This online reading highlights the four goal areas of Communication, Cultures, Connections, and Comparisons. Students are able to communicate about this reading in 1 of 3 ways. First, you can ask them to work in pairs or small groups and have them research one of the profiled actors. You can bring the information to class, they can bring the information to class, or you can take them to the language lab for research. The discussions that they have about the actors satisfy Standard 1.1. The reading they are doing in Spanish contributes to Standard 1.2. If you have them present the information they have read as a group or turn in a report of the information, it addresses Standard 1.3. If you have time to show a film, or film clip, from one of these actors, you can also use that as a starting point for discussion, assignments, and presentations. Students see the products and perspectives (Standard 2.2) through the contributions that Hispanics have made to the film industry. They can connect the new information to what they might have known about the actor(s) or topics discussed in the movie (Standard 3.2) and think about it in the context of learning Spanish. (The films by directors Pedro Almodóvar and Alfonso Cuarón are especially useful for Standard 3.2). Students can make comparisons between Spanish and English (subtitled movies work well to show the difference between translation and interpretation) and the cultural differences they see in the films (Standards 4.1 and 4.2).

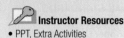

Instructor Resources

• PPT, Extra Activities

EXPANSION for 5-22 through 5-24

Other practice for ordinal numbers could include having students complete lists such as: *El primer día de la semana es lunes, el segundo día es martes*, etc., *El primer mes es enero, el segundo mes es…* , etc. You can start them with an example, and they can continue the list.

ANSWERS to 5-23

1. *Answers may vary.*
2. *Answers may vary.*
3. El tercer mes del año es marzo y el sexto es junio.
4. El séptimo día de la semana es el domingo (en los países hispanohablantes).
5. El primer presidente de los Estados Unidos se llama George Washington.
6. *Answers may vary.*

FOLLOW-UP for 5-24

You may choose to do both *Pasos 2* and *3* as whole-class activities by creating the list of 10 best movies and then ordering the list together.

`4:00` **5-22** **Orden de preferencia** Asigna un orden de preferencia a las actividades de la lista: desde la más importante (primero) hasta la menos importante (octavo). Después, comparte tu lista con un/a compañero/a usando oraciones completas. ■

MODELO   *Primero, me gusta ver una película con mi actor favorito, Colin Firth. Segundo, quiero visitar a mis hermanos. Tercero, prefiero…*

1. ir a un concierto de tu conjunto favorito   _____
2. visitar a tus amigos   _____
3. ver una película con tu actor/actriz favorito/a   _____
4. leer una novela buena   _____
5. ir a un partido de fútbol americano   _____
6. estudiar para un examen   _____
7. visitar Costa Rica   _____
8. conocer al presidente de los Estados Unidos   _____

Capítulo Preliminar A. Los días, los meses y las estaciones, pág. 20 del eText.

`2:00` **5-23** **Preguntas de trivia** Túrnense para hacerse y contestar las siguientes preguntas. ■

1. ¿En qué piso está tu clase de español?
2. ¿A qué hora es tu primera clase los lunes? ¿Y la segunda?
3. ¿Cuál es el tercer mes del año? ¿Y el sexto?
4. ¿Cuál es el séptimo día de la semana?
5. ¿Cómo se llama el primer presidente de los Estados Unidos?
6. ¿Cómo se llama la cuarta persona de la tercera fila (*row*) en la clase de español?

Estrategia

Remember that when asked a question with *tu/tus*, you need to answer *mi/mis*.

`6:00` Workbooklet **5-24** **La lista de los mejores** ¿Cuáles son las mejores películas para los estudiantes de tu clase? ■

Paso 1   Entrevista a cinco estudiantes y pregúntales cuáles son sus opiniones sobre las tres películas mejores. Usa las palabras **primera, segunda** y **tercera.**

Paso 2   Con el/la profesor/a, haz una lista de las **diez** películas más populares de la clase.

Paso 3   Organiza por orden de preferencia la lista de las películas más populares de la clase. Escribe el número ordinal apropiado para cada película.

PELÍCULAS FAVORITAS	ESTUDIANTE 1	ESTUDIANTE 2	ESTUDIANTE 3	ESTUDIANTE 4	ESTUDIANTE 5
PRIMERA					
SEGUNDA					
TERCERA					

8 GRAMÁTICA

Hay que trabajar. ¡No hay que ser perezoso!

05-38 to 05-40

Hay que + infinitivo
Stating what needs to be accomplished

So far when you have wanted to talk about what someone should do, needs to do, or has to do, you have used the expressions **debe, necesita,** or **tiene que.** The expression **hay que** + *infinitive* is another way to communicate responsibility, obligation, or the importance of something. **Hay que** + *infinitive* means:

> *It is necessary to . . .*
> *You must . . .*
> *One must/should . . .*

Para ser un músico bueno **hay que** ensayar mucho.
Hay que terminar nuestro trabajo antes de ir al cine.
Hay que ver la nueva película de Almodóvar.

To be a good musician it is necessary to rehearse a lot.
We must finish our work before we go to the movies.
You must see the new Almodóvar film.

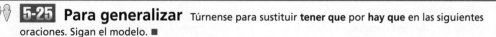

5-25 **Para generalizar** Túrnense para sustituir **tener que** por **hay que** en las siguientes oraciones. Sigan el modelo. ■

MODELO   E1:   Tenemos que consultar al empresario.
           E2:   *Hay que consultar al empresario.*

1. Ustedes tienen que sacar un CD con estas canciones nuevas.
2. Marisol, tú tienes que ser más paciente si quieres conseguir buenas entradas para ese concierto.
3. Mamá, ¡tienes que conocer la música de este conjunto nuevo!
4. Jorge y Catrina, ustedes tienen que hacer una gira con su grupo de jazz.
5. Rafael, tienes que visitar a tu hermana porque ella quiere ensayar contigo.
6. Enrique, tú tienes que leer los mensajes que escriben tus aficionados.

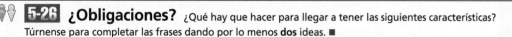

5-26 **¿Obligaciones?** ¿Qué hay que hacer para llegar a tener las siguientes características? Túrnense para completar las frases dando por lo menos **dos** ideas. ■

MODELO   E1:   Para ser un pintor excelente…
           E2:   Para ser un pintor excelente *hay que pintar mucho y hay que ser muy creativo.*

Para ser…

1. un músico impresionante…
2. un político honesto…
3. un cantante estupendo…
4. un director de cine sorprendente…
5. una actriz conmovedora…
6. una novelista entretenida…

Instructor Resources
• PPT, Extra Activities

METHODOLOGY • Chunking
You will note that *¡Anda! Curso elemental* presented *tener + que + infinitive* separately from *hay que + infinitive.* Once again, the purpose is to chunk information so that the students focus on smaller bits, giving them one way to express an idea and then providing them with another way to vary their repertoire.

NOTE for *Hay que + infinitivo*
For a quick drill that reinforces the use of the infinitive after *hay que,* have students make a list of 10 infinitives. Then in pairs, they take turns calling out an infinitive while their partners must quickly make an expression with *hay que,* e.g., *ensayar* ➔ *Hay que ensayar.*

EXPANSION for 5-26
Ask students to create sentences with *hay que* for these additional people:
un/a estudiante muy bueno/a…
un/a profesor/a memorable…
unos padres perfectos…
un/a companero/a de cuarto excelente…
un/a novio/a increíble…

METHODOLOGY • Higher-Order Thinking
Activities **5-26** and **5-27** require students to use critical thinking as well as to tap their previously learned vocabulary from other chapters. The aim is for your students to generate sentences such as:
    Un político: *Hay que leer y escribir mucho. También hay que estudiar y escuchar a la gente.*

Instructor Resources
• PPT, Extra Activities

HERITAGE LANGUAGE LEARNERS

Activity **5-27** is particularly good for heritage language learners, since they may be able to take more risks with the language. You may want them to share their sentences with the entire class so that all students can benefit from their linguistic creativity.

METHODOLOGY • *Personal a*

You may choose to present exceptions to the rule given to students regarding the personal *a,* e.g., *Tengo un hermano,* or talk about variations in the Spanish-speaking world. Your own personal philosophy, and your knowledge of your students and their abilities, will be your guide when making these types of decisions.

[4:00] **5-27 Y todos necesitamos...** ¿Qué debemos hacer para tener un futuro mejor? Compartan sus ideas y comuniquen sus resultados a la clase usando **tres** oraciones completas. ■

MODELO   E1:   Hay que...
         E2:   *Hay que respetar* (respect) *y ayudar a las personas mayores.*

[3:00]   **9 GRAMÁTICA**   05-41 to 05-43   *¡Hola!* Spanish/English Tutorials

Los pronombres de complemento directo y la "a" personal
Expressing *what* or *whom*

Direct objects receive the action of the verb and answer the questions ***What?*** or ***Whom?*** Note the following examples.

> **A:** I need to do *what?*
> **B:** You need to buy *the concert tickets* by Monday.
> **A:** Yes, I do need to buy *them.*
>
> **A:** I have to call *whom?*
> **B:** You have to call *your agent.*
> **A:** Yes, I do have to call *him.*

¿Mi trompeta y mi guitarra? Sí, las tengo.

Note the following examples of *direct objects* in Spanish.

María toca **dos instrumentos** muy bien.	*María plays two instruments very well.*
Sacamos **un CD** el primero de septiembre.	*We are releasing a CD the first of September.*
¿Tienes **las entradas**?	*Do you have the tickets?*
No conozco a **Benicio del Toro.**	*I do not know Benicio del Toro.*
Siempre veo a **Selena Gómez** en la televisión.	*I always see Selena Gómez on television.*

> **NOTE:** In **Capítulo 4,** you learned that to express knowing a person, you put **"a"** after the verb (*conocer + a* + person). Now that you have learned about direct objects, a more global way of stating the rule is: When direct objects refer to *people,* you must use the personal **"a."** Review the following examples.
>
> | **People** | **Things** |
> |---|---|
> | ¡Veo **a** *Cameron Díaz*! | ¡Veo *el coche* de Cameron Díaz! |
> | Hay que ver **a** *mis padres*. | Hay que ver *la película*. |
> | ¿**A** qué *actores* conoces? | ¿Qué *ciudades* conoces? |

(continued)

As in English, we can replace direct objects nouns with **direct object pronouns.** Note the following examples.

María **los** toca muy bien.	*María plays them very well.*
Lo sacamos el primero de septiembre.	*We are releasing it the first of September.*
¿**Las** tienes?	*Do you have them?*
No **lo** conozco.	*I do not know him.*
Siempre **la** veo en la televisión.	*I always see her on television.*

In Spanish, direct object pronouns *agree in gender and number with the nouns they replace.* The following chart lists the direct object pronouns.

Singular		Plural	
me	*me*	**nos**	*us*
te	*you*	**os**	*you all*
lo, la	*you*	**los, las**	*you all*
lo, la	*him, her, it*	**los, las**	*them*

Placement of direct object pronouns

Direct object pronouns are:

1. Placed before the verb.
2. Attached to *infinitives* or to the *present participle* (**-ando, -iendo**).

¿Tienes los discos compactos?	→	Sí, **los** tengo.
Tengo que traer los instrumentos.	→	**Los** tengo que traer. / Tengo que traer**los.**
Tiene que llevar su guitarra.	→	**La** tiene que llevar. / Tiene que llevar**la.**

—¿Por qué estás escribiendo una canción para tu madre?

—**La** estoy escribiendo porque es su cumpleaños. / Estoy escribiéndo**la** porque es su cumpleaños.

NOTE for os
You may wish to remind your students about *vosotros.* Also, remember that the *vosotros* forms are presented as a point of information in the charts, but they are not practiced in the activities.

NOTE for *Placement of direct object pronouns*
¡Anda! Curso elemental will present more information regarding accent marks in relation to direct and indirect objects in *Capítulo 10,* when commands are introduced.

METHODOLOGY •
Differentiated Instruction

Differentiated instruction is when you tailor your lessons for your different types of learners. The number of types of learners and their preferences depend on which research you are consulting. Some sources maintain that there are 4 different types of learning styles, some say 7 or 8, and still others claim that there are more than 20! As instructors, what we need to remember is that students learn in different ways and progress at different rates. When assessing the progress of your students, it is important to know that for some of your students, their best performance will be to give multiple answers, while for others, their best will be one complete sentence. Differentiating instruction, in part, means to tailor our lessons so that all of our students, no matter what their style or talents, will be successful.

ANSWERS to 5-29
All answers can be either sí *or* no.
1. ...la limpio
2. ...lo arreglo
3. ...los lavo
4. ...las guardo
5. ...los sacudo
6. ...las hago
7. ...la preparo
8. ...la pongo
9. ...los ayudo
10. ...te invito

ANSWERS to 5-30
1. Sí, lo conozco.
2. Sí, la traigo.
3. Sí, la saben.
4. Sí, los traemos.
5. Sí, las quiero.
6. Sí, lo oigo.
7. Sí, te vamos a necesitar. / Sí, vamos a necesitarte.
8. Sí, me va a anunciar. / Sí, va a anunciarme.

Capítulo 2. Presente indicativo de verbos regulares, pág. 67 del eText.

[2:00] **5-28 ¿Estás listo?** ¿Estás preparado/a para el concierto de Perrozompopo? Túrnate con un/a compañero/a para revisar la lista, esta vez usando **lo, la, los** o **las.** ■

MODELO
E1: confirmar *la hora* del concierto
E2: *La confirmo hoy.*

1. comprar *las entradas* Las compro.
2. invitar *a mis amigos* Los invito.
3. leer *el artículo* de *The New York Times* sobre Perrozompopo Lo leo.
4. compartir (*share*) *el artículo y los CD de Perrozompopo* con mis amigos Los comparto.
5. preparar *comida* para un pícnic La preparo.
6. traer *la cámara* La traigo.

Capítulo 3. Los quehaceres de la casa, pág. 109 del eText.

[2:00] **5-29 ¿Hay deberes?** El concierto de Perrozompopo fue increíble, pero hay que volver al mundo real. Siempre hay trabajo, sobre todo en la casa. Túrnate con un/a compañero/a para hacer y contestar las siguientes preguntas. ■

MODELO
E1: ¿Lavas los pisos?
E2: *Sí, los lavo. / No, no/nunca los lavo.*

1. ¿Limpias la cocina?
2. ¿Arreglas tu cuarto?
3. ¿Lavas los platos?
4. ¿Guardas tus cosas?
5. ¿Sacudes los muebles?
6. ¿Haces las camas?
7. ¿Preparas la comida?
8. ¿Pones la mesa?
9. ¿Nos ayudas a arreglar el jardín?
10. ¿Me invitas a un concierto?

[3:00] **5-30 Una hora antes** Carlos Santana, como muchos músicos, es una persona muy organizada. Antes de cada concierto repasa con su ayudante (*assistant*) personal todos los preparativos (*preparations*). Aquí tienes las preguntas del ayudante. Contesta como si fueras (*as if you were*) Santana, usando **lo, la, los** o **las.** ■

MODELO
E1: ¿Tienes tu anillo (*ring*) de la buena suerte?
E2: *Sí, lo tengo.*

1. Juan está enfermo. ¿Conoces al trompetista que toca esta noche con el conjunto?
2. ¿Traes tu guitarra nueva?
3. ¿Los cantantes saben la letra de la canción nueva?
4. ¿Traemos todos los trajes (*suits, outfits*)?
5. ¿Quieres unas botellas de agua (*water*)?
6. ¿Oyes al público aplaudir?
7. ¿Me van a necesitar después del concierto?
8. ¿El empresario te va a anunciar?

Carlos Santana

5-31 Mis preferencias Túrnense para hacerse y contestar las siguientes preguntas usando **el pronombre de complemento directo** correcto. ■

MODELO   E1: ¿Lees los poemas de Rubén Darío? ¿Por qué?

    E2: *No, no los leo. No los leo porque no los conozco.*

1. ¿Escuchas música clásica? ¿Por qué?
2. ¿Tu amigo y tú tienen ganas de ver una película de acción de Matt Damon? ¿Por qué?
3. ¿Tus amigos ven todas las películas de Penélope Cruz? ¿Por qué?
4. ¿Escuchas música jazz en tu iPod? ¿Por qué?
5. ¿Tocas un instrumento? ¿Por qué?

ESCUCHA

 Planes para un concierto

05-44 to 05-46

Estrategia	Use all clues available to you	it is important to read them
Anticipating content	to anticipate what you are about to hear. That includes photos, captions, and body language if you are looking at the individual(s) speaking. If there are written synopses,	in advance. Finally, if you are doing listening activities such as these, look ahead at the comprehension questions to give you an idea of the topic and important points.

5-32 Antes de escuchar Mira la foto y contesta las siguientes preguntas. ■

1. ¿Quiénes están en la foto?
2. ¿De qué hablan Eduardo y Cisco?

 5-33 A escuchar Escucha la conversación entre Eduardo y Cisco y averigua cuál es el tema (*topic; gist*). Después, escucha una vez más para contestar las siguientes preguntas. ■

Eduardo y Cisco

1. ¿Quién va al concierto de los Black Eyed Peas?
2. ¿Qué música prefiere Cisco?
3. Deciden no estudiar. ¿Adónde van a ir?

 5-34 Después de escuchar Describe una canción que te guste en **tres** oraciones y dibuja un cuadro (*picture*) que la represente. Preséntaselo a un/a compañero/a para ver si puede adivinar la canción. ■

CAPÍTULO 5

SECTION GOALS for *Escucha*
By the end of the *Escucha* section, students will be able to:
• practice anticipating content.
• summarize the main idea of the conversation.
• describe their favorite songs and create drawings to illustrate them.

NATIONAL STANDARDS
Communication
Capítulo 5 introduces a new listening strategy: anticipating content. Communication Standard 1.2 emphasizes understanding and interpretation of spoken Spanish. After listening, students discuss in small groups what they have heard. They can then describe their favorite types of music, musical groups, and/or songs. Conversations take place in pairs, allowing students to practice interpersonal communication, Standard 1.1.

AUDIOSCRIPT for 5-33

EDUARDO: Oye, ¿vas al concierto de los Black Eyed Peas el viernes?
CISCO: No, tengo que trabajar. ¿Tú vas a ir?
EDUARDO: Sí. Me gusta mucho la cantante del grupo. El último CD es fenomenal, ¿sabes?
CISCO: Sí, y dicen que sacan un CD nuevo el mes que viene.
EDUARDO: ¿Te gusta el rock?
CISCO: Sí, pero prefiero el jazz.
EDUARDO: ¿Tienes un conjunto favorito de jazz?
CISCO: Pues… el Grupo Pat Metheny. Wynton Marsalis, Nestor Torres, Norah Jones —son todos increíbles. ¿Cuál es tu conjunto favorito de rock?
EDUARDO: Hummm. Hay muchos muy buenos… U2, Coldplay, Molotov…
CISCO: Mira, vamos al Club Ritmo ahora. Siempre ponen una música muy buena.
EDUARDO: ¿Sí? Pues vamos. ¡Esta noche no estudiamos!

ANSWERS to 5-33
1. Eduardo
2. el jazz
3. Van al Club Ritmo.

SECTION GOALS for
¡Conversemos!
By the end of the *¡Conversemos!* section, students will be able to:

- share opinions about music and cinema.
- compare and contrast the United States, Mexico, Spain, Honduras, Guatemala, and El Salvador.

NATIONAL STANDARDS
Communication, Communities
The *¡Conversemos!* section affords students the opportunity to communicate in extended discourse in Spanish (Standard 1.3). Students can also be using the language in the community or simulating a real-life scenario (Standard 5.3).

NOTE for 5-36
This activity is a good opportunity to incorporate the C for Comparisons of cultures. You may have students work from the knowledge they have or make this more of a project by asking them to research music and cinema facts for each of the countries to add to what they have already learned.

ADDITIONAL ACTIVITY for
¡Conversemos!

El concierto del año Ganaron entradas para un concierto y ahora tienen que decidir qué artista o grupo quieren ver. Cada estudiante debe escribir diez oraciones sobre el/la artista o el conjunto que quieren ver y deben incluir información sobre el estilo de música, qué instrumentos tocan, quién toca cada instrumento, etc. Luego, decidan juntos qué concierto van a ver.

¡CONVERSEMOS!

 5-35 En mi opinión Hay un programa en el canal *E!* donde las personas expresan sus gustos y opiniones sobre la música y el cine ¡y tu compañero/a y tú van a participar esta semana! Entrevista a tu compañero/a sobre sus opiniones de: los mejores grupos, las mejores películas, los mejores actores y actrices. Luego, cambien de papel. ■

 5-36 Comparaciones Con un/a compañero/a, compara los Estados Unidos, México, España, Honduras, Guatemala y El Salvador incluyendo la música y el cine, cuando sea posible. Usa información de los capítulos anteriores (*previous chapters*) e información de otras fuentes (*sources*). ■

MODELO   *Los países son similares y diferentes. Por ejemplo, hablan español en todos los países. España tiene influencia árabe en ciudades como (like) Granada. México no tiene influencia árabe pero sí tiene influencia de los aztecas. La música popular es similar, pero la música folklórica…*

ESCRIBE

Una reseña (*A review*)

05-48

Estrategia	Reviewing the writing of a classmate teaches you valuable editing skills that can improve your classmate's paper as well as serve to	build your confidence in your own writing by enhancing the content and syntax of your work, as well as boost your critical thinking skills.
Peer review/editing		

5-37 Antes de escribir Piensa en una película que te gusta mucho. Anota algunas ideas sobre los aspectos que te gustan más de esa película. ▪

- ¿Qué tipo de película es?
- ¿Para qué grupo(s) es apropiada?
- ¿Cuál es el tema?
- ¿Tiene una lección para el público?

5-38 A escribir Organiza tus ideas y escribe una reseña (*review*), como una de las de **5-20**, de **cuatro** a **seis** oraciones. Puedes usar las siguientes preguntas para organizar tu reseña. ▪

1. ¿Cómo se llama la película?
2. ¿De qué género es?
3. ¿Cómo la describes?
4. ¿A quiénes les va a gustar? ¿Por qué?
5. ¿La recomiendas? ¿Por qué?

5-39 Después de escribir En grupos de tres compartan sus reseñas. Revisen las ideas tanto de la gramática como del vocabulario. Hagan los cambios necesarios. Después, tu profesor/a va a leer las reseñas. La clase tiene que adivinar cuáles son las películas. ▪

¿Cómo andas? II

Having completed **Comunicación II**, I now can . . .

	Feel confident	Need to review
• share information about movies and television programs (p. 127)	☐	☐
• describe Hispanic influences in North American film (p. 129)	☐	☐
• rank people and things (p. 129)	☐	☐
• state what needs to be accomplished (p. 131)	☐	☐
• express *what* or *whom* (p. 132)	☐	☐
• anticipate content when listening (p. 135)	☐	☐
• communicate about music and film (p. 136)	☐	☐
• write a movie review and practice peer editing (p. 137)	☐	☐

SECTION GOALS for Escribe
By the end of the *Escribe* section, students will be able to:
- organize their writing by brainstorming their favorite aspects of a movie.
- write a movie review.
- support the reasons why they like or dislike a particular film.
- engage in peer review/editing.

NATIONAL STANDARDS
Communication, Connections, Communities
Una reseña integrates several standards. Writing the movie review and then listening to the teacher read the reviews to the class uses Standard 1.2, because students are demonstrating comprehension of spoken Spanish. If the instructor required that students present their movie reviews as documents to be read by others or heard by others, that activity would satisfy Standard 1.3. If students had a copy of a movie review from a newspaper or magazine in Spanish, they could compare the types of information and expressions between reviews they have seen (e.g., "two thumbs up" or the letter grading system) in English and those in Spanish (Standard 4.2). The differences in the reviews and rating systems would provide a basis for them to make connections between the Hispanic cultures and their own (Standard 3.2). They now would have the information necessary to decide whether they would like to see a Hispanic film, based on what others have said about the film (Standard 5.1).

METHODOLOGY •
Differentiating Instruction
Some of your students will need some additional assistance with this writing. One way to assist them is to direct them to **5-20** so that they can consult the realia for some ideas on how to proceed.

METHODOLOGY • Peer Editing
Peer editing can be a valuable tool if students are properly prepared for the task. First the instructor must determine the approach and the focus of the editing. Generally peer review is carried out in small groups of students who may either read their own papers aloud or read peer papers silently. It is good for students to have a list of questions or a rubric to guide them through the critique of a classmate's writing. Tasks for the reviewer may involve careful consideration of specifics of grammar and spelling or they may involve responding to a series of questions like the following:

1. Did the author follow the prompt? Should the author add or delete details/sentences?
2. Is the draft well organized?
3. Did the author choose the correct word(s)? Are there words with which you are not familiar?
4. What suggestions for changes do you have?

For more information on designing and implementing peer review, you may want to refer to: Byrd, D. R. (2003). Practical Tips for Implementing Peer Editing Tasks in the Foreign Language Classroom. *Foreign Language Annals*, 36(3), 434–431.

SECTION GOALS for *Cultura*
By the end of the *Cultura* section, students will be able to:
• locate Nicaragua's lakes and volcanoes on a map.
• explain what *ticos* are.
• identify the national symbol of Costa Rica.
• list main exports and industries of Costa Rica.
• summarize the significance of the Panama Canal.
• identify *Los kunas* and their handicraft.
• compare and contrast Nicaragua, Costa Rica, and Panama.

NATIONAL STANDARDS
Cultures, Comparisons
The cultural information about Nicaragua, Costa Rica, and Panama highlights Standards 2.1 and 2.2. Students read about each country, what makes that country unique, and some of the daily activities and products the country is known for. The cultural information presented in each chapter allows students to make comparisons among the Hispanic countries and their own countries (Standard 4.2), as well as comparisons between the Hispanic countries presented here and in earlier chapters. They learn how geography, climate, exports, and natural resources contribute to the differences among the Hispanic countries, and how those countries differ from the United States or their countries of origin.

NOTE for *El volcán San Cristóbal*
Known as "The Land of Lakes and Volcanoes," besides its 2 large lakes (Lago Managua and Lago Nicaragua), Nicaragua has many active volcanoes including Cerro Negro, Concepción, Masaya, Momotombo, San Cristóbal, and Telica. Of these, San Cristóbal is the highest and Masaya is the most active.

NOTE for *La Concha Acústica*
This acoustical shell that sits on the shore of Lake Managua was built in 2004 by American artist Glen Howard Small. In the form of a wave, the shell appears to surge from the lake, perfectly framing the concerts and other cultural events that take place there.

Cultura
Nicaragua

05-49

Mauricio Morales Prado

Les presento mi país

Mi nombre es Mauricio Morales Prado y soy de Managua, Nicaragua. Mi país es conocido como la tierra de volcanes y lagos (*lakes*). Hay dos lagos principales y muchos volcanes. Siete están activos todavía y de ellos, San Cristóbal es el más alto y Masaya es el más activo. **¡Localiza estos volcanes en el mapa!** Mi familia y yo somos muy aficionados a la música. Vamos frecuentemente a los conciertos en La Concha Acústica en el Lago Managua. **¿Asistes a conciertos con tu familia o amigos?**

Teatro Nacional Rubén Darío, Managua

El volcán San Cristóbal

La Concha Acústica, Managua

HONDURAS
Río Coco
Cayos Miskitos
Puerto Cabezas
NICARAGUA
Matagalpa
Mar Caribe
▲San Cristóbal
León ▲Momotombo
Managua ▲Masaya   Bluefields   Islas del Maíz
Granada   Lago de Nicaragua
OCÉANO PACÍFICO
COSTA RICA
Río San Juan

ALMANAQUE

Nombre oficial:	República de Nicaragua
Gobierno:	República
Población:	5.995.928 (2010)
Idiomas:	español (oficial); miskito, otros idiomas indígenas
Moneda:	Córdoba (NIO)

¿Sabías que...?
• El Lago de Nicaragua es el único lago de agua dulce (*fresh water*) del mundo donde se encuentran tiburones (*sharks*) y atunes.
• El 23 de diciembre del año 1972, un terremoto (*earthquake*) desastroso de 6,5 en la escala Richter destruyó (*destroyed*) la ciudad de Managua.

Preguntas
1. ¿Por qué se llama Nicaragua la tierra de lagos y volcanes?
2. ¿Qué tiene el Lago de Nicaragua de especial?
3. ¿Cuáles son dos lugares en Managua adonde va la gente para eventos culturales? ¿Puedes nombrar algunos posibles eventos culturales para esos dos lugares?

 Amplía tus conocimientos sobre Nicaragua en MySpanishLab.

138

NOTE for *El Lago Managua*
El Lago Managua, also known as El Lago Xolotlán, covers an area of 400 square miles, measuring 16 miles from north to south and 36 miles from east to west. Managua, the capital of Nicaragua, lies on the lake's southern shore while the Momotombo volcano is on the northwestern shore. The Tipitapa River connects the lake to Lake Nicaragua.

NOTE for *El Teatro Nacional Rubén Darío*
Named for the world-renowned Nicaraguan poet Rubén Darío, this national theater located in Managua opened in 1969. It houses theater productions, concerts, opera, ballet, art exhibitions, and many other cultural events. The theater's main hall, with its outstanding acoustics, holds 1,200 seats.

Costa Rica

05-50

Laura Centeno Soto

Les presento mi país

Mi nombre es Laura Centeno Soto y soy *tica*. *Ticos* es el apodo (*nickname*) que tenemos todos los costarricenses. Soy de Guaitil, un pueblo muy pequeño entre varios parques nacionales y famoso por su cerámica. Uno de los pueblos más famosos por su artesanía, sobre todo por la carreta, un símbolo nacional de Costa Rica, es Sarchí. **¿Cuáles son algunas artesanías producidas donde tú vives?** Si piensas visitar Costa Rica, te recomiendo una visita a nuestros parques nacionales. Son bonitos y tienen flora y fauna únicas en el mundo. **¿Cuál es tu parque favorito?** ¡Costa Rica es pura vida!

El café es un producto principal de exportación

Una carreta pintada de Sarchí

El ecoturismo es muy importante para la economía de Costa Rica.

NICARAGUA

Río San Juan

Mar Caribe

Poás

COSTA RICA

Arenal

Puntarenas

Alajuela

Irazú

San José

Cartago

Limón

Golfo de Nicoya

Puerto Quepos

PANAMÁ

Golfito

OCÉANO PACÍFICO

ALMANAQUE

Nombre oficial: República de Costa Rica
Gobierno: República democrática
Población: 4.516.220 (2010)
Idiomas: español (oficial); inglés
Moneda: Colón (CRC)

¿Sabías que...?

• El ejército (*army*) se abolió en Costa Rica en el año 1948. Los recursos monetarios desde aquel entonces apoyan (*support*) el sistema educativo. A causa de su dedicación a la paz (*peace*), la llaman "La Suiza de Centroamérica".

Preguntas

1. ¿Qué artesanía es un símbolo nacional costarricense?
2. ¿Cuál es uno de los productos de exportación importantes de Costa Rica? ¿Qué otros países exportan productos similares?
3. ¿Qué otra industria es importante para la economía de Costa Rica?

 Amplía tus conocimientos sobre Costa Rica en MySpanishLab.

 Instructor Resources
• Text images (maps), Video resources

NOTE for *Ecoturismo*
Ecotourism is big business in Costa Rica. Because the geography, flora, and fauna are so varied, there is something for everyone, such as beautiful beaches, rain and cloud forests, volcanoes, two- and three-toed sloths, howler monkeys, butterflies, tapirs, and green turtles and their nesting sites. In recent years, sailing through the trees on zip lines or walking through tree canopies over hanging bridges have been two popular diversions offered to tourists. You and your students can research additional information on the Internet by using the key words *Costa Rica* and *ecotourism*.

NOTE for *La carreta*
The oxcart has played a big role in Costa Rica's economic history and traditions. Originally the oxcart was the only method for transporting coffee beans to coastal commerce centers. Because coffee was the economic livelihood of many farmers, the carts were extremely important. Eventually, the owners began to paint them to indicate their regions, their towns, and their own distinct personalities. These painted carts are rarely seen now, but they remain a cultural symbol and are a source of pride for many Costa Ricans, reflecting their history and industriousness. They were declared a national symbol on March 22, 1988.

NOTE for *El café*
Costa Rican coffee ranks among the finest in the world. Costa Rican soil is perfect for coffee growing. Volcanic ashes and rich organic matter help retain humidity and facilitate oxygenation, resulting in a slight hint of acidity in the coffee's flavor.

139

Instructor Resources
• Text images (maps), Video resources

NOTE for *El Canal de Panamá*
The Panama Canal reverted to Panamanian ownership and directorship on December 31, 1999. The canal greatly decreases the travel time from Atlantic Ocean destinations to Pacific Ocean ones; the trip was also much safer than going around the tip of South America. Five years after the takeover by Panama, the canal was profitable and the accident rate had been reduced.

SUGGESTION for *El Canal de Panamá*
We believe in the need to use English at some points so that the students will have the richest experience possible. These brief questions bring forward the National Foreign Language Standards of Cultures, Comparisons, and Connections since, through culture, they have students use knowledge from political science/history and make cultural comparisons. Ask students: *Why is this canal so strategically important? Why is the Panama Canal economically important?* Ask whether anyone has ever been through the canal or through a system of locks (e.g. from lake to lake).

NOTE for *Los kunas*
The Kuna Indians live in the Islas San Blas and in the province of Darién. The Kuna society is a matriarchal one; when a couple marries, the man moves to the woman's household. Kuna women are known for their colorful traditional dress that includes the *mola*, insets on both the front and back of a blouse with intricate patterns and/or designs. These are made by interleaving several layers of different colored cloth and cutting out shapes accordingly. This handicraft is highly prized and is a symbol of this indigenous culture.

NOTE for *El Panamá Viejo*
Panamá Viejo, the oldest European settlement on the Pacific Coast, was founded in 1519 by the conquistador Pedrarias Dávila, or Pedro Arias de Ávila. A UNESCO World Heritage Site, Panamá Viejo is situated northeast of downtown Panama City. Once a thriving city of reportedly 10,000 inhabitants, it was a major center for merchants and landowners. The town was damaged in the 1621 earthquake, suffered additional damage by fire in 1644, and then was devastated in 1671 during Sir Henry Morgan's invasion, and was never rebuilt.

Panamá

CULTURA • CULTURA • CULTURA • CU ... RA • CULTU

Magdalena Quintero de Gracia

Les presento mi país

Mi nombre es Magdalena Quintero de Gracia y soy de Colón, una ciudad y puerto en la costa caribeña de Panamá. Mi país es famoso por el canal y mi ciudad está muy cerca de su entrada (*entrance*) atlántica. **¿Qué sabes tú de la historia del canal?** La economía de Panamá se basa principalmente en el sector de los servicios, la banca, el comercio y el turismo. Los turistas van al canal y también a las Islas San Blas. Allí pueden apreciar la artesanía de las mujeres indígenas. Los kunas son un grupo de indígenas que viven en este lugar y las mujeres hacen *molas* como parte de su ropa tradicional.

El Canal de Panamá

Una mujer kuna vende molas, artesanía tradicional.

Las ruinas del Panamá Viejo

ALMANAQUE

Nombre oficial: República de Panamá
Gobierno: Democracia constitucional
Población: 3.410.676 (2010)
Idiomas: español (oficial), inglés, otros idiomas indígenas
Moneda: Balboa (PAB)

¿Sabías que...?
• Richard Halliburton nadó el canal en el año 1928 y la tarifa fue (*was*) 36 centavos. La tarifa más alta fue $141.344,91 para el crucero (*cruise ship*) Crown Princess.
• Hay un palíndromo famoso en inglés asociado con el canal: *A man, a plan, a canal:* ¡Panamá!

Preguntas
1. ¿Por qué es importante el canal?
2. Compara Panamá con Costa Rica y Nicaragua. ¿En qué son similares? ¿En qué son diferentes?
3. Compara Panamá, Costa Rica y Nicaragua con México. ¿En qué son similares? ¿En qué son diferentes?

Amplía tus conocimientos sobre Panamá en MySpanishLab.

140

NOTE for *Palíndromo*
A palindrome is a "word, phrase, verse, or sentence which reads the same backward or forward" (*American Heritage Dictionary*, 1982). A very famous one that appears in *The American Heritage Dictionary* is "A man, a plan, a canal, Panama!" Another palindrome in Spanish is *oso*.

SUGGESTION for *Las molas*
A brief English discussion of *molas* might include the following questions: *What is traditional clothing like in indigenous groups in the United States? (Possible answer: Some indigenous groups have animal skins or woven fabrics. The skins are natural tones, and the woven fabrics can be bright or more subdued, depending on the vegetation available for dying.) How does it compare with the molas? (Possible answer: They can be as colorful, depending on the dying materials available in nature. They reflect the culture with either geometric shapes or those of flora or fauna.)*

¡Hola!
eText p. 198   05-54

Ambiciones siniestras

EPISODIO 5

Lectura y video

Y por fin, ¿cómo andas?

	Feel confident	Need to review
Having completed this chapter, I now can . . .		
Comunicación I		
• discuss music (p. 116)	☐	☐
• practice pronouncing diphthongs and linking words (MSL/SAM)	☐	☐
• identify people and things (Part I) (p. 119)	☐	☐
• identify people and things (Part II) (p. 121)	☐	☐
• explain how something is done (p. 122)	☐	☐
• describe what is happening at the moment (p. 124)	☐	☐
Comunicación II		
• share information about movies and television programs (p. 127)	☐	☐
• rank people and things (p. 129)	☐	☐
• state what needs to be accomplished (p. 131)	☐	☐
• express *what* or *whom* (p. 132)	☐	☐
• anticipate content when listening (p. 135)	☐	☐
• communicate about music and film (p. 136)	☐	☐
• write a movie review and practice peer editing (p. 137)	☐	☐
Cultura		
• discuss Hispanic music in the United States (p. 122)	☐	☐
• describe Hispanic influences in North American film (p. 129)	☐	☐
• list interesting facts about Nicaragua, Costa Rica, and Panama (pp. 138–140)	☐	☐
Ambiciones siniestras		
• anticipate content when reading and discover what Cisco does in his search for Eduardo (p. 141)	☐	☐
• find out who is the second student to disappear (p. 141)	☐	☐
Comunidades		
• use Spanish in real-life contexts (SAM)	☐	☐

NATIONAL STANDARDS
Communication
The material presented online in *Ambiciones siniestras* is well aligned with the Communication Goal. Standard 1.2 emphasizes comprehension and interpretation of written and spoken Spanish, as is presented in the *Lectura* and the video episode. The *Después de leer* activity can be implemented using partners, so students discuss the content and provide and obtain information (Standard 1.1). An additional activity (a jigsaw or information gap activity) might require them to listen for specific things, get together, and help each other to fill in the information that the other person has about a character or an event. You could also use the Videoscript, and have students present it as if they were each character in *Ambiciones siniestras*, revealing some "secret" information that the students might not have understood. The presentations about the characters align with Standard 1.3, the presentational mode.

 Instructor Resources
• Video script

SECTION GOALS for *Lectura y video* (Online)
By the end of the *Lectura y video* section, students will be able to:
• implement reading strategies such as anticipating content, skimming, scanning, and identifying content.
• predict what might happen in the next reading of *Ambiciones siniestras*.
• discuss possible theories regarding Eduardo's whereabouts.
• report the events of the videoconference.
• predict what secrets Lupe might be hiding.

NOTE for *Lectura y video*
Activity answers for online content can be found on the next page for quick reference.

RECAP OF *AMBICIONES SINIESTRAS* Episodio 4 (Online)
Lectura: In the reading from *Capítulo 4, Las apariencias engañan*, Marisol and Lupe worked on a sociology project at Lupe's apartment. Marisol revealed a lot of information about where she lived, but Lupe would only say that she lived outside of Akron, Ohio. While Lupe took a break from the project to make a phone call, Marisol decided to read what Lupe had written on her computer screen. Marisol discovered that Lupe wasn't writing about Akron, but rather Los Angeles.
Video: In the *Capítulo 4* video episode, *¿Quiénes son en realidad?*, we learned that Eduardo is very passionate about volunteering for children's organizations in other countries. He tried to get Cisco to consider volunteering, but Cisco was more focused on the mysterious codes on his paper. Eduardo picked up the codes and Cisco yelled, *¡No toques mis cosas nunca más! ¿Me oyes?* When Cisco left the room to answer a phone call, Eduardo snooped through Cisco's things and discovered that the finalists' names appeared. He mumbled *¿Concurso falso?* He took some of Cisco's papers and left. Later we saw Eduardo type an e-mail to Sr. Verdugo.

METHODOLOGY • Checking for Comprehension in English
When encouraging students to hypothesize regarding what will happen, it is acceptable to encourage them to brainstorm in English.

VOCABULARIO ACTIVO

El mundo de la música	The world of music
el/la artista	artist
la batería	drums
el/la baterista	drummer
el/la cantante	singer
el concierto	concert
el conjunto	group; band
el/la empresario/a	agent; manager
la gira	tour
las grabaciones	recordings
la guitarra	guitar
el/la guitarrista	guitarist
el/la músico/a	musician
la música	music
la orquesta	orchestra
el/la pianista	pianist
el piano	piano
el tambor	drum
el/la tamborista	drummer
la trompeta	trumpet
el/la trompetista	trumpet player

Algunos verbos	Some verbs
dar un concierto	to give/perform a concert
ensayar	to practice/rehearse
grabar	to record
hacer una gira	to tour
sacar un CD	to release a CD
tocar	to play (a musical instrument)

Algunos géneros musicales	Some musical genres
el jazz	jazz
la música clásica	classical music
la música folklórica	folk music
la música popular	pop music
la música rap	rap music
la ópera	opera
el rock	rock
la salsa	salsa

Algunos adjetivos	Some adjectives
apasionado/a	passionate
cuidadoso/a	careful
fino/a	fine; delicate
lento/a	slow
suave	smooth

Otras palabras útiles	Other useful words
el/la aficionado/a	fan
la fama	fame
el género	genre
la habilidad	ability; skill
la letra	lyrics
el ritmo	rhythm
la voz	voice

El mundo del cine	The world of cinema
el actor	actor
la actriz	actress
la entrada	ticket
la estrella	star
la pantalla	screen
una película…	a … film; movie
de acción	action
de ciencia ficción	science fiction
documental	documentary
dramática	drama
de guerra	war
de humor	funny; comedy
de misterio	mystery
musical	musical
romántica	romantic
de terror	horror

Los números ordinales	Ordinal numbers
primer, primero/a	first
segundo/a	second
tercer, tercero/a	third
cuarto/a	fourth
quinto/a	fifth
sexto/a	sixth
séptimo/a	seventh
octavo/a	eighth
noveno/a	ninth
décimo/a	tenth

Otras palabras útiles	Other Useful Words
el estreno	opening
la película	film; movie
una película…	a … movie
aburrida	boring
animada	animated
conmovedora	moving
creativa	creative
deprimente	depressing
emocionante	moving
entretenida	entertaining
épica	epic
de espanto	scary
estupenda	stupendous
imaginativa	imaginative
impresionante	impressive
sorprendente	surprising
de suspenso	suspenseful
trágica	tragic

Algunos verbos	Some verbs
estrenar una película	to release a film/movie
presentar una película	to show a film/movie

143

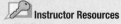 **Instructor Resources**
• IRM: Syllabi and Lesson Plans

NATIONAL STANDARDS

COMUNICACIÓN

• To describe your family and other families (Communication, Cultures, Comparisons)

• To relate information about your school and campus (Communication, Comparisons)

• To impart information about homes that you and your friends like and dislike (Communication, Comparisons)

• To offer opinions on what will take place in the future (Communication)

• To reveal what you and others like to do and what you need to do (Communication)

• To report on service opportunities in your community (Communication, Connections, Communities)

• To discuss music, movies, and television (Communication, Connections, Comparisons)

• To engage in additional communication practice (Communication)

CULTURA

• To share information about Hispanic cultures in the United States, Mexico, Spain, Honduras, Guatemala, El Salvador, Nicaragua, Costa Rica, and Panama (Communication, Cultures, Comparisons)

• To compare and contrast the countries you learned about in *Capítulos 1–5* (Cultures, Comparisons)

• To explore further cultural themes (Cultures)

AMBICIONES SINIESTRAS

• To review and create with *Ambiciones siniestras* (Communication)

COMUNIDADES

• To use Spanish in real-life contexts (Communities)

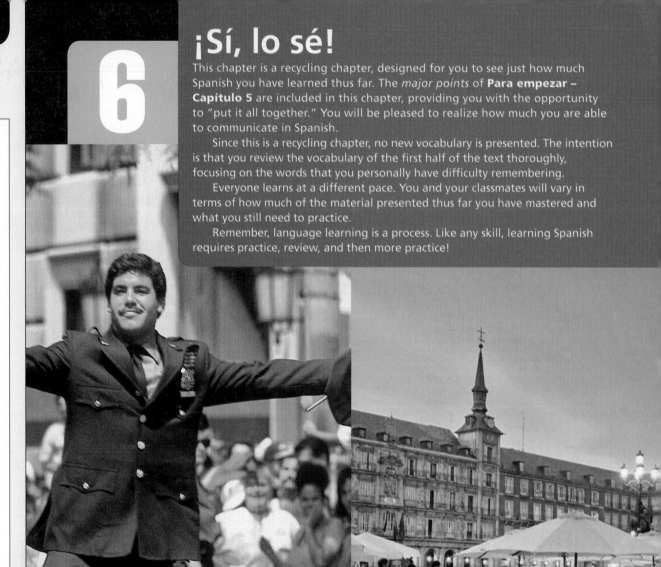

6

¡Sí, lo sé!

This chapter is a recycling chapter, designed for you to see just how much Spanish you have learned thus far. The *major points* of **Para empezar – Capítulo 5** are included in this chapter, providing you with the opportunity to "put it all together." You will be pleased to realize how much you are able to communicate in Spanish.

Since this is a recycling chapter, no new vocabulary is presented. The intention is that you review the vocabulary of the first half of the text thoroughly, focusing on the words that you personally have difficulty remembering.

Everyone learns at a different pace. You and your classmates will vary in terms of how much of the material presented thus far you have mastered and what you still need to practice.

Remember, language learning is a process. Like any skill, learning Spanish requires practice, review, and then more practice!

144

METHODOLOGY • Research Guiding ¡Anda!

The programs *¡Anda! Curso elemental* and *¡Anda! Curso intermedio* are written based not only on the National Standards but also on extensive research that impacts language learning. Reading more on the topics will help to deepen understanding of the instructional delivery topics and can create excellent collegial discussions. For example, for those wishing to know more

about spiraling, please consult the work of Robert Gagné, American educational psychologist (1916–2002) whose "Nine Events of Instruction" remains a foundation of instructional delivery. Other topics of interest may be the theory of multiple intelligences proposed by Howard Gardner in 1983 or Carol Ann Tomlinson's writings on differentiated instruction.

METHODOLOGY • Philosophy on Recycling

This chapter is unique in *¡Anda! Curso elemental* because it provides yet another opportunity for students to demonstrate the Spanish language they have acquired. In this chapter, *¡Anda! Curso elemental* has synthesized the main points of the first 5 chapters in a recycled format for students to practice the new skills they are learning. You will note that all of these

activities have the students *put it all together;* in other words, *all of the activities in Capítulo 6 are communicative.* There are no discrete point, mechanical activities. Instead, we direct the students to make use of the activities in MySpanishLab or to repeat the activities in their *Student Activities Manual,* the Extra Activities folder under Instructor's Resources, or in the textbook itself for mechanical practice.

Another way to use this chapter is to assign the activities while you are teaching each individual chapter. For example, you may have students who would benefit by additional communicative activities in addition to the *¡Conversemos!* activities. Since the Chapter 6 communicative activities have been separated by chapter, it makes it easy for you to assign them.

OBJETIVOS

COMUNICACIÓN

To describe your family and other families

To relate information about your school and campus

To impart information about homes that you and your friends like and dislike

To offer opinions on what will take place in the future

To reveal what you and others like to do and what you need to do

To report on service opportunities in your community

To discuss music, movies, and television

To engage in additional communication practice (SAM)

CULTURA

To share information about Hispanic cultures in the United States, Mexico, Spain, Honduras, Guatemala, El Salvador, Nicaragua, Costa Rica, and Panama

To compare and contrast the countries you learned about in **Para empezar – Capítulo 5**

To explore further cultural themes (SAM)

AMBICIONES SINIESTRAS

To review and create with **Ambiciones siniestras**

COMUNIDADES

To use Spanish in real-life contexts (SAM)

145

METHODOLOGY • Prioritizing Review Topics

Prior to beginning the activities in this chapter, if your students choose (or you strongly encourage them) to gain more mechanical practice, repeating the activities they have already done both in the ¡Anda! Curso elemental textbook and in their Student Activities Manual is an excellent start for their review. Redoing activities already done is an important review tool that is based on learning theory. This works for the following reasons: First, they are already familiar with the context of the activity, and know what they got correct and missed the first time; hence they are able to observe whether they have improved. They also are repeating the activities on a different level. Since they have already completed the activity, these repetitions go to a meta-analysis level, where they need to analyze why they continue to miss certain items. The same learning theory concept is similar in most fields/professions. For example, in the culinary arts, chefs are expected to perform the same preparations, such as cutting vegetables, in precisely the identical uniform way time and again. In music, the same scales and arpeggios are practiced over and over.

Finally, if you have advanced or heritage language learners, you may wish to skip this chapter or assign it as extra practice that the students can do by themselves.

METHODOLOGY • Organizing a Review for Students

Researchers and reviewers of ¡Anda! Curso elemental agree. After giving the students strategies on how to conduct an overall review, this chapter is organized by beginning with communicative and engaging activities that focus on grammar and vocabulary beginning with Capítulo Preliminar A. The review continues to move through the chapters, ending with Capítulo 5. This is followed by Un poco de todo, a more comprehensive review, truly putting it all together, combining all of the chapters. Finally, there is a review of countries presented in Capítulos 1–5.

METHODOLOGY • Recycling vs. Reviewing

In ¡Anda! Curso elemental, recycling up to this point has meant taking previously learned material and recombining it with new material. This concept is supported by Gagné's learning concept of spiraling information. In Capítulo 6, we are not presenting any new material, but rather recombining what your students have already learned and expanding the level. This also constitutes recycling. The concept of review is revisiting a topic, much like one does before an exam. Review is best illustrated in Capítulo 4 (Un repaso de ser y estar), as well as this chapter. No new information is introduced in a review, nor is there any true spiraling. Instead, a review affords students the opportunity to practice in a systematic fashion.

METHODOLOGY • Prioritizing Review Topics

You will note that the authors of ¡Anda! Curso elemental have listed only 5 grammar topics that we denote as major and upon which we are encouraging our students to focus the majority of their review time. Students become overwhelmed when told that everything is major. They then tend to make poor choices regarding where to focus the majority of their time when reviewing. Truth be told, we believe there to be one major, overarching grammar concept, which can be broken down into subparts: present tense of regular, irregular, and stem-changing verbs. If students are able to express themselves correctly using a richness of verbs in a wide array of topics, we believe the first semester has been successful. We have listed the other 4 as "icing on the cake." Please understand that we are not diminishing the importance of concepts such as noun and adjective agreement or the differences between saber and conocer. What we are saying is that if students were to communicate with a sympathetic native speaker, they would still be understood even with mistakes in those areas. We have used as our guide descriptors such as the ACTFL Proficiency Guidelines as well as the Spanish Advanced Placement descriptors. Also guiding us is the fact that when constructing final exams, the vast majority of points fall into the present tense category.

SUGGESTION for *Prioritizing Review Topics*
If you hold review sessions or if you have students such as tutors or academic support staff that offer review sessions, suggest that students generate their questions about particular points before coming to the review. An idea to consider is that the students provide evidence of their preparation for the review session. It can serve as their "admission ticket" to the review.

METHODOLOGY •
Differentiated Instruction
Differentiated instruction is when you tailor your lessons for your different types of learners. The number of types of learners and their preferences depend on which research you are consulting. Some sources maintain that there are four different types of learning styles, some say 7 or 8, and still others claim that there are more than 20! As instructors, what we need to remember is that students learn in different ways and progress at different rates. When assessing the progress of your students, it is important to know that for some of your students, their best performance will be to give multiple answers, while for others, their best will be one complete sentence. Differentiating instruction, in part, means to tailor our lessons so that all of our students, no matter what their style or talents, will be successful.

PLANNING AHEAD
You may wish to refer students to *Appendix 1, Capítulo 6,* where they can find a list of the grammar points reviewed in this chapter.

METHODOLOGY • Organizing a Review
¡Anda! Curso elemental is combining three chapters in this initial section for one important reason: Although there are a number of concepts and vocabulary words that appear in *Capítulo Preliminar A* and *Capítulo 1,* only 3 main verbs are introduced: *ser, tener,* and an abbreviated introduction of *gustar.* After completing *Capítulo 5,* your students already have a wide array of verbs and vocabulary at their fingertips. To require them to use only three in order to practice the family does not allow them to be as creative as possible. Also notice that we are suggesting that they can use verbs and vocabulary beyond *Capítulo 2.* You can differentiate instruction by directing specific students to focus on chapters beyond *Capítulo 2* if you wish.

Organizing Your Review

There are processes used by successful language learners for reviewing a world language. The following tips can help you organize your review. There is no one correct way, but these are some suggestions that will best utilize your time and energy.

1 Reviewing Strategies

1. Make a list of the *major* topics you have studied and need to review, dividing them into three categories: *vocabulary, grammar,* and *culture.* These are the topics on which you need to focus the majority of your time and energy.
Note: The two-page chapter openers can help you determine the *major* topics.
2. Allocate a minimum of an hour each day over a period of time to review. Budget the majority of your time for the major topics. After beginning with the most important grammar and vocabulary topics, review the secondary/supporting grammar topics and the culture. Cramming the night before a test is *not* an effective way to review and retain information.
3. Many educational researchers suggest that you start your review with the most recent chapter, or in this case, **Capítulo 5.** The most recent chapter is the freshest in your mind, so you tend to remember the concepts better, and you will experience quick success in your review.
4. Spend the most amount of time on concepts in which you determine *you* need to improve. Revisit the self-assessment tools **Y por fin, ¿cómo andas?** in each chapter to see how you rated yourself. Those tools are designed to help you become good at self-assessing what you need to work on the most.

2 Reviewing Grammar

1. When reviewing grammar, begin with the *major* points, that is, begin with the *present tense* of regular, irregular, and stem-changing verbs. After feeling confident with using the major grammar points correctly, proceed to the additional grammar points and review them.
2. Good ways to review include redoing activities in your textbook, redoing activities in your Student Activities Manual, and (re)doing activities on MySpanishLab.

3 Reviewing Vocabulary

1. When studying vocabulary, it is usually most helpful to look at the English word and then say or write the word in Spanish. Make a special list of words that are difficult for you to remember, writing them in a small notebook or in an electronic file. Pull out your list every time you have a few minutes (in between classes, waiting in line at the grocery store, etc.) to review the words. The **Vocabulario activo** pages at the end of each chapter will help you organize the most important words of each chapter.
2. Saying vocabulary (which includes verbs) out loud helps you retain the words better.

4 Overall Review Technique

1. Get together with someone with whom you can practice speaking Spanish. If you need something to spark the conversation, take the drawings from each vocabulary presentation in *¡Anda! Curso elemental* and say as many things as you can about each picture. Have a friendly challenge to see who can make more complete sentences or create the longest story about the pictures. This will help you build your confidence and practice stringing sentences together to speak in paragraphs.
2. Yes, it is important for you to know "mechanical" pieces of information such as verb endings, or how to take a sentence and replace the direct object with a pronoun, *but* it is *much more important* that you are able to take those mechanical pieces of information and put them all together, creating meaningful and creative samples of your speaking and writing on the themes of the first half of the textbook.
3. You are well on the road to success if you can demonstrate that you can speak and write in paragraphs, using a wide variety of verbs and vocabulary words correctly. Keep up the good work!

METHODOLOGY • Self-Assessment and Instructor's Use of Rubrics (Online)
Assessing student performance is an important task that we instructors perform. Students need to know in advance what is acceptable versus unacceptable work. It is important that students are provided in advance with the rubrics so that they are clear regarding our expectations.

The rubrics provided online in eText are meant to be used either as is or to act as a guide for you. The suggestion is that 3 = A; 2 = B; 1 = C; 0 = D/F. Also notice that there is a place for you to assess effort.

As instructors, we know that there will be some students who look for and take the easy way out, even though they may have the ability. These can be gifted students or heritage language learners who choose not to work to their potential.

The effort rating is a way of encouraging those students as well as giving credit to students who struggle but are working above and beyond their level of ability. These students deserve to be rewarded for their efforts.

You may wish to add other categories such as pronunciation to the rubric.

Un poco de todo

06-21 to 06-34

 6-15 **¡Ganaste la lotería!** Ganaste (*You won*) un millón de dólares en la lotería y te invitan a un programa de televisión para explicar qué vas a hacer con el dinero. Dile al/a la entrevistador/a (tu compañero/a) qué vas a hacer con el dinero en por lo menos **diez** oraciones. Después cambien de papel (*Take turns playing each role*). ■

 6-16 **Busco ayuda...** Con el dinero que ganaste en la lotería, decides buscar un ayudante personal (*personal assistant*) para ayudarte con los quehaceres de la casa y con algunos asuntos (*matters*) de tu trabajo. Entrevista a un/a compañero/a que hace el papel de ayudante. Después cambien de papel. ■

MODELO   E1:   *Debe mandar mis cartas y escribir unos emails.*

           E2:   *Bueno, pero no limpio las ventanas.*

           E1:   *¿Cómo? ¿No las limpia? ¿Pasa la aspiradora?*

           E2:   ...

6-17 **Mi horario para la semana** Crea un horario para una semana ideal durante el verano. Usa por lo menos **diez** verbos diferentes para explicar lo que tienes que hacer. Comparte tu horario con un/a compañero/a. ■

junio

L	M	M	J	V	S	D
	1	2	3	4	5	6
7	8	9	10	11	12	13
14	15	16	17	18	19	20
21	22	23	24	25	26	27
28	29	30				

julio

L	M	M	J	V	S	D
			1	2	3	4
5	6	7	8	9	10	11
12	13	14	15	16	17	18
19	20	21	22	23	24	25
26	27	28	29	30	31	

agosto

L	M	M	J	V	S	D
						1
2	3	4	5	6	7	8
9	10	11	12	13	14	15
16	17	18	19	20	21	22
23	24	25	26	27	28	29
30	31					

METHODOLOGY • Peer Editing

Activities **6-18, 6-19, 6-20,** and **6-21** provide starting points for simple narrations about familiar topics. You might assign these activities for homework so that each student has something written for class. Instead of correcting the writing assignments yourself, have your students peer edit. Peer editing affords students the opportunity to read carefully in order to help their classmates. For your students who need to be reminded about peer editing, suggest that they consult the *Estrategia* for the *Escribe* section of *Capítulo 5,* p. 194.

METHODOLOGY • Quantifying Minimum Expectations

You will note that we frequently include the minimum number of sentences expected of the students in both speaking and writing activities. If students do not know what these minimum expectations are, many will be happy with mediocre production. And they are not always the weaker students! Most of us have had bright students who are lazy and only willing to do "the minimum." Hence it is necessary for instructors to let students know what their expectations are and to encourage students to exceed the minimum.

Having provided this rationale, the decision is ultimately yours. You may choose (a) to use what we have recommended; (b) to require a different minimum level of production; or (c) not to state the level of language production. You will notice that some of the directions in this chapter are intentionally following (c). These are instructional delivery decisions that all of us must make based on a wide variety of differentiated objectives.

SUGGESTION for 6-19

For **6-19,** you may want to provide students with a free-verse poem in English to activate schemata.

6-18 Mis planes para el verano Escribe un email a un/a compañero/a de **ocho** a **diez** oraciones sobre lo que vas a hacer este verano: **cuándo, dónde** y **con quién.** ■

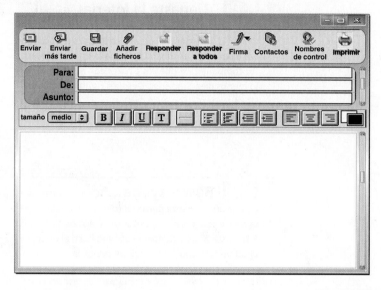

6-19 Para la comunidad Escribe un poema en verso libre o una canción sobre el voluntariado y sus beneficios para los que dan y para los que reciben ayuda. ■

6-20 Mi comunidad Túrnense para describir detalladamente su comunidad o la de la foto. Incluyan en su descripción oral detalles de su pueblo o ciudad (edificios, lugares de diversión, etc.), su casa y también las oportunidades que existen para hacer trabajo voluntario. Finalmente, hagan sus presentaciones para un grupo cívico como los Rotarios (*Rotary Club*). ■

México D.F.

6-21 **El juego de la narración** Túrnense para crear una narración oral sobre **Ambiciones siniestras.** ¡Incluyan muchos detalles! ◼

MODELO   E1:   Ambiciones siniestras *es un misterio muy imaginativo.*
             E2:   *Hay seis estudiantes que se llaman…*
             E1:   …

Cisco   Eduardo   Manolo   Alejandra   Lupe   Marisol

Estrategia

The ability to retell information is an important language-learning strategy. Practice summarizing or retelling in your own words in Spanish the events from *Ambiciones siniestras,* chapter by chapter. Set a goal for yourself of saying or writing at least 5 important events in each episode that move the story along. Another technique is to recap as if you were retelling the story to another student who was absent.

6-22 **¿Me quiere?** Cisco, de **Ambiciones siniestras,** le escribe un correo electrónico a la chica que conoció (*he met*) en el concierto. En el email habla de sus planes para el fin de semana y la invita a acompañarlo (*accompany him*). Escribe ese mensaje en **diez** oraciones como si fueras (*as if you were*) Cisco. ◼

MODELO

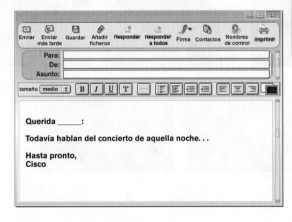

NOTE for 6-21
Students can begin the activity by brainstorming, jotting down the basic plot so far. They can then refer to this list to keep them on track as they add details in their oral narrations.

METHODOLOGY • Activities related to *Ambiciones siniestras*
A technique frequently used in literature classes (both beginning and advanced) is for students to retell stories / literature in their own words and in their own order. Research reports that students learn best from other students, and activities such as **6-21** afford students the opportunity to learn from their peers. Peers also stimulate each other and they are subtly encouraged to achieve higher levels.

6-23 Su versión En **6-21**, narraron (*you narrated*) una versión del cuento **Ambiciones siniestras**. Ahora es su turno como escritores. Sean muy creativos y creen su propia (*own*) versión creativa. Su instructor les va a explicar cómo hacerlo. Empiecen con la oración del modelo. ¡Diviértanse! ∎

MODELO   *Hay seis estudiantes de tres universidades.*

6-24 Tu propia película Eres cinematógrafo y puedes crear tu propia versión de **Ambiciones siniestras**. Primero, pon las fotos en el orden correcto y luego escribe el diálogo para la película. Luego, puedes filmar tu versión. ∎

6-25 **Los hispanos en los Estados Unidos** Escribe **cinco** influencias hispanas en los Estados Unidos. ■

MODELO   1. *St. Augustine fue fundada por los españoles en el año 1565.*

Workbooklet

6-26 **Aspectos interesantes** Escribe por lo menos **tres** cosas interesantes sobre cada uno de los siguientes países. ■

MÉXICO	ESPAÑA	HONDURAS	GUATEMALA

EL SALVADOR	NICARAGUA	COSTA RICA	PANAMÁ

6-27 **Un agente de viajes** Durante el verano tienes la oportunidad de trabajar en una agencia de viajes (*travel agency*). Tienes unos clientes que quieren visitar un país hispanohablante. Escoge uno de los países que estudiamos y recomienda el país en por lo menos **seis** oraciones. ■

6-28 **Mi país favorito** Describe tu país favorito entre los que hemos estudiado (*we have studied*). En por lo menos **ocho** oraciones explica por qué te gusta y lo que encuentras interesante e impresionante de ese país. ■

6-29 **Compáralos** Escoge dos países que estudiamos y escribe las diferencias y semejanzas (*similarities*) entre los dos. ■

MODELO   *México es un país grande en Norteamérica y Nicaragua es más pequeño que México y está en Centroamérica.*

CAPÍTULO 6

NOTE for 6-30

¡A jugar! is based on *Jeopardy!* a highly popular, long-running television quiz show in the United States. The premise of the game is that the contestant sees the answer and must formulate the appropriate question. The "answers" are grouped by categories and each "answer" has a dollar value. Easier answers have lower dollar values. In almost every community across the United States, it is on every night of the week for 30 minutes. This game show phenomenon has been wildly successful in Spanish classrooms for decades as a review tool. It provides students with a motivating way to review categories, helps them to organize material thematically, and forces them to create questions—a skill that the research says students seldom perform since they are usually answering our questions! Use the *¡Anda! Curso elemental* transparencies/images in MSL that accompany this activity to make this activity even more enjoyable and realistic.

 6-30 **¡A jugar!** En grupos de tres o cuatro, preparen las respuestas para las siguientes categorías de *¿Lo sabes?,* un juego como *Jeopardy!,* y después las preguntas correspondientes. Pueden usar valores de dólares, pesos, euros, etc. ¡Buena suerte! ■

CATEGORÍAS

VOCABULARIO	VERBOS	CULTURA
la vida estudiantil	verbos regulares	Estados Unidos
las materias y las especialidades	verbos irregulares	México
los deportes y los pasatiempos	**saber** y **conocer**	España
la casa y los muebles	**ser** y **estar**	Honduras
los quehaceres de la casa	**ir**	Guatemala
el cine	**ir** + **a** + infinitivo	El Salvador
la música	**estar** + **-ando, -iendo**	Nicaragua
el voluntariado		Costa Rica
		Panamá

MODELOS

CATEGORÍA: LA VIDA ESTUDIANTIL

Respuesta: en la residencia estudiantil
Pregunta: *¿Dónde viven los estudiantes?*

CATEGORÍA: LOS DEPORTES Y LOS PASATIEMPOS

Respuesta: Albert Pujols
Pregunta: *¿Quién juega al béisbol muy bien?*

¿LO SABES?

| MÉXICO | ESPAÑA | HONDURAS | GUATEMALA |

NOTE for 6-30
The images in this activity are as follows:
¿Lo sabes?

México: (top) Artesanía de Oaxaca (bottom) La biblioteca de la Universidad Nacional Autónoma de México

España: (top) Una tortilla española (bottom) La Pedrera (la Casa Milá) en Barcelona

Honduras: (top) Un charancaco *(basilisk)* de la Isla Roatán (bottom) Las ruinas de Copán

Guatemala: (top) Tikal (bottom) Antigua

¿Lo sabes? Doble

El Salvador: (top) Pupusas
(bottom) La playa El Sunzal

Nicaragua: (top) Volcán San Cristóbal
(bottom) La Concha
Acústica

Costa Rica: (top) El ecoturismo
(bottom) Una carreta

Panamá: (top) El Canal de Panamá
(bottom) Una mujer kuna

Y por fin, ¿cómo andas?

	Feel confident	Need to review
Having completed this chapter, I now can . . .		

Comunicación

- describe my family and other families ☐ ☐
- relate information about my school and campus ☐ ☐
- impart information about homes that my friends and I like and dislike ☐ ☐
- offer opinions on what will take place in the future ☐ ☐
- reveal what I and others like to do and what we need to do ☐ ☐
- report on service opportunities in my community ☐ ☐
- discuss music, movies, and television ☐ ☐
- engage in additional communication practice (SAM) ☐ ☐

Cultura

- share information about the Spanish-speaking world in the United States, Mexico, Spain, Honduras, Guatemala, El Salvador, Nicaragua, Costa Rica, and Panama ☐ ☐
- compare and contrast the countries I learned about in **Para empezar – Capítulo 5** ☐ ☐
- explore further cultural themes (SAM) ☐ ☐

Ambiciones siniestras

- review and create with **Ambiciones siniestras** ☐ ☐

Comunidades

- use Spanish in real-life contexts (SAM) ☐ ☐

Instructor Resources

• IRM: Syllabi and Lesson Plans

NATIONAL STANDARDS

COMUNICACIÓN I

• To discuss food (Communication, Cultures, Comparisons)
• To pronounce the different sounds of **r** and **rr** (Communication)
• To communicate with less repetition (Communication)
• To describe things that happened in the past (Part I) (Communication)
• To describe things that happened in the past (Part II) (Communication)
• To engage in additional communication practice (Communication)

COMUNICACIÓN II

• To explain food preparation (Communication, Cultures, Communities)
• To express things that happened in the past (Communication)
• To explain restaurant activity (Communication)
• To combine listening strategies (Communication)
• To communicate about food shopping and party planning (Communication)
• To relate a memory (Communication)
• To engage in additional communication practice (Communication)

CULTURA

• To compare and contrast eating habits (Cultures, Comparisons)
• To survey foods from different parts of the Hispanic world (Cultures, Comparisons)
• To list interesting facts about this chapter's featured countries: Chile and Paraguay (Cultures, Comparisons)
• To explore further the chapter's cultural themes (Cultures)

AMBICIONES SINIESTRAS

• To predict what will happen in a reading and discover the voice-mail message that frightens Cisco (Connections, Communication)
• To determine who has received the riddle and what they have figured out so far (Communication)

COMUNIDADES

• To use Spanish in real-life contexts (Communication, Communities)

7 ¡A comer!

Comer bien es un gran placer (*pleasure*). Dentro del mundo hispanohablante hay una tremenda variedad de comidas (*foods*) y la comida tiene una función social muy importante.

PREGUNTAS

1 ¿Cuáles son tus platos (*dishes*) favoritos?

2 ¿Hay alguna comida típica de la región donde vives tú? ¿Cuáles son algunas comidas típicas de los Estados Unidos?

3 ¿Qué platos de otras culturas te gustan? ¿Qué platos hispanos te gustan?

156

SECTION GOALS for *Chapter opener*
By the end of the Chapter opener section, students will be able to:
• discuss their favorite dishes.
• identify regional and national cuisines of the United States.
• report about their favorite ethnic foods.

NATIONAL STANDARDS
Communities
If you have a large Hispanic population in your area, this chapter lends itself well to several service learning ideas. If you have a farmer's market or Hispanic district where local goods are sold, students can volunteer their time assisting the merchants and customers as they shop. If you have many Hispanic-owned restaurants or local businesses where the employees speak Spanish, your students could shadow someone who interacts with the Spanish-speaking public. Social services agencies that provide meals or grocery shopping services to those members of the Spanish-speaking community who are confined to homes would also be appropriate. Other suggestions include collecting food for a food bank on behalf of your Spanish class, bringing in recipes in Spanish that students can make and deliver to nursing homes, churches, after-school programs or housing projects, or inviting community members to dine at the campus. If you do not have a Hispanic population in your area, you could plan a "Taste of Hispanic Foods" night and have students prepare the Spanish language recipes you provide for a battered women's shelter, a soup kitchen, or some other social service organization in your community.

✓	OBJETIVOS	CONTENIDOS	
	COMUNICACIÓN I		
	To discuss food	**1** Food	158
	To pronounce the different sounds of **r** and **rr**	**Pronunciación:** The different pronunciations of **r** and **rr**	MSL/SAM
	To communicate with less repetition	**2** Review of the direct object	163
	To describe things that happened in the past (Part I)	**3** The preterit tense (Part I)	164
	To describe things that happened in the past (Part II)	**4** The preterit tense (Part II)	166
	To engage in additional communication practice	**Heritage Language**	SAM
	COMUNICACIÓN II		
	To explain food preparation	**5** Food preparation	171
	To express things that happened in the past	**6** Irregular verbs in the preterit tense	173
	To explain restaurant activity	**7** In the restaurant	178
	To combine listening strategies	**Escucha:** Food shopping **Estrategia:** Combining strategies	182
	To communicate about food shopping and party planning	**¡Conversemos!**	183
	To relate a memory	**Escribe:** A description **Estrategia:** Topic sentence and conclusion	184
	To engage in additional communication practice	**Heritage Language**	SAM
	CULTURA		
	To compare and contrast eating habits	**NOTA CULTURAL** Las comidas en el mundo hispano	162
	To survey foods from different parts of the Hispanic world	**NOTA CULTURAL** La comida hispana	173
	To list interesting facts about this chapter's featured countries: Chile and Paraguay	**CULTURA** Chile y Paraguay	185–186
	To explore further the chapter's cultural themes	**MÁS CULTURA**	SAM
	AMBICIONES SINIESTRAS		
	To predict what will happen in a reading, and discover the voice-mail message that frightens Cisco	**EPISODIO 7** **Lectura:** El rompecabezas **Estrategia:** Predicting	187
	To determine who has received the riddle, and what they have figured out so far	**Video:** ¡Qué rico está el pisco!	187
	COMUNIDADES		
	To use Spanish in real-life contexts	**Experiential Learning:** La comida en varios países	SAM
		Service Learning: Tu comunidad	SAM

157

NOTE for *Chapter opener*
If your campus has a diverse student population and the students are familiar with different types of ethnic foods, you will want to anticipate the kinds of cuisine they might mention so you can tell them how to say those foods in Spanish.

NOTE for *Contenidos*
The Heritage Language activities, available in the Student Activities Manual (SAM), are not only for heritage learners, but for all of your students. The activities either require students to reflect on the usage of Spanish, or to use Spanish in ways that encompass all of the 5 Cs. The end product will vary from student to student, which is an expected outcome of performance-based activities.

HERITAGE LANGUAGE LEARNERS
Ask your heritage language learners whether there is a specific *comida casera* they enjoy and what ingredients they use to make the dish. If the vocabulary differs from that of the *Vocabulario activo*, ask them to explain how the dish is made and whether the products are available in American grocery stores.

METHODOLOGY • *¡Anda! Curso elemental*
If you are new to using the *¡Anda! Curso elemental* program, please refer to the preface where we describe our philosophy of language education. These teacher annotations will assist you as you progress through the rest of the program to help your students acquire Spanish and become effective communicators in the language. Also, please remember that the questions that follow the brief reading on this page are meant to start with what the students already know (activating their prior knowledge), and help to entice them to learn more about the topic. We suggest you spend no more than 5–7 minutes on the chapter openers.

WARM-UP for *Chapter opener*
Students are already familiar with the word *comer,* introduced in *Capítulo 2.* This is a good opportunity to ask them to think about the types of foods and Hispanic dishes they have already learned about in previous chapters.

METHODOLOGY • Making Topics Relevant for Students
The text and questions for this chapter opener are completely in Spanish, just as in *Capítulos 4* and *5.* Note that the questions begin with your learners and their preferences, a technique we have learned from educational philosopher John Dewey. Try having your students turn to their partners and answer the questions in pairs. Then have them share the answers their partners gave. This has them practice listening and also paraphrasing.

21ST CENTURY SKILLS • JOHN DEWEY
Educational philosopher John Dewey (1859–1952) had a profound effect on the U.S. educational system in the most positive of ways. A man well before his time, he had insight into many of the issues that would later develop in the world of education. For example, he maintained that all learners would need to take an interdisciplinary approach to learning. *¡Anda!* is based heavily on the philosophies of this visionary man.

EXPANSION for *Preguntas*
Ask students whether they are aware of dishes with the same names that are prepared differently. You may want to tell them about the difference between *la tortilla mexicana* (of corn or flour) and *la tortilla española* (potato omelet).
    You may also want to ask your students the following questions:
1. *En tu experiencia, ¿a qué tipo de comida se refiere la expresión "Spanish food"?*
2. *¿Hay restaurantes hispanos en nuestra ciudad? ¿Qué platos tienen?*

🔑 **Instructor Resources**
• Textbook images, Extra Activities

SECTION GOALS for
Comunicación I

By the end of the *Comunicación I* section, students will be able to:

• compare main dishes and cuisine from the United States and Hispanic countries.
• express preferences about food.
• categorize food into appropriate breakfast, lunch, or dinner menus.
• pronounce the letters *r* and *rr* properly.
• describe how the schedule for mealtimes differs between the United States and some Hispanic countries.
• narrate events and actions that occurred in the preterit tense.
• identify verbs with spelling changes in the preterit.
• select key words that trigger the use of the preterit.
• review the forms, uses, and placement of direct object pronouns.

NOTE for *La comida*

The Spanish language is rich with vocabulary for food and there are many variations among countries and regions. Refer students to the *También se dice…* section in Appendix 3 for additional words.

METHODOLOGY •
Assessment

In *Capítulo 1*, we talked about the fact that assessment comes in a variety of forms. The two basic categories are *formal* and *informal*. *Formal* assessment includes the end-of-chapter written and oral tests. It also includes periodic quizzes that you may give. *Informal* assessment is the daily process that we use as instructors to evaluate the progress of our students. Some of us give class participation grades. The authors suggest a class participation grade that includes students using the target language throughout the class and the effort the students put into their assignments.

METHODOLOGY •
Assessment Domains

As previously noted, there are two main types of assessment: *formal* and *informal*. Within those two types, there are three domains/modes by which we can assess our students: *interpretive, interpersonal,* and *presentational*. When students read a passage, as with the Chapter opener, and then respond to comprehension and critical thinking questions, you are employing the *interpretive* mode. When students work in pairs / groups, you are able to assess them in the *interpersonal* mode. Finally, when students present an assignment to a partner / group, or the class, it constitutes the *presentational* mode.

Comunicación I

1 VOCABULARIO

🔊 📖
07-01 to 07-07

5:00

La comida Discussing food

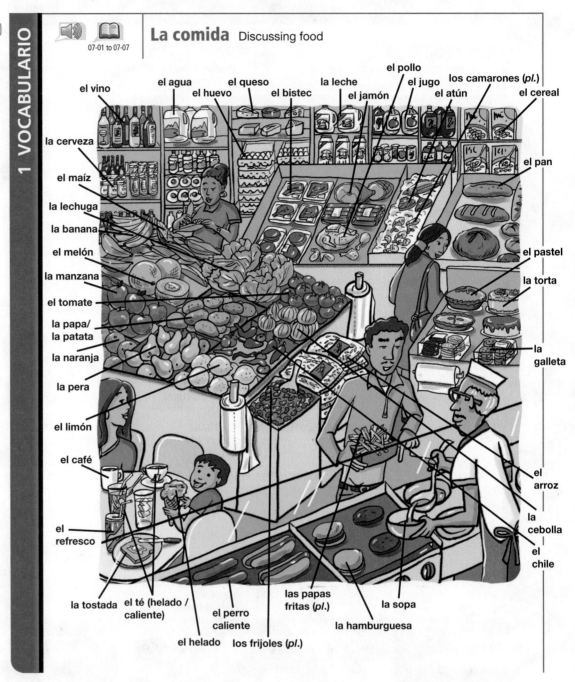

METHODOLOGY • Teaching Vocabulary

Research concludes that learning vocabulary is best achieved when images are associated with the target words rather than learning from lists of words that are not illustrated. The "Where's Waldo?" style images created for presenting the thematic chapter vocabulary in *¡Anda! Curso elemental* are intentionally rich. They are best appreciated either online or in transparency format where the images are enlarged from the print format. What may initially be difficult to discern will be clarified when the learner makes the connection to the artwork.

NOTE for *La comida*

Almorzar, introduced in *Capítulo 4,* is included in this list of new verbs to emphasize the connection between the noun for each meal and its corresponding verb.

NOTE for *La comida*

You may want to remind students that in *Capítulo 2* they learned "tomar" as "to drink" as well as "to take."

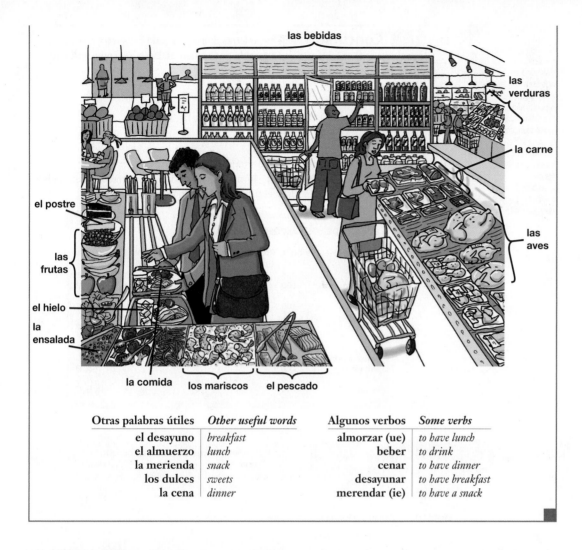

las bebidas

las verduras

la carne

las aves

el postre

las frutas

el hielo

la ensalada

la comida   los mariscos   el pescado

Otras palabras útiles	Other useful words	Algunos verbos	Some verbs
el desayuno	breakfast	almorzar (ue)	to have lunch
el almuerzo	lunch	beber	to drink
la merienda	snack	cenar	to have dinner
los dulces	sweets	desayunar	to have breakfast
la cena	dinner	merendar (ie)	to have a snack

PRONUNCIACIÓN

The different pronunciations of r and rr

¡Hola!

07-08 to 07-11

Go to MySpanishLab / Student Activities Manual to learn about the letters *r* and *rr*.

SECTION GOALS for *Pronunciación*

By the end of the *Pronunciación* section, students will be able to:
- distinguish between the sounds for *r* and *rr*.
- spell words correctly by hearing the *r* sound or the *rr* sound.

METHODOLOGY • Making Students Accountable for Their Own Learning

By creating a student-centered class, you reinforce the fact that your students are ultimately accountable for their own learning.

METHODOLOGY • Organizing the Student-Centered Classroom

When we say that *¡Anda! Curso elemental* supports and helps create a student-centered classroom, we mean that the presentations and activities afford students the maximum amount of time to practice Spanish in a classroom-controlled setting. Having your students work with partners provides them with an increased amount of time to speak Spanish. What follows are some ideas to help you maximize the effectiveness of your student-centered class.

1. Change partners daily. This gives all students the opportunity to work with everyone in the class on multiple occasions. Some days you can place two strong students together; other days you can pair a strong and a weak student. Still other days you may choose to pair students with similar hobbies or interests. You can also pair students randomly or in fun ways, such as according to their birth dates or their favorite colors.

2. You may wish to assign a variety of pair activities on the board at the beginning of the class so that students may work with their partners in 15–20 minute intervals. This might mean assigning up to 10 activities that the groups can work on at their own pace.

3. During pair work, students need to know that they are accountable for staying on task and for performing up to your expectations. Therefore, after 15–20 minute intervals, you may choose to have several groups report on some of their responses.

4. You may be familiar with the term *classroom management (discipline) by proximity*. You will have pairs of students that will find it difficult to stay on task. As you circulate around the room while the students are working together, make a point of positioning yourself frequently in close proximity to the pairs that need more monitoring.

5. Making class participation a significant component of the final grade for the class helps to keep students on task. When students understand that you expect them to speak in Spanish, to take turns, and to work well with others, AND that you will be grading them on their classroom behavior, it helps them understand the importance of their work in the classroom.

6. Not all groups will finish all items of all activities during a class period. That is fine, since students have been moving at the pace necessary for them to learn. During a subsequent class period when students are working with new partners, you can have a list of review pair activities that students can work on if they finish early. These would be the communicative activities at the end of each *chunk*. Even though your students are repeating an activity that they may have already done, the fact that they are working with a new partner and a new context will help to retain their interest.

Fíjate

Although *agua* and *ave* are feminine nouns, the masculine singular article *el* is used with them (*el agua, el ave*), as a way to separate and differentiate the similar stressed vowel sounds in each word (*la* and *a*). *Las* is used with the plurals of these words (*las aguas, las aves*). All adjectives describing these words are feminine (*el agua fría / las aguas frías*).

 7-1 **Concurso** Escoge **cinco** letras diferentes. Bajo cada letra escribe todas las palabras del vocabulario de **La comida** que recuerdes. Después, compara tu lista con la de un/a compañero/a. ■

MODELO	a	d	p
	arroz	desayuno	papas fritas
	agua	dulce	

 7-2 **¡Ay, las calorías!** Túrnense para decir a qué comida corresponden las siguientes descripciones. Usen el cuadro de los valores nutritivos. ■

CUADRO DE LOS VALORES NUTRITIVOS

Comida	Calorías	Proteínas (gramos)	Grasas (gramos)	Carbohidratos (gramos)	Vitaminas
bistec	455	27	36	0	A, B
hamburguesa con queso	950	50	60	54	B
jugo de naranja	100	1	0	16	A, B, C
naranja	50	1	0	16	A, B, C
pan	150	6	2	38	B
papa	100	3	0	23	B, C
perro caliente	200	5	14	1	B, C
salmón	200	24	10	0	A, B
torta	455	4	13	76	A, B, C
lechuga	10	1	0	2	A, B, C

 Capítulo Preliminar A. Los números 0–30, pág. 16 del eText; Capítulo 1. Los números 31–100, pág. 47 del eText; Capítulo 2. Los números 100–1.000, pág. 72 del eText.

Estrategia

¡Anda! Curso elemental has provided you with recycling references to help guide your continuous review of previously learned material. Make sure to consult the indicated pages if you need to refresh your memory about numbers.

MODELO   E1: *Esta comida tiene mucha agua, es verde y tiene diez calorías.*
         E2: *Es la lechuga.*

Esta comida tiene...

1. 60 gramos (*grams*) de grasas, 50 gramos de proteínas y 950 calorías. la hamburguesa con queso
2. muchas proteínas, es un pescado y tiene 200 calorías. el salmón
3. vitamina C, es una verdura y tiene 100 calorías. la papa
4. muchos carbohidratos y 150 calorías. el pan
5. 27 gramos de proteínas, es una carne y tiene 455 calorías. el bistec
6. 50 calorías y es una fruta. la naranja
7. 16 gramos de carbohidratos y es una bebida. el jugo de naranja
8. las vitaminas B y C, sólo un gramo de carbohidratos y 14 gramos de grasa. el perro caliente

NATIONAL STANDARDS
Communication
Activity **7-4** is an excellent opportunity for students to communicate meaningful preferences. Also, if you are beginning a new semester and have new students, the next activity is a good way to help them get acquainted and build classroom community.

The interpersonal communicative activities like **7-4,** in which students are working together to piece together information, promote Standard 1.1. They are engaging in conversations, providing and obtaining information, and exchanging their opinions about their eating habits and foods they like or dislike. If you ask students to write down their daily eating schedules and menus and to present them to the class, you can satisfy Standard 1.3 as well.

EXPANSION for 7-4
You may wish to have each student interview another student so that when reporting, he/she will say, *Él/Ella…*

Capítulo 2. El verbo *gustar*. pág. 80 del eText.

   7-3 **¿Cuáles son tus preferencias?** ¿Qué comidas te gustan? ■

Workbooklet

Paso 1   Completa el cuadro según tus preferencias.

Estrategia
You may want to talk about foods that are not included here. Refer to the *También se dice…* section in Appendix 3 for additional vocabulary.

1. Las carnes, las aves, el pescado y los mariscos que…	
a. más me gustan son…	b. menos me gustan son…
1.	1.
2.	2.
2. Las frutas y verduras que…	
a. más me gustan son…	b. menos me gustan son…
1.	1.
2.	2.

Paso 2   Ahora, compara tus preferencias con las de los compañeros de la clase: ¿Cuáles son sus comidas favoritas? ¿Qué comidas les gustan menos?

MODELO   E1:   *¿Cuál es tu carne favorita?*

E2:   *No me gusta la carne, pero me gusta mucho el pollo. ¿Y a ti?*

Capítulo Preliminar A. La hora, pág. 18 del eText; Capítulo Preliminar A. Los días, los meses y las estaciones, pág. 20 del eText.

   7-4   **La dieta de Nico**   Nico es un estudiante universitario de Santiago de Chile. Mira lo que (*what*) come normalmente y cuándo lo come. Después completa los siguientes pasos. ■

Workbooklet

Fíjate
The word *galleta* means both *cookie* and *cracker*.

Fíjate
While *patata* is used in Spain, *papa* is widely used in Latin America.

LA DIETA DE NICO

	DESAYUNO	ALMUERZO	MERIENDA	CENA
	8:30	12:00	5:30	8:00
DÍA 1:	té con galletas	ensalada, arroz con pollo y uvas	manzana	atún con una ensalada de lechuga con tomate y fruta
DÍA 2:	té y pan con mantequilla	sopa, tortilla de papas y flan	galletas	pan con mermelada

Paso 1   Ahora completa el cuadro con tu información.

TU DIETA

	DESAYUNO	ALMUERZO	MERIENDA	CENA
DÍA 1:				
DÍA 2:				

Paso 2   Con un/a compañero/a, comparen su información con la de Nico.

MODELO   E1:   *Yo nunca tomo té en el desayuno. Generalmente desayuno más temprano que Nico. ¿Y tú?*

E2:   *Yo desayuno a las siete y media y generalmente como huevos y tostadas.*

Vocabulario útil	
más temprano que	*earlier than*
más tarde que	*later than*

Paso 3 Miren la pirámide de alimentación para determinar si todos los grupos están representados en sus dietas.

MODELO E1: *Comemos pan en el desayuno y a veces en la cena.*

E2: *Comemos papas y ensaladas de lechuga y tomate, pero no comemos muchas otras verduras.*

E1: *Tienes razón, pero comemos mucha fruta…*

  7-5 ¿Qué comes tú? Entrevista a un/a compañero/a usando las siguientes preguntas. ■

1. ¿Comes bien o mal? Explica.
2. ¿Qué tipo de comida prefieres?
3. ¿Qué te gusta merendar?
4. ¿Qué comidas tienen vitamina C y calcio?
5. ¿Qué comidas tienen mucha proteína?
6. ¿Qué comidas no te gustan?

NOTA CULTURAL

¡Hola!   eText p. 261   07-12   **Las comidas en el mundo hispano**

NOTE for *Nota cultural.*
See eText pg. 261 for complete *Nota cultural* reading and *Preguntas.*

2 GRAMÁTICA

Repaso del complemento directo
Communicating with less repetition

07-13 to 07-17 Spanish/English Tutorials

¿Postre? Tenemos...

¡Los quiero todos!

In **Capítulo 5** you learned to use **direct object pronouns** in Spanish. Return to pages 132–133 for a quick review, then answer the following questions:

¡Explícalo tú!

1. What are **direct objects**? What are **direct object pronouns**?
2. What are the pronouns (forms)? With what must they agree?
3. Where are direct object pronouns placed in a sentence?

✓ Check your answers to the preceding questions in Appendix 1.

7-6 Las dietas ¿Piensas mucho en lo que comes? ■

Paso 1 Subraya (*Underline*) los complementos directos en las siguientes preguntas. Compara tus respuestas con las de un/a compañero/a.

MODELO ¿Conoces <u>la dieta Weight Watchers</u>?

1. ¿Sigues la dieta Nutrisystem?
2. ¿Prefieres los postres de chocolate?
3. ¿Sabes preparar bien el arroz?
4. ¿Comes muchas frutas diferentes?
5. ¿Preparas los huevos con queso?
6. ¿Lavas la lechuga bien antes de comerla?

Paso 2 Ahora contesten juntos las preguntas de Paso 1, usando los pronombres de complemento directo en sus respuestas.

MODELO E1: ¿Conoces <u>la dieta Weight Watchers</u>?

E2: *Sí, la conozco. / No, no la conozco.*

Instructor Resources
• PPT, Extra Activities

NOTE for *Repaso del complemento directo*
Direct object pronouns are reviewed here and recycled throughout the chapter in anticipation of the presentation of indirect object pronouns in *Capítulo 8*.

EXPANSION for 7-7
Have students create their own lists of food and drink items, then circulate among their classmates asking how often they eat / drink them.

METHODOLOGY • Grammar Presentations
Grammar presentations in *¡Anda! Curso elemental* are done deductively, inductively, or in a combination of both. With a *deductive* approach students are given the rules / forms and apply them in practice. With an *inductive* approach students are given examples of a grammar concept and, through the use of guiding questions, formulate the rule in their own words. Another way of saying this is that they construct their own knowledge. The research reports that students learn best from inductive grammar approaches by remembering and internalizing the rules better. So you might ask, why not present *all* grammar inductively? The main reason is that the inductive approach takes more time, and some grammar points may not merit the additional time.

NOTE for *Gramática*
This is an inductive grammar presentation in which the students are given examples of a grammar concept and through the use of guiding questions, they formulate the rule in their own words. Research indicates that students remember and internalize grammar rules better when they construct their own knowledge.

SUGGESTION for *El pretérito*
Orally or in writing, explain your daily routine for your students. Then, repeat the routine, this time in the preterit to share what you did yesterday. Be careful to use only verbs that are regular in the preterit. Have students repeat the things you did to you.

3:00   **7-7** ## Las buenas decisiones
Túrnense para expresar cómo les gusta tomar las siguientes comidas y bebidas y con qué frecuencia las toman. ∎

nunca	algunas veces	generalmente	constantemente	siempre

MODELO   E1: *la torta*
          E2: *La como con helado. La como algunas veces. / No la como nunca.*

1.

2.

3.

4.

5.

6.

3:00 **3 GRAMÁTICA**

07-18 to 07-22   *¡Hola!* Spanish/English Tutorials

El pretérito (Parte I)
Describing things that happened in the past

Up to this point, you have been expressing ideas or actions that take place in the present and future. To talk about something you did or something that occurred in the past, you can use the **pretérito** (*preterit*). Below are the endings for regular verbs in the **pretérito**.

Los verbos regulares
Note the endings for regular verbs in the **pretérito** below and answer the questions that follow.

🔑 **Instructor Resources**
• PPT, Extra Activities

	-ar: comprar	-er: comer	-ir: vivir
yo	compré	comí	viví
tú	compraste	comiste	viviste
Ud.	compró	comió	vivió
él/ella	compró	comió	vivió
nosotros/as	compramos	comimos	vivimos
vosotros/as	comprasteis	comisteis	vivisteis
Uds.	compraron	comieron	vivieron
ellos/as	compraron	comieron	vivieron

¡Explícalo tú!

1. What do you notice about the endings for **-er** and **-ir** verbs?
2. Where are accent marks needed?

✔ Check your answers to the preceding questions in Appendix 1.

Estrategia

Remember that there are two types of grammar presentations in *¡Anda!*:

1. You are given the grammar rule.
2. You are given guiding questions to help *you* construct the grammar rule, and state the rule in your own words.

—¿Dónde está el vino que **compré** ayer?
—Mis primos **bebieron** la botella entera anoche.
—¿Ah, sí? ¿**Comieron** ustedes en casa?
—No, **comimos** en un restaurante chino. ¡Ellos **terminaron** el vino antes de salir a cenar!

Where is the wine that I bought yesterday?
My cousins drank the whole bottle last night.
Really? Did you all eat at home?
No, we ate at a Chinese restaurant. They finished the wine before we went out to dinner!

[3:00] **7-8** **De la teoría a la práctica** Write six different infinitives on six small pieces of paper. Next, on six different small pieces of paper, write six different subject pronouns. Take turns selecting a paper from each pile and give the correct **pretérito** form of the verb. After several rounds, write another six verbs. ■

[3:00] 👥 **7-9** *Tic-tac-toe* Make a grid, like one for tic-tac-toe. With a partner, select one **-ar** verb. Write a different preterit form of the verb in each blank space on your grid. Each of you should write each preterit form with a different pronoun. Do not show your partner what you have written. Take turns randomly selecting pronouns and say the corresponding verb forms. When you say a form of the verb that your partner has, your partner marks an X over the word. The first person to get three X's either vertically, horizontally, or diagonally wins the round. After doing a round with **-ar** verbs, repeat with **-er** and **-ir** verbs. ■

MODELO   E1: *tú comiste*
            E2: (marks X over *tu comiste*)

tú comiste	ellos comieron	ellas comieron
yo comí	Uds. comieron	nosotros comimos
él comió	Ud. comió	ella comió

NOTE for 7-8
You may want to assign the preparation for this activity as homework. Not only will this make the implementation of this activity more efficient, but it will also help students anticipate one of the many activities they will be completing in class.

7-10 Cocinero/a Tu compañero/a y tú van a preparar una cena especial para sus amigos. Para saber si todo está listo, túrnense para contestar las siguientes preguntas usando el pretérito y un pronombre de complemento directo (**lo, la, los, las**). ∎

MODELO   E1:   ¿Compraste la carne?
               E2:   *Sí, la compré.*

1. ¿Compraste los refrescos?
2. ¿Cocinaste tus platos (*dishes*) favoritos?
3. ¿Preparaste una mesa bonita?
4. ¿Limpiaste el comedor?
5. ¿Mandaste las invitaciones?

7-11 Una comida Escribe un párrafo sobre una comida que preparaste para un amigo. Usa por lo menos **cinco** verbos en el pretérito. Lee tu párrafo a un/a compañero/a de clase y comparen sus experiencias. ∎

4 GRAMÁTICA

 ¡Hola!
07-23 to 07-26   Spanish/English Tutorials

El pretérito (Parte II)
Describing things that happened in the past

Los verbos que terminan en *-car, -zar* y *-gar* y el verbo *leer*

Several verbs have small spelling changes in the preterit. Look at the following charts.

> **Fíjate**
> The *-ar* and *-er* stem-changing verbs in the present tense do not have stem changes in the preterit. There may be spelling changes, however, as with *empezar* and *jugar*.

Hoy corrí cinco millas, jugué al tenis, toqué el piano por dos horas, leí una novela, empecé la tarea para la clase de español. . .

Instructor Resources
• PPT, Extra Activities

tocar (c → qu)	
yo	toqué
tú	tocaste
Ud.	tocó
él/ella	tocó
nosotros/as	tocamos
vosotros/as	tocasteis
Uds.	tocaron
ellos/ellas	tocaron

* (**sacar** and **buscar** have the same spelling change)

empezar (z → c)	
yo	empecé
tú	empezaste
Ud.	empezó
él/ella	empezó
nosotros/as	empezamos
vosotros/as	empezasteis
Uds.	empezaron
ellos/ellas	empezaron

* (**comenzar** and **organizar** have the same spelling change)

jugar (g → gu)	
yo	jugué
tú	jugaste
Ud.	jugó
él/ella	jugó
nosotros/as	jugamos
vosotros/as	jugasteis
Uds.	jugaron
ellos/as	jugaron

* (**llegar** has the same spelling change)

leer (i → y)	
yo	leí
tú	leíste
Ud.	leyó
él/ella	leyó
nosotros/as	leímos
vosotros/as	leísteis
Uds.	leyeron
ellos/as	leyeron

* (**creer** and **oír** have the same spelling change)

—**Toqué** la guitarra con el conjunto de mariachi en un restaurante mexicano anoche.

I played the guitar with a mariachi band at a Mexican restaurant last night.

—¿A qué hora **empezaste**?

At what time did you begin?

—**Empecé** a las nueve.

I began at nine.

—¿**Jugaron** tus hermanos al béisbol hoy?

Did your brothers play baseball today?

—No, **leyeron** un libro de recetas porque van a preparar una cena especial para nuestros padres.

No, they read a recipe book because they are going to prepare a special dinner for our parents.

Some things to remember:

1. With verbs that end in **-car,** the **c** changes to **qu** in the **yo** form to preserve the sound of the hard **c** of the infinitive.
2. With verbs that end in **-zar,** the **z** changes to **c** before **e.**
3. With verbs that end in **-gar,** the **g** changes to **gu** to preserve the sound of the hard **g** (**g** before **e** or **i** sounds like the **j** sound in Spanish).
4. For **leer, creer,** and **oír,** change the **i** to **y** in the third-person singular and plural.

[3:00] **7-12** **¡Apúrate!** One person makes a ball out of a piece of paper, says a subject pronoun and a verb in its infinitive form, and tosses the ball to someone in the group. That person catches it, gives the corresponding form of the verb in the preterit, then says another pronoun and tosses the ball to someone else. ■

MODELO   E1: *yo; comprar*

E2: *compré; ellas escribir*

E3: *escribieron; usted comer*

E4: *comió;…*

[4:00] **7-13** **Creaciones**

Paso 1   Combinen elementos de las tres columnas para escribir **ocho** oraciones que describan lo que hicieron las siguientes personas.

MODELO   Yolanda   comprar   mucho helado
Yolanda compró mucho helado.

Yolanda	beber	la televisión durante la cena
usted	limpiar	cuatro botellas de agua
los estudiantes	preparar	mucho helado
yo	buscar	dos hamburguesas con queso
mi mejor amigo y yo	leer	la cocina después del almuerzo
tú	ver	una cena deliciosa
mis primos	comprar	el restaurante La Frontera
el/la profesor/a	comer	sobre el gran cocinero Emeril Lagasse

Paso 2   Túrnense para preguntarse cuándo ocurrió cada actividad mencionada en **Paso 1**.

E1: *¿Cuándo compró Yolanda mucho helado?*

E2: *Compró mucho helado ayer. / Lo compró ayer.*

Fijate

In the list of *Vocabulario útil*, note that for the words "last weekend" (*el fin de semana pasado*), the adjective *pasado* agrees with the masculine noun *el fin* and not *semana*. In contrast, for "last week" (*la semana pasada*), the word "last" agrees with the feminine noun *semana*.

Vocabulario útil	
anoche	*last night*
anteayer	*the day before yesterday*
ayer	*yesterday*
el año pasado	*last year*
el fin de semana pasado	*last weekend*
el martes / viernes / domingo, etc., pasado	*last Tuesday / Friday / Sunday, etc.*
la semana pasada	*last week*

NOTE for 7-13
This activity provides an opportunity to practice listening. In pairs, have students take turns reading their sentences aloud. As one reads, the other traces a light line connecting the appropriate items from each column. You may also want students to write some of their sentences on the board for follow-up.

EXPANSION for 7-13
Activity **7-13** can be turned into a writing activity if, once the answers from the chart are compiled, you assign an expansion paragraph to each student who answered a topic affirmatively. If students answered that they ate in a restaurant last Saturday, for example, you could ask them for more details in the preterit, such as what they ordered, whether they spoke with the waiter, whether they left a tip, how the food tasted, etc.

EXPANSION for 7-13
Have each student write a sentence about something they have done recently. Collect the slips of paper and read them to the class, having students guess who wrote each one.

Capítulo 3. La casa, pág. 98 del eText; Capítulo 3. Los quehaceres de la casa, pág. 109 del eText.

[4:00] **7-14** Los quehaceres de Inés

Paso 1 Escribe una oración sobre cada quehacer que terminó Inés.

MODELO *Inés barrió el suelo.*

1. la ropa
2. la aspiradora
3. el baño
4. los muebles
5. la basura
6. el armario

Paso 2 Comparte tus oraciones con un/a compañero/a.

MODELO E1: el suelo

E2: *Inés barrió el suelo.*

E1: *Inés…*

Paso 3 Túrnense para decir qué hizo Inés en el centro después de terminar sus quehaceres. Sigan el modelo.

MODELO E1: el correo

E2: *Compró sellos.*

1. la librería
2. el cine
3. el banco
4. el cibercafé
5. la biblioteca
6. el café
7. el supermercado
8. la tienda

[4:00] **7-15** ¿Y cuándo…? Entrevista a un/a compañero/a para saber cuándo ocurrieron las siguientes cosas. ■

MODELO ¿Cuándo… (tú) comprar la lechuga?

E1: *¿Cuándo compraste la lechuga?*

E2: *La compré el sábado pasado.*

¿Cuándo…?

1. (tú) tocar el piano tocaste / toqué
2. (tus amigos) visitar a sus padres visitaron / visitaron
3. (tú) comprar un CD nuevo compraste / compré
4. (tus amigos y tú) comer un plato increíble en un restaurante comieron / comimos
5. (tú) empezar tus estudios universitarios empezaste / empecé
6. (tu profesor/a) leer una novela de John Grisham leyó / leyó
7. (tus amigos y tú) bailar el tango bailaron / bailamos
8. (ustedes) invitar a un amigo a una fiesta invitaron / invitamos

Capítulo 2. La formación de preguntas, pág. 70 del eText; Capítulo 5. Los pronombres de complemento directo, pág. 189 del eText.

5:00   Workbooklet   **7-16** **¿Te puedo hacer una pregunta?** Entrevista a cinco estudiantes diferentes y anota sus respuestas (**sí** o **no**). Después, compara tus respuestas con las de los otros estudiantes de la clase. ¿Cuáles son las tendencias? ◼

MODELO   arreglar el cuarto hoy

TÚ: *¿Arreglaste tu cuarto hoy?*

E1: *Sí, lo arreglé.*

E2: *No, no lo arreglé.*

E3: *Sí, arreglé mi cuarto.*

E4: *No, no arreglé mi cuarto.*

E5: *No, yo no lo arreglé, pero mi compañero lo arregló.*

	E1	E2	E3	E4	E5
1. arreglar el cuarto hoy					
2. comer en un restaurante el sábado pasado					
3. estudiar anoche					
4. lavar los platos ayer					
5. hablar por teléfono con los padres anteayer					
6. jugar al golf el verano pasado					
7. escribir un ensayo para la clase de inglés la semana pasada					
8. terminar la tarea para la clase de español anoche					

¿Cómo andas? I

	Feel confident	Need to review
Having completed **Comunicación I**, I now can . . .		
• discuss food (p. 158)	☐	☐
• pronounce the different sounds of **r** and **rr** (MSL/SAM)	☐	☐
• discuss eating habits (p. 162)	☐	☐
• communicate with less repetition using direct object pronouns (p. 163)	☐	☐
• describe things that happened in the past (Part I) (p. 164)	☐	☐
• describe things that happened in the past (Part II) (p. 166)	☐	☐

Comunicación II

3:00

5 VOCABULARIO

07-27 to 07-30

La preparación de las comidas
Explaining food preparation

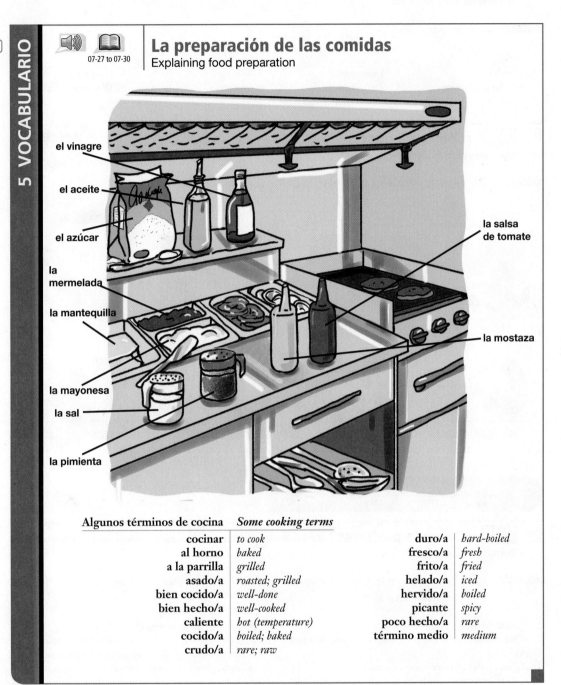

el vinagre

el aceite

el azúcar

la mermelada

la mantequilla

la mayonesa

la sal

la pimienta

la salsa de tomate

la mostaza

Algunos términos de cocina	*Some cooking terms*		
cocinar	*to cook*	**duro/a**	*hard-boiled*
al horno	*baked*	**fresco/a**	*fresh*
a la parrilla	*grilled*	**frito/a**	*fried*
asado/a	*roasted; grilled*	**helado/a**	*iced*
bien cocido/a	*well-done*	**hervido/a**	*boiled*
bien hecho/a	*well-cooked*	**picante**	*spicy*
caliente	*hot (temperature)*	**poco hecho/a**	*rare*
cocido/a	*boiled; baked*	**término medio**	*medium*
crudo/a	*rare; raw*		

7-17 La asociación Digan una palabra o expresión que asocian con cada condimento, especia o término de la siguiente lista. ■

MODELO   E1: picante

            E2: *salsa*

1. frito/a
2. la salsa de tomate
3. crudo/a
4. la mayonesa
5. el azúcar
6. a la parrilla
7. fresco/a
8. al horno
9. la mostaza
10. la mantequilla

7-18 ¡Cómo me gustan! Digan cómo les gusta preparar las siguientes comidas. ■

MODELO   *Me gustan los perros calientes a la parrilla con mostaza y salsa de tomate.*

1.   2.   3.   4.

5.   6.   7.   8.

♻ Capítulo 4. Los verbos con cambio de raíz, pág. 142 del eText, Capítulo 5. Los pronombres de complemento directo, pág. 189 del eText.

7-19 ¿Cómo lo prefieres? Entrevista a un/a compañero/a para conocer sus preferencias. Después cambien de papel. ■

MODELO   E1: ¿Cómo prefieres tu hamburguesa?

            E2: *La quiero término medio.*

1. ¿Cómo prefieres tu bistec?
2. ¿Qué condimentos usaste la última vez que comiste el bistec?
3. ¿Cómo pides tu refresco, con o sin hielo?
4. ¿Cómo preparaste los huevos la última vez que los comiste?
5. ¿Cómo prefieres la pizza?
6. ¿Cómo tomaste el té la última vez que lo bebiste, helado o caliente? ¿Lo tomaste con o sin azúcar?
7. ¿Cómo prefieres la sopa, con mucha o poca sal?
8. ¿Cómo tomaste el café esta mañana?

NOTA CULTURAL

¡Hola!
eText p. 271   07-31

La comida hispana

NOTE for *Nota cultural.*
See eText pg. 271 for complete *Nota cultural* reading and *Preguntas.*

8:00

6 GRAMÁTICA

07-32 to 07-37   Spanish/English Tutorials   ¡Hola!

Algunos verbos irregulares en el pretérito
Describing things that happened in the past

In **Comunicación I** you learned about verbs that are regular in the **pretérito** and others that have spelling changes. The following verbs are *irregular* in the **pretérito**; they follow patterns of their own. Study the verb charts to determine the similarities and differences among the forms.

Ayer anduvimos diez millas.

	andar (*to walk*)	estar	tener
yo	anduve	estuve	tuve
tú	anduviste	estuviste	tuviste
Ud.	anduvo	estuvo	tuvo
él/ella	anduvo	estuvo	tuvo
nosotros/as	anduvimos	estuvimos	tuvimos
vosotros/as	anduvisteis	estuvisteis	tuvisteis
Uds.	anduvieron	estuvieron	tuvieron
ellos/ellas	anduvieron	estuvieron	tuvieron

—El lunes pasado llegamos a Santiago y **anduvimos** mucho por la ciudad.
—¿**Estuvieron** en un restaurante o bar interesante?
—Sí, **tuvimos** mucha suerte y comimos en el mejor restaurante de la ciudad.

Last Monday we arrived in Santiago and walked a lot throughout the city.
Were you all in an interesting restaurant or bar?

Yes, we were very lucky and we ate at the best restaurant in the city.

	conducir (*to drive*)	traer	decir
yo	conduje	traje	dije
tú	condujiste	trajiste	dijiste
Ud.	condujo	trajo	dijo
él/ella	condujo	trajo	dijo
nosotros/as	condujimos	trajimos	dijimos
vosotros/as	condujisteis	trajisteis	dijisteis
Uds.	condujeron	trajeron	dijeron
ellos/as	condujeron	trajeron	dijeron

Fíjate
Note that the third-person plural ending of *conducir, decir,* and *traer* is *-eron.*

(continued)

ANSWERS to *Nota cultural* (Online)
1. *Answers may vary.*
2. *Possible answer:* La comida del Caribe tiene / lleva muchos condimentos y el arroz, el plátano, los mariscos y los frijoles son importantes. El arroz y los frijoles también son importantes en los países centroamericanos y en México. La comida de Sudamérica tiene mucha carne.

METHODOLOGY • The Preterit
The authors have chosen to present these irregular verbs together with regular verbs for more varied and richer practice. You may choose to divide the verbs into two or three groups and have students practice the forms with mechanical activities like **7-8.** For students who need additional practice, refer them to MySpanishLab, the Electronic Activities Cache, or the Student Activities Manual.

SUGGESTION for *Algunos verbos irregulares en el pretérito*
If you think now is an appropriate time, point out to your students that the verbs *querer* and *saber* change meaning in the preterit. For example, in the preterit, *querer* usually means "tried to," *no querer* means "refused," and *saber* means "found out."

NATIONAL STANDARDS
Cultures, Comparisons
The online reading, *La comida hispana,* provides cultural information about various Spanish-speaking regions throughout the world. Students learn about the main dishes, the ingredients, and the seasonings commonly used in Hispanic cooking. This information explains how the geographic location affects the diet and food choices, determining which ingredients and products are readily available. Students see how geography and climate affect the practices, the products, and the perspectives of Hispanic cultures (Standards 2.1, 2.2). There is great variety in the Hispanic diet, and the reading offers a brief outline of how food differs across the regions of Spain, Mexico, the Caribbean, and South America. Students can compare how *la comida hispana* differs from their own diet, and they can also compare how it varies across Spanish-speaking countries (Standard 4.2).

NOTE for *La comida hispana* (Online)
The authors understand that this chapter deals with the preterit tense and ideally the *Nota cultural* reading would incorporate that form. The nature of cultural notes, however, generally dictate that they be written in the present tense. For readings that contextualize both the grammar and the vocabulary of the chapter, be sure to assign and discuss the *Ambiciones siniestras* episodes.

NOTE for *Nota cultural* (Online)
You may choose to supplement your discussion with information about Hispanic foods in the U.S., perhaps contrasting "tex-mex" food with authentic Mexican food, and African influences on Hispanic food (*Afromestizo* cooking).

EXPANSION for *La comida hispana* (Online)
Additional questions to ask your students are:
1. ¿Dónde preparan muchos platos con arroz?
2. ¿Cuál es una de las especialidades de España? ¿Cuáles son algunos de los ingredientes de los platos típicos de México?
3. ¿Por qué crees que comen tanta (so much) carne de res en Uruguay y Argentina?
4. ¿Cuáles son algunos platos típicos de la región donde vives? ¿Y en la región dónde vive tu familia?

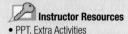
Instructor Resources
• PPT, Extra Activities

SUGGESTION for *Algunos verbos irregulares*
You may want to relate the following "experience" or create one of your own, using the irregular verbs presented. You can then have students make lists of the verb forms they hear, answer comprehension questions, or create an "experience" of their own with the verbs.

Ayer fue un día muy interesante. Por la mañana conduje al campo donde anduve cinco millas. Vi muchos animales y pude tomar muchas fotos. Mis amigos vinieron conmigo y trajeron un picnic fabuloso. Prepararon unos sándwiches de jamón y queso, ensalada de fruta y limonada. El almuerzo fue delicioso. Después de almorzar dormimos la siesta. ¡Luego anduvimos otras cinco millas!

—¿**Condujiste** de Santiago a Valparaíso?
—No pude conducir porque no **traje** mi licencia.
—¿Qué te **dijeron** en la agencia Avis?

Did you drive from Santiago to Valparaíso?
I couldn't drive because I didn't bring my driver's license.
What did they tell you at the Avis (car rental) agency?

	ir	ser
yo	fui	fui
tú	fuiste	fuiste
Ud.	fue	fue
él/ella	fue	fue
nosotros/as	fuimos	fuimos
vosotros/as	fuisteis	fuisteis
Uds.	fueron	fueron
ellos/as	fueron	fueron

Fíjate
Note that *ser* and *ir* have the same forms in the preterit. You must rely on the context of the sentence or conversation to determine the meaning.

—¿Cómo **fue** el viaje a Chile?
—¡**Fue** increíble! Después de Valparaíso **fuimos** a Patagonia.

How was the trip to Chile?
It was incredible! After Valparaíso, we went to Patagonia.

	dar	ver	venir
yo	di	vi	vine
tú	diste	viste	viniste
Ud.	dio	vio	vino
él/ella	dio	vio	vino
nosotros/as	dimos	vimos	vinimos
vosotros/as	disteis	visteis	vinisteis
Uds.	dieron	vieron	vinieron
ellos/as	dieron	vieron	vinieron

	hacer	querer
yo	hice	quise
tú	hiciste	quisiste
Ud.	hizo	quiso
él/ella	hizo	quiso
nosotros/as	hicimos	quisimos
vosotros/as	hicisteis	quisisteis
Uds.	hicieron	quisieron
ellos/as	hicieron	quisieron

Fíjate
The third-person singular form of *hacer* has a spelling change (*c* to *z*): *hizo*.

	poder	poner	saber
yo	pude	puse	supe
tú	pudiste	pusiste	supiste
Ud.	pudo	puso	supo
él/ella	pudo	puso	supo
nosotros/as	pudimos	pusimos	supimos
vosotros/as	pudisteis	pusisteis	supisteis
Uds.	pudieron	pusieron	supieron
ellos/as	pudieron	pusieron	supieron

— En Santiago **vimos** a mucha gente de la familia de Carlos.
— Sí, ¿y les **diste** los regalos que tu familia mandó?
— Mi madre **vino** con nosotros y ella misma **pudo** darles los regalos.
—¿Qué **hiciste** después de visitar a la familia de Carlos?

In Santiago we saw a lot of people in Carlos's family.
Yes, and did you give them the gifts your family sent?
My mother came with us and she was able to give them the gifts herself.
What did you do after visiting Carlos's family?

Verbos con cambio de raíz

The next group of verbs also follows its own pattern. In these stem-changing verbs, the first letters next to the infinitives, listed in parentheses, represent the present-tense spelling changes; the last letter indicates the spelling change in the **él/ella** and **ellos/ellas** forms of the **pretérito**.

¿Cuántas horas durmió anoche?

Por lo menos doce.

	dormir (o → ue → u)	pedir (e → i → i)	preferir (e → ie → i)
yo	dormí	pedí	preferí
tú	dormiste	pediste	preferiste
Ud.	durmió	pidió	prefirió
él/ella	durmió	pidió	prefirió
nosotros/as	dormimos	pedimos	preferimos
vosotros/as	dormisteis	pedisteis	preferisteis
Uds.	durmieron	pidieron	prefirieron
ellos/as	durmieron	pidieron	prefirieron

Fíjate

The -ir stem-changing verbs are irregular in the third-person singular and plural forms only.

—Cuando fuiste al restaurante en Valparaíso, ¿qué **pediste**?
— **Pedí** carne de res, pero mi madre **prefirió** pescado. Y después de comer mi madre **durmió** la siesta.

What did you order when you went to the restaurant in Valparaíso?
I ordered beef, but my mother preferred fish. And after eating, my mother took a nap.

 7-20 **Más práctica** Repite el juego de verbos de la actividad **7-8**, esta vez usando los verbos irregulares. ∎

 7-21 **¿Qué dijo?** Form groups of at least six students and sit in a circle. **Estudiante 1** starts by saying his/her name and something that he/she did yesterday, last week, or last year. **Estudiante 2** gives his/her name, says something he/she did, and then tells what the preceding person (**Estudiante 1**) did. **Estudiante 3** tells his/her name, says what he/she did, and then tells what **Estudiante 2** and **Estudiante 1** did (in that order). Follow the model. ∎

MODELO
E1: *Soy Fran y ayer fui a un restaurante mexicano.*
E2: *Soy Tom y ayer jugué al tenis. Fran fue a un restaurante mexicano.*
E3: *Soy Chris y ayer tuve que preparar la cena. Tom jugó al tenis y Fran fue a un restaurante mexicano.*

NOTE for 7-21
As you monitor this activity, pay special attention to student pronunciation, making note of the most serious, or most common, errors. At the end of the activity, go over the mistakes with your students, modeling the correct pronunciation. In this way, this activity may also serve as focused pronunciation practice.

NOTE for 7-21
You may wish to offer students some options for stating that they do not remember. For example, they can turn to the appropriate student and ask *¿Qué dijiste?* or *Repite, por favor.* Another possibility is to tell students that it is okay to prompt each other when a member of the circle forgets. You can also move to the next student, thus eliminating group members until one or two students are left.

NOTE for 7-21
You may wish to make this a writing activity: The first person writes a sentence, passes it to the next, who adds a sentence, and so on. This could be a competition to see which group has the most correct sentences after a 4- or 5-minute period.

NOTE for 7-21
Activity **7-21** encourages active listening. Discourage students from taking notes but rather have them prompt each other when help is needed.

⏰ 8:00 🍦🍦 **7-22** **El mercado** El año pasado, Amanda fue estudiante de intercambio y vivió con una familia en Asunción. Completa el siguiente párrafo sobre su primera visita al mercado y después compártelo con un/a compañero/a. ■

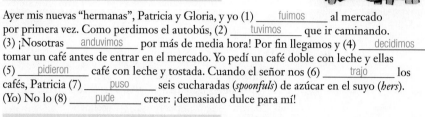

andar	traer	decidir	ir
pedir	poder	poner	tener

Ayer mis nuevas "hermanas", Patricia y Gloria, y yo (1) ___fuimos___ al mercado por primera vez. Como perdimos el autobús, (2) ___tuvimos___ que ir caminando. (3) ¡Nosotras ___anduvimos___ por más de media hora! Por fin llegamos y (4) ___decidimos___ tomar un café antes de entrar en el mercado. Yo pedí un café doble con leche y ellas (5) ___pidieron___ café con leche y tostada. Cuando el señor nos (6) ___trajo___ los cafés, Patricia (7) ___puso___ seis cucharadas (*spoonfuls*) de azúcar en el suyo (*hers*). (Yo) No lo (8) ___pude___ creer: ¡demasiado dulce para mí!

comprar	decir	estar	poner
ser	tomar	ver	volver

Al entrar en el mercado, yo (9) ___vi___ un montón (*a pile*) de verduras y frutas de muchos colores brillantes. (10) ___Fue___ impresionante. Después yo les (11) ___tomé___ varias fotos a las chicas. Primero compramos una lechuga, dos cebollas, ajo, medio kilo de zanahorias y un pimiento verde. Hablamos unos cinco minutos con la vendedora sobre su sobrina. Ella (12) ___estuvo___ seis meses en los Estados Unidos como estudiante de intercambio. Después miramos las frutas y por fin escogimos dos melones y medio kilo de peras. Las chicas (13) ___pusieron___ las verduras en el bolso grande y la fruta en el bolso más pequeño. Entonces pasamos a la parte del pescado donde nosotras (14) ___compramos___ atún. La señora lo envolvió (*wrapped*) en papel antes de ponerlo en una bolsa de plástico. Hicimos las compras en menos de media hora. A las nueve y cuarto les (15) ___dijimos___ adiós a todos y (16) ___volvimos___ a casa... esta vez en autobús.

⏰ 8:00 🍦🍦 **7-23** **¿Hay rutina en tu semana?** ¿Cuántas veces hiciste cada una de estas cosas la semana pasada? ■

Paso 1 Di las respuestas a las siguientes preguntas, según el modelo.

MODELO ver una película en la televisión

E1: La semana pasada, ¿cuántas veces viste una película en la televisión?

E2: *Vi una película en la televisión una vez (dos veces, tres veces, etc.).*

La semana pasada, ¿cuántas veces... ?

1. hacer la tarea
2. dar la respuesta correcta en clase
3. venir a la clase de español
4. conducir a la universidad
5. dormir ocho horas
6. andar por el centro
7. ir al cine
8. jugar un deporte
9. ver un partido en la televisión
10. comer comida rápida

Paso 2   Pídele a tu compañero/a que adivine (*guess*) cuántas veces hiciste las actividades del **Paso 1.** Sigue el modelo.

MODELO   E1: *La semana pasada, ¿cuántas veces piensas que (yo) hice la tarea?*

E2: *Pienso que la hiciste tres veces.*

E1: *Sí, tienes razón. ¡La hice tres veces!*

E1: *¿Cuántas veces piensas que fui al cine?*

E2: *Pienso que no fuiste.*

E1: *No, no tienes razón. Fui una vez.*

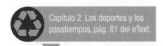

Capítulo 2. Los deportes y los pasatiempos, pág. 81 del eText.

 7-24 ¿Adónde fui? Hazle a tu compañero/a las siguientes preguntas para averiguar adónde fue de vacaciones. Después, cambien de papel. (**¡OJO!** *Before asking the last question, try to guess where he or she went.*) ■

MODELO   E1: *¿Fuiste en verano?*

E2: *No, fui en otoño. / Sí, fui en verano.*

1. ¿Fuiste a la playa? Fui
2. ¿Visitaste un museo? Visité
3. ¿Viste un partido de béisbol? Vi
4. ¿Montaste en bicicleta? Monté
5. ¿Qué compraste? Compré
6. ¿Comiste mariscos? Comí
7. ¿Tomaste el sol? Tomé

8. ¿Jugaste al golf? Jugué
9. ¿Nadaste? Nadé
10. ¿Dormiste en un hotel? Dormí
11. ¿Jugaste al tenis? Jugué
12. ¿Fuiste a un parque? Fui
13. ¿Qué más hiciste? *Answers may vary.*
14. ¿Adónde fuiste? Fui

Workbooklet

7-25 Chismes (*Gossip*) Imagina que eres el/la editor/a de la columna de chismes de un periódico. Escribe en el recuadro en la página 178 tus respuestas a las siguientes preguntas. Después, entrevista a tres compañeros/as y anota sus respuestas. ¿Están de acuerdo? ■

1. ¿Qué película tuvo mucho éxito el año pasado?
2. ¿Qué actor salió en una película que **no** tuvo éxito?
3. ¿Qué miembro del gobierno (*member of the government*) dijo algo tonto?
4. ¿Quién hizo un CD recientemente?
5. ¿Cuál de tus amigos estuvo en la playa recientemente?
6. ¿Quién vino tarde a la clase una vez?
7. ¿Quién no trajo sus libros a clase?
8. ¿Quién les dio un examen muy difícil la semana pasada?

YO	ESTUDIANTE 1	ESTUDIANTE 2	ESTUDIANTE 3
1.			
2.			
3.			
4.			
5.			
6.			
7.			
8.			

SUGGESTION for *En el restaurante*

You might want to add the word *cash* to your payment options. You can say *dinero en efectivo* for those students who pay for their meals in cash. You might also add the word *un descuento* for the university establishments that offer a discount to students with photo identification.

SUGGESTION for *En el restaurante*

You may want to ask your students the following questions:

¿Cuáles restaurantes en esta ciudad son caros?
¿Cuáles restaurantes tienen comida barata?
¿Cuánto dinero das de propina cuando comes en un restaurante?
¿Cuáles restaurantes tienen un menú grande?
¿Tienen especialidades de la casa en tus restaurantes favoritos?
¿Qué te dice el camarero cuando te sirve la comida?
¿Qué le dices al camarero cuando terminas la comida y quieres salir?

4:00

7 VOCABULARIO

07-38 to 07-42

En el restaurante Explaining restaurant activity

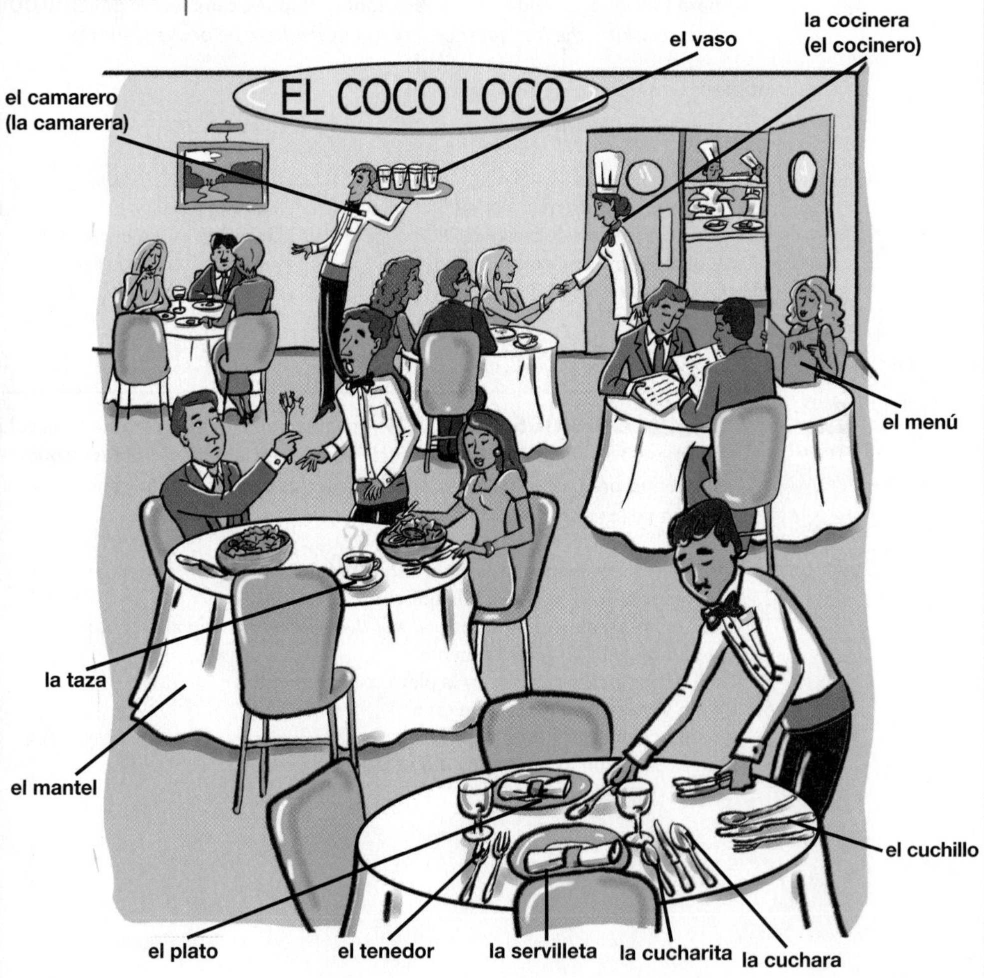
el vaso
la cocinera
(el cocinero)
EL COCO LOCO
el camarero
(la camarera)
el menú
la taza
el mantel
el cuchillo
el plato
el tenedor
la servilleta
la cucharita
la cuchara

Otras palabras y expresiones útiles	Other words and useful expressions	Algunos verbos	Some verbs
barato/a	cheap	pagar	to pay
¡Buen provecho!	Enjoy your meal!	pedir	to order
caro/a	expensive	reservar una mesa	to reserve a table
el/la cliente/a	customer; client		
la especialidad de la casa	specialty of the house		
La cuenta, por favor.	The check, please.		
la propina	tip		
la tarjeta de crédito	credit card		
la tarjeta de débito	debit card		

Workbooklet

7-26 La organización es clave Juntos escriban las siguientes categorías: **cosas en la mesa, pedir y pagar** y **personas en el restaurante.** Después, organicen el vocabulario de **En el restaurante** bajo esas categorías. ■

NOTE for 7-26
This activity can also be done as a class. Have one student be the scribe for each list, with classmates supplying the items.

MODELO	COSAS EN LA MESA	PEDIR Y PAGAR	PERSONAS EN EL RESTAURANTE
	el cuchillo	la propina	el camarero

7-27 ¿Cómo se dice? Túrnense para decir qué palabra o frase corresponde a las siguientes descripciones. ■

MODELO   E1: el "Gran Especial"

E2: *la especialidad de la casa*

> **Estrategia**
>
> As you acquire more Spanish in each chapter, try to write definitions in Spanish of your new vocabulary words as in the model. Learning new vocabulary will become easier the more you practice. Also, it will help you use your new vocabulary in sentences.

1. persona que sirve la comida el/la camarero/a
2. dinero que das por buen servicio la propina
3. lista de comidas y bebidas el menú
4. es necesario para limpiar las manos la servilleta
5. persona que prepara la comida en un restaurante el/la cocinero/a
6. es necesario para comer *Frosted Flakes* una cuchara/cucharita, la leche
7. es necesario para beber café una taza
8. persona que come en el restaurante el/la cliente/a

NOTE for 7-28
Activity **7-28** also encourages active listening, as students must pay careful attention to replicate their partners' drawings.

EXPANSION for 7-28
Have students bring in photos of well-set tables to describe in pairs or small groups. Also, in pairs, one student can describe his/her photo while the other student sketches what he/she hears, then switch roles. This works well as a listening comprehension activity.

Capítulo 2. El verbo *estar*, pág. 76 del eText;
Capítulo 3. *Hay*, pág. 119 del eText.

`5:00` 👥 **7-28** **Una mesa bien puesta**   Dibuja la mesa de tu familia o de la familia de un/a buen/a amigo/a para una cena especial con todo bien puesto (*well set*). Ahora, sin mostrar tu dibujo, descríbeselo a un/a compañero/a mientras él/ella lo dibuja. ¿Lo dibujó bien? Luego cambien de papeles. ∎

Vocabulario útil	
al lado (de)	*beside; next to*
a la izquierda (de)	*to the left (of)*
a la derecha (de)	*to the right (of)*
cerca (de)	*near*
debajo (de)	*under; underneath*
encima (de)	*on top of; above*

`3:00` 👥 **7-29** **¿Qué pasó?**   Miren el dibujo en la página 178 y digan por lo menos **cinco** oraciones acerca de lo que pasó anoche en el restaurante El Coco Loco. ∎

7:00

7-30 ¿Me puede servir...? Vas con dos amigos/as al restaurante más popular de Asunción para cenar. ■

Paso 1   Miren el menú y determinen qué van a pedir sabiendo que tienen 60.000 guaraníes para pagar.

EL RESTAURANTE
BUEN PROVECHO

SOPAS Y CREMAS
Sopa de cebolla gratinada	15.500 PYG
Sopa de pescado	32.000
Sopa de pollo y verduras	27.000
Consomé de pollo	17.000

ENSALADAS
Mixta de verduras	19.500
Ensalada de jamón, pollo o atún	45.000
Ensalada de frutas	35.000

SÁNDWICHES CALIENTES
Sándwich de queso	36.000
Sándwich de pollo, jamón y queso	48.000
Sándwich de jamón	38.000

SÁNDWICHES FRÍOS
Sándwich de pollo, tomate y lechuga	43.000
Sándwich de ensalada de pollo	45.000
Sándwich de jamón y queso	46.000

HELADOS Y POSTRES
Tres Marías	14.500
Helado de chocolate	12.000
Helado especial	12.000
Flan de la casa	14.500

BEBIDAS Y REFRESCOS
Café	5.500
Vaso de leche	6.600
Chocolate en taza	7.200
Té caliente	5.500
Té frío	5.500
Refrescos fríos	7.000
Cervezas	12.500
Copa de vino	14.000

Paso 2   Ahora, utilizando esa información, realicen (*act out*) una escena en un restaurante para la clase. Una persona debe ser el/la camarero/a y las otras personas deben ser los clientes.

Capítulo 2. Presente indicativo de verbos regulares, pág. 67 del eText.

10:00

7-31 De compras en el mercado Algunos estudiantes van a hacer el papel de vendedores y otros de clientes. Tu profesor/a te va a dar una lista de los productos que tienes para vender o de los que necesitas comprar. Los vendedores deben ganar cincuenta mil guaraníes y los clientes sólo pueden gastar cincuenta mil guaraníes. Va a haber competencia entre los vendedores y sí, ¡puedes regatear (*bargain; negotiate the price*)! ■

NATIONAL STANDARDS
Communication, Cultures, Communities
Ordering from the menu in **7-30** gives your learners the opportunity to use language in a real context and to experience the Spanish language from a part of the Spanish-speaking world that is apart from the usual. If your community has restaurants with cuisine from the Spanish-speaking world, encourage your students to use their Spanish when ordering from the menu.

EXPANSION for 7-31
This activity can also center on a restaurant experience with some students acting as patrons and others as owners or servers. The patrons could have a certain amount to spend and the owners or servers must try to convince the patrons to order specific items (or to mount the largest bill possible). Students could create sample menus for homework or work together in groups in class.

NOTE and INSTRUCTIONS for 7-31
This activity takes a bit of planning, but is well worth the effort. Half the class will be vendors, while the other half will be shoppers. There should be 2 meat and poultry vendors, 2 fruit and vegetable vendors, 2 bakery vendors, and 2 vendors of housewares. You may add other vendors, depending on the size of your class. The pairs of vendors sell the same types of goods but with some different varieties and/or slightly different prices. The shoppers should be given a context; for example, they may be shopping for a party or a holiday meal.

Ideally, the shops can be positioned in front of chalkboards so that the vendors can draw signs and advertisements. You can also provide them with pictures of products that are typical for their shops. The shopping lists should have drawings to represent what can be purchased, with the amounts written to the side. Shoppers may add to the lists, or simply create their own based on the type of meals or parties they choose to prepare. Encourage bargaining.

With regard to recycling prior concepts that the students have already learned, they should review and practice greetings, numbers, and interrogatives, as well as food vocabulary.

- Sample of partial list for shopper:

14 huevos	1 mantel
3 pollos	12 tenedores
2 jamones	6 cucharas
1 kilo de papas	6 tenedores
1 lechuga	servilletas de papel
3 tomates	pan para 12 personas
1 kilo de uvas	pasteles para 12 personas

- Sample of partial list for vendors (in kilos except where indicated):

huevos	$,50 each
pollo	$2,00
jamón	$12,00
bistec	$6,50
lechuga	$,40
tomates	$,30
uvas	$,40
pan	$,20 per loaf

Attempt to make the prices as realistic as possible. Also, to keep with the country / regional theme of this chapter, you may want the prices to reflect the Chilean peso or the Paraguayan guaraní. Consult the Internet for current conversion rates.

SECTION GOALS for *Escucha*

By the end of the *Escucha* section, students will be able to:

- combine the listening strategies they have been using in *Capítulos 1–5*.
- answer pre-listening questions in Spanish.
- predict what they are going to hear.
- determine the purpose of the conversation.
- decide whether certain statements about the conversation are true or false.
- recreate the conversation by acting out the roles.

ANSWERS to 7-32

1. Está en el mercado. Hace las compras.
2. *Answers may vary.*
3. *Answer may include:* necesito vocabulario para la comida, los números, saludos y despedidas, etc.

AUDIOSCRIPT for 7-33

VENDEDOR:	Muy buenos días, señora. ¿Cómo le puedo servir hoy?
MADRE:	Hola, Sr. Gómez. Tengo una lista bastante larga, pero de usted sólo necesito unas cuantas cosas.
VENDEDOR:	Dígame. Vamos a ver.
MADRE:	Pues, necesito leche, mantequilla, una docena de huevos grandes —me gustan los blancos— y queso fresco.
VENDEDOR:	Muy bien. ¿Necesita un galón de leche?
MADRE:	Sí, por favor.
VENDEDOR:	Perdone, pero no tengo huevos blancos hoy. Sólo tengo los marrones. ¿Está bien?
MADRE:	Bueno, entonces sólo quiero seis. ¿Mañana va a tener los blancos?
VENDEDOR:	Sí, por supuesto. Aquí tiene los huevos. Y el queso, ¿cuánto necesita? (*pause as if reaching for the cheese and indicating an amount*) ¿Así está bien?
MADRE:	Sí. Sólo quiero un poco. Lo necesito para un plato nuevo que quiero preparar de verduras al horno con una salsa de queso.
VENDEDOR:	Excelente.
MADRE:	¿Cuánto es?
VENDEDOR:	A ver —la leche, dos setenta y cinco; la mantequilla, uno cincuenta; seis huevos, 70 centavos; y el queso, uno noventa y cinco… (*pause*) son seis dólares noventa centavos.
MADRE:	Aquí lo tiene. Ahora necesito comprar las verduras.
VENDEDOR:	Muy bien. Gracias, señora. ¡Qué le vaya bien!
MADRE:	Adiós. Hasta mañana.

Las compras en el mercado

07-43

Estrategia

Combining strategies

To begin the new term it is useful to review and combine all the listening strategies you have practiced thus far. Remember to use all clues available to you to anticipate what you are about to hear, including photos, captions, and pre-listening synopses or questions. If you are performing a listening activity like the one to follow, also look ahead at the comprehension questions. Once you have an idea of the context, consider what you already know about it. Taking time to think about and practice these specific strategies will enhance your ability to listen effectively.

7-32 Antes de escuchar Contesta las siguientes preguntas. ■

1. Mira la foto. ¿Dónde está la mujer? ¿Qué hace?
2. ¿Haces las compras (*Do you shop*) en un mercado como este, donde hay muchos vendedores en un solo lugar, o en un supermercado?
3. ¿Qué tipo de vocabulario necesitas saber para poder hacer las compras en un mercado?

7-33 A escuchar Escucha la conversación entre la madre de Alejandra y un vendedor para averiguar el propósito (*purpose*) de la conversación. Después, escucha una vez más para contestar las siguientes preguntas. ■

1. ¿Qué compra? Marca (✓) delante de los ingredientes o condimentos que ella compra.

✓	mantequilla	____	vinagre
____	azúcar	✓	huevos
✓	queso	____	pan
____	mayonesa	✓	leche

2. Determina si las siguientes oraciones son ciertas (**C**) o falsas (**F**).
   a. La madre necesita ingredientes para preparar un plato nuevo. C
   b. El Sr. Gómez tiene huevos blancos y marrones. F
   c. La madre compra seis huevos. C
   d. El Sr. Gómez también vende verduras. F
   e. El Sr. Gómez tiene todo lo que la madre necesita comprar. F

7-34 Después de escuchar Realiza (*Act out*) con un/a compañero/a la escena entre la madre y el Sr. Gómez. ■

NATIONAL STANDARDS
Communication

The conversation in the *Escucha* section requires that students combine previously learned listening strategies such as using clues, anticipating content, previewing comprehension questions, using prior knowledge about the content, and practicing focused listening. The dialogue provides spoken Spanish, and students then understand and interpret the conversation between Alejandra's mother and the vendor (Standard 1.2). The pre-listening and post-listening activities also encourage interpersonal communication if students work in pairs or small groups (Standard 1.1). When students reenact the scene between the mother and Sr. Gómez and present the scene to the class, they use Standard 1.3, the presentational mode of communication.

SUGGESTION for 7-34

You may want to extend this activity by bringing in props and setting the classroom up like a market. You can assign students different roles as vendors and customers, provide shopping lists and fake money, etc.

¡CONVERSEMOS!

07-44

7-35 De compras Descríbele a un/a compañero/a lo que compraste la última vez que fuiste al supermercado. Di por lo menos **diez** oraciones e incluye detalles como los siguientes: ∎

- Lo que (no) tuviste que comprar (*tener que + infinitivo*)
- Los precios de la comida y de las bebidas
- Quien preparó la comida y cómo la preparó

Tu compañero/a va a comparar lo que él/ella compró con tus compras.

7-36 ¡Qué fiesta! Colin Cowie, un famoso organizador de fiestas para las grandes estrellas de Hollywood, te contrató para ayudarle a planear una fiesta para tu músico o actor favorito. Descríbele a un/a compañero/a (Colin Cowie) en por lo menos **diez** oraciones todo lo que tuviste que hacer. Incluye la comida que compraste, lo que preparaste para comer, cómo pusiste la mesa, quiénes vinieron a la fiesta, etc. Tu compañero/a (Colin Cowie) va a decirte si le gustó lo que hiciste. ∎

SECTION GOALS for ¡Conversemos!
By the end of the *¡Conversemos!* section, students will be able to:
- share past shopping experiences in the presentational and interpersonal modes.
- create scenarios in the past that involve party planning in the presentational and interpersonal modes.
- utilize previously learned / recycled vocabulary and grammatical concepts such as object pronouns.

HERITAGE LANGUAGE LEARNERS
For your heritage language learners who already know the commands, suggest they create a cooking show similar to shows on the Food Network or Cooking Channel.

ESCRIBE

Una descripción
07-45 to 07-46

Estrategia		
Topic sentence and conclusion	In writing for any audience, it is important to both capture the interest of the reader with a strong topic sentence, preparing him/her	for what he/she is about to read, and end with a strong conclusion, restating or summarizing the main points for the reader.

7-37 **Antes de escribir**   Piensa en el mejor día festivo que pasaste. Haz una
lista de los siguientes detalles: ■

- las personas con quienes celebraste o las que fueron a la fiesta
- lo que comieron y bebieron
- las cosas que hicieron
- los regalos que dieron y recibieron

7-38 **A escribir**   Ahora, usando los detalles de la lista, escribe un párrafo bien
desarrollado (*well developed*) sobre ese día, con introducción y conclusión. ■

7-39 **Después de escribir**   En grupos de cuatro o cinco estudiantes, lean
los párrafos de la actividad **7-38.** Ofrezcan (*Offer*) ideas a sus compañeros para mejorar su
trabajo. Después, escriban la versión final para entregársela (*turn it in*) a su profesor/a. ■

¿Cómo andas? II

	Feel confident	Need to review
Having completed **Comunicación II,** I now can . . .		
• explain food preparation (p. 171)	☐	☐
• survey foods from different parts of the Hispanic world (p. 173)	☐	☐
• express things that happened in the past using irregular forms (p. 173)	☐	☐
• explain restaurant activity (p. 178)	☐	☐
• combine listening strategies (p. 182)	☐	☐
• communicate about food shopping and party planning (p. 183)	☐	☐
• relate a memory (p. 184)	☐	☐

07-47 to 07-48

Les presento mi país

Gino Breschi Arteaga

Mi nombre es Gino Breschi Arteaga y soy de Viña del Mar, Chile. Viña del Mar es una ciudad turística en la costa y tiene una playa hermosa. El país es muy largo y estrecho, con un promedio (*average*) de 180 kilómetros de ancho (*wide*) y aproximadamente 4.300 kilómetros de largo. Al oeste, tenemos el océano Pacífico y al este, la cordillera majestuosa de los Andes, donde hay unas minas impresionantes de carbón, oro, cobre y otros minerales importantes. **¿Prefieres vivir cerca del océano o de las montañas?** Al norte, está el desierto de Atacama, el más árido del mundo. Al sur, hay una serie de glaciares en parques nacionales. Estudié geografía y ahora trabajo para el Ministerio del Medio Ambiente, específicamente con la división que supervisa el manejo (*management*) de las áreas protegidas, como el glaciar San Rafael. **¿Cuáles áreas están protegidas en tu país?**

La playa en Viña del Mar

El pastel de choclo es un plato favorito de los chilenos

El glaciar San Rafael, Patagonia

Isla de Pascua

ALMANAQUE

Nombre oficial: República de Chile
Gobierno: República
Población: 16.746.491 (2010)
Idioma: español
Moneda: Peso chileno ($)

¿Sabías que...?

• Además del (*In addition to*) desayuno, el almuerzo y la cena, los chilenos toman una merienda llamada "las onces", que comen entre las 4:00 y las 7:00 de la tarde.

• El baile nacional de Chile es la cueca. Este baile se inspira en el rito de cortejo (*courting*) del gallo (*rooster*) y la gallina (*hen*).

Preguntas

1. ¿Qué extremos geográficos y climatológicos se mencionan? ¿Hay algo parecido en los Estados Unidos?

2. ¿Qué tipos de minas hay en Chile? ¿Hay minas parecidas en los Estados Unidos?

3. Un plato popular en Chile es el pastel de choclo. ¿Cuáles son unos platos populares donde tú vives?

 Amplía tus conocimientos sobre Chile en MySpanishLab.

185

SECTION GOALS for *Cultura*
By the end of the *Cultura* section, students will be able to:
• report about some geographical features of Chile.
• discuss some Chilean cultural practices such as *las onces*.
• identify Chile's national dance.
• explain the role of Paraguay's indigenous people and their language.
• compare Chile and Paraguay.
• highlight the foods and crops important to Paraguay.

NATIONAL STANDARDS
Cultures, Comparisons
The *Les presento mi país* reading about Chile and Paraguay enhances students' prior knowledge about South American countries. The Cultures Goal states that students "gain knowledge and understanding of the cultures of the world." The cultural information highlights both Standards 2.1 and 2.2 because it provides insight into the practices, products, and perspectives of the Chilean people, the Paraguayan people, and the Guaraní. For example, from the reading students learn about *las onces, la cueca,* the crops such as *la mandioca* and *la batata,* and refreshments like *el tereré.* Students can compare how Chile and Paraguay differ from their own culture, how Chile and Paraguay differ from each other, and how these South American countries differ from other Spanish-speaking countries (Standard 4.2).

NOTE for *El pastel de choclo*
El pastel de choclo mixes meat and vegetables in a corn casserole.

NOTE for *Las onces*
Las onces, las once, or *la once,* as it is also referred to, probably originated from a mid-morning snack, much along the lines of "*elevenses*" in England. Due to changes in the workday schedule, it gradually worked its way to the afternoon as a snack. Typical fare for *las onces* is coffee or tea, and some sort of bread or bun with butter, jam, or marmalade, but it could be as elaborate as a ham sandwich and cookies, for example.

NOTE for *La cueca*
La cueca is the national dance of Chile. It represents the courtship of a rooster and a hen. The man is the rooster and dresses like a *huaso,* a Chilean cowboy. The woman is obviously the hen, and dresses in a folkloric costume as well.

SUGGESTION for *La cueca*
Ask students about folkloric dances in the United States and their origins (or folkloric dances from their own countries, if they are not from the United States: e.g., square dancing, Irish contra-dancing, etc.).

NOTE for *Chile*
The 2010 Chilean mining accident, also known as "Los 33," began as a large cave-in at the San José gold and copper mine in northern Chile on August 5, 2010. The 33 miners, who were trapped 2,300 feet underground, endured 69 days before being rescued on October 13, 2010. Once they were found to be alive, a borehole was established through which food and other provisions were passed to sustain the miners.

EXPANSION for *Chile*
You may choose to have your students further investigate the Chilean mining accident.

ADDITIONAL ACTIVITY for *Cultura*
 Have your students do the following web activity to learn more about *la cueca.*
¿Sabes bailar algún baile folclórico? Busca en el Internet cómo se baila la cueca y da una demostración en la clase. (Palabras clave: la cueca, cómo se baila, instrucciones para bailar la cueca)

Map labels: Arica, Iquique, BOLIVIA, BRASIL, San Pedro, PARAGUAY, Antofagasta, Lascar, ARGENTINA, La Serena, Viña del Mar, URUGUAY, Valparaíso, Santiago, Concepción, Río Bío Bío, Puerto Montt, Isla de Chiloé, Archipiélago de Los Hornos, Estrecho de Magallanes, Isla Grande de Tierra del Fuego, Punta Arenas, Cabo de Hornos, OCÉANO PACÍFICO, CORDILLERA DE LOS ANDES

NOTE for El Chaco
El Chaco, or *El Gran Chaco*, is a vast area of empty plains and forests. (The name *Chaco* supposedly comes from the Quechuan word for *great hunting ground*). It contains several of Paraguay's national parks and biological reserves. It is a prime area for ecotourism due to the variety of flora and fauna located there: e.g., the jaguar, the tapir, the elusive guanaco, the maned wolf, and the giant armadillo. It is also home to many aviary species, including the flamingo and the ostrich-like rhea or *ñandú*, which is endangered.

NOTE for La Represa Hidroeléctrica de Itaipú
The Itaipú Hydroelectric Dam is a joint venture of enormous proportions between Brazil and Paraguay. Construction began in 1975 and was completed in 1991. Harnessing the hydroelectric potential of the Paraná River, this dam and power plant provide more than 80% of the electrical power consumption of Paraguay and more than 25% of that of Brazil. It has become a huge tourist attraction.

NOTE for Tereré
Tereré is the cold infusion form of yerba mate, the grass-like tea that is the preferred drink in Paraguay, Uruguay, and Argentina. When it is hot, it is called *mate*; as a cold drink, it is called *tereré*.

NOTE for Remedios caseros
Beliefs in herbal and folk remedies abound in Paraguay. Sometimes they are combined with modern medical practices, depending on the person with an ailment, his/her background, and his/her geographic location—rural populations being more prone to these practices. Nevertheless, in the marketplaces in Asunción, a modern capital city, medicine women set up their stalls and do brisk business.

EXPANSION for Preguntas
Additional questions to ask your students are:
1. *¿Qué significa ser bilingüe?*
2. *¿Qué idiomas hablan los paraguayos? ¿Qué idiomas hablan los canadienses? ¿Los puertorriqueños?*
3. *¿Dónde vive la mayoría de los paraguayos? ¿Por qué piensas que es así?*
4. *¿Cómo se compara la comida paraguaya con la comida de otros países hispanos?*

Cultura
Paraguay

07-49 to 07-50

Sandra Manrique Esquivel

Les presento mi país

Mi nombre es Sandra Manrique Esquivel y vivo en Villa Rica, Paraguay. Como un gran porcentaje de los paraguayos, soy bilingüe: hablo español y guaraní. **¿En qué otros países hay una población bilingüe?** El guaraní es el idioma hablado por los indígenas originales del país: los guaraníes. Hoy día, el noventa por ciento de los paraguayos somos **mestizos,** una mezcla (*mixture*) de los indígenas y los conquistadores españoles. Los indígenas cultivaron la mandioca (*yucca*), la batata (*yam*), el maíz y la yerba mate entre otras cosechas (*crops*). Villa Rica es importante por la producción de tabaco y yerba mate. Durante el día, se ve a los paraguayos tomando su **tereré,** una infusión fría de yerba mate. **¿Qué refresco te gusta tomar?**

La Represa Hidroeléctrica de Itaipú, en la frontera entre Paraguay y Brasil

El ñandú es una especie de ave nativa y amenazada (*endangered*) de El Chaco

El tereré, una infusión fría de yerba mate, es la bebida preferida en Paraguay

ALMANAQUE

Nombre oficial:	República del Paraguay
Gobierno:	República constitucional
Población:	6.375.830 (2010)
Idiomas:	español (oficial); guaraní (oficial)
Moneda:	Guaraní (G)

¿Sabías que...?

• Muchos paraguayos son aficionados a los remedios caseros (*home-made remedies*), por ejemplo los usos de la planta guaraná, un arbusto (*bush; shrub*) indígena, para calmar los nervios y ayudar con la digestión.

• El Chaco cubre el 60% de la superficie de Paraguay pero contiene solamente un 2% de la población del país.

Preguntas

1. ¿Qué comidas se comen en Paraguay?
2. ¿Por qué son bilingües muchos paraguayos?
3. ¿En qué aspectos son Chile y Paraguay diferentes y similares? ¿Cómo se comparan con los otros países que hemos estudiado?

 Amplía tus conocimientos sobre Paraguay en MySpanishLab.

 ADDITIONAL ACTIVITY for Cultura
Have your students do the following research on the Internet.
1. ¿Qué piensas de los remedios caseros? ¿Prefieres las curas alternativas o ir al médico? ¿Por qué?
   Busca en el Internet más información sobre los remedios caseros y la clasificación de alimentos en la medicina herbal. (Palabras clave: la medicina herbal o alternativa, los remedios caseros)

2. La represa de Itaipú es un proyecto de construcción enorme. ¿Hay algún proyecto de este tipo en los Estados Unidos? ¿Por qué se llevaron a cabo estos proyectos? ¿Cuáles son los beneficios y las desventajas para los países? (Palabras clave: represas estadounidenses, proyectos hidroeléctricos, energía eléctrica)

Ambiciones siniestras

EPISODIO 7

¡Hola!
eText p. 286   07-53 to 07-54

Lectura y video

Y por fin, ¿cómo andas?

Having completed this chapter, I now can . . .

	Feel confident	Need to review
Comunicación I		
• discuss food (p. 158)	☐	☐
• pronounce **r** and **rr** correctly (MSL/SAM)	☐	☐
• communicate with less repetition using direct object pronouns (p. 163)	☐	☐
• express things that happened in the past (Part I) (p. 164)	☐	☐
• describe things that happened in the past (Part II) (p. 166)	☐	☐
Comunicación II		
• explain food preparation (p. 171)	☐	☐
• express things that happened in the past using irregular forms (p. 173)	☐	☐
• explain restaurant activity (p. 178)	☐	☐
• combine listening strategies (p. 182)	☐	☐
• communicate about food shopping and party planning (p. 183)	☐	☐
• relate a memory (p. 184)	☐	☐
Cultura		
• compare and contrast eating habits (p. 162)	☐	☐
• survey foods from different parts of the Hispanic world (p. 173)	☐	☐
• list interesting facts about this chapter's featured countries: Chile and Paraguay (pp. 185–186)	☐	☐
Ambiciones siniestras		
• predict what will happen in a reading and discover the voice-mail message that frightens Cisco (p. 187)	☐	☐
• determine who has received the riddle, and what they have figured out so far (p. 187)	☐	☐
Comunidades		
• use Spanish in real-life contexts (SAM)	☐	☐

Video: In *Episodio 5, Se conocen*, the characters finally met each other via a video conference organized by Cisco. Cisco read Eduardo's e-mail confronting el Sr. Verdugo about a fake contest, and found the names of the other finalists. Manolo revealed to Alejandra that Cisco was his cousin. When the finalists met online, they discovered that Eduardo was missing. Lupe seemed aloof, as if she had something to hide, and at the end of the video Alejandra's picture faded. We learned that Alejandra might have been taken by force by a mysterious stranger.

NOTE for 7-42, *Lectura* (Online)
In an attempt to contextualize the use of the preterit, in *Episodio 7* it was necessary to also use the imperfect in a few of the comprehension questions in **7-42** and **7-44**. You may want to point out to students that this is a preview of the other past tense they will learn in *Capítulo 8* and that they will practice when to use each past tense in *Capítulo 9*.

VOCABULARIO ACTIVO

Las carnes y las aves — *Meat and poultry*

las aves	poultry
el bistec	steak
la carne	meat
la hamburguesa	hamburger
el jamón	ham
el perro caliente	hot dog
el pollo	chicken

El pescado y los mariscos — *Fish and seafood*

el atún	tuna
los camarones (*pl.*)	shrimp
el pescado	fish

Las frutas — *Fruit*

la banana	banana
el limón	lemon
la manzana	apple
el melón	melon
la naranja	orange
la pera	pear
el tomate	tomato

Las verduras — *Vegetables*

la cebolla	onion
el chile	chili pepper
la ensalada	salad
los frijoles (*pl.*)	beans
la lechuga	lettuce
el maíz	corn
la papa/la patata	potato
las papas fritas (*pl.*)	french fries; potato chips
la verdura	vegetable

Los postres — *Desserts*

los dulces	candy; sweets
las galletas	cookies; crackers
el helado	ice cream
el pastel	pastry; pie
el postre	dessert
la torta	cake

Las bebidas — *Beverages*

el agua (con hielo)	water (with ice)
el café	coffee
la cerveza	beer
el jugo	juice
la leche	milk
el refresco	soft drink
el té (helado / caliente)	tea (iced / hot)
el vino	wine

Más comidas — *More foods*

el arroz	rice
el cereal	cereal
el huevo	egg
el pan	bread
el queso	cheese
la sopa	soup
la tostada	toast

Las comidas — *Meals*

el almuerzo	lunch
la cena	dinner
la comida	food; meal
el desayuno	breakfast
la merienda	snack

188

HERITAGE LANGUAGE LEARNERS
If you have heritage language learners in your class who have a grasp of the preterit and the imperfect, you may wish to ask them to answer the questions in **7-44** Online in those tenses.

Verbos — *Verbs*

almorzar (ue)	*to have lunch*
andar	*to walk*
beber	*to drink*
cocinar	*to cook*
conducir	*to drive*
cenar	*to have dinner*
desayunar	*to have breakfast*
merendar	*to have a snack*

Los condimentos y las especias — *Condiments and spices*

el aceite	*oil*
el azúcar	*sugar*
la mantequilla	*butter*
la mayonesa	*mayonnaise*
la mermelada	*jam; marmalade*
la mostaza	*mustard*
la pimienta	*pepper*
la sal	*salt*
la salsa de tomate	*ketchup*
el vinagre	*vinegar*

Algunos términos de cocina — *Cooking terms*

a la parrilla	*grilled*
al horno	*baked*
asado/a	*roasted; grilled*
bien cocido/a	*well done*
bien hecho/a	*well cooked*
caliente	*hot (temperature)*
cocido/a	*boiled; baked*
crudo/a	*rare; raw*
duro/a	*hard-boiled*
fresco/a	*fresh*
frito/a	*fried*
helado/a	*iced*
hervido/a	*boiled*
picante	*spicy*
poco hecho/a	*rare*
término medio	*medium*

En el restaurante — *In the restaurant*

el/la camarero/a	*waiter/waitress*
el/la cliente/a	*customer; client*
el/la cocinero/a	*cook*
la cuchara	*soup spoon; tablespoon*
la cucharita	*teaspoon*
el cuchillo	*knife*
la especialidad de la casa	*specialty of the house*
el mantel	*tablecloth*
el menú	*menu*
el plato	*plate; dish*
la propina	*tip*
la servilleta	*napkin*
la tarjeta de crédito	*credit card*
la tarjeta de débito	*debit card*
la taza	*cup*
el tenedor	*fork*
el vaso	*glass*

Verbos — *Verbs*

pagar	*to pay*
pedir	*to order*
reservar una mesa	*to reserve a table*

Otras palabras útiles — *Other useful words*

anoche	*last night*
anteayer	*the day before yesterday*
el año pasado	*last year*
ayer	*yesterday*
barato/a	*cheap*
¡Buen provecho!	*Enjoy your meal!*
caro/a	*expensive*
cerca (de)	*near*
debajo (de)	*under; underneath*
encima (de)	*on top (of); above*
el fin de semana pasado	*last weekend*
el… (jueves) pasado	*last . . . (Thursday)*
La cuenta, por favor.	*The check, please.*
la semana pasada	*last week*
más tarde que	*later than*
más temprano que	*earlier than*

Instructor Resources
• IRM: Syllabi and Lesson Plans

NATIONAL STANDARDS

COMUNICACIÓN I

• To describe clothing (Communication, Cultures, Comparisons)
• To pronounce *ll* and *ñ* correctly (Communication)
• To state to whom and for whom things are done (Communication)
• To express likes, dislikes, needs, etc. (Communication)
• To convey information about people and things (Communication, Comparisons)
• To engage in additional communication practice (Communication)

COMUNICACIÓN II

• To provide details about clothing (Communication)
• To relate daily routines (Communication)
• To share about situations in the past and how things used to be (Communication)
• To guess the meanings of unfamiliar words, when listening, from the context (Communication, Connections)
• To communicate about clothing and fashion (Communication)
• To write an e-mail, practicing circumlocution (Communication, Cultures, Comparisons, Connections, Communities)
• To engage in additional communication practice (Communication)

CULTURA

• To recount information about a Spanish clothing company (Communication, Cultures, Connections, Comparisons)
• To consider shopping practices in the Spanish-speaking countries (Communication, Cultures, Connections, Comparisons)
• To share important facts about Argentina and Uruguay (Cultures, Comparisons)
• To explore the chapter's cultural themes further (Cultures)

AMBICIONES SINIESTRAS

• To deduce the meanings of unfamiliar words, and explain the significance of the latest e-mail (Connections, Communication)
• To reveal secrets regarding Lupe (Communication)

COMUNIDADES

• To use Spanish in real-life contexts (Communities)

8 ¿Qué te pones?

En los países hispanohablantes la gente lleva (*wear*) ropa (*clothing*) muy similar a la que llevan por todo el mundo pero también se usa ropa más tradicional. Por ejemplo, en México se encuentran sarapes, ponchos y huaraches y en Colombia usan ruanas (ponchos) y alpargatas (*espadrilles*).

PREGUNTAS

1 ¿Qué tipo de ropa te gusta? ¿Prefieres la ropa formal o la ropa informal? ¿Qué ropa llevas normalmente?

2 ¿Te interesa la moda (*fashion*)? ¿Te gusta experimentar con diferentes estilos de ropa? Explica.

3 ¿Cómo influye el lugar donde vive una persona en la ropa que lleva?

190

SECTION GOALS for *Chapter opener*

By the end of the Chapter opener section, students will be able to:
• describe clothing preferences
• discuss how where one lives may affect how he/she dresses

NATIONAL STANDARDS
Communities

If you have a large Hispanic community in your area, you might ask students to volunteer their time at a local church, women's shelter, or other social service agency that collects clothing. There are several organizations throughout the United States, such as Dress for Success, Goodwill, and the Salvation Army, that accept clothing donations for resale. Some churches and welfare agencies collect new and gently used items of clothing for redistribution. If you have a children's hospital, cancer treatment facility, or hospice in the area, you might consider asking students to collect clothing that can be turned into quilt squares. Then students can cut the squares for hand or machine piecing. Donate the quilts to children, the homeless, senior citizens, relatives of hospice patients, or animal shelters.

191

NATIONAL STANDARDS
Cultures
It is important to reinforce the idea that students around the Spanish-speaking world share the same clothing "uniform" of jeans/slacks and T-shirts/shirts. Too often American students have the stereotypical notion that indigenous clothing is the only way of dressing. Nevertheless, it is important to share photos of indigenous peoples from the Spanish-speaking world so that your students will have a clearer picture of the diversity of *los hispanohablantes*. Activity **8-3** involves students describing the dress of indigenous people from different parts of Latin America, as depicted in the photos on p. 296.

NOTE for *Chapter opener*
You may wish to ask your students to give their impressions regarding the photo for this chapter opener. Also, have the students read the objectives for the chapter silently. We suggest you spend no more than 5 to 7 minutes on Chapter openers.

PLANNING AHEAD
Inform students that they will need to bring in photos of fashion models from magazines, catalogs, or the Internet for **8-22.** You will want to have extras on hand for the students who have trouble gathering the materials or forget to bring them to class.

METHODOLOGY • Contrasting and Comparing
Whenever possible, every effort will be made to have students make comparisons between the culture of their homes / university communities and what they are currently learning. Additionally, as appropriate, students will be asked to compare what they are currently learning with what they learned in previous chapters.

METHODOLOGY • Making Topics Relevant for Students
The opening questions for each chapter begin with your learners and their preferences, something that we have learned from educational philosopher John Dewey. Try having your students turn to a partner and answer the questions in pairs. Then have them share the answers their partners gave. This has them practice listening and paraphrasing.

METHODOLOGY • Meaningful Learning
One purpose of the discussion questions is to begin with a topic with which your students are familiar so they can see how the major theme of the chapter relates to their lives. This facilitates learning by encouraging active mental participation in relating new material to existing knowledge, the basic tenet of Ausubel's "meaningful learning" (Ausubel, D. *Educational Psychology: A cognitive view.* New York: Holt, Rinehart & Winston 1968).

NOTE for *Chapter opener*
Although *Capítulo 8* presents one primary vocabulary focus, clothing, it is rich in grammatical content. The chapter activities recycle the new vocabulary throughout, allowing students greater focus on the grammatical constructions (see *Contenidos*) while solidifying the ample list of new vocabulary words.

NOTE for *Chapter opener*
The authors have incorporated a great deal of recycling from previous chapters in *Capítulo 8*: *La hora, Los días y las estaciones, Ir + a+ infinitive, El pretérito, Los verbos irregulares del pretérito, Los quehaceres de la casa, El mundo de la música,* and *La casa.*

NOTE for *Chapter opener*
Ask students what they and their friends typically wear when they go to different places, e.g., a club to dance, a movie, a sporting event, an elegant restaurant, etc.

NOTE for *Chapter opener*
Bring in photos of famous designers from the Spanish-speaking world for discussion. Assign students to research designers such as Carolina Herrera, Toledo, Narciso Rodríguez, Custodio y David Dlmau, Adolfo Domínguez, Silvia Tcherassi, and Óscar de la Renta.

Instructor Resources
• Textbook images, Extra Activities

SECTION GOALS for
Comunicación I
By the end of the *Comunicación* section, students will be able to:
• talk about what people are wearing.
• pronounce the letters *ll* and *ñ* correctly.
• describe a Spanish clothing company.
• identify the indirect object in a sentence and substitute it with an indirect object pronoun.
• use the verb *gustar* and similar verbs with indirect object pronouns to express likes and dislikes.
• combine direct object pronouns and indirect object pronouns with infinitives or with present participles in a sentence.

NATIONAL STANDARDS
Communication, Cultures, Comparisons
Talking about clothing always lends itself to lively classroom discussions, since virtually everyone enjoys talking about and sharing opinions about clothes. As the chapter continues and students learn the imperfect tense, talking about what they used to wear recycles the clothing vocabulary.

La ropa is a topic to which students can relate. The pair activities focus on communication in the interpersonal mode (Standard 1.1), and the topic of clothing lends itself well to more creative outlets, such as a fashion show. If students become the models and announcers and narrate what each person wears as he or she walks the catwalk, you are engaging in Standard 1.3, the presentational mode. The cultural readings provide a basis for understanding the practices and perspectives (Standard 2.1) and the products and perspectives (Standard 2.2) of Hispanic people. As students discuss what types of clothing exist in the Hispanic world, what purpose a particular clothing item serves, who makes the item, and who wears the item and once they understand the cultural differences, they can compare how the concepts of clothing and fashion differ in the United States and the Hispanic world (Standard 4.2).

METHODOLOGY •
Constructing Knowledge
Since the 1940s and 1950s, educational researchers have explored how we learn and what assists in learning. When learners *construct knowledge,* the knowledge becomes internalized and transfers into long-term memory. On the other hand, memorizing lists, for example, goes into short-term memory but usually does not transfer into long-term memory. There are learning tools that help students retain information, such as mnemonic devices and connecting vocabulary with

Comunicación I

1 VOCABULARIO

7:00 08-01 to 08-07

La ropa Describing clothing

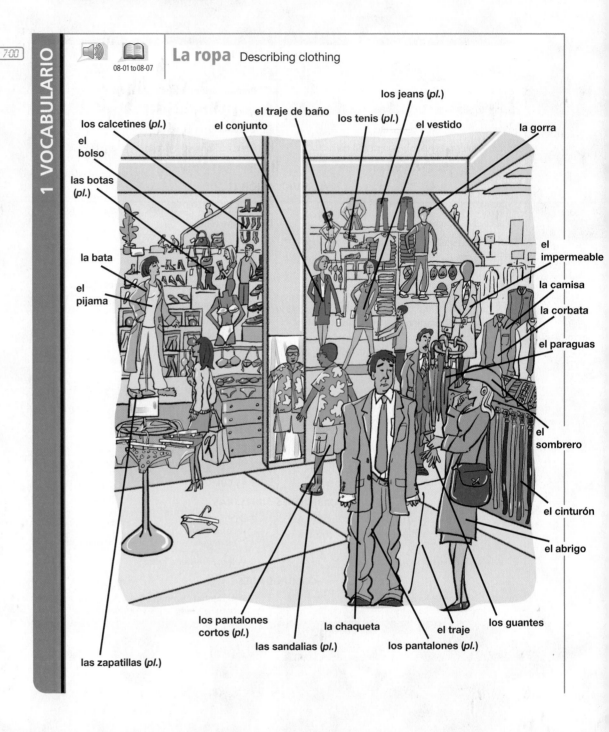

- los calcetines (*pl.*)
- el bolso
- las botas (*pl.*)
- la bata
- el pijama
- el conjunto
- el traje de baño
- los jeans (*pl.*)
- los tenis (*pl.*)
- el vestido
- la gorra
- el impermeable
- la camisa
- la corbata
- el paraguas
- el sombrero
- el cinturón
- el abrigo
- los pantalones cortos (*pl.*)
- la chaqueta
- el traje
- los guantes
- las sandalias (*pl.*)
- los pantalones (*pl.*)
- las zapatillas (*pl.*)

visual images. The "Where's Waldo?"–style composite visuals that *¡Anda! Curso elemental* employs to introduce vocabulary help students learn the new words. The students may need to consult with the *Vocabulario activo* pages at the end of the chapter to clarify / negotiate meaning, but that task helps them associate a visual image with a vocabulary word and acquire the meaning. These visuals will be excellent to use when you are introducing or practicing new tenses, since the students will have already associated these verbs with the images.

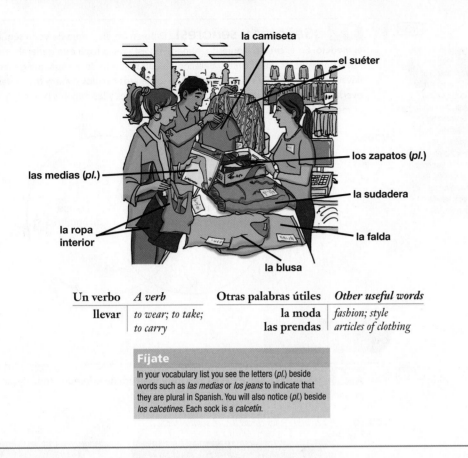

la camiseta

el suéter

los zapatos (*pl.*)

las medias (*pl.*)

la sudadera

la ropa interior

la falda

la blusa

Un verbo	*A verb*	Otras palabras útiles	*Other useful words*
llevar	*to wear; to take; to carry*	la moda	*fashion; style*
		las prendas	*articles of clothing*

Fíjate

In your vocabulary list you see the letters (*pl.*) beside words such as *las medias* or *los jeans* to indicate that they are plural in Spanish. You will also notice (*pl.*) beside *los calcetines*. Each sock is a *calcetín*.

METHODOLOGY • Introducing Lexical Variants
Every effort has been made to introduce highly common vocabulary and to limit the number of words per chapter so as not to overwhelm your students. In this chapter and others, it is highly appropriate to direct your heritage language learners and advanced beginners to explore the *También se dice…* section in Appendix 3 for additional vocabulary.

SECTION GOALS for *Pronunciación*
By the end of the *Pronunciación* section, students will be able to:
• pronounce the letters *ll* and *ñ* correctly.
• practice pronunciation skills using *dichos* and *refranes*.

PRONUNCIACIÓN

08-08 to 08-10

The letters *ll* and *ñ*

Go to MySpanishLab / Student Activities Manual to learn about the letters *ll* and *ñ*.

4:00   **8-1**   **Categorías**   Escribe todas las palabras nuevas del vocabulario que corresponden a las siguientes categorías. Luego, compara tu lista con la de un/a compañero/a. ■

¿Qué ropa usas para… ?   *Answers will vary but may include:*

1. hacer ejercicio y jugar a los deportes   el traje de baño, los pantalones cortos, la sudadera, los tenis
2. ir a la cama   la bata, el pijama, las zapatillas
3. cubrir (*to cover*) los pies (*feet*)   las zapatillas, los zapatos, los tenis, las botas, las sandalias, los calcetines, las medias
4. ir a clase   los jeans, los tenis, la camiseta, la sudadera
5. trabajar en una oficina   el traje, los pantalones largos, la camisa, la corbata, la falda, la blusa, la chaqueta, el conjunto, el vestido

METHODOLOGY • Direction Lines

Direction lines for the activities in *Capítulo 8* are exclusively in Spanish if they are *i + 1*. As a reminder, the nomenclature *i + 1* comes from the research by Stephen Krashen and his Input Hypothesis, which is a part of his Monitor Theory of Language Acquisition (see Krashen, Stephen. *Principles and Practice in Second Language Acquisition.* New York: Pergamon Press, 1982, pp. 9–32). The Input Hypothesis states that learners can comprehend input (words) based on words that they already know plus a few additional words that they may not know, but can intuit meaning from context. Any more than *i + 1* causes confusion, and in the case of many learners, they shut down due to frustration and cannot comprehend anything.

METHODOLOGY • Teacher Talk

In the classroom, although we simplify our language when we speak, attempting to stay within the range of *i + 1* (see preceding Methodology note), we should strive to deliver our speech at a speed that is as close to natural as possible. As the semester progresses, that speed will gradually increase.

21ST CENTURY SKILLS • WORLD LANGUAGES SKILLS MAP

World languages is a core subject for 21st century preparation. Sample objectives and activities at the ACTFL Novice, Intermediate, and Advanced levels were created based on the Partnership for 21st Century Skills. The skills developed by ACTFL are as follows: communication, collaboration, critical thinking and problem solving, creativity and innovation, information literacy, media literacy, technology literacy, flexibility and adaptability, initiative and self-direction, social and cross-cultural skills, productivity and accountability, leadership and responsibility, The full map can be found at www.P21.org.

METHODOLOGY • Small Group Work

¡Anda! Curso elemental is based on research. One important body of research deals with pair and cooperative learning. It states that students learn best from other students. Hence, this program has numerous pair and small group activities. Remember that it is ideal to change student pairs and groups daily. There are endless creative ways to pair students that can simultaneously review concepts. For example, pair students by their clothing and ask *¿Quién lleva tenis?* Students raise their hands to acknowledge that they are wearing such

Fijate

You have noticed that *¡Anda! Curso elemental* makes extensive use of pair and group work in the classroom to provide you with many opportunities during the class period to practice Spanish. When working in pairs or groups, it's imperative that you make every effort to speak only Spanish.

   **8-2** **¡Señoras y señores!** Dibujen un diagrama de Venn según el modelo. En el círculo izquierdo, hagan una lista de la ropa que generalmente llevan las mujeres. En el círculo derecho, hagan una lista de la ropa que generalmente llevan los hombres. En el centro donde se juntan los círculos (*where the circles overlap*), hagan una lista de la ropa que los hombres y las mujeres llevan. ¿Que lista es más larga? ■

MODELO

la ropa de mujeres

la ropa que sirve para hombres y mujeres

la ropa de hombres

Capítulo 3. Los colores, pág. 111 del eText.

8-3 **¿Cómo se visten?** Túrnense para describir qué ropa llevan las personas en las fotos. ■

MODELO   *El hombre y los chicos llevan sombreros…*

Estrategia

Remember that adjectives describe nouns and agree in number (singular / plural) and gender (masculine / feminine) with the nouns they are describing.

an item. This technique tests listening comprehension. Then pair students who are wearing those items of clothing, or pair students wearing opposites, like shorts versus long pants or light blue shirts versus dark blue. Once students are paired, instruct/remind students that they should introduce themselves, ask how their partner is feeling, and ask another question or two, such as *¿De dónde eres? ¿Cuál es tu especialidad?* or *¿Dónde vives?* before beginning the class activities.

HERITAGE LANGUAGE LEARNERS

Have students discuss indigenous dress of the different Spanish-speaking countries with which they are familiar.

[5:00] **8-4 El juego del viaje (*travel*)**

¿Te gusta viajar? Formen un círculo de cinco estudiantes o más. Primero, decidan dónde quieren ir de viaje. Después, túrnense para decir sus nombres y un artículo de ropa que quieren llevar. Cada estudiante tiene que repetir lo que dijeron los estudiantes anteriores. **¡OJO!** Si no recuerdan (*If you don't remember*), tienen que preguntar: **¿Qué dijiste, por favor?** o **¿Puedes repetir, por favor?** ◼

MODELO   Vamos a Cancún.

E1: *Soy Beverly y voy a llevar un traje de baño.*

E2: *Soy Tim y voy a llevar una camiseta blanca. Beverly va a llevar un traje de baño.*

E3: *Soy Kelly y voy a llevar una chaqueta. Tim va a llevar una camiseta blanca. Beverly va a llevar un traje de baño.*

E4: …

Estrategia

It is important to be supportive of your fellow classmates during these activities, which includes making suggestions and helpful comments and corrections. Because you will be learning from each other, it is good to know the following expressions to help you interact with each other:

(No) Estoy de acuerdo.	*I agree. / I don't agree.*
Yo pienso que es…	*I think it's . . .*
¿No debería ser…?	*Shouldn't it be . . . ?*

 Capítulo Preliminar A. Los días, los meses y las estaciones, pág. 20 del eText.

[5:00] **8-5 Señora, ¿qué debo llevar?**

Trabajas para una agencia de viajes y, para ayudar a tus clientes, tienes que preparar una lista de la ropa que deben llevar a cada destino (*destination*). Compara tu lista con la de un/a compañero/a. ◼

MODELO   La República Dominicana en agosto
los trajes de baño, los pantalones cortos, las camisetas, los jeans, los tenis y el paraguas

1. Argentina en julio
2. Costa Rica en junio
3. México en septiembre
4. Cuba en diciembre
5. Uruguay en marzo
6. España en febrero

Fíjate

Remember that the seasons south of the equator are the opposite of those in the northern hemisphere, so that when it is summer in the northern hemisphere it is winter in the southern hemisphere.

Capítulo 3. Los colores, pág. 111 del eText; Capítulo 4. *Ir + a + infinitivo*, pág. 147 del eText; Capítulo 5. Los pronombres de complemento directo, pág. 189 del eText; Capítulo 7. El pretérito, pág. 263 del eText.

Workbooklet

Fíjate
The expression *acabar de + infinitive* means *to have just done something*. Use this expression in the present tense when you want to refer to the very recent past. As in the *modelo*, this expression is useful for establishing a context for the use of the preterit.

8-6 ¿Tienes un presupuesto (*budget*)? Completa el siguiente cuadro con las prendas que acabas de comprar (*have just bought*) y con las que necesitas comprar. Luego, comparte tus respuestas con un/a compañero/a. ∎

MODELO *Acabo de comprar una blusa blanca muy elegante. La compré en Macy's la semana pasada. Pagué cuarenta y cinco dólares. Necesito comprar una falda negra.*

ACABO DE COMPRAR...	LO(S)/LA(S) COMPRÉ...	PAGUÉ...	VOY A / NECESITO COMPRAR...
1. una blusa blanca	en Macy's	$45	una falda negra
2.			
3.			

NOTA CULTURAL

eText p. 298 08-11 to 08-12

Zara: la moda internacional

NOTE for *Nota cultural*
See eText pg. 298 for complete *Nota cultural* reading and *Preguntas*.

2 GRAMÁTICA

 ¡Hola!
08-13 to 08-17 Spanish/English Tutorials

Los pronombres de complemento indirecto
Stating to whom and for whom things are done

The indirect object indicates *to whom* or *for whom* an action is done. Note these examples:

A: My mom bought this dress *for whom*?
B: She bought this dress *for you*.
A: Yes, she bought *me* this dress.

Review the chart of the indirect object pronouns and their English equivalents:

¿Éste es el vestido que mi madre me compró?

Los pronombres de complemento indirecto

me	*to / for me*
te	*to / for you*
le	*to / for you* (Ud.)
le	*to / for him, her*
nos	*to / for us*
os	*to / for you all* (vosotros)
les	*to / for you all* (Uds.)
les	*to / for them*

¡Explícalo tú!

Now study the sentences and answer the questions that follow.

Mi madre	**me**	compra mucha ropa.
Mi madre	**te**	compra mucha ropa.
Mi madre	**le**	compra mucha ropa a usted.
Mi madre	**le**	compra mucha ropa a mi hermano.
Mi madre	**nos**	compra mucha ropa.
Mi madre	**os**	compra mucha ropa.
Mi madre	**les**	compra mucha ropa a ustedes.
Mi madre	**les**	compra mucha ropa a mis hermanos.

In each of the above sentences:

1. Who is *buying* the clothing?
2. Who is *receiving* the clothing?

 Check your answers to the preceding questions in Appendix 1.

Now, look at the following examples. Identify the **direct objects** and the **indirect object pronouns**.

¿Me traes la falda gris?	*Will you bring me the gray skirt?*
Su novio le regaló la chaqueta más formal.	*Her boyfriend gave her the more formal jacket.*
Mi hermana me compró la blusa elegante.	*My sister bought me the elegant blouse.*
Nuestra compañera de cuarto nos lavó la ropa.	*Our roommate washed our clothes for us.*

Some things to remember:

1. Like direct object pronouns, indirect object pronouns *precede* verb forms and can also be *attached to infinitives and present participles* (**-ando, -iendo**).

¿**Me** quieres dar la chaqueta? ¿Quieres dar**me** la chaqueta?	*Do you want to give me the jacket?*
¿**Me** vas a dar la chaqueta? ¿Vas a dar**me** la chaqueta?	*Are you going to give me the jacket?*
¿**Me** estás dando la chaqueta? ¿Estás dánd**ome** la chaqueta?	*Are you giving me the jacket?*
Manolo **te** puede comprar la gorra en la tienda. Manolo puede comprar**te** la gorra en la tienda.	*Manolo can buy you the cap at the store.*
Su hermano **le** va a regalar una camiseta. Su hermano va a regalar**le** una camiseta.	*Her brother is going to give her a T-shirt.*

2. To clarify or emphasize the indirect object, a prepositional phrase (**a** + *prepositional pronoun*) can be added, as in the following sentences. Clarification of **le** and **les** is especially important since they can refer to different people (*him, her, you, them, you all*).

Le presto el abrigo **a él** pero no **le** presto nada **a ella.**	*I'm loaning him my coat, but I'm not loaning her anything.* (clarification)
¿**Me** preguntas **a mí**?	*Are you asking me?* (emphasis)

> **Fíjate**
> Remember that indirect object pronouns indicate to whom (*a quién*) and for whom (*para quién*) something is done.

3. It is common for Spanish speakers to include both an indirect object noun and pronoun in the same sentence, especially when the third person form is used. This is most often done to clarify or emphasize something.

[4:00] **8-7** **Amigos perfectos** Cuando sus mejores amigos celebran sus cumpleaños, tu compañero/a y tú siempre organizan las fiestas. Juntos escriban oraciones sobre las cosas que hacen, usando **me, te, nos, le** y **les.** ■

MODELO   E1:   yo / preparar / las fiestas de cumpleaños / para mis amigos

             E2:   *Yo preparo las fiestas de cumpleaños <u>para mis amigos</u>.* / *<u>Les</u> preparo las fiestas.*

1. yo / preparar / una fiesta sorpresa (*surprise*) / para él
2. yo / mandar / invitaciones / a todos nuestros amigos
3. mis amigos y yo / comprar / unos regalos cómicos / para ella
4. yo / hacer / una torta / para nosotros
5. mis amigos / dar / unas flores bonitas / a mi madre
6. nosotros / cantar / a nuestro amigo / una canción especial

[5:00]   **8-8** **¿Qué me recomienda?** Una persona hace el papel de consejero/a y la otra de estudiante de primer año (*freshman*). Deben hacer y contestar las siguientes preguntas según el modelo. Luego, cambien de papel. ■

MODELO   E1:   ¿Me recomienda usted la clase de Conversación 101?

             E2:   *No, no le recomiendo esa clase. Le recomiendo la clase de civilización española.*

1. ¿Me está pidiendo usted información sobre mi familia?
2. ¿Me recomienda usted algunas clases fáciles?
3. ¿Me ayuda usted con mis estudios?
4. ¿Me recomienda usted jugar algún deporte?
5. ¿Me recomienda usted hablar con mis profesores fuera de clase?
6. ¿Me recomienda usted la cafetería?

Capítulo 3. Los quehaceres de la casa, pág. 109 del eText; Capítulo 7. El pretérito, pág. 263 del eText.

 5:00

8-9 **¡Qué suerte!** Haz una lista de por lo menos **cuatro** cosas que tú hiciste por tu compañero/a de cuarto o tu familia la semana pasada. Después, haz otra lista de tres o cuatro cosas que esa persona hizo por ti. Compara tu lista con la de un/a compañero/a. ■

MODELO E1: *A mi compañero de cuarto le arreglé la sala, le contesté el teléfono…*

E2: *Mi compañera de cuarto me buscó unos libros en la biblioteca. También me preparó la comida…*

 Capítulo 7. El pretérito, pág. 263 del eText.

5:00

8-10 **Los regalos** ¿Te regalaron muchas cosas este año? ¿Regalaste muchas cosas tú? Escribe una lista de **cuatro** regalos que te dieron y de **cuatro** cosas que tú les regalaste. Luego, comparte tu lista con un/a compañero/a según el modelo. ¡Hay que ser creativos! ■

MODELO E1: *Le di una corbata a mi padre.*

E2: *¿Ah sí? ¿De qué color? ¿Le gustó a tu padre?*

E1: *Sí, le gustó mucho la corbata azul. Y mis padres me regalaron una bicicleta.*

E2: *¡Qué suerte! ¿Te gusta montar en bicicleta?*

Fíjate

As in English, there are word "families." *El regalo* (noun) means "gift" and *regalar* (verb) means "to give a gift."

ADDITIONAL ACTIVITY for *Los pronombres de complemento indirecto*

¡Qué consejos! Los consejeros normalmente les dan mucha información a los estudiantes nuevos durante la orientación. De los siguientes comentarios posibles, ¿cuáles son probables y cuáles son improbables?

MODELO
Les digo que tenemos una universidad muy buena.
E1: *Nos dice que tenemos una universidad muy buena. Es probable.*

1. Les pido información sobre sus familias.
2. Les pregunto cuáles son sus especialidades.
3. Les doy las reglas (*rules*) de la universidad.
4. Les prometo mi ayuda.
5. Les recomiendo la cafetería.
6. También les recomiendo el restaurante El Pollo Loco.
7. Les explico que no deben (*should not, must not*) estudiar mucho.
8. Les recomiendo clases fáciles.
9. Les digo que pueden salir hasta muy tarde todas las noches.
10. Les digo que no tienen que regresar a la residencia hasta las dos de la mañana.
11. Finalmente, les recomiendo que tomen una clase de español.

NOTE for 8-10
You may wish to prepare a list of possible "presents" for the students to choose from if time is a factor.

3 GRAMÁTICA

  ¡*Hola!* Spanish Tutorial
08-18 to 08-21

3:00

Gustar y verbos como *gustar*
Expressing likes, dislikes, needs, etc.

¡Me encanta el vestido!

As you already know, the verb **gustar** is used to express likes and dislikes. **Gustar** functions differently from other verbs you have studied so far.

• The person, thing, or idea that is liked is the *subject* (S) of the sentence.
• The person who likes the other person, thing, or idea is the *indirect object* (IO).

Consider the chart below:

(A mí)	**me**	gusta el traje.	_I_ like the suit.
(A ti)	**te**	gusta el traje.	_You_ like the suit.
(A Ud.)	**le**	gusta el traje.	_You_ like the suit.
(A él)	**le**	gusta el traje.	_He_ likes the suit.
(A ella)	**le**	gusta el traje.	_She_ likes the suit.
(A nosotros/as)	**nos**	gusta el traje.	_We_ like the suit.
(A vosotros/as)	**os**	gusta el traje.	_You_ (all) like the suit.
(A Uds.)	**les**	gusta el traje.	_You_ (all) like the suit.
(A ellos/as)	**les**	gusta el traje.	_They_ like the suit.

Note the following:

1. The construction **a** + *pronoun* (**a mí, a ti, a él,** etc.) or **a** + *noun* is optional most of the time. It is used for clarification or emphasis. Clarification of **le gusta** and **les gusta** is especially important since the indirect object pronouns **le** and **les** can refer to different people (*him, her, you, them, you all*).

A él le gusta llevar ropa cómoda. (clarification)	*He likes to wear comfortable clothes.*
A Ana le gusta llevar pantalones cortos. (clarification)	*Ana likes to wear shorts.*
Me gustan esos pantalones largos.	*I like those long pants.*
A mí me gustan más esos cortos. (emphasis)	*I like those short ones even more.*

2. Use the plural form **gustan** when what is liked (the subject of the sentence) is plural.

Me gusta **el traje.**	→	Me gusta**n los trajes.**
I like the suit.		*I like the suits.*

3. To express the idea that one likes *to do* something, **gustar** is followed by an infinitive. In that case you always use the singular **gusta,** even when you use more than one infinitive in the sentence:

Me gusta ir de compras por la mañana.	*I like to go shopping in the morning.*
A Pepe **le gusta leer** revistas de moda y **llevar** ropa atrevida.	*Pepe likes to read fashion magazines and wear daring clothing.*
Nos gusta llevar zapatos cómodos cuando hacemos ejercicio.	*We like to wear comfortable shoes when we exercise.*

The verbs listed below function like **gustar:**

encantar	*to love; to like very much*
fascinar	*to fascinate*
hacer falta	*to need; to be lacking*
importar	*to matter; to be important*
molestar	*to bother*

Me encanta ir de compras.
A Doug y a David **les fascina** la tienda de ropa
    Rugby.
¿**Te hace falta** dinero para comprar el vestido?
A Juan **le importa** el precio de la ropa,
    no la moda.
Nos molestan las personas que llevan sandalias
    en invierno.

I love to go shopping. (I like shopping very much.)
The Rugby clothing store fascinates (is fascinating to)
    Doug and David.
Do you need (are you lacking) money to buy the dress?
The price of the clothing, not the style, matters
    (is important) to Juan.
People who wear sandals in the winter bother us.

Capítulo 5. El mundo de la
música, pág. 172 del eText.

[5:00] **8-11** **Hablando de la música...** A Jaime y a Celia les gusta
mucho la música. Completa las siguientes oraciones para descubrir sus preferencias.
Después, comparte tu párrafo con un/a compañero/a. ∎

MODELO   A nosotros *nos fascina* (fascinar) la música rap.

A nosotros (1) __nos__ __encanta__ (encantar) la música rock. A mí (2) __me__ __gustan__
(gustar) los grupos como AC/DC y Metallica. Mi cantante favorito es Dave Matthews y
(3) __me__ __gusta__ (gustar) su grupo también. A Celia (4) __le__ __fascina__ (fascinar)
el grupo Nickleback. Celia tiene casi todos los CD pero, (5) __le__ __hace falta__ (hacer falta)
uno que se llama *Running with Dark Horse*. A nuestros compañeros (6) __les__ __molesta__
(molestar) tener que escuchar nuestra música favorita. Ellos prefieren la música jazz.
A Celia y a mí no (7) __nos__ __importa__ (importar) su opinión, ¡somos amigos pero no
nos tienen que gustar las mismas cosas siempre!

ADDITIONAL ACTIVITY for
Gustar y verbos como gustar

Ideas incompletas Completa las
siguientes oraciones. Después,
compártelas con un/a compañero/a.

1. En invierno me encanta(n)…
2. A mis profesores les molesta(n)…
3. A mi mejor amigo/a no le
   importa(n)…
4. A los estudiantes de español les
   fascina(n)…
5. A mis compañeros de clase y a mí
   nos hace(n) falta…

NOTE for Gustar *y verbos*
***como* gustar**
The authors have chosen to introduce
a manageable number of verbs at this
point. You may prefer to add some
additional verbs such as *aburrir, faltar,
interesar,* and *parecer*. Students will
practice *quedar bien* and *quedar mal* in
Comunicación II.

EXPANSION for 8-11
Challenge students to create as many
sentences as they can in a set amount of
time with *gustar* and *gustar*-type verbs
using music as the context. Then give
students another context and repeat.

METHODOLOGY • Practice in the Classroom

METHODOLOGY • Practice in the Classroom

Up to this point, we have spent a good deal of time addressing the benefits of pair and group work. Practice is the way that students gain confidence as well as improve their speaking skills. Another piece of research states that if "students can say it, they can write it." This research comes from the literature of English as a Second Language (ESL), as well as literacy literature. It states that an individual usually cannot write at a higher level than he/she can speak. Yes, there are some exceptions to this rule, but for the most part this is true. Think about your students in the past. The best writers tend to have the best verbal skills. This does not mean that their spelling will be perfect, but they should be able to express themselves. Hence, we encourage you to give your students as many opportunities as possible to use Spanish in the classroom.

FOLLOW-UP for 8-12

Once students have paired up and shared their opinions about the clothing, have them report what they have learned about their partner's opinions to the class. Do they share the same opinions?

8-12 ¿Qué opinas? Da tu opinión sobre esta ropa poniendo una equis (**X**) en la columna apropiada de cada hilera (*row*). Luego, comparte tu opinión con un/a compañero/a. ■

MODELO   E1: *¿Te fascinan los vestidos de Carolina Herrera?*
            E2: *Sí, me fascinan. / No, no me importan mucho. / No sé, no los conozco.*

	(NO) ME FASCINA(N)	(NO) ME ENCANTA(N)	NO ME IMPORTA(N) MUCHO	NO LO(S)/LA(S) CONOZCO
1. los vestidos de Carolina Herrera				
2. un traje de Armani				
3. una camisa y corbata de Zara				
4. una sudadera				
5. un conjunto				

Capítulo 2. Las materias y las especialidades, pág. 62 del eText; En la universidad, pág. 74 del eText; Los deportes y los pasatiempos, pág. 81 del eText.

Workbooklet

8-13 En mi opinión... ¿Qué te gusta y no te gusta de tu universidad? ■

Paso 1   Completa el siguiente cuadro según tu opinión.

ME MOLESTA(N)...	ME ENCANTA(N)...	NOS HACE(N) FALTA...
1.	1.	1.
2.	2.	2.
3.	3.	3.

Paso 2   Ahora, circula por la clase para pedirles a tres compañeros sus opiniones.

MODELO   E1 (Tú): *¿Qué te molesta?*
                E2: *Me molesta la comida de la cafetería.*

A _____ LE MOLESTA(N)...	A _____ LE ENCANTA(N)...	NOS HACE(N) FALTA...
1.	1.	1.
2.	2.	2.
3.	3.	3.

4 GRAMÁTICA

08-22 to 08-26

Spanish Tutorial

Los pronombres de complemento directo e indirecto usados juntos
Conveying information about people and things

You have worked with two types of object pronouns, direct and indirect. Now, note how they are used together in the same sentence.

¡Me encanta la elegante blusa verde!

¿Sí, amor? Pues, entramos. Te la compro ahora mismo.

Paula **nos** está devolviendo **las botas**.
Paula is giving us back the boots.
→ Paula **nos las** está devolviendo.
Paula is giving them back to us.

Ella nunca **nos** presta **sus zapatos**.
She never loans us her shoes.
→ Ella nunca **nos los** presta.
She never loans them to us.

Paula **me** pide **el bolso** ahora.
Paula is asking me for my purse now.
→ Paula **me lo** pide ahora.
Paula is asking me for it now.

Mi novio **me** compró **una blusa blanca**.
My boyfriend bought me a white blouse.
→ Mi novio **me la** compró.
My boyfriend bought it for me.

(continued)

METHODOLOGY • Review of the present tense

You may wish to remind your students that the present tense in Spanish can be translated in three ways, e.g., *Presto* = "I loan"; "I do loan"; "I am loaning."

METHODOLOGY • Instructors' Influence on Students' Self-Esteem

Using object pronouns designates a certain level of language sophistication and requires practice on the part of native English speakers. This concept, just like any grammar concept, should never be introduced as "difficult," nor as instructors should we ever say something is "easy." There are two problems with using those qualifiers:

1. If a concept is truly challenging, it will set up an instant bias in most students and may set them up for failure. They are sure they will never understand, and it raises Krashen's Affective Filter.

2. There may be grammar points that we instructors consider "easy," but inevitably there are students who do not find them to be so. When we announce something is "easy" and students do not instantly understand the concept, they feel defeated.

These kinds of instructor comments, although well intended, tend to do harm to a student's self-esteem.

METHODOLOGY • The Natural Approach

This sequence of activities is a good example of the Natural Approach for language acquisition, taking students from simple questions requiring a mechanical type of response to longer sentences.

ANSWERS to 8-14

1. Yo le di unos jeans la semana pasada. / Yo se los di la semana pasada.
2. Mis padres le regalaron un traje formal el año pasado. / Mis padres se lo regalaron el año pasado.
3. Yo le lavé la ropa anteayer. / Yo se la lavé anteayer.
4. Antonio me pidió dinero para comprar una gorra anoche. / Antonio me lo pidió anoche.
5. Antonio y yo les dijimos la verdad sobre el accidente ayer. / Antonio y yo se la dijimos ayer.

¡Explícalo tú!

1. You know that direct and indirect objects come after verbs. Where do you find the direct and indirect object pronouns?
2. Reading from left to right, which pronoun comes first (direct or indirect)? Which pronoun comes second?

 Check your answers for the preceding questions in Appendix 1.

¡OJO! A change occurs when you use **le** or **les** along with a direct object pronoun that begins with **l**: (**lo, la, los, las**): **le** or **les** changes to **se**.

le → se

Paula le pide el bolso a mi hermana.	→ Paula se lo pide.
Su novio no le compró una chaqueta.	→ Su novio no se la compró.
Su novio le va a comprar un traje.	→ Su novio se lo va a comprar.

les → se

Paula les devuelve las botas.	→ Paula se las devuelve.
Yo le presto mis zapatos.	→ Yo se los presto.
Paula nunca les presta sus cosas.	→ Paula nunca se las presta.

Direct and indirect object pronouns may also be attached to infinitives and present participles. Note that when attached, an accent is placed over the final vowel of the infinitive and the next-to-last vowel of the participle.

¿Aquel abrigo? Mi madre **me lo** va a comprar.
¿Aquel abrigo? Mi madre va a comprár**melo**.   *That coat over there? My mother is going to buy it for me.*

Me lo está comprando ahora.
Está comprándo**melo** ahora.   *She is buying it for me now.*

Capítulo 7. El pretérito, pág. 263 del eText; Algunos verbos irregulares en el pretérito, pág. 272 del eText.

8-14 Combinaciones Escribe oraciones completas sobre lo que dijo Pablo sobre su hermano Antonio. Sigue el modelo, primero usando el complemento indirecto y después los pronombres de complemento indirecto y directos juntos. Comparte tus oraciones con un/a compañero/a. ■

MODELO   Mi hermano Antonio / prestar / (a mí) / sus zapatos favoritos / ayer
*Mi hermano Antonio **me** prestó **sus zapatos favoritos** ayer.*
*Mi hermano Antonio **me los** prestó ayer.*

1. Yo / dar / (a Antonio) / unos jeans / la semana pasada
2. Mis padres / regalar / (a Antonio) / un traje formal / el año pasado
3. Yo / lavar / la ropa / (a Antonio) / anteayer
4. Antonio / pedir / dinero para comprar una gorra / (a mí) / anoche
5. Antonio y yo / decir / la verdad sobre el accidente / (a nuestros padres) / ayer

`4:00`   **8-15** **Antonio, ¿me prestas...?** Ahora Pablo va a una fiesta y quiere usar la ropa de su hermano Antonio. Túrnense para hacer los papeles de Pablo y Antonio usando los pronombres de complemento directo e indirecto. ■

MODELO prestar / un abrigo
E1 (Pablo): *¿Me prestas el abrigo?*
E2 (Antonio): *Sí, te lo presto. / No, no te lo presto.*

1. prestar / los zapatos negros
2. prestar / la corbata azul
3. prestar / una camiseta blanca y una camisa azul de manga larga (*long sleeved*)
4. prestar / el cinturón negro
5. prestar / tu abrigo nuevo

`4:00`   **8-16** **Mis recomendaciones** ¿Qué recomiendas? Lee la lista y pon una equis (**X**) en la columna apropiada. Después, comparte tus opiniones con un/a compañero/a según el modelo. ■

Workbooklet

MODELO los libros de Tom Clancy (a tus primas)
E1: *¿Les recomiendas los libros de Tom Clancy a tus primas?*
E2: *No, no se los recomiendo.*

	SÍ	NO
1. las novelas de Stephen King (a tus tíos)		
2. la música de Eminem (a tu compañero/a de cuarto)		
3. el restaurante Taco Bell (a nosotros)		
4. la tienda Macy's (a tu amiga que no tiene mucho dinero)		
5. la película *Drácula* (a tus primos de cinco años)		
6. Disney World (a tu hermano)		
7. el Museo de Arte Moderno (a tu profesor/a)		
8. la clase de español (a tu mejor amigo/a)		

EXPANSION for 8-17
Have students create a new set of questions between employer and employee beginning with a different phrase (or a variety of phrases), e.g., *¿Me puede decir por qué usted no me contestó los emails que le mandé ayer? (No se los contesté porque no tuve tiempo.) ¿Me puede decir por qué no me trajo el periódico esta mañana? (No se lo traje porque no lo pude encontrar.) ¿Me puede decir por qué no me dio la información sobre el nuevo cliente? (No se la di porque el nuevo cliente decidió no trabajar con nosotros.) ¿Me puede decir por qué no me buscó unas recepcionistas nuevas? (No se las busqué porque tuve que hacer muchas otras cosas esta semana.)* You may also want to change the scenario to designer / model, restaurant cook / waiter, professor / student, parent / child, etc.

EXPANSION for 8-17
After completing this activity, have students role-play the situations between the assistant and his/her boss.

ANSWERS to 8-17
1. Sí, se lo puedo traer. / Sí, puedo traérselo.
2. Sí, se los puedo comprar. / Sí, puedo comprárselos.
3. Sí, se los puedo arreglar. / Sí, puedo arreglárselos.
4. Sí, se lo puedo buscar. / Sí, puedo buscárselo.
5. Sí, se la puedo reservar. / Sí, puedo reservársela.
6. Sí, se las puedo comprar. / Sí, puedo comprárselas.

 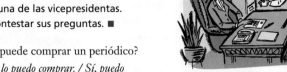

8-17 ¿En qué puedo servirle?

Acabas de empezar una pasantía (*internship*). En vez de (*Instead of*) tareas asociadas con la profesión que te interesa seguir, te dan el trabajo de ayudante de una de las vicepresidentas. Túrnense para contestar sus preguntas. ■

MODELO   E1: ¿Me puede comprar un periódico?

E2: *Sí, se lo puedo comprar. / Sí, puedo comprárselo.*

Estrategia

Remember that when addressing an employer, you would use *usted*, not *tú*. Also, be sure to practice both ways of structuring the sentence with two object pronouns, as in the *modelo*.

1. ¿Me puede traer un café?
2. ¿Me puede comprar los boletos (*tickets*) para un viaje a Nueva York?
3. ¿Me puede arreglar los apuntes y los papeles para la reunión de esta tarde?
4. ¿Me puede buscar un artículo en el periódico?
5. ¿Me puede reservar una mesa en un restaurante elegante para esta noche?
6. ¿Me puede comprar unas rosas para la recepcionista? Es su cumpleaños hoy.

¿Cómo andas? I

Having completed **Comunicación I,** I now can . . .

	Feel confident	Need to review
• describe clothing (p. 192)	☐	☐
• pronounce the letters *ll* and *ñ* (MSL / SAM)	☐	☐
• recount information about a Spanish clothing company (p. 196)	☐	☐
• state to whom and for whom things are done (p. 196)	☐	☐
• express likes, dislikes, needs, etc., (p. 200)	☐	☐
• convey information about people and things (p. 203)	☐	☐

Comunicación II

5 VOCABULARIO

3:00

08-27 to 08-29

Las telas y los materiales
Providing details about clothing

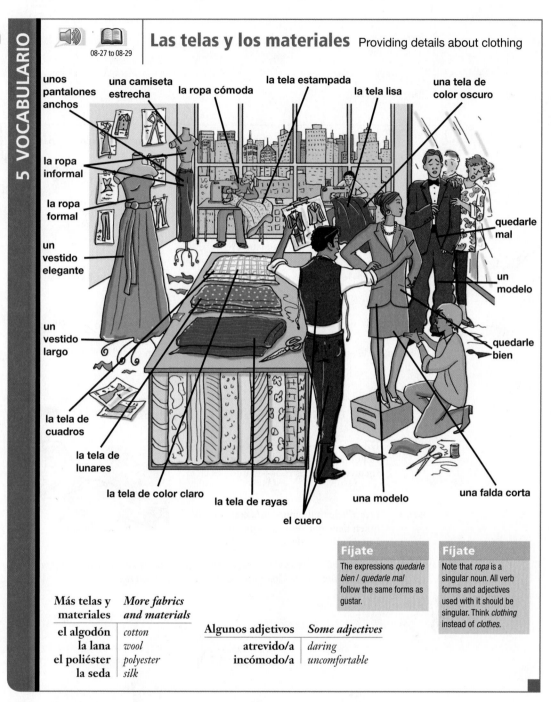

- unos pantalones anchos
- una camiseta estrecha
- la ropa cómoda
- la tela estampada
- la tela lisa
- una tela de color oscuro
- la ropa informal
- la ropa formal
- un vestido elegante
- un vestido largo
- la tela de cuadros
- la tela de lunares
- la tela de color claro
- la tela de rayas
- el cuero
- una modelo
- una falda corta
- quedarle mal
- un modelo
- quedarle bien

Fíjate
The expressions *quedarle bien* / *quedarle mal* follow the same forms as *gustar*.

Fíjate
Note that *ropa* is a singular noun. All verb forms and adjectives used with it should be singular. Think *clothing* instead of *clothes*.

Más telas y materiales	*More fabrics and materials*
el algodón	*cotton*
la lana	*wool*
el poliéster	*polyester*
la seda	*silk*

Algunos adjetivos	*Some adjectives*
atrevido/a	*daring*
incómodo/a	*uncomfortable*

ADDITIONAL ACTIVITY for *Las telas y los materiales*

👥 **¿Tienes una memoria fotográfica?** Mira alrededor de la clase por quince segundos. Cierra los ojos y en un minuto, describe con detalles quién lleva puesto qué. Di por lo menos cinco oraciones. Túrnense.

MODELO
Mark lleva una camiseta estampada y unos pantalones negros. Brenda lleva unas botas negras, una falda y un suéter. Julie lleva unos tenis, unos jeans y una chaqueta azul. Los tenis son amarillos. La chaqueta es estrecha e informal.

🔑 **Instructor Resources**
- Textbook images, Extra Activities

SECTION GOALS for *Comunicación II*
By the end of the *Comunicación* section, students will be able to:
- describe textures and patterns of articles of clothing and suggest appropriate clothing for different seasons and occasions.
- discuss their daily routines using reflexive and non-reflexive verbs.
- describe shopping centers in Latin America.
- use the imperfect forms for regular and irregular verbs correctly.
- explain when to use the imperfect.
- recognize key words that signal the imperfect.
- narrate what they used to do as children using the imperfect.

METHODOLOGY • Teaching Vocabulary
Help students organize the new vocabulary by using drawings, examples, and semantic maps. For teaching *la tela*, for example, you could bring in clothing made of each fabric and allow them to feel the texture as you explain what each word is. You could point out the patterns of students' clothing or draw examples on the board of *cuadros, lunares,* and *rayas.* Find photos that illustrate the adjectives or draw stick figures on the board and describe each item. You could also organize the vocabulary by theme, such as fabric, and draw a thematic map on the board to help them organize their learning.

CAPÍTULO 8

[1:00] **8-18** **Los opuestos** Túrnense para decir el opuesto de cada una de las siguientes palabras. ∎

1. ancho
2. formal
3. quedarle bien
4. claro
5. corto
6. liso

[2:00] **8-19** **Definiciones** Túrnense para elegir una palabra o expresión para completar cada oración. ∎

1. Cuando hace mucho frío, prefiero llevar un abrigo de…
   a. rayas   b. poliéster   (c.) lana
2. El padre de Ana está furioso porque ella salió de casa con un vestido muy…
   a. elegante   (b.) atrevido   c. ancho
3. La tela de __algodón__ viene de una planta.
   a. algodón   b. cuero   c. poliéster
4. A mi madre no le importa mucho __la moda__. Siempre prefiere llevar ropa cómoda y barata.
   a. el modelo   b. la moda   c. la seda
5. Mi padre dice que quiere proteger (*protect*) los animales. Por eso nunca lleva ropa…
   a. lisa   b. estampada   (c.) de cuero
6. A mi amigo le encanta la ropa __oscura__ porque dice que "su color" es el negro.
   a. lisa   b. clara   c. oscura

[6:00] **8-20** **¡A dibujar!** Completa los siguientes pasos. ∎

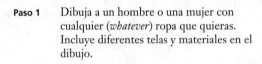

Paso 1   Dibuja a un hombre o una mujer con cualquier (*whatever*) ropa que quieras. Incluye diferentes telas y materiales en el dibujo.

Paso 2   Descríbele tu dibujo a un/a compañero/a, quien tiene que dibujar lo que tú le dices. Luego cambien de papel.

MODELO   *El hombre lleva un sombrero negro muy elegante. Lleva un traje azul oscuro muy elegante, una camisa blanca y una corbata azul con rayas rojas…*

8-21 **¿Cuál es tu conjunto favorito?** Usa las siguientes
preguntas para entrevistar a un/a compañero/a sobre su conjunto favorito. ■

1. ¿Cuál es tu conjunto favorito?
2. ¿De qué color es?
3. ¿De qué tela es?
4. ¿De qué estilo es?
5. ¿Lo compraste tú? Si no, ¿quién te lo compró?
6. ¿Cuándo lo compraste o cuándo te lo compraron?
7. ¿Dónde lo compraste o dónde te lo compraron?
8. ¿Cuándo lo llevas?
9. ¿Por qué te gusta tanto?

  8-22 **¿Qué está de moda?** Trae a la clase tres o cuatro fotos de
modelos (pueden ser de una revista [*magazine*], un catálogo o del Internet).
Túrnate con un/a compañero/a para describir en por lo menos **tres** oraciones la
ropa que llevan los modelos. Digan qué ropa les gusta más y qué ropa no les gusta.
¿Están de acuerdo? ■

MODELO   *La primera modelo de Carolina Herrera lleva un vestido corto. Es negro y muy*
           elegante. Su bolso es beige y es pequeño…

 **8-23** **¿Quién puede ser?** Escoge a una persona de tu clase y piensa en
la ropa que lleva incluyendo el estilo (*style*), el color y la tela. Describe **cuatro** de sus
prendas a tu compañero/a, quien tiene que adivinar a quién describes. Túrnense para
describir a **tres** compañeros de clase. ■

Capítulo 3. Los colores,
pág. 111 del eText.

MODELO   E1:   *Esta persona lleva unos pantalones largos de rayas blancas, una camiseta*
                 oscura, una chaqueta informal y unos tenis blancos.
           E2:   *Es Mayra.*

METHODOLOGY • Visual Organizers
It is helpful to have a file of pictures of clothing from magazines, preferably mounted on stiff paper. These can be used in a variety of ways, from activities like **8-22** to warm-ups for class. If you do not have pictures already collected and in your files, have students gather them for you.

6 GRAMÁTICA

Las construcciones reflexivas   Relating daily routines

08-30 to 08-35   Spanish/English Tutorials

Study the captions for the following drawings.

In each drawing:

• Who is performing / doing the action?
• Who or what is receiving the action?

When the subject both performs and receives the action of the verb, a reflexive verb and pronoun are used.

• Which of the drawings and captions demonstrate reflexive verbs?

Look at the following chart: the reflexive pronouns are highlighted.

La fiesta **los** despierta.   Alberto **la** acuesta.   Beatriz **lo** lava.

Raúl y Gloria **se** despiertan.   Alberto **se** acuesta.   Beatriz **se** lava.

Reflexive pronouns

Yo	me	divierto	en las fiestas.
Tú	te	diviertes	en las fiestas.
Usted	se	divierte	en las fiestas.
Él / Ella	se	divierte	en las fiestas.
Nosotros	nos	divertimos	en las fiestas.
Vosotros	os	divertís	en las fiestas.
Ustedes	se	divierten	en las fiestas.
Ellos / Ellas	se	divierten	en las fiestas.

Reflexive pronouns follow the same rules for position as other object pronouns. Reflexive pronouns:

1. precede conjugated verbs.
2. can be attached to *infinitives* and *present participles* (**-ando, -iendo**).

Te vas a dormir.
Vas a dormir**te**.   } *You are falling asleep.*

¿**Se** van a dormir esta noche?
¿Van a dormir**se** esta noche?   } *Are they going to fall asleep tonight?*

¿**Se** están durmiendo?
¿Están durmiéndo**se**?   } *Are you all falling asleep?*

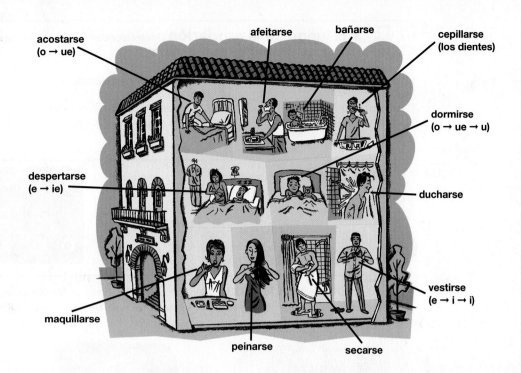

acostarse (o → ue) · **afeitarse** · **bañarse** · **cepillarse (los dientes)** · **dormirse (o → ue → u)** · **despertarse (e → ie)** · **ducharse** · **maquillarse** · **peinarse** · **secarse** · **vestirse (e → i → i)**

Algunos verbos reflexivos

acordarse de (o → ue)	to remember	**ponerse (nervioso/a)**	to get (nervous)
arreglarse	to get ready	**probarse (o → ue) la ropa**	to try on clothing
callarse	to get / keep quiet	**quedarse**	to stay; to remain
divertirse (e → ie → i)	to enjoy oneself; to have fun	**quitarse (la ropa)**	to take off (one's clothes)
irse	to go away; to leave	**reunirse**	to get together;
lavarse	to wash oneself		to meet
levantarse	to get up; to stand up	**sentarse (e → ie)**	to sit down
llamarse	to be called	**sentirse (e → ie → i)**	to feel
ponerse (la ropa)	to put on (one's clothes)		

Note: To identify all of the previous verbs as *reflexive*, the infinitives end in **-se.**

Estrategia
When a new infinitive is presented, if it is a stem-changing verb, the irregularities will be given in parentheses. For example, if you see *divertirse (e → ie → i)* you know that this infinitive is an -*ir* stem-changing verb, that the first "e" in the infinitive changes to "ie" in the present indicative, and that the "e" changes to "i" in the third-person singular and plural of the preterit.

Fíjate
Some verbs change their meanings slightly between non-reflexive and reflexive verbs, for example: *dormir* (to sleep) and *dormirse* (to fall asleep); *ir* (to go) and *irse* (to leave).

METHODOLOGY • Recycling
This is a good opportunity to recycle and remind students what the **e → ie → i** notation means.

METHODOLOGY • Reviewing and Recycling Grammatical Concepts
You may wish to have a warm-up each day at the beginning of class in which you select different verbs and vocabulary words from this and previous chapters. For example, you can do a quick mechanical drill with the forms of different tenses, such as the *pretérito* from *Capítulo 7*. You can also end a class with a quick mechanical drill. These quick reviews should last no more than 2 minutes.

ADDITIONAL ACTIVITY for *Las construcciones reflexivas*
El juego de la pelota En grupos de cuatro a seis estudiantes, van a tirar (*throw*) una pelota de papel. Turnándose, una persona del grupo nombra uno de los verbos reflexivos y un sujeto, y tira la pelota a un/a compañero/a. Si el/la compañero/a dice la forma correcta, gana un punto y tiene que continuar el juego. Cuando terminen, jueguen otra vez con los verbos en el pretérito.

MODELO
E1: ducharse… yo (tira la pelota)
E2: *me ducho*
E2: vestirse… mi madre (tira la pelota)
E3: *mi madre se viste*
E3: acordarse… tú (tira la pelota)
E4: *te acuerdas*

NOTE for 8-25

INSTRUCTIONS: Draw a 9-square tic-tac-toe board and write a different reflexive verb in each of the 9 squares. With a partner, and without showing your squares, play tic-tac-toe. For example, your partner says one of the verbs. If the verb is in your square, mark an X on the verb; if not, you don't have to do anything. Now you have to say one of your verbs, and you take turns until one of you has 3 Xs in a row going horizontally, vertically, or diagonally.

NOTE for 8-25

You may wish to tell your students that Tic-tac-toe is "Tres en raya" or "Taeti"

METHODOLOGY • Pair Work

You will want to identify daily who is Student "A" and who is Student "B," and then ask Student "A" to do the even-numbered items while Student "B" does the odd items. It is important for you to tell students explicitly to take turns when working in pairs. If not, one student may tend to monopolize the pair work.

NOTE for 8-26

You may wish to begin this activity by having students change the preterit forms of the reflexive verbs into the present tense.

TPR ACTIVITY for 8-26

Use **8-26** as a model to narrate a typical day using reflexive verbs. You can talk about your day or what we do, as in *primero nos despertamos y nos levantamos,* and have students act out the actions along with you. If you add extra information that is not in the book, make sure you write down those verbs so they can see them as they act out the day.

HERITAGE LANGUAGE LEARNERS

Have each student create his/her own complete "Un día en la vida" for a particular day and time of the year, school-related or not. Then collect their "lists" and read them aloud as they guess who wrote each one. Finally, discuss the similarities and differences in their days.

ANSWERS for 8-26

El día de María
1. Se levantó.
2. Se duchó.
3. Se secó.
4. Se maquilló. / Se vistió.
5. Se maquilló. / Se vistió.
6. Antes de irse a la universidad, se acordó de la tarea que no hizo para su clase de historia.
7. Llegó a la clase de historia y se quitó el abrigo.

⏱ 3:00   👥 **8-24** **El juego de la asociación** Juntos decidan qué verbos reflexivos asocian con las siguientes palabras y expresiones. ■

1. no decir nada   callarse
2. una silla   sentarse
3. recordar algo   acordarse
4. tener sueño   dormirse
5. no recordar algo   olvidarse de

6. triste o alegre, por ejemplo   ponerse / sentirse
7. un sombrero   ponerse
8. estar sucio   lavarse / ducharse / bañarse
9. no ir a ningún lugar   quedarse

⏱ 5:00   👥 **8-25** **¡Batalla!** Va a jugar con un/a compañero/a a *tic-tac-toe.* Escuchen mientras el/la profesor/a les explica el juego. ■

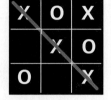

♻ Capítulo 7. El pretérito, pág. 263 del eText; Algunos verbos irregulares en el pretérito, pág. 272 del eText.

⏱ 3:00   👥 **8-26** **Un día en la vida** Ordena las actividades diarias de María y Tomás, estudiantes universitarios en Argentina, de forma cronológica. Luego, compara tu lista con la de un/a compañero/a. ■

El día de María
1. Antes de irse a la universidad, se acordó de la tarea que no hizo para su clase de historia.
2. Se duchó.
3. Se maquilló.
4. Llegó a la clase de historia y se quitó el abrigo.
5. Se vistió.
6. Se secó.
7. Se levantó.

El día de Tomás
1. Se acostó tarde.
2. Se levantó rápidamente a las ocho.
3. Se despertó tarde.
4. No se durmió inmediatamente.
5. Se divirtió con sus amigos.
6. Después de las clases se fue con los amigos para pasar el fin de semana en la playa.
7. Se fue para la clase de química.

♻ Capítulo Preliminar A. La hora, pág. 18 del eText.

⏱ 4:00   👥 **8-27** **Un día normal** Escribe por lo menos **cinco** actividades que haces normalmente y a qué hora las haces. Usa verbos reflexivos. Después, comparte tu lista con un/a compañero/a. ■

El día de Tomás
1. Se despertó tarde.
2. Se levantó rápidamente a las ocho.
3. Se fue para la clase de química.
4. Después de las clases se fue con los amigos para pasar el fin de semana en la playa.
5. Se divirtió con sus amigos.
6. Se acostó tarde.
7. No se durmió inmediatamente.

NOTE for 8-27

You may choose to make **8-27** a writing activity:

MODELO   *Me despierto a las ocho y me levanto inmediatamente. Después…*

EXPANSION for 8-27

You may wish to ask your students about their daily routines this morning and last night: e.g., *¿Qué hiciste esta mañana? ¿Qué hiciste anoche?*

`4:00` **8-28** **Para conocerte mejor** Túrnense para hacerse esta entrevista y conocer mejor sus hábitos. ∎

MODELO
    E1: ¿Qué te pones para ir al cine?

    E2: *Me pongo los jeans con una camiseta. ¿Y tú? ¿Qué te pones?*

    E1: *Generalmente me pongo pantalones con una blusa o un suéter.*

    E2: ¿Qué…?

1. ¿Qué te pones cuando sales con esa "persona especial"?
2. Cuando estás durmiéndote, ¿te acuerdas de las cosas que no hiciste durante el día?
3. ¿Cómo te diviertes?
4. Si tienes tiempo, ¿con quién(es) te reúnes?
5. ¿Cuándo te pones nervioso/a?
6. ¿Cuándo te sientes feliz?

`5:00` **8-29** **Mímica** Hagan mímica (*charades*) en grupos de cuatro. Túrnense para escoger un verbo reflexivo para representar al grupo. El grupo tiene que adivinar qué verbo es. Sigan jugando hasta que cada estudiante represente **cuatro** verbos diferentes. ∎

`7:00` **8-30** **¿Conoces bien a tus compañeros?** Trabaja en grupos de cuatro para hacer esta actividad. ∎

Paso 1 Un/a compañero/a debe salir de la sala de clase por un momento. Los otros estudiantes escriben **cinco** preguntas sobre la vida diaria del/de la compañero/a, usando los verbos reflexivos.

MODELO *¿A qué hora te despiertas?*
¿Te duchas todos los días?

Paso 2 Antes de entrar el/la compañero/a, el grupo de estudiantes debe adivinar cuáles van a ser las respuestas a esas preguntas.

MODELO *Se despierta a las siete.*
Sí, se ducha todos los días.

Paso 3 Entra el/la compañero/a y los otros le hacen las preguntas.

Paso 4 Comparen las respuestas del grupo con las del/de la compañero/a. ¿Tenían razón? Pueden repetir la actividad con los otros miembros del grupo.

NOTA CULTURAL

¡Hola!
eText p. 316   08-36   **Los centros comerciales en Latinoamérica**

NOTE for *Nota cultural*
See eText pg. 316 for complete *Nota cultural* reading and *Preguntas.*

7 GRAMÁTICA

 ¡Hola! Spanish/English Tutorials
08-37 to 08-41

5:00

El imperfecto
Sharing about situations in the past and how things used to be

In **Capítulo 7** you learned how to express certain ideas and notions that happened in the past with the preterit. Spanish has another past tense, **el imperfecto,** that *expresses habitual or ongoing past actions, provides descriptions,* or *describes conditions.*

Cuando Pepe vivía en la playa, nadaba en el mar todas las mañanas.

	-ar: hablar	-er: comer	-ir: vivir
yo	hablaba	comía	vivía
tú	hablabas	comías	vivías
Ud.	hablaba	comía	vivían
él, ella	hablaba	comía	vivía
nosotros/as	hablábamos	comíamos	vivíamos
vosotros/as	hablabais	comíais	vivíais
Uds.	hablablan	comían	vivían
ellos/as	hablaban	comían	vivían

Estrategia

Focus on the forms and when to use the *imperfecto*. Note that the *-er* and *-ir* forms are exactly the same, and that they have accents in every form. Also note that in the *-ar* verbs the *nosotros/nosotras* form has an accent.

There are only *three irregular verbs* in the imperfect: **ir, ser,** and **ver.**

	ir	ser	ver
yo	iba	era	veía
tú	ibas	eras	veías
Ud.	iba	era	veía
él, ella	iba	era	veía
nosotros/as	íbamos	éramos	veíamos
vosotros/as	ibais	erais	veíais
Uds.	iban	eran	veían
ellos/as	iban	eran	veían

The imperfect is used to:

1. provide background information, set the stage, or express a condition that existed

Llovía mucho.
Era una noche oscura y nublada.
Estábamos en el segundo año de la universidad.
Adriana **estaba** enferma y no **quería** levantarse.

It was raining a lot.
It was a dark and cloudy night.
We were in our second year of college.
Adriana was ill and didn't want to get up / get out of bed.

Fíjate

Repeated actions are usually expressed in English with *used to...* or *would...*

2. describe habitual or often repeated actions

Íbamos al centro comercial todos los viernes. Nos **divertíamos** mucho.
Cuando **era** pequeño, Lebron **jugaba** al básquetbol por lo menos dos horas al día.
Mis padres siempre **se vestían muy bien** los domingos para ir a la iglesia.

We went (used to go) to the mall / shopping district every Friday. We had a lot of fun.
When he was little, Lebron played (used to play) basketball for at least two hours a day.
My parents always dressed very well on Sundays to go to church.

Instructor Resources
• PPT, Extra Activities

Some words or expressions for describing habitual and repeated actions are:

a menudo	*often*	muchas veces	*many times*
casi siempre	*almost always*	mucho	*a lot*
frecuentemente	*frequently*	normalmente	*normally*
generalmente	*generally*	siempre	*always*
mientras	*while*	todos los días	*every day*

3. express *was* or *were* + *-ing*

¿**Dormías**?   *Were you sleeping?*
Me duchaba cuando Juan llamó.   *I was showering when Juan called.*
Alberto **leía** mientras Alicia **escuchaba** música.   *Alberto was reading while Alicia was listening to music.*

4. tell time in the past

Era la una y yo todavía **estudiaba**.   *It was 1:00 and I was still studying.*
Eran las diez y los niños **dormían**.   *It was 10:00 and the children were sleeping.*

[3:00] 👥 **8-31** **La práctica** Repitan el juego de la actividad **7-8** en la página 165, esta vez para practicar el imperfecto. ∎

[5:00] 👥 **8-32** **Cuando era joven** Completa el párrafo sobre Eva Perón para saber cómo pudo ser su vida cuando era joven. Después, compara tus respuestas con las de un/a compañero/a. ∎

ayudar	encantar	gustar	poder	querer
preferir	sentirse	ser	tener	trabajar

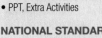

María Eva Duarte, como primero se llamaba, nació en una provincia de Buenos Aires en el año 1919. Cuando (1) ___tenía___ seis o siete años su padre murió. Eva y sus cuatro hermanos (2) __se sentían__ muy tristes y la vida (3) ___era___ muy difícil para ellos porque les faltaban dinero y comida. La madre (4) __trabajaba__ como costurera (*seamstress*) y los niños la (5) __ayudaban__ en la casa. Nos imaginamos que a Eva le (6) __encantaba__ el verano cuando (7) ___podía___ estar en casa con sus hermanos. No le (8) __gustaban__ las muñecas y (9) __prefería__ inventar juegos o imaginar situaciones diferentes. Parece que desde el principio (*from the start*) Eva (10) __quería__ ser actriz.

NATIONAL STANDARDS
Communication
Students tend to build confidence with the imperfect tense since there are so few irregulars. The activities that use the imperfect facilitate communication between classmates by engaging them in conversations in which they provide and obtain information, express feelings and emotions, and share opinions (Standard 1.1). Many activities can be tailored to meet the other Communication Standards by modifying the instructions. For example, when reading in Spanish about Eva Perón (**8-32**), your students could pick out the imperfect verbs that deal with her childhood (Standard 1.2). The other questions that refer to childhood and past schooling could be turned into presentations by asking students to bring in photos and narrate portions of their childhoods or activities siblings used to do (Standard 1.3). This can be done as a writing project or as an oral presentation.

Fíjate

In **8-33**, you see the word *el colegio.* Remember that *colegio* is a false cognate in Spanish; it can mean *school* or *high school.*

8-33 En el colegio... ¿Qué hacías cuando estabas en el colegio? ¿Con qué frecuencia? Escribe una equis (**X**) en la columna apropiada de cada hilera (*row*). Luego, compara tus respuestas con las de un/a compañero/a. ∎

MODELO   E1: *¿Escuchabas música de Cristina Aguilera?*

E2: *No, nunca escuchaba música de Cristina Aguilera. / Sí, a veces escuchaba música de Cristina Aguilera.*

	TODOS LOS DÍAS	MUCHAS VECES	A VECES	NUNCA
1. escuchar música de Cristina Aguilera				
2. nadar en la playa				
3. leer obras de Shakespeare				
4. bañarse por la noche				
5. acostarse temprano				
6. dormirse en las clases				
7. ponerse nervioso/a antes de un examen				
8. reunirse con los amigos				
9. vestirse como querías				
10. querer ir a la escuela				
11. levantarse muy tarde				
12. no hacer nada por la noche				

 Capítulo 3. La casa, pág. 98 del eText; Los colores, pág. 111 del eText.

8-34 Mi primera casa ¿Cómo era tu primera casa o la casa de tu amigo/a? Descríbesela a un/a compañero/a dándole por lo menos **cinco** detalles. Luego, cambien de papel. ∎

MODELO   *Mi primera casa estaba en una ciudad pequeña. Tenía dos dormitorios. La cocina era amarilla. El comedor blanco y la sala azul eran pequeños. Tenía solamente (only) un baño.*

8-35 **¡Cómo cambia la vida!** Miren el dibujo y escriban **siete** oraciones que contesten la pregunta "¿cómo era la vida en los años setenta?". Usen verbos como **tener, estar, ser, haber, ayudar, limpiar** y **jugar.** ¡Sean creativos! ■

Workbooklet

 8-36 **Preguntas personales** Cuando tenían dieciséis años, ¿qué hacían tus compañeros/as de clase? Circula por la clase para preguntárselo. ■

MODELO
E1: ¿Jugabas al fútbol con los amigos?
E2: *Sí, jugaba todos los días después de salir del colegio.*
E3: *Sí, jugaba con el equipo del colegio.*
E4: *No, nunca jugaba al fútbol. No me gustaba.*

	ESTUDIANTE 1:	ESTUDIANTE 2:	ESTUDIANTE 3:
1. ¿Te quedabas en casa los fines de semana?			
2. ¿Qué hacías los fines de semana?			
3. ¿Manejabas (*Did you drive*)?			
4. ¿Tenías coche (*car*)?			
5. ¿Trabajabas?			
6. ¿Qué hacías cuando hacía mal tiempo?			
7. ¿Qué hacías cuando hacía buen tiempo?			
8. ¿Qué hacías cuando tenías dinero?			
9. ¿Qué hacías cuando no tenías dinero?			
10. ¿Qué hacías para divertirte?			

ADDITIONAL ACTIVITY for *El imperfecto*

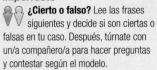

¿Cierto o falso? Lee las frases siguientes y decide si son ciertas o falsas en tu caso. Después, túrnate con un/a compañero/a para hacer preguntas y contestar según el modelo.

MODELO
E1: *Antes de venir a la universidad, ¿vivías en un apartamento?*
E2: *No, no vivía en un apartamento. Vivía con mis padres en una casa.*

Antes de venir a la universidad...
1. vivir en un apartamento
2. tener una mascota (*pet*)
3. ver mucho la televisión
4. gustarte comer verduras
5. ser un/a buen/a estudiante
6. tener muchos amigos
7. estudiar todo el tiempo
8. tener mucho dinero para gastar
9. llevar pantalones cortos
10. tocar un instrumento
11. sacar la basura
12. manejar mucho

ESCUCHA

En el centro comercial

08-42 to 08-43

Estrategia

Guessing meaning from context

You do not need to know every word to understand a listening passage or to get the gist of a conversation. Think about the overall message, then use the surrounding words or sentences to guess at meaning.

8-37 **Antes de escuchar** Beatriz, la prima de Marisol, es estudiante de intercambio en Buenos Aires. Va de compras con su "hermana" argentina, Luz. Están en la tienda Zara, comprando ropa. ■

1. ¿Cómo es la tienda Zara?
2. ¿Piensas que ir de compras a Zara en Buenos Aires es igual que ir de compras a Zara en Nueva York (o en cualquier otra ciudad)?

Beatriz y Luz van de compras.

 8-38 **A escuchar** Completa las siguientes actividades. ■

1. Escucha la conversación entre Beatriz y Luz y después selecciona la opción que mejor conteste la pregunta.

   ¿De qué se trata (*What is the gist of*) la conversación?

   _____ a. A Beatriz no le gustan las blusas de la tienda y tampoco la tienda. Jamás va de compras allí.

   _____ b. A Beatriz le encanta el dependiente. Vive cerca de Luz.

   _____ c. A Luz le gustan los perros negros. Alguien tiene un perro que se llama Toro o posiblemente Goro.

2. Escucha una vez más y termina las siguientes oraciones.

   a. Marisol y Beatriz visitaron una de las tiendas Zara… (dónde y cuándo)
   b. Marisol y Beatriz no compraron nada porque…
   c. Luz no quiere comprar la blusa de seda o la falda de lana porque…
   d. Beatriz reconoce (*recognizes*) al dependiente porque…

3. ¿Qué significa "dependiente"?

 8-39 **Después de escuchar** En grupos de tres, realicen (*act out*) la escena entre Beatriz, Luz y el dependiente. ■

¡CONVERSEMOS!
08-44

8-40 **Los modelos** Crea un desfile de moda (*fashion show*) con un/a compañero/a. Describe la ropa que lleva tu compañero/a. Si quieres, trae fotos de ropa de unas revistas y descríbela como si fueras un comentarista de moda para *Style.com*. Incluye **por lo menos diez** oraciones. ■

8-41 **¿Qué llevaban?** Piensa en la ropa que tus amigos, tu familia y tú llevaban cuando eran más jóvenes. ¿Cómo se compara el estilo de antes con el estilo de ahora? Describe con detalles la ropa que se llevaba en **por lo menos diez** oraciones. ■

SECTION GOALS for ¡Conversemos!
By the end of the ¡Conversemos! section, students will be able to:
- describe clothing in the presentational and interpersonal modes.
- discuss past clothing styles and compare them to present styles in the presentational and interpersonal modes.
- utilize previously learned/recycled vocabulary and grammatical concepts such as *gustar* and *gustar*-type verbs and the imperfect form.

NOTE for ¡Conversemos!
Creating a fashion show in class is excellent for communication practice. Among the many options, one is to have students write up their own descriptions and then wear what they describe to class. Another option is to have students give their written descriptions to classmates to be read as they model their outfits.

SECTION GOALS for *Escribe*

By the end of the *Escribe* section, students will be able to:
- pre-write by brainstorming childhood activities.
- organize their pre-writing.
- write an e-mail about childhood memories.
- listen to what other people wrote and guess who wrote each narration.
- practice circumlocution.

NATIONAL STANDARDS
Communication

The *Escribe* section focuses on communication in the presentational mode (Standard 1.3) when students listen to the instructor read aloud the writing samples from various students. The activity can be modified to include interpretation of written Spanish (Standard 1.2): e.g., you could write a brief narration of your childhood for your students to read. By working in groups and discussing their writing before handing it in, students practice interpersonal communication (Standard 1.1). The writing exercise reinforces the sound writing practices they have learned when writing in English: pre-writing, organizing, and brainstorming (Standard 4.1).

NOTE for *Estrategia*

While we generally associate circumlocution with speaking, it is a useful skill to develop for writing as well. While some writing assignments are completed over time and allow for revisions, others are more impromptu and are completed in class. Developing this skill in writing will make students less dependent on dictionaries and will allow the skill to transfer easily to speaking.

NOTE for *Estrategia*

After presenting the strategy of circumlocution, you may wish to have students revisit an activity in the *¡Conversemos!* section to practice the strategy orally.

ALTERNATE ACTIVITY for *Escribe*

The writing exercise in the *Escribe* section can be expanded to include other topics. One such topic could be that of one's first best friend. You can assign this writing exercise for homework and collect the assignment. Sometimes assignments that require students to reveal personal information are better suited for homework than for sharing with the class. Another topic that would work well would be their first pet.

ESCRIBE

08-45

Un email

Estrategia		
Circumlocution	It is common when learning a language not to know or remember the exact word(s) you need to communicate an idea. Thinking of another way to express something is called *circumlocution*—essentially using several words to describe something simple.	For example, if you don't know or remember the word for "tía," you could say "la hermana de mi padre." If you can't remember the word for "cine," you could get your point across by writing "todos los sábados íbamos al centro para ver una película."

8-42 Antes de escribir ¿Qué te gustaba hacer de niño/a? ¿Te levantabas temprano para jugar con tus amigos? ¿Tus padres te dejaban comer caramelos y otros dulces a menudo? Haz una lista de las **ocho** cosas que más te gustaba hacer cuando eras niño/a, usando "circumlocution" cuando sea necesario. ▪

8-43 A escribir Organiza tus ideas y escribe un email a tu hermano/a (o a tu mejor amigo/a), recordando las cosas que hacías en tu niñez. ▪

8-44 Después de escribir Tu profesor/a va a leer los emails a la clase para ver si ustedes pueden adivinar quiénes los escribieron. ▪

¿Cómo andas? II

	Feel confident	Need to review
Having completed **Comunicación II**, I now can . . .		
• provide details about clothing (p. 207)	☐	☐
• relate daily routines (p. 210)	☐	☐
• consider shopping practices in the Spanish-speaking countries (p. 213)	☐	☐
• share about situations in the past and how things used to be (p. 214)	☐	☐
• guess the meanings of unfamiliar words, when listening, from the context (p. 218)	☐	☐
• communicate about clothing and fashion (p. 219)	☐	☐
• write an e-mail, practicing circumlocution (p. 220)	☐	☐

10:00   08-46 to 08-48

Les presento mi país

Mi nombre es María Graciela Martelli Paz y vivo en Rosario, una ciudad cerca de Buenos Aires. Realmente soy porteña (*una persona de Buenos Aires*) porque nací allí. Mi primer apellido es italiano porque mis abuelos paternos eran de Nápoles. Muchos argentinos tienen apellidos italianos a causa de la gran inmigración europea a fines del siglo diecinueve. **¿De qué herencia sos vos, che?** Mi país es grande y la geografía es muy variada: desde la montaña más alta del hemisferio occidental, el Cerro Aconcagua, hasta la ciudad más sureña (*del sur*) del mundo, Ushuaia. También tenemos lugares naturales como los glaciares, las pampas, la región de la Patagonia, las cataratas del Iguazú y unas playas hermosas, como la de Mar del Plata. **¿Qué regiones y riquezas naturales hay en tu país?**

María Graciela
Martelli Paz

las cataratas del Iguazú en la frontera con Brasil y Argentina

el tango en San Telmo, un antiguo barrio en la capital

galerías Pacífico en la calle Florida

OCÉANO PACÍFICO

PARAGUAY   BRASIL

Salta   Formosa
San Miguel
de Tucumán

Córdoba   URUGUAY
Cerro   Mendoza   Rosario
Aconcagua Buenos Aires La Plata
                Río de
        PAMPAS la Plata
                Mar del Plata
        Bahía Blanca

Río Negro

                OCÉANO
                ATLÁNTICO

Ushuaia

ALMANAQUE

Nombre oficial:	República de Argentina
Gobierno:	República
Población:	41.343.203 (2010)
Idioma:	español
Moneda:	Peso argentino ($)

¿Sabías que...?

- El **lunfardo** es un dialecto o jerga que tuvo su origen en los barrios de Buenos Aires a finales del siglo XIX. Es la lengua del tango y también la jerga de las prisiones a principios del siglo XX. Se forman palabras diciendo las sílabas al revés (*reversing the syllables*): "tango" en lunfardo es *gotán*.

Preguntas

1. ¿Cuáles son tres de las distintas regiones geográficas del país? Cuando es verano en Argentina, ¿en qué estación estamos aquí? ¿Por qué?
2. ¿Dónde puedes ir de compras en Buenos Aires?
3. ¿Qué tiene Argentina en común con otros países de Sudamérica?

Amplía tus conocimientos sobre Argentina en MySpanishLab.

NOTE for *Les presento mi país*
While *voseo*, the use of the pronoun *vos* for second person singular, is widespread throughout many parts of Latin America, it is very widespread in Argentina. Though it is not taught in Spanish textbooks in the United States, millions of people in the Southern Cone and elsewhere use this linguistic form on a daily basis.

EXPANSION for *Preguntas*
Additional questions include: *¿Cómo se usa la palabra "che" en Argentina? ¿Por qué se dice que Buenos Aires es una ciudad cosmopolita? ¿Qué es el lunfardo?*

SECTION GOALS for *Cultura*
By the end of the *Cultura* section, students will be able to:
- explain the ethnic roots represented in Argentina.
- describe the geographical diversity of Argentina.
- discuss the climate and culture of Uruguay.
- compare Argentina and Uruguay, and also these two countries with previously featured countries.

NATIONAL STANDARDS
Cultures, Comparisons
In *Les presento mi país*, the readings highlight the unique features of Argentina and Uruguay. Students learn about the culture of these two countries (Standard 2.1), and with the information presented they can make comparisons about how these countries differ from the United States (Standard 4.2). One comparison they learn is that many Italians immigrated to Argentina and therefore many Argentines have Italian surnames; also, Italian cuisine has been incorporated into the Argentine and Uruguayan diet. In Uruguay there is a temperate climate, which differs from the extreme temperature variations in regions across the United States.

NOTE for *Les presento mi país*
One of the goals of *¡Anda! Curso elemental* is to expose students to new countries, ways of living, and ways of thinking. For many, this may be their first exposure to foreign cultures so a sampling of each country of focus is important as an introduction to the Spanish-speaking world. You may choose to highlight different points for these countries, given your background and interests. For example, you may choose to emphasize the history of Argentina touching on Evita Perón, los gauchos, Borges, etc., or spend more time on the national issues that Argentina and Uruguay face today.

NOTE for *Les presento mi país*
People from the city of Buenos Aires are called *porteños*. They are said to have their own mannerisms and idiomatic expressions as well as accent. The pronunciation of *y* and *ll* are closer to the *sh* sound in English than in Spanish elsewhere.

NOTE for *Les presento mi país*
Argentines use *che* to call attention to people, to begin sentences, as a nickname, and as a sentence interjection. It is an all-purpose word. In some indigenous languages, it means "man" or "people." It was, of course, the nickname of Ernesto Guevara, the revolutionary from Rosario, Argentina.

NOTE for *Montevideo*
Montevideo, Uruguay, is the southernmost capital in South America. This vibrant city lies on the northeastern bank of the Río de la Plata, the river that separates the southern coast of Uruguay from the northern coast of Argentina. With a rich culture influenced by many European immigrants, it is also an important center of commerce and higher education in Uruguay.

SUGGESTION for *Montevideo*
Ask students what influences might occur by having Montevideo just across the river from Argentina. Ask them whether they know of other cities that are located at the mouths of rivers, or are even split by them, and how they might be different from cities that are land locked.

NOTE for *Punta del Este*
Punta del Este is one of the most popular resorts in all of South America. It is a mecca for glamorous tourists who enjoy golfing, casinos, beautiful beaches, and other resort pastimes.

SUGGESTION for *Punta del Este*
Ask students: What are some famous resorts in the United States? Are some more exclusive than others? Why do they think that happens?

NOTE for *El chivito*
El chivito is a steak sandwich that contains cheese, ham, bacon, tomatoes, eggs, lettuce, and mayonnaise. It is the Uruguayan version of "fast food," and is quite popular. Another typical dish is *asado,* also common in Argentina. Italian food is also popular, due to the large number of people of Italian descent in the country.

SUGGESTION for *El chivito*
Ask students: What is our most common fast food? (hamburgers); Do we have food in common with other cultures, or is it exclusively "United Statesian"?

Uruguay

08-46 to 08-47, 08-49

Les presento mi país

Francisco Tomás Bacigalupe Bustamante

Mi nombre es Francisco Tomás Bacigalupe Bustamante, aunque de pequeño me llamaban Paquito. Soy de Montevideo, la capital de Uruguay. Mi país es pequeño, pero también es tranquilo y bonito. La mayoría de la población, el ochenta por ciento, vive en los centros urbanos. El clima es templado (no hace mucho calor ni mucho frío) y es perfecto para nuestras playas increíbles. Cuando era niño las playas eran nuestro destino favorito para ir de vacaciones. **¿Dónde ibas tú de vacaciones?** Tenemos mucho en común con nuestros vecinos los argentinos: el tango, la yerba mate, los gauchos y una dieta que contiene mucha carne. También comemos mucha pizza y pasta, debido a nuestra herencia italiana. **¿Qué comida de otros países te gusta comer?**

Punta del Este es un balneario (*resort*) muy turístico.

El chivito es un plato típico uruguayo.

el puerto de Montevideo

ALMANAQUE

Nombre oficial: República Oriental del Uruguay
Gobierno: República democrática
Población: 3.510.386 (2010)
Idiomas: español (oficial); portuñol/brasilero
Moneda: Peso uruguayo ($U)

¿Sabías que...?
• Debido al índice de alfabetización (*literacy*), el clima agradable y templado, la belleza del paisaje y la hospitalidad de la gente, a Uruguay se le conoce como "la Suiza de América".

Preguntas
1. ¿Dónde vive la mayoría de los uruguayos?
2. Muchos uruguayos son de herencia italiana. ¿En qué se ve esta herencia?
3. ¿Qué tiene en común Uruguay con su país vecino Argentina?

Amplía tus conocimientos sobre Uruguay en MySpanishLab.

EXPANSION for *Preguntas*
Additional questions to ask your students are:
1. *¿Cómo es Uruguay? ¿Por qué crees que la mayoría de la gente vive en los centros urbanos?*
2. *¿Qué plato de "comida rápida" es típico en Uruguay? ¿Cómo se compara este plato con la "comida rápida" estadounidense? ¿Y con la comida de los otros países que hemos estudiado?*

¡Hola!
eText p. 326   08-52 to 08-53

Ambiciones siniestras

EPISODIO 8

Lectura y video

Y por fin, ¿cómo andas?

	Feel confident	Need to review
Having completed this chapter, I now can . . .		

Comunicación I

- describe clothing (p. 192)
- pronounce *ll* and *ñ* correctly (MSL / SAM)
- state to whom and for whom things are done (p. 196)
- express likes, dislikes, needs, etc. (p. 200)
- convey information about people and things (p. 203)

Comunicación II

- provide details about clothing (p. 207)
- relate daily routines (p. 210)
- share about situations in the past, and how things used to be (p. 214)
- guess the meanings of unfamiliar words, when listening, from the context (p. 218)
- communicate about clothing and fashion (p. 219)
- write an e-mail, practicing circumlocution (p. 220)

Cultura

- recount information about a Spanish clothing company (p. 196)
- consider shopping practices in Spanish-speaking countries (p. 213)
- share important facts about this chapter's featured countries: Argentina and Uruguay (pp. 221–222)

Ambiciones siniestras

- deduce the meanings of unfamiliar words in a reading passage and explain the significance of the latest e-mail from Sr. Verdugo (p. 223)
- reveal secrets regarding Lupe (p. 223)

Comunidades

- use Spanish in real-life contexts (SAM)

EXPANSION for 8-45 (Online)
Additional questions to ask your students are:
    ¿Quién puede ser el hombre que deja el mensaje en el contestador automático?
    ¿Dónde piensas que están Eduardo y Alejandra? ¿Qué pasó con ellos?

METHODOLOGY • Reading
¡Anda! Curso elemental supports both top-down and bottom-up approaches to reading. In the top-down, or reader-driven, approach, the pre-existing knowledge the reader brings to the text is critical to comprehension. The

Antes de leer section supports this approach. The text-driven, or bottom-up, approach relies on the decoding of words, phrases, and sentences.

NATIONAL STANDARDS
Communication, Comparisons
Note that the online readings are kept at a level of comprehensible input that entices the students to read. Also, follow-up questions encourage students to think beyond the content of the story and make informed guesses about what they would do in the same circumstance.

CAPÍTULO 8

🔑 **Instructor Resources**
- Video script

SECTION GOALS for *Lectura y video* (Online)
By the end of the *Lectura y video* section, students will be able to:
- utilize the new reading strategy of guessing from the context.
- apply the new strategy in combination with the previous strategies.
- narrate the main events of the reading.
- review the events of the previous episode.
- retell the main points of the story.
- predict future events.

NOTE for *Lectura y video*
Activity answers for online content can be found on the next page for quick reference.

RECAP of *AMBICIONES SINIESTRAS Episodio 7* (Online)
Lectura: In *Capítulo 7, El rompecabezas,* Cisco called Manolo to check on Alejandra and learned that no one had heard from her. Cisco went to his favorite restaurant to do some thinking and received a phone call from a man who said he would have two days to solve a riddle or Eduardo would die. Upon further investigation, Cisco learned from Manolo that he too had received the mysterious phone call. When Manolo called Alejandra, he heard a man's voice on her answering machine.
Video: In *Episodio 7, ¡Qué rico está el pisco!,* Cisco organized a videoconference about Eduardo's and Alejandra's disappearances. Both Cisco and Lupe acted very mysteriously when asked about the disappearances. It appeared that Lupe was hiding her true identity, and that Cisco knew more about the disappearances than he was letting on. At the end of the episode, Cisco suspected that the answer to the riddle was Chile, and he wondered if Sr. Verdugo could be holding Eduardo in Chile.

NATIONAL STANDARDS
Communication
The *Lectura* online provides authentic text in Spanish that students have to read and interpret for understanding (Standard 1.2). The video provides listening practice as students interpret what is happening and why, and how these actions might affect future actions (Standard 1.2). The new strategy, guessing meaning from the context, prepares students to become more efficient readers as they scan for the main ideas and supporting ideas for enhanced understanding. If students work together to discuss the comprehension questions, they engage in conversations and provide and obtain information (Standard 1.1).

VOCABULARIO ACTIVO

La ropa	Clothing
el abrigo	overcoat
la bata	robe
la blusa	blouse
el bolso	purse
las botas (*pl.*)	boots
los calcetines (*pl.*)	socks
la camisa	shirt
la camiseta	T-shirt
la chaqueta	jacket
el cinturón	belt
el conjunto	outfit
la corbata	tie
la falda	skirt
la gorra	cap
los guantes	gloves
el impermeable	raincoat
los jeans (*pl.*)	jeans
las medias (*pl.*)	stockings; hose
la moda	fashion
los pantalones (*pl.*)	pants
los pantalones cortos (*pl.*)	shorts
el paraguas	umbrella
el pijama	pajamas
las prendas	articles of clothing
la ropa interior	underwear
las sandalias (*pl.*)	sandals
el sombrero	hat
la sudadera	sweatshirt
el suéter	sweater
los tenis (*pl.*)	tennis shoes
el traje	suit
el traje de baño	swimsuit; bathing suit
el vestido	dress
las zapatillas (*pl.*)	slippers
los zapatos (*pl.*)	shoes

Algunos verbos	Some verbs
llevar	to wear; to take; to carry
prestar	to loan; to lend

Algunos verbos como *gustar*	Verbs similar to gustar
encantar	to love; to like very much
fascinar	to fascinate
hacer falta	to need; to be lacking
importar	to matter; to be important
molestar	to bother

Las telas y los materiales	Fabrics and materials
el algodón	cotton
el cuero	leather
la lana	wool
el poliéster	polyester
la seda	silk
la tela	fabric

Algunos adjetivos	Some adjectives
ancho/a	wide
atrevido/a	daring
claro/a	light (colored)
cómodo/a	comfortable
corto/a	short
de cuadros	checked
de lunares	polka-dotted
de rayas	striped
elegante	elegant
estampado/a	print; with a design or pattern
estrecho/a	narrow; tight
formal	formal
incómodo/a	uncomfortable
informal	casual
largo/a	long
liso/a	solid-colored
oscuro/a	dark

Otra palabra útiles	Another useful word
el/la modelo	model

Un verbo	A verb
quedarle bien / mal	to fit well / poorly

Algunos verbos reflexivos	Some reflexive verbs
acordarse de (o → ue)	to remember
acostarse (o → ue)	to go to bed
afeitarse	to shave
arreglarse	to get ready
bañarse	to bathe
callarse	to get / keep quiet
cepillarse (el pelo, los dientes)	to brush (one's hair, teeth)
despertarse (e → ie)	to wake up; to awaken
divertirse (e → ie → i)	to enjoy oneself; to have fun
dormirse (o → ue → u)	to fall asleep
ducharse	to shower
irse	to go away; to leave
lavarse	to wash oneself
levantarse	to get up; to stand up
llamarse	to be called
maquillarse	to put on make up
peinarse	to comb one's hair
ponerse (la ropa)	to put on (one's clothes)
ponerse (nervioso/a)	to get (nervous)
probarse (o → ue) la ropa	to try on clothing
quedarse	to stay; to remain
quitarse (la ropa)	to take off (one's clothes)
reunirse	to get together; to meet
secarse	to dry off
sentarse (e → ie)	to sit down
sentirse (e → ie → i)	to feel
vestirse (e → i → i)	to get dressed

Instructor Resources
• IRM: Syllabi and Lesson Plans

NATIONAL STANDARDS

COMUNICACIÓN I

- To describe the human body (Communication)
- To pronounce the letters *d* and *t* (Communication)
- To share about people, actions, and things (Communication)
- To explain ailments and treatments (Communication)
- To make emphatic and exclamatory statements (Communication)
- To engage in additional communication practice (Communication, Communities)

COMUNICACIÓN II

- To narrate in the past (Communication)
- To explain how long something has been going on and how long ago something occurred (Communication, Communities)
- To ask yourself questions when listening to organize and summarize what you hear (Communication, Connections)
- To communicate about ailments and healthy living (Communication)
- To write a summary, sequencing past events (Communication, Comparisons)
- To engage in additional communication practice (Communication, Communities)

CULTURA

- To relate the importance of water in maintaining good health (Communication, Connections)
- To consider pharmacies in Spanish-speaking countries and how they differ from those in the United States (Communication, Comparisons, Connections)
- To list important information about this chapter's featured countries: Peru, Bolivia, and Ecuador (Communication, Cultures, Connections, Comparisons)
- To explore further the chapter's cultural themes (Communication, Cultures)

AMBICIONES SINIESTRAS

- To create check questions to facilitate comprehension when reading, and give details about the new e-mail message (Communication, Connections)
- To discover the progress the characters are making in deciphering the new riddle (Communication)

9 Estamos en forma

Todos queremos tener una buena calidad de vida y prolongarla lo más posible. No podemos cambiar nuestra herencia genética transmitida de padres a hijos, pero sí tenemos control sobre decisiones que pueden afectar nuestro estilo de vida: el ejercicio, la dieta, la prevención de accidentes y el uso de sustancias adictivas como el tabaco.

PREGUNTAS

1 ¿Vives una vida sana (*healthy*)? ¿Qué haces (o no haces) para tener una vida más sana?

2 ¿Qué tipo de ejercicio te gusta hacer?

3 ¿Cuáles son algunas de las decisiones específicas que tomamos que pueden afectar nuestra salud (*health*)?

226

COMUNIDADES
• To use Spanish in real-life contexts (Communities)

SECTION GOALS for *Chapter opener*
By the end of the Chapter opener section, students will be able to:
• list environmental and personal factors that contribute to longevity.
• compare healthy lifestyle choices with unhealthy choices.
• narrate how their choices contribute to or detract from living healthily.

OBJETIVOS	CONTENIDOS	

NATIONAL STANDARDS
Communities

This chapter is about health and wellness. If you have a health/wellness major at your school (especially nutrition/dietetics or exercise science) you could ask a faculty member to provide materials that your students could translate and use to make presentations to the Hispanic community about topics such as MyPlate, the food pyramid, diet, exercise, and preventive medical care. They could get healthy recipes and translate those into Spanish for the Spanish-speaking community as well. You could also ask local health clinics or doctors' offices if they have simple materials or signs they would like to post in Spanish, such as to whom to make checks, the rules of the office regarding the use of cell phones, or fees for certain services like flu shots or copies of forms. If you have a sizable Hispanic community, you could ask the hospital for upcoming wellness programs and have students make flyers in Spanish, posting the details of the events. As always, use good judgment when thinking of service projects, remember the skill level of your students, and consider how they could serve the community.

METHODOLOGY • Teacher Talk

In the classroom, although we simplify our language when we speak, attempting to stay within the range of *i + 1*, we should strive to deliver our speech at a speed that is as close to natural as possible. As the semester progresses, that speed gradually increases.

SECTION GOALS for
Comunicación I
By the end of the first *Comunicación* section, students will be able to:
• identify body parts and things associated with the human body.
• pronounce the letters *d* and *t* correctly.
• match body parts with clothing items worn on the body.
• review formation and placement of direct and indirect object pronouns and reflexive pronouns.
• describe ailments and medical treatments for ailments.
• tell where to go to treat certain symptoms and explain what symptoms they have.
• read about the importance of water to health.
• use *qué* and *cuánto* for exclamations.

NATIONAL STANDARDS
Communication
Talking about how one feels appeals to the basic sense that we all have; we love to talk about ourselves! Your students will enjoy the associated activities that help them acquire the vocabulary. The vocabulary associated with *El cuerpo humano* and *Algunas enfermedades y tratamientos médicos* is rich with communicative possibilities because the topic is universal. Most of the activities are for pairs and small groups: thus, students are engaging in interpersonal communication (Standard 1.1). If you have students play doctor and patient, pretending to have ailments, or act out ailments you suggest, you satisfy Standard 1.3, the presentational mode. You could bring in the Spanish dosage instructions from packages of over-the-counter medications for students to read and discuss, and that would meet Standard 1.2, the interpretive mode. You could also read the instructions to them and use that as a listening activity.

Comunicación I

1 VOCABULARIO

09-01 to 09-07

El cuerpo humano — Describing the human body

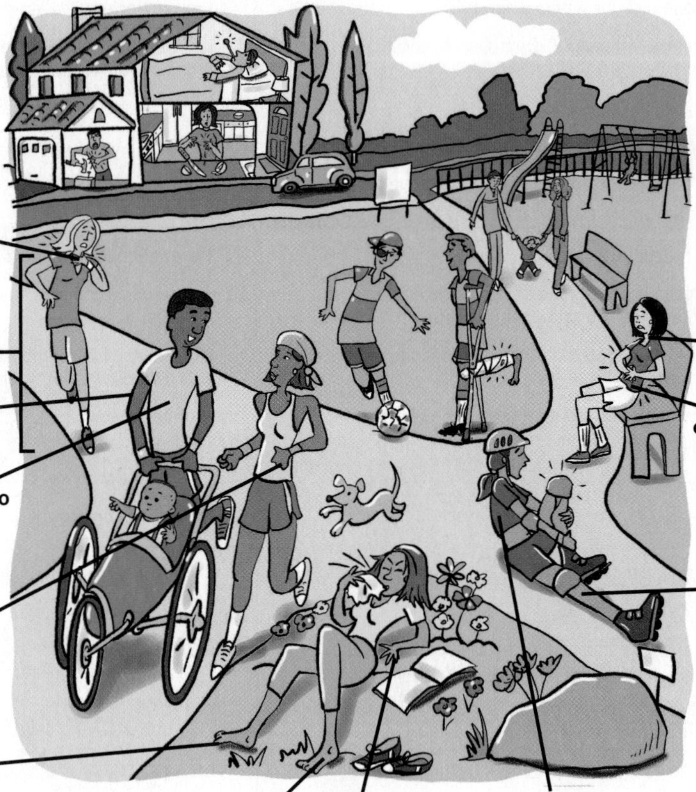

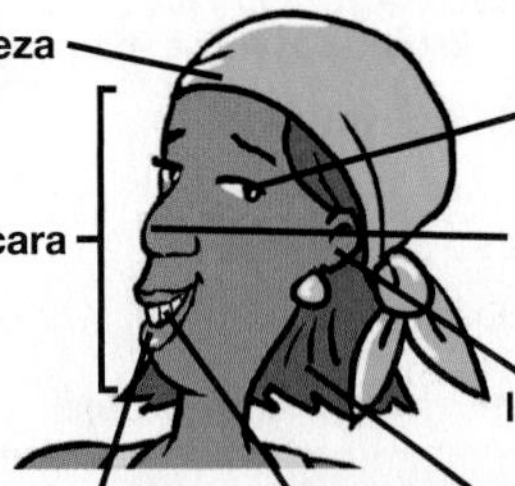

la garganta
el cuerpo
el brazo
el pecho
la mano
el dedo (del pie)
el pie
el dedo (de la mano)
la espalda
la pierna
el estómago
el cuello

la cabeza
el ojo
la cara
la nariz
la oreja
la boca
el diente
el pelo

Otras palabras útiles	Other useful words
la cintura	*waist*
el corazón	*heart*
el oído	*inner ear*
la salud	*health*
la sangre	*blood*

Algunos verbos	Some verbs
doler (ue)	*to hurt*
estar enfermo/a	*to be sick*
estar sano/a; saludable	*to be healthy*
ser alérgico/a (a)	*to be allergic (to)*

PRONUNCIACIÓN

The letters *d* and *t*

Go to MySpanishLab / Student Activities Manual to learn about the letters *d* and *t*.

¡Hola!
09-08 to 09-11

4:00 **9-1** **Simón dice** Escuchen mientras su instructor/a les da las instrucciones de esta actividad. ■

 Capítulo 8. La ropa, pág. 294 del eText.

2:00 **9-2** **¿Cómo nos vestimos?** Túrnense para decir qué partes del cuerpo asocian con la ropa indicada. ■

MODELO   E1: los zapatos
          E2: *los pies*

1. las botas   los pies
2. los guantes   las manos
3. los pantalones   las piernas
4. la gorra   la cabeza
5. la corbata   el cuello
6. la camiseta   el pecho/la espalda
7. los tenis   los pies
8. la chaqueta   el pecho/la espalda/los brazos

2:00 **9-3** **Categorías** Juntos escriban todas las palabras del vocabulario nuevo que corresponden a las siguientes partes del cuerpo. ■

MODELO   E1: la cabeza
          E2: *la cara, el pelo*, etc.

1. la cabeza
2. de la cintura para arriba (*from the waist up*)
3. de la cintura para abajo (*from the waist down*)
4. la cara

2:00 **9-4** **¿Cómo se escribe?** Escribe la primera y la última letra de una de las palabras del vocabulario. Un/a compañero/a tiene que terminarla. Túrnense para practicar la ortografía de por lo menos **ocho** palabras. ■

MODELO   E1: e _ _ _ _ _ a
          E2: e s p a l d a

CAPÍTULO 9

SECTION GOALS for *Pronunciación*
By the end of the *Pronunciación* section, students will be able to:
• pronounce the letters *d* and *t* correctly.
• practice pronunciation skills using *dichos* and *refranes*.

INSTRUCTIONS for 9-1
Play *Simón dice* with your students to practice the body parts. Here are the instructions for how to play the game:
    Tell students that they should all obey you if you first say the words "Simón dice" and that they are out of the game if they follow an order that doesn't begin with "Simón dice," or if they fail to do what Simón says to do.
    Begin by saying something like, "Simón dice, tócate la cabeza." Look to make sure all have touched their heads. Give another order such as, "Simón dice, tócate el brazo." Check again. Continue giving orders. Mix it up and say something like, "levanta la mano derecha," without the preface "Simón dice." Call out the players who raise their right hands. Play until one person is left. That is the winner.

METHODOLOGY • Pairing Students
What follows are some suggestions for pairing students using the body parts:
1. You will need one small piece of paper for each student. Write different body parts on half of the slips. On the other half of the slips, write related body parts or other words. For example, you might write *las manos* on one slip, and *los dedos* on another; *el ojo* on one, and *ver* on yet another. Put your slips of paper in a hat, box, or bag, and let each student draw a paper. Then tell them to get up and find the person who has the body part / word most closely "related" to their own. This is a critical thinking activity.
2. Again, you will need one slip of paper for each student in your class. Write the first part of a word on one slip, and finish word on a second slip. For example, one slip might have *ca* … and its mate would have … *ra*. Another pair could be *estó* … and its partner would be … *mago*.
3. A third way is to write a body part on one slip and draw it on another (or cut the pictures out of a magazine). For example, on one slip of paper you write *la nariz* and on its match you draw (or cut out) a nose.
    You will want to collect these slips of paper at the end of the activity so that you can reuse them in the future. A good way to organize them is to put them in sandwich bags and mark on the bags what vocabulary topic they are and to which chapter they correspond in *¡Anda! Curso elemental.*

INSTRUCTIONS for 9-7
This activity has two parts. Draw a monster on the board, a transparency, etc., and have students work in pairs with one student facing the drawing and the other with his/her back to the drawing. The student facing the drawing describes what he/she sees (the instructor's drawing) and the other student draws it. When finished, the student compares the drawing he/she created with the original and then the students switch places and repeat the activity.

SUGGESTION for 9-7
Make your "monster" as unusual as you like, since the more you deviate from a real person, the more closely the student who is drawing must listen to his/her partner. Perhaps the monster you draw has 1 eye, 3 noses, 2 mouths, 1 tooth, 1 big ear, 1 small ear, 3 legs, and 5 hearts. If you have an odd number of students, 1 pair has to draw while the third student gives directions. Also, you may ask the extra student to draw the second monster after you have modeled the procedure. You may wish to teach additional words like *cuadrado, círculo, línea, triángulo,* etc. Finally, encourage the student giving the directions *not* to use his/her hands since this is a listening activity and he/she needs to work toward making himself/herself understood. By the way, this is a very popular activity with students and instructors alike. The students feel a real sense of accomplishment when they are able to carry on extended descriptions.

NOTE for 9-7
The objective of this activity is for students to listen to each other and to instantly demonstrate comprehension via the drawing. If the student who has his/her back to the *monstruo* does not understand, he/she must ask questions for clarification. Although couched in an enjoyable context where students are practicing their new vocabulary, the objective is much more important. Your students are communicating on an interpersonal level in an attempt to be mutually understood.

2:00 **9-5** **¿Qué te duele?** Con un/a compañero/a, creen preguntas y respuestas para ver lo que les duele a las siguientes personas. ■

Fíjate
The verb *doler* functions like *gustar.*
Me duelen los brazos.
My arms hurt (me).

MODELO a Ricardo / los brazos
 E1: *¿Qué le duele a Ricardo?*
 E2: *Le duelen los brazos.*

1. A Julia / la cabeza ¿Qué le duele? Le duele la cabeza.
2. A Marco y a Miguel / las piernas ¿Qué les duele? Les duelen las piernas.
3. A ti / el estómago ¿Qué te duele? Me duele el estómago.
4. A tu primo / la garganta ¿Qué le duele a tu primo? Le duele la garganta.
5. A ustedes / los ojos ¿Qué les duele? Nos duelen los ojos.

4:00 **9-6** **Una obra de arte** Miren el cuadro y descríbanlo usando las siguientes preguntas como guía. ■

Capítulo 3. *Hay*, pág. 119 del eText.

Fíjate
Note that *la mano* is irregular; it ends in *o* but the word is feminine.

1. ¿Cuántas personas hay en el cuadro? dos
2. ¿Cuántas caras hay? cuatro
3. ¿Cuántas manos pueden ver? seis
4. ¿Cuántos ojos pueden ver? cinco
5. ¿Cuántas narices hay? cuatro
6. ¿Qué otras cosas ven en el cuadro? pelo, cabezas, etc.
7. Estas personas son… madre e hijo
8. El cuadro representa… *Answers may vary.*

6:00 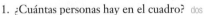 **9-7** **¿Es un monstruo o una obra de arte?** Su instructor/a va a dibujar un monstruo. Descríbele a un/a compañero/a cómo es el monstruo y él/ella tiene que dibujarlo. Al terminar, cambien de papel para describir un monstruo nuevo. ■

Estrategia
Being an "active listener" is an important skill in any language; it means that you have heard and understood what someone is saying. Being able to demonstrate that you have understood correctly, as in reproducing this drawing of the monster, helps you practice and perfect the skill of active listening.

El monstruo tiene…

a la derecha	a la izquierda	encima de	debajo de

ADDITIONAL ACTIVITY for *El cuerpo humano*
The following activity requires markers (or crayons) and end roll or butcher-type paper. If your institution does not have any paper readily available, you can acquire end rolls from your local newspaper. Newspapers usually donate end rolls to educators.

Vamos a dibujar Su profesor/a les va a dar un papel largo y unos marcadores (*markers*). Una persona del grupo va a acostarse (*lie down*) encima del papel. Otra persona va a trazar una línea (*trace*) alrededor del/de la compañero/a. Después, cada persona en el grupo tiene que marcar (*label*) por lo menos tres partes del cuerpo.

09-12 to 09-17 Spanish/English Tutorials

2 GRAMÁTICA

Un resumen de los pronombres de complemento directo e indirecto y reflexivos

Sharing about people, actions, and things

¡Mamá! ¡La muñeca! ¡Me la robó!

You have already learned the forms, functions, and positioning of the *direct* and *indirect object pronouns*, as well as the *reflexive pronouns*. The following is a review:

 Instructor Resources
• PPT, Extra Activities

METHODOLOGY • Recycling and Spiraling
We firmly believe in recycling and spiraling. *Recycling* concepts means bringing them back for additional practice, usually including new vocabulary or additional grammar concepts. *Spiraling* means taking an already introduced concept (or vocabulary) and taking it to new and higher levels. It can mean the incorporation of higher order/critical thinking skills. In *Capítulo 9*, we recycle/spiral the direct, indirect, and reflexive pronouns, a grammar concept that is always important to practice because the placement of the pronouns differs from that in English.

NOTE for *Un resumen de los pronombres de complemento directo e indirecto y reflexivos*
This grammar chunk is designed to help students "put it all together" with regard to object pronouns. You may want to send students back to the original presentations for additional practice.

NOTE for *Un resumen de los pronombres de complemento directo e indirecto y reflexivos*
This grammar presentation provides an opportunity to review not only the object pronouns and reflexive pronouns, but also verb phrases: *ir + a + infinitive* and the present progressive tense.

LOS PRONOMBRES DE COMPLEMENTO **DIRECTO**	LOS PRONOMBRES DE COMPLEMENTO **INDIRECTO**	LOS PRONOMBRES **REFLEXIVOS**
Direct object pronouns tell *what* or *who* receives the action of the verb. They replace direct object nouns and are used to avoid repetition.	Indirect object pronouns tell *to whom* or *for whom* something is done or given.	Reflexive pronouns indicate that the *subject* of a sentence or clause *receives the action of the verb.*

me	*me*	**me**	*to/for me*	**me**	*myself*
te	*you*	**te**	*to/for you*	**te**	*yourself*
lo, la	*you*	**le (se)**	*to/for you*	**se**	*yourself*
lo, la	*him/her/it*	**le (se)**	*to/for him/her*	**se**	*himself/herself*
nos	*us*	**nos**	*to/for us*	**nos**	*ourselves*
os	*you (all)*	**os**	*to/for you (all)*	**os**	*yourselves*
los, las	*you (all)*	**les (se)**	*to/for you (all)*	**se**	*yourselves*
los, las	*them/you*	**les (se)**	*to/for them/you*	**se**	*themselves/yourselves*

Compré la medicina ayer. **La** compré en la Farmacia Fénix. Tengo que dárse**la** a mi hijo.

I bought the medicine yesterday.
I bought it it at Fénix Pharmacy.
I have to give it to my son.

Le compré la medicina ayer. **Le** voy a dar la medicina esta noche.

I bought him the medicine yesterday.
I am going to give him the medicine tonight.

Me cepillo los dientes tres veces al día.

I brush my teeth three times a day.

Remember the following guidelines on position and sequence:

Position

• Object pronouns and reflexive pronouns come **before** the verb.

El doctor Sánchez **le** dio una inyección a David.   *Dr. Sánchez gave David a shot.*

Después **se** sintió aliviado.   *Then he felt relieved.*

(continued)

• Object pronouns and reflexive pronouns can also be placed before or be attached to the end of:

a. infinitives

La enfermera **me** va a llamar. }
La enfermera va a llamar**me**. } *The nurse is going to call me.*

Después **se** va a ir a su casa. }
Después va a ir**se** a su casa. } *Then she is going to go home.*

b. present participles (*-ando, -endo,* and *-iendo*)

La está tomando ahora. }
Está tomándo**la** ahora. } *He is taking it now.*

Se está poniendo nervioso. }
Está poniéndo**se** nervioso. } *He is getting nervous.*

Sequence

• When a direct (DO) and indirect object (IO) pronoun are used together, ***the indirect object precedes the direct object.***

• If both the direct and the indirect object pronouns begin with the letter "*l*" the indirect object pronoun changes from **le** or **les** to **se,** as in the following example.

Quiero mandar la carta al director ahora.   *I want to send the letter to the director now.*
          ↓   ↓   ↓   ↓
         DO   IO   DO   IO
         la   le (se)

         IO   DO
         se   la

Se la quiero mandar ahora mismo. }
Quiero mandár**sela** ahora mismo. } *I want to send it to him right now.*

 Capítulo 1. Los adjetivos descriptivos, pág. 43 del eText.

Capítulo 1. Los adjetivos descriptivos, pág. 43 del eText.

 **9-8** **Un animal muy extraño**

[3:00]

Juntos respondan a las siguientes oraciones exclamativas con el pronombre de complemento directo apropiado y un adjetivo. ■

MODELO   E1: ¡Mira la nariz!
             E2: *Sí, la tiene muy grande (pequeña/fea/ bonita…).*

Fijate
In Spanish, an animal's legs are referred to as *patas. Pierna(s)* is only used for people.

1. ¡Mira la boca!
2. ¡Mira las orejas!
3. ¡Mira los dientes!
4. ¡Mira las patas!

5. ¡Mira la cabeza!
6. ¡Mira el estómago!
7. ¡Mira la cara!
8. ¡Mira el cuello!

EXPANSION for 9-8
Have your students each draw their own *animal muy extraño*, and repeat **9-8**, using their own drawings.

EXPANSION for 9-8
Challenge students to bring in photos of the strangest animals they can find for the class to describe. Then take a class vote to determine which is the strangest.

EXPANSION for 9-8
Have students describe their favorite animals, and have their classmates guess which animals they are describing.

Capítulo 8. *Gustar* y verbos como *gustar*, pág. 302 del eText.

`3:00` `9-9` **Las preferencias** Escribe oraciones completas usando los pronombres de complemento indirecto. Después compara tus oraciones con las de un/a compañero/a. ∎

MODELO   A Betty / gustar despertarse temprano
              A Betty le gusta despertarse temprano.

1. A mis padres / importar el dinero A mis padres les importa el dinero.
2. A mí / molestar las personas irresponsables (A mí) Me molestan las personas irresponsables.
3. A Manolo / encantar las novelas de Mario Vargas Llosa A Manolo le encantan las novelas de Mario Vargas Llosa.
4. A nosotros / hacer falta estudiar mucho más (A nosotros) Nos hace falta estudiar mucho más.
5. A nuestro/a profesor/a / fascinar el cine japonés (A nuestro/a profesor/a) Le fascina el cine japonés.

`7:00` `9-10` **En el restaurante** ¿Qué les pasó ayer a Paco y a Pati en el Restaurante Boca Grande? ∎

Paso 1   Completa las siguientes oraciones con los pronombres de complemento directo, indirecto o reflexivo apropiados. Después, compara tus respuestas con las de un/a compañero/a.

Paco y Pati se conocieron en el gimnasio hace varias semanas. Anoche decidieron salir juntos. Llegaron al restaurante con mucha hambre. (1) ____Se, R____ sentaron en una mesa grande al lado de las ventanas. Primero pidieron el menú. El camarero (2) ____se, IO____ (3) ____lo, DO____ trajo en seguida (inmediatamente). Después, (4) ____les, IO____ recomendó unos platos muy ricos. Paco pidió un bistec para él y a Pati (5) ____le, IO____ pidió pollo asado con ajo. ¡Pati no (6) ____lo, DO____ podía creer! ¡Paco ni (7) ____le, IO____ preguntó qué quería! Ella (8) ____se, R____ sentía muy incómoda —ningún hombre, excepto su padre, (9) ____la, DO____ había tratado (*had treated*) así antes. Pati (10) ____se, R____ calló mientras Paco hablaba de su día, su trabajo y su familia. Cuando por fin el camarero (11) ____les, IO____ sirvió la comida, Pati miró su plato y (12) ____se, R____ levantó gritando. ¡Su plato era del "Menú para niños"!

Paso 2   Digan qué tipo de pronombre usaron en cada oración.

CAPÍTULO 9

EXPANSION for 9-9
Have students replace the subjects of each of these sentences with as many options as possible, and then complete new sentences.

MODELO
A mis padres/importar el dinero.
A mis padres/importar la salud.
A mis padres les importa la salud.

NOTE for 9-9
You may want to share with students that Mario Vargas Llosa is a Peruvian author and Nobel Prize winner.

METHODOLOGY • Oral Practice
Research strongly supports our belief that classroom time should be spent engaging the students almost exclusively in meaningful *oral* activities. You have noted that virtually all of the activities in *¡Anda! Curso elemental* are meant to be done orally, in pairs or groups. This is to maximize students' opportunities to speak and use Spanish in *i + 1* settings that help build their confidence in the language. Research confirms that strong oral skills translate into better writing skills. Therefore, we need to provide our students with a controlled environment in class to practice speaking so that outside of class they will be more successful and confident writers.

EXPANSION for 9-10
You may want to also use the passage as a reading comprehension activity, and ask the following questions:
1. ¿Dónde se conocieron Pati y Paco?
2. ¿Adónde fueron después?
3. ¿Quién pidió la comida? ¿Qué pidió?
4. ¿Por qué se enojó Pati?

EXPANSION for 9-10
You may want to convert **9-10** into a TPR activity. Choose three students to play the roles of Paco, Pati, and the waiter. Either call on students to read each sentence, or do the reading yourself, sentence by sentence. As each sentence is being read, the students perform the actions, providing a visual representation of how direct object, indirect object, and reflexive pronouns work.

Capítulo 4. *Ir + a +* infinitivo, pág. 147 del eText;
Capítulo 5. El presente progresivo, pág. 180 del eText.

9-11 ¿Quién…? Jacobo está enfermo y no puede levantarse de la cama. Es un poco exigente (*demanding*) y quiere saber quiénes lo van a atender (*wait on him*). Contesta sus preguntas y después comparte tus respuestas con un/a compañero/a. ■

MODELO ¿Quién va a traerme la tarea? (hermano)
Tu hermano te la va a traer. / Tu hermano va a traértela.

1. ¿Quién va a traerme los libros que pedí? (Patricia) Patricia te los va a traer. / Patricia va a traértelos.
2. ¿Quién está comprándome la medicina que necesito? (Marcelo) Marcelo te la está comprando. / Marcelo está comprándotela.
3. ¿Quién me va a limpiar el cuarto? (Guadalupe y Lina) Guadalupe y Lina te lo van a limpiar. / Guadalupe y Lina van a limpiártelo.
4. ¿Quién me está lavando la ropa? (tu madre) Tu madre te la está lavando. / Tu madre está lavándotela.
5. ¿Quién está preparándome la comida? (Tina y Luisa) Tina y Luisa te la están preparando. / Tina y Luisa están preparándotela.
6. ¿Quién me va a hacer la tarea? (nadie) Nadie te la va a hacer. / Nadie va a hacértela.

9-12 Hay que ayudar a Pepito Pepito tiene tres años y necesita ayuda para hacerlo todo. Túrnense para formar los pedidos (*requests*) del niño y las respuestas. ■

MODELO los dedos / limpiar
E1: *¿Me los limpias?*
E2: *Sí, te los limpio.*

1. el pelo / secar ¿Me lo secas? / Sí, te lo seco.
2. las manos / lavar ¿Me las lavas? / Sí, te las lavo.
3. las orejas / limpiar ¿Me las limpias? / Sí, te las limpio.
4. los dientes / cepillar ¿Me los cepillas? / Sí, te los cepillo.
5. los ojos / mirar ¿Me los miras? / Sí, te los miro.

3 VOCABULARIO

5:00

09-18 to 09-23

Algunas enfermedades y tratamientos médicos
Explaining ailments and treatments

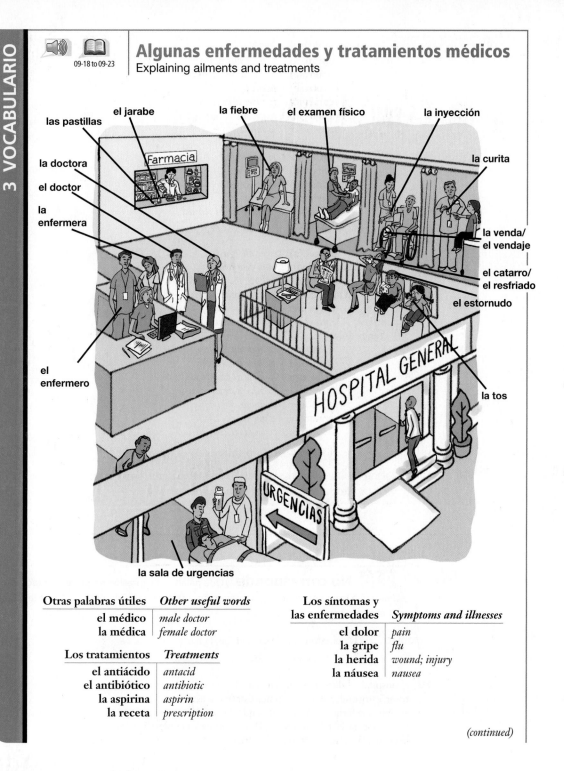

las pastillas · el jarabe · la fiebre · el examen físico · la inyección

Farmacia

la doctora
el doctor
la enfermera

la curita

la venda/
el vendaje

el catarro/
el resfriado

el estornudo

el enfermero

HOSPITAL GENERAL

la tos

URGENCIAS

la sala de urgencias

Otras palabras útiles	Other useful words
el médico	male doctor
la médica	female doctor

Los tratamientos	Treatments
el antiácido	antacid
el antibiótico	antibiotic
la aspirina	aspirin
la receta	prescription

Los síntomas y las enfermedades	Symptoms and illnesses
el dolor	pain
la gripe	flu
la herida	wound; injury
la náusea	nausea

(continued)

Instructor Resources
• Textbook images, Extra Activities

NATIONAL STANDARDS
Communication, Comparisons, Connections
The vocabulary about illness, injury, and explaining symptoms to medical personnel encompasses many of the National Standards. Any of the pair or small group activities that require students to engage in conversations, provide and obtain information, express their feelings and emotions, and exchange opinions address Standard 1.1. The idea of using verbs reflexively and non-reflexively or the concept of using articles with body parts instead of using possessive adjectives helps students see the differences between Spanish and English. They make comparisons (Standard 4.1) between how they express pain or discomfort in Spanish and in English. They are able to connect their prior knowledge of science/health with the new vocabulary in Spanish.

SUGGESTION for *Algunas enfermedades y tratamientos médicos*
Ask students to describe the emergency room scene.

SUGGESTION for *Algunas enfermedades y tratamientos médicos*
As a listening exercise, you may want to ask students true/false questions about the drawing:
1. La mujer en la bata rosada tiene un brazo roto.
2. La niña de la camiseta anaranjada se cortó el dedo.
3. Los doctores llevan batas blancas.
4. La mujer de la camiseta rosada se rompió la pierna.
5. El señor en la silla de ruedas (*wheelchair*) recibe una inyección.
6. Los niños están muy enfermos y necesitan tratamiento urgentemente.

Algunos verbos	Some verbs
acabar de + infinitivo	*to have just finished + (something)*
caer(se)	*to fall down*
cortar(se)	*to cut (oneself)*
curar(se)	*to cure; to be cured*
enfermar(se)	*to get sick*
estornudar	*to sneeze*
evitar	*to avoid*
guardar cama	*to stay in bed*
lastimar(se)	*to get hurt*
mejorar(se)	*to improve; to get better*
ocurrir	*to occur*
quemar(se)	*to burn; to get burned*
romper(se)	*to break*
tener...	
alergia (a)	*to be allergic (to)*
(un) catarro, resfriado	*to have a cold*
(la/una) gripe	*to have the flu*
una infección	*to have an infection*
tos	*to have a cough*
un virus	*to have a virus*
tener dolor de...	
cabeza	*to have a headache*
espalda	*to have a backache*
estómago	*to have a stomachache*
garganta	*to have a sore throat*
toser	*to cough*
tratar de	*to try to*
vendar(se)	*to bandage (oneself); to dress (a wound)*

Fíjate

A verb with *se* in parentheses indicates that it can be also used as a reflexive verb.

quemar(se): Ayer me quemé. (reflexive)   *Yesterday I burned myself.*
Ayer quemé los papeles viejos.   *Yesterday I burned the old papers.*

`2:00` **9-13** **No corresponde** ¿Qué palabra o expresión no pertenece (*doesn't belong*) a cada uno de los siguientes grupos de palabras? Túrnense para leer la lista y contestar. ■

MODELO   E1:   el estómago, la cara, el ojo, la nariz
            E2:   *el estómago*

1. el hospital, el doctor, el enfermero, el oído   el oído
2. toser, estornudar, la receta, tener catarro   la receta
3. el jarabe, la farmacia, las pastillas, quemarse   quemarse
4. lastimarse, la sala de urgencias, la tos, romperse la pierna   la tos
5. la venda, la herida, cortarse, el resfriado   el resfriado

Workbooklet `5:00`

9-14 Algunos tratamientos ¿Adónde tienes que ir para poder curarte o buscar tratamiento para las siguientes condiciones? Pon una equis (**X**) en la columna apropiada. Después, túrnate con un/a compañero/a para decir adónde van. ◾

MODELO   un brazo roto (*broken*)
E1:   *Si tengo un brazo roto, voy a la sala de urgencias.*

CONDICIÓN	A LA CAMA	A LA FARMACIA	AL CONSULTORIO DEL MÉDICO	AL HOSPITAL	A LA SALA DE URGENCIAS
1. tos					
2. náusea					
3. (la) gripe					
4. (un) dolor de garganta					
5. una infección de la sangre					
6. una herida en la pierna					
7. (un) catarro					
8. fiebre					

`4:00` **9-15 ¿Por qué?** Túrnense para describir lo que les pasa a estas personas y ofrecer una causa posible de su(s) problema(s). ◾

MODELO  *Selena tiene una herida porque se cortó con un cuchillo.*

Selena

1.
Antonio

2.
Umberto y Ricardo

3.
Juliana y Memo

4.
María Jesús

5.
Rafael

9-16 El soroche El verano pasado Nina fue a Bolivia como voluntaria para ayudar a construir una escuela en el altiplano (*high plateau*). ∎

El altiplano en los Andes de Bolivia

Paso 1 Juntos terminen la conversación entre Nina y su padre con las palabras de la lista.

corazón	enfermedad	evitar	me duele
mejorar	náusea	pastillas	estómago

NINA: Hola, papá.

PAPÁ: ¡Ay, Nina! ¿Cómo estás, hija? ¿Llegaste bien?

NINA: Sí. Ayer llegamos bien pero hoy me siento enferma. (1) _Me duele_ la cabeza. No me duele mucho el (2) _estómago_ pero tengo (3) _náusea_ cuando pienso en la comida —me entran ganas (*I get the urge*) de vomitar.

PAPÁ: Pobrecita. ¿Qué te pasa? ¿Comiste ayer?

NINA: Sí, un poco. Pero desde que (*since*) llegamos no tengo mucha hambre.

PAPÁ: ¿Tienes otros síntomas?

NINA: Sí. El (4) _corazón_ me late (*is beating*) rápidamente y no puedo respirar (*breathe*) muy bien. ¿Crees que tengo alguna (5) _enfermedad_?

PAPÁ: Nina, me parece que tienes soroche.

NINA: ¿Soroche? ¿Qué es eso?

PAPÁ: Es el mal de altura (*altitude sickness*). Debes empezar a sentirte mejor (*better*) en un par de días. Mientras tanto, necesitas intentar relajarte, tomar mucha agua y (6) _evitar_ el alcohol y el tabaco. También puedes tomar unas (7) _pastillas_ de ibuprofeno y beber un té medicinal hecho de (*made from*) hojas de coca (*coca leaves*).

NINA: Gracias, papá. Ya que entiendo qué me ocurre, creo que me voy a (8) _mejorar_ pronto.

Paso 2 Ahora, contesten las siguientes preguntas.

1. ¿Qué es el soroche?
2. ¿Cuáles son los síntomas?
3. ¿Qué tratamiento le recomienda su papá?

9-17 ¿Qué debemos hacer? En grupos de cuatro o cinco, cada estudiante escribe dos enfermedades u otros problemas médicos que tuvo, acaba de tener o que podría (*could*) tener. Después túrnense para compartir la información mientras los compañeros dicen lo que debe hacer. ■

MODELO
E1: *Tengo una pierna rota.*
E2: *Debes ir a la sala de urgencias.*
E3: *Debes guardar cama.*
E4: *Debes tomar medicina para el dolor.*

  9-18 Para evitar lo inevitable ¿Cómo tratan de evitar tus compañeros las siguientes enfermedades y condiciones? Circula por la clase para hacerles las siguientes preguntas. Necesitas **tres** respuestas para cada pregunta. ■

Workbooklet

MODELO
TÚ: ¿Cómo tratas de evitar el dolor de garganta?
E1: *Bebo mucho jugo de naranja.*
E2: *Llevo una bufanda (scarf) en el cuello.*
E3: *Tomo mucha vitamina C.*

1. ¿Cómo tratas de evitar el dolor de cabeza?	4. ¿Cómo evitas enfermarte?
E1: _____	E1: _____
E2: _____	E2: _____
E3: _____	E3: _____
2. ¿Cómo tratas de evitar el dolor de estómago?	5. ¿Cómo evitas cortarte?
E1: _____	E1: _____
E2: _____	E2: _____
E3: _____	E3: _____
3. ¿Cómo tratas de evitar el dolor de espalda?	6. ¿Cómo evitas caerte?
E1: _____	E1: _____
E2: _____	E2: _____
E3: _____	E3: _____

NOTA CULTURAL

¡Hola!
eText 346   09-24 to 09-25

El agua y la buena salud

NOTE for *Nota cultural*
See eText pg. 346 for complete *Nota cultural* reading and *Preguntas*.

ANSWERS to *Nota cultural* (Online)
1. El cuerpo contiene mucha agua, pero cada día elimina de 500 a 700 centímetros cúbicos al sudar.
2. Todos los órganos del cuerpo funcionan mejor; beber agua es bueno para la piel y el pelo; beber agua ayuda a eliminar toxinas del cuerpo.

21ST CENTURY SKILLS • SOCIAL AND CROSS-CULTURAL SKILLS
All activities in *¡Anda!*, including the information gap activities in which students need to circulate throughout the class build social and cross-cultural skills. The activities require students to listen and speak at appropriate times as well as be respectful of their classmates. By changing partners frequently (if not daily) students learn to work with a wide range of people.

METHODOLOGY • Reading (Online)
Always activate students' schemata, that is, tap into their pre-existing knowledge, prior to assigning a reading. For example, prepare students for this reading online by asking them what they usually drink, how much water they drink per day, and in what ways they think water is important to our health. You may also want to pick out a few key words from the reading and ask students what they mean.

NATIONAL STANDARDS
Communication, Cultures, Connections
The cultural reading online about *El agua y la buena salud* encompasses Communication and Connections. Students read and interpret the text (Standard 1.2). Students have prior knowledge about the benefits of water from their science and health courses, so they are able to connect what they read in Spanish to what they learned in those disciplines (Standard 3.1).

HERITAGE LANGUAGE LEARNERS
You may wish to assign heritage language learners or advanced learners the project of researching water issues in Latin America.

HERITAGE LANGUAGE LEARNERS
Your heritage language learners or advanced students may enjoy researching Spanish health issues on the Internet. Some of the more interesting sites for them may be online Spanish magazines and health-related websites. Students can take advantage of this wealth of information for writing reports or sending e-mails to other students, to name just a few activities.

Instructor Resources
• PPT, Extra Activities

NATIONAL STANDARDS
Communication
Making exclamations enriches the ability of the language learner to communicate in an expressive manner. The exclamatory phrases beginning with *¡qué!* or *¡cuánto!* provide a basis for communicating in natural contexts, as native speakers do. These expressions allow students to express their feelings and emotions and exchange opinions with others about their likes and dislikes (Standard 1.1). The exclamatory phrases are an easy way to communicate with native speakers and to be understood in multiple contexts.

4 GRAMÁTICA

2:00 | 09-26 to 09-29

 ¡Qué! y ¡cuánto! Making emphatic and exclamatory statements

¡Qué catarro! ¿Cuándo te refriaste?

Me levanté así (*like this*) esta mañana.

So far you have used **qué** and **cuánto** as interrogative words, but these words can also be used in exclamatory sentences.

—Felipe, **¡qué** fiebre tienes!   *Felipe, what a fever you have!*
—María, **¡cuánto** estornudas!   *María, you are sneezing so much!*

—Mi cabeza, **¡qué** dolor!   *My head—what pain!*
—**Cuánto** lo siento.   *I'm so sorry. (How sorry I am.)*

—**¡Qué** susto! ¡Se cortó el dedo!   *What a scare! He cut his finger!*
—Se ve muy mal. **¡Qué** feo!   *It looks really bad. How awful! (It looks awful/ugly.)*

—**¡Qué** doctor! Le salvó la vida.   *What a doctor! He saved his life.*
—**Cuánto** se lo agradezco.   *I'm so thankful. (How grateful I am.)*

Note that in the examples above, **cuánto** accompanies *verbs* and is masculine and singular. When **cuánto** accompanies *nouns* it must agree with them in gender and number:

—**¡Cuántas** recetas y todavía estoy tosiendo!   *So many prescriptions and I am still coughing!*
—Sí, y **¡cuántos** estudiantes con la misma infección!   *Yes, and so many students with the same infection!*

3:00 | **9-19** **¿Cómo respondes?** Elige la respuesta apropiada para cada comentario. Después, comparte tus respuestas con un/a compañero/a. ■

1. __d__ ¡Ay, el estómago!   a. ¡Qué feo!
2. __c__ Su novia se graduó con honores.   b. ¡Cuánto trabajo!
3. __h__ Pepe me compró veinticuatro rosas rojas.   c. ¡Qué inteligente!
4. __e__ Esta comida es deliciosa.   d. ¡Cuánto me duele!
5. __f__ Este doctor es el novio de aquella enfermera.   e. ¡Cuánto me gusta!
6. __g/b__ Mi madre preparó tapas para cincuenta personas.   f. ¡Qué interesante!
7. __a__ Tiene la cara de un monstruo.   g. ¡Cuánta comida!
8. __b__ Tengo que leer dos libros para mi clase de historia y preparar un informe.   h. ¡Qué romántico!

3:00 **9-20** **¡El amor es increíble!** Juntos respondan a estas situaciones. Pueden utilizar las siguientes expresiones o pueden responder con sus propias expresiones. ■

¡Qué (mala) suerte!	¡Qué cruel!	¡Qué dolor!
¡Qué horrible!	¡Qué romántico!	¡Cuánto tiempo!
¡Qué triste!	¡Qué interesante!	

1. Mis padres celebran este mes su aniversario de boda —¡25 años ya!
2. Félix, no te quiero desilusionar (*disappoint*) después de tantos meses juntos, pero quiero salir con otros hombres.
3. Silvia es la mujer más increíble del mundo. Quiero ser más que su novio. Quiero pasar mi vida con ella.
4. Nadie quiere salir conmigo (*with me*). Nadie me mira. Me gusta ir al cine, comer en buenos restaurantes, ir a partidos de básquetbol, bailar —pero no me gusta hacer estas cosas solo (*alone*).
5. Soy muy joven para tener novia. Me divertí contigo (*with you*) anoche en la fiesta pero me divierto con muchas mujeres…
6. Adriano es el hombre perfecto para mí. Es muy respetuoso y me trata bien siempre.

3:00 **9-21** **¿Qué tiene?** ¿Cómo responden ustedes a las siguientes situaciones? ■

MODELO   E1:   Tito está muy mal porque tiene un dolor terrible de estómago.

         E2:   *¡Cuánto le duele!*

         E1:   Yo no puedo hablar porque estoy tosiendo mucho.

         E2:   *¡Qué tos tienes!*

1. No puedo respirar, me duele la garganta, estornudo todo el tiempo y no tengo hambre. ¡Qué catarro/resfriado tienes!
2. A mi hermano siempre le ocurre algo malo: se cae, se rompe algo… ¡Qué mala suerte tiene!
3. ¡Ay! Necesito un antiácido ahora mismo, por favor. ¡Cuánto te duele el estómago!
4. Mi abuelo acaba de salir del hospital después de pasar mucho tiempo allí. No tiene seguro médico (*health insurance*). ¡Qué caro! ¡Cuánto dinero le va a costar!
5. Tú tienes mucha fiebre y te duele el cuerpo. ¡Qué enfermo/a estoy!

¿Cómo andas? I

	Feel confident	Need to review
Having completed **Comunicación I,** I now can . . .		
• describe the human body (p. 228)	☐	☐
• pronounce the letters **d** and **t** (MSL / SAM)	☐	☐
• share about people, actions, and things (p. 231)	☐	☐
• explain ailments and treatments (p. 235)	☐	☐
• relate the importance of water in maintaining good health (p. 239)	☐	☐
• make emphatic and exclamatory statements (p. 240)	☐	☐

SECTION GOALS for
Comunicación II
By the end of the second *Comunicación* section, students will be able to:
• explain the uses of the preterit and imperfect.
• identify key words that trigger the preterit or imperfect.
• contrast the use of the preterit or imperfect in a sentence.
• narrate a story in the past tense.
• discuss the role of pharmacies in the Spanish-speaking world.
• use expressions with *hacer.*

NATIONAL STANDARDS
Communication
Learning the differences between the preterit and the imperfect may be one of the greater challenges for your students in the first year of Spanish. *¡Anda! Curso elemental* makes strong use of enjoyable activities to help students acquire the concept.
    The narration of events in the past tense, using either the preterit or imperfect, allows for greater flexibility in communication. When students engage in conversations about activities that they used to do as children, or what they did last week, they are communicating in the interpersonal mode (Standard 1.1). If they read a story in Spanish, written in the past tense, they are using Standard 1.2, and if they listen to the story, as well as read it, they have met the Standard. If they narrate a past tense event and present it to the class either orally or as a written story, that addresses Standard 1.3—the presentational mode.

METHODOLOGY • Chunking
¡Anda! Curso elemental believes in the pedagogical concept of "chunking." *Chunking* means taking large, broad concepts and breaking them into manageable chunks. This is what we have done with the important grammar concept of the past tense. In *Capítulo 7,* the preterit was introduced; in *Capítulo 8,* the imperfect. Now in this chapter we review the formation of these two tenses, and then proceed to contrast their uses, breaking them into manageable rules.

Comunicación II

5 GRAMÁTICA

[5:00]

 📖 ¡Hola!
09-30 to 09-35   Spanish/English Tutorials

El pretérito y el imperfecto   Narrating in the past

Fuimos a Cuzco y subimos a Machu Picchu. Hacía buen tiempo.

In **Capítulos 7** and **8** you learned about two aspects of the past tense in Spanish, **el pretérito** and **el imperfecto,** which are not interchangeable. Their uses are contrasted below.

THE **PRETERIT** IS USED:	THE **IMPERFECT** IS USED:
1. To relate an event or occurrence that refers to *one specific time in the past* • **Fuimos** a Cuzco el año pasado. *We went to Cuzco last year.* • **Comimos** en el restaurante El Sol y **nos gustó** mucho. *We ate at El Sol restaurant and liked it a lot.*	**1.** To express *habitual* or often *repeated actions* • **Íbamos** a Cuzco todos los veranos. *We used to go to Cuzco every summer.* • **Comíamos** en el restaurante El Sol todos los lunes. *We used to eat at El Sol Restaurant every Monday.*
2. To relate an act *begun or completed in the past* • **Empezó** a llover. *It started to rain.* • **Comenzaron** los juegos. *The games began.* • La gira **terminó.** *The tour ended.*	**2.** To express *was/were + -ing* • **Llovía** sin parar. *It rained without stopping.* • **Comenzaban** los juegos cuando llegamos. *The games were beginning when we arrived.* • La gira **transcurría** sin ningún problema. *The tour continued without any problems.*
3. To relate a *sequence of events or actions,* each completed and moving the narrative along toward its conclusion • **Llegamos** en avión, **recogimos** las maletas y **fuimos** al hotel. *We arrived by plane, picked up our luggage, and went to the hotel.* • Al día siguiente **decidimos** ir a Machu Picchu. *The next day we decided to go to Machu Picchu.* • **Vimos** muchos ejemplos de la magnífica arquitectura incaica. Después **anduvimos** un poco por el camino de los incas. **Nos divertimos** mucho. *We saw many examples of the magnificent Incan architecture. Afterward we walked a bit on the Incan road. We had a great time.*	**3.** To provide *background* information, set the stage, or express a pre-existing condition • **Era** un día oscuro. **Llovía** de vez en cuando. *It was a dark day and it rained once in a while.* • Los turistas **llevaban** pantalones cortos y lentes de sol. *The tourists were wearing shorts and sunglasses.* • El camino **era** estrecho y **había** muchos turistas. *The path was narrow and there were many tourists.*

SUGGESTION for *El pretérito y el imperfecto*
Begin each class with directed questions using both the *pretérito* and the *imperfecto.* Some sample questions include: *¿A qué hora te acostaste anoche? ¿A qué hora te acostabas el verano pasado? ¿Qué te pusiste ayer? ¿Qué te ponías cuando tenías cinco años?,* etc.

SUGGESTION for *El pretérito y el imperfecto*
To assist in remembering the *pretérito* and *imperfecto* and the rules for each, have students recall humorous stories from their childhoods. Have students write their stories in English and decide which verbs in their stories would be *preterit* and which would be *imperfect.* They can use the examples from their humorous stories to help them remember which to use and why.

THE **PRETERIT** IS USED:

4. To relate an action that took place within a specified or *specific amount* (segment) *of time* **Caminé** (por) dos horas. *I walked for two hours.* **Hablamos** (por) cinco minutos. *We talked for five minutes.* **Contemplaron** el templo un rato. *They contemplated the temple for a while.* **Viví** en Ecuador (por) seis años. *I lived in Ecuador for six years.*	**Fíjate** The use of *por* is optional in these cases.

THE **IMPERFECT** IS USED:

4. To *tell time* in the past
Era la una.
It was 1:00.
Eran las tres y media.
It was 3:30.
Era muy tarde.
It was very late.
Era la medianoche.
It was midnight.

5. To describe physical and emotional states or characteristics
Después del viaje **queríamos** descansar. Yo **tenía** dolor de cabeza y no **me sentía** muy bien.
After the trip we wanted to rest. I had a headache and did not feel well.

WORDS AND EXPRESSIONS THAT COMMONLY SIGNAL:

PRETERIT	IMPERFECT
anoche	a menudo
anteayer	cada semana/mes/año
ayer	con frecuencia
de repente (*suddenly*)	de vez en cuando (*once in a while*)
el fin de semana pasado	frecuentemente
el mes pasado	mientras
el lunes pasado/el martes pasado, etc.	muchas veces
esta mañana	siempre
una vez, dos veces, etc.	todos los lunes/martes, etc.
	todas las semanas
	todos los días/meses/años

NOTE: The **pretérito** and the **imperfecto** can be used in the same sentence.

Veían la televisión cuando **sonó** el teléfono.   *They were watching television when the phone rang.*

In the preceding sentence, an action was going on (**veían**) when it was interrupted by another action (**sonó el teléfono**).

ADDITIONAL ACTIVITY for
El pretérito y el imperfecto
What follows is an additional activity that can help to ease students into using the preterit and the imperfect correctly. It is intentionally in English so that students are able to connect how the preterit and imperfect relate to expressing the past in English.
Una mañana muy extraña Lee el siguiente texto sobre una experiencia muy extraña. Señala si cada verbo debe estar en pretérito (P) o imperfecto (I) y explica por qué.

MODELO
1. <u>was</u> (P/I) #4 *(To relate an action that took place within a specified or specific amount [segment] of time—"yesterday morning.")*

Yesterday morning (1) <u>was</u> (P/I) strange. When I (2) <u>woke up</u> (P/I), I (3) <u>was feeling</u> (P/I) a little sick. My head (4) <u>was hurting</u> (P/I) and my back (5) <u>ached</u> (P/I) as well. The weather (6) <u>was</u> (P/I) damp and cold so I (7) <u>was</u> (P/I) not anxious to get out of bed. Suddenly I (8) <u>heard</u> (P/I) a crash. I (9) <u>glanced</u> (P/I) at the clock and (10) <u>saw</u> (P/I) that it (11) <u>was</u> (P/I) already 8:45. My roommate always leaves by 8:00, so I (12) <u>believed</u> (P/I) that I (13) <u>was</u> (P/I) alone. I (14) <u>jumped</u> (P/I) out of bed and (15) <u>ran</u> (P/I) to the window. I (16) <u>didn't see</u> (P/I) anything unusual. I (17) <u>was thinking</u> (P/I) I (18) <u>should look</u> (P/I) around outside when I (19) <u>heard</u> (P/I) an eerie sound, like a cross between a whimper and a howl.

By that time my head (20) <u>was throbbing</u> (P/I) along with my back, but I (21) <u>could not pay attention</u> (P/I) to the pain. I (22) <u>struggled</u> (P/I) to overcome it so I (23) <u>could focus</u> (P/I) on the situation at hand. Without grabbing a coat, I (24) <u>ran</u> out the door. I (25) <u>did not realize</u> (P/I) that the wooden steps (26) <u>were</u> (P/I) icy and I immediately (27) <u>slipped</u> (P/I) and (28) <u>fell</u> (P/I). I (29) <u>banged</u> (P/I) both my back and my head on the hard, wooden steps. I (30) <u>screamed</u> (P/I) loudly but (31) <u>did not feel</u> (P/I) the fall because to my right there (32) <u>was</u> (P/I) a big black bear digging in our garbage can. He (33) <u>was staring</u> (P/I) at me, apparently (34) <u>feeling</u> (P/I) just as startled as I (35) <u>was</u> (P/I). At exactly the same moment we (36) <u>began</u> (P/I) to back away from each other—me up the steps and the bear away from the garbage can. As I (37) <u>was reaching</u> (P/I) up to open the screen door, the bear (38) <u>turned</u> (P/I) and (39) <u>ran</u> (P/I).

Once I (40) <u>calmed</u> (P/I) down I (41) <u>realized</u> (P/I) that I (42) <u>was</u> no longer <u>feeling</u> (P/I) pain. The fear and the hard fall had cured me!

9-22 Una (muy) breve historia de los incas ¿Qué sabes sobre los incas? Completa los siguientes pasos. ■

Machu Picchu, la ciudad perdida de los incas   El imperio de los incas

Paso 1   Lee el siguiente fragmento.

El imperio de los incas <u>fue</u> uno de los imperios más importantes de las civilizaciones precolombinas. <u>Se encontraba</u> (*It was located*) en lo que es hoy Perú, Bolivia, el norte de Chile y parte de Ecuador. El imperio <u>se dividía</u> en tres partes iguales: una tercera parte <u>pertenecía</u> (*pertained/belonged to*) a los indígenas y <u>pasaba</u> de padre a hijo; otra tercera parte <u>era</u> del Inca, o sea, del Gobierno; la otra tercera parte <u>pertenecía</u> a la Iglesia.

Los incas <u>adoraban</u> al hijo del Sol. Según la leyenda (*legend*), el hijo <u>cayó</u> en algún lugar cerca del lago Titicaca. Con él <u>llegó</u> su hermana y según la leyenda, ellos <u>eran</u> los padres de todos los incas. Esta civilización <u>practicaba</u> sacrificios de animales y algunas veces sacrificios humanos. También le <u>ofrecían</u> objetos preciosos y joyas (*jewels*) al Sol. El último cacique (o jefe político) famoso de los incas <u>fue</u> Atahualpa.

Paso 2   Subrayen los verbos.

Paso 3   Digan cuáles son **pretéritos** y cuáles son **imperfectos** y expliquen por qué se usaron cada uno de estos tiempos verbales.

9-23 Un cuento de hadas En grupos de tres o cuatro personas, pongan las siguientes oraciones en orden cronológico para terminar el cuento de Ricitos de Oro (*Goldilocks*). Después, analicen los usos **del pretérito** y **el imperfecto** dentro del cuento y expliquen por qué usaron cada uno de estos tiempos verbales. ■

[4:00]

Había una vez una niña muy curiosa. Un día, mientras caminaba por el bosque, encontró una casa muy bonita. En la casa vivían tres osos. Mientras los osos no estaban…

9	Los osos la asustaron (*scared her*).
3	Entró en el dormitorio de los osos.
7	Mientras ella dormía entraron los osos.
10	La niña se levantó y salió corriendo de la casa.
2	Tenía sueño.
4	Buscó una cama.
1	La niña entró en la casa.
5	Vio que una cama era muy grande, otra era muy pequeña y la otra tenía el tamaño perfecto.
8	Encontraron a la niña dormida en la cama.
6	Se acostó.

Capítulo 8. Las construcciones reflexivas, pág. 312 del eText.

9-24 En el consultorio Completa el siguiente pasaje con la forma correcta **del pretérito** o **el imperfecto** de cada verbo entre paréntesis. Después, comparte las respuestas con un/a compañero/a y explícale por qué usaste el pretérito o el imperfecto. ■

[6:00]

Ayer en el consultorio del Dr. Fuentes (1. haber) __había__ mucha actividad. Muchos pacientes (2. esperar) __esperaban__ al médico y yo no (3. encontrar) __encontraba__ dónde sentarme. Dos horas (4. pasar) __pasaron__ lentamente. (5. Ser) __Eran__ las once cuando por fin la recepcionista me (6. llamar) __llamó__ y la enfermera (7. salir) __salió__ para buscarme. Juntas (8. entrar) __entramos__ al cuarto donde (9. estar) __estaba__ el médico. El Dr. Fuentes (10. levantarse) __se levantó__ y me (11. mirar) __miró__ con mucha curiosidad. (12. Empezar) __Empezó__ a examinarme y a hacerme preguntas.

Yo (13. ponerse) __me puse__ nerviosa y (14. callarse) __me callé__. Sólo (15. esperar) __esperaba__ un examen anual típico pero las preguntas (16. ser) __eran__ demasiado específicas. Por ejemplo, me (17. preguntar) __preguntó__ si (18. sentirse) __me sentía__ mareada (*faint*) por la mañana y si (19. comer) __comía__ bien cuando (20. tener) __tenía__ hambre.

Por fin (21. darse cuenta [*to realize*]: yo) __me di cuenta__ de lo que (22. ocurrir) __ocurría__. ¡El Dr. Fuentes (23. pensar) __pensaba__ que yo (24. estar) __estaba__ embarazada (*pregnant*)! Por lo visto la enfermera (25. equivocarse [*to be mistaken*]) __se equivocó__ y ¡le (26. dar) __dio__ al médico la información de otra paciente!

The reason for using a common fairy tale known by most students in **9-23** is that they know the story and can focus on the order, noting whether the verbs are providing conditions/description (*imperfecto*) or moving the story along (*pretérito*).

EXPANSION for 9-23
To make sure that your students have understood the story, you can check their understanding with the following comprehension questions.
1. ¿Quién entró en la casa?
2. ¿Dónde estaban los propietarios de la casa?
3. ¿Dónde se acostó Ricitos de Oro?
4. ¿Por qué seleccionó esa cama?
5. Mientras Ricitos dormía, ¿quiénes llegaron?
6. ¿Por qué estaba asustada?
7. ¿Qué le pasó a Ricitos al final?

FOLLOW-UP to 9-23
Have students write an alternate ending to the story. They could write what happened from the point when the three bears arrived home, or a sequel to Goldilocks—her adventures in the forest, and how she spent her time in the woods after running away from the bears' house.

EXPANSION for 9-23
Strip Stories A variation to practice both grammar and reading comprehension is to create or borrow an appropriate (*i* + *1*) story and write each sentence, or a small group of sentences, on slips of paper. In groups, students must put the strips of paper in chronological order.

EXPANSION for 9-25
Have students ask these questions of 2–3 other students. Then have a few volunteers report their findings to the class, changing the verb forms to *él/ella* or *ellos/ellas,* as appropriate.

NOTE for 9-26
Research shows it is important to always begin with what the student knows. For that reason we have chosen the story of Cinderella for students to retell, using the preterit and imperfect. After practicing with retelling a familiar story, they are ready to move on to narrating their own personal stories.

EXPANSION for 9-26
Have students present **9-26** as short skits to the class.

ADDITIONAL ACTIVITY for
El pretérito y el imperfecto
Find a simple story in Spanish (it could be a children's book that is familiar to your students) or translate a simple story from English to Spanish. Provide a list of verbs in the infinitive form. Ask students to fold a notebook page in half and first write all the verbs in the story in the preterit. Then on the other side of the page have them write the verbs in the imperfect. Then, you read them the story, having them circle which verb form was correct, or ask them to choose which verb form is correct. Finally, have them state the reason why the verb was preterit or imperfect, based on the rules they learned.

[4:00] **9-25** ### En el pasado Termina las siguientes oraciones. Después, compártelas con un/a compañero/a. ■

MODELO   Cuando era niño/a…

E1: *Cuando era niño, hacía ejercicio todos los días. Y tú, ¿qué hacías?*

E2: *Cuando era niña, siempre jugaba en el parque con mi hermana.*

1. Cuando era niño/a…
2. Cuando tenía dieciséis años, frecuentemente…
3. Una vez el verano pasado…
4. Ayer tenía ganas de _____ pero…
5. Anoche…
6. Cuando vivía con mis padres, todas las semanas…

[5:00] **9-26** ### Nuestro cuento En grupos de tres, van a contar una historia (en el pasado) basada en los dibujos. Al terminar van a compartir sus historias con los otros miembros de la clase. ■

Estrategia
In this variation of "Cinderella," remember to use the *imperfect* for *description* and *background* information. Use the *preterit* for *sequences of actions.*

La Cenicienta

NOTE for 9-27
This medical form is similar to what a student might encounter in a real-life emergency room visit. While at first glance the activity may appear labor intensive, in reality the form can be completed quickly, allowing plenty of time for *Pasos 2* and *3*.

Workbooklet

9-27 Y en el hospital Imagina que trabajas como enfermero/a en la sala de urgencias de un hospital. Un día entra un joven de unos veinte años con unos síntomas raros. ■

Paso 1   Llena el siguiente formulario médico para el joven enfermo como si fueras un/a enfermero/a.

FORMULARIO MÉDICO

Por favor complete este formulario con la mayor precisión posible. Toda la infomación en este formulario es confidencial y será utilizada en caso de emergencia. Por favor escriba legiblemente.

HISTORIA MÉDICA

Nombre _____
Dirección _____
Ciudad y estado _____
Código postal _____
Número de teléfono _____
Edad _____
Fecha de nacimiento _____
Sexo _____ Peso _____ Altura _____
Grupo sanguíneo _____

1. ¿Está bajo tratamiento por alguna enfermedad? Explique._____
_____

2. ¿Toma algún tipo de medicamento? _____
_____

3. ¿Tiene algún tipo de alergia?_____
_____

4. ¿Ha tenido cirugía alguna vez?_____
_____

CONDICIONES MÉDICAS

Por favor marque cualquier enfermedad que haya tenido en el pasado y la fecha en que comenzó.

_____artritis	_____asma	_____dolor de espalda
_____mareos	_____tos crónica	_____dolor de pecho
_____diabetes	_____epilepsia	_____fracturas
_____dolor de cabeza	_____hernia	_____presión alta

¿Ha tenido otra condición que no hemos mencionado?_____
_____

Paso 2   Crea **seis** preguntas para determinar cuál es su problema, según el modelo.

MODELO   E1:   ¿Dar / todos sus datos / en recepción?

            E2:   *¿Dio todos sus datos en recepción?*

1. ¿Cuándo / llegar / la sala de urgencias?   ¿Cuándo llegó Ud. a la sala de urgencias?
2. ¿Cuándo / empezar / a dolerle?   ¿Cuándo le empezó a doler?
3. ¿Qué / hacer / cuando / empezar / a dolerle?   ¿Qué hacía cuando le empezó a doler?
4. ¿Quién / estar / con Ud.?   ¿Quién estaba con Ud.?
5. ¿Cómo / sentirse / cuando / acostarse / anoche?   ¿Cómo se sentía Ud. cuando se acostó anoche?
6. ¿Qué / causar / el dolor?   ¿Qué le causó el dolor?

Paso 3   Crea un diálogo con un/a compañero/a entre el joven y el/la enfermero/a usando las preguntas que escribiste.

9-28 La última vez que nos enfermamos Túrnense para describir la última vez que ustedes, un amigo, o un pariente se enfermaron. ■

- ¿Cuándo fue?
- ¿Cómo se sentían?
- ¿Cuáles fueron los síntomas?
- Si fueron al médico, ¿qué les hizo? ¿Qué les dijo?
- ¿Les recetó (recetar = *to prescribe*) algo? ¿Cuánto pagaron por la visita? Si no fueron al médico, ¿qué hicieron para curarse?
- ¿Cuánto tiempo duró (durar = *to last*) la enfermedad?

> **Fíjate**
> Use the term *médico* when referring to the profession of a doctor. Use *doctor* for the title of the person.
> *El doctor Ramírez es un médico excelente.*

9-29 ¿Y ayer? Descríbele a un/a compañero/a tu día de ayer en por lo menos **cinco** oraciones. ■

MODELO   *Ayer hacía mal tiempo cuando me desperté. No quería levantarme, pero por fin salí de la cama y fui a mi clase de español. El profesor nos dio mucha tarea. Luego fui a la biblioteca. Estudiaba cuando llegó mi mejor amigo Jeff.*

> **Fíjate**
> When the preterit and imperfect are used together in narratives in which events are retold, you will notice that the *imperfect* provides the background information such as the time, weather, and location. The *preterit* relates the specific events that occurred.

Capítulo 5. El mundo del cine, pág. 184 del eText.

9-30 Luces, cámara, acción ¿Te gustan las películas? ¿Vas al cine a menudo? Cuéntale (*Narrate*) a un/a compañero/a una película que hayas visto (*you have seen*) últimamente. Usa por lo menos **siete** oraciones. ¡Recuerda! Generalmente **el imperfecto** se usa para la descripción y **el pretérito** para la acción. ■

NOTA CULTURAL

¡Hola!
eText 356   09-36

Las farmacias en el mundo hispanohablante

NOTE for *Nota cultural*
See eText pg. 356 for complete *Nota cultural* reading and *Preguntas*.

6 GRAMÁTICA

[4:00]

09-37 to 09-40   Spanish Tutorial

Expresiones con *hacer* Explaining how long something has been going on and how long ago something occurred

The verb **hacer** means *to do* or *to make*. You have also used **hacer** in idiomatic expressions dealing with weather. There are some additional special constructions with **hacer** that deal with time. **Hace** is used:

1. to discuss an action that began in the past but is still going on in the present.

> **hace** + *period of time* + **que** + *verb in the present tense*

Hace cuatro días **que** tengo la gripe.
Hace dos años **que** soy enfermera.

I've had the flu for four days (and still have it).
I've been a nurse for two years.

(continued)

 CAPÍTULO 9

Instructor Resources
• PPT, Extra Activities

NOTE for *Nota cultural* (Online)
You may want to share the following information with students regarding health systems in Spanish-speaking countries.

En el mundo hispano hay una variedad de sistemas de salud:
• nacionales de salud pública con cobertura (*coverage*) para todos.
• privados para la gente con mayores recursos (*greater financial resources*).
• mixtos (público y privado) con todo rango (*level*) de servicios según el nivel económico del paciente.
• de cobertura (*coverage*) para los trabajadores que contribuyen al seguro social (pero también hay opciones para las personas que no tienen recursos propios).

NATIONAL STANDARDS
Communication, Comparisons, Connections
The cultural reading online, *Las farmacias en el mundo hispanohablante*, provides the context for Communication, Comparisons, and Connections. Students are reading an authentic text that requires them to understand and interpret written Spanish (Standard 1.2), but if you read it aloud to them for listening comprehension, you could satisfy written and spoken Spanish. When students discuss the differences between Latin American pharmacies and American pharmacies, they engage in conversations in the interpersonal mode (Standard 1.1) and compare the cultural differences between pharmacies (Standard 4.2). Students use their background information about what role pharmacies have in the United States and they connect this knowledge to their understanding of how pharmacies in Latin America operate (Standard 3.2).

Answers to *Nota cultural* (Online)
1. Es una farmacia que está abierta 24 horas del día/nunca cierra. Algunas farmacias en los Estados Unidos son farmacias de turno o de guardía (como Walgreens).
2. En las farmacias hispanas tradicionales puedes pedir consejo a los farmacéuticos y conseguir medicina sin receta (como los antibióticos), pero sólo venden medicina, no lo gran variedad de productos que compramos en las farmacias de los Estados Unidos.

2. to ask how long something has been going on.

> **cuánto (tiempo)** + **hace** + **que** + *verb in present tense*

¿Cuántos años **hace que** estudias medicina? — *How many years have you been studying medicine?*
¿Cuánto tiempo **hace que** estudias medicina? — *How long have you been studying medicine?*
¿Cuántos meses **hace que** tu abuela guarda cama? — *How many months has your grandmother been staying in bed?*
¿Cuánto tiempo **hace que** tu abuela guarda cama? — *How long has your grandmother been staying in bed?*

3. in the preterit to tell how long ago something happened.

> **hace** + *period of time* + **que** + *verb in the preterit*

Hace cuatro años **que** empecé a estudiar medicina. — *I began to study medicine four years ago.*
Hace seis años **que** me mudé aquí para estudiar. — *I moved here six years ago to study.*

or

> *verb in the preterit* + **hace** + *period of time*

Empecé a estudiar medicina **hace** cuatro años. — *I began to study medicine four years ago.*
Me mudé aquí **hace** seis años. — *I moved here six years ago.*

Note that in this construction **hace** can either precede or follow the rest of the sentence. When it follows, **que** is not used.

4. to ask how long ago something happened.

> **cuánto (tiempo)** + **hace** + **que** + *verb in preterit*

¿Cuánto tiempo **hace que** empezaste a estudiar medicina? — *How long ago did you begin to study medicine?*
¿Cuánto tiempo **hace que** te enfermaste? — *How long ago did you get sick?*

9-31 ¿Qué pasa? Juntos completen el diálogo entre Julián, Mari Carmen y su mamá con las palabras apropiadas. ■

Julián, ¡ese sofá es horrible!

MAMÁ: Julián (1) ¿ __Cuánto__ tiempo hace (2) ___que___ vives en esta casa?

JULIÁN: Bueno, creo que (3) ___hace___ unos dos años que vivo aquí.

MAMÁ: Y (4) ¿ __cuánto__ __tiempo__ __hace__ que tienes ese sofá? Está muy sucio.

JULIÁN: No sé, mamá. Fue un regalo de un amigo. Lo tenía en su apartamento.

MAMÁ: Creo que (5) ___hace___ por lo menos diez años (6) ___que___ tiene esas manchas (*stains*) negras. ¡Es horrible!

JULIÁN: Mamá, (7) ___hace___ media hora (8) ___que___ criticas mi casa y…

MARI CARMEN: ¡Mamá! (9) ¡ ___Hace___ cinco minutos (10) ___que___ te estoy llamando! ¡Tráeme agua!

Workbooklet

9-32 Firma aquí Circula por la clase hasta encontrar a un estudiante que pueda contestar afirmativamente tus preguntas. ■

Fíjate

Note that *cuánto* agrees with the amount of time: *cuánto tiempo; cuántas semanas/horas; cuántos años/días.*

MODELO   empezar a estudiar español hace menos de (*less than*) un año

E1:   *¿Empezaste a estudiar español hace menos de un año?*

E2:   *No, empecé a estudiar español hace dos años.*

E1:   (a otro estudiante) *¿Empezaste a estudiar español hace menos de un año?*

E3:   *Sí, empecé a estudiar español hace seis meses.*

E1:   *Muy bien. Firma (Sign) aquí por favor.*

Janet

1. empezar a estudiar español hace menos de un año	_____
2. graduarse de la escuela secundaria (*high school*) hace dos años	_____
3. conocer a su mejor amigo/a hace muchos años	_____
4. ver una película de terror hace dos o tres semanas	_____
5. ir a un concierto hace uno o dos meses	_____
6. tomar café hace una hora	_____
7. comer en un restaurante elegante hace unos días	_____
8. hacer ejercicio hace unas horas	_____
9. hablar con alguien de su familia hace una semana	_____
10. enfermarse hace una semana	_____

NOTE for 9-32

Encourage students to move around the room, asking questions to as many different classmates as possible. You may want to make this a competition—the student who gets the most signatures in the amount of time you set wins.

5:00 **9-33** **Conversando** Habla con varios compañeros de clase utilizando las siguientes preguntas para guiar la conversación. ∎

1. ¿Cuánto tiempo hace que vives en este estado (*state*)? ¿Dónde vivías antes?
2. ¿Cuánto tiempo hace que estudias en esta universidad? ¿En qué año te gradúas?
3. ¿Cuánto tiempo hace que conoces a tu mejor amigo/a? ¿Dónde lo/la conociste?
4. ¿Cuánto tiempo hace que viste a tus padres? ¿Volviste a casa o te visitaron?
5. ¿Cuánto tiempo hace que fuiste al médico? ¿Qué te recomendó?

ESCUCHA

Síntomas y tratamientos

09-41 to 09-43

Estrategia	A useful tool for boosting comprehension is asking yourself check questions to help you organize	information and summarize what you have heard. You will practice this strategy in the **A escuchar** section.
Asking yourself questions		

9-34 Antes de escuchar Marisol no se siente bien y llama a su madre para pedirle consejo. Cuando tú no te sientes bien, ¿qué haces generalmente: llamas al médico, hablas con un/a amigo/a, llamas a tu madre u otro pariente o te cuidas solo/a (*take care of yourself*)? ∎

Marisol llama a su madre.

9-35 A escuchar Completen las siguientes actividades. ∎

1. La conversación entre Marisol y su madre se divide en tres partes. Escucha la primera parte y después escoge la pregunta que mejor resuma (*summarizes*) lo que escuchaste. Repite el proceso con cada parte.

   PRIMERA PARTE
   a. ¿Por qué llama Marisol a su madre?
   b. ¿Cuáles son los síntomas de Marisol?
   c. ¿Qué hizo Marisol cuando se levantó?

   SEGUNDA PARTE
   a. ¿Con quiénes salió Marisol anoche?
   b. ¿A Marisol le gustan las galletas?
   c. ¿Qué comió Marisol anoche?

   TERCERA PARTE
   a. ¿Debe ir a clase?
   b. ¿Debe comer mucho hoy?
   c. ¿Qué puede hacer Marisol para sentirse mejor?

 2. Escucha una vez más para averiguar si escogiste las preguntas apropiadas. Compáralas con las de un/a compañero/a. Expliquen por qué son las mejores preguntas.

3. Ahora escucha la conversación por última vez para contestar las siguientes preguntas.
   a. ¿Por qué llama Marisol a su madre? Llama a su madre porque no se siente bien y no sabe qué hacer.
   b. ¿Cuáles son sus síntomas? Le duele mucho la cabeza y el estómago. No tiene ganas de comer.
   c. ¿Qué comió Marisol anoche? Comió dos hamburguesas con queso y papas fritas, helado y galletas.
   d. ¿Cuál es el consejo de su mamá? Le dice que no debe comer mucho pero debe beber mucha agua y té. Si come, debe comer cosas ligeras como sopa, arroz y fruta.

  9-36 Después de escuchar Realicen la escena entre Marisol y su madre. ∎

SECTION GOALS for *Escucha*
By the end of the *Escucha* section, students will be able to:
• incorporate previously presented listening strategies with new strategies.
• apply the new strategy of asking themselves questions for comprehension checks.
• practice pre-listening skills to organize the information they are about to hear.
• act out the scene they have just heard.

NATIONAL STANDARDS
Communication, Connections
The new strategy of listening and asking themselves questions reinforces the ability to be a good listener. All interpersonal communication with pairs or groups requires the ability to listen well and follow a conversation (Communication Standard 1.1). Standard 1.2 focuses on interpreting and understanding spoken Spanish on a variety of topics. Standard 1.3 also focuses on presenting information to an audience of listeners, and, as other people present to the class, students have to apply their strategies as they listen and check their comprehension. The ability to be a good listener is interdisciplinary, as many classes are lecture based. Students transfer their strategies for listening in Spanish to other courses and can apply the new strategy of asking themselves questions to check their comprehension (Standard 3.1).

NOTE for *Escucha*
For the *Escucha* section, you will need to pause the CD after each part (*primera, segunda, tercera*) so that students can choose the question that best summarizes what they heard. Tell your students that they will be listening in small chunks and that you will stop the audio after each part to check their comprehension. If your students do the *Escucha* section at home, please ask them to pause the CD.

AUDIOSCRIPT for 9-35
PRIMERA PARTE
MARISOL: Hola, mamá. ¿Cómo estás?
MAMÁ: Bien, hija. ¿Cómo estás tú hoy?
MARISOL: Bueno, por eso te llamo. No me siento muy bien.
MAMÁ: ¿Ah sí? ¿Qué te pasa? ¿Estás enferma?
MARISOL: Sí, anoche no dormí bien y cuando me desperté esta mañana, me dolían mucho la cabeza y el estómago.
MAMÁ: Pues... ¿comiste algo cuando te levantaste?
MARISOL: No, mamá. No tengo ganas de comer nada.
MAMÁ: ¿Tomaste una aspirina o un Tylenol?
MARISOL: No. Todavía no.
(15 second pause)

SEGUNDA PARTE
MAMÁ: Vamos a ver... ¿qué comiste anoche?
MARISOL: Salí con unos amigos. Primero cenamos en el restaurante Hamburger Shack. Comí dos hamburguesas con queso y unas papas fritas. Después caminamos al centro y compramos helado. A las diez fuimos al apartamento de Tina y comimos chocolate con galletas.
MAMÁ: Marisol, ¿cuántas galletas comiste?
MARISOL: No sé... quizás seis o siete. Tú sabes que me encantan las galletas.
MAMÁ: Sí, hija. Pero eso es mucha comida en muy poco tiempo. Por eso te sientes mal.
(15 second pause)

TERCERA PARTE
MARISOL: ¿Qué puedo hacer? Tengo clase en dos horas.
MAMÁ: Primero debes tomar un té caliente, como un té de manzanilla. Si no te hace sentir mejor, puedes tomar un Alka Seltzer.
MARISOL: Gracias, mamá. Voy a mirar a ver si tengo Alka Seltzer aquí. Estoy segura de que tengo té.
MAMÁ: Muy bien, hija. Y Marisol...
MARISOL: ¿Sí?
MAMÁ: No debes comer mucho hoy. Tienes que beber mucha agua, y té también, si quieres. Además, debes comer cosas ligeras como sopa, arroz y fruta.
MARISOL: ¡Gracias, mamá! Adiós. ¡Te quiero!
MAMÁ: Bueno, cuídate. Adiós, hija. ¡Un beso!

¡CONVERSEMOS!

 9-37 Los pacientes Tienes un trabajo como voluntario/a en un hospital. Describe a tres pacientes (ficticios) con quienes estuviste ayer. Tu compañero/a te hace las siguientes preguntas para guiar tu descripción: ■

1. ¿Cómo son?
2. ¿Cuáles son las enfermedades o condiciones de los pacientes?
3. ¿Qué tratamientos recibieron?

Incluye por lo menos **diez** oraciones en tu descripción.

 9-38 ¿Qué hicieron? Piensa en alguien que conoces que antes no vivía una vida sana, pero que recientemente cambió su vida. Descríbele a tu compañero/a de clase qué hacía antes y qué hizo para cambiar. Piensa bien si debes usar **el pretérito** o **el imperfecto** para explicar su situación. Tu compañero/a te va a hacer preguntas para clarificar y recibir más información. ■

ESCRIBE

09-45

Un resumen

Estrategia	When writing a summary in Spanish about things that occurred in the past, you must choose appropriately between the preterit and the imperfect. For example, if you are relating a chain or sequence of events—actions that occurred one after the other—you will most likely need to use the preterit. If you	are describing situations, what used to happen, or what was going on when something else happened, you will most likely use the imperfect. At this stage of your learning, it is a good idea to bookmark the list of words and expressions that commonly signal the preterit and the imperfect on page 352 to also help guide you.
Sequencing events		

9-39 Antes de escribir Piensa en el Episodio 8 de **Ambiciones siniestras.**
Haz una lista de los **ocho** acontecimientos (*events*) más importantes de *¿Quién fue?* y *El misterio crece.* ▪

9-40 A escribir Escribe un resumen del Episodio 8 de **Ambiciones siniestras,** utilizando tu lista e incorporando un poco de descripción sobre los personajes y la escena: dónde estaban, qué hacían, cómo se sentían, etc. ▪

9-41 Después de escribir Comparte tu resumen con un/a compañero/a. ¿Tienen el mismo contenido? Enfóquense en los verbos. ¿Usaron de manera correcta el pretérito y el imperfecto? ▪

¿Cómo andas? II

	Feel confident	Need to review
Having completed **Comunicación II,** I now can . . .		
• narrate in the past (p. 242)	☐	☐
• consider pharmacies in Spanish-speaking countries and how they differ from those in the United States (p. 249)	☐	☐
• explain how long something has been going on and how long ago something occurred (p. 249)	☐	☐
• ask myself questions when listening to organize and summarize what I hear (p. 253)	☐	☐
• communicate about ailments and healthy living (p. 254)	☐	☐
• write a summary, sequencing past events (p. 255)	☐	☐

SECTION GOALS for *Escribe*
By the end of the *Escribe* section, students will be able to:
• review the events from *Episodio 8* of *Ambiciones siniestras* and write a synopsis in Spanish.
• sequence events.
• embellish the events they brainstormed to include a more detailed description of the events.
• compare their summaries with their classmates' summaries.
• write the story in the past tense, practicing the uses of the preterit and imperfect.
• edit the events based on feedback from their classmates or their instructor.

NATIONAL STANDARDS
Communication, Comparisons
Students write their summary of the *Episodio 8* events in the past tense. When they share their narrations with the class, it becomes the presentational mode of communication (Standard 1.3). You could turn the activity into a jigsaw; you tell them what happened in English (10 sentences), one student writes the even events and the other student writes the odd events. They then meet in pairs or small groups to discuss the story (Standard 1.1). They use their past tense narrations to compare which form (preterit or imperfect) is more appropriate, based on how they would say the sentence in English. They process and compare their understanding of the past tense with their understanding of the English past tense (Standard 4.1).

SECTION GOALS for *Cultura*
By the end of the *Cultura* section, students will be able to:
• discuss the geography of Peru.
• highlight geographical and historical sites in Peru.
• contrast Peru with Bolivia.
• identify the indigenous people of Bolivia.
• describe the indigenous ruins in Bolivia.
• explain how Bolivia differs from other South American countries.
• describe the geographical variation in Ecuador.
• explain the role of the shaman.
• make comparisons between Peru, Bolivia, and Ecuador.

NATIONAL STANDARDS
Communication, Cultures, Connections, Comparisons
The readings from *Les presento mi país* relate to Communication, Cultures, Connections, and Comparisons. The readings encompass interpretive communication because students are reading written Spanish and they have to interpret and understand the information (Standard 1.2). If you also read the cultural notes aloud, they would be interpreting and understanding spoken Spanish (Standard 1.2). Your students are engaging in interpersonal communication when discussing the readings in small groups and answering the questions that follow (Standard 1.1). The readings about Peru, Bolivia, and Ecuador explain how the cultures differ between the three countries, and students can relate to how the cultural differences shape the practices, perspectives, and products of the countries (Standards 2.1, 2.2). These cultural differences provide the basis for making comparisons between these cultures and the cultures of the United States (Standard 4.2). Students can also make connections between their studies in history, geography, and science to the new information about Peru, Bolivia, and Ecuador.

NOTE for *Les presento mi país*
The University of San Marcos was founded May on 12, 1551, by an order of Dominican friars; it is the oldest university in Latin America.

NOTE for *Miraflores*
An upscale neighborhood of Lima, this area is known for its excellent shopping, restaurants, parks, and beaches. It is also a cultural center with many art galleries and theaters.

09-46 to 09-47

Les presento mi país

Diana Ávila Peralta

Mi nombre es Diana Ávila Peralta y soy de Ayacucho, Perú. Estudio historia en la Universidad Nacional Mayor de San Marcos en Lima y mientras estudio, vivo con unos parientes en Miraflores, un barrio de la capital. **¿Dónde viven los estudiantes de tu universidad generalmente?** Quiero ser profesora porque me fascina la historia de mi país y quiero compartir mi pasión con otras personas. Hay muchas ruinas de la civilización incaica en Perú. **¿Qué sabes de la historia de tu país y sus pueblos antiguos?** Perú es un país de extremos geográficos: tenemos la costa, al nivel del mar, los Andes, montañas impresionantes, cañones profundos, la selva y los principios del río Amazonas con flora y fauna magníficas. ¡Puedes mantenerte en forma caminando por estas regiones!

Las líneas de Nazca

Loros en la selva amazónica

Miraflores, en las afueras de Lima, Perú

ALMANAQUE

Nombre oficial:	República del Perú
Gobierno:	República constitucional
Población:	29.907.003 (2010)
Idiomas:	español (oficial); quechua (oficial); idiomas indígenas
Moneda:	Nuevo sol (S/)

¿Sabías que...?
• Las líneas de Nazca, que se encuentran en un desierto del sur del país, son un enigma. Consisten en una serie de dibujos de diferentes animales, plantas y flores, y figuras geométricas que se reconocen solamente desde el aire.
• Hay casi 3,5 millones de llamas en los Andes.

Preguntas
1. ¿Por qué Diana quiere ser profesora?
2. ¿Por qué se dice que Perú es un país de geografía muy variada?
3. ¿Qué otros países comparten algunas de las características geográficas de Perú?

 Amplía tus conocimientos sobre Perú en MySpanishLab.

256

NOTE for *Las líneas de Nazca*
Las líneas de Nazca are still a mystery today. There are hundreds of different figures, plus additional cross-hatching lines, spread out over an area of 400 square miles. Some of the figures are distinctive (e.g., a monkey, a hummingbird, a spider, flowers), and others are difficult to decipher even now. Several theories exist as to the origin and meaning of the lines.

NOTE for *La selva amazónica*
It has been reported that the Andes Mountain range and the Amazon rainforest are home to more than half of the world's species of flora and fauna. The Scarlet Macaw is a member of the parrot family. Known for their vibrant colors and loud call, these birds can be seen gathering by the hundreds on the clay cliffs of the Amazon River where they feed on the rich minerals found there. Macaws build their nests high up in the canopy trees of the Amazon rainforest and mate for life. They can reach 32 inches long, more than half of which consists of a pointed tail, and an average weight of about 2.2 lbs.

Bolivia

09-46, 09-48

Les presento mi país

Jorge Gustavo
Salazar

Mi nombre es Jorge Gustavo Salazar y soy de Sucre, una de las dos capitales de mi país y la sede (*headquarters*) constitucional donde se mantiene el Tribunal Supremo de Bolivia. La Paz, la capital administrativa, es la capital más alta del mundo, a unos 3.650 m.s.n.m. en los Andes. **¿A qué altura está tu ciudad?** La gente indígena constituye más del cincuenta por ciento de la población del país, y muchos viven en el altiplano, un área cerca del lago Titicaca, que es el lago navegable más alto del mundo. En el altiplano se encuentran las ruinas de una civilización antigua preincaica, anterior a los aymara, que pueblan la región hoy en día. **¿Hay ruinas de antiguas civilizaciones cerca de donde tú vives?**

> **Fíjate**
>
> The abbreviation *m.s.n.m.* means *metros sobre nivel del mar,* or meters above sea level.

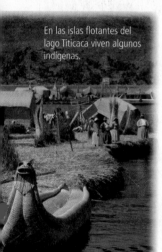

En las islas flotantes del lago Titicaca viven algunos indígenas.

Una mujer aymara con ropa tradicional

Unas chullpas en el altiplano

ALMANAQUE

Nombre oficial:	República de Bolivia
Gobierno:	República
Población:	9.947.418 (2010)
Idiomas:	español (oficial); quechua (oficial); aymara (oficial)
Moneda:	Boliviano (Bs)

¿Sabías que...?

- La papa, nativa de Sudamérica, es un alimento básico en Bolivia. Se cultivan más de doscientos tipos de papa en el país.
- Aunque no tiene salida al mar, Bolivia tiene una fuerza marina: la Armada Boliviana.

Preguntas

1. ¿Por qué crees que Bolivia tiene tres idiomas oficiales?
2. ¿Qué distinción tiene La Paz como capital?
3. ¿Qué riesgo para la salud (*health risk*) comparten Bolivia y Perú?

 Amplía tus conocimientos sobre Bolivia en MySpanishLab.

257

 Instructor Resources
- Text images (maps), Video resources

NOTE for *Los aymaras*
The Aymara indigenous people have a distinctive style of dress. The women wear layers of bright skirts (called *polleras*) and bowler hats. The hat is worn to the side of her head if the woman is unmarried, and in the center if she is married. The men wear striped ponchos and woven hats with earflaps, called *chullos*. The earflaps are a necessity for protection against the cold in the regions where they live.

SUGGESTION for *Aymaras*
Ask students: Do we have regional or indigenous costumes in the United States? Do we have a way of telling someone's civil status from apparel or some outward appearance (e.g., wedding rings)?

NOTE for *El lago Titicaca*
Lake Titicaca is the highest navigable lake in the world at 12,500 feet (3,810 meters). The Floating Islands of the Uros are here. These islands are constructed from layers of totora reeds, which are replaced from the top while those underneath decompose. The Uros people live on the islands and visitors are welcome, but you have to keep moving in order not to sink!

SUGGESTION for *El lago Titicaca*
Ask students whether they can imagine living on a floating island. What would that be like? Would the sensation be like sleeping on a waterbed?

NOTE for *Las chullpas*
Chullpas, ancient Aymara burial towers, can be found across the *Altiplano* in Bolivia and Peru. Corpses, placed in fetal position, were entombed along with some personal belongings. In the northern part of the *Altiplano* the *chullpas* are circular and made of stone while those in the southern part are rectangular and made of adobe.

NOTE for *La papa*
The potato is originally from South America, and scores of varieties are cultivated in Andean countries. It is a staple in the diet of Bolivians. Another staple is an Incan grain, *quinoa*. This grain has been called "the most complete protein" food and is extremely nutritious. Bolivians have their own version of "hot sauce" called *la llagua*. This is a condiment found on tables everywhere in Bolivia and consists of tomatoes, onions, and very hot peppers called *locotos*.

NOTE for *Los tsáchilas*
The Tsáchilas or *Colorados* are a distinctive indigenous group in the province of Pichincha, some 40 miles west of Quito. Although many of their traditions are being lost due to the encroachment of modernization and the lure of the big cities for the younger members of the community, this group maintains some easily recognizable traits. The men wear a rectangular piece of cloth, navy blue and white striped, which resembles a skirt. They shave their heads up to the crown, maintaining the hair on top rather long. This is then coated with a mixture of a vaseline-like substance tinted with the *achiote* seed, which makes it bright orange-red. The women weave a cloth of many colors for their skirts and wear necklaces of glass beads. Both sexes paint their bodies with black lines. The shamans of the Tsáchilas are well known for their knowledge and use of medicinal plants.

SUGGESTION for *Los tsáchilas*
Ask students: Why is it hard to maintain tribal or community customs in the present day? What do you think of shamans? Can they cure people? Why do you think they can or can't?

SUGGESTION for *El sombrero panamá*
Ask students: Can you think of other products or practices that have geographic misnomers, e.g., have names that do not truly reflect their origins (e.g., the Russian flu, which didn't begin in Russia, but was first documented there)?

NOTE for *El sombrero panamá*
Despite the name, Panama hats (*el sombrero panamá*) are made only in Ecuador. They are woven by hand from the toquilla plant. Monticristi and Jipijapa are two places where the hats are made. The true Panama hat is woven so tightly that it passes the water test: Turn the hat upside down and pour water into it. The best hats yield not a drop of water leaking out!

NOTE for *Las islas Galápagos*
The Galapagos Islands are an archipelago of volcanic islands that lie approximately 500 miles off the coast of Ecuador. Some 23,000 inhabitants live in this Ecuadorian province that encompasses a biological marine reserve and a national park. The islands are well known for their wildlife and the vast number of endemic species.

CULTURA • CULTURA • CULTURA • CULTURA

Ecuador

09-46, 09-49

Les presento mi país

Yolanda Pico Briones

Mi nombre es Yolanda Pico Briones y soy de Quito, la capital de Ecuador. Mi país tiene tres diferentes tipos de geografía: la costa, la sierra y el oriente o la selva. La población, principalmente mestiza e indígena, se concentra en la sierra y la costa. **¿Dónde vive la mayoría de la población en tu país?** Uno de los grupos indígenas de Ecuador son los tsáchilas, también llamados "los colorados", debido a la costumbre de los hombres de pintarse (*dye*) el pelo de color rojo. Los chamanes (*shamans*) de esta tribu tienen gran conocimiento de las plantas medicinales y, por lo tanto, tienen mucho poder en la comunidad. **¿Es popular la medicina alternativa donde tú vives?**

Las islas Galápagos

Las Islas Galápagos

Un sombrero panamá

Las plantas medicinales son importantes en la medicina alternativa.

ALMANAQUE

Nombre oficial:	República del Ecuador
Gobierno:	República
Población:	14.790.608 (2010)
Idiomas:	español (oficial), quechua y otros idiomas indígenas
Moneda:	El dólar estadounidense ($)

¿Sabías que...?

• El famoso sombrero panamá es en realidad de Ecuador.
• El volcán Cotopaxi se considera el volcán activo más alto del mundo.

Preguntas

1. ¿Cuál es una costumbre de los tsáchilas?
2. ¿Qué tiene Ecuador en común geográficamente con Perú y Bolivia?
3. ¿En qué otros países se encuentra un gran porcentaje de mestizos e indígenas?

 Amplía tus conocimientos sobre Ecuador en MySpanishLab.

258

NOTE for *Las islas Galápagos*
Charles Darwin spent a good deal of time studying the vast array of animal species found there during the voyage of the *Beagle*. His collections and observations contributed to Darwin's theory of natural selection.

¡Hola!
eText 366   09-52

Ambiciones siniestras

EPISODIO 9

Lectura y video

Y por fin, ¿cómo andas?

	Feel confident	Need to review
Having completed this chapter, I now can . . .		
Comunicación I		
• describe the human body (p. 228)	☐	☐
• pronounce the letters **d** and **t** (MSL / SAM)	☐	☐
• share about people, actions, and things (p. 231)	☐	☐
• explain ailments and treatments (p. 235)	☐	☐
• make emphatic and exclamatory statements (p. 240)	☐	☐
Comunicación II		
• narrate in the past (p. 242)	☐	☐
• explain how long something has been going on and how long ago something occurred (p. 249)	☐	☐
• ask myself questions when listening to organize and summarize what I hear (p. 253)	☐	☐
• communicate about ailments and healthy living (p. 254)	☐	☐
• write a summary, sequencing past events (p. 255)	☐	☐
Cultura		
• relate the importance of water in maintaining good health (p. 239)	☐	☐
• consider pharmacies in Spanish-speaking countries and how they differ from those in the United States (p. 249)	☐	☐
• list important information about this chapter's featured countries: Peru, Bolivia, and Ecuador (pp. 256–258)	☐	☐
Ambiciones siniestras		
• create check questions to facilitate comprehension when reading, and give details about the new e-mail message (p. 259)	☐	☐
• discover the progress the characters are making in deciphering the new riddle (p. 259)	☐	☐
Comunidades		
• use Spanish in real-life contexts (SAM)	☐	☐

NATIONAL STANDARDS
Communication, Comparisons
Note that the online readings are kept at a level of comprehensible input that entices the students to read. Also, the follow-up questions encourage your students to think beyond the content of the story and make informed guesses about what they would do in the same circumstances. The *Ambiciones siniestras* reading for *Capítulo 9* focuses on asking questions while reading. If students work together and discuss the questions as they read, they are communicating interpersonally (Standard 1.1). The students can also make comparisons between the past tense in English and the preterit and imperfect in Spanish (Standard 4.1) as they read the story and decide why parts of the story required the preterit or the imperfect.

NATIONAL STANDARDS
Communication, Connections
The reading and writing activities from *Ambiciones siniestras* are designed to practice the new strategy of asking oneself questions. Students read the passage or engage in pre-writing activities that facilitate their communication in Spanish (Standard 1.2), and if they communicate with others in the interpersonal mode, they also apply Standard 1.1. They can use this new strategy and apply it to other subjects as they read for comprehension (Standard 3.1) while they strengthen their reading skills and increase their comprehension in other disciplines.

CAPÍTULO 9

SECTION GOALS for *Lectura y video* (Online)
By the end of the *Lectura y video* section, students will be able to:
• use the new strategy, asking themselves questions as they read the passage.
• incorporate familiar reading strategies with the new reading strategy.
• recall the events from *Episodio 8* and make predictions about what will happen in *Episodio 9*.
• summarize the main events from the story.
• answer pre-viewing questions.
• make predictions about what will happen
• based on the previous episode.

NOTE for *Lectura y video*
Activity answers for online content can be found on the next page for quick reference.

EXPANSION for *Antes de leer* (Online)
Have students retell *Ambiciones siniestras* from the first lesson (reading and video) through *Capítulo 8* by revisiting the summaries they wrote for the *Escribe* section. They could work in pairs, comparing their summaries.

RECAP of
AMBICIONES SINIESTRAS
Episodio 8 (Online)

Lectura: In *Ambiciones siniestras, Capítulo 8,* Marisol read her e-mail and discovered that someone had solved the puzzle, and she received a new puzzle to solve. As she read her e-mail, the phone rang and it was Manolo. Marisol confessed that she thought Lupe was Sr. Verdugo, and Manolo told her that he thought Cisco was Sr. Verdugo. They decided not to call the police and hung up. Marisol saw a new e-mail message from an unfamiliar sender, read the message, and screamed.

Video: Marisol received a threatening message over e-mail. Manolo called Lupe and she revealed that she solved the puzzle. She had photos of Alejandra and Eduardo from wherever they were being held, but the other characters do not know that she has the information. Toward the end of their conversation it appeared as if someone had been listening to their entire conversation. Lupe realized something important, packed a suitcase, and added a gun to her suitcase. Manolo called Cisco to tell him that Lupe solved the puzzle and their call was dropped. We saw Cisco find a paper he was looking for, change his clothes, and then he finished getting dressed and walked out.

SUGGESTION for *Lectura*
You may want to explain that *Verdugo* means "tormenter."

ANSWERS to 9-43, *Lectura* (Online)

1. c
2. a
3. *Possible answers include:*
   ¿Cómo está Manolo hoy?
   ¿Por qué Cisco llama a Manolo?
   ¿Por qué Marisol llama a Manolo?
   ¿Tienen tiempo para descifrar el rompecabezas?
   ¿Qué oportunidad les da el Sr. Verdugo?
   ¿Cómo les amenaza?
   ¿Qué hace Manolo después de leer el mensaje?

ANSWERS to 9-44, *Lectura* (Online)

1. No saben si ellos también van a desaparecer.
2. Durmió mal y le duele el cuerpo. También está asustado.
3. Cisco y Marisol llaman a Manolo para saber si él recibió y leyó el mensaje nuevo.
4. Dice que pueden trabajar juntos y que él los está vigilando.
5. El Sr. Verdugo dice que los está vigilando y que es "capaz de todo".

ANSWERS to 9-46, *Video* (Online)

1. Estaban en la biblioteca.
2. Trataban de descifrar el rompecabezas.
3. Tenía un libro de Perú que hablaba de la cordillera de los Andes, una zona de gran altura.
4. Lupe dijo que todos los países de los Andes, Chile, Argentina, Perú, Bolivia, Ecuador, Colombia y Venezuela tienen grandes alturas.
5. Decidieron llamarlos para compartir sus ideas sobre el rompecabezas.
6. Dijo que es una frase famosa que dijo Eva Perón, la esposa del Presidente argentino Juan Perón.
7. Manolo propuso dividir el trabajo — la tercera pista para las chicas y la cuarta para Cisco y él.
8. Tenían doce horas.
9. Marisol no se encontraba bien y Lupe le dijo que pensaba que Cisco no les estaba diciendo la verdad. Cisco la oyó decirlo.

VOCABULARIO ACTIVO

El cuerpo humano	*The human body*
la boca	*mouth*
el brazo	*arm*
la cabeza	*head*
la cara	*face*
la cintura	*waist*
el corazón	*heart*
el cuello	*neck*
el cuerpo	*body*
el dedo (de la mano)	*finger*
el dedo (del pie)	*toe*
el diente	*tooth*
la espalda	*back*
el estómago	*stomach*
la garganta	*throat*
la mano	*hand*
la nariz	*nose*
el oído	*inner ear*
el ojo	*eye*
la oreja	*ear*
el pecho	*chest*
el pelo	*hair*
el pie	*foot*
la pierna	*leg*

Algunos verbos	*Some verbs*
doler (ue)	*to hurt*
estar enfermo/a	*to be sick*
estar sano/a; saludable	*to be healthy*
ser alérgico/a (a)	*to be allergic (to)*

Otras palabras útiles	*Other useful words*
la salud	*health*
la sangre	*blood*

Algunas enfermedades y tratamientos médicos	*Illnesses and medical treatments*
el antiácido	*antacid*
el antibiótico	*antibiotic*
la aspirina	*aspirin*
el catarro / el resfriado	*cold*
la curita	*adhesive bandage*
el/la doctor/a	*doctor*
el dolor	*pain*
el/la enfermero/a	*nurse*
el estornudo	*sneeze*
el examen físico	*physical exam*
la farmacia	*pharmacy*
la fiebre	*fever*
la gripe	*flu*
la herida	*wound; injury*
el hospital	*hospital*
la inyección	*shot*
el jarabe	*cough syrup*
el/la médico/a	*doctor*
la náusea	*nausea*
las pastillas	*pills*
la receta	*prescription*
la sala de urgencias	*emergency room*
la tos	*cough*
la venda / el vendaje	*bandage*

260

Algunos verbos	Some verbs
acabar de + *infinitivo*	*to have just finished + (something)*
caer(se)	*to fall down*
cortar(se)	*to cut (oneself)*
curar(se)	*to cure; to be cured*
enfermar(se)	*to get sick*
estornudar	*to sneeze*
evitar	*to avoid*
guardar cama	*to stay in bed*
lastimar(se)	*to get hurt*
mejorar(se)	*to improve; to get better*
ocurrir	*to occur*
quemar(se)	*to burn; to get burned*
romper(se)	*to break*
tener…	
alergia (a)	*to be allergic (to)*
(un) catarro, resfriado	*to have a cold*
(la/una) gripe	*to have the flu*
una infección	*to have an infection*
tos	*to have a cough*
un virus	*to have a virus*
tener dolor de…	*to have a…*
cabeza	*headache*
espalda	*backache*
estómago	*stomachache*
garganta	*sore throat*
toser	*to cough*
tratar de	*to try to*
vendar(se)	*to bandage (oneself); to dress (a wound)*

Instructor Resources
• IRM: Syllabi and Lesson Plans

NATIONAL STANDARDS

COMUNICACIÓN I

• To discuss modes of transportation (Communication, Comparisons)
• To pronounce the letters *b* and *v* (Communication)
• To influence others and give advice (Communication)
• To give orders and instructions (Communication)
• To engage in additional communication practice (Communication, Communities)

COMUNICACIÓN II

• To share about travel (Communication)
• To state what belongs to you and others (Communication)
• To compare people, places, and things (Communication, Comparisons)
• To focus on linguistic cues (Communication, Connections)
• To communicate about travel plans (Communication)
• To write and present a report using linking words (Communication, Cultures, Connections)
• To engage in additional communication practice (Communication, Communities)

CULTURA

• To list some public transportation options and discuss procedures for getting a driver's license (Communication, Cultures, Connections, Comparisons)
• To investigate travel and tourism opportunities in Venezuela (Communication, Cultures)
• To impart important facts about this chapter's featured countries: Colombia and Venezuela (Communication, Cultures, Comparisons)
• To explore further the chapter's cultural themes (Communication, Cultures)

AMBICIONES SINIESTRAS

• To determine when it is appropriate to skip unfamiliar words and to discover the truth about what Cisco knows (Communication, Comparisons)
• To confirm that Lupe is not who she appears to be (Communication)

COMUNIDADES

• To use Spanish in real-life contexts (Communities)

10 ¡Viajemos!

¿Te gusta viajar (*travel*)? ¿Adónde? ¿Cómo? ¿Cuándo? Exploremos muchas opciones. ¡Viajemos!

PREGUNTAS

1 Cuando viajas, ¿adónde vas generalmente?

2 ¿Cuándo viajas? ¿Por qué?

3 En el futuro, ¿adónde quieres ir?

262

SECTION GOALS for *Chapter opener*
By the end of the Chapter opener section, students will be able to:
• list preparations of smart travelers.
• make suggestions for planning a trip.

NATIONAL STANDARDS
Communities
There are several service learning options available for integrating travel, transportation, and the use of Spanish. If you have a large Hispanic population, you could plan a travel fair, where students have a table or booth for each Spanish-speaking country. You could invite community members from those countries to represent their countries of origin with realia, photos, souvenirs,

artifacts, or food. This could be done during the day, during your class time, at night, or on a weekend. Students could research the countries of their Hispanic partners and act as the travel agents for the public, offering advice for what to see, excursions to take, and general travel tips. If you do not have a large Hispanic population, you could ask the students to do research as if they were travel agents and offer a "get to know my country" event where community members could find out what each Spanish-speaking country has to offer tourists. Students could research the current cost of travel, immunizations, and documentation required, and the best places to see; they could also plan a virtual trip using the Internet.

EXPANSION for *Preguntas*
Ask your students the following questions: *¿Tuviste problemas alguna vez en un viaje? Explica. ¿Qué puedes hacer para evitar ese problema en futuros viajes?*

PLANNING AHEAD
Assign **10-31** several days in advance, so that students can plan well their sentences.

METHODOLOGY • Student Motivation
Motivation plays a large role in learning another language. All of the activities in *¡Anda! Curso elemental* focus on having students interact with each other in a non-threatening and highly engaging way. You should notice your students becoming more and more comfortable and confident as they learn Spanish. This chapter continues our goal of providing students with fun, enjoyable opportunities to practice Spanish with their classmates.

SECTION GOALS for *Comunicación I*

By the end of the *Comunicación* section, students will be able to:

- discuss different modes of transportation.
- identify the parts of a car and their functions.
- pronounce the letters *b* and *v* correctly.
- give affirmative and negative *tú* commands.
- give affirmative and negative *Ud.* and *Uds.* commands.
- contrast public transportation options in the United States and abroad, and report about learning how to drive in Colombia.

NATIONAL STANDARDS
Communication

The vocabulary and activities in this section are highly motivational since a number of the transportation words are cognates. Also, it is very easy for students to access and use this vocabulary in real-life situations using the Internet, since there is an abundance of travel web sites for each country.

Depending on where one lives, there are multiple modes of transportation available. In the large cities, people walk or use public transportation such as trains or buses, whereas in small cities and suburbs many people drive cars. In *Capítulo 10*, students learn about different modes of transportation and how in many Hispanic countries there is a greater reliance on public transportation than on cars. They are able to make comparisons (Standard 4.2) about how transportation options differ among countries.

The vocabulary in *Capítulo 10* is focused on transportation, the parts of a car, and verbs associated with driving and maintaining vehicles. Students communicate in the interpersonal mode when they identify the parts of a car and discuss proper car maintenance (Standard 1.1). They can use this information, coupled with commands, to express themselves to others (rental car agents, mechanics, police, cab drivers, chauffeurs, bus drivers, etc.) about their transportation needs when traveling abroad (Standard 2.2). Students are able to connect what they already know about transportation and car parts with the new information they have learned in Spanish (Standard 3.1).

Comunicación I

1 VOCABULARIO

7:00 🔊 📖 10-01 to 10-08

Los medios de transporte   Discussing modes of transportation

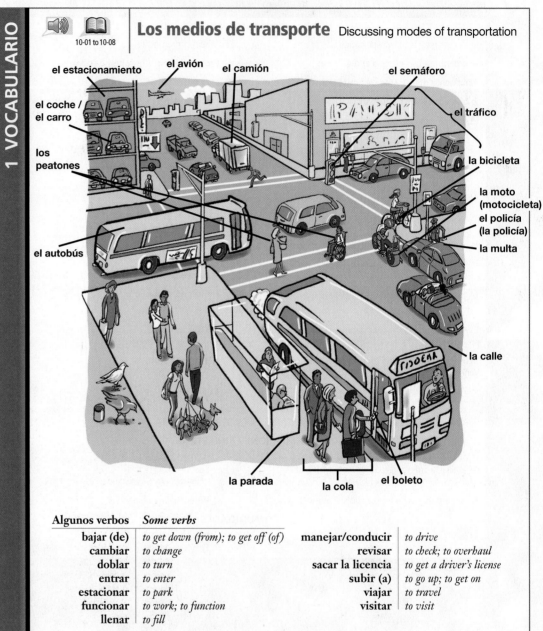

el estacionamiento · el avión · el camión · el semáforo · el tráfico · el coche / el carro · la bicicleta · los peatones · la moto (motocicleta) · el policía (la policía) · la multa · el autobús · la calle · la parada · la cola · el boleto

Algunos verbos	*Some verbs*		
bajar (de)	*to get down (from); to get off (of)*	**manejar/conducir**	*to drive*
cambiar	*to change*	**revisar**	*to check; to overhaul*
doblar	*to turn*	**sacar la licencia**	*to get a driver's license*
entrar	*to enter*	**subir (a)**	*to go up; to get on*
estacionar	*to park*	**viajar**	*to travel*
funcionar	*to work; to function*	**visitar**	*to visit*
llenar	*to fill*		

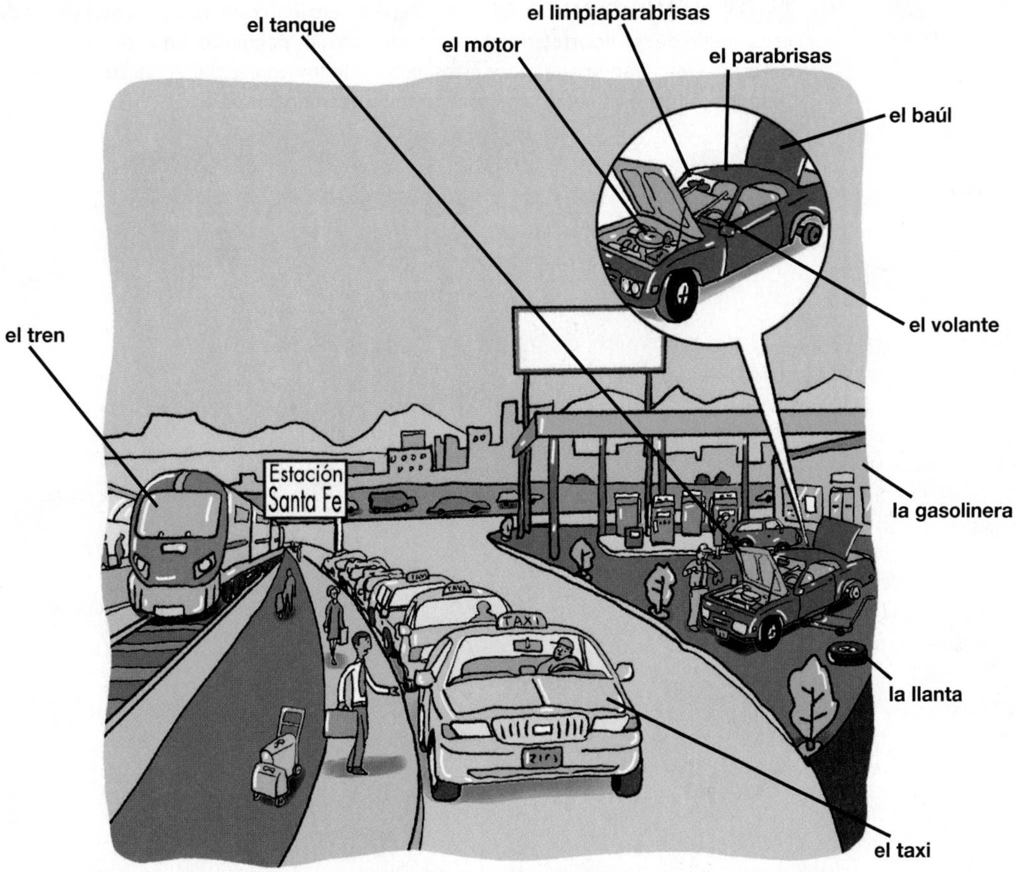

el tanque
el limpiaparabrisas
el motor
el parabrisas
el baúl
el volante
el tren
Estación
Santa Fe
TAXI
la gasolinera
la llanta
el taxi

Otras palabras útiles	*Other useful words*
el aire acondicionado	*air conditioning*
la autopista	*highway; freeway*
el barco	*boat*
la calefacción	*heat*
la licencia (de conducir)	*driver's license*
la llave	*key*
el metro	*subway*
el ruido	*noise*
el taller mecánico	*auto repair shop*

PRONUNCIACIÓN

The letters *b* and *v*

¡Hola! 10-09 to 10-12

Go to MySpanishLab / Student Activities Manual to learn about the letters *b* and *v*.

NOTE for *Los medios de transporte*

If you wish, point out other ways of saying some of the following vocabulary. For example: *el autobús/camión (Mex.)/guagua (Caribe); el coche/el carro/el auto; el boleto/el billete.* If you choose to expand their knowledge by explaining that different countries have different ways of saying things, we recommend that you explain to beginning students that they will still be understood using the basic vocabulary we are presenting in *¡Anda! Curso elemental.* Otherwise, they will become frustrated, thinking that native speakers in country X will not understand them. As always, remind them of the *También se dice…* section in Appendix 3.

SECTION GOALS for *Pronunciación*

By the end of the *Pronunciación* section, students will be able to:

- pronounce the letters *b* and *v* correctly.
- state the rules that state when the *v* is pronounced like *b.*
- pronounce some popular *dichos y refranes* with *v* and *b* sounds in them.

5:00   Workbooklet

10-1 ¿Qué tienen en común?

Escriban características específicas de cada medio de transporte en cada uno de los círculos pequeños. En el círculo grande del centro, escriban lo que todos estos medios de transporte tienen en común. Después comparen su diagrama con los de otros compañeros. ■

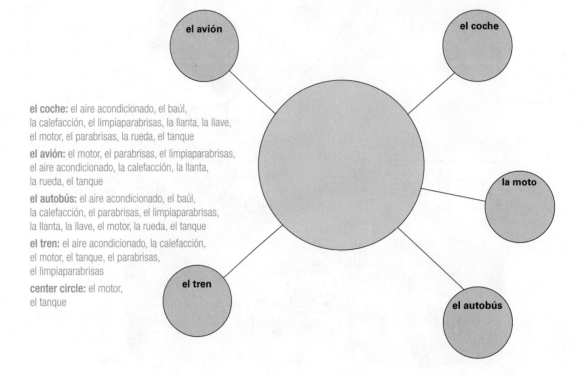

el coche: el aire acondicionado, el baúl, la calefacción, el limpiaparabrisas, la llanta, la llave, el motor, el parabrisas, la rueda, el tanque

el avión: el motor, el parabrisas, el limpiaparabrisas, el aire acondicionado, la calefacción, la llanta, la rueda, el tanque

el autobús: el aire acondicionado, el baúl, la calefacción, el parabrisas, el limpiaparabrisas, la llanta, la llave, el motor, la rueda, el tanque

el tren: el aire acondicionado, la calefacción, el motor, el tanque, el parabrisas, el limpiaparabrisas

center circle: el motor, el tanque

4:00

10-2 ¿Es verdad?

Decide si las siguientes oraciones son ciertas (**C**) o falsas (**F**). Si son falsas, corrígelas (*correct them*). Compara tus respuestas con las de un/a compañero/a. ■

MODELO   Un carro tiene seis llantas.
E1: *Un carro tiene seis llantas.*
E2: *Falso. Un carro tiene cuatro llantas.*

1. Hay semáforos en las autopistas. F   en las calles
2. Para llegar a la universidad yo puedo tomar el autobús o ir a pie. C/F
3. Ir en avión es más rápido que ir en tren. C
4. Un coche no puede funcionar sin limpiaparabrisas. F   un motor, gasolina, etc.
5. Hay que cambiar el aceite de un coche cada 100.000 millas. F   de cada 3.000 a 5.000
6. Puedes llenar el tanque con gasolina en la gasolinera. C
7. Usamos la calefacción en el verano. F   Usamos la calefacción en el invierno.
8. Si manejamos muy rápido el policía nos puede dar una llave. F   una multa

`6:00` 👥 **10-3** **¿Cómo vas?** Completa los siguientes pasos. ▪

Paso 1   Pon una equis (X) en la columna apropiada. Después, pregúntale a un/a compañero/a qué medios de transporte usa él/ella.

¿QUÉ USAS...?	A MENUDO	A VECES	NUNCA
bicicleta			
autobús			
avión			
carro			
tren			

MODELO   E1:   *¿Qué medio de transporte usas a menudo?*

                 E2:   *Uso el autobús a menudo. ¿Y tú?*

                 E1:   *Uso el carro.*

                 E2:   *¿Qué medio de transporte usas a veces?*

                 E1:   *Uso la bicicleta a veces. ¿Y tú?*

Paso 2   Túrnense para hacerse y contestar las siguientes preguntas.

               ¿Qué medio de transporte usas...

1. más?
2. menos?
3. para ir a la universidad?
4. para ir al centro comercial?
5. para ir a visitar a tus amigos?
6. para ir a la casa de tus padres o de unos parientes?
7. para ir a Los Ángeles?
8. para ir a Caracas, Venezuela?
9. para ir a Europa?

`6:00` 👥 **10-4** **Cinco preguntas** En grupos de tres o cuatro estudiantes, escriban **cinco** preguntas interesantes relacionadas con **Los medios de transporte**. Después, para cada pregunta, deben escoger a una persona de otro grupo para contestarla. ▪

MODELO   GRUPO 1:   *¿Cambiaste el aceite del coche la semana pasada?*

       GRUPO 2 (PHILIP):   *No, no cambié el aceite la semana pasada, pero tengo que cambiarlo pronto.*

       GRUPO 1:   *¿Viajaste a México el verano pasado?*

       GRUPO 2 (GENA):   *Sí, fui a Cancún con mi familia.*

METHODOLOGY • Following Up Activities

As always, it is important to follow up pair and group work by altering the activity to the level of the class. Following up student work has many benefits. For example, it:

- lets students know their work is important.
- allows students to check their work.
- lets you know what students understand and don't understand.
- gives students the opportunity to "report back" using different forms of the verbs.
- provides you with the opportunity to ask expansion questions

METHODOLOGY • Holding Students Accountable

When following up activities you may ask students to report on the responses of other students. For example, in **10-3,** students report on their partners' use of modes of transportation. After one or two students report you could ask: *María, ¿cómo viene Tom a la clase de español?* or *¿Cómo vienen Tom y Sara a la clase de español?* This is great listening practice and encourages students to pay attention.

METHODOLOGY • Formulating Questions

Activity **10-4** gives students the opportunity to create questions to ask of other students. Research states that language students have a difficult time formulating questions since they have little practice; it is usually the teacher asking the questions. Asking questions incorporates higher order thinking since the group of students then needs to hypothesize the answer that their classmate will give.

NOTE for 10-5
As with all activities like **10-5,** insist that students answer truthfully, the purpose being that students will need to interact with a variety of others in the class.

ADDITIONAL ACTIVITY for
Los medios de transporte
You may choose to use this activity as a teacher-led listening activity or as a paired activity.

¿Cierto o falso? Decidan si las siguientes oraciones son ciertas (**C**) o falsas (**F**).

1. Se compra la gasolina en galones en los Estados Unidos.
2. Se puede manejar sin llantas.
3. Cuesta más viajar en avión que viajar por autobús.
4. Hay que tener una licencia especial para conducir una moto.
5. Cuesta menos comprar un coche con aire acondicionado.
6. Las llaves sirven para abrir el baúl.
7. Se puede estacionar en la autopista.
8. Un coche puede funcionar sin aceite.

ANSWERS:
1. C
2. F
3. C
4. C
5. F
6. C/F
7. F
8. F

Workbooklet

Estrategia
When performing a signature search (or *Firma aquí*) activity, remember to circulate around the classroom, speaking to many different classmates. You should try to have a different student's signature for each item.

10-5 Firma aquí Circula por la clase hasta encontrar a un estudiante que pueda contestar afirmativamente a tu pregunta. **¡OJO!** Debes usar **el pretérito** en la mayoría de las preguntas. ■

MODELO   manejar un camión el verano pasado
E1: *¿Manejaste un camión el verano pasado?*
E2: *Sí, manejé un camión el verano pasado.*
E1: *Pues, firma aquí.*
___*Rosario*___

manejar un camión el verano pasado	ir a una gasolinera esta mañana	saber manejar un barco
tener más de tres llaves contigo	ir a la universidad por la autopista.	tener un coche sin (*without*) calefacción
perder las llaves alguna vez	viajar a algún lugar exótico durante las últimas vacaciones	recibir una multa el año pasado
tener un accidente de coche en los últimos dos años	llevar el coche al taller mecánico el mes pasado	viajar en tren el año pasado

---

 10-6 ¡No funciona! Necesitan llevar su coche a un mecánico. Hagan los papeles del conductor y el mecánico. Tienen que descubrir qué problema tiene el coche, hablar de posibles soluciones y decidir cuánto tiempo se necesita para repararlo. ■

2 GRAMÁTICA

6:00

10-13 to 10-18 Spanish/English Tutorials

¡Hola!

Los mandatos informales

Influencing others and giving advice

¡A la derecha, Pepe! Dobla a la derecha, no a la izquierda...

When you need to give orders, advise, or ask people to do something, you use commands. If you are addressing a friend or someone you normally address as **tú,** you use informal commands. You have been responding to **tú** commands since the beginning of *¡Anda! Curso elemental*: **escucha, escribe, abre tu libro en la página,** etc.

1. The affirmative *tú* command form is the same as the *él, ella, Ud.* form of the present tense of the verb:

Infinitive		Present tense	Affirmative *tú* command
llen**ar**	él, ella, Ud.	llen**a**	llen**a**
le**er**	él, ella, Ud.	le**e**	le**e**
ped**ir**	él, ella, Ud.	pid**e**	pid**e**

Llena el tanque.	*Fill the tank.*
Dobla a la derecha.	*Turn to the right.*
Conduce con cuidado.	*Drive carefully.*
Pide permiso.	*Ask permission.*

There are eight common verbs that have irregular affirmative *tú* commands:

decir	→	**di**	ir	→	**ve**	salir → **sal**	tener → **ten**
hacer	→	**haz**	poner	→	**pon**	ser → **sé**	venir → **ven**

Sé respetuoso con los peatones.	*Be respectful of pedestrians.*
Ten cuidado al conducir.	*Be careful when driving.*
Ven al aeropuerto con tu pasaporte.	*Come to the airport with your passport.*
Pon las llaves en la mesa.	*Put the keys on the table.*

(continued)

CAPÍTULO 10

 Instructor Resources
• PPT, Extra Activities

NATIONAL STANDARDS
Communication
Students enjoy learning the command forms since it provides them the linguistic opportunity to give directions to others. The communicative activities related to the parts of a car and the vocabulary about driving offer a starting point for conversation. Most students are aware of the responsibilities of driving and maintaining a car, and they are able to state their likes and dislikes about driving and practice posing questions to their classmates (Standard 1.1).

NOTE for *Los mandatos informales*
You may wish to point out that accent marks are not needed when one pronoun is attached to a command of one syllable; for example, *ponlo, dime,* etc.

NOTE for *Los mandatos informales*
As stated at the beginning of *¡Anda! Curso elemental*, the forms of *vosotros* are not practiced. If you wish to include them here, please do so.

SUGGESTION for *Los mandatos informales*
Drill *tú* commands by saying an infinitive and having the students tell you the command.

ADDITIONAL ACTIVITY for *Los mandatos informales*
¿Qué hago? Di las formas afirmativas y negativas de los mandatos informales de los siguientes verbos.

MODELO
E1: *beber*
E2: *¡Bebe! ¡No bebas!*

1. hablarme
2. comer
3. tomarla
4. llevarlo
5. usarlas
6. estudiar menos
7. ser bueno
8. ponerlo aquí
9. salir temprano
10. venir ahora
11. tenerlo
12. hacerlo
13. decírmelo
14. dormirse
15. vestirse

EXPANSION for *Los mandatos informales*
You may have a favorite song in Spanish that has familiar commands. Make a copy of the lyrics and use correction fluid to cover up the command forms. Make copies for each student. Tell them they will be listening for the *tú* commands. These are engaging for students, since many songs have lyrics such as *don't leave me, come back, kiss me,* etc.

EXPANSION for *Los mandatos informales*
Pair students so that one student is taking the driving test and the other student is the test administrator. Provide students with selected verbs that they might encounter (*doblar a la derecha, doblar a la izquierda, ir más despacio, tener cuidado, seguir recto,* etc.), have them form commands that the driving instructor/test administrator tells the student, and have the student act out the actions as he/she hears the commands.

NOTE for *Los mandatos informales*
In keeping with our philosophy of presenting new information in manageable chunks, we have opted to not present all irregular forms of the negative *tú* commands at this point. Additional irregular forms will be presented in the *Los mandatos formales* presentation, including *dé, esté vaya, sepa, sea,* etc. If you feel that your students would benefit by practicing these additional forms at this point, please feel free to present them.

2. To form the negative *tú* (informal) commands:

1. Take the **yo** form of the present tense of the verb.
2. Drop the **-o** ending.
3. Add ***-es*** for **-ar** verbs, and add ***-as*** for **-er** and **-ir** verbs.

Infinitive	Present tense		Negative *tú* command
llen**ar**	yo llen**ø**	+ es	no llenes
le**er**	yo le**ø**	+ as	no leas
ped**ir**	yo pid**ø**	+ as	no pidas

No llen**es** el tanque.	*Don't fill the tank.*
No dobl**es** a la derecha.	*Don't turn to the right.*
No conduzc**as** muy rápido.	*Don't drive very fast.*
No pid**as** permiso.	*Don't ask permission.*

Fíjate
The verb *conducir* has an irregular *yo* form, similar to *conocer* (conocer → cono**zc**o; conducir → condu**zc**o).

Verbs ending in **-car, -gar,** and **-zar** have a spelling change in the negative **tú** command. These spelling changes are needed to preserve the sounds of the infinitive endings.

Fíjate
These are the same spelling changes with which you were presented when you learned the irregular preterit tense of these verbs.

Infinitive	Present tense		Negative *tú* command
sa**car**	yo saco	**c → qu**	no saques
lle**gar**	yo llego	**g → gu**	no llegues
empe**zar**	yo empiezo	**z → c**	no empieces

3. Object and reflexive pronouns are used with *tú* commands in the following ways:

a. They are *attached* to the ends of *affirmative* commands. When the command is made up of more than two syllables after the pronoun(s) is/are attached, a written accent mark is placed over the stressed vowel.

Se me pinchó una llanta. **¡Cámbiamela!**	*I got a flat tire. Change it for me!*
Tu bicicleta no funciona. **Revísala.**	*Your bike does not work. Check it.*
Me gusta tu coche. **Préstamelo.**	*I like your car. Lend it to me.*
Es tarde. **Duérmete** mientras conduzco.	*It's late. Sleep while I drive.*

b. They are placed *before negative* **tú** commands.

No se nos pinchó una llanta. ¡No **me la** cambies!	*We don't have a flat tire.* *Don't change it for me!*
Tu bicicleta funciona. No **la** revises.	*Your bicycle works.* *Don't check it.*
No me gusta tu coche. No **me lo** prestes.	*I don't like your car.* *Don't lend it to me.*
Es tarde. No **te duermas** mientras conduces.	*It's late. Don't fall asleep while you drive.*

NOTE for 10-8
You may prefer to offer additional practice with the command forms prior to adding all the pronouns by taking advantage of the suggestions and additional activities offered in the instructor annotations for this section, the Extra Activities folder under Instructor Resources, and on MySpanishLab.

[3:00] **10-7 ¿Qué diría el profesor?** Túrnense para decir cuál de los dos mandatos diría (*would say*) un/a profesor/a de una escuela de conducir. ■

MODELO a. Toma apuntes mientras hablo.
b. No tomes apuntes mientras hablo.
E1: *Toma apuntes mientras hablo.*

1.(a) Estudia las reglas (*rules*) en el manual de conducir.   b. No estudies las reglas.
2. a. Ven tarde a la clase.   (b) No vengas tarde a la clase.
3.(a) Lee el manual con cuidado.   b. No leas el manual con cuidado.
4.(a) Practica fuera de la clase.   b. No practiques fuera de la clase.
5. a. Ponte nervioso/a.   (b) No te pongas nervioso/a.
6.(a) Conduce con cuidado.   b. No conduzcas con cuidado.
7. a. Sal de la clase antes de tiempo.   (b) No salgas de la clase antes de tiempo.
8.(a) Trae tu manual a clase.   b. No traigas tu manual a clase.

[3:00] **10-8 Hazlo, por favor** Túrnense para expresar mandatos afirmativos y negativos usando los pronombres de complemento directo. ■

Capítulo 5. Los pronombres de complemento directo, pág. 189 del eText.

MODELO esperar el autobús
E1: *¡Espéralo!*
E2: *¡No lo esperes!*

Estrategia
For activities like **10-8** you can take turns by having one student do the even-numbered items while the other does the odd-numbered ones. Or, one can give the affirmative commands while the other gives the negatives; then switch roles.

1. tomar el autobús
2. prestarme las llaves
3. conducir el carro
4. usar la calefacción
5. hacer ruido
6. limpiar el parabrisas
7. subir la ventana
8. estacionar el coche en el garaje
9. buscar un estacionamiento

ANSWERS to 10-8
1. ¡Tómalo! ¡No lo tomes!
2. ¡Préstamelas! ¡No me las prestes!
3. ¡Condúcelo! ¡No lo conduzcas!
4. ¡Úsala! ¡No la uses!
5. ¡Hazlo! ¡No lo hagas!
6. ¡Límpialo! ¡No lo limpies!
7. ¡Súbela! ¡No la subas!
8. ¡Estaciónalo en el garaje! ¡No lo estaciones en el garaje!
9. ¡Búscalo! ¡No lo busques!

[3:00] **10-9 El sobrinito** Tu hermana está enferma y necesita ir al médico. Tú tienes que quedarte en su casa con Abel, su hijo de cuatro años. Dile lo que puede y no puede hacer en las siguientes situaciones. ■

MODELO Abel quiere comer un plato de donas (*donuts*).
¡No comas todas las donas!

Abel quiere...
1. mirar un programa de *Sesame Street* ¡Mira Sesame Street!
2. llamar por teléfono a Big Bird ¡No llames a Big Bird!
3. dibujar en la pared ¡No dibujes en la pared!
4. limpiar su cuarto ¡Limpia tu cuarto!
5. mirar una película de terror ¡No mires la película de terror!
6. poner el gato (*cat*) en la lavadora ¡No pongas el gato en la lavadora!
7. beber una Coca-Cola ¡No bebas Coca-Cola!
8. dormir la siesta ¡Duerme la siesta!

21ST CENTURY SKILLS • LIFE AND CAREER SKILLS
The Partnership for 21st Century Skills requires that education include preparing students for the world of work. That includes the skills of managing goals and time, working independently, and being self-directed learners. *¡Anda!* provides Estrategias at the point of need to help learners become successful, independent, life-long learners. Perhaps more important are the curricular suggestions for *¡Anda!* users, one of which is assigning topics like grammar presentations and cultural readings to be done before class. This approach ensures the creation of independent, self-directed learners.

[4:00] **10-10 ¡Ayúdame!** ¡Tu compañero/a de apartamento te vuelve loco/a! ■

Paso 1 Usa los siguientes verbos para decirle lo que debe y no debe hacer y compara tus respuestas con las de un/a compañero/a.

MODELO no poner tus libros en mi cama
No pongas tus libros en mi cama.

1. no dormirse en el sofá No te duermas en el sofá.
2. sacar la basura Saca la basura.
3. no comer en la sala No comas en la sala.
4. no beber de mi vaso No bebas de mi vaso.
5. decirme la verdad siempre Dime la verdad siempre.
6. no vestirse en la cocina No te vistas en la cocina.
7. tener más paciencia con mi gato Ten más paciencia con mi gato.
8. no invitar siempre a los amigos después de las once de la noche No invites siempre a tus amigos después de las once de la noche.

Paso 2 Para cada mandato negativo que dieron juntos, den otra alternativa.

MODELO E1: *No pongas tus libros en mi cama.*
E2: *Ponlos en la mesa.* Answers will vary.

[5:00] **10-11 ¡Una fiesta!** Tu compañero/a y tú organizan una fiesta para sus amigos. Tienen mucho que hacer: limpiar el apartamento, organizar la música, comprar y preparar la comida, vestirse, etc. Un amigo se ofrece a ayudarles. Hagan una lista de las cosas que él puede hacer. ■

MODELO

1. Organiza los CD.

[5:00] **10-12 El transporte** Revisa el vocabulario de **Los medios de transporte.** Escoge seis de los verbos y haz una lista de mandatos afirmativos y negativos, usando los verbos. ¡Sé creativo! Después, comparte tu lista con un/a compañero/a. ■

MODELO revisar → *Revisa el motor de tu coche.*

Instructor Resources
• PPT, Extra Activities

3 GRAMÁTICA

10-19 to 10-22   Spanish/English Tutorials

Los mandatos formales   Giving orders and instructions

When you need to influence others by making a request, giving advice, giving instructions, or giving orders to people you normally treat as **Ud.** or **Uds.**, you are going to use a different set of commands: **formal** commands. The forms of these commands are similar to the negative **tú** command forms.

¡Volaba!

Muéstreme su licencia, por favor.

¿Iba muy rápido, señor policía?

1. **To form the *Ud.* and *Uds.* commands:**
   1. Take the **yo** form of the present tense of the verb.
   2. Drop the **-o** ending.
   3. Add **-e(n)** for **-ar** verbs, and add **-a(n)** for **-er** and **-ir** verbs.

Infinitive	Present tense		*Ud.* commands	*Uds.* commands
limpi**ar**	yo limpi**ø**	+ e(n)	(no) limpie	(no) limpien
le**er**	yo le**ø**	+ a(n)	(no) lea	(no) lean
ped**ir**	yo pid**ø**	+ a(n)	(no) pida	(no) pidan

Llene el tanque. **Llénelo.**	*Fill up the tank. Fill it.*
No limpie el parabrisas. **No lo limpie.**	*Don't clean the windshield. Don't clean it.*
Conduzca el camión. **Condúzcalo.**	*Drive the truck. Drive it.*
No ponga esa gasolina cara en el coche.	*Don't put that expensive gasoline in the car.*
No la ponga en el coche.	*Don't put it in the car.*
Traiga su licencia. **Tráigala.**	*Bring your license. Bring it.*
No busquen sus llaves. **No las busquen.**	*Don't look for your keys. Don't look for them.*

¡Explícalo tú!

1. Where do the object pronouns appear in affirmative commands? Where do they appear in negative commands? In what order?
2. Why are there written accents added to some of the commands and not to others?

✓ Check your answers to the preceding questions in Appendix 1.

2. Verbs ending in *-car*, *-gar*, and *-zar* have a spelling change in the *Ud.* and *Uds.* commands. These spelling changes are needed to preserve the sounds of the infinitive endings.

Infinitive	Present tense		Ud/Uds. commands
sa**car**	yo sa**c**o	c → qu	saque(n)
lle**gar**	yo lle**g**o	g → gu	llegue(n)
empe**zar**	yo empie**z**o	z → c	empiece(n)

(continued)

NOTE for *Los mandatos formales*
The formal commands are introduced at this point since the students have already begun the imperative with the familiar commands. Note that students have already seen some formal commands in *Capítulo Preliminar A.* The formal commands provide pre-practice for the subjunctive. Students are now able to perform the imperative with both singular and plural subjects.

NOTE for *Los mandatos formales*
Remind students that the verbs that are stem-changing in the present tense also have stem changes in the command forms, e.g., *pedir* → *pida*, *dormir* → *duerma*, *volver* → *vuelva*, etc.

NOTE for *Los mandatos formales*
Remind students that *conducir* has an irregular *yo* form and it maintains this change in the negative *tú* command. This is also true for the rest of the verbs with irregular *yo* forms that you have learned thus far (*hacer, conocer, decir, poner,* etc.).

NOTE for *Gramática*
This is an inductive grammar presentation in which the students are given examples of a grammar concept and, through the use of guiding questions, they formulate the rule in their own words. Research indicates that students remember and internalize grammar rules better when they construct their own knowledge.

3. These verbs also have irregular forms for the *Ud./Uds.* commands:

dar	→ **dé(n)**	ir	→ **vaya(n)**	ser	→ **sea(n)**
estar	→ **esté(n)**	saber	→ **sepa(n)**		

Finally, compare the forms of the *tú* and *Ud./Uds.* commands:

	Tú commands affirmative	negative	*Ud./Uds.* commands affirmative	negative
hablar	habla	no hables	hable(n)	no hable(n)
comer	come	no comas	coma(n)	no coma(n)
pedir	pide	no pidas	pida(n)	no pida(n)

Capítulo 8. Las construcciones reflexivas, pág. 312 del eText.

[4:00] **10-13** **Consejos** Dos estudiantes de intercambio (*exchange students*) van a llegar a tu universidad y necesitan tu ayuda con lo que deben y no deben hacer antes de venir a los Estados Unidos. Hazles una lista con tus consejos y comparte la lista con un/a compañero/a. ■

MODELO E1: acostarse temprano la noche antes de viajar

E2: *Acuéstense temprano la noche antes de viajar.*

1. levantarse temprano el día del viaje
2. preparar el equipaje (*luggage*) el día anterior
3. llevar ropa cómoda
4. no ponerse nervioso/a

5. evitar el alcohol
6. tener su pasaporte a mano (*on hand*)
7. sentarse en el asiento correcto
8. dormirse en el avión

Capítulo 9. Un resumen de los pronombres de complemento directo, indirecto y reflexivos, pág. 337 del eText.

[7:00] **10-14** **La multa** Termina el diálogo entre Mayra y el policía. Después presenta la escena con un/a compañero/a. ■

MAYRA: Buenas noches. ¿Iba muy rápido, señor policía?

POLICÍA: Sí, señorita. (1) _Muéstreme_ (mostrarme) su licencia, por favor.

MAYRA: Aquí la tiene (*here you go*), señor. Sé que la foto es muy mala.

POLICÍA: No (2) _se preocupe_ (preocuparse). Ahora, (3) _cuénteme_ (contarme), señorita: ¿A qué velocidad (*speed*) iba?

MAYRA: Pues… la verdad es que no estoy segura. (4) _Dígamelo_ (decírmelo) usted.

POLICÍA: Iba a ochenta kilómetros por hora y el límite aquí es sesenta y cinco.

MAYRA: ¡Ay! ¡Mi padre me va a matar! Por favor, no (5) __me dé__ (darme) una multa.
Lo siento. Le aseguro que voy a manejar mucho más lento ahora.

POLICÍA: No es mi decisión. Es la ley (*law*).

MAYRA: Entonces, por lo menos no (6) __escriba__ (escribir) ochenta kilómetros por hora en la multa.
(7) __Ponga__ (poner) setenta, por favor.

POLICÍA: No puedo hacer eso. Bueno, (8) __tómela__ (tomarla).

MAYRA: (*silencio*)

POLICÍA: Y no (9) __maneje__ (manejar) tan rápido en el futuro. (10) __Tenga__ (tener) más cuidado.

10-15 **El transporte rápido** El Transmilenio es
un sistema de transporte masivo de pasajeros (*passengers*) en
autobús que permite llegar rápidamente a cualquier (*any*) lugar
de la ciudad de Bogotá. Lee las siguientes reglas del Transmilenio
y completa la lista con mandatos formales. Luego, compártela
con un/a compañero/a. ■

entrar	llevar	pagar	pararse (*to stand*)
permitir	respetar	evitar	transitar (*to enter/exit*)

MODELO   Siempre *evite* correr.

- Instrucciones para el uso adecuado (*suitable*) del sistema:

1. Cuando espere al autobús, __párese__ detrás de la línea
   amarilla de seguridad.
2. Antes de entrar, __permita__ que salgan los pasajeros.
3. __Pague__ con su tarjeta al entrar.
4. Al usar las rampas, túneles o plataformas, __transite__ por la derecha.
5. No __lleve__ paquetes (*packages*) grandes ni mascotas (*pets*).
6. No __entre__ en el autobús bebiendo o fumando ni en estado de embriaguez (*intoxication*).
7. __Respete__ las sillas azules que son para personas con discapacidad, mujeres embarazadas, niños pequeños y
   ancianos.

NOTA CULTURAL

¡Hola!
eText 386

10-23

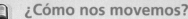
¿Cómo nos movemos?

NOTE for Nota cultural
See eText pg. 386 for complete *Nota cultural* reading and *Preguntas*.

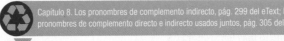

Capítulo 8. Los pronombres de complemento indirecto, pág. 299 del eText; Los pronombres de complemento directo e indirecto usados juntos, pág. 305 del eText.

⏱ 4:00

10-16 La gasolinera Ustedes acaban de llegar a una gasolinera con taller mecánico. Túrnense para decirle al mecánico lo que necesitan. ∎

MODELO   No pueden abrir el baúl.
Ábranos el baúl, por favor. / Ábranoslo, por favor.

1. Necesitan gasolina.
2. El parabrisas está sucio.
3. El limpiaparabrisas no funciona.
4. El motor tiene un ruido extraño.
5. Las llantas necesitan aire.
6. El aceite está sucio.

Capítulo 2. La sala de clase, pág. 65 del eText.

⏱ 3:00

10-17 ¿Cómo contestaría tu profe de español? Túrnense para hacer los papeles de profesor/a (**P**) y estudiante (**E**). ∎

MODELO   E: ¿Debemos hacer la tarea para mañana?
              P: *Sí, hagan la tarea para mañana. / Sí, háganla para mañana.*

1. ¿Debemos traer el cuaderno a la clase?
2. ¿Podemos llegar cinco minutos tarde?
3. ¿Hay que hablar en español todo el tiempo?
4. ¿Tenemos que tomar un examen pasado mañana?
5. ¿Podemos usar nuestros apuntes durante el examen?
6. ¿Está bien si no venimos a clase mañana?
7. ¿Podemos desayunar en la sala de clase?
8. ¿Buscamos la lectura en el Internet?
9. ¿Empezamos la tarea en clase?
10. ¿Podemos salir temprano?

Capítulo 3. La casa, pág. 98 del eText; Los muebles y otros objetos de la casa, pág. 106 del eText; Los quehaceres de la casa, pág. 109 del eText.

⏱ 5:00

10-18 ¡A su servicio! Ustedes son compañeros/as de apartamento y acaban de ganar el concurso ¡A su servicio! Reciben como premio la ayuda de Jaime, un mayordomo (*butler*), por una semana. Díganle **ocho** cosas que quieren que haga (*you want him to do*) para ayudarlos hoy con los quehaceres. Después, díganle **tres** cosas que no debe hacer. ∎

MODELO   *Jaime, saque la basura, por favor.*

¿Cómo andas? I

	Feel confident	Need to review
Having completed **Comunicación I,** I now can . . .		
• discuss modes of transportation (p. 264)	☐	☐
• pronounce the letters **b** and **v** (MSL / SAM)	☐	☐
• influence others and give advice (p. 269)	☐	☐
• give orders and instructions (p. 273)	☐	☐
• list some public transportation options and discuss procedures for getting a driver's license (p. 275)	☐	☐

Comunicación II

5:00

10-24 to 10-29

El viaje   Sharing about travel

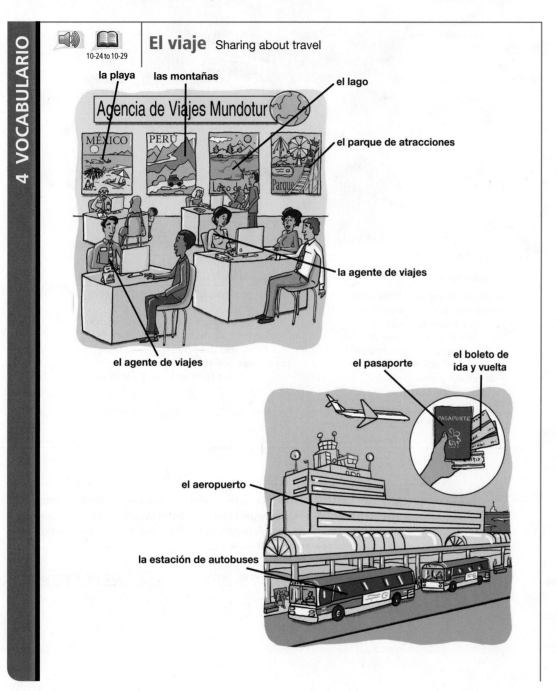

la playa

las montañas

el lago

Agencia de Viajes Mundotur

MÉXICO

PERÚ

el parque de atracciones

la agente de viajes

el agente de viajes

el pasaporte

el boleto de ida y vuelta

el aeropuerto

la estación de autobuses

SECTION GOALS for
Comunicación II

By the end of the *Comunicación II* section, students will be able to:

• talk about traveling and planning trips.
• read about vacation opportunities in Venezuela.
• state what belongs to someone using possessive pronouns.
• make equal and unequal comparisons and use comparatives and superlatives.

NATIONAL STANDARDS
Communication

We have broken the vocabulary dealing with travel into manageable chunks. Students will be able to recycle the vocabulary they learned in the first *Comunicación* section.

The communicative activities allow students to converse about their travel plans and all things associated with going on a trip. Most of the activities require students to engage in conversations, provide and obtain information, express feelings and emotions, and exchange opinions (Standard 1.1).

METHODOLOGY •
Pronunciation

As always, pronounce the words and have students repeat them after you. Remember that it is important to say the words several times and have the students repeat after you each time. It is excellent for modeling, along with their laboratory exercises.

SUGGESTION for *El viaje*

Practice the vocabulary with directed questions, such as *¿Tienes un pasaporte? ¿Tuviste que comprar boletos para un viaje?, ¿para tomar el autobús para venir a la universidad? ¿Prefieres ir a un lago o a las montañas para pasar un fin de semana tranquilo?*, etc.

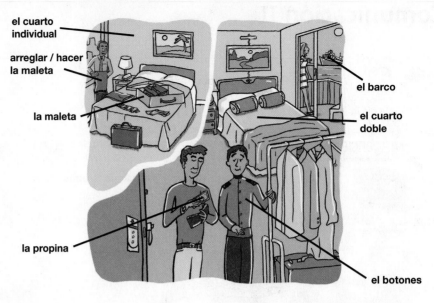

Otras palabras útiles	*Other useful words*	Algunos verbos útiles	*Some useful verbs*
la agencia de viajes	*travel agency*	caminar, ir a pie	*to walk; to go on foot*
la estación de tren	*train station*	dejar	*to leave*
el extranjero	*abroad*	ir de vacaciones	*to go on vacation*
la recepción	*front desk*	ir de viaje	*to go on a trip*
la reserva	*reservation*	irse del hotel	*to leave the hotel; to check out*
el sello	*postage stamp*	registrarse (en el hotel)	*to check in*
la tarjeta postal	*postcard*	volar (o → ue)	*to fly; to fly away*
las vacaciones	*vacation*		
los viajeros	*travelers*		
el vuelo	*flight*		

   10-19 **Categorías** Tienes tres minutos para escribir todas las palabras que pertenecen (*pertain*) a las siguientes categorías. No debes repetir palabras. Después, compara tus listas con las de un/a compañero/a. Date un punto por cada palabra que tienes que tu compañero/a no tiene. ■

EL AEROPUERTO	EL HOTEL	LAS VACACIONES

[4:00] **10-20** **La competencia** En grupos de cuatro o cinco estudiantes, escriban la oración más larga (y lógica) posible usando las palabras nuevas de **El viaje.** ∎

[7:00]

Workbooklet

Capítulo 7. El pretérito, pág. 263 del eText.

10-21 **¿Quiénes lo hacen?** Circula por la clase hasta encontrar a un/a estudiante que pueda contestar afirmativamente a tu pregunta. **¡OJO!** Debes usar el pretérito (P) en algunas de las preguntas. ∎

MODELO   ¿Quién…?

siempre dejar una buena propina para el/la camarero/a (*housekeeper*) cuando va a un hotel

TIFFANY: *¿Siempre dejas una buena propina para el camarero cuando vas a un hotel?*

ROB: *Sí, siempre dejo una buena propina.*

TIFFANY: *Pues, firma aquí.*

                Rob
        —————————————

¿QUIÉN…?		
siempre dejar una buena propina para el/la camarero/a cuando va a un hotel _____	ir a un parque de atracciones el año pasado _____	viajar al extranjero _____
ir a la playa el verano pasado _____	volar en avión _____	recibir tarjetas postales _____
quedarse en un hotel elegante una vez _____	esquiar en las montañas _____	tener más de dos maletas _____

[3:00] **10-22** **Antes de ir** Tu amigo tiene que ir a Venezuela para una reunión (*meeting*) de negocios. Dale **cinco** consejos sobre lo que debe o no debe hacer para prepararse para el viaje y compara tu lista con la de tu compañero/a. ∎

MODELO   1. *Busca tu pasaporte.*

ADDITIONAL ACTIVITY for *El viaje*

 ¿Adónde van? Ustedes trabajan en una agencia de viajes y un/a cliente quiere ir de viaje a la isla de Margarita en Venezuela. Tiene un presupuesto de 2.000 dólares.

Paso 1 Escriban una conversación entre el/la agente de viajes y el/la cliente. Incluyan:
1. como mínimo dos preguntas sobre las preferencias del cliente.
2. los planes —el destino, cómo va a viajar, cuánto cuesta el boleto, qué puede hacer y ver allí y qué ropa necesita para hacer la maleta.

Paso 2 Realicen la escena para la clase.

While the students are writing, circulate often among them to offer suggestions and make corrections. That way, when they present their skits there won't be as many errors. You may also have them turn the skits in, correct them, and give them back the following class for students to act out. How you handle *Paso 2* will determine the amount of time you need to set aside for the activity.

NOTE for 10-22
The authors have used Venezuela as the destination in this activity because it is one of the countries highlighted in this chapter. You may prefer to assign a different country or allow students to decide where the friend must go on the business trip.

NOTE for 10-23

Prior to preparing the interview, you may want to show your students on a world map where the Seven Summits are located. You may also want to investigate Jordan Romero's latest adventures to include in the information you provide. You may even choose to have students research Jordan Romero on the Internet and bring their own facts to share with the class.

NOTE for 10-23

Share the following information with your students as either a listening or a reading passage:

Jordan Romero (n. el 12 de julio del año 1996), en Bear Lake, California, es un joven extraordinario. El 22 de mayo del año 2010, junto con su padre y un equipo, se convirtió en la persona más joven en escalar el monte Everest. Así, con sólo trece años cumplió la meta de escalar las "Siete cumbres" (*Seven Summits*). Cuando tenía sólo 10 años, subió al Kilimanjaro (África, 5.981 metros) en julio del año 2006. En abril del año 2007, alcanzó el Kosciuszko (Australia continental, 2.228 metros), y el mismo año subió también al Elbrus (Europa, 5.642 metros) y al Aconcagua (Sudamérica, 6.962 metros). En el año 2008 completó la ascensión al monte McKinley (Norteamérica, 6.236 metros) y en septiembre del año 2009, al Carstensz Pyramid (Oceanía, 4.884 metros).

NATIONAL STANDARDS
Communication, Cultures

The *Nota cultural* reading online, *Venezuela, país de aventuras*, addresses Standard 1.2, the interpretive mode. Students read about the adventure activities in Venezuela, and they have to interpret and understand the reading. If they discuss the questions that follow with partners for comprehension and elaboration, they engage in interpersonal communication (Standard 1.1). The reading provides new information about things to see and do in Venezuela, and they can compare Venezuela and its culture to vacation places in the United States. Through the reading, they learn about the culture of the people whose language they are learning (Standard 2.1).

ANSWERS to *Nota cultural* (Online)

1. En el Canaima puedes ver el Salto Ucaima y el Salto Ángel. En los tepuyes puedes subir el Pico Humboldt. En la isla de Margarita puedes disfrutar de todos los deportes de agua, pescar, jugar al golf y explorar las playas.
2. *Answers may vary.*
3. *Answers may vary.*

  10-23 ## Un joven increíble Su profesor/a les va a dar información sobre Jordan Romero, un alpinista mexicoamericano muy interesante. Luego, van a preparar una entrevista entre Jordan y un/a reportero/a. Completen los siguientes pasos. ■

Paso 1 Preparen una lista de preguntas para Jordan.

MODELO
1. ¿Cuándo y dónde naciste?
2. ¿Cuándo empezaste a hacer alpinismo?

Paso 2 Inventen respuestas lógicas a las preguntas.

MODELO
E1: *¿Cuándo y dónde naciste?*
E2: *Nací en Bear Lake, California, el doce de julio del año 1996.*

Paso 3 Hagan los papeles de Jordan y el/la reportero/a.

  10-24 ## Las mejores vacaciones Piensa en tus mejores vacaciones al contestar las siguientes preguntas. Después, circula por la clase para entrevistar a tus compañeros/as. ■

1. ¿Adónde fuiste?
2. ¿Cómo viajaste?
3. ¿Dónde te quedaste?
4. ¿Cuánto tiempo estuviste allí?
5. ¿Qué hiciste durante aquellas vacaciones especiales?
6. ¿A quién le mandaste una tarjeta postal?, ¿una tarjeta electrónica?

NOTA CULTURAL

¡Hola!
eText 391   10-30

Venezuela, país de aventuras

NOTE for *Nota cultural*
See eText pg. 391 for complete *Nota cultural* reading and *Preguntas*.

EXPANSION for *Preguntas* (Online)

Ask your students the following questions:

1. ¿Qué esperas encontrar en un hotel de lujo?
2. Cuándo vas a un viaje de aventuras, ¿prefieres un hotel de lujo o prefieres acampar/hacer camping y dormir debajo de las estrellas al aire libre? ¿Por qué?

5 GRAMÁTICA

10-31 to 10-33 ¡Hola!
Spanish/English Tutorials

Otras formas del posesivo
Stating what belongs to you and others

¿Dónde están tus llaves? Tengo las mías aquí.

Pues, las llaves mías deben estar en el carro.

You have already learned how to say *my, your, his, ours,* etc.
(**mi/s, tu/s, su/s, nuestro/a/os/as, vuestro/a/os/as, su/s**).
In Spanish you can also show possession with the long (or
stressed) forms, the equivalents of the English *of mine, of yours,
of his, of hers, of ours,* and *of theirs.*

	Singular		Plural		
	Masculine	Feminine	Masculine	Feminine	
	mío	mía	míos	mías	*mine*
	tuyo	tuya	tuyos	tuyas	*yours* (fam.)
	suyo	suya	suyos	suyas	*his, hers, yours* (for.), *theirs* (form.)
	nuestro	nuestra	nuestros	nuestras	*ours*
	vuestro	vuestra	vuestros	vuestras	*yours* (fam.)

Study the following examples.

Mi coche funciona bien.   **El coche mío** funciona bien.   **El mío** funciona bien.
Nuestros boletos cuestan   **Los boletos nuestros** cuestan   **Los nuestros** cuestan mucho.
mucho.   mucho.
¿Dónde están **tus** llaves?   ¿Dónde están **las llaves tuyas**?   ¿Dónde están **las tuyas**?
Su multa es de $100.   **La multa suya** es de $100.   **La suya** es de $100.

¡Explícalo tú!

Compare the possessives in the sentences above.

1. What is the position of each possessive in the left-hand column? the middle column?
2. How do the possessive adjectives and pronouns agree?
3. What do the sentences in the column on the right mean? What has been removed from
   each previous sentence?

✔ Check your answers to the preceding questions in Appendix 1.

*Note that the third-person forms (**suyo/a/os/as**) can have more than one meaning. To avoid
confusion, you can use:

                            article + noun + de + subject pronoun:
                          ⎧ el coche de él/ella
el coche suyo   ⎨ el coche de Ud.
                          ⎪ el coche de ellos/ellas
                          ⎩ el coche de Uds.

CAPÍTULO 10

 Instructor Resources
• PPT, Extra Activities

**METHODOLOGY •
Differentiated Instruction**
Differentiating instruction can take the
form of utilizing different methods or
having different assignments that are
leveled for different abilities or interests.
In the interest of differentiation, if you
have students who are at risk of not
achieving a high level of success, the
long form of possessive adjectives and
possessive pronouns is not an essential
grammatical concept and one that
can be skipped for them. They already
have one way of expressing possession
from *Capítulo 1,* and at this point in
the chapter, you could ask them to
review *Capítulo 1,* and then hold them
accountable for just that way of forming
the possessive.

SUGGESTION for *Otras formas
del posesivo*
Have students engage in a round of
verbal "one-upmanship." One student
begins by describing a common
possession, in very general terms. The
next student describes to a partner his/
hers and goes one better. This continues
until nothing can be added, and then
another round begins. Students are
encouraged to embellish the truth!
E1: *Tengo una bicicleta roja.*
E2: *La mía es roja y tiene ruedas
      especiales.*
E3: *La mía es una bicicleta de carrera y
      puede ir muy rápido.*
E4: *La mía me costó mil dólares y…*

NOTE for *Gramática*
This is an inductive grammar
presentation in which the students
are given examples of a grammar
concept and, through the use of guiding
questions, they formulate the rule in
their own words. Research indicates
that students remember and internalize
grammar rules better when they
construct their own knowledge.

NATIONAL STANDARDS
Communication
The activities that accompany the presentation of possessive pronouns help students master speech typical of native speakers. They have already learned the possessive adjectives and how to use *de* for possession, and now they have learned another way to express possession. The activities recycle the possessive adjectives in combination with the new material, and students are able to communicate in the interpersonal mode (Standard 1.1) about what they and others possess.

SUGGESTION for 10-25
You may want to begin the activity by having students identify the possessive adjectives in the conversation by underlining them.

EXPANSION for 10-25
Ask students to create a list of their 5 favorite possessions. Then have them circulate around the room and offer those possessions to other students.
E.g., Mi iPod negro.→ ¿Quieres el iPod negro mío?
No, no quiero el iPod tuyo. / Sí, quiero el iPod tuyo.

EXPANSION for 10-26
Ask students to point out and discuss the clothing they and their classmates are wearing using possessive forms.

⏱ 3:00 👥👥 **10-25 Entre hermanos**

Cambia todos los posesivos a la forma nueva (larga) en la conversación entre Marco y Mari. Después compara los cambios con los de un/a compañero/a. ■

MODELO El problema que tienes con tu coche es serio.
El problema que tienes con el coche tuyo es serio.

MARCO: Mari, parece que tu llanta pierde aire.

MARI: Ah, ¿sí? Tampoco funciona bien mi coche.

MARCO: Pues, mi mecánico es muy bueno.

MARI: Gracias, pero pienso llevar el coche a nuestro mecánico. Hace muchos años que Tom y yo lo conocemos.

MARCO: ¿Él tiene su negocio en la calle Bolívar?

MARI: Sí, y trabaja con uno de sus hermanos.

MARCO: ¿Puedes usar uno de sus coches mientras arregla el tuyo?

MARI: Sí, pero prefiero sacar tu BMW del garaje. Nunca lo manejas.

MARCO: Escucha, hermana. Ese BMW es un tesoro (*treasure*) y nadie lo maneja.

♻ Capítulo 8. La ropa, pág. 294 del eText; Las telas y los materiales, pág. 309 del eText.

⏱ 4:00 👥👥 **10-26 ¡Problemas!** Están de viaje con algunos de sus mejores amigos. El hotel les lavó la ropa pero ahora ustedes no saben de quiénes son las prendas. Túrnense para hacer y contestar las preguntas de Ana, quien está intentando organizar la ropa. ■

MODELO E1 (ANA): Los calcetines rojos, ¿son tuyos? (de Felipe)

E2: *No, son de Felipe.*
Los calcetines son suyos.

1. Los pantalones cortos azules, ¿son tuyos? (de Tina) No, son de Tina. Los pantalones (cortos azules) son suyos.
2. La camisa de rayas, ¿es mía? (de Susana) No, es de Susana. La camisa (de rayas) es suya.
3. Los calcetines estampados, ¿son tuyos? (mío) Sí, son míos. Los calcetines (estampados) son míos.
4. La chaqueta negra, ¿es tuya? (de Felipe) No, es de Felipe. La chaqueta (negra) es suya.
5. El suéter de algodón, ¿es tuyo? (mío) Sí, es mío. El suéter (de algodón) es mío.
6. Las camisetas blancas, ¿son tuyas? (de Tina) No, son de Tina. Las camisetas (blancas) son suyas.

Instructor Resources
• PPT, Extra Activities

[5:00]   **10-27** **Personalmente...** Termina las siguientes oraciones sobre tu mejor amigo/a y tú y después compártelas con un/a compañero/a. ■

1. El mejor amigo mío…
2. La casa suya…
3. La especialidad mía…
4. La materia favorita suya…
5. El restaurante favorito nuestro…
6. A los otros amigos nuestros les encanta(n)…

 6 GRAMÁTICA

[6:00]

  ¡Hola! Spanish/English Tutorials
10-34 to 10-39

El comparativo y el superlativo
Comparing people, places, and things

El comparativo

Just as English does, Spanish uses comparisons to specify which of two people, places, or things has a lesser, equal, or greater degree of a particular quality.

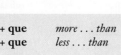
No tengo tantas maletas como tú.

1. **The formula for comparing unequal things follows the same pattern as in English:**

más + *adjective/adverb/noun* + **que**	*more . . . than*
menos + *adjective/adverb/noun* + **que**	*less . . . than*

El Hotel Hilton es **más** caro **que** el Motel 6.   *The Hilton is **more** expensive **than** Motel 6.*
El Motel 6 hace reservas **más** rápidamente **que** el Hotel Hilton.   *Motel 6 makes reservations **faster than** the Hilton.*
En esta ciudad hay **menos** hoteles **que** moteles.   *In this city there are **fewer** hotels **than** motels.*

• When comparing numbers, **de** is used instead of **que**:

El Hilton de Bogotá tiene **más de** doscientos cuartos.   *The Bogotá Hilton has **more than** two hundred rooms.*

2. **The formula for comparing two or more *equal* things also follows the same pattern as in English:**

tan + *adjective/adverb* + **como**	*as . . . as*
tanto(a/os/as) + *noun* + **como**	*as much/many . . . as*

La agencia de viajes Mundotur es **tan** conocida **como** Meliá.   *The Mundotur travel agency is **as** well known **as** Meliá.*
Estos vuelos son **tan** caros **como** esos.   *These flights are **as** expensive **as** those.*
Mi coche va **tan** rápido **como** un Ferrari.   *My car is **as** fast **as** a Ferrari.*
No tengo **tantas** maletas **como** tú.   *I don't have **as many** suitcases **as** you (do).*
No hay **tanto** tráfico **como** ayer.   *There isn't **as much** traffic **as** yesterday.*

NATIONAL STANDARDS
Communication, Comparisons
In *Capítulo 10*, students learn how to compare things that are similar and dissimilar. They also learn how to form comparatives and superlatives. This new information allows for greater depth of conversation with others when they express their feelings and emotions and exchange opinions. They can discuss familiar topics in Spanish with classmates (Standard 1.1), and, if they travel abroad, they can form useful questions, such as where the cheapest place to stay is, or what restaurant has the best food. If they are deciding between two things featured in their guidebooks, they can ask which one is better. The new grammar allows them to compare how to phrase comparisons in English and Spanish (Standard 4.1).

SUGGESTION for *El comparativo y el superlativo*
Use your students and objects in the classroom to demonstrate forming comparisons and superlatives. Have two students stand up. Offer a couple of comparisons as a model (e.g., *Mary es más baja que Gena. El pelo de Gena es tan rubio como el pelo de Mary.*). Then have students create as many comparisons of equality and inequality as possible on their own. Together, create superlative statements about the students and the classroom. Another great topic for comparison is your institution with a rival institution.

NOTE for *El comparativo y el superlativo*
You may want to point out to students that *tan* is an adverb and therefore its form does not change, while *tanto* is an adjective, and as such, must agree with the noun that follows it.

El superlativo

1. To compare three or more people or things, use the superlative. The formula for expressing the superlative is:

> **el, la, los, las** (*noun*) + **más/menos** + *adjective* (+ **de**)

La agencia de viajes Viking es **la** agencia **más** popular **de** nuestro pueblo.

The Viking Travel Agency is the most popular (travel) agency in our town.

—¿Es el aeropuerto Hartsfield de Atlanta **el** aeropuerto **más** concurrido **de** los Estados Unidos?

Is Atlanta's Hartsfield Airport the busiest airport in the United States?

—Sí, ¡y el aeropuerto de mi ciudad es **el menos** concurrido!

Yes, and my city's airport is the least busy!

2. The following adjectives have irregular comparative and superlative forms.

Adjective		Comparative		Superlative	
bueno/a	*good*	**mejor**	*better*	**el/la mejor**	*the best*
malo/a	*bad*	**peor**	*worse*	**el/la peor**	*the worst*
joven	*young*	**menor**	*younger*	**el/la menor**	*the youngest*
viejo/a	*old*	**mayor**	*older*	**el/la mayor**	*the eldest*

Comparative:

Mi clase de español es **mejor que** mis otras clases.   *My Spanish class is better than my other classes.*

Superlative:

Mi clase de español es **la mejor de** mis clases.   *My Spanish class is the best (one) of my classes.*

10-28 ¿Cierto o falso? ¿Qué sabes de la geografía? Indica si las siguientes oraciones son ciertas (C) o falsas (F); si son falsas, corrígelas. Después, comparte tus oraciones con las de un/a compañero/a siguiendo el modelo. ■

MODELO   México es más grande que Uruguay.

E1: *¿Es México más grande que Uruguay?*

E2: *Sí. México es mucho más grande que Uruguay. ¿Es Chile tan grande como Argentina?*

E1: *No. Chile es más pequeño que Argentina, pero creo que es tan grande como Venezuela.*

1. México es más pequeño que Colombia. F   México es más grande que Colombia.
2. Venezuela es casi tan grande como Colombia. C
3. Panamá es más grande que Venezuela. F   Panamá es más pequeño que Venezuela.
4. De estos países, Panamá es el más pequeño. C
5. Colombia es más grande que los Estados Unidos. F Colombia es más pequeño que los Estados Unidos.
6. Caracas es tan grande como México, D.F.
   F   Caracas no es tan grande como México, D.F.

Capítulo 1. Los adjetivos descriptivos, pág. 43 del eText.

10-29 ¡Así son! Cada persona tiene su opinión. Vamos a descubrir sus opiniones. ■

Paso 1   Con un/a compañero/a, hagan una lista de tres o cuatro adjetivos para describir a la persona de cada categoría.

MODELO   persona de la clase

E1: *alto/a, interesante*

E2: *cómico/a, simpático/a*

1. actriz de la televisión
2. actor del cine
3. jugador de fútbol/béisbol/tenis/etc.
4. cantante de rock/jazz/ópera
5. profesor/a de la universidad
6. persona de la política

Paso 2   Ahora creen preguntas y luego respuestas para cada categoría.

E1: *¿Quién es la persona más alta de la clase?*

E2: *Catalina es la persona más alta de la clase.*

NOTE for 10-28
This may be a good time to revisit Spanish-speaking countries and their capitals for a quick review.

EXPANSION for 10-28
Lead students in making comparisons between the countries they have studied this term, incorporating the facts they have learned.

EXPANSION for 10-28
Encourage students to make 5 additional comparisons and 2 superlative statements using the map.

7:00

Workbooklet

10-30 **¿El mejor o el peor?** Circula por la clase para averiguar qué opinan los estudiantes sobre "los mejores" y "los peores". Necesitas al menos **dos** opiniones para cada categoría. ■

Estrategia
You can also use the following expressions to express your opinions: *Pienso que…, Creo que…, Estoy de acuerdo, No estoy de acuerdo,* and *En mi opinión…*

MODELO E1: *¿Cuál es el mejor supermercado?*
E2: *En mi opinión, Whole Foods es el mejor supermercado. Y tú, ¿qué piensas?*
E1: *Creo que el mejor supermercado es Kroger.*

	ESTUDIANTE 1	ESTUDIANTE 2
1. el mejor supermercado		
el peor supermercado		
2. el mejor almacén		
el peor almacén		
3. el mejor restaurante		
el peor restaurante		
4. el mejor aeropuerto		
el peor aeropuerto		
5. el mejor hotel		
el peor hotel		
6. el mejor parque de atracciones		
el peor parque de atracciones		
7. la mejor playa		
la peor playa		
8. el mejor lugar para la luna de miel (*honeymoon*)		
el peor lugar para la luna de miel		
9. la mejor aerolínea (*airline*)		
la peor aerolínea		
10. el mejor coche		
el peor coche		

8:00

10-31 **Adivina, adivinanza** Trae un objeto personal a la clase y escribe **cuatro** oraciones sobre él, usando las formas comparativas. No digas el nombre de tu objeto. Lee las oraciones en grupos de cuatro o cinco estudiantes para ver si los compañeros pueden adivinar (*guess*) lo que es. ■

Estrategia
One way to approach **10-31** is to arrange your clues from most general to most specific.

MODELO un bolígrafo
E1: 1. Es más grande que un anillo.
2. Es tan importante como un libro.
3. Es menos largo que mi zapato.
4. Seguramente ustedes lo usan tanto como yo.
5. Es tan útil como un lápiz.
E2: *¡Es un bolígrafo!*

10-32 **El transporte** Habla con un/a compañero/a sobre todos los medios de transporte que usan o han usado (*have used*) y compárenlos, pensando en los aspectos positivos y negativos de cada uno. ∎

MODELO   E1: *Uso el coche más que el metro pero el metro es más rápido que el coche.*

          E2: *Nunca voy en metro porque no hay metro en mi ciudad. Voy mucho en autobús porque es más barato que un taxi y es más rápido que mi bicicleta.*

 Capítulo 7. El pretérito, pág. 263 del eText; Algunos verbos irregulares en el pretérito, pág. 272 del eText; Capítulo 8. El imperfecto, pág. 317 del eText; Capítulo 9. El pretérito y el imperfecto, pág. 349 del eText.

  10-33 **Los mejores recuerdos (*memories*)** Escoge uno de los siguientes temas y descríbele la situación a un/a compañero/a. Debes mencionar cuándo y dónde ocurrió, quiénes estaban contigo y qué pasó. Túrnense. ∎

1. el mejor regalo que recibí
2. el mejor regalo que regalé (*gave*)
3. el mejor día de mi vida
4. el peor día de mi vida
5. las mejores vacaciones que tomé
6. las peores vacaciones que tomé

ESCUCHA

Las vacaciones

10-40 to 10-41

Estrategia

Listening for linguistic cues

You can enhance comprehension by listening for linguistic cues. For example, verb endings can tell you who is participating and whether the incident is taking place now, already took place in the past, or will take place in the future.

10-34 **Antes de escuchar** Los amigos de Manolo están en una fiesta. Oyen por casualidad una conversación entre varias personas sobre algunos viajes que ya tomaron y otros viajes que quieren tomar en el futuro. ■

1. ¿Cuáles fueron tus viajes más memorables?
2. ¿Hay un viaje en particular que le puedes recomendar a un/a amigo/a?
3. ¿A dónde quieres ir en tu próximo viaje?

Memo, Cristina y Rosa hablan de unos viajes interesantes.

10-35 **A escuchar**

Paso 1 Escucha la conversación entre Memo, Cristina y Rosa para tener una idea general de lo que dicen.

Paso 2 Cristina habla de Venezuela. Escucha otra vez y apunta todos los verbos que puedas que ella usa. ¿Cuál es el tiempo verbal que usa más? Entonces, es un viaje que...
   a. hizo ya.
   b. va a hacer.
   c. quiere hacer.

Paso 3 Escucha una vez más para poder completar la siguiente actividad.
   1. ¿Quién sale mañana para Colombia? Escribe los verbos que usa esta persona para hablar de su viaje.
   2. ¿Habla Rosa de un viaje que hizo ya, va a hacer o quiere hacer? ¿Cómo lo sabes?

10-36 **Después de escuchar** En grupos de tres o cuatro estudiantes, hablen de dos o tres lugares turísticos diferentes que conozcan (*you know*). ¿Qué tienen en común? ■

¡CONVERSEMOS!
10-42

SECTION GOALS for
¡Conversemos!
By the end of the *¡Conversemos!* section,
students will be able to:
- create an itinerary for an employer and give directions about the impending trip using presentational and interpersonal modes.
- plan an ideal trip with a person of choice and then explain what must be done in preparation, using presentational and interpersonal modes.
- utilize previously learned/recycled vocabulary and grammatical concepts such as formal and informal commands.

10-37 **Ayudante indispensable**
Tu jefe/a viaja mucho para el negocio y necesita que
tú le hagas los arreglos (*make the arrangements*)
para su próximo viaje a Colombia. Crea un itinerario
para tu jefe/a y dile lo que necesita hacer y
cuándo, usando por lo menos **siete** mandatos. Tu
compañero/a de clase va a ser el/la jefe/a y tiene que
responder a tus arreglos, usando mandatos cuando
sea necesario. ¿Van a usar mandatos formales o
informales? ■

10-38 **¡Buen viaje!** Tienes fondos (*funds*) sin límite para tus próximas
vacaciones. Planea un viaje para tu compañero/a de clase y tú. Después, descríbele el viaje
a tu compañero/a y dile qué necesita hacer y cuándo, usando por lo menos **siete** mandatos.
Tu compañero/a tiene que responder, también usando mandatos cuando sea necesario.
¿Van a usar mandatos formales o informales? ■

ESCRIBE

Un reportaje

10-43

Estrategia		
Using linking words	Linking words help you connect ideas and sentences so you can communicate more effectively. As you write your travel review, practice linking your ideas and sentences. Linking words	you know include *y, o, pero, porque, que, cuando, antes de, después de, durante, para empezar, entonces, antes, después, de repente, finalmente, al final, por fin,* and *mientras*.

 10-39 Antes de escribir Escoge un lugar turístico de Colombia o Venezuela e investígalo en el Internet. Toma apuntes sobre los aspectos que encuentres más interesantes del lugar. ■

10-40 A escribir Organiza tus ideas y escribe un reportaje para una revista turística que incluya como mínimo la siguiente información: ■

1. dónde está
2. cómo llegar allí
3. qué actividades se pueden hacer
4. dónde uno puede quedarse (hotel de lujo, etc.)

5. el precio del viaje
6. este lugar es más interesante que…
7. este lugar es más/menos barato que…
8. este lugar es el más _____ porque…

 10-41 Después de escribir Presenta tu reportaje a los compañeros de clase. Después de todas las presentaciones deben votar para elegir los **tres** lugares que desean visitar. ■

¿Cómo andas? II

Having completed **Comunicación II**, I now can . . .

	Feel confident	Need to review
• share about travel (p. 277)	☐	☐
• investigate travel and tourism opportunities in Venezuela (p. 280)	☐	☐
• state what belongs to me and others (p. 281)	☐	☐
• compare people, places, and things (p. 283)	☐	☐
• focus on linguistic cues (p. 288)	☐	☐
• communicate about travel plans (p. 289)	☐	☐
• write and present a report using linking words (p. 290)	☐	☐

Cultura
Colombia

A • CULTURA • CULTURA • CULTUR[...]ULTURA •

10-44 to 10-46

Les presento mi país

Rosa María Gutiérrez Murcia

Mi nombre es Rosa María Gutiérrez Murcia y soy de Medellín, la segunda ciudad de Colombia. El setenta y cinco por ciento de la población colombiana se concentra en los centros urbanos y las regiones montañosas del país. En Medellín disfrutamos del único sistema de metro del país que proporciona transporte a la gente que vive en las afueras de la ciudad. **¿Qué tipos de transporte público hay en tu pueblo o ciudad?** Bogotá tiene el sistema más extenso de ciclorrutas (caminos para bicicletas) del país; gracias a él, la gente puede circular y disfrutar de los espacios públicos y verdes de la capital. Mi país es muy bello y tiene muchas atracciones para los turistas. Además, es el único país de Sudamérica que tiene costa en el Océano Pacífico y en el Mar Caribe.

Bogotá, Colombia

La Catedral de Sal de Zipaquirá

El Museo del Oro en Bogotá

ALMANAQUE

Nombre oficial: República de Colombia
Gobierno: República
Población: 44.205.293 (2010)
Idioma: español
Moneda: Peso colombiano (COP/$)

¿Sabías que...?

- En Zipaquirá, Colombia, hay una catedral única. ¡La catedral está situada a 600 pies adentro de una montaña de sal!
- Simón Bolívar es conocido por ser *El Libertador*. Se considera un héroe en Colombia, Venezuela, Ecuador, Perú, Panamá y Bolivia, entre otros países hispanoamericanos.

Preguntas

1. ¿Qué tiene Colombia que no tiene ningún otro país del continente?
2. ¿Cómo se comparan los medios de transporte de Medellín y Bogotá con los de tu área?
3. ¿Qué tienen en común Colombia, Perú y Chile?

 Amplía tus conocimientos sobre Colombia en MySpanishLab.

291

Map labels
Mar Caribe
Barranquilla
Cartagena
Calamar
PANAMÁ
Bucaramanga
OCÉANO PACÍFICO
Medellín
Zipaquirá
VENEZUELA
Río Meta
Bogotá
Buenaventura
Río Magdalena
Cali
Río Guaviare
COLOMBIA
Mitú
ECUADOR
CORDILLERA DE LOS ANDES
Río Caquetá
PERÚ
BRASIL
Río Putumayo
BRASIL

NOTE for *Les presento mi país*
The discovery of oil reserves in Venezuela in the early 20th century has had a major impact on the Venezuelan economy. Venezuela relies heavily on its oil reserves to keep its economy booming. Projected oil income is looking to new methods of extracting valuable minerals from the earth. The Oil Belt of the Orinoco, *La Faja del Orinoco*, is an example of an oil reserve that is coming into increasing importance for its deposits of extra heavy crude oil and bitumen, both products that will be commercially producible and will contribute to the world oil reserves.

NOTE for *La Universidad Central de Venezuela*
Founded in 1721, the Universidad Central de Venezuela is the oldest university in Venezuela and one of the oldest in Latin America. It is a public institution with more than 60,000 students and 8,000 professors. UNESCO has designated it a World heritage Site, or *Patrimonio de la Humanidad* in Spanish.

SUGGESTION for *La Universidad Central de Venezuela*
Additional questions to ask your students are: How many students attend your university? How many professors do you think are employed there? Do students live in dorms or in apartments or with family members, as in many Latin American countries?

NOTE for *La arepa, el pabellón criollo y la hallaca*
The *arepa* is the "bread" of Venezuela. Made with corn meal, it is served plain, stuffed, or filled with cheese, beans, meat, or just about anything. It is eaten as an accompaniment, as a main course, or as "fast food" on the run. The *pabellón criollo* is a dish of shredded beef, black beans (*caraotas negras*), rice, and fried plantains. The *hallaca* is a traditional Christmas confection, a mixture of chopped beef, chicken, pork, onions, green peppers, tomatoes, raisins, olives, and spices mixed into corn dough. It is then wrapped in banana leaves and steamed.

METHODOLOGY • Cultural Expansion
Many countries in the Spanish-speaking world have constantly changing political and economic conditions. We recommend that you have your students consult the Internet to research the latest news taking place in Venezuela and Colombia.

CULTURA • CULTURA • CULTURA • CU

Venezuela

10-44 to 10-45, 10-47

Joaquín Navas Posada

Les presento mi país

Mi nombre es Joaquín Navas Posada y soy de Maracaibo, Venezuela. Hace dos años que vivo con mi hermano mayor y su esposa en la capital, Caracas, porque estudio arte en la Universidad Central de Venezuela. Mi hermano es ingeniero y trabaja en la industria petrolera. Venezuela es miembro de la Organización de Países Exportadores de Petróleo, conocida como la OPEP. **¿Qué papel tiene Venezuela en la OPEP?** Me encanta vivir con mi hermano porque es el mejor cocinero de Venezuela y sabe preparar todas las comidas tradicionales venezolanas como las arepas, las hallacas y el pabellón criollo! ¡Qué ricos! Vivir en la capital, es decir, en la costa, es muy agradable, porque hay mucho que hacer, tanto para nosotros como para los turistas.

Caracas tiene cuatro millones de habitantes.

Las arepas, un plato típico venezolano

Mar Caribe · OCÉANO ATLÁNTICO · Esmeralda · Isla de Margarita · Caracas · Maracaibo · Barcelona · Barquisimeto · Tucupita · Barinas · Mérida · Río Orinoco · Río Apure · San Fernando de Apure · Ciudad Bolívar · VENEZUELA · GUYANA · COLOMBIA · Río Orinoco · BRASIL

La industria petrolera es muy importante para la economía venezolana.

ALMANAQUE

Nombre oficial:	República Bolivariana de Venezuela
Gobierno:	República federal
Población:	27.223.228 (2010)
Idiomas:	español (oficial); lenguas indígenas
Moneda:	Bolívar (BOB)

¿Sabías que...?

• El Salto Ángel, a unos 978 metros de altura, es la catarata más alta del mundo. El agua cae desde la cima del Auyan-tepuy, que está en el Parque Nacional Canaima, en el sureste del país.
• En Mérida hay una heladería que ha figurado en el libro Mundial de Récords Guinness por el mayor número de helados: tienen más de 600 sabores. Por costumbre hay 110 sabores disponibles diariamente.

Preguntas

1. ¿Dónde vive Joaquín? ¿Le gusta? Explica.
2. ¿Cuál es la base principal de la economía venezolana actualmente?
3. La bandera de Venezuela es muy parecida a la de Colombia y a la de Ecuador. ¿Por qué piensas que es así? ¿En qué se diferencian las banderas y a qué se deben estas diferencias?

 Amplía tus conocimientos sobre Venezuela en MySpanishLab.

292

¡Hola!
eText 404 10-50 to 10-51

Ambiciones siniestras

EPISODIO 10

Lectura y video

SECTION GOALS for *Lectura y video* **(Online)**
By the end of the *Lectura y video* section, students will be able to:
- apply the new reading strategy, skipping words.
- integrate the new strategy with other reading strategies.
- preview the reading and make predictions.
- comprehend the main idea of the passage.
- implement the new strategy, listening for linguistic cues, when the characters are talking.
- contrast their previous predictions with what really happened in the episode.
- predict what will happen in the next video.
- summarize the main events.

Y por fin, ¿cómo andas?

Having completed this chapter, I now can . . .

	Feel confident	Need to review

Comunicación I
- discuss modes of transportation (p. 264) ☐ ☐
- pronounce the letters **b** and **v** (MSL / SAM) ☐ ☐
- influence others and give advice (p. 269) ☐ ☐
- give orders and instructions (p. 273) ☐ ☐

Comunicación II
- share about travel (p. 277) ☐ ☐
- state what belongs to me and others (p. 281) ☐ ☐
- compare people, places, and things (p. 283) ☐ ☐
- focus on linguistic cues (p. 288) ☐ ☐
- communicate about travel plans (p. 289) ☐ ☐
- write and present a report using linking words (p. 290) ☐ ☐

Cultura
- list some public transportation options and discuss procedures for getting a driver's license (p. 275) ☐ ☐
- investigate travel and tourism opportunities in Venezuela (p. 280) ☐ ☐
- impart important facts about this chapter's featured countries: Colombia and Venezuela (pp. 291–292) ☐ ☐

Ambiciones siniestras
- determine when it is appropriate to skip unfamiliar words and to discover the truth about what Cisco knows (p. 293) ☐ ☐
- confirm that Lupe is not who she appears to be (p. 293) ☐ ☐

Comunidades
- use Spanish in real-life contexts (SAM) ☐ ☐

NOTE for *Lectura y video*
Activity answers for online content can be found on the next page for quick reference.

NATIONAL STANDARDS
Communication
Ambiciones siniestras engages students because they want to know more about this sinister plot. As the readings use more complex Spanish, students may encounter unfamiliar words. The new strategy of skipping unfamiliar words allows them to read for the gist of the passage so they do not miss the plot. This strategy facilitates their communicative skills in reading (Standard 1.2), because they cannot comprehend or interpret a text if they do not have the tools or strategies to help them negotiate meaning. They can apply the strategy of listening for linguistic cues from the *Escucha* section as they listen to the characters in *Ambiciones siniestras* discuss how to proceed with Sr. Verdugo's puzzle (Standard 1.2). When students can understand what they have read, heard, and seen with others, they can engage in conversations in the interpersonal mode (Standard 1.1).

NOTE for *Episodio 10* **(Online)**
In a Ponzi scheme, named for Italian Charles Ponzi, a fraudulent operator offers an unusually high return to investors on an initial investment. The extremely high returns advertised (and paid) necessitate an ever-increasing flow of money from investors to keep the scam going, and greed fuels investing more money. The scheme collapses either by the police being notified or by the Ponzi operator disappearing with the money. In 2009, Bernard Madoff was convicted of the largest Ponzi scheme ever, with losses estimated at $65 billion dollars.

RECAP of *AMBICIONES SINIESTRAS Episodio 9* **(Online)**
Lectura: At separate times, Cisco and Marisol called Manolo to alert him that they had received another clue from Sr. Verdugo. Manolo logged on to his e-mail and was frightened to see the next clue. He was supposed to call Marisol back after reading the e-mail, but he did not.
Video: Lupe, Marisol, Cisco, and Manolo organized a videoconference. Lupe and Marisol were in the library working to solve the puzzle that Sr. Verdugo sent. The four of them discussed possible answers, and tensions were building. Lupe suspected that Cisco knew more than he was letting on, and at the end of the episode he told them he had something to confess.

METHODOLOGY • Checking for Comprehension in English
When encouraging students to hypothesize regarding what will happen, it is acceptable to encourage them to brainstorm in English.

ANSWERS to 10-44, *Lectura*
(Online)

1. Les confesó que sabía más de lo que dijo y que Eduardo encontró los papeles de Cisco y le mandó un email al Sr. Verdugo antes de desaparecer.
2. Era una conspiración Ponzi.
3. Querían saber si Eduardo pudo hablar con las autoridades antes de desaparecer, si salió en busca del Sr. Verdugo y qué tiene que ver Alejandra con todo esto.
4. Lupe
5. Miró la pantalla de la computadora, escribió algo y empezó a marcar.

ANSWERS to 10-46, *Video*
(Online)

1. Marisol
2. Le dice que no, que es peligroso.
3. Parece que un hombre la está persiguiendo/vigilando.
4. Le mandan un email con la respuesta al Sr. Verdugo. Luego tienen una videoconferencia con Manolo y Cisco y les dan la solución.
5. Quiere llamar a la policía.
6. Marisol dice que hay cosas que no tienen sentido, que sabe que Lupe miente sobre quién es y también sobre su vida.
7. Lupe dice que va a ser sincera y saca una pistola.

VOCABULARIO ACTIVO

El transporte	Transportation
el autobús	*bus*
el avión	*airplane*
la bicicleta	*bicycle*
el camión	*truck*
el carro / el coche	*car*
el metro	*subway*
la moto(cicleta)	*motorcycle*
el taxi	*taxi*
el tren	*train*

Otras palabras útiles	Other useful words
la autopista	*highway; freeway*
el boleto	*ticket*
la calle	*street*
la cola	*line (of people)*
el estacionamiento	*parking*
la gasolinera	*gas station*
la licencia (de conducir)	*driver's license*
la multa	*traffic ticket; fine*
la parada	*bus stop*
el peatón	*pedestrian*
el/la policía	*policeman/policewoman*
el ruido	*noise*
el semáforo	*traffic light*
el taller mecánico	*auto repair shop*
el tráfico	*traffic*

Algunas partes de un vehículo	Parts of a vehicle
el aire acondicionado	*air conditioning*
el baúl	*trunk*
la calefacción	*heat*
el limpiaparabrisas	*windshield wiper*
la llanta	*tire*
la llave	*key*
el motor	*motor; engine*
el parabrisas	*windshield*
el tanque	*gas tank*
el volante	*steering wheel*

Algunos verbos útiles	Some useful verbs
arreglar / hacer la maleta	to pack a suitcase
bajar (de)	to get down (from); to get off (of)
cambiar	to change
caminar, ir a pie	to walk; to go on foot
dejar	to leave
doblar	to turn
entrar	to enter
estacionar	to park
funcionar	to work; to function
ir de vacaciones	to go on vacation
ir de viaje	to go on a trip
irse del hotel	to leave the hotel; to check out
llenar	to fill
manejar / conducir	to drive
registrarse (en el hotel)	to check in
revisar	to check; to overhaul
sacar la licencia	to get a driver's license
subir (a)	to go up; to get on
viajar	to travel
visitar	to visit
volar (o → ue)	to fly; to fly away

El viaje	The trip
el aeropuerto	airport
la agencia de viajes	travel agency
el/la agente de viajes	travel agent
el barco	boat
el boleto de ida y vuelta	round-trip ticket
la estación (de tren, de autobús)	(train, bus) station
el extranjero	abroad
la maleta	suitcase
el pasaporte	passport
la reserva	reservation
el sello	postage stamp
la tarjeta postal	postcard
las vacaciones	vacation
los viajeros	travelers
el vuelo	flight

El hotel	The hotel
el botones	bellman
el cuarto doble	double room
el cuarto individual	single room
la recepción	front desk

Algunos lugares	Some places
el lago	lake
las montañas	mountains
el parque de atracciones	theme park
la playa	beach

295

Instructor Resources
• IRM: Syllabi and Lesson Plans

11 El mundo actual

¿Qué peligros existen hoy en día para el medio ambiente (*environment*)? Hay más de 5.000 especies de animales en peligro (*danger*) de extinción, el 70% del aire en las ciudades está contaminado, y las selvas (*jungles*), las cuales contienen más del 50% de todas las especies de plantas y animales existentes, se reducen drásticamente cada año.

PREGUNTAS

1 ¿Dónde hay selvas tropicales?

2 ¿Puedes nombrar algunos animales que están en peligro de extinción?

3 ¿Dónde está contaminado el aire en los Estados Unidos?

296

SECTION GOALS for *Chapter opener*
By the end of the Chapter opener section, students will be able to:
• discuss the environment and the dangers facing it.
• list factors that contribute to deforestation.

EXPANSION for *Preguntas*
These questions are simpler than usual because students do not yet have the vocabulary to respond to higher-level questions on this topic in Spanish. By the end of the chapter, you may want to bring them back to the chapter opener and ask:
1. ¿Qué factores contribuyen a la contaminación del aire?
2. ¿Cómo podemos todos (individuos, ciudades, estados y naciones) contribuir a la mejora del medio ambiente?

OBJETIVOS	CONTENIDOS	
COMUNICACIÓN I		
To describe animals and their habitats	**1** Animals	298
To pronounce words following the rules for accentuation and stress	**Pronunciación:** Review of word stress and accent marks	MSL / SAM
To share details about the environment	**2** The environment	302
To comment on what is necessary, possible, probable, and improbable	**3** The subjunctive	305
To engage in additional communication practice	**Heritage Language**	SAM
COMUNICACIÓN II		
To discuss government and current affairs	**4** Politics	312
To express time, deadlines, movement, destination, means, purpose, etc.	**5** **Por** and **para**	315
To specify location and other information	**6** Prepositions and pronouns that follow them	317
To provide more information about location, time, and other subjects	**7** Infinitives that follow prepositions	321
To listen to a radio announcement and practice using visual organizers to enhance comprehension	**ESCUCHA:** A political announcement **Estrategia:** Using visual organizers	323
To communicate about world issues	**¡Conversemos!**	324
To employ persuasive writing to create a public announcement	**ESCRIBE:** A public service announcement **Estrategia:** Persuasive writing	325
To engage in additional communication practice	**Heritage Language**	SAM
CULTURA		
To describe El Yunque, the rain forest of Puerto Rico	**NOTA CULTURAL** El Yunque: tesoro tropical	305
To relate specific facts about politics in the Spanish-speaking world	**NOTA CULTURAL** La política en el mundo hispano	314
To share important facts about Cuba, Puerto Rico, and the Dominican Republic	**CULTURA** Cuba, Puerto Rico, and La República Dominicana	326–328
To explore further the chapter's cultural themes	**MÁS CULTURA**	SAM
AMBICIONES SINIESTRAS		
To use visual organizers when reading, and explain who Lupe really is	**EPISODIO 11** **Lectura:** *Celia* **Estrategia:** *Using visual organizers*	329
To relate what happened to Eduardo and Alejandra	**Video:** *El desenlace*	329
COMUNIDADES		
To use Spanish in real-life contexts	**Experiential Learning:** El medio ambiente **Service Learning:** En tu comunidad	SAM SAM

297

21ST CENTURY SKILLS • WORLD LANGUAGES SKILLS MAP

A world language skills map was created that incorporates all of the 21st century skills identified by the Partnership for 21st Century Skills. The map illustrates sample outcomes for the skills in ACTFL terms. Examples of the skills are provided in the Novice, Intermediate, and Advanced ranges. This tool is available at www.P21.org.

EXPANSION for *Preguntas*

Additional questions to ask your students are: *¿Por qué es tan importante proteger las selvas? ¿Por qué es la destrucción de la selva tropical tan peligrosa para el mundo?*

WARM-UP for *Chapter opener*
This chapter is about the environment and all aspects related to being responsible citizens in a global village. Start out by asking your students how they contribute to or detract from the well-being of the environment. What changes do they think each person can make to help make the environment cleaner and safer for future generations? Ask your students what endangered animals they can name and where those animals are found.

NOTE for *Chapter opener*
Draw a semantic map or word web on the board and discuss the categories of animals (mammals, reptiles, birds, amphibians) and list the endangered animals from each group. You could also brainstorm things like ethanol fuels, wind power, cisterns, hybrid cars, bamboo, etc., that students can list as responsible choices that individuals and government could make in the future.

NATIONAL STANDARDS
Communities
Depending on the area in which you live, you might want to consider the following service learning options. If you have a large Hispanic population, you could team up with a local school, zoo, or animal sanctuary and start an environmental campaign about the dangers facing humans and animals and how the Hispanic community can band together to make small changes for big gains (recycling, using less electricity, carpooling, using environmentally friendly products, etc.). Students could partner with the science faculty and other students at your school to make presentations (in Spanish) to the Hispanic community about endangered natural resources and how each community member can do his or her part to preserve nature and the environment. If you do not have a large Hispanic population in your community, students could campaign to have local businesses sell green merchandise and set up recycling projects in your community. You could report the results in Spanish on your school web site. At your university, you could invite the community to a showing of a documentary on environmental issues as a solo project or as part of Earth Week, or whatever science-themed activities your school does, and discuss the film and its implications in Spanish after the viewing. You might also hold a fundraiser and have your students donate the money to "sponsor" an animal at a local zoo or aquarium (many animals in danger of extinction can be sponsored for as little as $20—check with your local animal welfare agency for details). The animal can be one that is indigenous to a Spanish-speaking country.

Instructor Resources
• Textbook images, Extra Activities

SECTION GOALS for
Comunicación I
By the end of the *Comunicación* section, students will be able to:
• name different types of animals and organize them into categories.
• state the rules for accents.
• discuss the environment and natural disasters.
• plan ways to conserve and protect the environment.
• locate El Yunque and describe highlights of the rain forest.
• differentiate between the indicative and the subjunctive moods.
• form the present subjunctive of regular and irregular verbs.
• use the subjunctive to express opinions, doubt, and probability, as well as wishes and hopes.
• give advice to others using the subjunctive.

NATIONAL STANDARDS
Communication, Cultures, Connections, Comparisons, Communities
In this final chapter of new material in *¡Anda! Curso elemental,* students are now able to combine a great deal of basic language and express thoughtful ideas, both in speaking and in writing. This chapter lends itself well to comparisons of the United States and Hispanic cultures, while connecting to other disciplines such as environmental science, government, biology, and the like.

    This chapter encompasses all 5 Goal Areas of the National Standards. Students communicate in the interpersonal mode (Standard 1.1) when they share their opinions with others about environmental issues in the United States and abroad and possible solutions for a changing population and environment. If students present their ideas for preserving habitats and improving air quality to an audience, they are communicating in the presentational mode (Standard 1.3). They have to consider how the practices and perspectives of Hispanic people and their cultures affect the environment (for example, in the El Yunque rainforest or in South America) (Standard 2.1). The environment is something that students study in political science, geography, business, religion, science, sociology, and numerous other disciplines. They take the knowledge they have learned from these courses and make connections (Standards 3.1 and 3.2), using Spanish to express their opinions regarding possible solutions, while also considering

how the cultures of Spanish-speaking people affect the environment. They might consider, for example, how in the United States there is a greater dependence on oil than in Hispanic countries, and how transportation choices affect the environment; this allows them to compare how people in the United States and Hispanic countries differ (Standard 4.2). Finally, if your students participate in environmental campaigns by reading, attending meetings, or traveling abroad, they can use their Spanish to participate in the communities in which they live or in the communities to which they travel (Standard 5.1).

Comunicación I

1 VOCABULARIO

7:00   11-01 to 11-05

Los animales   Describing animals and their habitats

Los animales de la granja

el bosque
el toro
las vacas
las moscas
el árbol
el cerdo
los insectos
el conejo
el hoyo
el lago
el caballo
el mosquito
el perro
la gallina
el ratón
el gato
la rana
la rata
el pez

Otras palabras útiles	Other useful words
los animales de la granja	farm animals
los animales domésticos / las mascotas	domesticated animals; pets
la granja / la finca	farm

Algunos verbos	Some verbs
cuidar	to take care of
preocuparse (por)	to worry about; to concern oneself with

Los animales salvajes

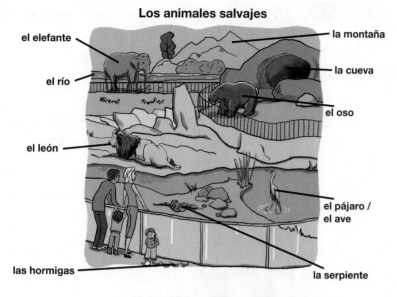

el elefante

el río

el león

las hormigas

la montaña

la cueva

el oso

el pájaro /
el ave

la serpiente

Otras palabras útiles	Other useful words
los animales salvajes	*wild animals*
los animales en peligro de extinción	*endangered species*
el bosque	*forest*
el océano	*ocean*
peligroso/a	*dangerous*
la selva	*jungle*

PRONUNCIACIÓN

Review of Word Stress and Accent Marks

¡Hola!

Go to MySpanishLab / Student Activities Manual to review word stress and accent marks.

11-06 to 11-10

3:00

Workbooklet

11-1 **La fauna** Organiza los animales del vocabulario con un/a compañero/a según las siguientes categorías: **insecto, reptil, mamífero, ave** y **anfibio.** ∎

INSECTO	REPTIL	MAMÍFERO	AVE	ANFIBIO

CAPÍTULO 11

METHODOLOGY • Critical Thinking Skills
There are numerous ways to incorporate higher-order/critical-thinking skills when studying animals. One is to have students categorize the animals in a variety of manners, such as those that live in water, on land, and in trees; carnivores versus herbivores; domestic versus wild; those that live in the mountains, on the plains; and so on. Other fun ways to review the animals are to play charades, Pictionary, and hangman.

ADDITIONAL ACTIVITY for
Los animales

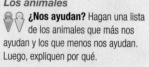 **¿Nos ayudan?** Hagan una lista de los animales que más nos ayudan y los que menos nos ayudan. Luego, expliquen por qué.

MODELO   *La vaca nos ayuda porque nos da leche.*
El mosquito no nos ayuda porque trae enfermedades y nos molesta.

SECTION GOALS for
Pronunciación
By the end of the *Pronunciación* section, students will be able to:
- use written accent marks correctly.
- identify the stress in a word.
- pronounce words correctly following the rules for accentuation.
- differentiate between one-syllable words that have accents and those that do not.

NOTE for *Pronunciación*
In the experience of the authors, word stress and rules for written accents merit revisiting, especially after students have built a substantial vocabulary and have worked with commands and object pronouns. This review allows students to *put it all together.*

⏲ 2:00 👥 **11-2** **¿Dónde viven?** Digan en qué lugar viven los siguientes animales. ■

1. __e__

a. la selva

2. __a__

b. un lago

3. __f__

c. una granja

4. __d__

d. el bosque

5. __b__

e. un hoyo

6. __c__

f. un árbol

⏲ 3:00 👥 **11-3** **¿Qué sabemos?** Termina las siguientes oraciones con lo que sabes de los animales y dónde viven. Después compara tus oraciones con las de un/a compañero/a. ■

♻ Capítulo 10. El comparativo y el superlativo, pág. 394 del eText.

MODELO   Los insectos más molestos son…
Los insectos más molestos son las moscas y los mosquitos.

1. Los animales de la granja más grandes son…
2. Los animales de la granja más pequeños son…
3. Los animales domésticos más comunes en mi familia y entre mis amigos son…
4. El animal salvaje más peligroso es…
5. El animal salvaje más grande es…
6. Los animales del bosque más interesantes son…

Capítulo 8, *Gustar* y verbos como *gustar*, pág. 302 del eText.

NOTE for 11-4
Prior to beginning **11-4,** you may want students to brainstorm first, and create a group list of any new vocabulary they may want to use. Also make this a circumlocution exercise by guiding them through how to express their ideas using words they know. You can refer students to the *Escribe* section on circumlocution in *Capítulo 8.*

3:00 **11-4** **Las preferencias** Completa los siguientes pasos. ■

Estrategia
When you write in Spanish you are not expected to be as articulate as you are in your native language. Try to limit, as much as possible, your responses to the vocabulary you know, and as always, you can circumlocute (see *Capítulo 8, Escribe* section).

Paso 1 Escribe los nombres de los **tres** animales que más te gustan y de los **tres** que menos te gustan y explica por qué. Usa verbos como **gustar, fascinar, encantar, hacer falta** y **molestar.** Después, comparte tus respuestas con un/a compañero/a.

MODELO *El animal que más me gusta es el caballo porque es muy fuerte y me encanta montar a caballo (go horseback riding). También me gustan los gatos y los perros porque puedo tenerlos en casa. Los tres animales que menos me gustan son... porque...*

Paso 2 Presenten sus respuestas a los compañeros de la clase. ¿Cuál es el animal que más les gusta? ¿Y el que menos les gusta?

METHODOLOGY • Follow-Up to Group Work
It is important to monitor group work closely for many reasons: to keep students on task, check for understanding, guide and answer questions, and determine how best to follow up the activity. While monitoring group work for **11-5,** note which items students find most amusing or interesting. Have groups present those responses, rather than taking the time to have each group report on all the items.

5:00
Workbooklet

11-5 **¿Qué opinas?** Circula por la clase para averiguar (*find out*) con quiénes asocian tus compañeros las siguientes actividades. ■

Estrategia
Remember that when completing signature search activities like **11-5,** it is important to move quickly around the room, trying to get as many different signatures as possible, while asking and answering all questions in Spanish.

MODELO tener miedo de las serpientes

    E1: *Hola Sarah. ¿Quién tiene miedo de las serpientes?*

    E2: *Hola Tomás. Mi madre tiene mucho miedo de las serpientes.*

¿QUIÉN...?		
tener miedo de las serpientes	ver un oso el año pasado	gustarle los perros
E1: La madre de Sarah	E1: _____	E1: _____
E2: _____	E2: _____	E2: _____
E3: _____	E3: _____	E3: _____
tener un animal doméstico	odiar los insectos	saber ordeñar (*to milk*) una vaca
E1: _____	E1: _____	E1: _____
E2: _____	E2: _____	E2: _____
E3: _____	E3: _____	E3: _____
ver un elefante o un león	gustarle cuidar animales	tener un caballo
E1: _____	E1: _____	E1: _____
E2: _____	E2: _____	E2: _____
E3: _____	E3: _____	E3: _____

⏱ 5:00 👥 **11-6 Una encuesta** ¿Qué experiencias tienen ustedes con los animales? ■

Paso 1 Háganse preguntas sobre los siguientes animales.

MODELO los perros

E1: *Sarah, ¿tienes perros?*

E2: *Sí, tengo dos perros. Se llaman Duke y Spot. ¿Y ustedes?*

E3: *Sí, en mi casa tenemos dos perros grandes. Se llaman Sissie y Pepper. Son viejos porque ya tienen ocho años.*

E4: *Nosotros no tenemos perrros. Tenemos dos gatos que se llaman Snuggles y Lucky.*

E1: *Tengo un perro pequeño. Es chihuahua y se llama Bullet…*

1. los perros	4. los caballos	7. los osos
2. los gatos	5. los pájaros	8. las vacas
3. las ranas	6. las serpientes	9. ¿?

Paso 2 Organicen las respuestas y compártanlas con los otros grupos.

MODELO *En nuestro grupo todos tenemos perros menos Jack. Los perros se llaman Duke, Spot, Sissie, Pepper y Bullet. Jack tiene dos gatos…*

⏱ 4:00 🔊 📖
11-11 to 11-18

2 VOCABULARIO

El medio ambiente Sharing details about the environment

Los desastres

- la inundación
- la contaminación
- el huracán
- el derrame de petróleo
- el terremoto
- el tornado
- la tormenta
- el incendio
- el tsunami
- el derrame de petróleo

EXPANSION for *El medio ambiente*
Give students 3 or 4 minutes to study the list of new words. Then have them close their books and in 3 minutes write all the words they can remember. You may wish to make this a competition by asking who has the longest list.

EXPANSION for *El medio ambiente*
Ask students for details on specific occurrences of the natural disasters listed.

MODELO

El derrame de petróleo:
Un ejemplo ocurrió en los Estados Unidos en el año 2010 en el Golfo de México que afectó principalmente la costa de Luisiana, Mississippi y Florida.

SUGGESTION for *El medio ambiente*
Ask students what is involved in cleanup after specific disasters.

SUGGESTION for *El medio ambiente*
Have students rank by least harmful to most harmful the things human beings do to harm the environment.

El reciclaje

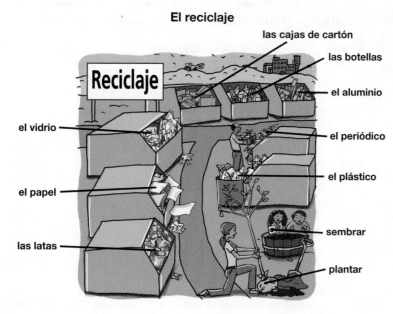

las cajas de cartón
las botellas
el aluminio
el vidrio
el periódico
el plástico
el papel
sembrar
las latas
plantar

El planeta	The planet
el cielo	sky; heaven
la naturaleza	nature
el recurso natural	natural resource
la selva (tropical)	jungle; (tropical) rain forest
la tierra	land; soil
la Tierra	Earth

Otras palabras útiles	Other useful words
el aire	air
la basura	garbage
la calidad	quality
la ecología	ecology
puro/a	pure
el vertedero	dump
vivo/a	alive; living

Los desastres	Disasters
la destrucción	destruction
el efecto invernadero	global warming
la lluvia ácida	acid rain
la tragedia	tragedy

Algunos verbos	Some verbs
botar	to throw away
contaminar	to pollute
evitar	to avoid
hacer daño	to (do) damage; to harm
matar	to kill
proteger	to protect
reciclar	to recycle
reforestar	to reforest
reutilizar	to reuse

2:00   **11-7 Asociaciones** Túrnense para decir qué asocian con cada una de las siguientes palabras o expresiones. ■

MODELO   E1: reutilizar
          E2: *reciclar*

1. la basura
2. hacer daño
3. el recurso natural
4. puro
5. proteger
6. la lluvia ácida

EXPANSION for *El medio ambiente*
This vocabulary lends itself to practicing affirmative and negative commands by creating sentences about what one should do to protect the environment and should not do to avoid harming it.

ADDITIONAL ACTIVITY for *El medio ambiente*
¿Cómo aprendemos? Mira el vocabulario de *El medio ambiente* y sigue los pasos:
Paso 1. Escribe una lista de las palabras que ya conoces.
Paso 2. Escribe una lista de las palabras que son cognados.
Paso 3. Escribe una lista de las palabras que ya asocias con imágenes (piensas en la palabra y "ves" el objeto o la acción) o nombres específicos (el huracán Irene) o situaciones (la lluvia ácida destruye los árboles donde vivo).
Paso 4. Escribe las palabras que quedan que no están en tus listas.
Paso 5. Comparte tus listas con un/a compañero/a. Después, hablen de estratégias para aprender y recordar las palabras del Paso 4.

`3:00` **11-8** **¿Qué es...?** Aquí tienen las definiciones. ¿Cuáles son las palabras? ■

MODELO E1: lo opuesto de contaminado

  E2: *puro*

1. plantar árboles donde antes los había reforestar
2. el estudio de la protección del medio ambiente la ecología
3. un lugar designado donde botamos la basura el vertedero
4. no botar; buscar un uso nuevo para una lata, botella, etc. reutilizar
5. estas plantas grandes protegen la Tierra de la potencia del sol los árboles
6. ensuciar el agua o el aire contaminar
7. lo opuesto de muerto vivo
8. el posible resultado de la contaminación del aire el efecto invernadero

`3:00` **11-9** **Hay que reciclar** ¿Qué hacen tu familia, tu comunidad y tu universidad para proteger el medio ambiente? Explícale a un/a compañero/a quién hace qué para proteger el medio ambiente. Después, cambien de papel. ■

MODELO *Yo voy a la universidad en bicicleta para evitar la contaminación del aire. Mi familia y yo reciclamos el plástico. Mi pueblo ofrece programas de prevención contra incendios. La universidad dio un seminario sobre el efecto invernadero y la destrucción de la capa de ozono.*

`5:00` **11-10** **Entrevista** Circula por la clase haciéndoles a tus compañeros las siguientes preguntas. ■

1. ¿Cuáles son los recursos naturales más importantes donde vivimos?
2. ¿Dónde está el vertedero más cerca de aquí?
3. ¿Qué haces con tu basura?

4. Dónde podemos reciclar en nuestra universidad?
5. ¿Qué reciclamos en nuestra universidad?
6. ¿Cómo es la calidad del aire donde vivimos?

`12:00` **11-11** **El reportaje** ¿Cómo podemos proteger el medio ambiente? ■

Paso 1 Escribe un párrafo de **seis** a **ocho** oraciones sobre qué podemos hacer en el futuro para proteger el medio ambiente. Puedes usar las ideas de la siguiente lista.

- sembrar muchas plantas
- reciclar y/o reutilizar el plástico, el vidrio, el papel y el cartón
- usar carros eléctricos
- proteger los animales en peligro de extinción
- apoyar las instituciones de conservación de los recursos naturales

- proteger la selva tropical
- reforestar los bosques
- usar el carro lo menos posible
- usar energía solar
- no prender (*turn on*) a menudo el aire acondicionado

MODELO *Para evitar la destrucción de los bosques y la selva tropical, no debemos cortar más árboles. En el futuro, debemos plantar más árboles para reforestar el bosque…*

Paso 2 Después, en grupos pequeños, comparen sus oraciones y juntos escriban un reportaje corto con sus recomendaciones para proteger el medio ambiente.

NOTA CULTURAL

 El Yunque: tesoro tropical

eText 419   11-19 to 11-20

NOTE for *Nota cultural*
See eText pg. 419 for complete *Nota cultural* reading and *Preguntas*.

3 GRAMÁTICA

5:00

 ¡Hola!
11-21 to 11-25   Spanish/English Tutorials

El subjuntivo Commenting on what is necessary, possible, probable, and improbable

In Spanish, *tenses* such as the present, past, and future are grouped under two different moods, the **indicative** mood and the **subjunctive** mood.

Up to this point you have studied tenses grouped under the *indicative* mood (with the exception of commands) to report what happened, is happening, or will happen. The *subjunctive* mood, on the other hand, is used to express doubt, insecurity, influence, opinion, feelings, hope, wishes, or desires that can be happening now, have happened in the past, or will happen in the future. In this chapter you will learn the present tense of the *subjunctive mood*.

Es una lástima que no quieran reciclar el plástico, el vidrio, el aluminio y el papel.

Present subjunctive

To form the subjunctive, take the **yo** form of the present indicative, drop the final **-o,** and add the following endings.

Fíjate

You are already somewhat familiar with the subjunctive forms from your practice with *usted* (*¡Estudie!*) and negative *tú* (*¡No hables!*) commands.

Present indicative	*yo* form		Present subjunctive
estudiar	estudiø	+ e	estudie
comer	comø	+ a	coma
vivir	vivø	+ a	viva

(continued)

NATIONAL STANDARDS
Communication, Communities
The subjunctive affords students the opportunity to express needs, wants, and desires in a linguistically sophisticated way. From an oral and written proficiency standpoint, use of the subjunctive helps elevate the level of an individual's performance in the language.

METHODOLOGY • Chunking
You will note that, yet again, *¡Anda! Curso elemental* is taking a complex concept, the subjunctive, and breaking it down into "bite-size" chunks that make learning possible for students.

METHODOLOGY • Affective Filter
With regard to motivation, it is important not to say that the subjunctive is "complex," "difficult" or "complicated." Those words set a bias for some students, in which they tell themselves that they will not be able to comprehend. Nor is it ever appropriate to qualify something as "easy." What might be easy for one learner could be difficult for another. If an instructor says something is easy, and a student does not understand, he/she loses self-esteem and Krashen's affective filter will come into play.

	estudiar	comer	vivir
yo	estudie	coma	viva
tú	estudies	comas	vivas
Ud.	estudie	coma	viva
él, ella	estudie	coma	viva
nosotros/as	estudiemos	comamos	vivamos
vosotros/as	estudiéis	comáis	viváis
Uds.	estudien	coman	vivan
ellos/as	estudien	coman	vivan

Irregular forms

- Verbs with irregular **yo** forms maintain this irregularity in all forms of the present subjunctive. Note the following examples.

	conocer	hacer	poner	venir
yo	conozca	haga	ponga	venga
tú	conozcas	hagas	pongas	vengas
Ud.	conozca	haga	ponga	venga
él, ella	conozca	haga	ponga	venga
nosotros/as	conozcamos	hagamos	pongamos	vengamos
vosotros/as	conozcáis	hagáis	pongáis	vengáis
Uds.	conozcan	hagan	pongan	vengan
ellos/as	conozcan	hagan	pongan	vengan

- Verbs ending in **-car, -gar,** and **-zar** have a spelling change in all present subjunctive forms, in order to maintain the sound of the infinitive.

		Present indicative	Present subjunctive
buscar	c → qu	yo busco	busque
pagar	g → gu	yo pago	pague
empezar	z → c	yo empiezo	empiece

	buscar	pagar	empezar
yo	busque	pague	empiece
tú	busques	pagues	empieces
Ud.	busque	pague	empiece
él, ella	busque	pague	empiece
nosotros/as	busquemos	paguemos	empecemos
vosotros/as	busquéis	paguéis	empecéis
Uds.	busquen	paguen	empiecen
ellos/as	busquen	paguen	empiecen

Stem-changing verbs

In the present subjunctive, stem-changing **-ar** and **-er** verbs make the same vowel changes that they do in the present indicative: **e → ie** and **o → ue.**

	pensar (e → ie)	poder (o → ue)
yo	piense	pueda
tú	pienses	puedas
Ud.	piense	pueda
él, ella	piense	pueda
nosotros/as	pensemos	podamos
vosotros/as	penséis	podáis
Uds.	piensen	puedan
ellos/as	piensen	puedan

The pattern is different with the **-ir** stem-changing verbs. In addition to their usual changes of **e → ie, e → i,** and **o → ue,** in the **nosotros** and **vosotros** forms the stem vowels change **ie → i** and **ue → u.**

	sentir (e → ie, i)	dormir (o → ue, u)
yo	sienta	duerma
tú	sientas	duermas
Ud.	sienta	duerma
él, ella	sienta	duerma
nosotros/as	sintamos	durmamos
vosotros/as	sintáis	durmáis
Uds.	sientan	duerman
ellos/as	sientan	duerman

The **e → i** stem-changing verbs keep the change in all forms.

	pedir (e → i, i)
yo	pida
tú	pidas
Ud.	pida
él, ella	pida
nosotros/as	pidamos
vosotros/as	pidáis
Uds.	pidan
ellos/as	pidan

(continued)

NOTE for *El subjuntivo*
¡Anda! Curso elemental is research based and coordinated with the National Standards. In addition, hundreds of reviewers were consulted, and they determined that the present subjunctive should at least be introduced in the first year. This chapter's theme lends itself well to expressing opinions, making suggestions and recommendations, and finding solutions to problems. These types of language skills are important to communication, especially in the interpersonal mode (Standard 1.1) and when making presentations (Standard 1.3). Students learned the commands in previous chapters and therefore already learned how to form subjunctive endings. A more in-depth treatment of the subjunctive continues in *¡Anda! Curso intermedio.*

NOTE for *El subjuntivo*
You may have learned these fixed expressions as impersonal expressions with *ser*. In *¡Anda! Curso elemental,* we have chosen to simply call them, "fixed expressions," under the headings of opinions, doubts, probabilities, wishes, desires, and hopes. This eliminates any confusion between "personal" and "impersonal," because these expressions can be used regardless of the relationship to the speaker.

Irregular verbs in the present subjunctive

- The following verbs are irregular in the subjunctive.

	dar	estar	saber	ser	ir
yo	dé	esté	sepa	sea	vaya
tú	des	estés	sepas	seas	vayas
Ud.	dé	esté	sepa	sea	vaya
él, ella	dé	esté	sepa	sea	vaya
nosotros/as	demos	estemos	sepamos	seamos	vayamos
vosotros/as	deis	estéis	sepáis	seáis	vayáis
Uds.	den	estén	sepan	sean	vayan
ellos/as	den	estén	sepan	sean	vayan

Dar has a written accent on the first- and third-person singular forms (**dé**) to distinguish them from the preposition **de.** All forms of **estar,** except the **nosotros** form, have a written accent in the present subjunctive.

Using the subjunctive

One of the uses of the subjunctive is with fixed expressions that communicate opinion, doubt, probability, and wishes. They are always followed by the subjunctive.

¡Es increíble que este capítulo sea el último!

Opinion

Es bueno / malo / mejor que…	*It's good / bad / better that . . .*
Es importante que…	*It's important that . . .*
Es increíble que…	*It's incredible that . . .*
Es una lástima que…	*It's a pity that . . .*
Es necesario que…	*It's necessary that . . .*
Es preferible que…	*It's preferable that . . .*
Es raro que…	*It's rare that . . .*

Doubt and probability

Es dudoso que…	*It's doubtful that . . .*
Es imposible que…	*It's impossible that . . .*
Es improbable que…	*It's unlikely that . . .*
Es posible que…	*It's possible that . . .*
Es probable que…	*It's likely that . . .*

Wishes and hopes

Ojalá (que)…   *Let's hope that . . . / Hopefully . . .*

Es necesario que protejamos los animales en peligro de extinción.

It's necessary that we protect endangered species.

Es una lástima que algunas personas no quieran reciclar el plástico, el vidrio, el aluminio y el papel.

It's a shame that some people don't want to recycle plastic, glass, aluminum, and paper.

Ojalá (que) haya menos destrucción del medio ambiente en el futuro.

Let's hope that there is less destruction of the environment in the future.

> **Fíjate**
> The expression *Ojalá* (*que*) comes from the Arabic expression meaning *May it be Allah's will.* The conjunction *que* is optional in this expression.

> **Fíjate**
> The subjunctive of *hay* is *haya*.

> **¡Explícalo tú!**
> 1. What is the difference between the subjunctive and the indicative moods?
> 2. What other verb forms look like the subjunctive?
> 3. Where does the subjunctive verb come in relation to the word **que**?
>
> ✓ Check your answers to the preceding questions in Appendix 1.

`5:00` **11-12 ¡Corre!** Escuchen mientras su profesor/a les explica cómo jugar con las formas de los verbos en el subjuntivo. ■

`4:00` **11-13 Opciones** Túrnense para crear oraciones completas usando los sujetos indicados en cada frase. ■

MODELO   Es preferible que ella / nosotros / tú (reciclar el vidrio)

    E1: *Es preferible que ella recicle el vidrio.*
    E2: *Es preferible que nosotros reciclemos el vidrio.*
    E3: *Es preferible que tú recicles el vidrio.*

1. Es dudoso que tú / Marta y yo / ella (reutilizar las botellas de plástico) reutilices / reutilcemos / reutilice
2. Es necesario que el gobierno / ellos / Uds. (reforestar los bosques) reforeste / reforesten / reforesten
3. Ojalá que ellos / él / nosotros (conservar las selvas tropicales) conserven / conserve / conservemos
4. Es posible que yo / tú / Uds. (poder evitar la lluvia ácida) pueda / puedas / puedan
5. Es importante que mi país / los jóvenes / nosotros (respetar la naturaleza) respete / respeten / respetemos
6. Es una lástima que papá / tú / tus hermanos (botar basura por las calles) bote / botes / boten

NOTE and INSTRUCTIONS for 11-12
11-12 is a fun way to practice verb forms.
INSTRUCTIONS: Have your students sit in rows. Each row is a team, so each team/row should have an equal number of people. Each person at the head of the row has a piece of paper with as many subject pronouns written on it as there are people in the row. Do not list the pronouns in their conjugation order.
Write any infinitive on the board. The first student writes the subjunctive form of that verb that corresponds to the first pronoun listed. That student then passes the sheet of paper over his/her head. The second student writes the correct form of the subjunctive of the second pronoun and passes the paper to the student sitting behind him/her. The process continues with all of the students in the row. The last student in the row brings the completed sheet to you. The first row to finish with all forms correct wins that round.
Additional rules:
1. After each round, have students each move back one seat, with the person in the last seat of the row moving to the front.
2. Allow any students to correct any forms that came before.

⏱ 5:00 👥👥 **11-14 El cocodrilo** Completa el siguiente párrafo con la forma correcta del verbo apropiado en el subjuntivo. Después, compara tus respuestas con las de un/a compañero/a. ■

El cocodrilo cubano

> **Fíjate**
> The *yo* form of the present tense (indicative mode) of *proteger* is *protejo*. Therefore, the subjunctive of *proteger* is *proteja, protejas*, etc.

| estar | proteger | haber | matar |
| poder | existir | ser | vivir |

Es raro que los cocodrilos (1) __vivan / existan__ en el hemisferio occidental. ¡Siempre pienso en el continente de África como hábitat para este animal! Es una lástima que el cocodrilo americano y el cocodrilo cubano (2) __estén__ en peligro de extinción. Es bueno que el cocodrilo americano (3) __exista / viva__ en varias partes del hemisferio (Florida, algunas islas del Caribe y varias zonas costeras del Golfo de México y el océano Pacífico), porque así tiene menos peligro de extinción que el cocodrilo cubano, el cual (*which*) existe solamente en el sureste de Cuba. Es posible que el cocodrilo americano (4) __sea__ peligroso para los humanos. Son tan grandes que pueden atacar y comer animales de gran tamaño cuando se acercan a beber agua. Es improbable que el cocodrilo cubano (5) __mate__ a una persona porque es mucho más pequeño y prefiere aves, pequeños mamíferos, peces y otros animales acuáticos. Es increíble que el cocodrilo americano (6) __pueda__ caminar distancias cortas, lo que significa que puede matar fuera del agua también. Es necesario que nosotros (7) __protejamos__ estos reptiles y ojalá que (8) __haya__ muchos más en el futuro.

📖 Workbooklet 👥👥 **11-15 Mis mejores consejos...** Completa el cuadro con tus mejores consejos.
⏱ 6:00 Después, comparte tu información con un/a compañero/a. ■

PARA PROTEGER LOS RÍOS Y LOS OCÉANOS	PARA EVITAR LA CONTAMINACIÓN DEL AIRE	PARA MANTENER LAS CALLES LIMPIAS
1. Es importante que no botemos la basura en los ríos.	1.	1.
2.	2.	2.
3.	3.	3.

⏱ 5:00 👥👥 **11-16 ¿Para quién es necesario que...?**
Túrnense para hacer y contestar las preguntas sobre las siguientes situaciones usando las expresiones de las páginas 308–309. ■

MODELO estudiar esta noche
  E1: *Es probable que estudie esta noche. ¿Y tú?*
  E2: *Tengo que estudiar, pero es posible que vaya al cine.*

1. estudiar este fin de semana
2. comer menos comida rápida
3. arreglar su cuarto
4. gastar menos dinero
5. buscar un/a nuevo/a compañero/a de cuarto
6. dormir más
7. sacar mejores notas
8. comprar un coche nuevo
9. reciclar más

4:00

11-17 Posibles determinaciones

¿Cuáles pueden ser tus determinaciones (*resolutions*) para el próximo año? Descríbelas y después compártelas con un/a compañero/a. ■

Estrategia

Take advantage of activities like **11-17** to challenge yourself to go beyond a simple answer, providing as much pertinent information as you can.

MODELO *Es mejor que no coma tanto chocolate el próximo año, pero es dudoso que pueda evitarlo. ¡Me fascina el chocolate! Es importante que haga más ejercicio. Es una lástima que no me guste hacerlo.*

12:00

11-18 Es importante que...

Juntos escojan una de las siguientes situaciones para desarrollar en forma de diálogo. Usando las expresiones que acaban de (*have just*) aprender, den consejos según la situación. Después, presenten el diálogo a los compañeros de clase. ■

Situación A:

La doctora Pérez es especialista en nutrición. María Cecilia es una joven universitaria de dieciocho años que va a hacerle una consulta a la doctora sobre cómo mejorar el cutis *(complexion)*.

Situación C:

El sargento López está enamorado de la linda Carolina, pero es tan tímido que nunca la invita a salir con él. Su amiga Carmen trata de ayudarlo.

Situación B:

Bruno quiere comprar un carro usado y le pide a su amigo Manolo, quien trabaja en una agencia de carros, que le ayude.

Situación D:

Patricio se mata estudiando para el examen de matemáticas. Un día antes del examen se da cuenta *(he notices)* de que no tenía un examen de matemáticas, ¡sino de español! Va a su consejero para ver qué le aconseja.

¿Cómo andas? I

Having completed **Comunicación I,** I now can . . .	Feel confident	Need to review
• describe animals and their habitats (pp. 298–299)	☐	☐
• pronounce words following the rules for accentuation and stress (MSL / SAM)	☐	☐
• share details about the environment (p. 302)	☐	☐
• describe El Yunque, the rain forest of Puerto Rico (p. 305)	☐	☐
• comment on what is necessary, possible, probable, and improbable (p. 305)	☐	☐

NOTE for 11-18

If you prefer, have students write a story rather than a dialogue. You may also want to brainstorm alternate situations with students to tailor the activity to your group.

ADDITIONAL ACTIVITY for *El subjuntivo*

Mis deberes Con un/a compañero/a, hagan una lista de por lo menos cinco cosas que deben hacer o que pueden ocurrir este fin de semana.

MODELO

Es necesario que estudiemos más este fin de semana. También es importante que vayamos al supermercado. Después de ir al supermercado, es necesario que limpiemos la cocina. Es probable que salgamos con nuestros amigos el sábado. Finalmente, es posible que nuestros padres vengan a visitarnos.

SECTION GOALS for
Comunicación II
By the end of the *Comunicación* section, students will be able to:

- discuss how governments are organized and administered.
- debate with others about politics and the environment.
- contrast the political history of the United States with that of Latin America and Spain.
- suggest ways to improve politics in the future.
- identify the uses of *por* and *para*.
- use common prepositions and prepositional phrases.
- form prepositions with the correct pronouns.
- explain where items are located in relation to one another using prepositions.
- use infinitives after prepositions.

NATIONAL STANDARDS
Communication, Cultures, Connections, Comparisons
This final vocabulary presentation in *¡Anda! Curso elemental* provides students with a sophisticated vocabulary that helps them talk and write about current events both in the United States and abroad. Since politics change so rapidly, you may want your students to check the web sites of Spanish-speaking countries to note their current political climates.

The vocabulary for *la política* allows students to talk about current events and reflect on the rapidly changing political policies and leaders. With this vocabulary, students can read news articles from Spanish-language web sites (Standard 1.2) using authentic text to read and interpret written Spanish. They can also engage in conversations with others in the interpersonal mode (Standard 1.1) about what is going on in the world, and they can present to an audience of listeners or readers about their political views (especially interesting during an election year) and debate important issues (Standard 1.3). They can use this information to analyze the cultural differences between the way the United States is governed and its relationship to other countries (Standards 2.1 and 2.2), and how the government affects the practices, products, and perspectives of the people. Students can make connections between their understanding of U.S. government and diplomatic and economic relationships with Hispanic countries (Standard 3.2). They can compare the government, election process, and rights of the people to see how the culture in the United States differs from Hispanic cultures and how they are governed (Standard 4.2).

Comunicación II

4 VOCABULARIO

7:00
11-26 to 11-29

La política Discussing government and current affairs

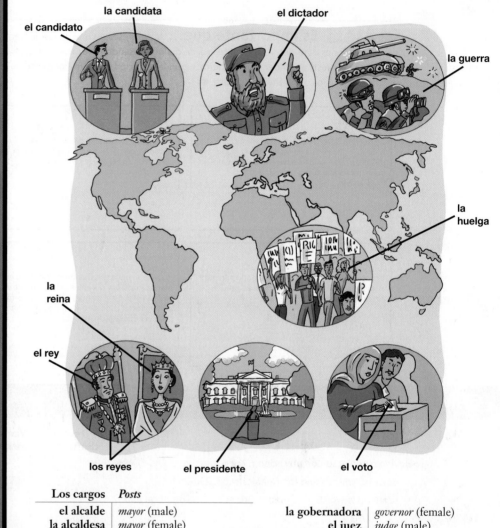

Los cargos	*Posts*		
el alcalde	*mayor* (male)	**la gobernadora**	*governor* (female)
la alcaldesa	*mayor* (female)	**el juez**	*judge* (male)
la dictadora	*dictator* (female)	**la jueza**	*judge* (female)
el diputado	*deputy; representative* (male)	**la presidenta**	*president* (female)
la diputada	*deputy; representative* (female)	**el senador**	*senator* (male)
el gobernador	*governor* (male)	**la senadora**	*senator* (female)

Las administraciones y los regímenes	*Administrations and regimes*
el congreso	*congress*
la democracia	*democracy*
la dictadura	*dictatorship*
el estado	*state*
el gobierno	*government*
la ley	*law*
la monarquía	*monarchy*
la presidencia	*presidency*

Las cuestiones políticas	*Political matters*
el bienestar	*well-being; welfare*
la corte	*court*
la defensa	*defense*
la delincuencia	*crime*
el desempleo	*unemployment*
la deuda (externa)	*(foreign) debt*
el impuesto	*tax*
la inflación	*inflation*
el juicio	*trial*

Algunos verbos	*Some verbs*
apoyar	*to support*
combatir	*to fight; to combat*
elegir	*to elect*
estar en huelga	*to be on strike*
llevar a cabo	*to carry out*
luchar	*to fight; to combat*
meterse en política	*to get involved in politics*
resolver (o → ue)	*to resolve*
votar	*to vote*

[5:00]   **11-19 Al revés** Generalmente ustedes reciben las definiciones y tienen que advinar la palabra o expresión. Esta vez van a elegir **seis** palabras o expresiones de **La política** y escribir las definiciones. ■

MODELO   el impuesto
El dinero que tenemos que pagar al gobierno cuando compramos algo. Es un porcentaje del costo.

[5:00] Workbooklet   **11-20 Batalla** Completa cada parte del cuadro con el nombre de un lugar o una persona según la descripción. Después, compara tus respuestas con las de un/a compañero/a. Dense un punto por cada acierto (*match*). ■

1. una reina	5. un país con alta inflación	9. el nombre del segundo presidente de los Estados Unidos
2. un estado en el Noreste	6. un país con baja inflación	10. el nombre de un senador de tu estado
3. un país con monarquía	7. una ciudad de los Estados Unidos con mucha delincuencia (*crime*)	11. el nombre de una guerra muy larga
4. un rey	8. un alcalde	12. un/a juez/a de la Corte Suprema de los Estados Unidos

NOTE for *La política*
Tell students that *el alcalde* has an irregular feminine counterpart, *la alcaldesa*. Another similar pair is *el rey* and *la reina*.

SUGGESTION for *La política*
Have students note how many of the words in this list are cognates. They may want to master these words first, and then add those that are unfamiliar to them.

NOTE for 11-19
Students may need additional guidance and support as they work through this activity. While a bit challenging for some, this activity is designed to help students develop the skill of circumlocution.

EXPANSION for 11-20
Have students share the reasoning behind their choices, e.g., why they believe a particular country has such a high rate of inflation or why President X was the best.

11-21 Reportando Imagínense que son periodistas y tienen que hacer un reportaje sobre unas charlas y discursos de unos políticos. Formen oraciones lógicas, añadiendo otras palabras cuando sea necesario. ■

 Capítulo 7. El pretérito, pág. 263 del eText; Algunos verbos irregulares en el pretérito, pág. 272 del eText.

MODELO encuesta / mostrar / el 65% de las personas / no votar / elecciones
La encuesta mostró que el 65% de las personas no votaron en las elecciones.

1. alcalde / no resolver / problemas / huelgas
2. jefe / partido politico / decir / (él) meterse en política / para combatir / alta inflación
3. senadora / confirmar / senado / votar por / nuevos impuestos
4. reyes / preocuparse por / bienestar / personas / provincias
5. presidente / dedicarse a / luchar contra / delincuencia, desempleo, deuda externa

NOTA CULTURAL

¡Hola! eText 428   11-30   **La política en el mundo hispano**

NOTE for *Nota cultural*
See eText pg. 428 for complete *Nota cultural* reading and *Preguntas*.

 11-22 ¿Qué sabes de…? Juntos contesten las siguientes preguntas para mostrar sus conocimientos políticos. ■

1. ¿En qué año fue la última campaña para la presidencia de los Estados Unidos?
2. ¿Cómo se llama el/la gobernador/a de tu estado?
3. ¿Quién fue un/a dictador/a infame? ¿De qué país? ¿Cuándo fue dictador/a?
4. ¿Qué países tienen un rey o una reina? ¿Cómo se llaman?
5. ¿Cuántos senadores hay en el senado de los Estados Unidos?
6. ¿Cuántos jueces hay en la Corte Suprema de los Estados Unidos?

 11-23 El futuro político Escribe algunas ideas sobre lo que debe pasar en el futuro en tu ciudad, estado, país o en el mundo. Después, en grupos de tres, escriban un párrafo colectivo para la clase. Usen las expresiones que requieren el subjuntivo cuando sea posible. ■

MODELO *Es necesario que los partidos políticos no combatan tanto entre sí* (among themselves). *También es importante que el presidente resuelva problemas económicos como la inflación. Es dudoso que podamos bajar la deuda nacional porque todos quieren dinero para sus programas.*

11-24 Los partidos políticos En grupos de cinco o seis estudiantes van a crear un partido político nuevo. Tienen que determinar el nombre del partido y el programa (*platform*). Después, presenten sus partidos a los otros grupos y juntos decidan cuál(es) de los partidos mejor representa(n) las opiniones de la clase. ■

NOTE for 11-24

If you find that **11-24** is too challenging for your students, you could start by brainstorming a list of local governmental issues or (non-partisan) problems that the community and/or your state face, and then have students react to the statements. Some ideas include general problems across the United States:

El desempleo en la Compañía X es muy alto.
Los empleados de la Fábrica X están en huelga.
Hay más problemas con el clima y la temperatura alta que en años previos.
En los Estados Unidos hay mucha basura y no hay suficiente reciclaje.

Por y para
Expressing time, deadlines, movement, destination, means, purpose, etc.

11-31 to 11-34

As you have seen, Spanish has two main words to express *for*: **por** and **para.** They have distinct uses and are not interchangeable.

¿Por cuánto tiempo ocupa el presidente la presidencia?

POR is used to express:

1. Duration of time (*during, for*)
El presidente ocupa la presidencia **por** cuatro años consecutivos.
The president holds the presidency for four consecutive years.
El alcalde habló **por** más de media hora.
The mayor spoke for more than a half hour.

2. Movement or location (*through, along, past, around*)
Los candidatos andan **por** la calle y hablan con la gente.
The candidates are going through the streets talking with the people.
El rey saluda **por** la ventana.
The king is waving through the window.

3. Motive (*on account of, because of, for*)
Decidimos meternos en política **por** nuestros hijos. Queremos asegurarles un futuro mejor.
We decided to get involved in politics because of our children. We want to assure them a better future.
En resumen, nos dijeron que hay que reciclar **por** el futuro de nuestro planeta.
In short, they told us that we must recycle for the future of our planet.

4. Exchange (*in exchange for*)
Gracias **por** su ayuda, señora Presidenta.
Thank you for your help, Madam President.
Limpiaron el vertedero **por** diez mil dólares.
They cleaned the dump for ten thousand dollars.

5. Means (*by*)
Los diputados discutieron los resultados de las elecciones **por** teléfono.
The representatives argued about the election results over the phone.
¿Los reyes van a viajar **por** barco o **por** avión?
Are the king and queen going to travel by ship or by plane?

PARA is used to express:

1. Point in time or a deadline (*for, by*)
Es dudoso que todos los problemas se solucionen **para** el final de su presidencia.
It is doubtful that all problems will be solved by the end of her presidency.
Es importante que bajemos los impuestos **para** el próximo año.
It is important that we lower taxes by next year.

2. Destination (*for*)
La reina sale hoy **para** Puerto Rico.
The queen leaves for Puerto Rico today.
Los diputados se fueron **para** el Capitolio.
The representatives left for the Capitol.

3. Recipients or intended person or persons (*for*)
Mi hermano escribe discursos **para** la gobernadora.
My brother writes speeches for the governor.
Necesitamos un avión **para** el dictador.
We need a plane for the dictator.

4. Comparison (*for*)
Para un hombre que sabe tanto de la política, no tiene ni idea sobre la delincuencia de nuestras calles.
For a man who knows so much about politics, he has no idea about the crime on our streets.
La tasa de desempleo es bastante baja **para** un país en desarrollo.
The unemployment rate is quite low for a developing country.

5. Purpose or goal (*to, in order to*)
Para recibir más votos, la candidata necesita proponer soluciones **para** los problemas con la deuda externa.
(In order) to receive more votes, the candidate needs to propose solutions for the problems with foreign debt.
Hay que luchar contra la contaminacón **para** proteger el medio ambiente.
One needs to fight pollution to protect the environment.

CAPÍTULO 11

🔑 **Instructor Resources**
• PPT, Extra Activities

NOTE for *Por y para*
Tell students that the reason *por* appears in parentheses in some of the examples is because it is optional.

NOTE for *Por y para*
Tell students to note that an infinitive is used when a verb comes immediately after *por* or *para* as well as after all other prepositions.

SUGGESTION for *Por y para*
You may wish to ask your students the following questions to practice *por* and *para*. Recycling previous vocabulary works well with this type of directed questions.
1. ¿Por cuánto tiempo estudiaste / hablaste por teléfono / hiciste ejercicio anoche / ayer / anteayer / durante el fin de semana?
2. ¿Por dónde hay un apartamento / un banco / un mercado / un restaurante?
3. ¿Para quién compras discos compactos?
4. ¿Qué tienes que hacer para sacar buenas notas / estar contento/a?

[3:00] **11-25 Los políticos** Hoy en día, los políticos son muy activos y están en todas partes. Completen las oraciones de manera lógica. ■

MODELO La candidata Dávila tuvo una entrevista y habló por…
La candidata Dávila tuvo una entrevista y habló por tres horas.

1. El alcalde dijo que se metió en política para…
2. Las diputadas Meana y Caballero dijeron que hay que elegir a un gobernador nuevo para…
3. Nuestro presidente les dio las gracias a las organizadoras por…
4. El dictador se comunicó por…
5. Después del discurso el rey salió para…
6. La senadora, acompañada por _____, caminó por…

[4:00] **11-26 Razones** Túrnense para decir para quiénes están haciendo ustedes las siguientes cosas. ■

Capítulo 5. El presente progresivo, pág. 180 del eText.

MODELO comprar / libro sobre la inflación
E1: *¿Para quién estás comprando el libro sobre la inflación?*
E2: *Estoy comprando el libro para mis padres.*

1. hacer / campaña
2. escribir / discurso
3. pedir / donación (*contribution*)
4. buscar / empleo
5. circular / peticiones
6. proteger / el medio ambiente

[7:00] **11-27 Mi hermana Leonor** Mi hermana Leonor me dio una gran sorpresa para mi cumpleaños. ■

Paso 1 Para saber qué pasó, completa cada espacio en blanco del siguiente párrafo con **por** o **para.**

Leonor, mi hermana, estuvo en mi casa (1) __por__ un mes el verano pasado. Vino (2) __para__ mi cumpleaños. Leonor llegó con tres maletas y una enorme caja misteriosa. El día de mi cumpleaños me dijo que (yo) tenía que estar lista (3) __para__ las cinco de la tarde. Efectivamente, a las cinco en punto estaba sentada en la sala cuando vi (4) __por__ la ventana a un grupo de amigos. Venían con un trío de guitarras. ¡Era una serenata (5) __para__ mí! ¡Qué emoción tan grande! La serenata comenzó y Leonor bajó (6) _____ la escalera con una caja.
—Es (7) __para__ ti —me dijo. La abrí y ¡qué sorpresa! Era una hamaca de yute (*jute hammock*) de la República Dominicana, donde Leonor había vivido (*had lived*) (8) __por__ varios meses.
—¡Una hamaca (9) __para__ el patio —exclamé— (10) __para__ leer y dormir al sol! ¡Qué delicia! —Y en seguida pregunté:— Pero, Leonor, ¿cómo trajiste esta hamaca desde Santo Domingo? ¿La trajiste (11) __por__ avión o la mandaste (12) __por__ correo?
Leonor se rió y me contestó: —(13) __para__ una hermana como tú, todo es posible. Me la traje en avión. (14) __para__ ser una caja tan grande la verdad es que no me causó tantos problemas. ¡Feliz cumpleaños!

Paso 2 Comparte tus respuestas con un/a compañero/a y explícale por qué usaste **por o para** en cada una.

11-28 Preguntas personales Túrnense para contestar las siguientes preguntas. ■

Capítulo 7. El pretérito, pág. 263 del eText; Algunos verbos irregulares en el pretérito, pág. 272 del eText; Capítulo 8. El imperfecto, pág. 317 del eText.

1. ¿Por cuánto tiempo viste las noticias en la televisión anoche?
2. ¿Por cuánto tiempo estudiaste anoche?
3. ¿Qué veías por la ventana de tu cuarto cuando eras joven?
4. Cuando estabas en la escuela primaria, ¿ibas al colegio en autobús, carro o a pie?
5. ¿Por quién votaste la primera vez que pudiste votar?
6. ¿Qué puede hacer un estudiante universitario para ser más activo en la política?
7. ¿Sabes si hay un centro de reciclaje por aquí? ¿Por dónde voy para llegar allí?
8. ¿Qué necesitamos hacer para evitar la contaminación?

6 GRAMÁTICA

11-35 to 11-37 Spanish/English Tutorials

Las preposiciones y los pronombres preposicionales
Specifying location and other information

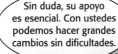

Sin duda, su apoyo es esencial. Con ustedes podemos hacer grandes cambios sin dificultades.

Besides the prepositions **por** and **para,** there is a variety of useful prepositions and prepositional phrases, many of which you have already been using throughout *¡Anda! Curso elemental.* Study the following list to review the ones you already know and to acquaint yourself with those that may be new to you.

a	*to; at*	**después de**	*after*
a la derecha de	*to the right of*	**detrás de**	*behind*
a la izquierda de	*to the left of*	**en**	*in*
acerca de	*about*	**encima de**	*on top of*
(a)fuera de	*outside of*	**enfrente de**	*across from; facing*
al lado de	*next to*	**entre**	*among; between*
antes de	*before (time/space)*	**hasta**	*until*
cerca de	*near*	**lejos de**	*far from*
con	*with*	**para**	*for; in order to*
de	*of; from; about*	**por**	*for; through; by; because of*
debajo de	*under; underneath*	**según**	*according to*
delante de	*in front of*	**sin**	*without*
dentro de	*inside of*	**sobre**	*over; about*
desde	*from*		

Instructor Resources
• PPT, Extra Activities

TPR ACTIVITY for *Las preposiciones*
Prepositions lend themselves well to TPR activities. These can be simple, like using classroom objects and giving amusing instructions for the students to follow, e.g., *Pon el lápiz encima de tu cabeza.*

If you want to incorporate world geography with the prepositions, have students work in groups with a map of South America and Central America, with the countries cut out into individual shapes. Create a new map by giving directions such as *Brasil está lejos de Honduras* or *Chile está cerca de Argentina* and have them put their new maps together. See which groups' maps match yours. You can also assign countries to individual students and, based on their classmates' suggestions, they form a "human" map of Central and South America.

NOTE for *Los pronombres preposicionales*
In addition to *conmigo* and *contigo*, you may choose to present the form *consigo.*

El centro de reciclaje está **a la derecha del** supermercado.	The recycling center is to the right of the supermarket.
La alcadesa va a hablar **acerca de** los problemas que tenemos con la protección del cocodrilo cubano.	The mayor is going to speak about the problems we are having with the protection of the Cuban crocodile.
Vimos un montón de plástico **encima del** papel.	We saw a mountain of plastic on top of the paper.
Quieren sembrar flores **enfrente del** vertedero.	They want to plant flowers in front of the dump.
El proyecto no puede tener éxito **sin** el apoyo del gobierno local.	The project cannot be successful without the support of the local government.

Los pronombres preposicionales

Study the list of pronouns that are used following prepositions.

Fíjate				
The list of pronouns that follow prepositions is the same as the list of subject pronouns, except for the first two (*mí* is used instead of *yo*, and *ti* instead of *tú*).	**mí**	*me*	**nosotros/as**	*us*
	ti	*you*	**vosotros/as**	*you*
	usted	*you*	**ustedes**	*you*
	él	*him*	**ellos**	*them*
	ella	*her*	**ellas**	*them*

Para mí, es muy importante resolver el problema de la lluvia ácida.	For me, it's really important to solve the problem of acid rain.
¿Qué candidato está sentado **enfrente de ti**?	Which candidate is seated in front of you?
Se fueron de la huelga **sin nosotros.**	They left the strike without us.
Trabajamos **con ellos** para proteger el medio ambiente.	We work with them to protect the environment.

Note that **con** has two special forms:

1. con + mí = **conmigo** *with me*
   —¿Vienes **conmigo** al discurso?
   Are you coming with me to the speech?

2. con + ti = **contigo** *with you*
   —Sí, voy **contigo.**
   Yes, I'm going with you.

4:00 🍦🍦 **11-29 Hablando del candidato** Termina la conversación
entre Celia y Manolo sobre el candidato Carlos Arroyo con los pronombres
preposicionales apropiados y después comparte tus respuestas con un/a
compañero/a. ∎

CELIA: Manolo, ¿qué opinas tú de (1) ___él___?

MANOLO: Pues, te digo que para (2) ___mí___ está muy claro.
El señor Arroyo no piensa en (3) ___nosotros___ ni en
nuestros problemas.

> **Fíjate**
> Remember that when *a + el* and *de + el* appear together in a sentence, you must use the contractions (*al, del*).

CELIA: Sí, siempre está con las personas ricas e influyentes
(*influential*), tratando de conseguir dinero de (4) ___ellos___ para su campaña.

MANOLO: También creo que vive parte del año aquí y parte en la costa. Para (5) ___mí___ eso significa que
quiere ser nuestro líder pero no quiere vivir con (6) ___nosotros___. ¿Y para (7) ___ti___, Celia?

CELIA: Creo que tienes razón. Me gusta hablar con ___tigo (contigo)___ (8) porque me haces pensar en las cosas que
no son tan obvias.

ADDITIONAL ACTIVITY for
Las preposiciones
In groups of 4 to 6 students, alternate
sending two students out of the room
while the remaining students in each
group hide an object. The students return
and the remaining students give clues for
finding the objects, using prepositions.

MODELO
(la mochila de Inés)
E1: *No está debajo del escritorio.*
E2: *Está delante de la profesora.*
E3: *Está a la derecha de Silvia.*
       …

3:00 **11-30 Descríbemelo** Juntos describan el dibujo usando las siguientes preposiciones. ■

MODELO   *El gato está al lado del árbol.*

1. al lado de
2. a la derecha de
3. a la izquierda de
4. cerca de

5. debajo de
6. delante de
7. detrás de
8. lejos de

5:00 **11-31 Una política joven** Completa
el párrafo sobre Martina Peña, una candidata nueva
en el mundo político, con las preposiciones de la
lista. Después compara tu párrafo con el de un/a
compañero/a. ■

a	antes de	con (2 veces)	de
después de	entre	sobre	sin

(1) ___Antes de___ meterse en la política. Martina compartió
sus ideas (2) ___con___ mucha gente. (3) ___Entre___ otras
personas se reunió (4) ___con___ políticos importantes
y, (5) ___de___ ellos, aprendió mucho (6) ___sobre___
el bienestar, los derechos humanos, la violencia, el
desempleo y la inflación. (7) ___Después de___ escuchar todo lo que tenían que decir, ella volvió
(8) ___a___ su casa y empezó a convertir sus ideas en discursos. El próximo paso fue
buscar apoyo y dinero. Sabía perfectamente que (9) ___sin___ ese apoyo no iba a ser
posible ganar las elecciones.

NOTE for 11-32
These buildings are historical sites located in Viejo San Juan, near El Castillo de San Felipe del Morro. Many of them are open to the public and serve as museums or tourist sites, while others are used for government business and officials.

NOTE for 11-32
Activity **11-32** lends itself well to a cultural expansion activity. Students can research San Juan sites such as El Morro on the Internet and present their findings to the class.

ADDITIONAL ACTIVITY for
Las preposiciones
En nuestra clase… Creen diez oraciones con preposiciones que describan su clase de español.

MODELO
Ryan se sienta al lado de George. / Los libros de mi profesor están encima de su escritorio. / Las ventanas están lejos de nosotros.

[8:00] **11-32** **¿Dónde están?**
Con un/a compañero/a, expliquen dónde están los siguientes lugares en El Viejo San Juan en Puerto Rico, usando siempre las preposiciones apropiadas. ■

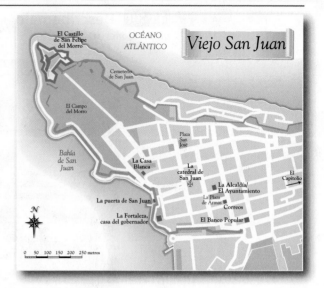

MODELO   E1: *¿Dónde está el Campo del Morro?*

E2: *Está entre el Castillo y La Casa Blanca, al lado del Cementerio de San Juan.*

1. La Fortaleza, casa del gobernador
2. El Capitolio, edificio de las oficinas de los senadores y representantes
3. La Plaza de Armas
4. El Castillo de San Felipe del Morro
5. La Casa Blanca, casa de la familia de Juan Ponce de León
6. La Alcaldía / El Ayuntamiento, edificio donde el alcalde tiene sus oficinas
7. Correos
8. El Banco Popular
9. La puerta de San Juan
10. La catedral de San Juan

[4:00] **11-33** **La universidad** Túrnense para explicar dónde están los siguientes lugares en su universidad. ■

Capítulo 2. En la universidad, pág. 74 del eText.

MODELO   *La biblioteca está detrás del centro estudiantil.*

1. la biblioteca
2. el gimnasio
3. el centro estudiantil
4. la librería
5. la cafetería
6. tu cuarto o residencia estudiantil
7. el centro de salud
8. el estadio de fútbol

[4:00] **11-34** **¿Con quién…?** Decide quién hace las siguientes actividades contigo y después comparte las respuestas con un/a compañero/a. ■

MODELO   E1: *¿Quién… habla contigo por teléfono todos los días?*

E2: *Mi madre habla conmigo por teléfono todos los días.*

¿Quién…?
1. viene a clase contigo Antes de comprar el boleto, tengo que ir al banco.
2. se sienta contigo en la sala de clase Después de ir al cuarto, tengo que pasar por recepción.
3. hace las actividades de clase contigo Después de llegar al aeropuerto, tengo que mostrar el pasaporte.
4. estudia contigo fuera de clase Antes de hacer la maleta, necesito lavar la ropa.
5. almuerza o cena contigo Antes de ir de vacaciones, necesito dejar el gato con mis padres.
6. sale contigo por la tarde (para ir al cine / bar / club de baile, etc.)

7 GRAMÁTICA

11-38 to 11-40

El infinitivo después de preposiciones

Providing more information about location, time, and other subjects

¡No me digas que todos tienen que comer antes de salir nosotros!

In Spanish, if you need to use a verb immediately after a preposition, it must always be in the **infinitive** form. Study the following examples:

Antes de reciclar las latas debes limpiarlas.
Después de pisar la hormiga la niña empezó a llorar.
Es fácil decidir **entre reciclar** y **botar**.

Necesitamos trabajar con personas de todos los países **para proteger** mejor la Tierra.
Ganaste el premio **por estar** tan interesado en el medio ambiente.
No podemos vivir **sin trabajar** juntos.

Before recycling the cans, you should clean them.
After stepping on the ant, the little girl began to cry.
It is easy to decide between recycling and throwing away.
We need to work with people from all countries in order to better protect the Earth.
You won the prize for being so interested in the environment.
We cannot live without working together.

Capítulo 10. El viaje, pág. 388 del eText.

4:00

11-35 **De viaje** Forma oraciones lógicas usando **antes de** o **después de**. Después, compártelas con un/a compañero/a. ■

MODELO   E1: salir / hacer la maleta

        E2: *Antes de salir, necesito hacer la maleta. / Antes de salir, tengo que hacer la maleta.*

1. comprar el boleto / ir al banco Antes de comprar el boleto, tengo que ir al banco.
2. pasar por recepción / ir al cuarto Después de ir al cuarto, tengo que pasar por recepción.
3. llegar al aeropuerto / mostrar el pasaporte Después de llegar al aeropuerto, tengo que mostrar el pasaporte.
4. hacer la maleta / lavar la ropa Antes de hacer la maleta, necesito lavar la ropa.
5. ir de vacaciones / dejar el gato con mis padres Antes de ir de vacaciones, necesito dejar el gato con mis padres.

Fíjate

The sentences for **11-35** can be written two ways. Start the sentence with *antes de* + *infinitive* or *después de* + *infinitive* and finish the sentence, as in *Antes de salir necesito hacer la maleta.* Or end the sentence with the prepositional phrase, e.g., *Necesito hacer la maleta antes de salir.*

 Instructor Resources
• PPT, Extra Activities

ADDITIONAL ACTIVITY for
El infinitivo después de preposiciones
Challenge groups of 3 to 4 students, to write the longest logical sentences possible, focusing on prepositions followed by infinitives.

ADDITIONAL ACTIVITY for
El infinitivo después de preposiciones
Have pairs of students each create a 15-second commercial for a product, service, or business. In their commercials, they must use 5 prepositions followed by infinitives. As an alternative, students could produce public service announcements related to protecting the environment, in which they use at least 5 prepositions followed by infinitives.

11-36 Lo que pasó con el perro Termina las siguientes oraciones de forma lógica según el modelo. Después, comparte tus respuestas con un/a compañero/a. ■

MODELO   E1:   Es importante que sepas que el perro se escapó para…

E2:   *Es importante que sepas que el perro se escapó para jugar con esa perra bonita del vecino.*

1. Es mejor que busquemos el perro antes de…
2. Es probable que el perro nos evite para…
3. Es posible que el perro tenga hambre después de…
4. Sí, es raro que no venga para…
5. Es dudoso que se vaya con otra persona después de…
6. Ojalá que lo encontremos sin…

  11-37 Mis decisiones Termina las siguientes oraciones y después compártelas con un/a compañero/a. ■

MODELO   E1:   No me voy de aquí sin…

E2:   *No me voy de aquí sin terminar la tarea.*

1. Necesito pensar en el futuro antes de…
2. Quiero hablar con mis padres / mi mejor amigo sobre…
3. Voy a buscar un trabajo después de…
4. Tengo que escoger entre…
5. Me quedo en este lugar hasta…
6. Después pienso ir a _____ para…

ESCUCHA

Un anuncio político

11-41 to 11-43

Estrategia	Once you know the topic or gist of a passage, it may be helpful to mentally organize what you are about to hear.	Determine whether a list, chart, or diagram could be useful in helping you keep track of the information.
Using visual organizers		

11-38 **Antes de escuchar** Fania Marte Lozada tiene un anuncio político en la radio. ■

1. ¿Qué es un anuncio político?
2. ¿Escuchaste alguna vez un anuncio político de un candidato en la radio o viste uno de estos anuncios en la televisión?
3. ¿Qué información contiene generalmente un anuncio de este tipo?

Fania Marte Lozada, candidata

11-39 **A escuchar** Completa los siguientes pasos. ■

1. Escucha el anuncio para sacar la idea general.
2. Decide de qué forma quieres organizar la información (*list, chart, diagram*, etc.).
3. Escucha otra vez para completar tu diagrama o lista con la información esencial.
4. Escucha una vez más para añadir algunos detalles.

11-40 **Después de escuchar** En grupos de tres o cuatro, compartan su información y juntos decidan si la Dra. Marte Lozada sería (*would be*) una buena alcaldesa. Expliquen. ■

SECTION GOALS for *Escucha*
By the end of the *Escucha* section, students will be able to:
- implement the new strategy, using visual organizers.
- incorporate previously learned listening strategies.
- listen for specific information.
- debate whether they think the candidate in the announcement would be a good mayor.

NATIONAL STANDARDS
Communication
The *Escucha* section introduces the new strategy of using visual organizers. This strategy complements the presentational mode very well (Standard 1.3), because students have a sketch of something they can talk or write about and present to an audience. The students practice their interpretive communication skills (Standard 1.2) as they listen to the passage and understand and interpret its meaning. The post-listening activity requires small group communication (Standard 1.1) as students discuss what they have heard and decide whether Dra. Marte Lozada would make a good mayor.

AUDIOSCRIPT for 11-39
Un anuncio de nuestra candidata Fania Marte Lozada
Compañeros y amigos:
  Lo que necesitamos es un alcalde honrado y dedicado, o mejor dicho, una alcaldesa honrada y dedicada. Señores, yo quiero ser su alcaldesa. Estoy convencida de que estoy bien calificada para el trabajo. Hace dieciséis años que vivo en este pueblo bello en el corazón de nuestra isla. Mis tres hijos se graduaron de la Escuela Josefina León Zayas y ahora estudian en la Universidad de Puerto Rico en Río Piedras.
  Algunos de ustedes me conocen como la doctora Marte Lozada puesto que soy pediatra. He tratado a casi todos los niños de Jayuya. También sirvo a nuestra comunidad como asesora para la Cruz Roja y presidenta de la organización Ambiente, PR. La salud de nuestros hijos, la protección del medio ambiente y la limpieza del mundo en que vivimos son mis grandes pasiones y van a ser mis prioridades como alcaldesa.
  Amigos, votar por mí es votar por el futuro de nuestras familias, nuestro pueblo y nuestra isla.

SECTION GOALS for
¡Conversemos!

By the end of the *¡Conversemos!* section, students will be able to:

- discuss environmental issues, along with potential solutions and funding sources using presentational and interpersonal modes.
- share information about a politically-related current event using presentational and interpersonal modes.
- utilize previously learned/recycled vocabulary and grammatical concepts such as the subjunctive mood, *por* and *para,* and other prepositions.

¡CONVERSEMOS!

11-44

 11-41 **Nuestro mundo**

Junto con un/a compañero/a, creen una conversación entre un ciudadano y un candidato sobre los problemas más críticos del medio ambiente y las posibles soluciones y fondos (*funding*). Necesitan incluir por lo menos **diez** oraciones y usar el **subjuntivo por lo menos cinco veces.** Después, presenten la entrevista para los compañeros de la clase. ■

 11-42 **La política** Tu compañero/a y tú son reporteros de noticias. Juntos creen un reportaje sobre algún aspecto de la política del mundo y de lo que pasó hoy. Incluyan por lo menos **diez** oraciones. ■

ESCRIBE

11-45

Un anuncio de servicio público

Estrategia	
Persuasive writing	In writing a public announcement, your goal is to influence the listeners to support your cause and become better environmentalists. To create the most effective announcement, consider the elements of persuasive writing: appeal to reason, emotions, and good character (ethical, morals, and concern for the well-being of the | audience); define any key terms that may not be clear; reference an authority and/or supporting evidence to back your claims; and anticipate counterarguments and address them. You must develop a rational argument, making sure the conclusion logically follows the claims you make.

11-43 **Antes de escribir** Vas a crear un anuncio de publicidad para la radio sobre algún aspecto de la protección del medio ambiente. Debe durar (*last*) unos quince segundos. Decide de qué quieres hablar y haz una lista de los puntos más importantes que quieres incluir. ■

11-44 **A escribir** Organiza tus ideas y escribe un anuncio. Debe estar dirigido (*directed*) a los adultos jóvenes. ■

 11-45 **Después de escribir** Presenta tu anuncio a los compañeros de clase. ■

¿Cómo andas? II

	Feel confident	Need to review
Having completed **Comunicación II**, I now can . . .		
• discuss government and current affairs (p. 312)	☐	☐
• relate specific facts about politics in the Spanish-speaking world (p. 314)	☐	☐
• express time, deadlines, movement, destination, means, purpose, etc. (p. 315)	☐	☐
• specify location and other information (p. 317)	☐	☐
• provide more information about location, time, and other subjects (p. 321)	☐	☐
• listen to a radio announcement and practice using visual organizers to enhance comprehension (p. 323)	☐	☐
• communicate about world issues (p. 324)	☐	☐
• employ persuasive writing to create a public announcement (p. 325)	☐	☐

CAPÍTULO 11

SECTION GOALS for *Escribe*
By the end of the *Escribe* section, students will be able to:
• write an advertisement for a target audience.
• practice persuasive writing strategies.
• create an advertisement that lasts 15 seconds.
• present the advertisement to their classmates.

NATIONAL STANDARDS
Communication, Connections, Communities
Writing an advertisement for the protection of the environment encompasses many Goal Areas. The writing and presenting satisfy the presentational mode, because they are writing and discussing what they have written to an audience of listeners/readers (Standard 1.3). In the writing process, if they work in pairs or groups, they engage in conversations, exchange ideas, express feelings and opinions, and provide and obtain information (Standard 1.1). They can begin the writing process in English to organize the structure of their ads and use their English public speaking skills to form a succinct argument about the environment. They are able to make connections with other disciplines like English, journalism, speech and debate, and public speaking when they write and perform their ads (Standard 3.1). As students realize that if they can write and perform an ad, typical of those they would hear on the radio, they can also listen for these ads in Spanish from a Spanish-speaking radio station or read them in print media, they discover that they can use their Spanish outside of the university setting, while forming part of the community (Standard 5.1).

NOTE for 11-45
You may choose to videotape the ads for students.

Instructor Resources
• Text images (maps), Video resources

SECTION GOALS for *Cultura*
By the end of the *Cultura* section, students will be able to:
• name the cultural influences in Cuba.
• list important agricultural products in Cuba.
• discuss the wildlife common to Cuba.
• identify the natural resources of Puerto Rico.
• state the relationship of Puerto Rico to the United States.
• report about the major products of the Dominican Republic.
• explain how the geography of the Dominican Republic differs from that of other Hispanic countries.
• contrast Cuba, Puerto Rico, and the Dominican Republic with other Hispanic countries.

NATIONAL STANDARDS
Communication, Cultures, Comparisons
Students read about three Hispanic countries: Cuba, Puerto Rico, and the Dominican Republic, in *Les presento mi país.* The reading provides written Spanish and students are able to interpret and understand the cultural information presented (Standard 1.2). They can discuss in pairs or small groups how the three featured countries differ and how they are different from other Hispanic countries they have learned about (Standard 1.1). The information explains how the cultures differ from country to country, and students can compare how the history and geography of these countries affect their products, practices, and perspectives (Standards 2.1 and 2.2). They can then make comparisons between the cultural practices of Cubans, Puerto Ricans, and Dominicans and how they are similar to or different from those of the United States (Standard 4.2).

NOTE for *Cultura*
You may live in a part of the country that has a large number of people whose heritage is Puerto Rican, Cuban, or Dominican. At this point in *Capítulo 11,* and as you approach the end of *¡Anda! Curso elemental,* you can include students from these countries in a discussion of their heritage, which will enrich the learning of the entire class.

SUGGESTION for *La Plaza de la Revolución*
Additional questions to ask your students are: *¿Qué lugares públicos en los Estados Unidos se usan para las demostraciones públicas, tanto políticas como de otro tipo?* (e.g., Times Square in NYC), *¿Cómo se honra en los Estados Unidos a los héroes políticos y militares?*

Cultura

Cuba

10:00   11-46 to 11-47

Les presento mi país

Alicia Ortega Mujica

Mi nombre es Alicia Ortega Mujica y soy de La Habana, la capital de Cuba. La mayoría de los cubanos tenemos herencia española, africana o una mezcla (*mixture*) de las dos. La influencia africana se nota sobre todo en la música cubana, especialmente en la salsa. Celia Cruz, "la reina de la salsa", siempre alababa estas raíces africanas en sus canciones. **¿Qué influencia africana se siente en la música de tu país?** Antes, la economía cubana dependía mayormente de la producción de azúcar, pero ahora el turismo es muy importante y el gobierno invierte recursos para desarrollar esa infraestructura a fin de (*in order to*) atraer más visitantes al país.

La Plaza de la Revolución

El ajiaco, un plato típico cubano

El Gran Teatro de La Habana y El Ballet Nacional de Cuba

ALMANAQUE

Nombre oficial:	República de Cuba
Gobierno:	Estado/Régimen comunista
Población:	11.477.459 (2010)
Idioma:	español
Moneda:	Peso cubano (CUP) y Peso convertible (CUC)

¿Sabías que...?
• El zunzuncito, el pájaro más pequeño del mundo, es endémico (*common*) de Cuba. Mide menos de seis centímetros y pesa menos de dos gramos. Es una especie de colibrí (*hummingbird*).

Preguntas
1. ¿Cuál es la composición étnica de la población cubana?
2. ¿Cuáles son las bases principales de la economía cubana?
3. ¿Qué tipo de música es popular en Cuba? ¿Es popular en otras partes del mundo?

Amplía tus conocimientos sobre Cuba en MySpanishLab.

326

EXPANSION for *El ajiaco*
Additional questions to ask your students are: *¿Tenemos una sopa nacional? ¿un plato nacional? ¿Cuál es tu sopa favorita? ¿cómo se prepara?*

SUGGESTION for *El Ballet Nacional de Cuba*
Additional questions to ask your students are: *¿Hay alguna compañía de ballet famosa en los Estados Unidos? Nombra algún bailarín famoso. ¿Adónde puedes ir a ver un ballet?*

Puerto Rico

11-46, 11-48

Les presento mi país

Pablo Colón Padín

Mi nombre es Pablo Colón Padín y soy de San Germán, Puerto Rico, conocido como la Ciudad de las Lomas (*hills*). Actualmente soy estudiante del Recinto Universitario de Mayagüez, donde han asistido, entre muchos otros, algunos ingenieros de NASA. **¿Te interesan los estudios del espacio y de los planetas?** El Observatorio de Arecibo, sitio del radiotelescopio de un solo plato más grande del mundo, está a unas setenta millas de mi universidad. También se puede estudiar una naturaleza muy diversa en mi isla: desde un área de cuevas del norte hasta El Yunque, bosque lluvioso del este. Puerto Rico es territorio de los Estados Unidos pero la cuestión de la independencia y la estadidad (*statehood*) se siguen debatiendo. **¿Qué opinas tú de esta cuestión?**

El radiotelescopio del Observatorio de Arecibo

Vista de San Juan, la capital

OCÉANO ATLÁNTICO

Isabela · Arecibo · San Juan · Bayamón · Río Piedras · Isla de Culebra · Mayagüez · PUERTO RICO · Ponce · Isla de Vieques

Mar Caribe

El coquí, el famoso símbolo de Puerto Rico

ALMANAQUE

Nombre oficial:	Estado Libre Asociado de Puerto Rico
Gobierno:	Territorio de los Estados Unidos; Estado Libre Asociado
Población:	3.978.702 (2010)
Idiomas:	español e inglés
Moneda:	Dólar estadounidense ($)

¿Sabías que...?

• Puerto Rico tiene tres bahías fosforescentes habitadas por millones de microorganismos (dinoflagelados) que emanan (*emanate*) luz cuando son alborotados (*stirred up*). Se puede observar este fenómeno por la noche. ¡Qué maravilla!

Preguntas

1. ¿Qué evidencia del desarrollo avanzado de las ciencias hay en Puerto Rico?
2. Describe la variedad natural de la isla.
3. ¿Hay otros países de Centroamérica que tienen bosques lluviosos?

 Amplía tus conocimientos sobre Puerto Rico en MySpanishLab.

327

CAPÍTULO 11

 Instructor Resources
• Text images (maps), Video resources

NOTE for *Vista de San Juan*
San Juan is located in the northern coastal plains in the Karstic region of Puerto Rico. (Karst contains such features as caves, sinkholes, springs, and sinking streams. These landforms are created by water dissolving the bedrock over many thousands of years.) San Juan is an excellent natural harbor. Founded in 1521, it is technically the oldest city in the United States, founded by Juan Ponce de León five years before he reached St. Augustine, FL. *La ciudad amurallada* is a nickname of San Juan.

EXPANSION for *Vista de San Juan*
Additional questions to ask your students are: *¿Hay alguna ciudad amurallada en los Estados Unidos? ¿Por qué crees que la muralla fue importante para San Juan en su momento?*

NOTE for *El coquí*
The *coquí* is the "national" frog, or symbol of Puerto Rico. It is a tiny amphibian of about 1 inch in length. About 16 different species live on the island, and 13 of those are found in *El Yunque*, the Caribbean National Forest. The *coquí* is so named because of the sound or call made by the male of the species at dusk: co-quí, co-quí.

EXPANSION for *El coquí*
Additional questions to ask your students are: *¿Cuál es el símbolo oficial de los Estados Unidos? ¿Había otros posibles "candidatos" cuando fue escogido? ¿Cuál prefieres tú y por qué?*

NOTE for *El radiotelescopio de Arecibo*
The single-dish radio telescope at the Arecibo Observatory is the largest of its kind in the world. This important scientific facility is open to scientists worldwide on the basis of competitive research proposals and projects. It is located at the National Astronomy and Ionosphere Center in Arecibo, Puerto Rico. It has even appeared in several movies: *GoldenEye* (James Bond), *Contact*, and *Species*. To learn more about this facility research it on the Internet.

EXPANSION for *El radiotelescopio de Arecibo*
Additional questions to ask your students are: *¿Qué instalaciones para la investigación científica hay en los Estados Unidos? ¿dónde están?* (e.g., NASA in Texas and NORAD in Colorado)

NOTE for *Los cigarros*
Tabacco is the Dominican Republic's oldest crop, cultivated by the Taino Indians before Columbus landed, and is a stable agricultural export. The Association of Cigar Producers (Procigar) estimates that more than 70,000 Dominicans make their living off the crop. The United States is the number one importer of Dominican cigars.

NOTE for *La Catedral Santa María La Menor*
Also known as the *Catedral Primada de América*, the church was begun in 1514 and completed in 1540. The architecture is a blend of Gothic, baroque, and plateresque styles and the façade is made of coral and limestone.

NOTE for *El merengue*
Merengue means whipped egg whites and sugar in Spanish, similar to the English word meringue. It is unclear as to why this name became the name of a style of music from the Dominican Republic. But, perhaps, we can trace its meaning to a dance move that resembles an egg beater in action.

This style of music was created by Ñico Lora in the 1920s and eventually became the country's national music and dance style. World-famous merengue singers include Los Hermanos Rosario, Juan Luis Guerra, Wilfredo Vargas, Sergio Vargas, Johnny Ventura, Kinito Mendez, Josie Esteban y la Patrulla 15, Pochy y su Cocoband, Fernando Villalona, Cuco Valoy, Elvis Crespo, Miriam Cruz y Las Chicas del Can, Conjunto Quisqueya, and Omega.

La República Dominicana

11-46, 11-49

Les presento mi país

Amparo Burgos Báez

Mi nombre es Amparo Burgos Báez y soy de la República Dominicana, que comparte la isla de La Española con Haití. Mi país es muy montañoso y áspero (*rough*), con cuatro sistemas principales de cordilleras (*mountain ranges*), pero también tiene unas playas increíbles de arena fina y agua cristalina. **¿Prefieres las montañas o la playa?** Uno de nuestros platos más típicos es *la bandera dominicana,* que consiste en arroz, habichuelas rojas, carne, ensalada y tostones (*plantain chips*)… Si nos visitas, vas a escuchar el merengue y la bachata con sus ritmos contagiosos. Otras aficiones del país son los deportes acuáticos y el béisbol. **¿Sabes qué jugadores dominicanos juegan para equipos estadounidenses?**

Santa María La Menor, la primera catedral del Nuevo Mundo

Los cigarros dominicanos son de los mejores del mundo.

El merengue, la música nacional

ALMANAQUE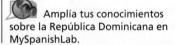

Nombre oficial: La República Dominicana
Gobierno: Democracia representativa
Población: 9.823.821 (2010)
Idioma: español (oficial)
Moneda: Peso dominicano ($RD)

¿Sabías que...?

• Cristóbal Colón descubrió la isla en su primer viaje y la nombró La Española. Santo Domingo fue la primera ciudad europea fundada en el Nuevo Mundo y hoy en día casi la mitad de la población vive ahí, en la capital.
• La mayoría de los beisbolistas hispanos en las Grandes Ligas son dominicanos.

Preguntas

1. ¿Cómo es la geografía dominicana y qué tiene de especial?
2. ¿Qué es "la bandera dominicana"?
3. ¿Qué tienen en común la República Dominicana y los otros países del Caribe que has estudiado?

 Amplía tus conocimientos sobre la República Dominicana en MySpanishLab.

eText 444 11-52

Ambiciones siniestras

EPISODIO 11

Lectura y video

Y por fin, ¿cómo andas?

	Feel confident	Need to review

Having completed this chapter, I now can . . .

Comunicación I

- describe animals and their habitats (pp. 298–299) ☐ ☐
- pronounce words following the rules for accentuation and stress (MSL / SAM) ☐ ☐
- share details about the environment (p. 302) ☐ ☐
- comment on what is necessary, possible, probable, and improbable (p. 305) ☐ ☐

Comunicación II

- discuss government and current affairs (p. 312) ☐ ☐
- express time, deadlines, movement, destination, means, purpose, etc. (p. 315) ☐ ☐
- specify location and other information (p. 317) ☐ ☐
- provide more information about location, time, and other subjects (p. 321) ☐ ☐
- listen to a radio announcement and practice using visual organizers to enhance comprehension (p. 323) ☐ ☐
- communicate about world issues (p. 324) ☐ ☐
- employ persuasive writing to create a public announcement (p. 325) ☐ ☐

Cultura

- describe El Yunque, the rain forest of Puerto Rico (p. 305) ☐ ☐
- relate specific facts about politics in the Spanish-speaking world (p. 314) ☐ ☐
- share important facts about Cuba, Puerto Rico, and the Dominican Republic (pp. 326–328) ☐ ☐

Ambiciones siniestras

- use visual organizers when reading, and explain who Lupe really is (p. 329) ☐ ☐
- relate what happened to Eduardo and Alejandra (p. 329) ☐ ☐

Comunidades

- use Spanish in real-life contexts (SAM) ☐ ☐

CAPÍTULO 11

SECTION GOALS for *Lectura y video* **(Online)**
By the end of the *Lectura y video* section, students will be able to:

- predict what will happen from the pre-reading questions.
- apply the new strategy, using visual organizers, as they read.
- compare and contrast the visual organizers they created with organizers their classmates created.
- brainstorm how they think the episode will end based on the information from the *Lectura*.
- reveal the ending of *Ambiciones siniestras*.
- discuss their opinions and feelings about the ending.
- summarize the plot from the first episode to the final episode.

NOTE for *Lectura y video*
Activity answers for online content can be found on the end vocabulary page for quick reference.

RECAP of
AMBICIONES SINIESTRAS
Episodio 10 **(Online)**
Lectura: In *Episodio 10* of *Ambiciones siniestras*, Cisco revealed that he had his doubts about el Sr. Verdugo, so he investigated further and wrote notes about his suspicions. Eduardo saw his notes, took them, sent the e-mail to Sr. Verdugo, and disappeared. Cisco read Eduardo's e-mail, but without the evidence, Cisco felt that he could not contact the police. Meanwhile, Lupe did not respond to the e-mail evidence, and while the others continued their videoconference, she wrote an e-mail to an unidentified person and dialed a number from her cell phone.
Video: In *Episodio 10*, *Falsas apariencias*, Marisol solved the last riddle and rushed off to Lupe's apartment to confront her about knowing more than she previously admitted. On the way, someone frightened Marisol. She arrived at Lupe's, and they sent an e-mail to el Sr. Verdugo, telling him that they had solved the riddle. They called for a videoconference with the others, and during the conference, Lupe stepped out to take a phone call. Marisol confronted Lupe about her mysterious behavior, and Lupe took out a gun as she started to explain. The videoconference went black.

NATIONAL STANDARDS
Communication, Comparisons
The new strategy of creating visual organizers facilitates comprehension of the *Ambiciones siniestras Lectura* and *Video*. Students are able to read the storyline, organize the new information, and see how it fits with the previous information from other chapters. The reading satisfies one part of Standard 1.2, in which students read to understand and interpret written Spanish. Students work together in pairs to answer the comprehension questions and compare their visual organizers (Standard 1.1), but if they present their visual organizers to the class and explain them in Spanish,

they would address Standard 1.3, the presentational mode. The use of visual organizers as a way of preparing for new content and structuring their learning can be applied to whatever other subject they might be studying. This new strategy allows them to make comparisons between their study skills in Spanish and English (Standard 4.1).

VOCABULARIO ACTIVO

Algunos animales — *Some animals*

el caballo	*horse*
el cerdo	*pig*
el conejo	*rabbit*
el elefante	*elephant*
la gallina	*chicken; hen*
el gato	*cat*
la hormiga	*ant*
el insecto	*insect*
el león	*lion*
la mosca	*fly*
el mosquito	*mosquito*
el oso	*bear*
el pájaro / el ave	*bird*
el perro	*dog*
el pez (*pl.*, los peces)	*fish*
la rana	*frog*
la rata	*rat*
el ratón	*mouse*
la serpiente	*snake*
el toro	*bull*
la vaca	*cow*

Algunos verbos — *Some verbs*

cuidar	*to take care of*
preocuparse (por)	*to worry about; to concern oneself with*

Las cuestiones políticas — *Political issues*

el bienestar	*well-being; welfare*
la defensa	*defense*
la delincuencia	*crime*
el desempleo	*unemployment*
la deuda (externa)	*(foreign) debt*
el impuesto	*tax*
la inflación	*inflation*

Otras palabras útiles — *Other useful words*

los animal domésticos / las mascotas	*domesticated animals; pets*
los animales en peligro de extinción	*endangered species*
los animales salvajes	*wild animals*
el árbol	*tree*
el bosque	*forest*
la cueva	*cave*
la finca	*farm*
la granja	*farm*
el hoyo	*hole*
el lago	*lake*
la montaña	*mountain*
el océano	*ocean*
peligroso/a	*dangerous*
el río	*river*
la selva	*jungle*

El medio ambiente — *The environment*

el aluminio	*aluminum*
la botella	*bottle*
la caja (de cartón)	*(cardboard) box*
la contaminación	*pollution*
el derrame de petróleo	*oil spill*
el huracán	*hurricane*
el incendio	*fire*
la inundación	*flood*
la lata	*can*
el periódico	*newspaper*
el plástico	*plastic*
el terremoto	*earthquake*
la tormenta	*storm*
el tornado	*tornado*
el tsunami	*tsunami*
el vidrio	*glass*

Algunos verbos — *Some verbs*

apoyar	*to support*
botar	*to throw away*
combatir	*to fight; to combat*
contaminar	*to pollute*
cuidar	*to take care of*
elegir	*to elect*
estar en huelga	*to be on strike*
evitar	*to avoid*
hacer daño	*to (do) damage; to harm*
llevar a cabo	*to carry out*
luchar	*to fight; to combat*
matar	*to kill*
meterse en política	*to get involved in politics*
plantar	*to plant*
proteger	*to protect*
reciclar	*to recycle*
reforestar	*to reforest*
reutilizar	*to reuse*
resolver (o → ue)	*to resolve*
sembrar (e → ie)	*to sow*
votar	*to vote*

La política — *Politics*

el alcalde / la alcaldesa	*mayor*
el/la candidato/a	*candidate*
el/la dictador/a	*dictator*
el/la diputado/a	*deputy; representative*
el/la gobernador/a	*governor*
la guerra	*war*
la huelga	*strike*
el/la juez/a	*judge*
el juicio	*trial*
el/la presidente/a	*president*
el rey / la reina	*king / queen*
el/la senador/a	*senator*

Las preposiciones — *Prepositions*

See page 317.

Las administraciones y los regímenes — *Administrations and regimes*

el congreso	*congress*
la corte	*court*
la democracia	*democracy*
la dictadura	*dictatorship*
el estado	*state*
el gobierno	*government*
la ley	*law*
la monarquía	*monarchy*
la presidencia	*presidency*
la provincia	*province*
la región	*region*
el senado	*senate*

Las elecciones — *Elections*

la campaña	*campaign*
el discurso	*speech*
la encuesta	*survey; poll*
el partido político	*political party*
el voto	*vote*

Otras palabras útiles — *Other useful words*

el aire	*air*
la basura	*garbage*
la calidad	*quality*
la capa de ozono	*ozone layer*
el cielo	*sky; heaven*
el desastre	*disaster*
la destrucción	*destruction*
la ecología	*ecology*
el efecto invernadero	*global warming*
la lluvia ácida	*acid rain*
la naturaleza	*nature*
el planeta	*planet*
puro/a	*pure*
el recurso natural	*natural resource*
la selva tropical	*jungle; (tropical) rain forest*
la Tierra	*Earth*
la tierra	*land; soil*
la tragedia	*tragedy*
el vertedero	*dump*
vivo/a	*alive; living*

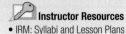

Instructor Resources
• IRM: Syllabi and Lesson Plans

NATIONAL STANDARDS

COMUNICACIÓN

• To communicate preferences regarding food and clothing (Communication)
• To relate ideas about past experiences and your daily routine (Communication)
• To convey information about people and things (Communication)
• To express ideas on topics such as health, travel, animals, the environment, and politics (Communication, Connections, Communities)
• To make requests and give advice using commands (Communication)
• To articulate desires and opinions on a variety of topics (Communication)

CULTURA

• To share information about Chile, Paraguay, Argentina, Uruguay, Perú, Bolivia, Ecuador, Venezuela, Colombia, Cuba, Puerto Rico, and La República Dominicana (Cultures, Comparisons, Communication)
• To compare and contrast the countries you learned about in *Capítulos 7–11* (Cultures, Comparisons)

AMBICIONES SINIESTRAS

• To go behind the scenes of *Ambiciones siniestras* (Communication)

COMUNIDADES

• To use Spanish in real-life contexts

12 Y por fin, ¡lo sé!

This final chapter is designed for you to see just how much Spanish you have acquired thus far. The *major points* of **Capítulos 7–11** are recycled in this chapter. No new vocabulary is presented.

All learners are different in terms of what they have mastered and what they still need to practice. Take the time with this chapter to determine what you feel confident with, and what you personally need to work on. And remember, language learning is a process. Like any skill, learning Spanish requires practice, review of the basics, and then more practice!

Before we begin revisiting the important grammar concepts, go to the end of each chapter, to the **Vocabulario activo** summary sections, and review the vocabulary that you have learned. Doing so now will help you successfully and creatively complete the following recycling activities. Consult the **Vocabulario activo** pages as needed as you progress through this chapter.

332

METHODOLOGY • Philosophy on Recycling

This chapter is unique in *¡Anda! Curso elemental* because it presents an opportunity for instructors and students to have yet another assessment regarding language acquired. In this chapter, *¡Anda!* has synthesized the main points of the final 5 chapters in a recycled format for students to practice the new skills they are learning. You will note that all of these activities have the students *put it all together*; in other words, *virtually all of the activities in Capítulo 12 are communicative*. There are no discrete-point mechanical

activities; some are structured, meaningful activities that help students build towards communicative practice. For mechanical practice, we direct students to make use of the activities in MySpanishLab, or to repeat the activities in their Student Activities Manual or in the textbook itself.

Finally, if you have advanced or heritage language learners, this is an excellent chapter for them, since most of the activities afford them the opportunity to be highly creative.

OBJETIVOS

COMUNICACIÓN

To communicate preferences regarding food and clothing

To relate ideas about past experiences and your daily routine

To convey information about people and things

To express ideas on topics such as health, travel, animals, the environment, and politics

To make requests and give advice using commands

To articulate desires and opinions on a variety of topics

CULTURA

To share information about Chile, Paraguay, Argentina, Uruguay, Perú, Bolivia, Ecuador, Venezuela, Colombia, Cuba, Puerto Rico, and La República Dominicana

To compare and contrast the countries you learned about in **Capítulos 7–11**

AMBICIONES SINIESTRAS

To go behind the scenes of **Ambiciones siniestras**

COMUNIDADES

To use Spanish in real-life contexts (SAM)

METHODOLOGY • Organizing a Review for Students
Researchers and reviewers of *¡Anda! Curso elemental* agree: after giving students strategies on how to conduct an overall review, this chapter is organized by beginning with communicative and engaging activities that focus on grammar and vocabulary from *Capítulo 7*. The recycling continues to move through the chapters, ending with *Capítulo 11*. This is followed by *Un poco de todo*, a more comprehensive review, after which students are truly *putting all the chapters together*. Finally, there is a recycling of countries presented in *Capítulos 7–11* as well as *Ambiciones siniestras*.

METHODOLOGY • Recycling vs. Reviewing
In *¡Anda! Curso elemental*, recycling has meant taking previously learned material and recombining it with new material. This concept is supported by Gagné's learning concept of spiraling information. The concept of *review* is revisiting a topic, much like one does before an exam. *Review* is best illustrated in *Capítulo 7 (Un repaso del complemento directo)*, as well as in this chapter. No new information is presented, but rather a review affords students the opportunity to practice in a systematic fashion.

PLANNING AHEAD
You may wish to point out to your students Appendix 1, *Capítulo 12*, where they can find a list of the grammar points reviewed in this chapter.

METHODOLOGY • Prioritizing Review Topics

You will note that *¡Anda! Curso elemental* has listed four grammar topics (*past tenses, pronouns, commands,* and *subjunctive*) that we denote as *major* and upon which we are encouraging our students to focus the majority of their review time. Students become overwhelmed when told that *everything* is major. They then tend to make poor choices on where to focus the majority of their time spent reviewing. Granted, those four topics are indeed major and need to be broken down into chunks by your students, so that the past tense becomes *preterit (regular* and *irregular verbs), imperfect (regular* and *irregular verbs),* and *when to use preterit/imperfect.* Then the pronouns are broken down into *direct object, indirect object,* and *reflexive pronouns.* The same breakdown continues with the *commands* and the *introduction to the subjunctive.* Our goal by listing *four* topics is to encourage students with the "you-can-do-it" kind of attitude as opposed to discouraging them from the task at hand. Also, many students may feel confident with some or all four of the overarching concepts from *Capítulos 7–11.* If we were to present this material focusing on the enormity of the task, many students would lose confidence and begin to doubt themselves. Doubting oneself is counterproductive to the task at hand.

Please understand that we are not diminishing the importance of concepts such as demonstrative adjectives or expressions with *hacer,* but what we are saying is that if students were to communicate with a sympathetic native speaker, they would still be understood even with mistakes in those areas. We have used as our guide the *ACTFL Proficiency Guidelines,* as well as the *Spanish Advanced Placement* descriptors. Also guiding us is the fact that, when constructing final exams, the vast majority of points fall into the *expressing oneself in the past, usage of pronouns, commands,* and *subjunctive* categories.

METHODOLOGY • Tools for Reviewing

If your students choose (or you strongly encourage them) to gain more mechanical practice, prior to beginning the activities in this chapter, have them repeat the activities they have already done in the *¡Anda! Curso elemental* textbook, in the Student Activities Manual and MySpanishLab. All are an excellent start for their review. Re-doing activities is an important review tool that is based on learning theory. This works for the

Organizing Your Review

There are processes used by successful language learners for reviewing a world language. The following tips can help you organize your review. There is no one correct way, but these are some suggestions that will best utilize your time and energy.

1 Reviewing Strategies

1. Make a list of the *major* topics you have studied and need to review, dividing them into categories: *vocabulary, grammar,* and *culture.* These are the topics where you need to focus the majority of your time and energy.
   Note: The two-page chapter openers can help you determine the *major* topics.
2. Allocate a minimum of an hour each day over a period of days to review. Budget the majority of your time with the major topics. After beginning with the major grammar and vocabulary topics, review the secondary/supporting grammar topics and the culture. Cramming the night before a test is *not* an effective way to review and retain information.
3. Many educational researchers suggest that you start your review with the most recent chapter, or for this review, **Capítulo 11.** The most recent chapter is the freshest in your mind, so you tend to remember the concepts better, and you will experience quick success in your review.
4. Spend the most amount of time on concepts in which you determine *you* need to improve. Revisit the self-assessment tools from **Y por fin, ¿cómo andas?** in each chapter to see how you rated yourself. Those tools are designed to help you become good at self-assessing what *you* need to work on the most.

2 Reviewing Grammar

1. When reviewing grammar, begin with the *major* points, that is, begin with the *preterit, imperfect, pronouns (direct, indirect, and reflexive), commands,* and the *subjunctive.* After feeling confident using the major grammar points correctly, then proceed with the additional grammar points and review them.
2. Good ways to review include redoing activities in your textbook, redoing activities in your Student Activities Manual, and (re)doing activities on MySpanishLab.

3 Reviewing Vocabulary

1. When studying vocabulary, it is usually most helpful to look at the English word, and then say or write the word in Spanish. Make a special list of words that are difficult for you to remember, writing them in a small notebook or in an electronic file. Pull out the notebook every time you have a few minutes (in between classes, waiting in line at the grocery store, etc.) to review the words. The **Vocabulario activo** pages at the end of each chapter will help you organize the most important words of each chapter.
2. Saying vocabulary (which includes verbs) out loud helps you retain the words better.

4 Overall Review Technique

1. Get together with someone with whom you can practice speaking Spanish. It is always good to structure the oral practice. If you need something to spark the conversation, take the drawings from each vocabulary presentation in *¡Anda! Curso elemental* and say as many things as you can about each picture. Have a friendly challenge to see who can make more complete sentences or create the longest story about the pictures. This will help you build your confidence and practice stringing sentences together to speak in paragraphs.
2. Yes, it is important for you to know "mechanical" pieces of information such as verb endings, or how to take a sentence and replace the direct object with a pronoun. *But,* it is *much more important* for you to be able to take those mechanical pieces of information and put them all together, creating meaningful and creative samples of your speaking and writing on the themes of **Capítulos 7–11.** Also remember that **Capítulos 7–11** are built upon previous knowledge that you acquired in the beginning chapters of *¡Anda! Curso elemental.*
3. You are on the road to success if you can demonstrate that you can speak and write in paragraphs, using a wide variety of verbs and vocabulary words correctly. Keep up the good work!

following reasons. First, students are already familiar with the context of the activities, know what they got correct and missed the first time, and hence are able to observe whether they have improved. They also are repeating the activities on a different level; since they have already completed the activities, these repetitions go to a meta-analysis level, in which they need to analyze why they continue to miss certain items. The same learning theory concept is similar in music, in which we practice the same scales and arpeggios over and over.

METHODOLOGY • Using This Chapter

Although most of the activities in this chapter utilize the pair icon, you will note that most can be done at home. You can choose whether you want these activities to be oral, written, or a combination of oral and written. You can also choose whether you want the activities to be prepared outside of class or done in class. The decisions are yours to personalize the chapter in a manner that best suits your needs and those of your students.

Un poco de todo

12-33 to 12-41

12-21 Nuestro medio ambiente y más aún Creen juntos un reportaje (*report*) para la televisión sobre uno de los siguientes temas. ∎

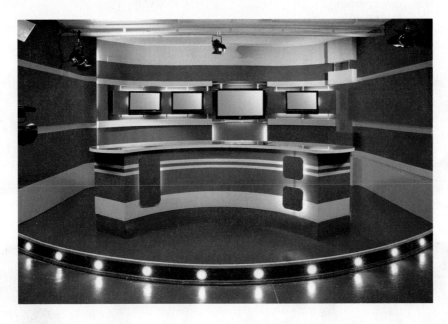

TEMAS

1. el medio ambiente
2. la política
3. el tiempo
4. el arte, la música, los deportes y otros eventos

NOTE for *Un poco de todo*
In the *Un poco de todo* section, each activity combines concepts from all of the previous chapters resulting in comprehensive, highly communicative review activities.

NOTE for *Un poco de todo*
In the *Un poco de todo* section, students put together all the information they have learned thus far. These activities show students how much they have progressed in their competence with Spanish and their ability to communicate. You might decide to film the *entrevistas* and *reportajes* as examples for future students, using the MediaShare feature in MySpanishLab. Additionally, these videos will demonstrate to your current students how much they have learned throughout the course. If you have "potential" Spanish minors/majors in the course, this would be useful for their language learning portfolio.

NOTE for *Un poco de todo*
Remind students that activities 12-1 to 12-20 can be found in the eText in MySpanishLab for additional practice.

SUGGESTION for 12-21
You may want to ask your students to make a PowerPoint presentation, video, or podcast based on this activity.

METHODOLOGY • Self-Assessment and Instructor's Use of Rubrics
Assessing student performance is an important task that we instructors perform. Students need to know in advance what is acceptable versus unacceptable work. It is important that students are provided in advance with the rubrics so that they are clear regarding our expectations.

The rubrics provided online in the eText are meant to be used either as is or to act as a guide for you. The suggestion is that 3 = A; 2 = B; 1 = C; 0 = D/F. Also notice that there is a place for you to assess effort. As instructors, we know that there will be some students who look for and take the easy way out, even though they may have the ability. These can be gifted students or heritage language learners who choose not to work to their potential. The effort rating is a way of encouraging those students as well as giving credit to students who struggle but are working above and beyond their level of ability. These students deserve to be rewarded for their efforts.

You may wish to add other categories such as pronunciation to the rubric as well.

12-22 **¿Cómo eres?** Conoces un poco a los estudiantes de los países que estudiamos en los capítulos anteriores. ¿Qué más quieres saber de ellos? Escribe por lo menos **diez** preguntas que quieras hacerles. Usa **el pretérito, el imperfecto** y **el subjuntivo** en tus preguntas. ■

MODELO
1. ¿Qué estudiaste el semestre pasado?
2. ¿Adónde fuiste el verano pasado?
3. ¿Es posible que viajes este verano?
4. …

Gino Breschi Arteaga

Sandra Manrique Esquivel

María Graciela Martelli Paz

Francisco Tomás Bacigalupe Bustamante

Diana Ávila Peralta

Jorge Gustavo Salazar

Yolanda Pico Briones

Rosa María Gutiérrez Murcia

Joaquín Navas Posada

Alicia Ortega Mujica

Pablo Colón Padín

Amparo Burgos Báez

12-23 **¿Sabías que...?** Completa los siguientes pasos. ■

Workbooklet

Paso 1 Escribe dos cosas interesantes que no sabías antes pero que aprendiste sobre cada uno de los siguientes países.

CHILE	PARAGUAY	ARGENTINA	URUGUAY
1.	1.	1.	1.
2.	2.	2.	2.

PERÚ	BOLIVIA	ECUADOR	COLOMBIA
1.	1.	1.	1.
2.	2.	2.	2.

VENEZUELA	CUBA	PUERTO RICO	LA REPÚBLICA DOMINICANA
1.	1.	1.	1.
2.	2.	2.	2.

Paso 2 Compara la información con el lugar donde vives. ¿Qué cosas son similares? ¿Qué diferencias hay?

SUGGESTION for 12-24
You may wish to make this a class
activity where students bring the *platos*
to class, along with the recipes. You
could compile the recipes to "publish" a
class cookbook. Your students could also
share the recipes with your school's food
service and perhaps have a Hispanic or
international foods day.

12-24 **¡A cocinar!** Vas a preparar una cena latina para tus amigos con platos representativos de varios países. Selecciona por lo menos **tres** platos y **una** bebida. Indica el país de origen de cada plato y los ingredientes. Si varios países comparten el plato, menciónalos también.

La parrillada

El chivito

EXPANSION for 12-25
Have students compare their chosen
symbols with symbols of their own
country.

12-25 **Los símbolos nacionales** Escoge **tres** países distintos y un símbolo para cada uno de ellos. Describe estos símbolos nacionales y habla de cómo y por qué son representativos del país. Después, haz una comparación entre los países y sus símbolos. ■

12-26 **¿El ecoturismo o una expedición antropológica?**
¡Qué suerte! Recibiste la distinción de ser el/la mejor estudiante de español y puedes elegir entre un viaje de ecoturismo o una expedición antropológica. Piensa en lo que aprendiste de cada país y decide adónde quieres ir para divertirte e investigar más. Después, describe el lugar específico que vas a visitar y di por qué, cómo, cuándo, etc. Si hay dos países con lugares similares, compáralos e indica por qué seleccionaste uno en particular. ■

12-27 **Tus propias ambiciones siniestras** ¡Ahora te toca a ti!

Episodio 12   Puedes seleccionar entre las siguientes actividades basadas en **Ambiciones siniestras.** ■

 1. Imagina que eres David Letterman o Cristina y que tienes la oportunidad de entrevistar a los actores de **Ambiciones siniestras.** Prepara la entrevista con un/a compañero/a.

2. Escribe tu propia versión resumida de **Ambiciones siniestras.** ¿Termina igual que el original? Compara tu versión con la de un/a compañero/a.

3. Escribe y filma **Ambiciones siniestras II.** Al final, ¿qué pasa con el Sr. Verdugo? Preséntale tu película a la clase.

CAPÍTULO 12

NOTE for 12-27
Episodio 12 is a behind-the-scenes compilation of *Ambiciones siniestras.* The video includes outtakes as well as interviews with the actors.

SUGGESTION for 12-27
Film your students' versions of *Ambiciones siniestras II* using the MediaShare feature in MySpanishLab and have the class vote on their favorite version.

NOTE to Instructors
To our esteemed colleagues: our most heartfelt thank you for using the *¡Anda! Curso elemental* instructional program. We encourage you to submit any comments or questions you may have to your local sales representative, or to the World Languages Division at Pearson Arts & Sciences. If you have enjoyed teaching with *¡Anda! Curso elemental* as much as we have enjoyed creating the program, please consider using *¡Anda! Curso intermedio* for your intermediate courses.

Y por fin, ¿cómo andas?

	Feel confident	Need to review
Having completed this chapter, I now can . . .		
Comunicación		
• communicate preferences regarding food and clothing	☐	☐
• relate ideas about past experiences and my daily routine	☐	☐
• convey information about people and things	☐	☐
• express ideas on topics such as health, travel, animals, the environment, and politics	☐	☐
• make requests and give advice using commands	☐	☐
• articulate desires and opinions on a variety of topics	☐	☐
Cultura		
• share information about Chile, Paraguay, Argentina, Uruguay, Perú, Bolivia, Ecuador, Venezuela, Colombia, Cuba, Puerto Rico, and La República Dominicana	☐	☐
• compare and contrast the countries I learned about in **Capítulos 7–11**	☐	☐
Ambiciones siniestras		
• go behind the scenes of **Ambiciones siniestras**	☐	☐
Comunidades		
• use Spanish in real-life contexts (SAM)	☐	☐

Appendix 1

Inductive Grammar Answers to
¡Explícalo tú! in the eText

Capítulo Preliminar A

12. Gustar

1. To say you like or dislike one thing, what form of **gustar** do you use?
   gusta
2. To say you like or dislike more than one thing, what form of **gustar** do you use?
   gustan

Capítulo 2

9. El verbo *gustar*

1. To say you like or dislike one thing, what form of **gustar** do you use?
   gusta
2. To say you like or dislike more than one thing, what form of **gustar** do you use?
   gustan
3. Which words in the examples mean *I?* **(Me)** *You?* **(Te)** *He/she?* **(le)**
4. If a verb is needed after **gusta/gustan,** what form of the verb do you use?
   the infinitive form of the verb

Capítulo 4

4. Los verbos con cambio de raíz

1. Which verb forms look like the infinitive **cerrar**?
   nosotros, vosotros
2. Which verb forms have a spelling change that differs from the infinitive **cerrar**?
   yo, tú, él, ella, usted, ellos, ellas, ustedes

1. Which verb forms look like the infinitive **pedir**?
   nosotros, vosotros
2. Which verb forms have a spelling change that differs from the infinitive **pedir**?
   yo, tú, él, ella, usted, ellos, ellas, ustedes

1. Which verb forms look like the infinitive **encontrar**?
   nosotros, vosotros
2. Which verb forms have a spelling change that differs from the infinitive **encontrar**?
   yo, tú, usted, él, ella, ustedes, ellos, ellas

A1

1. Which verb forms look like the infinitive **jugar**?
   nosotros, vosotros
2. Which verb forms have a spelling change that differs from the infinitive **jugar**?
   yo, tú, usted, él, ella, ustedes, ellos, ellas
3. Why does **jugar** not belong with the verbs like **encontrar**?
   because the change is *u → ue*, not *o → ue* like *encontrar*

To summarize . . .

1. What is a rule that you can make regarding all four groups of stem-changing verbs and their forms?
   ***Nosotros/vosotros* look like the infinitive. All the other forms have the spelling change.**
2. With what group of stem-changing verbs would you put **querer**?
   e → ie
3. With what group of stem-changing verbs would you put the following verbs:

demostrar	*to demonstrate*	**o → ue**
devolver	*to return (an object)*	**o → ue**
encerrar	*to enclose*	**e → ie**
perseguir	*to chase*	**e → i**

6. *Ir + a* + infinitivo

1. When do the actions in these sentences take place: in the *past*, *present*, or *future*?
   future
2. What is the first bold type verb you see in each sentence?
   a form of *ir*
3. In what form is the second bolded verb?
   infinitive
4. What word comes between the two verbs?
   a

   Does this word have an equivalent in English?
   no
5. What is your rule, then, for expressing future actions or statements?
   use a form of *ir + a* + infinitive

8. Las expresiones afirmativas y negativas

1. When you use a negative word (**nadie, nunca,** etc.) in a sentence, does it come before or after the verb?
   The negative word can go either before or after the verb.
2. When you use the word **no** and then a negative word in the same sentence, does **no** come before or after the verb?
   ***No* comes before the verb.**

   Where does the negative word come in these sentences?
   The negative word can go either before or after the verb.
3. Does the meaning change depending on where you put the negative word? (E.g., **Nadie llama** *versus* **No llama nadie.**)
   No, the meaning stays the same.

9. Un repaso de *ser* y *estar*

1. Why do you use a form of **ser** in the first sentence?
   because it is a characteristic that remains relatively constant
2. Why do you use a form of **estar** in the second sentence?
   because it describes a physical or personality characteristic that can change, or a change in condition

Capítulo 5

2. Los adjetivos demostrativos

1. When do you use **este, ese,** and **aquel**?
   when you want to point out *one* masculine person or object
2. When do you use **esta, esa,** and **aquella**?
   when you want to point out *one* feminine person or object
3. When do you use **estos, esos,** and **aquellos**?
   when you want to point out *two or more* masculine persons or objects, or a mix of masculine and feminine persons or objects
4. When do you use **estas, esas,** and **aquellas**?
   when you want to point out *two or more* feminine persons or objects

5. El presente progresivo

1. What is the infinitive of the first verb in each sentence that is in *italics*?
   estar
2. What are the infinitives of **haciendo, estudiando, escuchando, tocando, viendo,** and **escribiendo**?
   hacer, estudiar, escuchar, tocar, ver, escribir
3. How do you form the verb forms in **boldface**?
   Take the infinitive, drop the *-ar, -er,* or *-ir,* and add *-ando* or *-iendo*.
4. In this new tense, the *present progressive*, do any words come between the two parts of the verb?
   no
5. Therefore, your formula for forming the present progressive is:
   a form of the verb *estar* + a verb ending in *-ando* or *-iendo*

Capítulo 6

Major grammar points to be reviewed

1. Present tense of:
   Regular **-ar, -er, -ir** verbs
   Irregular verbs
   Stem-changing verbs e → ie, e → i, o → ue, u → ue
2. Future tense *ir + a + infinitive*
3. Use of direct object pronouns

A3

4. Correctly using **ser** and **estar**
5. Correctly using **gustar**

Major vocabulary to be reviewed

1. The *Vocabulario activo* at the end of each chapter

Major cultural information to be reviewed

1. At least two facts about each of the feature countries
2. At least one point about each of the two culture presentations in each chapter

Capítulo 7

2. Repaso del complemento directo

1. What are direct objects?
   Direct objects receive the action of verbs, answering the questions *what* and *whom*.
   What are direct object pronouns?
   Direct object pronouns replace direct objects.
2. What are the pronouns (forms)? With what must they agree?
   The pronoun forms are *me, te, lo, la, nos, los, las*. They must agree with direct objects.
3. Where are direct object pronouns placed in a sentence?
   They are placed either before verbs or attached to infinitives, *-ando*, or *-iendo*.

3. El pretérito (Parte I)

1. What do you notice about the endings for **-er** and **-ir** verbs?
   They are the same.
2. Where are accent marks needed?
   Accent marks are needed on the *yo* and *él/ella/usted* forms.

Capítulo 8

2. Los pronombres de complemento indirecto

1. Who is buying the clothing?
   Mi madre.
2. Who is receiving the clothing?
   Mi madre **me** compra mucha ropa.
   I am receiving the clothes.
   Mi madre **te** compra mucha ropa.

You are receiving the clothes.
Mi madre **le** compra mucha ropa a usted.
You are receiving the clothes.
Mi madre **le** compra mucha ropa a mi hermano.

My brother is receiving the clothes.
Mi madre **nos** compra mucha ropa.
We are receiving the clothes.
Mi madre **os** compra mucha ropa.

You all are receiving the clothes.
Mi madre **les** compra mucha ropa a ustedes.

You all are receiving the clothes.
Mi madre **les** compra mucha ropa a mis hermanos.
My brothers are receiving the clothes.

¿Me (i.o.) traes la falda gris (d.o.)?	*Will you bring me the gray skirt?*
Su novio le (i.o.) regaló la chaqueta mas formal (d.o.).	*Her boyfriend gave her the more formal jacket.*
Mi hermana me (i.o.) compró la blusa elegante (d.o.).	*My sister bought me the elegant blouse.*
Nuestra compañera de cuarto nos (i.o.) lavó la ropa (d.o.).	*Our roommate washed our clothes for us.*

4. Los pronombres de complemento directo e indirecto usados juntos

1. You know that direct and indirect objects come after verbs. Where do you find direct and indirect object pronouns?
   before verbs or attached to infinitives or present participles
2. Reading from left to right, which pronoun comes first (direct or indirect)? Which pronoun comes second?
   The indirect object pronoun comes first, and the direct object pronoun comes second.

6. Las construcciones reflexivas

In each drawing:

Who is performing / doing the action?
   a. La fiesta
   b. Alberto
   c. Beatriz
   d. Raúl y Gloria
   e. Alberto
   f. Beatriz

Who or what is receiving the action?
   a. neighbors
   b. daughter
   c. car
   d. Raúl and Gloria
   e. Alberto
   f. Beatriz

Which of the drawings and captions demonstrate reflexive verbs?
the bottom row (Raúl y Gloria se despiertan. / Alberto se acuesta. / Beatriz se lava.)

A5

Capítulo 10

3. Los mandatos formales

1. Where do the object pronouns appear in affirmative commands?
attached to the command
In negative commands?
before the command and not attached
In what order?
i.o. / d.o.
2. Why are there written accents on some of the commands and not on others?
because some commands would change pronunciation without the accent marks

5. Otras formas del posesivo

1. What is the position of each possessive in the left-hand column? the middle column?
before the noun; after the noun
2. How do the possessive adjectives and pronouns agree?
They agree in number and gender with the nouns they describe or replace.
3. What do the sentences mean in the column on the right?
Mine works fine; Ours cost a lot; Where are yours? His/hers/yours is $100.
What have you removed from the previous sentence?
the noun

Capítulo 11

3. El subjuntivo

1. What is the difference between the subjunctive and the indicative moods?
The subjunctive expresses concepts such as doubts, emotions, wishes, and desires. The indicative reports events and happenings.
2. What other verb forms look like the subjunctive?
The *Usted* and *Ustedes* (formal) commands.
3. Where does the subjunctive verb come in relation to the word **que?**
after the word *que*

Capítulo 12

Major grammar points to be reviewed

1. Past tenses:
Regular and irregular preterit
Regular and irregular imperfect
Uses of the preterit and imperfect
2. Pronouns:
Direct object
Indirect object
Reflexive
Placement of pronouns

3. Commands:
   Informal affirmative and negative
   Formal affirmative and negative
4. Subjunctive:
   Formation
   Usage

Major vocabulary to be reviewed

1. The *Vocabulario activo* at the end of each chapter

Major cultural information to be reviewed

1. At least two facts about each of the feature countries
2. At least one point about each of the two culture presentations in each chapter

A7

Appendix 2

Verb Charts

Regular Verbs: Simple Tenses

Infinitive Present Participle Past Participle	Indicative						Subjunctive		Imperative
	Present	Imperfect	Preterit	Future	Conditional		Present	Imperfect	Commands
hablar hablando hablado	hablo hablas habla hablamos habláis hablan	hablaba hablabas hablaba hablábamos hablabais hablaban	hablé hablaste habló hablamos hablasteis hablaron	hablaré hablarás hablará hablaremos hablaréis hablarán	hablaría hablarías hablaría hablaríamos hablaríais hablarían		hable hables hable hablemos habléis hablen	hablara hablaras hablara habláramos hablarais hablaran	habla (tú), no hables hable (usted) hablemos hablad (vosotros), no habléis hablen (Uds.)
comer comiendo comido	como comes come comemos coméis comen	comía comías comía comíamos comíais comían	comí comiste comió comimos comisteis comieron	comeré comerás comerá comeremos comeréis comerán	comería comerías comería comeríamos comeríais comerían		coma comas coma comamos comáis coman	comiera comieras comiera comiéramos comierais comieran	come (tú), no comas coma (usted) comamos comed (vosotros), no comáis coman (Uds.)
vivir viviendo vivido	vivo vives vive vivimos vivís viven	vivía vivías vivía vivíamos vivíais vivían	viví viviste vivió vivimos vivisteis vivieron	viviré vivirás vivirá viviremos viviréis vivirán	viviría vivirías viviría viviríamos viviríais vivirían		viva vivas viva vivamos viváis vivan	viviera vivieras viviera viviéramos vivierais vivieran	vive (tú), no vivas viva (usted) vivamos vivid (vosotros), no viváis vivan (Uds.)

Regular Verbs: Perfect Tenses

Indicative					Subjunctive	
Present Perfect	Past Perfect	Preterit Perfect	Future Perfect	Conditional Perfect	Present Perfect	Past Perfect
he hablado	había hablado	hube hablado	habré hablado	habría hablado	haya hablado	hubiera hablado
has comido	habías comido	hubiste comido	habrás comido	habrías comido	hayas comido	hubieras comido
ha vivido	había vivido	hubo vivido	habrá vivido	habría vivido	haya vivido	hubiera vivido
hemos	habíamos	hubimos	habremos	habríamos	hayamos	hubiéramos
habéis	habíais	hubisteis	habréis	habríais	hayáis	hubierais
han	habían	hubieron	habrán	habrían	hayan	hubieran

Irregular Verbs

Infinitive / Present Participle / Past Participle	Indicative					Subjunctive		Imperative
	Present	Imperfect	Preterit	Future	Conditional	Present	Imperfect	Commands
andar andando andado	ando andas anda andamos andáis andan	andaba andabas andaba andábamos andabais andaban	anduve anduviste anduvo anduvimos anduvisteis anduvieron	andaré andarás andará andaremos andaréis andarán	andaría andarías andaría andaríamos andaríais andarían	ande andes ande andemos andéis anden	anduviera anduvieras anduviera anduviéramos anduvierais anduvieran	anda (tú), no andes ande (usted) andemos andad (vosotros), no andéis anden (Uds.)
caer cayendo caído	caigo caes cae caemos caéis caen	caía caías caía caíamos caíais caían	caí caíste cayó caímos caísteis cayeron	caeré caerás caerá caeremos caeréis caerán	caería caerías caería caeríamos caeríais caerían	caiga caigas caiga caigamos caigáis caigan	cayera cayeras cayera cayéramos cayerais cayeran	cae (tú), no caigas caiga (usted) caigamos caed (vosotros), no caigáis caigan (Uds.)
dar dando dado	doy das da damos dais dan	daba dabas daba dábamos dabais daban	di diste dio dimos disteis dieron	daré darás dará daremos daréis darán	daría darías daría daríamos daríais darían	dé des dé demos deis den	diera dieras diera diéramos dierais dieran	da (tú), no des dé (usted) demos dad (vosotros), no deis den (Uds.)
decir diciendo dicho	digo dices dice decimos decís dicen	decía decías decía decíamos decíais decían	dije dijiste dijo dijimos dijisteis dijeron	diré dirás dirá diremos diréis dirán	diría dirías diría diríamos diríais dirían	diga digas diga digamos digáis digan	dijera dijeras dijera dijéramos dijerais dijeran	di (tú), no digas diga (usted) digamos decid (vosotros), no digáis digan (Uds.)

A9

Irregular Verbs (continued)

Infinitive / Present Participle / Past Participle	Indicative Present	Indicative Imperfect	Indicative Preterit	Indicative Future	Indicative Conditional	Subjunctive Present	Subjunctive Imperfect	Imperative Commands
estar / estando / estado	estoy / estás / está / estamos / estáis / están	estaba / estabas / estaba / estábamos / estabais / estaban	estuve / estuviste / estuvo / estuvimos / estuvisteis / estuvieron	estaré / estarás / estará / estaremos / estaréis / estarán	estaría / estarías / estaría / estaríamos / estaríais / estarían	esté / estés / esté / estemos / estéis / estén	estuviera / estuvieras / estuviera / estuviéramos / estuvierais / estuvieran	está (tú), no estés / esté (usted) / estemos / estad (vosotros), no estéis / estén (Uds.)
haber / habiendo / habido	he / has / ha / hemos / habéis / han	había / habías / había / habíamos / habíais / habían	hube / hubiste / hubo / hubimos / hubisteis / hubieron	habré / habrás / habrá / habremos / habréis / habrán	habría / habrías / habría / habríamos / habríais / habrían	haya / hayas / haya / hayamos / hayáis / hayan	hubiera / hubieras / hubiera / hubiéramos / hubierais / hubieran	
hacer / haciendo / hecho	hago / haces / hace / hacemos / hacéis / hacen	hacía / hacías / hacía / hacíamos / hacíais / hacían	hice / hiciste / hizo / hicimos / hicisteis / hicieron	haré / harás / hará / haremos / haréis / harán	haría / harías / haría / haríamos / haríais / harían	haga / hagas / haga / hagamos / hagáis / hagan	hiciera / hicieras / hiciera / hiciéramos / hicierais / hicieran	haz (tú), no hagas / haga (usted) / hagamos / haced (vosotros), no hagáis / hagan (Uds.)
ir / yendo / ido	voy / vas / va / vamos / vais / van	iba / ibas / iba / íbamos / ibais / iban	fui / fuiste / fue / fuimos / fuisteis / fueron	iré / irás / irá / iremos / iréis / irán	iría / irías / iría / iríamos / iríais / irían	vaya / vayas / vaya / vayamos / vayáis / vayan	fuera / fueras / fuera / fuéramos / fuerais / fueran	ve (tú), no vayas / vaya (usted) / vamos, no vayamos / id (vosotros), no vayáis / vayan (Uds.)
oír / oyendo / oído	oigo / oyes / oye / oímos / oís / oyen	oía / oías / oía / oíamos / oíais / oían	oí / oíste / oyó / oímos / oísteis / oyeron	oiré / oirás / oirá / oiremos / oiréis / oirán	oiría / oirías / oiría / oiríamos / oiríais / oirían	oiga / oigas / oiga / oigamos / oigáis / oigan	oyera / oyeras / oyera / oyéramos / oyerais / oyeran	oye (tú), no oigas / oiga (usted) / oigamos / oíd (vosotros), no oigáis / oigan (Uds.)

A10

Irregular Verbs (continued)

Infinitive / Present Participle / Past Participle	Indicative Present	Imperfect	Preterit	Future	Conditional	Subjunctive Present	Imperfect	Imperative Commands
poder pudiendo podido	puedo puedes puede podemos podéis pueden	podía podías podía podíamos podíais podían	pude pudiste pudo pudimos pudisteis pudieron	podré podrás podrá podremos podréis podrán	podría podrías podría podríamos podríais podrían	pueda puedas pueda podamos podáis puedan	pudiera pudieras pudiera pudiéramos pudierais pudieran	
poner poniendo puesto	pongo pones pone ponemos ponéis ponen	ponía ponías ponía poníamos poníais ponían	puse pusiste puso pusimos pusisteis pusieron	pondré pondrás pondrá pondremos pondréis pondrán	pondría pondrías pondría pondríamos pondríais pondrían	ponga pongas ponga pongamos pongáis pongan	pusiera pusieras pusiera pusiéramos pusierais pusieran	pon (tú), no pongas ponga (usted) pongamos poned (vosotros), no pongáis pongan (Uds.)
querer queriendo querido	quiero quieres quiere queremos queréis quieren	quería querías quería queríamos queríais querían	quise quisiste quiso quisimos quisisteis quisieron	querré querrás querrá querremos querréis querrán	querría querrías querría querríamos querríais querrían	quiera quieras quiera queramos queráis quieran	quisiera quisieras quisiera quisiéramos quisierais quisieran	quiere (tú), no quieras quiera (usted) queramos quered (vosotros), no queráis quieran (Uds.)
saber sabiendo sabido	sé sabes sabe sabemos sabéis saben	sabía sabías sabía sabíamos sabíais sabían	supe supiste supo supimos supisteis supieron	sabré sabrás sabrá sabremos sabréis sabrán	sabría sabrías sabría sabríamos sabríais sabrían	sepa sepas sepa sepamos sepáis sepan	supiera supieras supiera supiéramos supierais supieran	sabe (tú), no sepas sepa (usted) sepamos sabed (vosotros), no sepáis sepan (Uds.)
salir saliendo salido	salgo sales sale salimos salís salen	salía salías salía salíamos salíais salían	salí saliste salió salimos salisteis salieron	saldré saldrás saldrá saldremos saldréis saldrán	saldría saldrías saldría saldríamos saldríais saldrían	salga salgas salga salgamos salgáis salgan	saliera salieras saliera saliéramos salierais salieran	sal (tú), no salgas salga (usted) salgamos salid (vosotros), no salgáis salgan (Uds.)

A11

Irregular Verbs (continued)

Infinitive / Present Participle / Past Participle	Indicative					Subjunctive		Imperative
	Present	Imperfect	Preterit	Future	Conditional	Present	Imperfect	Commands
ser / siendo / sido	soy eres es somos sois son	era eras era éramos erais eran	fui fuiste fue fuimos fuisteis fueron	seré serás será seremos seréis serán	sería serías sería seríamos seríais serían	sea seas sea seamos seáis sean	fuera fueras fuera fuéramos fuerais fueran	sé (tú), no seas sea (usted) seamos sed (vosotros), no seáis sean (Uds.)
tener / teniendo / tenido	tengo tienes tiene tenemos tenéis tienen	tenía tenías tenía teníamos teníais tenían	tuve tuviste tuvo tuvimos tuvisteis tuvieron	tendré tendrás tendrá tendremos tendréis tendrán	tendría tendrías tendría tendríamos tendríais tendrían	tenga tengas tenga tengamos tengáis tengan	tuviera tuvieras tuviera tuviéramos tuvierais tuvieran	ten (tú), no tengas tenga (usted) tengamos tened (vosotros), no tengáis tengan (Uds.)
traer / trayendo / traído	traigo traes trae traemos traéis traen	traía traías traía traíamos traíais traían	traje trajiste trajo trajimos trajisteis trajeron	traeré traerás traerá traeremos traeréis traerán	traería traerías traería traeríamos traeríais traerían	traiga traigas traiga traigamos traigáis traigan	trajera trajeras trajera trajéramos trajerais trajeran	trae (tú), no traigas traiga (usted) traigamos traed (vosotros), no traigáis traigan (Uds.)
venir / viniendo / venido	vengo vienes viene venimos venís vienen	venía venías venía veníamos veníais venían	vine viniste vino vinimos vinisteis vinieron	vendré vendrás vendrá vendremos vendréis vendrán	vendría vendrías vendría vendríamos vendríais vendrían	venga vengas venga vengamos vengáis vengan	viniera vinieras viniera viniéramos vinierais vinieran	ven (tú), no vengas venga (usted) vengamos venid (vosotros), no vengáis vengan (Uds.)
ver / viendo / visto	veo ves ve vemos veis ven	veía veías veía veíamos veíais veían	vi viste vio vimos visteis vieron	veré verás verá veremos veréis verán	vería verías vería veríamos veríais verían	vea veas vea veamos veáis vean	viera vieras viera viéramos vierais vieran	ve (tú), no veas vea (usted) veamos ved (vosotros), no veáis vean (Uds.)

Stem-Changing and Orthographic-Changing Verbs

Infinitive Present Participle Past Participle	Indicative — Present	Imperfect	Preterit	Future	Conditional	Subjunctive — Present	Imperfect	Imperative — Commands
almorzar (ue) (c) almorzando almorzado	almuerzo almuerzas almuerza almorzamos almorzáis almuerzan	almorzaba almorzabas almorzaba almorzábamos almorzabais almorzaban	almorcé almorzaste almorzó almorzamos almorzasteis almorzaron	almorzaré almorzarás almorzará almorzaremos almorzaréis almorzarán	almorzaría almorzarías almorzaría almorzaríamos almorzaríais almorzarían	almuerce almuerces almuerce almorcemos almorcéis almuercen	almorzara almorzaras almorzara almorzáramos almorzarais almorzaran	almuerza (tú), no almuerces almuerce (usted) almorcemos almorzad (vosotros), no almorcéis almuercen (Uds.)
buscar (qu) buscando buscado	busco buscas busca buscamos buscáis buscan	buscaba buscabas buscaba buscábamos buscabais buscaban	busqué buscaste buscó buscamos buscasteis buscaron	buscaré buscarás buscará buscaremos buscaréis buscarán	buscaría buscarías buscaría buscaríamos buscaríais buscarían	busque busques busque busquemos busquéis busquen	buscara buscaras buscara buscáramos buscarais buscaran	busca (tú), no busques busque (usted) busquemos buscad (vosotros), no busquéis busquen (Uds.)
corregir (i, i) (j) corrigiendo corregido	corrijo corriges corrige corregimos corregís corrigen	corregía corregías corregía corregíamos corregíais corregían	corregí corregiste corrigió corregimos corregisteis corrigieron	corregiré corregirás corregirá corregiremos corregiréis corregirán	corregiría corregirías corregiría corregiríamos corregiríais corregirían	corrija corrijas corrija corrijamos corrijáis corrijan	corrigiera corrigieras corrigiera corrigiéramos corrigierais corrigieran	corrige (tú), no corrijas corrija (usted) corrijamos corregid (vosotros), no corrijáis corrijan (Uds.)
dormir (ue, u) durmiendo dormido	duermo duermes duerme dormimos dormís duermen	dormía dormías dormía dormíamos dormíais dormían	dormí dormiste durmió dormimos dormisteis durmieron	dormiré dormirás dormirá dormiremos dormiréis dormirán	dormiría dormirías dormiría dormiríamos dormiríais dormirían	duerma duermas duerma durmamos durmáis duerman	durmiera durmieras durmiera durmiéramos durmierais durmieran	duerme (tú), no duermas duerma (usted) durmamos dormid (vosotros), no durmáis duerman (Uds.)
incluir (y) incluyendo incluido	incluyo incluyes incluye incluimos incluís incluyen	incluía incluías incluía incluíamos incluíais incluían	incluí incluiste incluyó incluimos incluisteis incluyeron	incluiré incluirás incluirá incluiremos incluiréis incluirán	incluiría incluirías incluiría incluiríamos incluiríais incluirían	incluya incluyas incluya incluyamos incluyáis incluyan	incluyera incluyeras incluyera incluyéramos incluyerais incluyeran	incluye (tú), no incluyas incluya (usted) incluyamos incluid (vosotros), no incluyáis incluyan (Uds.)

A13

Stem-Changing and Orthographic-Changing Verbs (continued)

Infinitive / Present Participle / Past Participle	Indicative					Subjunctive		Imperative
	Present	Imperfect	Preterit	Future	Conditional	Present	Imperfect	Commands
llegar (gu) / llegando / llegado	llego / llegas / llega / llegamos / llegáis / llegan	llegaba / llegabas / llegaba / llegábamos / llegabais / llegaban	llegué / llegaste / llegó / llegamos / llegasteis / llegaron	llegaré / llegarás / llegará / llegaremos / llegaréis / llegarán	llegaría / llegarías / llegaría / llegaríamos / llegaríais / llegarían	llegue / llegues / llegue / lleguemos / lleguéis / lleguen	llegara / llegaras / llegara / llegáramos / llegarais / llegaran	llega (tú), no llegues / llegue (usted) / lleguemos / llegad (vosotros), no lleguéis / lleguen (Uds.)
pedir (i, i) / pidiendo / pedido	pido / pides / pide / pedimos / pedís / piden	pedía / pedías / pedía / pedíamos / pedíais / pedían	pedí / pediste / pidió / pedimos / pedisteis / pidieron	pediré / pedirás / pedirá / pediremos / pediréis / pedirán	pediría / pedirías / pediría / pediríamos / pediríais / pedirían	pida / pidas / pida / pidamos / pidáis / pidan	pidiera / pidieras / pidiera / pidiéramos / pidierais / pidieran	pide (tú), no pidas / pida (usted) / pidamos / pedid (vosotros), no pidáis / pidan (Uds.)
pensar (ie) / pensando / pensado	pienso / piensas / piensa / pensamos / pensáis / piensan	pensaba / pensabas / pensaba / pensábamos / pensabais / pensaban	pensé / pensaste / pensó / pensamos / pensasteis / pensaron	pensaré / pensarás / pensará / pensaremos / pensaréis / pensarán	pensaría / pensarías / pensaría / pensaríamos / pensaríais / pensarían	piense / pienses / piense / pensemos / penséis / piensen	pensara / pensaras / pensara / pensáramos / pensarais / pensaran	piensa (tú), no pienses / piense (usted) / pensemos / pensad (vosotros), no penséis / piensen (Uds.)
producir (zc) (j) / produciendo / producido	produzco / produces / produce / producimos / producís / producen	producía / producías / producía / producíamos / producíais / producían	produje / produjiste / produjo / produjimos / produjisteis / produjeron	produciré / producirás / producirá / produciremos / produciréis / producirán	produciría / producirías / produciría / produciríamos / produciríais / producirían	produzca / produzcas / produzca / produzcamos / produzcáis / produzcan	produjera / produjeras / produjera / produjéramos / produjerais / produjeran	produce (tú), no produzcas / produzca (usted) / produzcamos / producid (vosotros), no produzcáis / produzcan (Uds.)
reír (i, i) / riendo / reído	río / ríes / ríe / reímos / reís / ríen	reía / reías / reía / reíamos / reíais / reían	reí / reíste / rio / reímos / reísteis / rieron	reiré / reirás / reirá / reiremos / reiréis / reirán	reiría / reirías / reiría / reiríamos / reiríais / reirían	ría / rías / ría / riamos / riáis / rían	riera / rieras / riera / riéramos / rierais / rieran	ríe (tú), no rías / ría (usted) / riamos / reíd (vosotros), no riáis / rían (Uds.)

A14

Stem-Changing and Orthographic-Changing Verbs (continued)

Infinitive Present Participle Past Participle	Indicative					Subjunctive		Imperative
	Present	Imperfect	Preterit	Future	Conditional	Present	Imperfect	Commands
seguir (i, i) (ga) siguiendo seguido	sigo sigues sigue seguimos seguís siguen	seguía seguías seguía seguíamos seguíais seguían	seguí seguiste siguió seguimos seguisteis siguieron	seguiré seguirás seguirá seguiremos seguiréis seguirán	seguiría seguirías seguiría seguiríamos seguiríais seguirían	siga sigas siga sigamos sigáis sigan	siguiera siguieras siguiera siguiéramos siguierais siguieran	sigue (tú), no sigas siga (usted) sigamos seguid (vosotros), no sigáis sigan (Uds.)
sentir (ie, i) sintiendo sentido	siento sientes siente sentimos sentís sienten	sentía sentías sentía sentíamos sentíais sentían	sentí sentiste sintió sentimos sentisteis sintieron	sentiré sentirás sentirá sentiremos sentiréis sentirán	sentiría sentirías sentiría sentiríamos sentiríais sentirían	sienta sientas sienta sintamos sintáis sientan	sintiera sintieras sintiera sintiéramos sintierais sintieran	siente (tú), no sientas sienta (usted) sintamos sentid (vosotros), no sintáis sientan (Uds.)
volver (ue) volviendo vuelto	vuelvo vuelves vuelve volvemos volvéis vuelven	volvía volvías volvía volvíamos volvíais volvían	volví volviste volvió volvimos volvisteis volvieron	volveré volverás volverá volveremos volveréis volverán	volvería volverías volvería volveríamos volveríais volverían	vuelva vuelvas vuelva volvamos volváis vuelvan	volviera volvieras volviera volviéramos volvierais volvieran	vuelve (tú), no vuelvas vuelva (usted) volvamos volved (vosotros), no volváis vuelvan (Uds.)

A15

Appendix 3

También se dice...

Capítulo Preliminar A

Los saludos/*Greetings*

¿Cómo andas? *How are you doing?*
¿Cómo vas? *How are you doing?*
El gusto es mío. *Pleased to meet you; The pleasure is all mine.*
Hasta entonces. *Until then.*
¿Qué hubo? *How's it going? What's happening? What's new?*
¿Qué pasa? *How's it going? What's happening? What's new?*
¿Qué pasó? *How's it going? What's happening? What's new?*

Las despedidas/*Farewells*

Nos vemos. *See you.*
Que te vaya bien. *Hope everything goes well.*
Que tenga(s) un buen día. *Have a nice day.*
Vaya con Dios. *Go with God.*

Las presentaciones/*Introductions*

Me gustaría presentarle a... *I would like to introduce you to . . . (formal)*
Me gustaría presentarte a... *I would like to introduce you to . . . (familiar)*

Expresiones útiles para la clase/*Useful classroom expressions*

Preguntas y respuestas/*Questions and answers*

(No) entiendo. *I (don't) understand.*
¿Puede repetir, por favor? *Could you repeat, please?*

Expresiones de cortesía/*Polite expressions*

Muchas gracias. *Thank you very much.*
No hay de qué. *Not at all.*

Mandato para la clase/*Instruction for class*

Saque(n) un bolígrafo/papel/lápiz. *Take out a pen/a piece of paper/a pencil.*

Las nacionalidades/*Nationalities*

argentino/a *Argentinian*
boliviano/a *Bolivian*
chileno/a *Chilean*
colombiano/a *Colombian*
costarricense *Costa Rican*
dominicano/a *Dominican*
ecuatoriano/a *Ecuadorian*
guatemalteco/a *Guatemalan*
hondureño/a *Honduran*
nicaragüense *Nicaraguan*
panameño/a *Panamanian*
peruano/a *Peruvian*
uruguayo/a *Uruguayan*
venezolano/a *Venezuelan*

Expresiones del tiempo/*Weather expressions*

el arco iris *rainbow*
el chirimiri *drizzle (Spain)*
Está despejado. *It's clear.*
Hace fresco. *It's cool.*
Hay neblina/niebla. *It's foggy.*
la humedad *humidity*
los copos de nieve *snowflakes*
las gotas de lluvia *raindrops*
el granizo *hail*
el hielo *ice*
el huracán *hurricane*
la llovizna *drizzle*
el pronóstico *weather forecast*
el/los rayo/s, el relámpago *lightning*
la tormenta *storm*
el tornado *tornado*
el/los trueno/s *thunder*

Capítulo 1

La familia/*Family*

el/la ahijado/a *godchild*
el bisabuelo *great-grandfather*
la bisabuela *great-grandmother*
el/la cuñado/a *brother-in-law/sister-in-law*
la familia política *in-laws*
el/la hermanastro/a *stepbrother/stepsister*
el /la hijastro/a *stepson/stepdaughter*
el/la hijo/a único/a *only child*
la madrina *godmother*
el/la medio/a hermano/a *half brother/half sister*
los medios hermanos *half brothers and sisters*
la mami *Mommy; Mom (Latin America)*
el marido *husband*
la mujer *wife*
los nietos *grandchildren*
la nuera *daughter-in-law*
el padrino *godfather*

el papi *Daddy; Dad (Latin America)*
el pariente *relative*
el/la prometido/a *fiancé(e)*
los sobrinos *nieces and nephews*
el/la suegro/a *father-in-law/mother-in-law*
los suegros *in-laws*
la tatarabuela *great-great-grandmother*
el tatarabuelo *great-great-grandfather*
la tía abuela *great-aunt*
el tío abuelo *great-uncle*
el/la viudo/a *widower/widow*
el yerno *son-in-law*

Otra palabra útil/*Another useful word*

divorciado/a *divorced*

La gente/*People*

el bato *friend; guy (in SE USA slang)*
el/la chaval/a *young man/young woman (Spain)*
el chamaco *young man (Cuba, Honduras, Mexico, El Salvador)*
el/la fulano/a *unknown man/woman*

Los adjetivos/*Adjectives*

La personalidad y otros rasgos/*Personality and other characteristics*

amable *nice; kind*
bobo/a *stupid; silly*
el/la bromista *person who likes to play jokes*
cariñoso/a *loving; affectionate*
chistoso/a *funny*
cursi *pretentious; affected*
divertido/a *funny*
educado/a *well mannered; polite*

elegante *elegant*
empollón/ona *bookworm; nerd*
encantador/a *charming; lovely*
espabilado/a *smart; vivacious; alert (Latin America)*
frustrado/a *frustrated*
gracioso/a *funny*
grosero/a *unpleasant*
histérico/a *crazed*
impaciente *impatient*
indiferente *indifferent*
irresponsable *irresponsible*
malvado/a *evil; wicked*
majo/a *pretty; nice (Spain)*
mono/a *pretty; nice (Spain, Caribbean)*
odioso/a *unpleasant*
pesado/a *annoying person*
pijo/a *posh; snooty (Spain)*
progre *liberal; progressive (Spain)*
sabelotodo *know-it-all*
viejo/a *old*

Las características físicas/*Physical characteristics*

atlético/a *athletic*
bello/a *beautiful (Latin America)*
blando/a *soft*
esbelto/a *slender*
flaco/a *thin*
frágil *fragile*
hermoso/a *beautiful; lovely*
musculoso/a *muscular*
robusto/a *sturdy*

Otras palabras útiles/*Other useful words*

demasiado/a *too much*
suficiente *enough*

Capítulo 2

Las materias y las especialidades/*Subjects and majors*

la agronomía *agriculture*
la antropología *anthropology*
el cálculo *calculus*
las ciencias políticas *political sciences*
las comunicaciones *communications*
la contabilidad *accounting*
la economía *economics*
la educación física *physical education*
la enfermería *nursing*
la filosofía *philosophy*
la física *physics*
la geografía *geography*
la geología *geology*
la historia *history*
la ingeniería *engineering*
la literatura comparada *comparative literature*
el mercadeo *marketing (Latin America)*
la mercadotecnia (el márketing) *marketing (Spain)*

la medicina del deporte *sports medicine*
la química *chemistry*
los servicios sociales *social work*
la sociología *sociology*
la terapia física *physical therapy*

En la sala de clase/*In the classroom*

el aula *classroom*
el/la alumno/a *student*
la bombilla *light bulb*
la cámara proyectora *overhead camera*
el cielorraso *ceiling*
el enchufe *wall socket*
el interruptor *light switch*
las luces *lights*
el ordenador *computer (Spain)*
la pantalla *screen*
el proyector *projector*
la prueba *test*
el pupitre *student desk*

A17

el rotulador *marker*
el sacapuntas *pencil sharpener*
el salón de clase *classroom*
el suelo *floor*
la tarima *dais; platform*

Los verbos/*Verbs*

apuntar *to point*
asistir a clase *to attend class*
beber *to drink*
entrar *to enter*
entregar *to hand in*
mirar *to look; to observe*
prestar atención *to pay attention*
repasar *to review*
responder *to answer*
sacar *to take out*
sacar buenas/malas notas *to get good/bad grades*
tomar apuntes *to take notes*

Las palabras interrogativas/*Interrogative words*

¿Con cuánto/a/os/as? *With how many . . . ?*
¿Con qué? *With what . . . ?*
¿Con quién? *With whom . . . ?*
¿De dónde? *From where . . . ?*
¿De qué? *About what . . . ?*
¿De quién? *Of whom . . . ?*

Emociones y estados/*Emotions and states of being*

agotado/a *exhausted*
agradable *nice*
alegre *happy*
asombrado/a *amazed; astonished*
asqueado/a *disgusted*
asustado/a *scared*
deprimido/a *depressed*
desanimado/a *discouraged; disheartened*
disgustado/a *upset*
dormido/a *sleepy*
emocionado/a *moved; touched*
entusiasmado/a *delighted*
fastidiado/a *annoyed; bothered*
ilusionado/a *thrilled*
optimista *optimistic*
pesimista *pessimistic*
retrasado/a *late*
sonriente *smiling*
soñoliento/a *sleepy (Spain)*

Los lugares/*Places*

el apartamento estudiantil *student apartment*
el campo de fútbol *football field*
el campus *campus*
la cancha de tenis/baloncesto *tennis/basketball court*
la/s casa/s de hermandad/es *fraternity and sorority housing*
el centro comercial *mall*
el comedor estudiantil *student dining hall*
la habitación *room*
la matrícula *registration*

el museo *museum*
la oficina de consejeros *guidance/advising office*
el supermercado *supermarket*
el teatro *theater*

La residencia/*The dorm*

los bafles *speakers (Spain)*
el calendario *calendar*
la cama *bed*
el iPod *iPod*
el Internet *Internet*
las literas *bunkbeds*
la llave *memory stick*
la mesita de noche *nightstand*
el móvil *cell phone (Spain)*
la redacción/la composición *essay*
la tarjeta de crédito *credit card*
la tarjeta de identidad; el carnet *ID card*
los videojuegos *video games*

Los deportes y los pasatiempos/*Sports and pastimes*

cazar *to hunt*
conversar con amigos *to talk with friends*
escalar *to go mountain climbing*
esquiar *to ski*
estar en forma *to be in shape*
hablar por teléfono *to talk on the phone*
hacer alpinismo *to go hiking*
hacer footing *to go jogging (Spain)*
hacer gimnasia *to exercise*
hacer senderismo *to hike*
hacer pilates *to do Pilates*
hacer yoga *to do yoga*
ir al centro comercial *to go the mall; to go downtown*
ir a fiestas *to go to parties*
ir a un partido de... *to go to a . . . game*
jugar al ajedrez *to play chess*
jugar al boliche *to bowl*
jugar al ráquetbol *to play racquetball*
jugar a videojuegos *to play video games*
levantar pesas *to lift weights*
ver videos *to watch videos*
montar a caballo *to go horseback riding*
pasear *to go out for a ride; to take a walk*
pasear en barco *to sail*
ir a navegar *to sail*
pescar *to fish*
practicar boxeo *to box*
practicar ciclismo *to cycle*
practicar lucha libre *to wrestle*
practicar las artes marciales *to do martial arts*
salir a cenar/comer *to go out to dinner/eat*
tirar un platillo volador *to throw a Frisbee*

Palabras asociadas con los deportes y los pasatiempos/*Words associated with sports and pastimes*

el/la aficionado/a *fan*
el bate *bat*

el campo *field*
los libros de…
    acción *action books*
    aventura *adventure books*
    cuentos cortos *short stories*
    ficción (ciencia-ficción) *fiction (science fiction)*
    horror *horror books*

    misterio *mystery books*
    romance *romance books*
    espías *spy books*
el palo de golf *golf club*
la pista *track*
la pista y el campo *track and field (Spain)*
la raqueta *racket*

Capítulo 3

La casa/*The house*

la alcoba *bedroom*
el armario empotrado *closet (Spain)*
el ático *attic*
la bodega *cellar*
la buhardilla *attic*
el clóset *closet (Latin America)*
el corredor *hall*
el cuarto *bedroom*
el despacho *office*
el desván *attic*
el pasillo *hallway*
el patio *patio; yard*
el placar *closet (Argentina)*
el portal *porch*
el porche *porch*
la recámara *bedroom (Mexico)*
el salón *salon; lounge; living room*
el tejado *roof*
la terraza *terrace; porch*
el vestíbulo *entrance hall*

En la sala y el comedor/*In the living room and dining room*

la banqueta/el banquillo *small seating stool*
la estantería *bookcase*
la mecedora *rocking chair*
la moqueta *carpet (Spain)*

En la cocina/*In the kitchen*

el congelador *deep freezer*
el friegaplatos *dishwasher*
el frigorífico *refrigerator (Spain)*
el horno *oven*
el lavavajillas *dishwasher (Spain)*
el taburete *bar stool*

Otras palabras/*Other words*

el aparato eléctrico *electric appliance*
la chimenea *chimney*
la cómoda *dresser*
las cortinas *curtains*
el espejo *mirror*
el fregadero *sink*
los gabinetes *cabinets*

la lavadora *washer*
la secadora *dryer*
el librero *bookcase (Mexico)*
la nevera *refrigerator*
las persianas *shutters; window blinds*

En el baño/*In the bathroom*

la cisterna *toilet water tank*
el espejo *mirror*
los grifos *faucets*
la jabonera *soap dish*
el toallero *towel rack*

En el dormitorio/*In the bedroom*

el edredón *comforter*
la frazada *blanket (Latin America)*

Los quehaceres de la casa/*Household chores*

barrer *to sweep*
cortar el césped *to cut the grass*
fregar los platos *to wash the dishes*
fregar los suelos *to clean the floors*
guardar la ropa *to put away clothes*
lavar la ropa *to do laundry*
ordenar *to put in order*
planchar la ropa *to iron*
quitar el polvo *to dust*
recoger *to clean up in general*
recoger la mesa *to clean up after a meal*
regar las plantas *to water the plants*
sacudir las alfombras *to shake out the rugs*
sacudir el polvo *to dust*

Expresiones con *tener*/*Expressions with* tener

tener celos *to be jealous*
tener novio/a *to have a boyfriend/girlfriend*

Los colores/*Colors*

color café *brown*
púrpura *purple (Spain)*
azul/verde claro *light blue/green*
azul/verde oscuro *dark blue/green*
rosa *pink (Spain)*

A19

Capítulo 4

Lugares en una ciudad o pueblo/*Places in a city or town*

la alberca *swimming pool; sports complex (Mexico)*
el ambulatorio *medical center (not a hospital) (Spain)*
el aseo *public restroom*
la catedral *cathedral*
el campo de golf *golf course*
la capilla *chapel*
la clínica *clinic*
el consultorio *doctor's office*
el convento *convent*
la cuadra *block (Latin America)*
la ferretería *hardware store*
la fogata *bonfire*
la frutería *fruit store*
la fuente *fountain*
la gasolinera *gas station*

la heladería *ice cream shop*
la manzana *block (Spain)*
el mercadillo *open-air market*
la mezquita *mosque*
la papelería *stationary store*
la panadería *bread store*
la pastelería *pastry shop*
la pescadería *fish shop; fishmonger*
la piscina *pool*
el polideportivo *sports center*
el quiosco *newsstand*
los servicios *public restrooms*
la sinagoga *synagogue*
la tienda de juguetes *toy store*
la tienda de ropa *clothing store*
el zócalo *plaza (Mexico)*

Capítulo 5

El mundo de la música/*The world of music*

la musica...
    alternativa *alternative music*
    bluegrass *bluegrass music*
el coro *choir*
el cuarteto *quartet*
el equipo de cámara/sonido *camera/sound crew*
el/la mánager *manager*
el merengue *merengue*
la música popular *popular music*
el/la organista *organist*
la pandilla *gang; posse*
los/las seguidores/as *groupies*
el teclado *keyboard*

El mundo del cine/*The world of film*

Gente/*People*

el/la cinematógrafo/a *cinematographer*
el/la director/a *director*
el/la guionista *scriptwriter*

Las películas/*Movies*

el cortometraje *short (film)*
los dibujos animados *cartoons*
el guión *script*
el montaje *montage*

Capítulo 7

Las carnes y las aves/*Meats and poultry*

las aves de corral *poultry*
la carne de cerdo *pork*
la carne de cordero *lamb*
la carne de res *beef*
la carne molida *ground beef*
la carne picada *ground beef (Spain)*
el chorizo *highly seasoned pork sausage*
la chuleta *chop*
el chuletón *T-bone (Spain)*
el jamón serrano *prosciutto ham (Spain)*
el pavo *turkey*
la salchicha *sausage; hot dog*
el salchichón *spiced sausage (Spain)*
la ternera *veal*
el tocino *bacon*

El pescado y los mariscos/*Fish and seafood*

las almejas *clams*
las anchoas *anchovies*

los calamares *squid*
el cangrejo *crab*
el chillo *red snapper (Puerto Rico)*
las gambas *shrimp*
el huachinango *red snapper (Mexico)*
la langosta *lobster*
el lenguado *flounder*
la ostra *oyster*
el pulpo *octopus*
la sardina *sardines*

Las frutas/*Fruits*

el aguacate *avocado*
el albaricoque *apricot*
el ananá *pineapple (Latin America)*
el banano *banana; banana tree*
la cereza *cherry*
la china *orange (Puerto Rico)*
la ciruela *plum*
el durazno *peach*

la fresa *strawberry*
el melocotón *peach*
la papaya *papaya*
la piña *pineapple*
el pomelo *grapefruit*
la sandía *watermelon*
la toronja *grapefruit*

Las verduras/*Vegetables*

las aceitunas *olives*
la alcaparra *caper*
el apio *celery*
la berza *cabbage (Spain)*
el calabacín *zucchini*
la calabaza *squash; pumpkin*
los champiñones *mushrooms*
la col *cabbage*
la coliflor *cauliflower*
los espárragos *asparagus*
las espinacas *spinach*
los guisantes *peas*
las habichuelas *kidney beans*
los hongos *mushrooms (Latin America)*
la judías verdes *green beans*
el pepinillo *pickle*
el pepino *cucumber*
el pimiento *pepper*
el plátano *plantain*
el repollo *cabbage*
la salsa *sauce*
las setas *wild mushrooms (Spain)*
la zanahoria *carrot*

Los postres/*Desserts*

el arroz con leche *rice pudding*
la batida *milkshake*
el batido *milkshake (Spain)*
los bocaditos *bite-size sandwiches*
los bollos *sweet bread*
el bombón *sweets; candy*
el caramelo *sweets; candy*
los chocolates *chocolates*
los chuches *candies in general (Spain)*
la dona *donut*
el dónut *donut (Spain)*
el flan *caramel custard*
la natilla *custard*
los pastelitos *turnover; pastry; finger cakes*
la tarta *cake*

Las bebidas/*Beverages*

el champán *champagne*
la sidra *cider*
el zumo *juice (Spain)*

Más comidas/*More foods*

el ajo *garlic*
la avena *oatmeal*
el caldo *broth*
el consomé *clear soup*
los fideos *noodles (in soup)*
la harina *flour*

la jalea *jelly; marmalade (Spain, Puerto Rico)*
la margarina *margarine*
la miel *honey*
el pan dulce *sweet roll*
el panqueque *pancake*
las tortas americanas *pancakes (Spain)*

Las comidas/*Meals*

el aperitivo *appetizer*
las tapas *hors d'oeuvres*

Los condimentos y las especias/*Condiments and spices*

el aderezo *seasoning; dressing*
el aliño *seasoning; dressing (Spain)*

Algunos términos de la cocina/*Some cooking terms*

agregar *to add*
asar *to roast; to broil*
aumentar libras/kilos *to gain weight*
batir *to beat*
calentar *to heat*
derretir *to melt*
espesarse *to thicken*
freír *to fry*
mezclar *to mix*
revolver *to stir*
servir *to serve*
unir *to combine*
verter *to pour*

Otras palabras útiles/*Other useful words*

aclararse *to thin*
añadir *to add*
el batidor *beater*
la batidora *hand-held mixer*
la cacerola *saucepan*
cocer *to cook*
la copa *goblet; wine glass*
el cuenco *bowl; mixing bowl*
echar (algo) *to add*
el fuego (lento, mediano, alto) *(low, medium, high) heat*
la fuente *serving platter/dish*
el ingrediente *ingredient*
el kilogramo *kilogram (or 2.2 pounds)*
el nivel *level*
la olla *pot*
el pedazo *piece*
el platillo *saucer*
el plato hondo *bowl*
el plato sopero *soup bowl*
la receta *recipe*
recalentar *to reheat*
remover *to stir (Spain)*
la sartén *frying pan*
el/la sopero/a *soup serving bowl*

En el restaurante/*In the restaurant*

la cucharilla *teaspoon (Spain)*
el friegaplatos *dishwasher (person)*
el/la mesero/a *waiter/waitress (Latin America)*
el/la pinche *kitchen assistant*

A21

Capítulo 8

La ropa y la joyería/Clothing and jewelry

el albornoz *bathrobe (Spain)*
las alpargatas *espadrille shoes (Spain)*
el anorak *rain-proof coat*
los aretes *earrings*
la bolsa *bag*
la bufanda *scarf*
la capa de agua *raincoat (Puerto Rico)*
la cartera *pocketbook, purse*
el chubasquero *raincoat (Spain)*
el collar *necklace*
la correa *belt*
el gorro *wool cap; hat*
los mahones *jeans (Puerto Rico)*
las pantallas *earrings (Puerto Rico)*
el peine *comb*
la peinilla *comb (Latin America)*
los pendientes *earrings*
la pulsera *bracelet*
la sombrilla *parasol; umbrella*
los vaqueros *jeans*
las zapatillas de tenis *sneakers; tennis shoes (Spain)*

Más palabras útiles/More useful words

de buena/mala calidad *good/poor quality*
de goma *(made of) rubber*
de lino *(made of) linen*
de manga corta/larga/media *short/long/half sleeve*

de nilón *nylon*
de oro *(made) of gold*
de plata *(made) of silver*
de platino *platinum*
de puntitos *polka dotted*

Para comprar ropa/To go clothes shopping

el escaparate *store window*
el/la dependiente/a *clerk*
la ganga *bargain*
la liquidación *clearance sale*
el maniquí *mannequin*
el mostrador *counter*
la oferta *offer; sale*
la rebaja *sale; discount*
el tacón alto/bajo *high/low heel*
la venta *clearance sale*
la vitrina *store window*
los zapatos planos/de cuña *flat/wedge shoes*

Algunos adjetivos/Some adjectives

amplio/a *wide*
apretado/a *tight*

Un verbo reflexivo/A reflexive verb

desvestirse (e → i → i) *to get undressed*

Capítulo 9

El cuerpo humano/The human body

la arteria *artery*
el cabello *hair*
la cadera *hip*
la ceja *eyebrow*
el cerebelo *cerebellum*
el cerebro *brain*
la cintura *waist*
el codo *elbow*
la costilla *rib*
la frente *forehead*
el hombro *shoulder*
el hueso *bone*
el labio *lip*
la lengua *tongue*
las mejillas *cheeks*
la muñeca *wrist*
el músculo *muscle*
el muslo *thigh*
los nervios *nerves*
la pestaña *eyelash*
la piel *skin*
el pulmón *lung*
la rodilla *knee*
el talón *heel*

el trasero *buttocks (Spain)*
el tobillo *ankle*
la uña *nail*
las venas *veins*

Algunas enfermedades/Some illnesses

el alcoholismo *alcoholism*
la alta tensión *high blood pressure*
el ataque del corazón *heart attack*
la baja tensión *low blood pressure*
el cáncer *cancer*
la depresión *depression*
la diabetes *diabetes*
el dolor de cabeza *headache*
el/la drogadicto/a *drug addict*
la hipertensión *high blood pressure*
el infarto *heart attack*
la inflamación *inflammation*
el mareo *dizziness*
la narcomanía *drug addiction*
la presión alta/baja *high/low blood pressure*
la quemadura *burn*
el sarampión *measles*
el SIDA *AIDS*
la varicela *chicken pox*

Otros verbos útiles/*Other useful verbs*

contagiarse de *to catch (an illness)*
desmayarse *to faint*
desvanecerse *to faint*
doblarse *to sprain*
enyesar *to put on a cast*
fracturar(se) *to break; to fracture*
hacer gárgaras *to gargle*
hinchar *to swell*
pegársele *to catch something*
recetar *to prescribe*
respirar *to breathe*
sacar la sangre *to draw blood*
tomarle la presión *to take someone's blood pressure*
tomarle el pulso *to take someone's pulse*
tomarle la temperatura *to check someone's temperature*
torcerse *to sprain*
vomitar *to vomit*

la camilla *stretcher*
la cura *cure*
la dosis *dosage*
la enfermedad *illness*
las gotas para los ojos *eyedrops*
los medicamentos *medicines*
las muletas *crutches*
operar *to operate*
el/la paciente *patient*
la penicilina *penicillin*
el pulso *pulse*
las pruebas médicas *medical tests*
la radiografía *X-ray*
el resultado *result*
retorcerse *to sprain*
el termómetro *thermometer*
la tirita *bandage*
la vacuna *vaccination*

Otras palabras útiles/*Other useful words*

las alergias *allergies*
el antihistamínico *antihistamine*

Capítulo 10

El transporte y otras palabras/*Transportation and other words*

el aparcamiento *parking lot*
el atasco *traffic jam*
el billete *ticket*
el camino *dirt road*
el camión *bus (Mexico)*
la camioneta *pickup truck; van; station wagon*
el carnet *driver's license (Spain)*
la carretera *highway*
enviar *to send; to dispatch*
la goma *tire (Latin America)*
la guagua *bus (Caribbean)*
el guía *steering wheel*
el paso de peatones *crosswalk*
el seguro del coche *car insurance*
el tiquete *ticket*
la velocidad *speed*

Algunas partes de un vehículo/*Some parts of a car*

el acelerador *accelerator; gas pedal*
el cinturón de seguridad *seat belt*
el claxon *horn*
el espejo retrovisor *rearview mirror*
los frenos *brakes*
las luces *lights*

el maletero *car trunk (Spain)*
el parachoques *bumper*
la transmisión *transmission*

Un verbo útil/*A useful verb*

perderse *to get lost*

El viaje/*Travel*

los cheques de viajero *traveler's checks*
la dirección *address*
el equipaje *luggage*
la estampilla *(postage) stamp*
la oficina de turismo *tourist office*
el paquete *package*
el pasaje de ida y vuelta *round-trip ticket*
los pasajes *(travel) tickets*
el sobre *the envelope*

El hotel/*The hotel*

el/la camarero/a *service maid*
el/la guardia de seguridad *security guard*
el/la portero/a *doorman/woman*
el/la recepcionista *receptionist*
el servicio *room service (cleaning)*
el/la telefonista *telephone operator*

A23

Capítulo 11

Algunos animales/Some animals

la abeja *bee*
la ardilla *squirrel*
la ballena *whale*
la cabra *goat*
el cangrejo *crab*
el ciervo *deer*
el cochino *pig*
la culebra *snake*
el dinosaurio *dinosaur*
la foca *seal*
el gallo *rooster*
el gorila *gorilla*
la iguana *iguana*
la jirafa *giraffe*
el lobo *wolf*
el loro *parrot*
la mariposa *butterfly*
el marrano *pig*
el mono *monkey*
el nido *nest*
la oveja *sheep*
la paloma *pigeon; dove*
el pato *duck*
el puerco *pig*
el pulpo *octopus*
el puma *puma*
el rinoceronte *rhinoceros*
el saltamontes *grasshopper*
el tiburón *shark*
el tigre *tiger*
la tortuga *turtle*
el venado *deer*
el zorro *fox*

El medio ambiente/The environment

el aerosol *aerosol*
el agua subterránea *ground water*
la Antártida *Antarctica*
el Ártico *the Arctic*
la atmósfera *atmosphere*
el aumento *increase*
el bióxido de carbono *carbon dioxide*
el carbón *coal*
el central nuclear *nuclear plant*
el clorofluorocarbono *chlorofluorocarbon*
el combustible fósil *fossil fuel*
la cosecha *crop; harvest*
la descomposición *decomposition*
el desperdicio de patio *yard waste*
el ecosistema *ecosystem*
la energía *energy*
la energía eólica (molinos de viento) *wind power (windmills)*

la industria *industry*
insoportable *unbearable; unsustainable*
el medio ambiente *environment*
el oxígeno *oxygen*
el país *country*
el pesticida *pesticide*
el petróleo *petroleum*
la piedra *rock; stone*
las placas solares *solar panels*
la planta eléctrica *power plant*
el plomo *lead*
el polvo *dust*
el rayo de sol *ray of sunlight*
el rayo ultravioleta *ultraviolet ray*
el riesgo *risk*

Algunos verbos/Some verbs

atrapar *to trap*
conseguir *to achieve*
corroer *to corrode*
dañar *to damage*
desarrollar *to evolve; to develop*
descongelarse *to melt; melt down*
destruir *to destroy*
hacer huelga *to go on strike*
hundirse *to sink*
luchar en contra *to fight against*
prevenir *to prevent*
realizar *to achieve*
tirar *to throw away (Spain)*

La política/Politics

la constitución *constitution*
la ciudadanía *citizenship*
el/la ciudadano/a *citizen*
el/la congresista *congressman/woman*
el gobierno *the government*
la monarquía constitucional *constitutional monarchy*
el paro general *general strike*
el/la primer/a ministro/a *prime minister*
el/la secretario/a de estado *secretary of state*

Las cuestiones políticas/Political issues

el aborto *abortion*
el abuso de menores *child abuse*
el derecho de trabajadores *workers' rights*
la eutanasia *euthanasia*
el genocidio *genocide*
la inmigración ilegal *illegal immigration*
la pena capital *death penalty*
la seguridad social *social security*
la violencia doméstica *domestic violence*

Appendix 4

Spanish-English Glossary

A

a to; at (11); **~ cambio** in exchange (4, PB); **~ eso de** around (7); **~ fin de** in order to (11); **~ la derecha (de)** to the right (of) (3, 11); **~ la izquierda (de)** to the left (of) (3, 11); **~ la parrilla** grilled (7); **~ mano** on hand (10); **~ menudo** often (2, 3); **¿~ qué hora...?** At what time? (PA); **~ veces** sometimes; from time to time (2, 3, 4); **~ ver** let's see (2)

abarcar to encompass (5)

Abra(n) el libro en la página... Open your book to page . . . (PA)

abrazo, el hug (PA)

abrigo, el coat; overcoat (3, 8)

abrir to open (2)

abuelo/a, el/la grandfather/grandmother (1)

abuelos, los grandparents (1)

aburrido/a boring; bored (*with* **estar**) (1, 2, 5)

acabar con end (4)

acabar de + infinitivo to have just finished + (*something*) (3, 9)

aceite, el oil (7)

acerca de about (11)

acercar to approach (8)

acierto, el match (11)

acompañar to accompany (6)

acordarse (o, ue) de to remember (8)

acostarse (o, ue) to go to bed (8)

actor, el actor (5)

actriz, la actress (5)

además de furthermore; in addition to (2, 7)

Adiós. Good-bye. (PA)

adivinar to guess (7)

adjetivos, los adjectives (1)

administración de empresas, la business (2)

¿Adónde? To where? (2)

advertir to warn (8)

aerolínea, la airline (10)

aeropuerto, el airport (10)

afeitarse to shave (8)

aficionado/a, el/la fan (5)

afuera de outside of (11)

afueras, las outskirts (3)

agencia de viajes, la travel agency (6, 10)

agente de viajes, el/la travel agent (10)

agua, el water; **~ (con hielo)** water (with ice) (5, 7); **~ dulce** fresh water (5)

ahora now (PB)

aire, el air (11); **~ acondicionado** air conditioning (10)

al horno baked (7)

al lado (de) beside; next to (3, 11)

alborotado/a stirred up (11)

alcalde, el mayor (11)

alcaldesa, la mayor (11)

alebrijes, los painted wooden animals (2)

alemán/alemana German (PA)

alfabetazación, la literacy (8)

alfombra, la rug; carpet (3)

algo something; anything (4, PB)

algodón, el cotton (8)

alguien someone (4)

algún some; any (4)

alguno/a/os/as some; any (3, 4)

allá over there (*and potentially not visible*) (6)

allí there / over there (4, 6)

almacén, el department store (4)

almohada, la pillow (3)

almorzar (ue) to have lunch (4, 7)

almuerzo, el lunch (7)

alpargatas, las espadrilles (8)

altillo, el attic (3)

altiplano, el high plateau (9)

alto/a tall (1)

aluminio, el aluminum (11)

amarillo yellow (3)

ambulante roving (4)

amenaza, la threat (8)

amenazada endangered (7)

amigo/a, el/la friend (1)

amor, el love (4)

amueblado/a furnished (3)

anaranjado orange (3)

ancho wide (7, 8)

andar to walk (7)

anillo, el ring (5)

animada animated (5)

animal, el animal (11); **~ doméstico** domesticated animal; pet (11); **~ en peligro de extinción** endangered species (11); **~ salvaje** wild animal (11)

año pasado, el last year (7)

anoche last night (7)

ante before (6)

anteayer the day before yesterday (7)

anterior previous (5)

antes de before (time/space) (11)

antiácido, el antacid (9)

antibiótico, el antibiotic (9)

antiguo/a old (3)

antipático/a unpleasant (1)

anuncio, el ad (3)

apartamento, el apartment (2)

apasionado/a passionate (5)

apéndice, el appendix (4)

apodo, el nickname (5)

apoyar to support (5, PB, 11); **~ a un/a candidato/a** to support a candidate (4)

aprender to learn (2)

aprobado/a approved (10)

apuntes, los (*pl.*) notes (2)

aquel/la that, that one (*way over there/not visible*) (5)

aquellos/as that, those (*way over there/not visible*); those ones (5)

aquí here (6)

árbol, el tree (11)

arbusto, el bush; shrub (7)

armario, el armoire; closet; cabinet (3)

arquitectura, la architecture (2)

arreglar to straighten up; to fix (3); **~se** to get ready (8); **~ la maleta** to pack a suitcase (10)

arroz, el rice (7)

arte, el art (2)

artículo, el article (1); **~ definido** definite article (1); **~ indefinido** indefinite article (1)

A25

artista, el/la artist (5)
asado/a roasted; grilled (7)
áspero/a rough (11)
aspirina, la aspirin (9)
asunto, el matter (6)
asustado/a frightened (7)
asustar to scare (9)
atender to wait on (9)
aterredor/a frightening (9)
atletismo, el track and field (2)
atrevido/a daring (8)
atún, el tuna (7)
aumentar to grow (11)
autobús, el bus (10)
autopista, la highway; freeway (10)
ave, el bird (11)
averiguar to find out (4, PB)
aves, las poultry (7)
avión, el airplane (10)
ayer yesterday (7)
ayudante, el/la assistant (5)
ayudar to help (3); ~ a las personas mayores/los mayores to help elderly people (4)
azotar to whip (11)
azúcar, el sugar (7)
azul blue (3)

B

bailar to dance (2)
bajar (de) to get down (from); to get off (of) (10)
bajo/a short (1)
balcón, el balcony (3)
banana, la banana (7)
bañarse to bathe (8)
banco, el bank (4)
bañera, la bathtub (3)
baño, el bathroom (3)
bar, el bar (4)
barato/a cheap (7)
barco, el boat (4, 10, PB)
barro negro, el black clay (2)
Bastante bien. Just fine. (PA)
basura, la garbage (11)
bata, la robe (8)
batata, la yam (7)
batería, la drums (5)
baterista, el/la drummer (5)
baúl, el trunk (10)
beber to drink (7)
bebida, la beverage (7, PB)
beige beige (3)
bella beautiful (4)
besito, el little kiss (PA)

biblioteca, la library (2)
bicicleta, la bicycle (10)
bidet, el bidet (3)
bien: bien cocido/a well done (7); ~ hecho/a well cooked (7); ~, gracias. Fine, thanks. (PA)
bienestar, el well-being; welfare (11)
biología, la biology (2)
bistec, el steak (7)
blanco white (3)
blusa, la blouse (8)
boca, la mouth (9)
boda, la wedding (4, 6)
boleto, el ticket (8, 10); ~ de ida y vuelta round-trip ticket (10)
bolígrafo, el ballpoint pen (2)
bolso, el purse (8)
bondadoso/a kind (11)
bonito/a pretty (1)
borrador, el eraser (2)
bosque, el forest (11)
botar to throw away (11)
botas, las (pl.) boots (8)
botella, la bottle (11)
botones, el bellman (10)
brazo, el arm (9)
broma, la joke (3, 8)
buceo, el scuba diving (4)
¡Buen provecho! Enjoy your meal! (7)
bueno/a good (1, 10)
Buenos días. Good morning. (PA)
Buenas noches. Good evening. (PA)
Buenas tardes. Good afternoon. (PA)
bufanda, la scarf (9)
bullicio, el hubbub (4)
buscar to look for (4)

C

caballo, el horse (11)
cabeza, la head (9)
cada each (3)
cadena, la chain (3)
caer(se) to fall down (9)
café, el café (4, 7)
cafetería, la cafeteria (2)
caja, la (de cartón) (cardboard) box (11)
cajero automático, el ATM (4)
calcetines, los (pl.) socks (8)
calculadora, la calculator (2)
calefacción, la heat (10)
calidad, la quality (11)

caliente hot (temperature) (7)
callarse to get / keep quiet (8)
calle, la street (3, 10)
cama, la bed (3)
camarero/a, el/la waiter/waitress (7); housekeeper (10)
camarones, los (pl.) shrimp (7)
cambiar to change (10)
caminar to walk (2); to walk; to go on foot (10)
camión, el truck (10)
camisa, la T-shirt (5); shirt (8)
camiseta, la T-shirt (8)
campamento de niños, el summer camp (4)
campaña, la campaign (11)
campo, el country (3)
canadiense Canadian (PA)
candidato/a, el/la candidate (11)
cansado/a tired (2)
cantante, el/la singer (5)
capa de ozono, la ozone layer (11)
capítulo, el chapter (5)
cara, la face (9)
cargos, los posts (11)
carne, la meat (7); ~ de cerdo pork (7)
caro/a expensive (4, 7)
carro, el car (10)
casa, la house (3)
casado/a married (1)
cascada, la waterfall (10)
castillo, el castle (3)
catarro, el cold (9)
catorce fourteen (PA)
cebolla, la onion (7)
cena, la dinner (7)
cenar to have dinner (7)
centro, el downtown (4); ~ comercial mall; business/ shopping district (4); ~ estudiantil student center; student union (2)
cepillarse (el pelo, los dientes) to brush (one's hair, teeth) (8)
cerca (de) near (2, 7, 11)
cerdo, el pig (11)
cereal, el cereal (7)
cero zero (PA)
cerrar (ie) to close (4)
cerveza, la beer (7)
cestería, la basket making (2)
chamán, el shaman (9)
Chao. Bye. (PA)
chaqueta, la jacket (8)
chico/a, el/la boy/girl (1)

chile, el chili pepper (7)
chino/a Chinese (PA)
cibercafé, el Internet café (4)
cielo, el sky; heaven (11)
cien one hundred (2); ~ mil one hundred thousand (3); ~ millones one hundred million (3); ~ one hundred (1)
ciencias, las (pl.) science (2)
Cierre(n) el/los libros/s. Close your book/s. (PA)
cierto/a true (4)
cinco five (PA)
cincuenta fifty (1)
cine, el movie theater (4)
cintura, la waist (9); de la ~ para arriba from the waist up (9)
cinturón, el belt (8)
circular una petición to circulate a petition (4)
cita, la appointment (4, PB)
ciudad, la city (3, 4)
claro/a light (colored) (8)
cliente/a, el/la customer; client (7)
club, el club (4); ~ de campo country club (4)
coche, el car (8, 10)
cocido/a boiled; baked (7)
cocina, la kitchen (3)
cocinar to cook (7)
cocinero/a, el/la chef (4, 7)
cognado, el cognate (PA)
cola, la line (of people) (10)
colcha, la bedspread; comforter (3)
colgar to hang up (7)
colibrí, el hummingbird (11)
color, el color (3)
combatir to fight; to combat (11)
comedor, el dining room (3)
comenzar (ie) to begin (4)
comer to eat (2)
cómico/a funny; comical (1)
comida, la food; meal (7, PB)
¿Cómo? What? How? (PA, 2); ¿~ está usted? How are you? (for.) (PA); ¿~ estas? How are you? (fam.) (PA); ¿~ se dice... en españól? How do you say . . . in Spanish? (PA); ¿~ se llama usted? What is your name? (for.) (PA); ¿~ te llamas? What is your name? (fam.) (PA)
como like (5)
cómodo/a comfortable (8)
compañero/a de clase, el/la classmate (2)

compartir share (3, 5)
composición, la composition (2)
comprar to buy (2)
comprender to understand (2)
Comprendo. I understand. (PA)
computadora, la computer (2)
con with (11)
concierto, el concert (5)
concurso, el contest (3)
condimento, el condiment; seasoning (7)
conducción, la driving (10)
conducir to drive (7, 8, 10)
conejo, el rabbit (11)
congreso, el congress (11)
conjunto, el group; band (5); outfit (8)
conmigo with me (9)
conmovedora moving (5)
conocer to be acquainted with (3)
consejo, el advice (5)
contaminación, la pollution (11)
contaminar to pollute (11)
contar to narrate (9)
contemporáneo/a contemporary (3)
contento/a content; happy (2)
contestar to answer (2)
Conteste(n). Answer. (PA)
contigo with you (9)
corazón, el heart (9)
corbata, la tie (8)
cordillera, la mountain range (11)
corregir to correct (3, 10)
correo basura, el spam (3)
correos, el post office (4)
correr to run (2)
cortar(se) to cut (oneself) (9)
corte, la court (11)
cortejo, el courting (7)
corto/a short (8)
cosa, la thing (3)
cosecha, la crop (7)
costar (ue) to cost (4)
costurero/a, el/la tailor/ seamstress (8)
crear create (4)
creativa creative (5)
creer to believe (2)
crucero, el cruise ship (5)
crudo/a rare; raw (7)
cuaderno, el notebook (2)
cuadro, el picture; painting (3, 5)
cual which (11)
¿Cuál? Which (one)? (2); ¿~ es la fecha de hoy? What is today's date? (PA)

cualquier whatever (8)
¿Cuándo? When? (2)
¿Cuánto/a? How much?, How many? (2)
cuarenta forty (1)
cuarto, el room (2, 3); ~ doble double room (10); ~ individual single room (10)
cuarto/a fourth (5)
cuatro four (PA)
cuatrocientos four hundred (2)
cubano/a Cuban (PA)
cubrir to cover (8)
cuchara, la soup spoon; tablespoon (7)
cucharada, la spoonful (7)
cucharita, la teaspoon (7)
cuchillo, el knife (7)
cuello, el neck (9)
cuenta, la bill; account (4)
cuero, el leather (8)
cuerpo humano, el human body (9)
cuestiones políticas, las political issues (11)
cueva, la cave (11)
cuidadoso/a careful (5)
cuidar to take care of (3, 11)
culpable, el/la guilty (8)
curandero/a, el/la folk healer (4)
curar(se) to cure; to be cured (9)
curita, la adhesive bandage (9)
curso, el course (2)

D

dañar to hurt (11)
dar to give (3); to find (2); ~ un concierto to give/perform a concert (5); ~ vida give life (5)
de of; from; about (11); ~ cuadros checked (8); ¿~ dónde? From where? (2); ~ la mañana in the morning (PA); ~ la noche in the evening (PA); ~ la tarde in the afternoon (PA); ~ lunares polka-dotted (8); ~ nada. You're welcome. (PA); ¿~ qué se trata... ? What is the gist of . . . ? (8); ~ rayas striped (8); ~ repente suddenly (PB); ~ suspenso suspenseful (5)
debajo (de) under; underneath (7, 11)
deber, el obligation; duty (4); ~ ought to; should (4)
débil weak (1)

décimo/a tenth (**5**)
decir to say; to tell (**3**)
dedo, el (de la mano) finger (**9**);
~ **(del pie)** toe (**9**)
defensa, la defense (**11**)
dejar to leave (**10**)
delante de in front of (**11**)
delgado/a thin (**1**)
delincuencia, la crime (**11**)
demás, los others (**4**)
democracia, la democracy (**11**)
demostrar (ue) to demonstrate (**4**)
dentro de inside of (**11**)
deporte, el sport (**2**)
derecho, el law (**2**)
derrame de petróleo, el oil spill
(**11**)
desaparecer to disappear (**5**)
desaparecido/a missing (**9**)
desastre, el disaster (**11**)
desayunar to have breakfast (**7**)
desayuno, el breakfast (**7**)
descansar to rest (**7**)
desde from (**11**)
desempleo, el unemployment (**11**)
desfile de moda, el fashion show (**8**)
desilusionar to disappoint (**9**)
desordenado/a messy (**3**)
despedida, la farewell (**PA**)
despertador, el alarm clock (**2**)
despertarse (e, ie) to wake up; to
awaken (**8**)
después afterward (**6**); after (**11**)
destacar stand out (**5**); to
distinguish (**7**)
destino, el destination (**8**)
destrucción, la destruction (**11**)
destruir to destroy (**5**)
detrás (de) behind (**4, 11**)
deuda, la (externa) (foreign)
debt (**11**)
devolver (ue) to return
(an object) (**4**)
día, el day (**PA**); ~ **festivo**
holiday (**7**)
dibujo, el drawing (**3**)
dictador/a, el/la dictator (**11**)
dictadura, la dictatorship (**11**)
diente, el tooth (**9**)
diez ten (**PA**)
difícil difficult (**2**)
dinero, el money (**2**)
diputado/a, el/la deputy;
representative (**11**)
disco compacto, el (el CD) compact
disk, CD (**2**)

discurso, el speech (**11**)
discutir to discuss (**PB**)
diseñador/a, el/la designer (**8**)
disfrutar de enjoy (**4, PB**)
distraer to distract (**5**)
divertirse (e, ie) to enjoy oneself; to
have fun (**8**)
dividido por divided by (**1**)
doblar to turn (**10**)
doce twelve (**PA**)
doctor/a, el/la doctor (**9**)
doler (ue) to hurt (**9**)
dolor, el pain (**9**)
domingo, el Sunday (**PA**)
dona, la donut (**10**)
¿Dónde? Where? (**2**)
dormir (ue) to sleep (**4**); ~**se (o, ue)**
to fall asleep (**8**)
dormitorio, el bedroom (**3**)
dos two (**PA**)
dos millones two million (**3**)
doscientos two hundred (**2**)
ducha, la shower (**3**)
ducharse to shower (**8**)
dulce, el candy; sweets (**7**)
durante during (**PB**)
durar to last (**9, 11**)
duro/a hard-boiled (**7**)
DVD, el (*pl.* los DVD) DVD/s (**2**)

E

echar una siesta take a nap (**PB**)
ecología, la ecology (**11**)
edificio, el building (**2**)
efecto invernadero, el global
warming (**11**)
ejército, el army (**5**)
él he, him (**PA, 11**)
el/la/los/las the (**1**)
elecciones, las elections (**11**)
elefante, el elephant (**11**)
elegante elegant (**8**)
elegir to elect (**11**)
ella she (**PA**); her (**11**)
ellos/as they (**PA**); them (**11**)
emanar to emanate (**11**)
embarazada pregnant (**9**)
embriaguez, el intoxication (**10**)
emocionante moving (**5**)
emociones, las emotions (**2**)
empanada, la turnover (meat) (**7**)
empezar (ie) to begin (**4**)
empleado/a, el/la attendant (**12**)
empresario/a, el/la agent;
manager (**5**)

en in (**11**); ~ **frente de** in front of
(**2**); ~ **vez de** instead of (**8**)
encantar to love; to like very
much (**8**)
Encantado/Encantada. Pleased to
meet you. (**PA**)
encender to turn on (**9**)
encerrar (ie) to enclose (**4**)
encima (de) on top (of); above
(**3, 7, 11**)
encontrar (ue) to find (**4**)
encubierto/a undercover (**11**)
encuesta, la survey; poll (**11**)
endémico/a common (**11**)
enfermar(se) to get sick (**9**)
enfermedad illness (**9**)
enfermero/a, el/la nurse (**9**)
enfermo/a ill; sick (**2**)
enfrente (de) in front (of) (**4**); across
from; facing (**11**)
enojado/a angry (**2**)
ensalada, la salad (**7**)
ensayar to practice/rehearse (**5**)
ensayo, el essay (**2**)
enseñar to teach; to show (**2**)
entender (ie) to understand (**4**)
enterar to find out (**8, 10**)
entonces then (**6**)
entrada, la ticket (**5**); ~ **gratis** free
ticket (**5**); ~ entrance (**5**)
entrar to enter (**10**); ~ **ganas** get the
urge (**9**)
entre among; between (**4, PB, 11**)
entregar to turn in (**7**)
entretenerse to entertain oneself (**8**)
entretenido/a entertaining (**5**)
entrevista, la interview (**3**)
envolver to wrap (**7**)
épica epic (**5**)
equipaje, el luggage (**10**)
equipo, el team (**2**)
equivocarse to be mistaken (**9**)
es: ~ la... It's . . . o'clock. (**PA**);
~ **necesario que** it's necessary
that (**11**); ~ **una lástima** it's a
shame (**11**)
escalera, la staircase (**3, 11**)
esconder to hide (**8**)
escribir to write (**2**)
Escriba(n). Write. (**PA**)
escritorio, el desk (**2**)
escuchar: escuchar música to listen
to music (**2**)
Escuche(n). Listen. (**PA**)
escuela secundaria, la high
school (**9**)

ese/a that, that one (**5**)
esos/as those over there; those ones (**3, 5**)
espalda, la back (**9**)
español/española Spaniard (**PA**)
espantosa scary (**5**)
especialidad, la: ~ **de la casa** specialty of the house (**7**); ~**es** majors (**2**)
especias, las spices (**7**)
esperar to wait for; to hope (**2**)
esposo/a, el/la husband/wife (**1**)
Está nublado. It's cloudy. (**PA**)
estación, la (de tren, de autobús) (train, bus) station (**10**); ~ season (**PA**)
estacionamiento, el parking (**10**)
estacionar to park (**10**)
estadidad, la statehood (**11**)
estadio, el stadium (**2**)
estado, el state (**2, 9, 11**)
estadounidense (norteamericano/a) American (**PA**)
estafar to defraud (**10**)
estampado/a print; with a design or pattern (**8**)
estante, el bookcase (**3**)
estar to be (**2**); ~ **de acuerdo** to agree (**4**); ~ **en huelga** to be on strike (**11**); ~ **enfermo/a** to be sick (**9**); ~ **sano/a; saludable** to be healthy (**9**)
este/a this, this one (**5**)
estilo, el style (**8**)
esto this (**3**)
estómago, el stomach (**9**)
estornudar to sneeze (**9**)
estornudo, el sneeze (**9**)
estos/as these (**5**)
estrecho/a narrow; tight (**8**)
estrella, la star (**5**)
estrenar una película to release a film/movie (**5**)
estreno, el opening (**5**)
estudiante, el/la student (**2**)
estudiar to study (**2, 6**)
estufa, la stove (**3**)
estupendo/a stupendous (**5**)
evitar to avoid (**9, 11**)
evolucionar evolve (**5**)
examen, el exam (**2**); ~ **físico** physical exam (**9**)
exigente demanding (**9**)
experimentar to experience (**11**)
expresión, la expression (**PA**); ~ **de cortesía** polite expression (**PA**)

extranjero, el abroad (**10**)
extraño/a strange (**4**)

F

fabada, la bean stew (**7**)
fábrica, la factory (**8**)
fácil easy (**2**)
falda, la skirt (**8**)
faltar to miss (**4, PB**)
fama, la fame (**5**)
familia, la family (**1**)
farmacéutico/a, el/la pharmacist (**9**)
farmacia, la pharmacy (**9**)
fascinar to fascinate (**8**)
feliz happy (**2**)
feo/a ugly (**1**)
fiebre, la fever (**9**)
fiesta, la party (**3**)
fila, la row (**5**)
fin de semana, el weekend (**7**)
finalmente finally (**6**)
finca, la farm (**11**)
fino/a fine; delicate (**5**)
firma, la signature (**4**)
físico/a physical (**1**)
floreciente flourishing (**8**)
fondos, los funds (**10**)
formal formal (**8**)
foto, la photo (**1**)
francés/francesa French (PA)
fresco/a fresh (**7**)
frijoles, los (*pl.*) beans (**7**)
frito/a fried (**7**)
fruta, la fruit (**7**)
fuente, la source (**5, 9**)
fuera outside (**7**)
fuerte strong (**1**); loud (**3**)
funcionar to work; to function (**10**)

G

galleta, la cookie; cracker (**7**)
gallina, la chicken, hen (**7, 11**)
gallo, el rooster (**7**)
ganar to win (**6**)
garaje, el garage (**3**)
garganta, la throat (**9**)
gasolinera, la gas station (**10**)
gato, el cat (**10, 11**)
género, el genre (**5**)
gente, la people (**1**)
gimnasio, el gymnasium (**2**)
gira, la tour (**5**)
gobernador/a, el/la governor (**11**)
gobierno, el government (**11**)

gordo/a fat (**1**)
gorra, la cap (**8**)
grabación, la recording (**5**)
grabar to record (**5**)
Gracias. Thank you. (**PA**)
graduar to graduate (**11**)
gramo, el gram (**7**)
grande big; large (**1, 10**)
granja, la farm (**11**)
gripe, la flu (**9**)
gris gray (**3**)
gritar to scream (**8**)
guantes, los gloves (**8**)
guapo/a handsome/pretty (**1**)
guardar to put away; to keep (**3**); ~ **cama** to stay in bed (**9**)
guerra, la war (**11**)
guía, la guide (**5**)
guitarra, la guitar (**5**)
guitarrista, el/la guitarist (**5**)
gustar to like (**PA**)

H

habilidad, la ability; skill (**5**)
hablar to speak (**2**)
hace: ~ **buen tiempo.** The weather is nice. (**PA**); ~ **calor.** It's hot. (**PA**); ~ **frío.** It's cold. (**PA**); ~ **mal tiempo.** The weather is bad. (**PA**); ~ **sol.** It's sunny. (**PA**); ~ **viento.** It's windy. (**PA**)
hacer to do; to make (**3, 9**); ~ **artesanía** to make arts and crafts (**4**); ~ **daño** to (do) damage; to harm (**11**); ~ **ejercicio** to exercise (**2**); ~ **falta** to need; to be lacking (**8**); ~ **la cama** to make the bed (**3**); ~ **mímica** to play charades (**8**); ~ **una caminata** to take a walk (**4**); ~ **una gira** to tour (**5**); ~ **una hoguera** to light a campfire (**4**)
hamaca, la hammock (**11**)
hamburguesa, la hamburger (**7**)
hasta until (**11**); ~ **luego.** See you later. (**PA**); ~ **mañana.** See you tomorrow. (**PA**); ~ **pronto.** See you soon. (**PA**)
hay there is; there are (**2**); ~ **que +** **infinitivo** it is necessary . . . / you must . . . / one must/should . . . (**5**)
helado, el ice cream; iced (**7**)
herida, la wound; injury (**9**)
hermano/a, el/la brother/sister (**1**)
hermanos, los brothers and sisters; siblings (**1**)

A29

hervido/a boiled (**7**)
hijo/a, el/la son/daughter (**1**)
hijos, los sons and daughters; children (**1**)
hispanohablante Spanish-speaking (**3**)
hojalatería, la tin work (**2**)
¡Hola! Hi! (**PA**)
hombre, el man (**1**)
hora, la time (**PA**)
horario, el (de clases) schedule (of classes) (**2**, **6**)
hormiga, la ant (**11**)
hospital, el hospital (**9**)
hotel, el hotel (**10**)
hoyo, el hole (**11**)
huelga, la strike (**11**)
huevo, el egg (**7**)
humilde humble (**3**)
huracán, el hurricane (**11**)

I

idiomas, los (*pl.*) languages (**2**)
iglesia, la church (**4**)
Igualmente. Likewise. (**PA**)
imaginativo/a imaginative (**5**)
impermeable, el raincoat (**8**)
importar to matter; to be important (**8**)
impresionante impressive (**5**)
impuesto, el tax (**11**)
incendio, el fire (**11**)
incómodo/a uncomfortable (**8**)
incumbir to concern (**8**)
inflación, la inflation (**11**)
influyente influential (**11**)
informal casual (**8**)
informática, la computer science (**2**)
inglés/inglesa English (**PA**)
inodoro, el toilet (**3**)
insecto, el insect (**11**)
inteligente intelligent (**1**)
interesante interesting (**1**)
interesar to be interested in (**2**)
inundación, la flood (**11**)
invierno, el winter (**PA**)
involucrado/a involved (**11**)
inyección, la shot (**9**)
ir to go (**4**); **~ de camping** to go camping (**4**); **~ de compras** to go shopping (**2**); **~ de excursión** to take a short trip (**4**); **~ de vacaciones** to go on vacation (**10**); **~ de viaje** to go on a trip (**10**); **~se del hotel** to leave the hotel; to check out (**10**); **~se** to go away; to leave (**8**)

J

jamás never; not ever (*emphatic*) (**4**, **11**)
jamón, el ham (**7**)
japonés/japonesa Japanese (**PA**)
jarabe, el cough syrup (**9**)
jardín, el garden (**3**)
jazz, el jazz (**5**)
jeans, los (*pl.*) jeans (**8**)
joven young; young man/young woman (**1**, **10**)
joya, la jewel (**9**)
jueves, el Thursday (**PA**)
juez/a, el/la judge (**11**)
jugar (ue) to play (**4**); **~ al básquetbol** to play basketball; **~ al béisbol** to play baseball; **~ al fútbol** to play soccer; **~ al fútbol americano** to play football; **~ al golf** to play golf; **~ al tenis** to play tennis (**2**)
jugo, el juice (**7**)
juicio, el jury (**11**)

L

La cuenta, por favor. The check, please. (**7**)
laboratorio, el laboratory (**2**)
lado, el side (**2**)
lago, el lake (**5**, **10**, **11**)
lámpara, la lamp (**3**)
lana, la wool (**8**)
lápiz, el pencil (**2**)
largo/a long (**8**)
lastimar(se) to get hurt (**9**)
lata, la can (**11**)
latir to beat (heart) (**9**)
lavabo, el sink (**3**)
lavaplatos, el dishwasher (**3**)
lavar los platos to wash dishes (**3**); **~se** to wash oneself (**8**)
le to/for him, her (**8**)
Lea(n). Read. (**PA**)
leche, la milk (**7**)
lechuga, la lettuce (**7**)
leer to read (**2**)
lejos de far from (**2**, **11**)
lento/a slow (**3**, **5**)
león, el lion (**11**)
les to/for them (**8**)
letra, la lyrics (**5**)
levantarse to get up; to stand up (**8**)
ley, la law (**10**, **11**)
leyenda, la legend (**9**)

librería, la bookstore (**2**)
libro, el book (**2**)
licencia, la (de conducir) driver's license (**10**)
ligero/a light (**PB**)
limón, el lemon (**7**)
limpiaparabrisas, el windshield wiper (**10**)
limpiar to clean (**3**)
limpio/a clean (**3**)
lío, el mess (**9**)
liso/a solid-colored (**8**)
literatura, la literature (**2**)
llamarse to be called (**8**)
llanta, la tire (**10**)
llave, la key (**10**)
llegar to arrive (**2**)
llenar to fill (**10**)
llevar to wear; to take; to carry (**8**); **~ a alguien al médico** to take someone to the doctor (**4**); **~ a cabo** to carry out (**11**)
Llueve. It's raining. (**PA**)
lluvia, la rain (**PA**); **~ ácida** acid rain (**11**)
Lo sé. I know. (**PA**)
lo, la him, her, it, you (**5**)
loma, la hill (**11**)
loro, el parrot (**11**)
los, las them; you all (**5**)
lucha libre, la wrestling (**2**)
luchar to fight; to combat (**11**)
luego then (**6**)
lugar, el place (**2**)
lugareños, los locals (*pl.*) (**4**)
luna de miel, la honeymoon (**10**)
lunes, el Monday (**PA**)

M

madrastra, la stepmother (**1**)
madre, la mother (**1**)
maíz, el corn (**7**)
mal de altura, el altitude sickness (**9**)
maleta, la suitcase (**10**)
malo/a bad (**1**, **10**)
malvado/a evil (**10**)
mamá, la mom (**1**)
mandar una carta to send/mail a letter (**4**)
mandato, el instruction, command (**PA**)
mandioca, la yucca (**7**)
manejar to drive (**8**, **10**)
manejo, el management (**7**)
mano, la hand (**1**, **9**)

manta, la blanket (**3**)
mantel, el tablecloth (**7**)
mantequilla, la butter (**7**)
manzana, la apple (**7**)
mapa, el map (**2**)
maquillarse to put on make up (**8**)
marcar to dial (**9**)
mariscos, los seafood (**7**)
marrón brown (**3**)
martes, el Tuesday (**PA**)
más + *adjective/adverb/noun* + **que** more . . . than (**10**)
más plus (**1**); **~ o menos.** So-so. (**PA**); **~ tarde que** later than (**7**); **~ temprano que** earlier than (**7**)
mascota, la domesticated animal; pet (**10, 11**)
matar to kill (**11**)
matemáticas, las (*pl.*) mathematics (**2**)
materia, la subject (**2**)
material, el material (**8**)
mayonesa, la mayonnaise (**7**)
mayor old; older (**1**); the eldest (**10**); the largest (**5**); bigger (**10**)
mayordomo, el butler (**10**)
me me (**5**); to/for me (**8**)
Me llamo... My name is . . . (**PA**)
medianoche, la midnight (**PA**)
medias, las (*pl.*) stockings; hose (**8**)
medicina, la medicine (**2**)
médico/a, el/la doctor (**9**)
medio ambiente, el environment (**11**)
medio medium (**7**)
mediodía, el noon (**PA**)
mejor, el/la the best (**4, 10**); better (**10**); **~(se)** to improve; to get better (**9**)
melón, el melon (**7**)
menor smaller; younger; the smallest; the youngest (**10**)
menos + *adjective/adverb/noun* + **que** less . . . than (**10**)
menos minus (**1**)
mensaje, el message (**3**)
mentir (ie) to lie (**4**)
mentira, la lie (**5, 7**)
menú, el menu (**7**)
mercado, el market (**4**)
merendar to have a snack (**7**)
merienda, la snack (**7**)
mermelada, la jam; marmalade (**7**)
mes, el month (**PA**)
mesa, la table (**2**)
meterse en política to get involved in politics (**11**)
metro, el subway (**10**)

mexicano/a Mexican (**PA**)
mezcla, la mixture (**7**)
mí me (**11**)
mi, mis my (**1**)
microondas, el microwave (**3**)
mientras while (**2**)
miércoles, el Wednesday (**PA**)
mil one thousand (**2**)
milla, la mile (**PB**)
millón one million (**3**)
mío/a/os/as mine (**10**)
mirar to look at (**1**)
mochila, la bookbag; knapsack (**2**)
moda, la fashion (**8**)
modelo, el/la model (**8**)
moderno/a modern (**3**)
molestar to bother (**8**)
monarquía, la monarchy (**11**)
montaña, la mountain (**10, 11**)
montañoso/a mountainous (**4**)
montar: ~ (a caballo) to ride a horse (**11**); **~ en bicicleta** to ride a bike (**2**); **~ una tienda de campaña** to put up a tent (**4**)
montón, el pile (**7**)
morado purple (**3**)
morir (ue) to die (**4**)
mosca, la fly (**11**)
mosquito, el mosquito (**11**)
mostaza, la mustard (**7**)
mostrar (ue) to show (**4**)
moto(cicleta), la motorcycle (**1, 10**)
motor, el motor; engine (**10**)
muchacho/a, el/la boy/girl (**1**)
Mucho gusto. Nice to meet you. (**PA**)
mueble, el piece of furniture (**3**)
muebles, los furniture (*pl.*) (**3**)
muerto/a dead (**11**)
mujer, la woman (**1**)
multa, la traffic ticket; fine (**10**)
museo, el museum (**4**)
música, la music (**2**); **~ clásica** classical music (**5**); **~ folklórica** folk music (**5**); **~ popular** pop music (**5**); **~ rap** rap music (**5**)
musical musical (**5**)
músico/a, el/la musician (**5**)
muy very (**1**)
Muy bien. Really well. (**PA**)

N

nacionalidad, la nationality (**PA**)
nada nothing (**4**)
nadar to swim (**2**)

nadie no one; nobody (**4**)
naranja, la orange (**7**)
nariz, la nose (**9**)
narrar to narrate (**6**)
naturaleza, la nature (**11**)
náusea, la nausea (**9**)
necesitar to need (**2**)
negocio, el business (**8**)
negro black (**3**)
nervioso/a upset; nervous (**2**)
ni... ni neither . . . nor (**4**)
ni nor (**3**)
nieto/a, el/la grandson/ granddaughter (**1**)
nieve, la snow (**PA**)
nigeriano/a Nigerian (**PA**)
ningún none (**4**)
ninguno/a/os/as none (**3, 4**)
niño/a, el/la little boy/little girl (**1**)
no: ~ comprendo. I don't understand. (**PA**); **~ lo sé.** I don't know. (**PA**); **~.** No. (**PA**)
noreste, el northeast (**2**)
nos us (**5**); to/for us (**8**)
nosotros/as us (**PA**); we (**11**)
novecientos nine hundred (**2**)
noveno/a ninth (**5**)
noventa ninety (**1**)
novio/a, el/la boyfriend/girlfriend (**1**)
nube, la cloud (**PA**)
nuestro/a/os/as our/s (**1, 10**)
nueve nine (**PA**)
nuevo/a new (**3**)
número, el number (**PA**); **~ ordinal** ordinal number (**5**)
nunca never (**2, 3, 4**)

O

o... o either . . . or (**4**)
objeto, el object (**3**)
obtener to get (**10**)
océano, el ocean (**11**)
ochenta eighty (**1**)
ocho eight (**PA**)
ochocientos eight hundred (**2**)
octavo/a eighth (**5**)
ocurrir to occur (**9**)
oeste, el west (**2**)
oferta, la offer (**3**)
oficina, la office (**3**); **~ de correos** post office (**4**)
ofrecer offer (**2**)
oído, el inner ear (**9**)
oír to hear (**3**)
ojalá que let's hope (**11**)

ojear las vitrinas to window shop (8)
ojo, el eye (9)
once eleven (PA)
ópera, la opera (5)
oreja ear (9)
organizar to organize (4)
orgulloso/a proud (4)
orquesta, la orchestra (5)
os to/for you all (5, 8)
oscuro/a dark (8)
oso, el bear (11)
otoño, el fall (PA)
otro/a another (PA)

P

paciente, el/la patient (1)
padrastro, el stepfather (1)
padre, el father (1)
padres, los parents (1)
pagar to pay (7)
paisaje, el countryside (3)
pájaro, el bird (11)
palabra, la word (PA)
pan, el bread (7)
pantalla, la screen (5)
pantalones, los (*pl.*) pants (8);
    ~ cortos (*pl.*) shorts (8)
papá, el dad (1)
papa, la potato (7)
papas fritas, las (*pl.*) french fries;
    potato chips (7)
papel, el paper (2)
paquete, el package (10)
para for (PB); in order to (11)
parabrisas, el windshield (10)
parada, la bus stop (10)
paraguas, el umbrella (8)
pararse to stand (10)
parecer seem (4)
pared, la wall (2)
parientes, los relatives (*pl.*) (2)
parque, el park (4); **~ de atracciones**
    theme park (10)
parrillada, la mixed grill (7)
participar en una campaña política
    to participate in a political
    campaign (4)
partido político, el political party
    (11)
pasajero, el passenger (10)
pasaporte, el passport (10)
pasar: ~ to happen (PB); **~ la**
    aspiradora to vacuum (3)
pasatiempos, los pastimes (2)
pastel, el pastry; pie (7)

pastilla, la pill (9)
pata, la leg (of an animal) (9)
patata, la potato (7)
patinar to skate (2)
paz, la peace (5)
peatón, el pedestrian (10)
pecho, el chest (9)
pedagogía, la education (2)
pedido, el request (9)
pedir (i) to ask for (4); to order (7)
peinarse to comb one's hair (8)
película, la film (4, 5); **~ de acción**
    action movie (5); **~ de ciencia**
    ficción science fiction movie (5);
    ~ documental documentary (5);
    ~ dramática drama (5); **~ de**
    guerra war movie (5); **~ de humor**
    funny movie; comedy (5); **~ de**
    misterio mystery movie (5); **~**
    musical musical (5); **~ romántica**
    romantic movie (5); **~ de terror**
    horror movie (5)
peligro, el danger (11)
peligroso/a dangerous (8, 11)
pelo, el hair (9)
pelota, la ball (2)
pensar (ie) to think (4)
peor worse, the worst (4, 10)
pequeño/a small (1, 10)
pera, la pear (7)
perder (ie) to lose; to waste (4)
perdido/a lost (4)
perezoso/a lazy (1)
periódico, el newspaper (11)
periodismo, el journalism (2)
pero but (2)
perro: ~ dog (3, 11); **~ caliente** hot
    dog (7)
perseguir (i) to chase (4)
personalidad, la personality (1)
pertenecer to belong (9)
pesadilla, la nightmare (8)
pescado, el fish (7)
pésimo/a heavy; depressing (5)
peso corporal, el body weight (9)
pez, el (*pl.*, los peces) fish (11)
pianista el/la pianist (5)
piano, el piano (5)
picante spicy (7)
pie, el foot (8, 9)
pierna, la leg (9)
pijama, el pajamas (8)
pimienta, la pepper (7)
pintar to dye (9)
piso, el floor; story (3)
pista, la clue (5, 7)

pizarra, la chalkboard (2)
placer, el pleasure (7)
planeta, el planet (11)
planta baja, la ground floor (3)
plantar to plant (11)
plástico, el plastic (11)
plato, el plate; dish (7)
playa, la beach (10)
plaza, la town square (4)
pobre poor (1)
poco (un) (a) little (1); **~ hecho/a**
    rare (7)
poder to be able to (3)
policía, el policeman (10)
poliéster, el polyester (8)
política, la politics (11)
pollo, el chicken (7)
poner to put; to place (3); **~ la mesa**
    to set the table (3); **~se (la ropa)**
    to put on (one's clothes) (8); **~se**
    (nervioso/a) to get (nervous) (8)
por times; by (1); **~** for; through; by;
    because of (11); **~ favor.** Please.
    (PA); **~ lo menos** at least (3);
    ~ ciento percent (1); ¿**~ qué?**
    Why? (2)
portarse to behave (8)
postre, el dessert (7)
preferir (ie) to prefer (4)
preguntar to ask (a question) (2)
prenda, la article of clothing (8)
preocupado/a worried (2)
preocuparse (por) to worry about;
    to concern (11)
preparar to prepare; to get ready (2);
    ~ la comida to prepare a meal (3)
preparativo preparation (5)
presentación, la introduction (PA)
presentar una película to show a
    film/movie (5)
presentarlo to introduce (3)
presidencia, la presidency (11)
presidente/a, el/la president (11)
prestar to loan; to lend (8)
presupuesto, el budget (8)
primavera, la spring (PA)
primer first (5); **~ piso** second
    floor (3)
primero/a first (5)
primo/a, el/la cousin (1)
primos, los cousins (1)
principio, el start (8)
probarse (o, ue) la ropa to try on
    clothing (8)
profesor/a, el/la professor (2)
programa, el platform (11)

promedio, el average (7)
propina, la tip (7)
propio/a own (6)
proponer propose (5)
propósito, el purpose (7)
proteger to protect (11)
provincia, la province (11)
prueba, la proof (10)
psicología, la psychology (2)
pueblo, el town; village (4)
puerta, la door (2)
puertorriqueño/a Puerto Rican (PA)
puro/a pure (11)

Q

que what (3)
¿Qué? What? (2); **¿~ día es hoy?** What day is today? (PA); **¿~ es esto?** What is this? (PA); **¿~ hora es?** What time is it? (PA); **¿ ~ significa?** What does it mean? (PA); **¿~ tal?** How's it going? (PA); **¿~ tiempo hace?** What's the weather like? (PA)
quedar to stay (11)
quedarle bien / mal to fit well / poorly (8)
quedarse to stay; to remain (8)
quehaceres, los (*pl.*) chores (3)
quemar(se) to burn; to get burned (9)
querer to want; to love (2, 3)
queso, el cheese (7)
¿Quién/es? Who? (PA, 2)
quiero: ~ presentarle a... I would like to introduce you to . . . (*for.*) (PA); **~ presentarte a...** I would like to introduce you to . . . (*fam.*) (PA)
quince fifteen (PA)
quinientos five hundred (2)
quinto/a fifth (5)
quitarse (la ropa) to take off (one's clothes) (8)

R

radio, el/la radio (2)
rana, la frog (11)
rasgo, el characteristic (1)
rata, la rat (11)
ratón, el mouse (11)
realizar to act out (7)
rebozo, el poncho (8)
recepción, la front desk (10)

receta, la prescription (9)
recetar to prescribe (9)
recibir to receive (2)
reciclar to recycle (11)
recomendar (ie) to recommend (4)
reconocer to recognize (8)
recordar (ue) to remember (4)
recuerdo, el memento (3); memory (7)
recurso natural, el natural resource (11)
reforestar to reforest (11)
refresco, el soft drink (7)
refrigerador, el refrigerator (3)
regalo, el gift (8)
regatear to bargain (7)
regímenes, los regimes (11)
región, la region (11)
registrarse (en el hotel) to check in (10)
regresar to return (2)
Regular. Okay. (PA)
reina, la queen (11)
reírse to laugh (4)
reloj, el clock; watch (2)
remedio casero, el home-made remedy (7)
repartir comidas to hand out/deliver food (4)
repetir (i) to repeat (4)
Repita(n). Repeat. (PA)
reportaje, el report (12)
reproductor de CD/DVD, el CD/ DVD player (2)
requerir to require (11)
reseña, la review (PB, 5)
reserva, la reservation (10)
reservar una mesa to reserve a table (7)
resfriado, el cold (9)
residencia, la dorm (2); **~ estudiantil** dormitory (2)
resolver (o, ue) to resolve (11)
respetar to respect (5)
responsable responsible (1)
restaurante, el restaurant (4, 7)
resumir to summarize (9)
reunirse to get together; to meet (8)
reutilizar to reuse (11)
revisar to check; to overhaul (10)
revista, la magazine (8)
rey, el king (11)
rico/a rich (1)
riesgo, el risk (9)
río, el river (11)
ritmo, el rhythm (5)

rock, el rock (5)
rojo red (3)
rompecabeza, el riddle (7)
romper(se) to break (9)
ropa, la clothes; clothing (3, 8); **~ interior** underwear (8)
rosado pink (3)
roto broken (9)
ruido, el noise (3, PB, 10)

S

sábado, el Saturday (PA)
sábana, la sheet (3)
saber to know (4)
sacar: ~ la basura to take out the garbage (3); **~ la licencia** to get a driver's license (10); **~ un CD** to release a CD (5)
sacudir los muebles to dust (3)
sal, la salt (7)
sala, la: ~ de clase classroom (2); **~ de urgencias** emergency room (9); **~** living room (3)
salir to leave; to go out (3)
salsa, la salsa (5); **~ de tomate** ketchup (7)
salud, la health (9)
saludo, el greeting (PA)
salvar to save (9)
sano/a healthy (9)
sandalia, la sandal (8)
sangre, la blood (9)
secarse to dry off (8)
seda, la silk (8)
sede, la seat (of government) (9)
seguir (i) to follow; to continue (doing something) (4)
según according to (3, 11)
segundo/a second (5)
segundo piso, el third floor (3)
seguridad, la security (2)
seguro médico, el health insurance (9)
seis six (PA)
seiscientos six hundred (2)
sello, el postage stamp (10)
selva, la jungle (11); **~ tropical** jungle; (tropical) rain forest (11)
semáforo, el traffic light (10)
semana, la week (PA); **~ pasada** last week (7)
sembrar (e, ie) to sow (11)
semejanza, la similarity (6)
semestre, el semester (2)
senado, el senate (11)

A33

senador/a, el/la senator (**11**)
señor, el (Sr.) man; gentleman; Mr. (**1**)
señora, la (Sra.) woman; lady; Mrs. (**1**)
señorita, la (Srta.) young woman; Miss (**1**)
sentarse (e, ie) to sit down (**8**)
sentido, el meaning (**3**)
sentir to feel (**PB**); **~se (e, ie)** to feel (**8**)
séptimo/a seventh (**5**)
ser to be (**PA**); **~ alérgico/a (a)** to be allergic (to) (**9**)
serpiente, la snake (**11**)
servilleta, la napkin (**7**)
servir (i) to serve (**4**)
sesenta sixty (**1**)
setecientos seven hundred (**2**)
setenta seventy (**1**)
sexto/a sixth (**5**)
si if (**4**)
Sí. Yes. (**PA**)
siempre always (**3, 4**)
siete seven (**PA**)
siglo, el century (**3**)
siguiente, el following (**3**)
silla, la chair (**2**)
sillón, el armchair (**3**)
simpático/a nice (**1**)
sin embargo nevertheless (**2, 3, 6**)
sin without (**4, PB, 11**)
sobre on; on top (of); over (**3, 4, 11**); **~ todo** above all (**5**)
sofá, el sofa (**3**)
sol, el sun (**PA**)
solamente only (**8**)
solicitud, la application (**2**)
solo alone (**9**)
sombrero, el hat (**8**)
son equals (**1**)
sopa, la soup (**7**)
sorprendente surprising (**5**)
sorpresa, la surprise (**8**)
sospechoso/a suspicious (**2**)
sótano, el basement (**3**)
Soy... I am . . . (**PA**)
su/s his, her, its, your, their (**1**)
suave smooth (**5**)
subir (a) to go up; to get on (**10**)
subrayar to underline (**7**)
sucio/a dirty (**3**)
sudadera, la sweatshirt (**8**)
suelo, el floor (**3**)
suéter, el sweater (**8**)
sunami, el tsunami (**11**)

supermercado, el supermarket (**4**)
surgir to emerge (**8**)
suspiro, el sigh (**11**)
suyo/a/os/as his, her/s, your/s (*for.*), their/s (**PB, 3, 10**)

T

tal vez perhaps (**3**)
taller mecánico, el auto repair shop (**10**)
también too; also (**2**)
tambor, el drum (**5**)
tamborista, el/la drummer (**5**)
tampoco nor (**7**)
tan such (**2**)
tan... como as . . . as (**1**)
tanque, el gas tank (**10**)
tanto many (**2**); so much (**9**)
tarde late (**3**)
tarea, la homework (**2**)
tarjeta, la: ~ de crédito credit card (**7**); **~ de débito** debit card (**7**); **~ postal** postcard (**4, 10**)
taxi, el taxi (**10**)
taza, la cup (**7**)
te to/for you (**5, 8**)
té, el (helado / caliente) tea (iced / hot) (**7**)
teatro, el theater (**4**)
techo, el roof (**3**)
tela, la fabric (**8**)
televisión, la television (**2**)
tema, el topic; gist (**5**)
temperatura, la temperature (**PA**)
templo, el temple (**4**)
temprano early (**3**)
tenedor, el fork (**7**)
tener to have (**1**); **~ alergia (a)** to be allergic (to) (**9**); **~ ... años** to be . . . years old (**3**); **~ calor** to be hot (**3**); **~ cuidado** to be careful (**3**); **~ dolor de cabeza** to have a headache (**9**); **~ dolor de estómago** to have a stomachache (**9**); **~ dolor de espalda** to have a backache (**9**); **~ éxito** to be successful (**3**); **~ ganas de + (infinitive)** to feel like + (verb) (**3**); **~ hambre** to be hungry (**3**); **~ (la/una) gripe** to have the flu (**9**); **~ miedo** to be afraid (**3**); **~ prisa** to be in a hurry (**3**); **~ que + (infinitive)** to have to + (verb) (**3**); **~ razón** to be right (**3**); **~ resfriado** to have a cold (**9**);

~ sed to be thirsty (**3**); **~ sueño** to be sleepy (**3**); **~ suerte** to be lucky (**3**); **~ tos** to have a cough (**9**); **~ (un) catarro** to have a cold (**9**); **~ un virus** to have a virus (**9**); **~ una infección** to have an infection (**9**); **~ vergüenza** to be embarrassed (**3**)
tenis, los (*pl.*) tennis shoes (**8**)
tercer, el: ~ piso fourth floor (**3**)
tercero/a third (**5**)
terminar to finish; to end (**2**)
terremoto, el earthquake (**5, 11**)
tesoro, el treasure (**10**)
ti you (**11**)
tiburón, el shark (**5**)
tienda, la store (**2**)
tierra, la land; soil (**11**)
Tierra, la Earth (**11**)
tío/a, el/la uncle/aunt (**1**)
tíos, los aunts and uncles (**1**)
tirar to throw (**9**)
tiza, la chalk (**2**)
tocador, el dresser (**3**)
tocar touch (**4**); **~** to play (a musical instrument) (**2, 5**)
todavía still (**4**)
tomar to take; to drink (**2**); **~ el sol** to sunbathe (**2**)
tomate, el tomato (**7**)
tonto/a silly; dumb (**1**)
tormenta, la storm (**11**)
tornado, el tornado (**11**)
torneo, el tournament (**4**)
toro, el bull (**11**)
torre, la tower (**3**)
torta, la cake (**7**)
tos, la cough (**9**)
toser to cough (**9**)
tostada, la toast (**7**)
trabajador/a hard-working (**1**)
trabajar to work (**2**); **~ como consejero/a** to work as a counselor (**4**); **~ como voluntario/a en la residencia de ancianos** to volunteer at a nursing home (**4**); **~ en política** to work in politics (**4**)
trabajo en prácticas, el internship (**8**)
tradicional traditional (**3**)
traer to bring (**3**)
tráfico, el traffic (**10**)
tragedia, la tragedy (**11**)
trágico/a tragic (**5**)
traje, el suit (**8**); outfit (**5**); **~ de baño** swimsuit; bathing suit (**8**)
transitar to enter/exit (**10**)

transporte, el transportation (**10**)
tratamiento médico, el medical treatment (**9**)
tratar de to try to (**3, 9**); to treat (**9**)
trece thirteen (**PA**)
treinta thirty (**PA**)
tren, el train (**10**)
tres three (**PA**)
trescientos three hundred (**2**)
triste sad (**2**)
trompeta, la trumpet (**5**)
trompetista, el/la trumpet player (**5**)
tú you (*fam.*) (**PA**)
tu, tus your (**1**)
turnarse to take turns (**3**)
tuyo/a/os/as yours (*fam.*) (**3, 10**)

U

un/una/unos/unas a, an, some (**1**)
uno one (**PA**)
usar to use (**2, 4, PB**)
uso adecuado, el suitable use (**10**)
usted/es you (*for.*) (**PA, 11**)
útil useful (**PA**)

V

vaca, la cow (**11**)
vacaciones, las vacation (**10**)

vaso, el glass (**7**)
Vaya(n) a la pizarra. Go to the board. (**PA**)
vehículo, el vehicle (**10**)
veinte twenty (**PA**)
venda, la bandage (**9**)
vendaje, el bandage (**9**)
vendar(se) to bandage (oneself); to dress (a wound) (**9**)
venir to come (**3**)
ventana, la window (**2**)
ver to see (**3**); **~ la televisión** to watch television (**2**)
verano, el summer (**PA**)
verbo, el verb (**1, 2**)
verde green (**3**)
verdura, la vegetable (**7**)
vertedero, el dump (**11**)
vestido, el dress (**8**)
vestirse (e, i) to get dressed (**8**)
vez, la time (**5**)
viajar to travel (**10**); **~ en canoa** to canoe (**4**)
viaje, el trip (**10**)
viajero/a, el/la traveler (**10**)
vidrio, el glass (**11**)
viejo/a old (**3, 10**)
viento, el wind (**PA**)
viernes, el Friday (**PA**)
vinagre, el vinegar (**7**)

vino, el wine (**7**)
visitar to visit (**10**)
vivir to live (**2**)
vivo/a alive; living (**11**)
volante, el steering wheel (**10**)
volar (o, ue) to fly; to fly away (**10**)
voluntariado, el volunteerism (**4**)
volver (ue) to return (**4**); **~ loco/a** to drive him/her crazy (**12**)
vosotros/as you (*fam. pl. Spain*) (**PA, 11**)
votar to vote (**11**)
voto, el vote (**11**)
voz, la voice (**5**)
vuelo, el flight (**10**)
vuestro/a/os/as your/s (*fam. pl. Spain*) (**1, 10**)

Y

y: ¿~ tú? And you? (*fam.*) (**PA**); **¿~ usted?** And you? (*for.*) (**PA**)
ya already (**4**); **~ no** no longer (**5**); **~ que** since (**1**)
yo I (**PA**)

Z

zapatillas, las (*pl.*) slippers (**8**)
zapatos, los (*pl.*) shoes (**8**)

A35

Appendix 5

English-Spanish Glossary

A

a un/una/unos/unas (**1**)
ability la habilidad (**5**)
able to, to be poder (**3**)
about acerca de (**11**); sobre (**4, 11**)
above all sobre todo (**5**)
abroad el extranjero (**10**)
aburrida boring (**5**)
accompany, to acompañar (**6**)
according to según (**3, 11**)
account la cuenta (**4**)
acid rain la lluvia ácida (**11**)
acquainted with, to be conocer (**3**)
across from enfrente de (**11**)
act out, to realizar (**7**)
actor el actor (**5**)
actress la actriz (**5**)
ad el anuncio (**3**)
adjectives los adjetivos (**1**)
administration la administración (**11**)
advice el consejo (**5**)
afraid, to be tener miedo (**3**)
after después de (**11**)
afterward después (**6**)
agent el/la empresario/a (**5**)
agree, to estar de acuerdo (**4**)
air el aire (**11**); **~ conditioning** el aire acondicionado (**10**)
airline la aerolínea (10)
airplane el avión (**10**)
airport el aeropuerto (**10**)
alarm clock el despertador (**2**)
alive vivo/a (**11**)
allergic (to), to be tener alergia (a) (**9**)
alone solo (**9**)
already ya (**4**)
also también (**2**)
altitude sickness el mal de altura (**9**)
aluminum el aluminio (**11**)
always siempre (**3, 4**)
American estadounidense (norteamericano/a) (**PA**)
among entre (**11**)
an un/una/unos/unas (**1**)
And you? ¿Y tú? (*fam.*) (**PA**); **And you?** ¿Y usted? (*for.*) (**PA**)
angry enojado/a (**2**)
animal animal (**11**)

animated animado/a (**5**)
another otro/a
answer, to contestar (**2**); **~.** Conteste(n). (**PA**)
ant la hormiga (**11**)
antacid el antiácido (**9**)
antibiotic el antibiótico (**9**)
any algún; alguno/a/os/as (**4**)
anything algo (**4**)
apartment el apartamento (**2**)
appendix el apéndice (**4**)
apple la manzana (**7**)
application la solicitud (**2**)
appointment la cita (**4**)
approach, to acercar (**8**)
approved aprobado/a (10)
architecture la arquitectura (**2**)
arm el brazo (**9**)
armchair el sillón (**3**)
armoire el armario (**3**)
army el ejército (**5**)
around a eso de (**7**)
arrive, to llegar (**2**)
art el arte (**2**)
article el artículo (**1**); **definite ~** el artículo definido (**1**); **indefinite ~** el artículo indefinido (**1**)
articles of clothing las prendas (**8**)
artist el/la artista (**5**)
as . . . as tan... como (**1**)
ask (a question), to preguntar (**2**); **to ~ for** pedir (i) (**4**)
aspirin la aspirina (**9**)
assistant la ayudante (**5**)
at least por lo menos (**3**)
At what time . . . ? ¿A qué hora... ? (**PA**)
ATM el cajero automático (**4**)
attendant el/la empleado/a (**12**)
attic el altillo (**3**)
aunt la tía (**1**)
auto repair shop el taller mecánico (**10**)
average el promedio (**7**)
avoid, to evitar (**9, 11**)
awaken, to despertarse (e, ie) (**8**)
away, to go irse (**8**)

B

back la espalda (**9**)
bad malo/a (**1, 10**)
baked al horno; cocido/a (**7**)
balcony el balcón (**3**)
ball la pelota (**2**)
ballpoint pen el bolígrafo (**2**)
banana la banana (**7**)
band el conjunto (**5**)
bandage (adhesive) la curita; el vendaje; la venda (**9**)
bandage (oneself), to vendar(se) (**9**)
bank el banco (**4**)
bar el bar (**4**)
bargain, to regatear (**7**)
basement el sótano (**3**)
basket making la cestería (**2**)
bathe, to bañarse (**8**)
bathroom el baño (**3**)
bathtub la bañera (**3**)
be, to estar (**2**); ser (**PA**)
beach la playa (**10**)
beans los frijoles (*pl.*) (**7**); **~ stew** la fabada (**7**)
bear el oso (**11**)
beat (*heart*), to latir (**9**)
beautiful bella (**4**)
because of por (**11**)
bed la cama (**3**)
bedroom el dormitorio (**3**)
bedspread la colcha (**3**)
beer la cerveza (**7**)
before ante (**6**); **~ (*time/space*)** antes de (**11**)
begin, to comenzar (ie); empezar (ie) (**4**)
behave, to portarse (**8**)
behind detrás de (**4, 11**)
beige beige (**3**)
believe, to creer (**2**)
bellman el botones (**10**)
belong, to pertenecer (**9**)
belt el cinturón (**8**)
beside al lado (de) (**3**)
best el/la mejor (1, 4, 10)
better mejor (**10**); **to get ~** mejorar(se) (**9**)
between entre (**4, 11**)
beverage la bebida (**PB, 7**)

bicycle la bicicleta (**10**)
bidet el bidet (**3**)
big grande (**1, 10**); **bigger** mayor (**10**); **biggest** el/la mayor (**10**)
bill la cuenta (**4**)
biology la biología (**2**)
bird el ave; el pájaro (**11**)
black negro (**2, 3**)
blanket la manta (**3**)
blood la sangre (**9**)
blouse la blusa (**8**)
blue azul (**3**)
boat el barco (**4, 10**)
body el cuerpo (**9**); **~ weight** el peso corporal (**9**)
boiled cocido/a; hervido/a (**7**)
book el libro (**2**); **~bag** la mochila (**2**); **~case** el estante (**3**); **~store** la librería (**2**)
boots las botas (*pl.*) (**8**)
bored (with *estar*) aburrido/a (**2**)
boring aburrido/a (**1**)
bother, to molestar (**8**)
bottle la botella (**11**)
box (*cardboard*) la caja (*de cartón*) (**11**)
boy el chico; el muchacho; **little ~** el niño (**1**); **~friend** el novio (**1**)
bread el pan (**7**)
break, to romper(se) (**9**)
breakfast el desayuno (**7**); **to have ~** desayunar (**7**)
bring, to traer (**3**)
broken roto (**9**)
brother el hermano (**1**)
brown marrón (**3**)
brush, to (*one's hair, teeth*) cepillarse (*el pelo, los dientes*) (**8**)
budget el presupuesto (**8**)
building el edificio (**2**)
bull el toro (**11**)
burn, to quemar(se) (**9**)
bus el autobús (**10**); **~ stop** la parada (**10**)
bush el arbusto (**7**)
business el negocio (**8**); **~** la administración de empresas (**2**); **~ / shopping district** el centro comercial (**4**)
but pero (**2**)
butler el mayordomo (**10**)
butter la mantequilla (**7**)
buy, to comprar (**2**)
by por (**1, 11**)
Bye. Chao. (**PA**)

C

cabinet el armario (**3**)
café el café (**4**)
cafeteria la cafetería (**2**)
cake la torta (**7**)
calculator la calculadora (**2**)
called, to be llamarse (**8**)
campaign la campaña (**11**)
can la lata (**11**)
Canadian canadiense (**PA**)
candidate el/la candidato/a (**11**)
candy los dulces (**7**)
canoe, to viajar en canoa (**4**)
cap la gorra (**8**)
car el coche (**8, 10**)
care for cuidar (**3**)
careful cuidadoso/a (**5**); **to be ~** tener cuidado (**3**)
carpet la alfombra (**3**)
carry, to llevar (**8**); **to ~ out** llevar a cabo (**11**)
castle el castillo (**3**)
casual informal (**8**)
cat el/la gato/a (**10, 11**)
cave la cueva (**11**)
CD/DVD player el reproductor de CD/DVD (**2**)
century el siglo (**3**)
cereal el cereal (**7**)
chain la cadena (**3**)
chair la silla (**2**)
chalk la tiza (**2**); **~board** la pizarra (**2**)
change, to cambiar (**10**)
chapter el capítulo (**5**)
characteristic el rasgo (**1**)
charades, to play hacer mímica (**8**)
chase, to perseguir (i) (**4**)
cheap barato/a (**7**)
check in, to registrarse (en el hotel) (**10**); **to ~ out** irse del hotel (**10**)
checked de cuadros (**8**)
cheese el queso (**7**)
chef el/la cocinero/a (**4**)
chest el pecho (**9**)
chicken el pollo (**7**); la gallina (**11**)
children los hijos (**1**)
chili pepper el chile (**7**)
Chinese chino/a (**PA**)
chores los quehaceres (**3**)
church la iglesia (**4**)
circulate a petition, to circular una petición (**4**)
city la ciudad (**3, 4**)

classmate el/la compañero/a de clase (**2**)
Classroom instructions (*commands*) Mandatos para la clase (**PA**)
classroom la sala de clase (**2**)
clay barro (**2**)
clean limpio/a (**3**); **to ~** limpiar (**3**)
client el/la cliente/a (**7**)
clock el reloj (**2**)
Close your book/s. Cierre(n) el/los libros/s. (**PA**)
close, to cerrar (ie) (**4**)
closet el armario (**3**)
clothes la ropa (**3**)
clothing la ropa (**3, 8**)
cloud la nube (**PA**)
club el club (**4**)
clue la pista (**5, 7**)
coat el abrigo (**3**)
coffee el café (**7**)
cognate el cognado (**PA**)
cold el catarro; el resfriado (**9**)
cold, to be tener frío (**3**); **to have a ~** tener (un) catarro; tener resfriado (**9**)
color el color (**3**)
comb one's hair, to peinarse (**8**)
combat, to combatir (**11**)
come, to venir (**3**)
comfortable cómodo/a (**8**)
comforter la colcha (**3**)
comical cómico/a (**1**)
common endémico/a (**11**)
compact disk el disco compacto (el CD) (**2**)
composition la composición (**2**)
computer la computadora (**2**); **~ science** la informática (**2**)
concern, to incumbir (**8**)
concert el concierto (**5**)
condiment el condimento (**7**)
congress el congreso (**11**)
contemporary contemporáneo/a (**3**)
content contento/a (**2**)
contest el concurso (**3**)
continue (*doing something*), to seguir (i) (**4**)
cook el/la cocinero/a (**7**)
cook, to cocinar (**3, 7**)
cookies las galletas (**7**)
corn el maíz (**7**)
correct, to corregir (**3, 10**)
cost, to costar (ue) (**4**)
cotton el algodón (**8**)

A37

cough, to toser (9); ~ **la tos** (9);
~ **syrup** el jarabe (9); **to have a**
~ tener tos (9)
country el campo (3); ~ **club** el club
de campo (4)
countryside el paisaje (3)
course el curso (2)
court la corte (11)
courting el cortejo (7)
cousin el/la primo/a (1)
cover, to cubrir (8)
cow la vaca (11)
crackers las galletas (7)
create crear (4)
creative creativo/a (5)
credit card la tarjeta de crédito (7)
crime la delincuencia (11)
crop la cosecha (7)
cruise ship el crucero (5)
Cuban cubano/a (PA)
cup la taza (7)
cure, to curar(se) (9)
customer el/la cliente/a (7)
cut (oneself), to cortar(se) (9)

D

dad el papá (1)
damage, to (do) hacer daño (11)
dance, to bailar (2)
danger el peligro (11)
dangerous peligroso/a (8, 11)
daring atrevido/a (8)
dark oscuro/a (8)
daughter la hija (1)
day el día (PA); **the ~ before**
yesterday anteayer (7)
dead muerto/a (11)
debit card la tarjeta de débito (7)
debt (*foreign*) la deuda (*externa*) (11)
defense la defensa (11)
defraud, to estafar (10)
delicate fino/a (5)
demanding exigente (9)
democracy la democracia (11)
demonstrate, to demostrar (ue) (4)
department store el almacén (4)
depressing pésimo/a (5)
deputy el/la diputado/a (11)
designer el/la diseñador/a (8)
desk el escritorio (2)
dessert el postre (7)
destination el destino (8)
destroy, to destruir (5)
destruction la destrucción (11)
dial, to marcar (9)

dictator el/la dictador/a (11); **~ship**
la dictadura (11)
die, to morir (ue) (4)
difficult difícil (2)
dining room el comedor (3)
dinner la cena (7); **to have ~** cenar (7)
dirty sucio/a (3)
disappear, to desaparecer (5)
disappoint, to desilusionar (9)
disaster el desastre (11)
discuss, to discutir (PB)
dish el plato (7); **~washer** el
lavaplatos (3)
distinguish, to destacar (7)
distract, to distraer (5)
divided by dividido por (1)
do, to hacer (3)
doctor el/la doctor/a; el/la médico/a (9)
documentary el documental (5)
dog el perro (3, 11)
domesticated animals los animales
domésticos (11)
donut la dona (10)
door la puerta (2)
dorm / dormitory la residencia (2)
double room el cuarto doble (10)
downtown el centro (4)
drama dramático/a (5)
drawing el dibujo (3)
dress (*a wound*), **to** vendar(se) (9)
dress el vestido (8)
dresser el tocador (3)
drink, to tomar (2); beber (7)
drive, to conducir (7, 10); manejar
(8); **to ~ him/her crazy** volver
loco/a (12)
driver's license la licencia (*de conducir*)
(10); **to get a ~** sacar la licencia (10)
driving la conducción (10)
drum el tambor (5)
drummer el/la baterista (5); el/la
tamborista (5)
drums la batería (5)
dry off, to secarse (8)
dumb tonto/a (1)
dump el vertedero (11)
during durante (PB)
dust, to sacudir los muebles (3)
duty el deber (4)
DVD el DVD (2)
dye, to pintar (9)

E

each cada (3)
ear la oreja (9); **ear** (*inner*) el oído (9)

earlier than más temprano que (7)
early temprano (3)
Earth la Tierra (11)
earthquake el terremoto (5, 11)
easy fácil (2)
eat, to comer (2)
ecology la ecología (11)
education la pedagogía (2)
egg el huevo (7)
eight hundred ochocientos (2)
eight ocho (PA)
eighteen diez y ocho (PA)
eighth octavo/a (5)
eighty ochenta (1)
either . . . or o... o (4)
eldest el/la mayor (10)
elect, to elegir (11)
elections las elecciones (11)
elegant elegante (8)
elephant el elefante (11)
eleven once (PA)
emanate, to emanar (11)
embarrassed, to be tener
vergüenza (3)
emerge, to surgir (8)
emergency room la sala de
urgencias (9)
emotions emociones (2)
enclose, to encerrar (ie) (4)
encompass, to abarcar (5)
end, to acabar con (4); terminar (2)
endangered amenazada (7);
~ species los animales en peligro
de extinción (11)
engine el motor (10)
English inglés/inglesa (PA)
Enjoy your meal! ¡Buen provecho! (7)
enjoy, to disfrutar de (4); **to**
~ oneself divertirse (e, ie) (8)
enter, to entrar (10)
enter/exit, to transitar (10)
entertain oneself, to entretenerse (8)
entrance la entrada (5)
entretenida entertaining (5)
environment el medio ambiente (11)
epic épica (5)
equals son (1)
eraser el borrador (2)
espadrilles las alpargatas (8)
essay el ensayo (2)
ever jamás (11)
evil malvado/a (10)
evolve, to evolucionar (5)
exam el examen (2)
exercise, to hacer ejercicio (2)
expensive caro/a (4, 7)

A38

experience, to experimentar (11)
expression la expresión (PA)
eye el ojo (9)

F

fabric la tela (8)
face la cara (9)
facing enfrente de (11)
factory la fábrica (8)
fall: ~ el otoño (PA); to ~ asleep
  dormirse (o, ue) (8); to ~ down
  caer(se) (9)
fame la fama (5)
family la familia (1)
fan el/la aficionado/a (5)
far from lejos de (2, 11)
Farewells Las despedidas (PA)
farm la finca; la granja (11)
fascinate, to fascinar (8)
fashion la moda (8); ~ show el desfile
  de moda (8)
fat gordo/a (1)
father el padre (1)
feel, to sentir (PB); sentirse (e, ie) (8)
fever la fiebre (9)
fifteen quince (PA)
fifth quinto/a (5)
fifty cincuenta (1)
fight, to luchar (11)
fill, to llenar (10)
film la película (4)
finally finalmente (6)
find out, to averiguar (PB, 4);
  enterar (8); enterarse (10)
find, to dar con (2); encontrar (ue) (4)
Fine, thanks. Bien, gracias. (PA)
fine: ~ fino/a (5); ~ la multa (10)
finger el dedo (de la mano) (9)
finish, to terminar (2); to have just
  ~ed + (something) acabar de +
  infinitivo (9)
fire el incendio (11)
first primer, primero/a (5)
fish el pez (pl., los peces) (7, 11)
fit well / poorly, to quedarle bien /
  mal (8)
five cinco (PA); ~ hundred
  quinientos (2)
fix, to arreglar (3)
flight el vuelo (10)
flood la inundación (11)
floor el piso (3); el suelo (3)
flourishing floreciente (8)
flu la gripe (9); to have the ~ tener
  (la/una) gripe (9)

fly la mosca (11)
fly, to volar (o, ue); to ~ away volar
  (o, ue) (10)
folk healer el/la curandero/a (4)
follow, to seguir (i) (4)
following el siguiente (3)
food la comida (7)
foot el pie (8, 9); to go on ~ ir a
  pie (10)
for para (PB, 11); por (11)
forest el bosque (11)
fork el tenedor (7)
formal formal (8)
forty cuarenta (1)
four cuatro (PA); ~ hundred
  cuatrocientos (2); ~ hundred
  thousand cuatrocientos mil (3)
fourteen catorce (PA)
fourth cuarto/a (5); ~ floor el tercer
  piso (3)
freeway la autopista (10)
French francés/francesa (PA)
french fries las papas fritas (pl.) (7)
fresh fresco/a (7)
Friday el viernes (PA)
fried frito/a (7)
friend el/la amigo/a (1)
frightened asustado/a (7)
frightening aterredor (9)
frog la rana (11)
From where? ¿De dónde? (2)
from: ~ desde (11); ~ time to time a
  veces (2); ~ about de (11)
front: ~ desk la recepción (10); in
  ~ (of) enfrente (de) (4)
fruit las frutas (7)
function, to funcionar (10)
funds los fondos (10)
funny cómico/a (1)
furnished amueblado/a (3)
furniture los muebles (3); piece of
  ~ el mueble (3)
furthermore además (2)

G

garage el garaje (3)
garbage la basura (11)
garden el jardín (3)
gas: ~ station la gasolinera (10);
  ~ tank el tanque (10)
genre el género (5)
gentleman el señor (Sr.) (1)
German alemán/alemana (PA)
get: to ~ obtener (10); to ~ dressed
  vestirse (e, i) (8); to ~ down (from)

  bajar (de) (10); to ~ (nervous)
  ponerse (nervioso/a) (8); to ~ off
  (of) bajar (de) (10); to ~ on subir
  (a) (10); to ~ ready preparar (2),
  arreglarse (8); to ~ the urge
  entrar ganas (9); to ~ together
  reunirse (8); to ~ up levantarse (8)
gift el regalo (8)
girl la chica; la muchacha; little ~ la
  niña (1); ~friend la novia (1)
gist el tema (5)
give, to dar (3); to ~ life dar vida (5);
  to ~ a concert dar un concierto (5)
glass el vaso (7); el vidrio (11)
global warming el efecto
  invernadero (11)
gloves los guantes (8)
go out, to salir (3)
Go to the board. Vaya(n) a la
  pizarra. (PA)
go: to ~ ir (4); to ~ camping ir de
  camping (4); to ~ shopping ir de
  compras (2); to ~ to bed acostarse
  (o, ue) (8); to ~ up subir (a) (10)
Good afternoon. Buenas tardes.
  (PA)
good bueno/a (1, 10); ~ -bye. Adiós.
  (PA); ~ evening. Buenas noches.
  (PA); ~ morning. Buenos días. (PA)
government el gobierno (11)
governor el/la gobernador/a (11)
graduate, to graduar (11)
gram el gramo (7)
granddaughter la nieta (1)
grandfather el abuelo (1)
grandmother la abuela (1)
grandparents los abuelos (1)
grandson el nieto
gray gris (3)
green verde (3)
Greetings Los saludos (PA)
grilled a la parrilla (7); asado/a (7)
ground floor la planta baja (3)
group el conjunto (5)
grow, to aumentar (11)
guess, to adivinar (7)
guide la guía (5)
guilty el/la culpable (8)
guitar la guitarra (5)
guitarist el/la guitarrista (5)
gymnasium el gimnasio (2)

H

hair el pelo (9)
ham el jamón (7)

hamburger la hamburguesa (**7**)
hammock la hamaca (**11**)
hand la mano (**1, 9**); **to ~ out food** repartir comidas (**4**)
handsome guapo
hang up, to colgar (**7**)
happen, to pasar (**PB**)
happy contento/a (**2**); feliz (**2**)
hard: ~ **-boiled** duro/a (**7**); ~ **-working** trabajador/a (**1**)
harm, to hacer daño (**11**)
hat el sombrero (**8**)
have, to tener (**1**); **to ~ a... -ache** tener dolor de... (**9**); **to ~ a backache** tener dolor de espalda (**9**); **to ~ fun** divertirse (e, ie) (**8**); **to ~ a headache** tener dolor de cabeza (**9**); **to ~ just** acabar de (**3**); **to ~ lunch** almorzar (ue) (**4**); **to ~ a stomachache** tener dolor de estómago (**9**); **to ~ + (verb) to** tener que + (infinitive) (**3**)
he él (**PA**)
head la cabeza (**9**)
headquarters la sede (**9**)
health la salud (**9**); ~ **insurance** seguro médico (**9**)
healthy sana (**9**); **to be ~** estar sano/a; saludable (**9**)
heart el corazón (**9**)
heat la calefacción (**10**)
heaven el cielo (**11**)
heavy pésimo/a (**5**)
help, to ayudar (**3**); **to ~ elderly people** ayudar a las personas mayores/los mayores (**4**)
hen la gallina (**7, 11**)
her ella (**11**)
here aquí (**6**)
Hi! ¡Hola! (**PA**)
hide, to esconder (**8**)
high school la escuela secundaria (**9**)
highway la autopista (**10**)
hill la loma (**11**)
him él (**11**)
him/her, to/for le (**8**)
him/her/it lo, la (**5**)
his/her/its su, sus (**1**)
his/her/s/your/s (for.) /their/s suyo/a/os/as (**3, 10**); suyo/a (**PB**)
hole el hoyo (**11**)
holiday el día festivo (**7**)
home-made remedy el remedio casero (**7**)
homework la tarea (**2**)
honeymoon la luna de miel (**10**)

hope, to esperar (**2**)
horse el caballo (**11**)
hose las medias (pl.) (**8**)
hospital el hospital (**9**)
hot dog el perro caliente (**7**)
hot, to be tener calor (**3**); ~ (temperature) caliente (**7**)
hotel el hotel (**10**); **to leave the ~** irse del hotel (**10**)
house la casa (**3**)
housekeeper el/la camarero/a (**10**)
how: ~? ¿Cómo? (**2**); ~ **are you?** ¿Cómo está usted? (for.) (**PA**); ~ **are you?** ¿Cómo estas? (fam.) (**PA**); ~ **do you say . . . in Spanish?** ¿Cómo se dice... en español? (**PA**); ~ **many?** ¿Cuántos/as? (**2**); ~ **much?** ¿Cuánto/a? (**2**); ~**'s it going?** ¿Qué tal? (**PA**)
hubbub el bullicio (**4**)
hug el abrazo (**PA**)
human body el cuerpo humano (**9**)
humble humilde (**3**)
hummingbird el colibrí (**11**)
hungry, to be tener hambre (**3**)
hurricane el huracán (**11**)
hurry, to be in a tener prisa (**3**)
hurt, to dañar (**11**); doler (ue) (**9**); **to get ~** lastimar(se) (**9**)
husband el esposo (**1**)

I

I: ~ yo (**PA**); ~ **am . . .** Soy... (**PA**); ~ **don't know.** No lo sé. (**PA**); ~ **don't understand.** No comprendo. (**PA**); ~ **know.** Lo sé. (**PA**); ~ **understand.** Comprendo. (**PA**); ~ **would like to introduce you to . . .** Quiero presentarle a... (for.) (**PA**); ~ **would like to introduce you to . . .** Quiero presentarte a... (fam.) (**PA**)
ice cream el helado (**7**)
iced helado/a (**7**)
if si (**4**)
ill enfermo/a (**2**)
illness la enfermedad (**9**)
imaginative imaginativo/a (**5**)
important, to be importar (**8**)
impressive impresionante (**5**)
improve, to mejorar(se) (**9**)
in en (**11**); ~ **addition to** además de (**7**); ~ **exchange** a cambio (**4**); ~ **front of** delante de (**11**), en frente de (**2**); ~ **order to** a fin de

(**11**); ~ **order to** para (**11**); ~ **the afternoon** de la tarde (**PA**); ~ **the evening** de la noche (**PA**); ~ **the morning** de la mañana (**PA**)
infection, to have an tener una infección (**9**)
inflation la inflación (**11**)
influential influyente (**11**)
injury la herida (**9**)
insect el insecto (**11**)
inside of dentro de (**11**)
instead of en vez de (**8**)
intelligent inteligente (**1**)
interested in, to be interesar (**2**)
interesting interesante (**1**)
Internet café el cibercafé (**4**)
internship el trabajo en prácticas (**8**)
interview la entrevista (**3**)
intoxication el embriaguez (**10**)
introduce, to presentar (**3**)
Introductions Las presentaciones (**PA**)
involved involucrado/a (**11**)
it is necessary . . . (you must . . . / one must/should . . .) hay que + infinitivo (**5**)
it's: ~ **a shame** es una lástima (**11**); ~ **cold.** Hace frío. (**PA**); ~ **cloudy.** Está nublado. (**PA**); ~ **hot.** Hace calor. (**PA**); ~ **necessary that** es necesario que (**11**); ~ **raining.** Llueve. (**PA**); ~ **sunny.** Hace sol. (**PA**); ~ **windy.** Hace viento. (**PA**); ~ **. . . o'clock.** Es la... / Son las... (**PA**)

J

jacket la chaqueta (**8**)
jam la mermelada (**7**)
Japanese japonés/japonesa (**PA**)
jazz el jazz (**5**)
jeans los jeans (pl.) (**8**)
jewel la joya (**9**)
joke la broma (**3, 8**)
journalism el periodismo (**2**)
judge el/la juez/a (**11**)
juice el jugo (**7**)
jungle la selva, la selva tropical (**11**)
jury el juicio (**11**)
Just fine. Bastante bien. (**PA**)

K

keep, to guardar (**3**)
ketchup la salsa de tomate (**7**)
key la llave (**10**)

kill, to matar (11)
kind bondadoso/a (11)
king el rey (11)
kiss el beso (1); **little ~** el besito (PA)
kitchen la cocina (3)
knapsack la mochila (2)
knife el cuchillo (7)
know, to saber (4)

L

laboratory el laboratorio (2)
lacking, to be hacer falta (8)
lady la señora (Sra.) (1)
lake el lago (5, 10, 11)
lamp la lámpara (3)
land la tierra (11)
languages los idiomas (*pl.*) (2)
large grande (1)
largest mayor (5)
last: to ~ durar (9, 11); **~ night** anoche (7); **~ week** la semana pasada (7); **~ weekend** el fin de semana pasado (7); **~ year** el año pasado (7)
late tarde (3)
later than más tarde que (7)
laugh, to reírse (4)
law el derecho (2); la ley (10, 11)
lazy perezoso/a (1)
learn, to aprender (2)
leather el cuero (8)
leave, to dejar (10); irse (8); salir (3)
left (of), to the a la izquierda (de) (3, 11)
leg (*of an animal*) la pata (9); la pierna (9)
legend la leyenda (9)
lemon el limón (7)
lend, to prestar (8)
less . . . than menos + *adjective/ adverb/noun* + que (10)
let's: ~ hope ojalá que (11); **~ see** a ver (2)
lettuce la lechuga (7)
library la biblioteca (2)
lie la mentira (5, 7); **to ~** mentir (ie) (4)
light a campfire, to hacer una hoguera (4)
light ligero (PB); **~** (*colored*) claro/a (8)
like very much, to encantar (8)
like, to gustar (PA)
like: ~ como (5); **to feel ~ +** (*verb*) tener ganas de + (*infinitive*) (3)
Likewise. Igualmente. (PA)

line (*of people*) la cola (10)
lion el león (11)
listen to music, to escuchar música (2)
Listen. Escuche(n). (PA)
literacy la alfabetización (8)
literature la literatura (2)
little (*a*) (un) poco (1)
live, to vivir (2)
living room la sala (3)
living vivo/a (11)
loan to, to prestar (8)
locals los lugareños (4)
long largo/a (8)
look: to ~ at mirar (1); **to ~ for** buscar (4)
lose, to perder (ie) (4)
lost perdido/a (4)
loud fuerte (3)
love el amor (4); **to ~** encantar (8); querer (3)
lucky, to be tener suerte (3)
luggage el equipaje (10)
lunch el almuerzo (7); **to have ~** almorzar (ue) (7)
lyrics la letra (5)

M

magazine la revista (8)
mail a letter, to mandar una carta (4)
majors las especialidades (2)
make, to hacer (3); **to ~ arts and crafts** hacer artesanía (4); **to ~ the bed** hacer la cama (3)
mall el centro comercial (4)
man el hombre; el señor (Sr.) (1)
management el manejo (7)
manager el/la empresario/a (5)
many tanto/a (2)
map el mapa (2)
market el mercado (4)
marmalade la mermelada (7)
married casado/a (1)
match el acierto (11)
material el material (8)
mathematics las matemáticas (*pl.*) (2)
matter: ~ el asunto (6); **to ~** importar (8)
mayonnaise la mayonesa (7)
mayor el alcalde/la alcaldesa (11)
me me (5); mí (11); **to/for ~** me (8)
meal la comida (PB, 7)
meaning sentido (3)
meat la carne (7)
medical treatment el tratamiento médico (9)

medicine la medicina (2)
medium término medio (7)
meet, to reunirse (8)
melon el melón (7)
memento el recuerdo (3)
memory el recuerdo (7)
menu el menú (7)
mess el lío (9)
message el mensaje (3)
messy desordenado/a (3)
Mexican mexicano/a (PA)
microwave el microondas (3)
midnight la medianoche (PA)
mile la milla (PB)
milk la leche (7)
mine mío/a/os/as (10)
minus menos (1)
miss, to faltar (4)
Miss la señorita (Srta.) (1)
missing desaparecido/a (9)
mistaken, to be equivocarse (9)
mixed grill la parrillada (7)
mixture la mezcla (7)
model el/la modelo (8)
modern moderno/a (3)
mom la mamá (1)
monarchy la monarquía (11)
Monday el lunes (PA)
money el dinero (2)
month el mes (PA)
more . . . than más + *adjective/adverb/ noun* + que (10)
mosquito el mosquito (11)
mother la madre (1)
motor el motor (10)
motorcycle la moto (1); la moto(cicleta) (10)
mountain la montaña (10, 11); **~ range** la cordillera (11)
mountainous montañoso/a (4)
mouse el ratón (11)
mouth la boca (9)
movie la película (4, 5); **action ~** una película de acción (5); **science fiction ~** una película de ciencia ficción (5); **war ~** una película de guerra (5); **comedy ~** una película de humor (5); **mystery ~** una película de misterio (5); **romantic ~** una película romántica (5); **horror ~** una película de terror (5); **~ theater** el cine (4)
moving conmovedor/a; emocionante (5)
Mr. Sr. (1)
Mrs. Sra. (1)

A41

much tanto/a (9)
museum el museo (4)
music la música (2, 5); classical ~ la música clásica (5); folk ~ la música folklórica (5); pop ~ la música popular (5); rap ~ la música rap (5)
musical musical (5)
musician el/la músico/a (5)
mustard la mostaza (7)
my mi, mis (1)
My name is . . . Me llamo... (PA)

N

napkin la servilleta (7)
narrate, to contar (9); narrar (6)
narrow estrecho/a (8)
nationality la nacionalidad (PA)
natural resource el recurso natural (11)
nature la naturaleza (11)
nausea la náusea (9)
near cerca de (2, 7, 11)
neck el cuello (9)
need, to hacer falta (8); necesitar (2)
neither . . . nor ni... ni (4)
nervous nervioso/a (2)
never jamás (4); nunca (2, 3, 4)
nevertheless sin embargo (2, 3, 6)
new nuevo/a (3)
newspaper el periódico (11)
next to al lado de (11)
nice simpático/a (1)
Nice to meet you. Mucho gusto. (PA)
nickname el apodo (5)
Nigerian nigeriano/a (PA)
nightmare la pesadilla (8)
nine nueve (PA); ~ hundred novecientos (2)
nineteen diez y nueve (PA)
ninety noventa (1)
ninth noveno/a (5)
no: ~ longer ya no (5); ~. No. (PA); ~ one nadie (4)
nobody nadie (4)
noise el ruido (PB, 3, 10)
none ninguna (3); ningún (4); ninguno/a/os/as (4)
noon el mediodía (PA)
nor ni (3); tampoco (7)
northeast el noreste (2)
nose la nariz (9)
not ever (emphatic) jamás (4)
notebook el cuaderno (2)
notes los apuntes (pl.) (2)

nothing nada (4)
now ahora (PB)
number el número (PA)
nurse el/la enfermero/a (9)

O

object el objeto (3)
obligation el deber (4)
occur, to ocurrir (9)
ocean el océano (11)
offer la oferta (3); to ~ ofrecer (2)
office la oficina (3)
often a menudo (2, 3)
oil el aceite (7); ~ spill el derrame de petróleo (11)
oír to hear (3)
Okay. Regular. (PA)
old antiguo/a (3); mayor (1); viejo/a (3, 10); ~er mayor (10)
on top (of) encima (de), sobre (3, 7, 11)
on: on sobre (3); ~ hand a mano (10)
one uno (PA); ~ hundred cien (1, 2); ~ hundred million cien millones (3); ~ hundred thousand cien mil (3); ~ million un millón (3); ~ thousand mil (2)
onion la cebolla (7)
only solamente (8)
Open your book to page . . . Abra(n) el libro en la página... (PA)
open, to abrir (2)
opening el estreno (5)
opera la ópera (5)
orange anaranjado (3); ~ la naranja (7)
orchestra la orquesta (5)
order, to pedir (7)
ordinal numbers los números ordinales (5)
organize, to organizar (4)
others los demás (4)
ought to deber (4)
our/s nuestro/a/os/as (1, 10)
outfit el conjunto (8); el traje (5)
outside fuera (7); ~ of (a)fuera de (11)
outskirts las afueras (3)
over sobre (3, 11); ~ there (and potentially not visible) allá (6)
overcoat el abrigo (8)
overhaul, to revisar (10)
own propio/a (6)
ozone layer la capa de ozono (11)

P

package el paquete (10)
pain el dolor (9)
painted wooden animals los alebrijes (2)
painting el cuadro (3)
pajamas el pijama (8)
pants los pantalones (pl.) (8)
paper el papel (2)
parents los padres (1)
park el parque (4)
park, to estacionar (10)
parking el estacionamiento (10)
parrot el loro (11)
participate in a political campaign, to participar en una campaña política (4)
party fiesta (3)
passenger el pasajero (10)
passionate apasionado/a (5)
passport el pasaporte (10)
pastimes los pasatiempos (2)
pastry el pastel (7)
patient paciente (1)
pay, to pagar (7)
peace la paz (5)
pear la pera (7)
pedestrian el peatón (10)
pencil el lápiz (2)
people la gente (1)
pepper la pimienta (7)
percent por ciento (1)
perhaps tal vez (3)
personality la personalidad (1)
pet la mascota (10); el animal doméstico (11)
pharmacist el/la farmacéutico/a (9)
pharmacy la farmacia (9)
photo la foto (1)
physical física (1); ~ exam el examen físico (9)
pianist el/la pianista (5)
piano el piano (5)
picture el cuadro (3, 5)
pie el pastel (7)
pig el cerdo (11)
pile el montón (7)
pill la pastilla (9)
pillow la almohada (3)
pink rosado (3)
place el lugar (2)
place, to poner (3)
planet el planeta (11)
plant, to plantar (11)
plastic el plástico (11)

plate el plato (**7**)
plateau (high) el altiplano (**9**)
platform el programa (**11**)
play, to jugar (ue) (**4**); **to ~ an instrument** tocar un instrumento (**2, 5**); **to ~ basketball** jugar al básquetbol; **to ~ baseball** jugar al béisbol; **to ~ soccer** jugar al fútbol; **to ~ football** jugar al fútbol americano; **to ~ golf** jugar al golf; **to ~ tennis** jugar al tenis (**2**)
Please. Por favor. (**PA**)
Pleased to meet you. Encantado/ Encantada. (**PA**)
pleasure el placer (**7**)
plus más (**1**)
policeman el policía (**10**)
Polite expressions Expresiones de cortesía (**PA**)
political: ~ issues las cuestiones políticas (**11**); **~ party** el partido político (**11**)
politics la política (**11**); **to get involved in ~** meterse en política (**11**)
polka-dotted de lunares (**8**)
poll la encuesta (**11**)
pollute, to contaminar (**11**)
pollution la contaminación (**11**)
polyester el poliéster (**8**)
poncho el rebozo (**8**)
poor pobre (**1**)
pork la carne de cerdo (**7**)
post office correos; la oficina de correos (**4**)
postage stamp el sello (**10**)
postcard la tarjeta postal (**4, 10**)
posts los cargos (**11**)
potato chips las papas fritas (*pl.*) (**7**)
potato la papa; la patata (**7**)
poultry las aves (**7**)
practice, to ensayar (**5**)
prefer, to preferir (ie) (**4**)
pregnant embarazada (**9**)
preparation preparativo (**5**)
prepare, to preparar (**2**); **to ~ a meal** preparar la comida (**3**)
prescribe, to recetar (**9**)
prescription la receta (**9**)
presidency la presidencia (**11**)
president el/la presidente/a (**11**)
pretty bonito/a, guapa (**1**)
previous anterior (**5**)
print with a design or pattern el/la estampado/a (**8**)
professor el/la profesor/a (**2**)
proof la prueba (**10**)

propose, to proponer (**5**)
protect, to proteger (**11**)
proud orgulloso/a (**4**)
province la provincia (**11**)
psychology la psicología (**2**)
Puerto Rican puertorriqueño/a (**PA**)
pure puro/a (**11**)
purple morado (**3**)
purpose el próposito (**7**)
purse el bolso (**8**)
put away, to guardar (**3**)
put, to poner (**3**)
put: to ~ on (*one's clothes*) ponerse (la ropa) (**8**); **to ~ on make up** maquillarse (**8**); **to ~ up a tent** montar una tienda de campaña (**4**)

Q

quality la calidad (**11**)
queen la reina (**11**)
Questions and answers Preguntas y respuestas (**PA**)
quiet, to keep callarse (**8**)

R

rabbit el conejo (**11**)
radio el/la radio (**2**)
rain la lluvia (**PA**); **~ forest** (*tropical*) la selva tropical (**11**)
raincoat el impermeable (**8**)
rare crudo/a; poco hecho/a (**7**)
rat la rata (**11**)
raw crudo/a (**7**)
read, to leer (**2**)
Read. Lea(n). (**PA**)
Really well. Muy bien. (**PA**)
receive, to recibir (**2**)
recognize, to reconocer (**8**)
recommend, to recomendar (ie) (**4**)
record, to grabar (**5**)
recordings las grabaciones (**5**)
recycle, to reciclar (**11**)
red rojo (**3**)
reforest, to reforestar (**11**)
refrigerator el refrigerador (**3**)
regime el regímen (**11**)
region la región (**11**)
rehearse, to ensayar (**5**)
relatives los parientes (**2**)
release a CD, to sacar un CD (**5**)
release a movie, to estrenar una película (**5**)
remain, to quedarse (**8**)

remember, to acordarse de (o, ue) (**8**); recordar (ue) (**4**)
repeat, to repetir (i) (**4**)
Repeat. Repita(n). (**PA**)
report el reportaje (**12**)
representative el/la diputado/a (**11**)
request el pedido (**9**)
require, to requerir (**11**)
reservation la reserva (**10**)
reserve a table, to reservar una mesa (**7**)
resolve, to resolver (o, ue) (**11**)
respect, to respetar (**5**)
responsible responsable (**1**)
rest, to descansar (**7**)
restaurant el restaurante (**4, 7**)
return, to regresar (**2**); volver (ue) (**4**); **to ~** (*an object*) devolver (ue) (**4**)
reuse, to reutilizar (**11**)
review la reseña (PB, **5**)
rhythm el ritmo (**5**)
rice el arroz (**7**)
rich rico/a (**1**)
riddle el rompecabeza (**7**)
ride: to ~ a bike montar en bicicleta (**2**); **to ~ a horse** montar (a caballo) (**11**)
right: to be ~ tener razón (**3**); **to the ~ (of)** a la derecha (de) (**3, 11**)
ring el anillo (**5**)
risk el riesgo (**9**)
river el río (**11**)
roasted asado/a (**7**)
robe la bata (**8**)
rock el rock (**5**)
roof el techo (**3**)
room el cuarto (**2, 3**); **~mate** el/la compañero/a de cuarto (**2**)
rooster el gallo (**7**)
rough áspero/a (**11**)
roving ambulante (**4**)
row la fila (**5**)
rug la alfombra (**3**)
run, to correr (**2**)

S

sad triste (**2**)
salad la ensalada (**7**)
salsa la salsa (**5**)
salt la sal (**7**)
sandals las sandalias (*pl.*) (**8**)
Saturday el sábado (**PA**)
save, to salvar (**9**)
say, to decir (**3**)
scare, to asustar (**9**)

A43

scarf la bufanda (9)
scary espantoso/a (5)
schedule el horario (6); ~ (of classes) el horario (de clases) (2)
science las ciencias (pl.) (2)
scream, to gritar (8)
screen la pantalla (5)
scuba diving el buceo (4)
seafood los mariscos (7)
seamstress la costurera (8)
season la estación (PA)
seasoning el condimento (7)
second segundo/a (5); ~ floor el primer piso (3)
security la seguridad (2)
see, to ver (3)
see: ~ you later. Hasta luego. (PA); ~ you soon. Hasta pronto. (PA); ~ you tomorrow. Hasta mañana. (PA)
seem, to parecer (4)
semester el semestre (2)
senate el senado (11)
senator el/la senador/a (11)
send a letter, to mandar una carta (4)
serve, to servir (i) (4)
set the table, to poner la mesa (3)
seven siete (PA); ~ hundred setecientos (2)
seventeen diez y siete (PA)
seventh séptimo/a (5)
seventy setenta (1)
shaman el chamán (9)
share, to compartir (3, 5)
shark el tiburón (5)
shave, to afeitarse (8)
she ella (PA)
sheet la sábana (3)
shirt la camisa (8)
shoes los zapatos (pl.) (8)
short bajo/a (1); corto/a (8)
shorts los pantalones cortos (pl.) (8)
shot la inyección (9)
should deber (4)
show, to enseñar (2); mostrar (ue) (4); to ~ a movie presentar una película (5)
shower la ducha (3); to ~ ducharse (8)
shrimp los camarones (pl.) (7)
shrub el arbusto (7)
siblings los hermanos (1)
sick, to be estar enfermo/a (2, 9); enfermar(se) (9)
side el lado (2)
sigh el suspiro (11)
signature la firma (4)

silk la seda (8)
silly tonto/a (1)
similarity la semejanza (6)
since ya que (1)
singer el/la cantante (5)
single room el cuarto individual (10)
sink el lavabo (3)
sister la hermana (1)
sit down, to sentarse (e, ie) (8)
six seis (PA); ~ hundred seiscientos (2)
sixteen diez y seis (PA)
sixth sexto/a (5)
sixty sesenta (1)
skate, to patinar (2)
skill la habilidad (5)
skirt la falda (8)
sky el cielo (11)
sleep, to dormir (ue) (4)
sleepy, to be tener sueño (3)
slippers las zapatillas (pl.) (8)
slow lento/a (3, 5)
small pequeño/a (1, 10); smaller menor (10); smallest el/la menor (10)
smooth suave (5)
snack la merienda (7); to have a ~ merendar (7)
snake la serpiente (11)
sneeze el estornudo (9); to ~ estornudar (9)
snow la nieve (PA)
socks los calcetines (pl.) (8)
sofa el sofá (3)
soft drink el refresco (7)
soil la tierra (11)
solid-colored liso/a (8)
some algún (4); alguno/a/os/as (3, 4); un/una/unos/unas (1)
someone alguien (4)
something algo (PB, 4)
sometimes a veces (2, 3, 4)
son el hijo (1)
sore throat el dolor de garganta (9)
So-so. Más o menos. (PA)
soup la sopa (7); ~ spoon la cuchara (7)
source la fuente (5, 9)
sow, to sembrar (e, ie) (11)
spam el correo basura (3)
Spaniard español/española (PA)
Spanish-speaking hispanohablante (3)
speak, to hablar (2)
specialty of the house la especialidad de la casa (7)
speech el discurso (11)
spices las especias (7)
spicy picante (7)

spoonful la cucharada (7)
sports los deportes (2)
spring la primavera (PA)
stadium el estadio (2)
staircase la escalera (3, 11)
stand: to ~ pararse (10); to ~ out destacar (5); to ~ up levantarse (8)
star la estrella (5)
start el principio (8)
state el estado (9, 11)
statehood la estadidad (11)
states (of being) los estados (2)
station (train, bus) la estación (de tren, de autobús) (10)
stay, to quedarse (8, 11); to ~ in bed guardar cama (9)
steak el bistec (7)
steering wheel el volante (10)
stepfather el padrastro (1)
stepmother la madrastra (1)
still todavía (4)
stirred up alborotado/a (11)
stockings las medias (pl.) (8)
stomach el estómago (9)
store la tienda (2)
storm la tormenta (11)
story el piso (3)
stove la estufa (3)
straighten up, to arreglar (3)
strange extraño (4)
street la calle (3, 10)
strike la huelga (11); to be on ~ estar en huelga (11)
striped de rayas (8)
strong fuerte (1)
student el/la estudiante (2); ~ center/ union el centro estudiantil (2)
study, to estudiar (2, 6)
stupendous estupendo/a (5)
style el estilo (8)
subject la materia (2)
subway el metro (10)
successful, to be tener éxito (3)
such tan (2)
suddenly de repente (PB)
sugar el azúcar (7)
suit el traje (5, 8); bathing ~ el traje de baño (8)
suitable use el uso adecuado (10)
suitcase la maleta (10); to pack a ~ arreglar/hacer la maleta (10)
summarize, to resumir (9)
summer el verano (PA); ~ camp el campamento de niños (4)
sun el sol (PA); to ~bathe tomar el sol (2)

Sunday el domingo (**PA**)
supermarket el supermercado (**4**)
support, to apoyar (**5, PB, 11**); **to ~ a candidate** apoyar a un/a candidato/a (**4**)
surprise la sorpresa (**8**)
surprising sorprendente (**5**)
survey la encuesta (**11**)
suspenseful de suspenso (**5**)
suspicious sospechoso/a (**2**)
sweater el suéter (**8**)
sweatshirt la sudadera (**8**)
sweets los dulces (**7**)
swim, to nadar (**2**); **~suit** traje de baño (**8**)

T

table la mesa (**2**)
tablecloth el mantel (**7**)
tablespoon la cuchara (**7**)
tailor el costurero (**8**)
take turns, to turnarse (**3**)
take, to tomar (**2**); llevar (**8**); **to ~ a nap** echar una siesta (**PB**); **to ~ a short trip** ir de excursión (**4**); **to ~ a walk** hacer una caminata (**4**); **to ~ care of** cuidar (**11**); **to ~ off** (*one's clothes*) quitarse (*la ropa*) (**8**); **to ~ out the garbage** sacar la basura (**3**); **to ~ someone to the doctor** llevar a alguien al médico (**4**)
tall alto/a (**1**)
tax el impuesto (**11**)
taxi el taxi (**10**)
tea (*iced/hot*) el té (*helado/caliente*) (**7**)
teach, to enseñar (**2**)
team el equipo (**2**)
teaspoon la cucharita (**7**)
television la televisión (**2**)
tell, to decir (**3**)
temperature la temperatura (**PA**)
temple el templo (**4**)
ten diez (**PA**)
tennis shoes los tenis (*pl.*) (**8**)
tenth décimo/a (**5**)
Thank you. Gracias. (**PA**)
that, that one (*way over there/not visible*) aquel/la; ese/a (**5**)
that, those (*way over there/not visible*); **those ones** aquellos/as (**5**)
the el/la/los/las (**1**); **~ check, please.** La cuenta, por favor. (**7**); **~ weather is bad.** Hace mal tiempo. (**PA**); **~ weather is nice.** Hace buen tiempo. (**PA**)

theater el teatro (**4**)
their su, sus (**1**)
them los, las (**5**); ellos/as (**11**); **to/for ~** les (**8**)
theme park el parque de atracciones (**10**)
then entonces, luego (**6**)
there / over there allí (**4, 6**)
there is / are hay (**2**)
these estos/as (**5**)
they ellos/as (**PA**)
thin delgado/a (**1**)
thing la cosa (**3**)
think, to pensar (ie) (**4**)
third tercer, tercero/a (**5**); **~ floor** el segundo piso (**3**)
thirsty, to be tener sed (**3**)
thirteen trece (**PA**)
thirty treinta (**PA, 1**); **~ thousand** treinta mil (**3**)
this esto (**3**)
this, this one este/a (**5**)
those over there; those ones esos/as (**3, 5**)
threat la amenaza (**8**)
three tres (**PA**); **~ hundred** trescientos (**2**)
throat la garganta (**9**)
through por (**11**)
throw, to tirar (**9**); **to ~ away** botar (**11**)
Thursday el jueves (**PA**)
ticket el boleto (**8, 10**), la entrada (**5**); **free ~** la entrada gratis (**5**); **round-trip ~** el boleto de ida y vuelta (**10**)
tie la corbata (**8**)
tight estrecho/a (**8**)
time la hora (**PA**)
time la vez (**5**)
times por (**1**)
tin work hojalatería (**2**)
tip la propina (**7**)
tire la llanta (**10**)
tired cansado/a (**2**)
to a (**11**); **~ where?** ¿Adónde? (**2**)
toast la tostada (**7**)
toe el dedo (del pie) (**9**)
toilet el inodoro (**3**)
tomato el tomate (**7**)
too también (**2**)
tooth el diente (**9**)
topic el tema (**5**)
tornado el tornado (**11**)
touch, to tocar (**4**)
tour la gira (**5**); **to ~** hacer una gira (**5**)

tournament el torneo (**4**)
tower la torre (**3**)
town el pueblo (**4**); **~ square** la plaza (**4**)
track and field el atletismo (**2**)
traditional tradicional (**3**)
traffic el tráfico (**10**); **~ light** el semáforo (**10**); **~ ticket** la multa (**10**)
tragedy la tragedia (**11**)
tragic trágico/a (**5**)
train el tren (**10**)
transportation el transporte (**10**)
travel, to viajar (**10**); **~ agent** el/la agente de viajes (**10**); **~ agency** la agencia de viajes (**6, 10**)
traveler el/la viajero/a (**10**)
treasure el tesoro (**10**)
treat, to tratar (**9**)
tree el árbol (**11**)
trip el viaje (**10**); **to go on a ~** ir de viaje (**10**)
truck el camión (**10**)
true cierto/a (**4**)
trumpet la trompeta (**5**); **~ player** el/la trompetista (**5**)
trunk el baúl (**10**)
try on clothing, to probarse (o, ue) la ropa (**8**)
try to, to tratar de (**3, 9**)
T-shirt la camiseta (**5, 8**)
tsunami el sunami (**11**)
Tuesday el martes (**PA**)
tuna el atún (**7**)
turn: to ~ doblar (**10**); **to ~ in** entregar (**7**); **to ~ on** encender (**9**)
turnover (*meat*) la empanada (**7**)
twelve doce (**PA**)
twenty veinte (**PA**)
two dos (**PA**); **~ hundred** doscientos (**2**); **~ million** dos millones (**3**); **~ thousand** dos mil (**3**)

U

ugly feo/a (**1**)
umbrella el paraguas (**8**)
uncle el tío (**1**)
uncomfortable incómodo/a (**8**)
under; underneath debajo (de) (**7, 11**)
undercover encubierto/a (**11**)
underline, to subrayar (**7**)
understand, to comprender (**2**); entender (ie) (**4**)
underwear la ropa interior (**8**)
unemployment el desempleo (**11**)

A45

unpleasant antipático/a (**1**)
until hasta (**11**)
upset nervioso/a (**2**)
us nos (**5**); nosotros/as (**11**); **to/for ~** nos (**8**)
use, to usar (**PB, 2**, 4)
useful útil (**PA**)

V

vacation las vacaciones (**10**); **to go on ~** ir de vacaciones (**10**)
vacuum, to pasar la aspiradora (**3**)
vegetable la verdura (**7**)
vehicle el vehículo (**10**)
verb el verbo (**1, 2**)
very muy (**1**)
village el pueblo (**4**)
vinegar el vinagre (**7**)
virus, to have a tener un virus (**9**)
visit, to visitar (**10**)
voice la voz (**5**)
volunteer at a nursing home, to trabajar como voluntario/a en la residencia de ancianos (**4**)
volunteerism el voluntariado (**4**)
vote el voto (**11**); **to ~** votar (**11**)

W

waist la cintura (**9**); **from the ~ up** de la cintura para arriba (**9**)
wait: to ~ for esperar (**2**); **to ~ on** atender (**9**)
waiter el camarero (**7**)
waitress la camarera (**7**)
wake up, to despertarse (e, ie) (**8**)
walk, to andar (**7**); caminar (**2**)
wall la pared (**2**)
want, to querer (**2, 3**)
war la guerra (**11**)
warn, to advertir (**8**)
wash: to ~ dishes lavar los platos (**3**); **to ~ oneself** lavarse (**8**)
waste, to perder (ie) (**4**)
watch el reloj (**2**)
watch television, to ver la televisión (**2**)
water el agua; **fresh ~** el agua dulce (**5**); **~ (with ice)** el agua (con hielo) (**7**)

waterfall la cascada (**10**)
we nosotros/as (**PA**)
weak débil (**1**)
wear, to llevar (**8**)
wedding la boda (**4**)
Wednesday el miércoles (**PA**)
week la semana (**PA**)
welfare el bienestar (**11**)
well: well cooked bien hecho/a (**7**); **~ done** bien cocido/a (**7**); **~ -being** el bienestar (**11**)
west el oeste (2)
what que (3)
what? ¿qué? (3); **~?** ¿Cómo? (**PA**); **~?** ¿Qué? (**2**); **~ day is today?** ¿Qué día es hoy? (**PA**); **~ does it mean?** ¿Qué significa? (**PA**); **~ is the gist of . . . ?** ¿De qué se trata... ? (**8**); **~ is this?** ¿Qué es esto? (**PA**); **~ is today's date?** ¿Cuál es la fecha de hoy? (**PA**); **~ is your name?** ¿Cómo se llama usted? (*for.*) (**PA**); **~ is your name?** (*fam.*) ¿Cómo te llamas? (**PA**); **~ time is it?** ¿Qué hora es? (**PA**); **~'s the weather like?** ¿Qué tiempo hace? (**PA**)
whatever cualquier (8)
When? ¿Cuándo? (**2**)
Where? ¿Dónde? (**2**)
which el cual (**11**); **~ (one/s)?** ¿Cuál/es? (**2**)
while mientras (2)
whip, to azotar (**11**)
white blanco (3)
Who? ¿Quién? (**PA, 2**); ¿Quiénes? (*pl.*) (**2**)
Why? ¿Por qué? (**2**)
wide ancho/a (**7, 8**)
wife la esposa (**1**)
wild animals los animales salvajes (**11**)
win, to ganar (6)
wind el viento (**PA**)
window la ventana (**2**); **to ~ shop** ojear las vitrinas (8)
windshield el parabrisas (**10**); **~wiper** el limpiaparabrisas (**10**)
wine el vino (**7**)
winter el invierno (**PA**)

with con (**11**); **~ me** conmigo (**9**); **~ oneself** consigo (**11**); **~ you** contigo (**9**); **~out** sin (**4, 11**)
woman la mujer (**1**); la señora (Sra.) (**1**)
wool la lana (**8**)
word la palabra (**PA**)
work, to funcionar (**10**), trabajar (**2**); **to ~ as a counselor** trabajar como consejero/a (**4**); **to ~ in politics** trabajar en política (**4**)
worried preocupado/a (**2**)
worry about, to preocuparse (por) (**11**)
worse peor (**10**)
worst el/la peor (**4, 10**)
wound la herida (**9**)
wrap, to envolver (**7**)
wrestling la lucha libre (**2**)
write, to escribir (**2**)
Write. Escriba(n). (**PA**)

Y

yam la batata (**7**)
years old, to be . . . tener... años (**3**)
yellow amarillo (**3**)
Yes. Sí. (**PA**)
yesterday ayer (**7**)
you te (**5**); ti (**11**); tú (*fam.*) (**PA**); usted/es (*for.*) (**PA, 11**); vosotros/as (*fam. pl. Spain*) (**PA, 11**); **~ all** os (**5**); **~ all** los, las (**5**); **to/for ~** te (**8**); **to/for ~ all** os (**8**)
young joven (**1, 10**); **~ man** el joven, el señor (Sr.) (**1**); **~ woman** la joven, la señorita (Srta.) (**1**); **~er** menor (**10**); **~est** el/la menor (**10**)
your (*for.*) su, sus (**1**); tu, tus (**1**); vuestro/a/os/as (*fam. pl. Spain*) (**1, 10**)
You're welcome. De nada. (**PA**)
yours (*fam.*) tuyo/a/os/as (**3, 10**)
yucca la mandioca (**7**)

Z

zero cero (**PA**)

Credits

Photo Credits

Page numbers given for all references correspond to the eText, available in MySpanishLab.

p. 2: Jack Hollingsworth/Photodisc/Thinkstock; **p. 4:** (l) Demetrio Carrasco/Dorling Kindersley; (c) Jupiterimages/Comstock/Thinkstock; (r) Digital Vision/Thinkstock; **p. 7:** (t) Stockbyte/Getty Images; (b) Comstock Images/Thinkstock; **p. 12:** Yuri Arcurs/Shutterstock; **p. 15:** Jupiterimages/Comstock/Thinkstock; **p. 16:** George Doyle/Stockbyte/Thinkstock; **p. 20:** (t) Stockbyte/Thinkstock; (1st row, left to right) Jupiterimages/Photos.com/Thinkstock; Jupiterimages/Comstock/Thinkstock; Pete Saloutos/Shutterstock; BananaStock/Thinkstock; (2nd row, left to right) James Woodson/Photodisc/Thinkstock; BananaStock/Thinkstock; Jupiterimages/Brand X Pictures/Thinkstock; BananaStock/Thinkstock; **p. 21:** Samot/Shutterstock; **p. 22:** (l) Medioimages/Photodisc/Thinkstock; (tr) David Kay/Shutterstock; (br) Eddie Gerald/Rough Guides/DK Images; **p. 26:** (t) Andi Berger/Shutterstock; (1st row, l) iofoto/Shutterstock; (1st row, c) Resnak/Shutterstock; (1st row, r) Brad Remy/Shutterstock; (2nd row, l) Jupiterimages/Comstock/Thinkstock; (2nd row, c) Brandon Seidel/Shutterstock; (2nd row, r) Saleeee/Shutterstock; (3rd row, l) Paul Yates/Shutterstock; (3rd row, c) olly/Shutterstock; **pp. 30–31:** Andresr/Shutterstock; **p. 35:** (t) monbibi/Shutterstock; (b) David Sacks/Lifesize/Thinkstock; **p. 45:** Rido/Shutterstock; **p. 46:** (t) Knotsmaster/Shutterstock; (b) Grigory Kubatyan/Shutterstock; **p. 50:** (l) Goodshoot/Thinkstock; (r) Comstock Images/Thinkstock; **p. 52:** (t) ImageryMajestic/Shutterstock; (c) Jeffery Allan Salter/Corbis SABA/Corbis Entertainment/Corbis; (cr) Aspen Photo/Shutterstock; (bl) Michael Moran/Dorling Kindersley; (bc) Samot/Shutterstock; **pp. 60–61:** Bill Perry/Shutterstock; **p. 64:** csp/Shutterstock; **p. 69:** Jack Hollingsworth/Photodisc/Thinkstock; **p. 72:** (tl) kaarsten/Shutterstock; (cr) Creatista/Shutterstock; **p. 73:** (l) Poprugin Aleksey/Shutterstock; (cl) John Foxx/Stockbyte/Thinkstock; (cr) Matthew Ward/Dorling Kindersley; (r) Comstock Images/Getty Images/Thinkstock; **p. 81:** (tl) Skylinephoto/Shutterstock; (tc) Stockbyte/Thinkstock; (tr) Jack Hollingsworth/Digital Vision/Thinkstock; (bl) Comstock/Thinkstock; (bc) Jupiterimages/Comstock/Thinkstock; (br) Donald Miralle/Lifesize/Thinkstock; **p. 82:** (1st row, l) Bikeriderlondon/Shutterstock; (1st row, c) Stockbyte/Thinkstock; (1st row, r) Stephen Mcsweeny/Shutterstock; (2nd row, l) BananaStock/Thinkstock; (2nd row, c) Digital Vision/Thinkstock; (2nd row, r) Stockbyte/Thinkstock; (3rd row, l) Poleze/Shutterstock; (3rd row, c) Maridav/Shutterstock; (3rd row, c) Daria Minaeva/Shutterstock; (4th row, l) Jupiterimages/Brand X Pictures/Thinkstock; **p. 83:** Stockbyte/Thinkstock; **p. 84:** John Gibson/AFP/Getty Images; **p. 86:** (t) Jack Hollingsworth/Photodisc/Thinkstock; (b) Jupiterimages/Comstock/Thinkstock; **p. 88:** (t) Jack Hollingsworth/Photodisc/Thinkstock; (cr) csp/Shutterstock; (b) csp/Shutterstock; **p. 89:** (t) Pixland/Thinkstock; (c) SoloHielo/Shutterstock; (b) Francesca Yorke/Dorling Kindersley; **pp. 96–97:** D. Heining-Boynton, HBPHOTOPRO.COM; **p. 100:** (tl) D. Heining-Boynton, HBPHOTOPRO.COM; (tc) Evok20/Shutterstock; (tr) gary yim/Shutterstock; (bl) javarman/Shutterstock; (bc) Jarno Gonzalez Zarraonandia/Shutterstock; (br) D. Heining-Boynton, HBPHOTOPRO.COM; **p. 104:** Mark Hayes/Shutterstock; **p. 105:** (t) D. Heining-Boynton, HBPHOTOPRO.COM; (b) D. Heining-Boynton, HBPHOTOPRO.COM; **p. 107:** HamsterMan/Shutterstock; **p. 111:** (1st row, l) D. Heining-Boynton, HBPHOTOPRO.COM; (1st row, c) D. Heining-Boynton, HBPHOTOPRO.COM; (1st row, r) D. Heining-Boynton, HBPHOTOPRO.COM; (2nd row, l) D. Heining-Boynton, HBPHOTOPRO.COM; (2nd row, c) D. Heining-Boynton, HBPHOTOPRO.COM; (2nd row, r) D. Heining-Boynton, HBPHOTOPRO.COM; (3rd row, l) D. Heining-Boynton, HBPHOTOPRO.COM; (3rd row, tc) Alberto Loyo/Shutterstock; (3rd row, bc) D. Heining-Boynton, HBPHOTOPRO.COM; (3rd row, r) D. Heining-Boynton, HBPHOTOPRO.COM; **p. 112:** D. Heining-Boynton, HBPHOTOPRO.COM; **p. 117:** (tl) D. Heining-Boynton, HBPHOTOPRO.COM; (tr) Natalia Belotelova/Shutterstock; (bl) Pres Panayotov/Shutterstock; (br) D. Heining-Boynton, HBPHOTOPRO.COM; **p. 119:** (t) D. Heining-Boynton, HBPHOTOPRO.COM; (b) D. Heining-Boynton, HBPHOTOPRO.COM; **p. 121:** Comstock/Thinkstock; **p. 122:** Photoroller/Shutterstock; **p. 124:** (t) Brand X Pictures/Thinkstock; (cr) Richard Wareham Fotografie/Alamy; (bl) Vinicius Tupinamba/Shutterstock; (br) imageZebra/Shutterstock; **p. 125:** (tl) Sillycoke/Shutterstock; (cl) D. Heining-Boynton, HBPHOTOPRO.COM; (cr) Joan Ramon Mendo Escoda/Shutterstock; (b) D. Heining-Boynton, HBPHOTOPRO.COM; **p. 126:** Pearson Education; **p. 128:** (l) Erin Baiano/Pearson Education/PH College; (c) Erin Baiano/Pearson Education/PH College; (r) Erin Baiano/Pearson Education/PH College; **pp. 132–133:** Grigory Kubatyan/Shutterstock; **p. 135:** (t) Peter Wilson/Dorling Kindersley; (bl) Stockbyte/Thinkstock; (br) olly/Shutterstock; **p. 136:** Suzanne Long/Shutterstock; **p. 137:** Jennifer Stone/Shutterstock; **p. 139:** Jupiterimages/Thinkstock; **p. 141:** Medioimages/Photodisc/Thinkstock; **p. 145:** ImageState Royalty Free/Alamy; **p. 146:** PhotoLibrary; **p. 148:** Jack Hollingsworth/Stockbyte/Thinkstock; **p. 151:** vadim kozlovsky/Shutterstock; **p. 153:** Pixland/Thinkstock; **p. 156:** Andresr/Shutterstock; **p. 157:** Pearson Education; **p. 158:** BananaStock/Thinkstock; **p. 161:** (t) Andresr/Shutterstock; (cl) Christopher Poe/Shutterstock; (cr) Dave Rock/Shutterstock; (b) John A. Anderson/Shutterstock; **p. 162:** (t) Jupiterimages/liquidlibrary/Thinkstock; (cl) Daniel Loncarevic/Shutterstock; (cr) Gugli/Dreamstime; (b) Mike Cohen/Shutterstock; **p. 163:** (t) iofoto/Shutterstock; (cl) rj lerich/Shutterstock; (bl) Yai/Shutterstock; (br) EpicStockMedia/Shutterstock; **p. 164:** Pearson Education; **p. 166:** (l, c, r) Pearson Education; **pp. 170–171:** AndrusV/Shutterstock; **p. 174:** (t) olly/Shutterstock; **p. 178:** (tr) JLC/ZOJ WENN Photos/Newscom; (bl) Miguel Campos/Shutterstock; (br) Helga Esteb/Shutterstock; **p. 186:** (tl) cinemafestival/Shutterstock; (cl) cinemafestival/Shutterstock; (bl) cinemafestival/Shutterstock; (br) DFree/Shutterstock; **p. 191:** (t) dwphotos/Shutterstock; (b) Dana Nalbandian/Shutterstock; **p. 192:** Pearson Education; **p. 193:** DeshaCAM/Shutterstock; **p. 195:** (t) Getty Images, Inc. – PhotoDisc; (cl) rj lerich/Shutterstock; (cr) rj lerich/Shutterstock; (b) Terry Honeycutt/Shutterstock; **p. 196:** (t) Kim Steele/Photodisc/Thinkstock;

Page numbers given for all references correspond to the eText, available in MySpanishLab.

(cl) Sandra A. Dunlap/Shutterstock; (cr) Brandon Stein/Shutterstock; (b) Brand X Pictures/Thinkstock; **p. 197:** (t) Jack Hollingsworth/Photodisc/Thinkstock; (cl) Paul Katz/Photodisc/Thinkstock; (cr) Chris Howey/Shutterstock; (b) rj lerich/Shutterstock; **p. 198:** Pearson Education; **p. 200:** (l, c, r) Pearson Education; **p. 204:** (l) Michael Moran/Dorling Kindersley; (r) Vinicius Tupinamba/Shutterstock; **p. 205:** (l) Daniel Loncarevic/Shutterstock; (r) Brandon Stein/Shutterstock; **p. 207:** (tl) Jack Hollingsworth/Thinkstock; (tr) Creatas Images/Thinkstock; (b) Ryan McVay/Photodisc/Getty Images; **p. 208** (1st row, l) ImageryMajestic/Shutterstock; (1st row, lc) Jack Hollingsworth/Photodisc/Thinkstock; (1st row, rc) Brand X Pictures/Thinkstock; (1st row, r) Andresr/Shutterstock; (2nd row, l) Jupiterimages/liquidlibrary/Thinkstock; (2nd row, lc) iofoto/Shutterstock; (2nd row, c) Getty Images, Inc. – PhotoDisc; (2nd row, rc) Kim Steele/Photodisc/Thinkstock; (2nd row, r) Jack Hollingsworth/Photodisc/Thinkstock; **p. 211:** Ian Tragen/Shutterstock; **p. 214:** Steve Mason/Getty Images; **p. 216:** Dwphotos/Shutterstock; **p. 219:** Frontpage/Shutterstock; **p. 220:** (all) Pearson Education; **p. 221:** (all) Pearson Education; **p. 222:** Santiago Cornejo/Shutterstock; **p. 223:** (bl) Joe Mercier/Shutterstock; (br) Aspen Photo/Shutterstock; **p. 224:** (t, 1st row, l) csp/Shutterstock; (t, 1st row, lc) D. Heining-Boynton, HBPHOTOPRO.COM; (t, 1st row, rc) John A. Anderson/Shutterstock; (t, 1st row, r) Daniel Loncarevic/Shutterstock; (t, 2nd row, l) csp/Shutterstock; (t, 2nd row, lc) D. Heining-Boynton, HBPHOTOPRO.COM; (t, 2nd row, rc) Dave Rock/Shutterstock; (t, 2nd row, r) Mike Cohen/Shutterstock; (b, 1st row, l) rj lerich/Shutterstock; (b, 1st row, lc) Terry Honeycutt/Shutterstock; (b, 1st row, rc) Brandon Stein/Shutterstock; (b, 1st row, r) Paul Katz/Photodisc/Thinkstock; (b, 2nd row, l) EpicStockMedia/Shutterstock; (b, 2nd row, lc) rj lerich/Shutterstock; (b, 2nd row, rc) Brand X Pictures/Thinkstock; (b, 2nd row, r) rj lerich/Shutterstock; **pp. 226–227:** Andresr/Shutterstock; **p. 228:** (tl) Jack Hollingsworth/Photodisc/Thinkstock; (tr) Corbis; (bl) Julie Keen/Shutterstock; (br) Digital Vision./Digital Vision/Thinkstock; **p. 229:** Creatas/Jupiter Images; **p. 236:** (l) Ilja Maå¡Åk/Shutterstock; (r) Pearson Education; **p. 238:** (l) D. Heining-Boynton, HBPHOTOPRO.COM; (r) russ witherington/Shutterstock; **p. 239:** (l) D. Heining-Boynton, HBPHOTOPRO.COM; (c) Pearson Education; (r) D. Heining-Boynton, HBPHOTOPRO.COM; **p. 240:** (l) Cheryl Casey/Shutterstock; (c) Giordano Aita/Shutterstock; (r) Michael Shake/Shutterstock; **p. 242:** Dean Mitchell/Shutterstock; **p. 243:** Jupiterimages/Thinkstock; **p. 246:** Creatas Images/Thinkstock; **p. 247:** Dario Sabljak/Shutterstock; **p. 248:** Barone Firenze/Shutterstock; **p. 250:** Marten Czamanske/Shutterstock; **p. 251:** Scott Leman/Shutterstock; **p. 252:** (all) Pearson Education; **pp. 254–255:** Jupiterimages/Goodshoot/Thinkstock; **p. 261:** Digital Vision/Thinkstock; **p. 262:** (t) catman/Shutterstock; (1st row, l) C.J. White/Shutterstock; (1st row, c) Digital Vision/Thinkstock; (1st row, r) Yellowj/Shutterstock; (2nd row, l) joingate/Shutterstock; (2nd row, c) Valentyn Volkov/Shutterstock; (2nd row, r) Michal Zajac/Shutterstock; **p. 264:** George Doyle/Thinkstock; **p. 267:** Yellowj/Shutterstock; **p. 270:** (t) Kiselev Andrey Valerevich/Shutterstock; (1st row, l) Valentyn Volkov/Shutterstock; (1st row, lc) Andrey Jitkov/Shutterstock; (1st row, rc) hfng/Shutterstock; (1st row, r) Robyn Mackenzie/Shutterstock; (2nd row, l) Shebeko/Shutterstock; (2nd row, lc) Denis Vrublevski/shutterstock; (2nd row, rc) epsylon_lyrae/Shutterstock; (2nd row, r) Ramon grosso dolarea/Shutterstock; **p. 271:** D. Heining-Boynton, HBPHOTOPRO.COM; **p. 279:** Comstock/Thinkstock; **p. 280:** D. Heining-Boynton, HBPHOTOPRO.COM; **p. 281:** Jupiterimages/Thinkstock; **p. 282:** (t) Deklofenak/Shutterstock; (b) Aleksey Kondratyuk/Shutterstock; **p. 284:** (t) Barbara Penoyar/Photodisc/Getty Images; (tr) Alexander Chaikin/Shutterstock; (l) D. Heining-Boynton, HBPHOTOPRO.COM; (br) Rhonda Klevansky/Getty Images; **p. 285:** (t) Andresr/Shutterstock; (c) iladm/Shutterstock; (bl) Pearson Learning Photo Studio; (br) Pixel1962/shutterstock; **p. 286:** Pearson Education; **p. 288:** (l, c, r) Pearson Education; **pp. 292–393:** Photos.com/Jupiterimages/Thinkstock; **p. 296:** (l) Suzanne Long/Shutterstock; (r) Joel Shawn/Shutterstock; **p. 297:** Brand X Pictures/Jupiterimages/Thinkstock; **p. 298:** Colin Sinclair/Dorling Kindersley; **p. 301:** Thomas Northcut/Photodisc/Thinkstock; **p. 304:** (t) NataliaYeromina/Shutterstock; (lc) Creatas/Thinkstock; (c) littleny/Shutterstock; (rc) Paul Sutherland/Digital Vision/Thinkstock; (b) Losevsky Pavel/Shutterstock; **p. 311:** (l) NataliaYeromina/Shutterstock; (l, inset) Doug James/Shutterstock; (r) lev radin/Shutterstock; **p. 316:** jorisvo/Shutterstock; **p. 318:** Pictorial Press Ltd/Alamy; **p. 319:** Linda Johnsonbaugh/Shutterstock; **p. 321:** Digital Vision/Thinkstock; **p. 322:** (t) lev radin/Shutterstock; (b) iofoto/Shutterstock; **p. 324:** (t) Jack Hollingsworth/Thinkstock; (tl) Larry Lee Photography/Corbis; (c) Demetrio Carrasco/Dorling Kindersley; (bl) Dale Mitchell/Shutterstock; **p. 325:** (t) Hans Neleman/Getty Images; (tl) Brand X Pictures/Thinkstock; (c) D. Heining-Boynton, HBPHOTOPRO.COM; (bl) SF photo/Shutterstock; **p. 326:** Pearson Education; **p. 328:** (l, c, r) Pearson Education; **pp. 332–333:** Andresr/Shutterstock; **p. 336:** Stephen Schildbach/Getty Images; **p. 340:** AVAVA/Shutterstock; **p. 344:** Guido Amrein, Switzerland/Shutterstock; **p. 346:** Stockbyte/Getty Images; **p. 351:** Galyna Andrushko/Shutterstock; **p. 352:** Regissercom/Shutterstock; **p. 355:** (t) Getty Images/Thinkstock; (b) BananaStock/Thinkstock; **p. 356:** TheThirdMan/Shutterstock; **p. 359:** Creatas/Jupiterimages/Thinkstock; **p. 360:** Pearson Education; **p. 361:** (t) Creatas Images/Thinkstock; (b) Andresr/Shutterstock; **p. 363:** (t) Maria Teijeiro/Photodisc/Thinkstock; (tl) Jarno Gonzalez Zarraonandia/Shutterstock.com; (c) terekhov igor/Shutterstock; (b) Maria Veras/Shutterstock; **p. 364:** (t) Andresr/Shutterstock; (l) gary yim/Shutterstock; (tc) Paul Clarke/Shutterstock; (bc) Jarno Gonzalez Zarraonandia/Shutterstock.com; **p. 365:** (t) Andresr/Shutterstock; (c) nouseforname/Shutterstock; (bl) Jacqueline Abromeit/Shutterstock; (br) Sofia/Shutterstock; **p. 366:** Pearson Education; **pp. 368:** (l, c, r) Pearson Education; **pp. 372–373:** Bryan Busovicki/Shutterstock; **p. 377:** Andresr, 2010/used under license from www.Shutterstock.com; **p. 378:** Ramona Heim/Shutterstock; **p. 382:** (t) Creatas Images/Thinkstock; (b) Stockbyte/Thinkstock; **p. 385:** (t) Stockbyte/Thinkstock; (b) gary yim/Shutterstock; **p. 386:** (t) Robert Kneschke/Shutterstock; (b) Noel Hendrickson/Thinkstock; **p. 387:** Thomas Northcut/Thinkstock; **p. 390:** John Foxx/Thinkstock; **p. 391:** (tl) Lysithee/Shutterstock; (r) Robert WrÃfÃ³blewski/Shutterstock; (bl) Attila JANDI/Shutterstock; **p. 393:** Digital Vision/Thinkstock; **p. 398:** Andrey Yurlov/Shutterstock; **p. 399:** Stockbyte/Getty Images; **p. 400:** (t) Dmitriy Shironosov/Shutterstock; (b) nito/Shutterstock; **p. 402:** (t) Stockbyte/Getty Images; (l) gary yim/Shutterstock; (tc) max blain/Shutterstock; (bc) javarman/Shutterstock; **p. 403:** (t) Rido/Shutterstock; (l) Alexander Chaikin/Shutterstock; (tc) D. Heining-Boynton, HBPHOTOPRO.COM; (bc) Andriy Markov/Shutterstock; **p. 404:** Pearson Education; **p. 406:** (l, c, r) Pearson Education; **pp. 410–411:** James Thew/Shutterstock; **p. 413:** Pan Xunbin/Shutterstock; **p. 414:** (top to bottom) Ng Yin Jian/Shutterstock; Lucky Business/Shutterstock; marilyn barbone/Shutterstock; Denis Pepin/Shutterstock; Narcis Parfenti/Shutterstock; Hintau Aliaksei/Shutterstock; **p. 415:** kaarsten/Shutterstock; **p. 419:** Colin D. Young/

Page numbers given for all references correspond to the eText, available in MySpanishLab.

Page numbers given for all references correspond to the eText, available in MySpanishLab.

Page numbers given for all references correspond to the eText, available in MySpanishLab.

Page numbers given for all references correspond to the eText, available in MySpanishLab.

Page numbers given for all references correspond to the eText, available in MySpanishLab.

Page numbers given for all references correspond to the eText, available in MySpanishLab.

ESTADOS
UNIDOS

Mexicali
Tijuana
Nogales
Ciudad Juárez

Río Bravo del Norte
Río Grande

Nuevo Laredo

Golfo de México

BAJA CALIFORNIA

Golfo de California

SIERRA MADRE OCCIDENTAL

SIERRA MADRE ORIENTAL

Monterrey

MÉXICO

Mérida

Península de Yucatán

Guadalajara

Comala
México, D.F.
Veracruz

Taxco

Palenque
Belice

Tikal
Belmopan
BELICE

Acapulco
Oaxaca

GUATEMALA

Quetzaltenango
Copán

Guatemala
Volcán Izalco
San Salvador

EL SALVADOR

OCÉANO
PACÍFICO

✪	Capital
•	Otras ciudades
▲	Volcán
∴	Ruinas

Islas Galápagos (Ec.)

México, América Central y el Caribe